CIVIL WAR
NAVIES
1855–1883

280x208 HB

THE U.S. NAVY WARSHIP SERIES

The Sailing Navy, 1775–1854
Civil War Navies, 1855–1883
The New Navy, 1883–1922

CIVIL WAR NAVIES
1855–1883

Paul H. Silverstone

Routledge
Taylor & Francis Group
New York   London

Routledge
Taylor & Francis Group
711 Third Avenue
New York, NY 10017

Routledge
Taylor & Francis Group
2 Park Square
Milton Park, Abingdon
Oxon OX14 4RN

Routledge is an imprint of Taylor & Francis Group, an Informa business

First issued in paperback 2016

© 2006 by Taylor & Francis Group, LLC

No part of this book may be reprinted, reproduced, transmitted, or utilized in any form by any electronic, mechanical, or other means, now known or hereafter invented, including photocopying, microfilming, and recording, or in any information storage or retrieval system, without written permission from the publishers.

Trademark Notice: Product or corporate names may be trademarks or registered trademarks, and are used only for identification and explanation without intent to infringe.

Library of Congress Cataloging-in-Publication Data

Silverstone, Paul H.
   Civil war navies, 1855-1883 / Paul H. Silverstone.
     p. cm.
   Includes bibliographical references and index.
   ISBN 0-415-97870-X (hb)
   1. United States. Navy--Lists of vessels. 2. Confederate States of America. Navy--Lists of vessels. 3. Warships--United States--History--19th century. 4. Warships--Confederate States of America--History. 5. United States--History--Civil War, 1861-1865--Naval operations. I. Title.

VA61.S54 2006
973.7'5--dc22
                                      2006002087

Visit the Taylor & Francis Web site at
http://www.taylorandfrancis.com

and the Routledge Web site at
http://www.routledge-ny.com

ISBN13: 978-0-415-97870-5 (hbk)
ISBN13: 978-1-138-99135-4 (pbk)

To the memory of Martin E. Holbrook,
who helped locate and identify many of the
photographs of this era and who was always
certain that a photograph of the CSS *Alabama*
would be discovered.

CONTENTS

Introduction	ix
Explanation of Data	xi
United States Navy Chronology, 1855–1883	xiii
Abbreviations	xvii
Naval Ordnance, 1855–1883	xix

PART I   UNITED STATES NAVY WARSHIPS

1	Armored Vessels	3
2	Unarmored Steam Vessels	13
3	Acquired Combatant Vessels	43
4	Service Vessels	77
5	Sailing Ships	93
6	The Mississippi River Fleet	109
7	United States Revenue Cutter Service	135
8	United States Coast Survey	143

PART II   CONFEDERATE STATES NAVY

Introduction to Part II		147
9	Armored Vessels	149
10	Unarmored Steam Vessels	157
11	Area Defense Forces	167
12	Privateers	189
13	Blockade Runners	191
14	Tenders	197
Appendix: List of Shipbuilders		199
Bibliography		203
Index		205

INTRODUCTION

As the drums of war sounded in North America in 1861, a great technological change was taking place in the realm of naval warfare. The introduction of the armored warship was only one aspect of this revolution at sea. Steam was well on its way to supplanting sail as the motive power for ships, and the first armored warships were already at sea. Larger and more powerful cannons were being developed using shells instead of solid shot. These developments changed not only the outward appearance of ships but also their capabilities and use as well as tactics at sea.

The United States Navy grew in size with the onset of war and continued to expand throughout the conflict. Prior to 1861 the duties of the Navy were restricted to protecting American interests abroad, a task which was handled by the forty-two ships in commission in March. Now it was called upon to provide ships to blockade the entire coast of the southern states from Hampton Roads to the Rio Grande as well as to protect American shipping abroad from Confederate commerce destroyers. It quickly became apparent that the strength of the Navy was totally inadequate for new and varied duties imposed by the war.

The Navy suffered its first losses with the withdrawal of many experienced Southern naval officers and the loss of the valuable ships, equipment, and facilities at its largest navy yard at Norfolk. Gideon Welles was appointed Secretary of the Navy by President Lincoln.

The United States Navy was the possessor of some fine new propeller-driven warships such as the frigates of the *Merrimack* class and the *Hartford*-class sloops, which, although having machinery problems, were greatly admired in naval circles.

Many vessels were required to enforce the blockade. Southern privateers and later raiders started to make war on American commerce on the high seas, and fast ships with high endurance were needed to protect merchant ships abroad.

As war loomed, many new ships were ordered including such revolutionary designs as the ironclad vessels *Monitor* and *New Ironsides*. Whole classes of new sloops and monitors were built; "90-day gunboats," double-enders, and others rapidly enlarged the fleet. Numerous merchant vessels of all sizes were requisitioned for use in the blockade to cover the long coastline and the major southern ports. To our eyes these quaint-looking vessels seem quite inadequate to have performed the arduous tasks they were assigned, yet they gave good service and won the day for the Union.

In addition, a fleet was created to fight on and take control of the inland rivers such as the Mississippi, the Cumberland, and the Tennessee. Here, too, ironclad ships were built and others converted; the strange shapes of these vessels belied their deadly strength. Initially it was the Army that built and converted river steamers to fighting vessels, but the Navy soon inherited this fleet to which were added many stern-wheel river steamers, lightly armored and fitted with guns; they became known as tinclads.

By 1863 the Navy had seized control of the major waterways. Using the rivers as highways into the interior of the South, the Navy and Army cooperated in expeditions and campaigns up the rivers, culminating in the capture of Vicksburg. The other major expedition was the Red River Campaign of 1864.

At first, the Confederate Navy obviously did not exist and had to make do with makeshift designs and conversions. Greatly hampered by lack of industrial capacity, it was unable to match the ship-building program of the North and tried by various devices to raise a fleet. Of great interest were the several ships built and purchased in Great Britain and France, only a few of which ever sailed under the Confederate flag. Some, however, such as the *Alabama* and *Shenandoah*, were responsible for a great deal of activity and many celebrated incidents of the war.

The United States Navy expanded greatly during the war. Construction of over 200 vessels was started, and 418 vessels were purchased. The roster of men in service, totaling 7,600 in 1861, increased to more than 51,000 in 1865.

The blockade of Southern ports ordered by President Lincoln in 1861 required a huge investment in resources of ships and men. Endless hours lengthened into days and months and years for the blockaders patrolling off the major ports such as Charleston and Wilmington.

In September 1861, the fleet was divided into four major commands. The Atlantic coast from Virginia to Key West, Florida was covered by the North and South Atlantic Blockading Squadrons. The East and West Gulf Blockading Squadrons covered the Gulf of Mexico coast from Key West to Brownsville, Texas. The success of the blockade can be seen by the numbers of ships captured and destroyed as reported in the *Annual Report of the Secretary of the Navy* for 1865.

	Captured	Destroyed
Steamers	210	85
Schooners	569	114
Sloops	139	32
Ships	13	2
Brigs	29	2
Barks	25	4
Yachts	2	—
Small boats	139	96
Rams	6	5
Gunboats	10	11
Others	7	—
Total	1149	351

The demobilization of the Navy swiftly followed the end of hostilities. Most of the purchased vessels and many of those built by the Navy were sold out of service by 1869, including practically all the river steamers. The merchant vessels had inferior machinery unsuitable for warships and went quickly. At the end of June 1865, the North and South Atlantic Squadrons were merged as were the East and West Gulf Squadrons. The Potomac Flotilla was disbanded on 31 July 1865 and the Mississippi Squadron two weeks later on 14 August. The Navy went back to its peacetime disposition with squadrons in Europe, the Far East, and South America.

The purpose of this book is to provide a single comprehensive source of definitive information on Civil War Navy vessels with details and brief war records of the ships. Despite the intense and continuing interest in the Civil War, the naval vessels of that conflict have not been as well described as those of other eras.

A major problem is that despite the variety of sources, there is much conflicting information. Systems of measuring ships — both tonnage and dimensions — varied, so the numbers given differ from source to source. One has no assurance that these figures are right or wrong, or if they are only reporting different measurements. Some judgment has been required to choose which of these various measurements should be used.

Similarly it has been difficult to identify some acquired ships as to their prior identity, name of builder, or even date of construction. This is particularly true of the Confederate ships for which records are few and sparse or even nonexistent.

In the matter of pictures, I have tried to illustrate the book with photographs only. For this period in which photography was still in its infancy, surprising gaps appear and some famous ships are unavailable in photographs. The *Merrimack* (later *Virginia*), it appears, was never photographed either before or after her conversion. Nevertheless, search has been crowned with success in finding photographs of some ships of which none was previously known. The late Martin Holbrook was instrumental in finding and identifying many of the pictures. In a few cases, however, we have been forced to use contemporary drawings to depict a ship's appearance.

Appreciation is extended to the following for assistance in obtaining information and photographs: Ernest Arroyo, Ian L. Buxton, Dr. Francis J. Ducoin, Kevin Foster, William Gladstone, Ian Grant, Charles R. Haberlein, Rowan M.B.H. Hackman, William Jurens, Charles Lawesson, Rear Admiral Lauren S. McCready, Dr. Charles Peery, Norman Polmar, William Rau.

EXPLANATION OF DATA

To make it easier to use this book and to identify the Navy's ships, the various types of vessels have been divided into categories based on mode of propulsion and size, as well as duties.

Navy-built ships are listed first, followed by those merchant ships acquired during the war for temporary service. The categories are arbitrary, and some may disagree with the placement of any particular ship. Each category is subdivided into separate sections for side-wheel and propeller steamers, which it is felt would be helpful to the reader, as is separating steam and sailing ships.

The larger acquired vessels were used as seagoing blockaders and as cruisers to search for Confederate raiders. Smaller vessels operated in coastal waters and the rivers and inlets of the southern Atlantic coast. As a distinct type, the former ferryboats are listed in one section. Ships that served principally in service roles are listed as auxiliaries and are in a separate section as are tugs. The ships of the inland Navy are listed in a separate section, Navy-built vessels first followed by those acquired and armed.

For Confederate ships, the task is much more difficult inasmuch as much information and many records are lacking. The Confederate Navy was not able to operate as a unified force, and ships, except in unusual cases, did not move from one area to another; therefore, the bulk of the ships are listed geographically by area of operation. To help the reader, exception is made to this order by listing together several distinct types such as armored vessels, ocean cruisers, torpedo boats, and government-operated blockade runners and not geographically. Most blockade runners were privately owned and therefore are not within the scope of this work; their listing must await another book.

The Confederate section is necessarily sparse as to information, both particulars and service record of ships. Many ships turn up in the records for one or a few occasions and then disappear. Often the vessel's antecedents or later history are unclear or unknown.

Because many Confederate ships remained in their own local area, sections are provided for each locality. These are: Louisiana, Texas, the Gulf Coast (Alabama, Mississippi, and the west coast of Florida), the Atlantic Coast (North and South Carolina, Georgia and the east coast of Florida), Virginia, and inland rivers.

In this book, information for ships built or acquired before 1855 is provided only where it pertains to the period after that year. Full particulars and earlier history may be found in the first volume of this series on the Sailing Navy.

Particulars are given for each ship as follows. For certain types of ships, such as sailing vessels and lesser Confederate vessels, the particulars are given in a single line without explanation.

Name: Navy name as completed with former names given below. Further changes of name, if any, are indicated in the service record with new Navy names in bold type.

Builder: Place where the ship was built followed by the builder's name, if known, in parentheses. The full name and location of most builders is given in the Appendix.

Construction dates: For Navy-built ships, dates given are for laying down of keel, launching, and commissioning. For acquired vessels, dates given are date of launching, acquisition by the Navy, and commissioning.

Tonnage: This figure is taken from various sources, many of which did not explain what formula of measurement was used. Merchant ships' measurement was usually expressed in *tons burden*, a measurement of the carrying capacity of the ship, which gives little guide to its size, and rules of its calculation varied widely. In 1864 a new uniform system of measurement was introduced that led to a more accurate figure and that could serve as a better guide to relative size. D = displacement, B = tons burden (old measurement), n/r = new register (1864 rules), GRT = British gross registered tonnage

Dimensions: Standard dimensions given in feet (') and inches ("), are length × beam × draft (or depth of hull, prefixed with "d"). Here, too, figures varied widely and were often published without explanation of the method of measurement. Where known, length is specified as overall (oa); between perpendiculars (bp), that is, between foreside of stem and aftside of rudder post; on deck (dk); or on the waterline (wl). On occasion an authoritative source has given a measurement of length without specific explanation; to guide the user of this book as to a possible discrepancy, it has been felt useful to provide this information followed by a U in parentheses (U). Where used with beam, (oa) refers to width including the paddle boxes.

Machinery: Mode of propulsion — propeller (screw) or side/stern wheels; number, type, and size of engines, and number of boilers where known; horsepower; and speed. Occasionally no indication as to type has been found and none is given. Older sources often delineate a two-cylinder engine as two engines, leading to some confusion. Propeller-driven ships generally, but not always, had direct-acting engines while side wheelers had beam engines. The diameter of the cylinder(s) and the length of the stroke of the piston are shown for the former in inches and for the latter in feet, e.g., (50" × 2'), following the type of engine. The symbol # indicates a disagreement in sources as to the mode of propulsion, particularly whether a river steamer had stern or side wheels. The maker of the machinery is noted in parentheses, if known ("bldr" indicates machinery manufactured by the builder).

Complement: Normal figure for officers and crew. For many ships, where sources vary, a range is given (e.g., 50/75). There was often a large variance in peacetime and wartime complements.

Armament: Original number and type of guns are given first. Later significant changes made during the war are given, with date, either by listing the entire complement of guns, or by indicating modifications as additions or subtractions from the previous armament shown. The date reflects the date of survey rather than when changes were actually made. Minor variations are not necessarily given. Guns were described by caliber (inches) or weight (pdr/pounder) of projectile. MLR = muzzle-loading rifle, SB = smoothbore, H = howitzer, M = mortar, R = rifle. The entry "4–32pdr/42" refers to four smoothbore guns of 42 cwt (hundredweight), a reference to the size of the cannon, firing 32-pound projectiles.

Armor (armored vessels only): Maximum or a range of thickness of the armor only is given.

Notes: Additional information pertaining to design, construction, or later modifications, acquisition, or earlier historical notes of interest, not included in other categories.

Service record: A capsule history of each ship's naval service showing assignment by station or squadron and war service, including participation in engagements, major damage to vessel, or loss. Changes in Navy name are given here. Also final disposition by the Navy: loss, sale, or transfer to another agency.

Ships captured: Names and dates of merchant ships captured or sunk, principally blockade runners for USN ships. Some prizes were credited to several ships acting together and so appear more than once. Ships named are sailing vessels unless indicated as steamers (str). Those ships destroyed are marked with an asterisk (*).

Later history: Brief details of the ship's career after leaving naval service including later merchant names, service in other government departments, or in foreign navies. The ultimate fate is given where known, or the year the ship disappeared from shipping registers (RR) or was sold to foreign buyers (S/F). Occasionally a date is given for the last published reference (SE = still existing).

UNITED STATES NAVY CHRONOLOGY, 1855-1883

Oct 1858	Expedition to Paraguay to demand retribution for attack on USS *Water Witch* in 1855, to Feb 1859.
25 Jun 1859	USS *Powhatan* assists in attack on Pei Ho forts, China.
24 Dec 1860	South Carolina secedes from the Union, followed by Mississippi (9 Jan), Florida (10 Jan), Alabama (11 Jan), Georgia (19 Jan), Louisiana (26 Jan), and Texas (1 Feb).
9 Jan 1861	Unarmed steamer *Star of the West*, with reinforcements for Fort Sumter, fired upon by shore batteries.
9 Feb 1861	Jefferson Davis elected president of the Confederacy.
4 Mar 1861	Abraham Lincoln inaugurated president of the United States.
12 Apr 1861	Fort Sumter fired upon, surrendered the next day; the opening shots of the Civil War.
17 Apr 1861	Virginia secedes.
19 Apr 1861	President Lincoln declares blockade of southern ports.
20 Apr 1861	Atlantic coast: Norfolk Navy Yard abandoned, USS *Merrimack* and eight other ships burned.
24 Apr 1861	USS *Constitution* left Annapolis for Newport, RI, with officers and midshipmen of the Naval Academy.
21 Jul 1861	Virginia: First Battle of Bull Run.
28-29 Aug 1861	Atlantic coast: Capture of Hatteras Inlet, NC, taken by joint army-navy operation under Dupont. Union strategy to seize important points along the coast to enforce the blockade.
4-10 Sep 1861	Inland waters: Grant's operation to seize mouths of Cumberland and Tennessee Rivers; *Tyler* & *Lexington* in action with CSS *Jackson* and against batteries at Hickman, K; seizure of Paducah, Ky.
16 Sep 1861	Ironclad Board recommends construction of three ironclads (*Monitor, New Ironsides, Galena*).
12 Oct 1861	Gulf coast: Engagement by CSS *Manassas* and squadron near Head of Passes, Miss., against Union squadron.
5-7 Nov 186	Atlantic coast: Engagement with CSN squadron and capture of Port Royal, SC.
8 Nov 1861	High seas: USS *San Jacinto* (Charles Wilkes) stopped British steamer *Trent* on the high seas and removed Confederate envoys James M. Mason and John Slidell, causing a serious international incident.
9 Nov 1861	Atlantic coast: Dupont's force took Beaufort, SC.
22-23 Nov 1861	Gulf coast: Bombardment of forts at Pensacola, FL.
25-28 Nov 1861	Atlantic coast: Bombardment of forts at St. Helena Sound: SC; capture of Tybee Island.
5-6 Dec 1861	Atlantic coast: Engagement with forts in Wassaw Sound, GA.
31 Dec 1861-2 Jan 1862	Atlantic coast: Army operations at Port Royal Ferry, SC.
11 Jan 1862	Inland waters: Engagement with CSN vessels near Lucas Bend, MO, Mississippi River.
6 Feb 1862	Inland waters: Fort Henry, TN, controlling the Tennessee River, captured by naval forces under Foote.
7-8 Feb 1862	Atlantic coast: Roanoke Island, NC, captured; engagement at Elizabeth City, 10 Feb.

6-11 Feb 1862	Inland waters: Expedition to Florence, AL, Tennessee River.
14 Feb 1862	Inland waters: Fort Donelson, TN, on Cumberland River, captured by forces under Foote and Grant.
17 Feb 1862	Atlantic coast: Ironclad CSS *Virginia* (ex-USS *Merrimack*) commissioned.
2-12 Mar 1862	Atlantic coast: Capture of Fernandina, FL and Brunswick, St.Simons and Jekyll Islands, GA.
8-9 Mar 1862	Atlantic coast: Battle of Hampton Roads. CSS *Virginia* attacks Union fleet, sinking USS *Cumberland* and *Congress*. On 9 Mar, USS *Monitor* and *Virginia* battle in the historic first engagement between ironclads.
14 Mar 1862	Atlantic coast: Capture of New Bern, NC.
15 Mar 1862	Inland waters: Siege of Island No.10 began, strategically located in Mississippi River at TN-KY border, which surrendered 7 Apr.
6-7 Apr 1862	Inland waters: Gunboats USS *Tyler* and *Lexington* supported Grant's army at Battle of Shiloh (Pittsburg Landing), TN.
13 Apr 1862	Inland waters: Bombardment of Fort Pillow, TN.
14-29 Apr 1862	Virginia: Army operations at Gloucester and York, VA.
18-28 Apr 1862	Gulf coast: Farragut in USS *Hartford* leads his squadron in bombardment of Forts Jackson and St. Philip below New Orleans in Mississippi River. Fleet ran past the forts on 24 Apr and engaged Confederate squadron.
26 Apr 1862	Gulf coast: New Orleans captured.
25-26 Apr 1862	Atlantic coast: Fort Macon, NC, surrendered to joint army-navy force.
8 May 1862.	Virginia: Union ships engage batteries at Sewells Point, on York River, as part of support of army operations.
10 May 1862	Gulf coast: Pensacola, FL., occupied.
10-11 May 1862	Inland waters: Engagement with enemy vessels and batteries at Fort Pillow, TN.
11 May 1862	Virginia: Confederates abandon Norfolk Navy Yard; CSS *Virginia* blown up to avoid capture.
13 May 1862	Inland waters: Occupation of Natchez, MS., as Farragut's fleet moved north.
17 May 1862	Virginia: Expedition up Pamunkey River, VA.
May 26, 1862	Inland waters: Bombardment of Grand Gulf, MS.
6 Jun 1862	Inland waters: Battle of Memphis involving Union ships and Ellet rams and the Confederate River Defense Fleet. All Confederate ships are destroyed; Ellet mortally wounded. Memphis taken.
17 Jun 1862	Inland waters: Expedition up White River to support army and bombardment of St. Charles, AR.
28 Jun 1862	Inland waters: Farragut's fleet moving north runs past batteries at Vicksburg and joins the flotilla upriver.
15 Jul 1862	Inland waters: Ironclad CSS *Arkansas* engages ships in Yazoo River, then attacks Union fleet in Mississippi above Vicksburg. Farragut's fleet moves south.
16 Jul 1862	David Farragut becomes first officer to hold the rank of rear admiral.
22 Jul 1862	Inland waters: Ironclad *Essex* and ram *Queen of the West* attack CSS *Arkansas* at Vicksburg.
16-22 Aug 1862	Inland waters: Expeditions up Yazoo River to Greenville, MS.
23 Aug 1862	High seas: New sloop USS *Adirondack* wrecked in Bahamas.
24 Aug 1862	High seas: CSS *Alabama* commissioned off Azores Islands. Raphael Semmes in command.
29-30 Aug 1862	Virginia: Second Battle of Bull Run.
4 Sep 1862	Gulf coast: CSS *Florida* ran blockade into Mobile Bay.
17 Sep 1862	Virginia: Battle of Antietam (Sharpsburg).
25 Sep 1862	Gulf coast: Bombardment of Sabine City, TX.
1 Oct 1862	Western Gunboat Flotilla transferred from the War Department to the Navy.
3 Oct 1862	Gulf coast: Attack on Galveston, TX. Surrendered on 9 Oct.
21 Nov-11 Dec 1862	Inland waters: Expedition up Yazoo River. Ironclad USS *Cairo* sunk by a torpedo, 12 Dec.
Dec 1862	Second attempt to take Vicksburg (land).
13 Dec 1862	Virginia: Battle of Fredericksburg.
23-28 Dec 1862	Inland waters: Expedition in Yazoo River, dragging for torpedoes, bombardments at Haynes Bluff and Drumgoulds Bluff.
31 Dec 1862	USS *Monitor* founders in tow off Cape Hatteras.
1862-63	High seas: Search in N. Atlantic for CSS *Florida* and *Alabama*.
1 Jan 1863	Emancipation Proclamation issued by Lincoln.
1 Jan 1863	Gulf coast: Confederates recapture Galveston, Tex. Gunboat *Harriet Lane* captured, *Westfield* sunk.
4-11 Jan 1863	Inland waters: Expedition up White River, bombardment and capture of Fort Hindman, AR.
11 Jan 1863	Gulf coast: Raider CSS *Alabama* sinks gunboat USS *Hatteras* off Galveston.
16 Jan 1863	Gulf coast: Raider CSS *Florida* ran blockade out of Mobile, AL.
27 Jan 1863	Atlantic coast: Monitors attack Fort McAllister, GA again on 1 Feb.
31 Jan 1863	Atlantic coast: Ironclads CSS *Palmetto State* and *Chicora* attack blockading fleet off Charleston.
3 Feb 1863	Inland waters: Defense of Fort Donelson against Confederate attack.
25 Feb 1863	Inland waters: Yazoo Pass Expedition withdrew 22 Mar.

United States Navy Chronology, 1855–1883   xv

28 Feb 1863	Atlantic coast: Monitor *Montauk* and others destroy blockade runner *Rattlesnake* at Fort McAllister.
14 Mar 1863	Inland waters: USS *Hartford* and *Albatross* pass batteries at Port Hudson, La. Frigate *Mississippi* sunk.
14-26 Mar 1863.	Inland waters: Expedition to Steele's Bayou, MS.
24 Feb 1863	Inland waters: USS *Indianola* sunk by CSS *Webb* and *Queen of the West* below Warrenton, MS.
11-23 Mar 1863	Inland waters: Yazoo Pass expedition, attack on Fort Pemberton, Tallahatchie River, start of Grant's campaign against Vicksburg.
31 Mar 1863	Inland waters: passage past Port Hudson, La., 14 Mar, north past Grand Gulf, MS, 19 Mar and run south.
3 Apr 1863	Inland waters: Expedition to burn Palmyra, TN.
7 Apr 1863	Atlantic coast: Monitors under Dupont attack forts in Charleston Harbor without success. USS *Keokuk*, damaged, sinks the next day.
16 Apr 1863	Inland waters: Gunboats and transports under Porter ran past batteries at Vicksburg.
29 Apr 1863	Inland waters: Porter's ships and Grant's troops force evacuation of Grand Gulf, MS.
29 Apr-2 May 1863	Inland waters: Feigned attack on Haynes' Bluff, MS., to prevent reinforcement of Grand Gulf.
2-4 May 1863	Virginia: Battle of Chancellorsville.
3-13 May 1863	Inland waters: Porter's expedition up Red River to Alexandria, LA.
18 May 1863	Inland waters: Capture of Haynes' Bluff, Yazoo River.
22 May 1863	Siege of Vicksburg begins. Bombardments continue through next two months.
20-31 May 1863	Inland waters: Expedition up Yazoo River; destruction of Yazoo City, NY.
17 Jun 1863	Atlantic coast: Monitors *Weehawken* and *Nahant* force surrender of ironclad *Atlanta* in Wassaw Sound, GA.
26 Jun 1863	High seas: Revenue cutter *Caleb Cushing* seized by boarders at Portland, ME.
28 Jun 1863	Inland waters: Bombarded Donaldsonville, LA.
1-3 Jul 1863	Virginia: Battle of Gettysburg.
4 Jul 1863	Inland waters: Surrender of Vicksburg.
9 Jul 1863	Inland waters: Port Hudson, LA., surrendered, completing Union control of the Mississippi River.
10 Jul 1863	Inland waters: Expedition to Trinity, LA., Red River.
13 Jul 1863	Inland waters: Expedition to capture Yazoo City, MS. 19 Confederate ships destroyed. Ironclad USS *Baron de Kalb* sunk by torpedo.
16 Jul 1863	High seas: USS Wyoming engaged batteries at Shimonoseki, Japan, and sank a steamer.
16 Jul 1863	Atlantic coast: Engaged batteries in Stono River, SC.
18 Jul 1863	Atlantic coast: Monitors under Dahlgren commence attack on Fort.Wagner, Charleston.
26-30 Jul 1863	Atlantic coast: Expedition in Chowan River, NC.
12-15 Aug 1863	Inland waters: Reconnaissance up White River, AR.
17 Aug 1863	Atlantic coast: Dahlgren renews attack on forts in Charleston Harbor. On 6 Sep Confederates evacuate Morris Island.
23 Aug 1863	Virginia: Confederate boats capture gunboats *Reliance* and *Satellite* in Rappahannock River.
29 Aug 1863	Atlantic coast: Confederate submarine *Hunley* sinks in Charleston harbor with all hands. Later salvaged.
8 Sep 1863	Gulf coast: Expedition to take Sabine Pass, TX. Gunboats *Clifton* and *Sachem* captured.
15 Oct 1863	Atlantic coast: Confederate submarine *Hunley* sinks for second time with all hands. Salvaged.
19-20 Sep 1863	Battle of Chickamauga.
... Oct 1863	High seas: British government seizes two ironclad rams built by Laird for the Confederate government.
27 Oct-3 Nov 1863	Gulf coast: Expedition to Brazos Santiago, Rio Grande, TX., to obtain position on the Mexican border.
23-25 Nov 1863	Battles of Chattanooga, Missionary Ridge, Lookout Mountain.
6 Dec 1863	Atlantic coast: Monitor *Weehawken* foundered in Charleston Harbor.
... Dec 1863	High seas: CSS *Alabama* arrives in Singapore.
2 Feb 1864	Atlantic coast: Confederates destroy gunboat USS *Underwriter* in Neuse River.
2-22 Feb-16 Apr 1864	Atlantic coast: Assault on Jacksonville, FL.
16-29 Feb 1864	Gulf coast: Bombardment of Fort Powell, Mobile Bay.
17 Feb 1864	Atlantic coast: Sloop *Housatonic* sunk off Charleston by spar torpedo of submarine torpedo boat CSS *Hunley*. *Hunley* foundered following the attack.
1-5 Mar 1864	Inland waters: Expedition up Black and Ouachita Rivers, LA.
12 Mar-16 May 1864	Inland waters: Red River Expedition. Fort de Russy, AR., captured. Water level in river dropped threatening to trap the fleet.
19 Apr 1864	Atlantic coast: Ironclad CSS *Albemarle* sorties and sinks gunboat USS *Southfield*, at Plymouth, NC.
5 May 1864	Atlantic coast: Engagements with CSS *Albemarle* at Plymouth, NC.
5-6 May 1864	Virginia: Battle of the Wilderness.
6-7 May 1864	Atlantic coast: CSS *Raleigh* engages Union ships off New Inlet, NC.

13 May 1864	Inland waters: Red River Expedition, last of ships trapped by low water escape downriver.
25-27 May 1864	Atlantic coast: Joint expedition up Ashepoo and S. Edisto Rivers, SC.
15-18 Jun 1864	Virginia: Siege of Petersburg begins.
19 Jun 1864	High seas: USS *Kearsarge* sinks CSS *Alabama* off Cherbourg.
4 Aug 1864	Virginia: Engaged battery near Harrison's Landing, VA.
5 Aug 1864	Gulf coast: Battle of Mobile Bay. Farragut's fleet bypasses Forts Morgan and Gaines and engages Confederate squadron. Monitor *Tecumseh* sunk; ironclad CSS *Tennessee* captured.
9-23 Aug 1864	Gulf coast: Bombardment of Fort Morgan, Mobile Bay, which finally surrenders.
2 Sep 1864	Sherman occupies Atlanta.
7 Oct 1864.	High seas: USS *Wachusett* captured CSS *Florida* in neutral harbor of Bahia, Brazil.
19 Oct 1864	High seas: CSS *Shenandoah* commissioned at sea off Madeira.
27 Oct 1864	Atlantic coast: Cushing destroys CSS *Albemarle* with spar torpedo, leading to recapture of Plymouth, NC.
27 Nov-30 Dec 1864	Atlantic coast: Expedition up Broad River, SC.
Dec 1864	Inland waters: Operations in Cumberland River, TN.
22 Dec 1864	Sherman captures Savannah.
24-25 Dec 1864	Atlantic coast: Unsuccessful attack on Fort Fisher, NC, by Porter and General Benjamin Butler.
13-15 Jan 1865	Atlantic coast: Second attack on Fort Fisher by Porter with 59 warships. Assault by troops under General Terry take the fort after a long bombardment, closing the port of Wilmington.
24 Jan 1865	Virginia: Engagement at Trent's Reach, James River, VA.
9 Feb 1865	Atlantic coast: Engagement with batteries in Togodo Creek, SC, near Charleston.
12-17 Feb 1865	Atlantic coast: Expedition to Bulls Bay, SC.
18 Feb 1865	Charleston surrenders.
18 Mar 1865	Gulf coast: Monitor *Milwaukee* sunk by torpedo in Blakeley River, AL. Monitor *Osage* sunk on 29 Mar.
23 Feb 1865	Atlantic coast: Expedition to Georgetown, SC.
Mar 1865	High seas: Escape of Confederate ironclad *Stonewall* from Ferrol, Spain.
9 Apr 1865	Lee surrenders at Appomattox.
24 Apr 1865	Gulf coast: CSS *Webb* in the Red River attempts to reach the open sea and is destroyed below New Orleans.
1-6 Jun 1865	Gulf coast: Expedition up Red River and capture of CSS *Missouri*.
5 Nov 1865	CSS *Shenandoah* arrives at Liverpool and surrenders to British authorities.
16 Dec 1866	USS *New Ironsides* destroyed by fire at Philadelphia.
28 Aug 1867	US flag raised over Midway Island.
18 Nov 1867	USS *Monongahela* wrecked in hurricane at Frederikstad, St. Croix. She was later refloated.
13 Aug 1868	USS *Wateree* cast ashore by tidal wave following earthquake at Arica, Peru.
21 Sep 1869	USS *Idaho* wrecked in typhoon off Yokohama, Japan.
24 Jan 1870	USS *Oneida* sunk in collision with British steamer *Bombay* off Yokohoma.
11-13 Aug 1870	USS *Palos* the first Navy ship to transit the Suez Canal.
1 Jun 1871	USS *Palos* and *Monocacy* fired upon by Korean fort. On 10 Jun Marines and sailors landed a destroyed fort.
29 Jun 1871	USS *Polaris* sailed from New York on Arctic exploration cruise. When the ship was overdue an expedition of three ships was sent north. *Polaris* was lost on 24 Oct 1872 off Greenland. 19 survivors of *Polaris* rescued 30 Apr 1873 after drifting 2,000 miles on an ice floe.
31 Oct 1873	American steamer *Virginius* captured by a Spanish warship while transporting arms to Cuban insurgents; 30 crew members were executed, which almost led to war with Spain.
24 Nov 1877	Gunboat USS *Huron* wrecked in a gale off Nags Head, NC.
7 Aug 1879	*Jeannette* expedition sailed from San Francisco for Arctic exploration which ended in tragedy. Ship was crushed by ice and sank 12 Jun 1881; all but 10 of crew died.
5 Aug 1882	First warships of the "New Navy" authorized by Congress.

ABBREVIATIONS

†	for further details see next volume	MLR	muzzle-loading rifle
*	destroyed (as to prizes taken)	mph	miles per hour
#	sources disagree as to type of propulsion	NAtlBS	North Atlantic Blockading Squadron
AtlBS	Atlantic Blockading Squadron	NHP	normal horsepower
B	burden (tonnage) (old measurement)	n/r	new register (tonnage) (1864 rules)
bldr	builder	NYd	Navy Yard
BLR	breach-loading rifle	oa	length overall
bp	length between perpendiculars	recomm	recommissioned
BU	broken up	RR	removed from shipping registers
comm	commissioned	SAtlBS	South Atlantic Blockading Squadron
CSN	Confederate States Navy	SB	smoothbore gun
CSS	Confederate States Ship	schr	schooner
cyl.	cylinder	SE	still existing
d	depth of hull	S/F	sold foreign
D	displacement (tonnage)	sqn	squadron
decomm	decommissioned	stn	station
dk	length on deck	str	steamer
EGulfBS	East Gulf Blockading Squadron	(U)	unknown
FFU	further fate unknown	USAT	U.S. Army Transport
GulfBS	Gulf Blockading Squadron	USCS	U.S. Coast Survey
GRT	gross registered tonnage (British)	USLHS	U.S. Light House Service
H	howitzer	USN	U.S. Navy
HMS	Her Majesty's Ship (Royal Navy)	USRC	U.S. Revenue Cutter
HP	horsepower	USS	U.S. Ship
IHP	indicated horsepower	WGF	Western Gunboat Flotilla
L	launched	WGulfBS	West Gulf Blockading Squadron
M	mortar	wl	length on waterline

NAVAL ORDNANCE, 1855–1883

Ordnance of the Civil War era differed from that in earlier inventories primarily by the introduction of rifled guns and elongated shell. The rifling of guns turned out to be a rather formidable technical challenge. More-or-less experimental rifled guns had become available in the early 1800s, but it was not until about 1850 that really practical weapons became available. The elongated projectiles used in rifled guns tended to be heavier than their spherical predecessors; this, coupled with the increased resistance as the projectile traveled up the bore, placed the gun — which was geometrically more complex to begin with — under greater strain. Further, in the absence of efficient and effective breech blocks, it still remained necessary to load most rifled guns through the muzzle, a comparatively complex and difficult process. Thus, although primitive breech-loading designs had been developed by 1861, almost all Civil War naval guns remained muzzle-loaders.

Guns were typically mounted on traditional carriages with wheeled trucks, or in so-called pivot mounts, where the gun and carriage rotated around a central pivot, usually recoiling on skids. A good deal of manhandling was still required to load and maneuver either type, and the number of men in the crew was usually closely related to the weight of the gun. A 3,000-lb 32 pdr might require a crew of seven, a 6,850-lb 32 pdr a crew of fifteen, and a 16,000-lb IX-inch a crew of twenty-five.

Smoothbores remained common throughout the war. Although a 64 pdr was available, for both North and South the 32 pdr remained the most common variant, available in a variety of sizes and usually mounted on conventional trucked carriages. The Confederacy also used a small number of prewar carronades.

In the North, rifled guns were primarily based on designs springing from the work of Robert P. Parrot and John A. Dahlgren. The Parrot gun, essentially a muzzle-loading cast-iron rifle, was marked by a single cylindrical, half-caliber-thick, wrought-iron band shrink-fitted around the breech. The projectile was typically shaped rather like a pistol bullet, and was one and one-half to three calibers long. These relatively expensive weapons were manufactured in a range of sizes, with the larger varieties and the 60 pdr — all of which were prone to bursting — typically available only later in the war. Broadly speaking, Dahlgren guns may be divided into three groups, small bronze boat howitzers and rifles, iron smoothbore guns, and iron rifles. Visually, these guns appear as slightly tapered cylinders in the smaller sizes, with the larger sizes typically exhibiting a slight well-blended swelling around the breech. The Union also employed a 17,000-lb 13-inch Knap mortar, a 4-foot-diameter monster mounted on a 12-foot-diameter carriage. Twenty pounds of powder took the 218-pound shell some 4,200 yards. In-bore shot travel was only about a yard.

The Confederacy, which tended to be more innovative than the Union, largely employed rifled guns based on designs by John M. Brooke. Like guns designed in the North, these were also reinforced by wrought-iron bands shrunk around the breech but almost always had more than one band, giving the reinforced area a "stepped" appearance in photographs. In spite of the blockade, the Confederacy was, for a time, also able to import a significant number of foreign guns, primarily from Britain. Many, though by no means all, were breech-loaders. The best of these was the breech-loading Armstrong gun, a built-up design made up of tubes manufactured from heavy metal coils. The Whitworth guns typically presented a very slim profile and were characterized by their unique hexagonal rifling system, which, of course, accommodated hexagonal projectiles. The Blakely gun appeared in a variety of external profiles. All of these guns delivered remarkable accuracy and range, but were relatively complex for the time. The North imported some too, but found little need to utilize them extensively.

The period between 1865 and 1874 was marked by systematic conversions of older smoothbore guns into (usually smaller caliber) rifled muzzle-loaders, the 11-inch Dahlgren, for example, being reduced to 8-inch caliber, in the process. This program was followed by a somewhat less successful one, which saw 60 and

100 pdr Brooke guns converted into breech-loaders. In 1878, the Navy began construction of a prototype 6-inch/24 (70 pdr) breech-loading rifle. The weapon, which stretched U.S. manufacturing capabilities to the limit, was not completed until 1883, and then only with significant British assistance.

GUN TABLES

The following tables have been compiled from a number of sources, but can only be considered representative. Technology was developing rapidly and innovation, experimentation, and modification remained the rule for both projectiles and guns throughout the war. Warren Ripley's *Artillery and Ammunition of the Civil War*, Spencer Tucker's *Arming the Fleet*, and Eugene Canfield's excellent summary in volume 3 of the *Dictionary of American Naval Fighting Ships* are highly recommended sources if more detail is required.

All-up weights of gun mountings are difficult to determine because carriage styles varied widely and since carriages have not proven nearly as durable as tubes, surviving examples are rare. All-up weights marked with an asterisk (*) are estimates based on the assumption that the carriage weighed one-third as much as the tube. Projectile weights and gun ranges have been omitted when the variety of projectiles fired would render a single table entry meaningless. Charge weights were typically about one-tenth of the projectile weight, and initial velocities were usually between 1,200 and 1,700 feet per second. Black powder propellant was universal.

32 pdr Smoothbores ("Shot") Guns: (Used by Both Union and Confederate Forces)

Size	Length (inches)	Weight (gun) (lbs)	Weight (all-up) (lbs)	Projectile weight (lbs)	Caliber (inches)	Range at 5° (yards)
27 cwt	81	3,024	4,030*	32	c. 6.35	1,470
32 cwt	92	3,584	4,780*	32	c. 6.35	1,600
42 cwt	107	4,704	6,275*	32	c. 6.35	1,750
46 cwt	115.5	5,152	6,869*	32	c. 6.35	
51 cwt	121	5,712	7,620*	32	c. 6.35	
57 cwt	125	6,384	8,510*	32	c. 6.35	2,730

Note: Projectile weights are for solid shot. Shell weighed 26 lbs.

Typical Parrott Guns (Union)

Size	Length (inches)	Weight (gun) (lbs)	Weight (all-up) (lbs)	Projectile weight (lbs)	Caliber (inches)	Range at 5° (yards)
10 pdr	78	890	1,200*	c. 10	2.9–3.0	1,850
20 pdr	91.5	1,750	2,350*	c. 19	3.67	1,900–2,100
30 pdr	132.5	3,550	4,700*	25–30	4.2	2,200
60 pdr	124	5,360	7,150*	55	5.3	(U)
100 pdr	155	9,700	13,000*	70–100	6.4	c. 2,250
8-inch (150 pdr)	162	16,300	22,000*	132–175	8.0	2,100

Typical Brooke Guns (Primarily Confederate)

Size	Length (inches)	Weight (gun) (lbs)	Weight(all-up) (lbs)	Projectile weight (lbs)	Caliber (inches)	Range at 5° (yards)
6.4-inch	143	10,700	14,250*	95	6.4	(U)
7.0-inch	147	15,300	20,400*	110	7.0	(U)
8.0-inch	(U)	(U)	(U)	117–157	8.0	(U)
10-inch SB	158.5	21,560	28,700	(U)	10.0	(U)
11-inch SB	170	23,610	31,500	(U)	11.0	(U)

*Actual projectile weights for Brooke guns were highly variable depending upon the design; measured values for recovered projectiles ranged from 73 to 169 lbs for the 7-inch, for example.

Typical Dahlgren Guns (Union):

Size	Length (inches)	Weight (gun) (lbs)	Weight (all-up) (lbs)	Projectile weight (lbs)	Caliber (inches)	Range (yards)
12 pdr boat howitzer rifle	63.5	880	1,175*	11	3.4	c. 1,750 at 5°
12 pdr boat howitzer*	39–63	300–750	800–1,500	12	4.62	c. 1,200 at 5°
24 pdr boat howitzer	67	1,310	1,750*	24	5.82	(U)
32 pdr	108	4,500	6,000*	32	6.4	(U)
50 pdr rifle	105	6,000	8,000*	50	5.1	(U)
80 pdr rifle	(U)	7,900	10,650*	80	6.0	(U)
150 pdr rifle	140	16,000	21,350*	150	7.5	(U)
VIII-inch	115.5	6,500	8,650*	52	8.0	2,600 at 10°
IX-inch	131.5	9,000	12,000*	70–90	9.0	3,450 at 15°
X-inch	146	12,000	16,000*	97–125	10.0	3,000 at 11°
XI-inch	161	15,700	21,000*	127–170	11.0	3,400 at 15°
XV-inch	162–178	42,000	56,000*	330–440	15–60	2,100 at 7°

*These weapons were provided in "light", "medium," and "heavy" variants, which explains the wide range in sizes and weights.

Whitworth Guns (Primarily Confederate)

Size	Length (inches)	Weight (gun) (lbs)	Weight (all-up) (lbs)	Proj. weight (lbs)	Caliber (inches)	Range (yards)
32 pdr	c. 100	3,360	4,480*	32	4.0	(U)
70 pdr	133	8,580	11,440*	70	5.0	(U)
120 pdr	c. 160	c. 15,000	20,000*	120	6.4	(U)

Blakely Guns (Primarily Confederate)

Size	Length (inches)	Weight (gun) (lbs)	Weight (all-up) (lbs)	Projectile weight (lbs)	Caliber (inches)	Range (yards)
4.5 inch	96	(U)	(U)	(U)	4.5	(U)
6.3 inch	88.5	(U)	(U)	(U)	6.3	(U)
100 pdr	c. 100	8,000	10,650*	100	6.4	(U)
120 pdr	119.5	9,600	12,800*	120	7.0	(U)
150 pdr	124	(U)	(U)	150	7.25	(U)
200 pdr	136	c. 17,000	22,660*	200	9.0	(U)
250 pdr	150.5	24,000	32,000*	250	11.0	(U)

PROJECTILES

The variety of projectiles utilized by the Union and Confederacy during the war defies succinct description. Experimentation was the rule, and there were, quite literally, hundreds of variants. Most guns could fire quite a variety of types. Solid round shot remained common. Round shells typically had wall thicknesses of about a quarter caliber, and came with a variety of fillings, only some of which were explosive. The old-style, cut wooden time fuzes had, in naval service, usually been replaced with metal designs by the time the war broke out; typical burn times were 5, 10, and 15 seconds. Concussion fuzes (initiated by the concussion of firing) were sometimes used, and percussion fuzes (activated by impact on the target) were common. The need to orient the fuze properly often demanded the addition of a sabot to a round-shot load; this was, of course, unnecessary with elongated shot.

Rifled projectiles were typically two to three calibers long and were often hollowed out to contain a bursting charge; if solid, they were known as "bolts" (so-called curved bolts were heavily cut away around the midsection, yielding an hourglass shape). Bolts used for punching armor were typically marked by slightly curved or flat chamfered noses; shells, none of which were designed to penetrate armor, typically had much more rounded or pointed profiles. The most successful Union elongated shell designs were the teardrop-shaped Schenkl shell with a papier-maché sabot, a splined tapered base, and stubs to engage the rifling; the Hotchkiss projectile, a three-part design with a sliding cup at the base that compressed a lead driving band into the rifling; and the Parrott projectile, equipped with an expanding cup at the base. Most Confederate shells were copies of the Parrott design; similar types were made by Read, Brooke, or Mullane, supplemented by a variety of British designs supplied by Armstrong, Blakely, and Whitworth. Projectiles for rifled guns were often grooved and shaped to mate with somewhat unconventional rifling designs used in the guns that fired them and/or to provide passages for the propellant flame to pass forward and ignite the fuzes. A few long, saboted, subcaliber anti-ironclad bolts, conceptually very advanced for the time, were used successfully by the North.

W. J. Jurens

PART I
United States Navy Warships

1
ARMORED VESSELS

By 1861, the first ironclad warships had been developed in France and Britain; the *Gloire* and *Warrior* were already afloat. Earlier, Robert L. Stevens had started construction of his giant unnamed ironclad warship, known to history as the *Stevens Battery*. This revolutionary design was modified from time to time, but the Navy refused further funds to complete this vessel and it was never finished.

The Navy ordered construction of three experimental ironclads of radically different design in 1861. The first of these revolutionized naval warfare. A low-draft ship without superstructure or rigging, it had only a revolving turret on a flush deck and was aptly described as "the cheese box on a raft." Designed by John Ericsson and named *Monitor*, it presented a very small target area by eliminating all top-hamper and having an extremely low freeboard. The ship was built extremely quickly being launched within 101 days of the keel being laid.

Following the *Monitor*'s stunning success in standing off the Confederate *Virginia* at Hampton Roads in March 1862, the Navy ordered many additional vessels of the Monitor type. The *Passaic* and *Canonicus* classes were basically modified repeat Monitors. Ericsson also designed the larger *Dictator* and the twin-turreted *Puritan*.

Other twin-turret monitors, *Onondaga* and the four near-sisters of the *Monadnock* class, were designed by others. Construction of the larger ocean-going *Kalamazoo* class was suspended at the end of the war and never resumed, as was the similar sized *Puritan*. Many of these ships were built with poorly seasoned timber that quickly deteriorated.

The *Puritan* and the four *Monadnock* class ships remained on the Navy List for many years by the subterfuge of "repairing" the old hulls while actually building new ones. As appropriations did not cover the cost of new monitors, old ships were turned over to the contractors as payment.

Not all the monitor designs were successful. A need for low-draft monitors for river operations led to the disastrous *Casco* class of twenty ships. Because of poor planning and erroneous calculations, they floated with their decks barely above water before being fitted with turrets and other heavy gear. Although a few served as torpedo boats without turrets, most were never used and all were scrapped within about ten years.

The second experimental ironclad ordered in 1861, the *New Ironsides*, was a more conventional armored broadside vessel. Speed was not considered important for the ship, but she suffered practically no damage from enemy fire although hit numerous times. The third vessel was the smaller *Galena*, whose armor proved inadequate against shore batteries; she was quickly converted to an unarmored corvette.

Another curious vessel produced at this time was the *Keokuk*, whose defense against shellfire was so poor that she sank the day after her first day under fire. The monster ironclad ram *Dunderberg*, a broadside vessel similar in design to the Confederate ironclads, was so delayed in construction that she was rejected by the Navy in 1865 and eventually sold to France. The screw frigate *Roanoke* was cut down to the gun deck, armored, and three turrets were mounted on the low hull. The conversion was not successful because the weight of the turrets was too great for the wooden hull.

Fig 1.1: Monitors laid up at Washington Navy Yard, 1866. The ship in the center is either *Casco* or *Chimo* completed without a turret. Right to left behind her are *Montauk*, *Saugus* and *Mahopac* which retain their Civil War distinguishing markings. (U.S. Naval Historical Center)

Fig 1.2: A closeup view of the *Monitor's* turret, 1862, looking forward. Some dents from her battle are visible in the turret. (U.S. Naval Historical Center)

Fig 1.3: The *Monitor* as depicted by Oscar Parkes showing the square funnels added behind the turret later in 1862. (U.S. Naval Historical Center, Norman Polmar Collection)

Of all the new designs, only the monitors seemed to be successful. At Charleston they proved their worth against land batteries; at Mobile Bay they led the fleet into battle. After the war they were laid up and kept as America's ace against foreign attack. Never the equal of foreign ocean-going ironclad warships, their continued existence led to a sense of false security. Some were recommissioned during the 1873 war scare caused by the *Virginius* Affair, and in 1898 those remaining were again commissioned to defend the East Coast against the threat of the Spanish fleet.

Despite many attempts to provide for modern warships, Congress remembered the successes of earlier decades and preferred to rely on the inadequate and obsolete monitors. When the first true American battleships were built, the *Indiana* class of 1890, they were described as coast defense battleships and had a monitorlike low freeboard.

MONITORS

Monitor

Name	Builder	Keel Laid	Launched	Comm.
Monitor	Greenpoint, N.Y. (Continental)	25 Oct 1861	30 Jan 1862	25 Feb 1862
Tonnage	987 tons D; 776 tons B			
Dimensions	179' (oa) × 41'6" × 10'6"			
Machinery	1 screw, Ericsson vibrating-lever (trunk) engine (36" × 2'2"), 2 boilers, IHP 320, 9 knots (Delamater)			
Complement	49			
Armament	2–11" SB guns			
Armor	8" turret, 4.5" sides, 2" deck, 9" pilot house			

Notes: The first ironclad warship built without rigging or sails. One of three experimental ironclads ordered in 1861. Designed by John Ericsson based on his design offered to Napoleon III in 1854. Spindle-type cylindrical turret built by Novelty Iron Works on iron hull (126' × 34') with overhanging armored deck. The iron hull was a box with flat bottom and pointed ends. Hurried to completion and towed to Hampton Roads with workmen still on board. Two square funnels added after March 1862.

Service record: Engaged CSS *Virginia* at Hampton Roads in first action between ironclads, Battle of Hampton Roads, Va., 9 Mar 1862. Engaged batteries at Sewells Point, Va., 8 May and at Drewry's Bluff, Va., 15 May 1862. Engagement with CSS *Teaser* in James River, Va., 4 Jul 1862. Foundered in gale off Cape Hatteras while under tow of USS *Rhode Island*, 31 Dec 1862 (16 lost). The ship's propeller was recovered in 1998, the engine in 2001, and the turret and cannons in 2003. They are on display at the Mariner's Museum.

Roanoke

Name	Converted by	Launched	Recommissioned
Roanoke	Novelty	13 Dec 1855	29 Jun 1863
Tonnage	6,300 tons		
Dimensions	278' (oa) 262'10" (bp) × 53'3" × 24'3", d 26'2"		
Machinery	1 screw, 2-cyl. horizontal direct acting engine, 5 boilers, IHP 997, 7 knots		
Complement	350		
Armament	(forward) 1–15" SB, 1–150 pdr MLR; (middle) 1–15" SB, 1–11" SB; (aft) 1–11" SB, 1–150 pdr MLR		
Armor	11" turrets, 4.5" sides, 3" ends, 2.25" deck, 9" pilot house		

Fig 1.4: The ironclad *Roanoke* out of commission at Brooklyn in 1865. Notice the different size gunports to accommodate the different caliber guns. At left is the receiving ship *Vermont*. (U.S. Naval Historical Center, Norman Polmar Collection)

Fig 1.5: The double-turret monitor *Onondaga* in the James River 1864.

Fig 1.6: The monitor *Camanche* in drydock at Mare Island. She was taken to California in parts and rebuilt there. (U.S. Naval Historical Center)

Notes: Converted from screw frigate cut down to gun deck and armor plated. Ram bow. The only monitor with three turrets; originally planned with four turrets but weight created too great a draft. Weight of turrets caused ship to roll excessively; wooden hull was not strong enough for their weight. Draft was too great for inshore operations but freeboard was too small for ocean cruising. The first ship with more than two turrets on centerline. The guns were arranged in the turrets as indicated above.

Service record: NAtlBS. Harbor defense ship, Hampton Roads 1863–65. Decomm 20 Jun 1865. Recomm 13 Jan 1874–12 Jun 1875. Sold 27 Sep 1883 and BU at Chester, Pa.

Onondaga

Name	Builder	Keel Laid	Launched	Comm.
Onondaga	Greenpoint, N.Y. (Continental)	1862	29 Jul 1863	24 Mar 1864

Tonnage	2,592 tons D; 1,250 tons B
Dimensions	226′(oa) × 51′5″ × 12′10″
Machinery	2 screws, 2 2-cyl. horizontal back-acting engines (30″ × 18′), 4 boilers, IHP 642 , 7 knots (Morgan)
Complement	130
Armament	2–15″ SB, 2–150 pdr MLR
Armor	11.75″ turrets, 5.5″ sides, 1″ deck

Notes: Built under contract by her designer G.W. Quintard. Iron hull with two turrets. Returned to Quintard 1867.

Service record: James River flotilla 1864–65. Engagements at Howlett's, Trent's Reach, Va., 21 Jun and at Dutch Gap, Va., 13 Aug 1864 and 16–18 Aug 1864. Engaged battery at Howlett's Farm, Va., 5–6 Dec 1864. Engagement at Trent's Reach, 24 Jan 1865. Decomm 8 Jun 1865. Sold to France 2 Mar 1867.

Later history: French *Onondaga*. BU 1903.

Passaic Class

Name	Builder	Keel Laid	Launched	Comm.
Camanche	San Francisco, Calif. (Donahue)	1862	14 Nov 1864	24 May 1865
Catskill	Greenpoint, N.Y. (Continental)	1862	16 Dec 1862	24 Feb 1863
Lehigh	Chester, Pa. (Reaney)	1862	17 Jan 1863	15 Apr 1863
Montauk	Greenpoint, N.Y. (Continental)	1862	9 Oct 1862	17 Dec 1862
Nahant	Boston, Mass. (City Point)	1862	7 Oct 1862	29 Dec 1862
Nantucket	Boston, Mass. (Atlantic)	1862	6 Dec 1862	26 Feb 1863
Passaic	Greenpoint, N.Y. (Continental)	1862	30 Aug 1862	25 Nov 1862
Patapsco	Wilmington, Del. (Harlan)	1862	27 Sep 1862	2 Jan 1863
Sangamon ex-Conestoga	Chester, Pa. (Reaney) (9 Sep 1862)	1862	27 Oct 1862	9 Feb 1863
Weehawken	Jersey City, N.J. (Secor)	17 Jun 1862	5 Nov 1862	18 Jan 1863

Tonnage	1,335 tons D; 844 tons B
Dimensions	200′ (bp) × 46′ × 11′6″
Machinery	1 screw, 2-cyl. Ericsson vibrating-lever (trunk) engine (40″ × 1′10″), 2 boilers. IHP 340, 7 knots [*Catskill, Montauk, Passaic*: Delamater; *Lehigh and Sangamon*: Morris Towne; *Camanche, Weehawken*: Colwell; others: Builder]
Complement	67/88
Armament	1–15″ SB, 1–11″ SB guns, except *Camanche*: 2–15″ SB *Catskill, Montauk, Nahant*: (Jan 1865) add 2–12 pdr MLR; all: (1873) 2–15″ SB
Armor	11″ turret, 5″ sides, 1″ deck, 8″ pilot house

Notes: Highly successful class designed by Ericsson, who wanted to name the first six *Impenetrable, Penetrator, Paradox, Gauntlet, Palladium,* and *Agitator*. Improved monitor with pilot house located on top of turret and a permanent smoke pipe. The first ships to mount the 15″ gun, which did not project from the turret. Gun ports had to be opened to reload guns, and turrets were liable to jam if struck near the base. Had colored bands on turrets to distinguish. After war, deck raised 15″.

Some units rebuilt 1871–75.

Service records

Camanche: Built by Secor in Jersey City, then shipped in parts to San Francisco aboard ship *Aquila*, which sank there at her pier 14 Nov 1863. Reassembled by Union Iron Works.†

Fig 1.7: Officers relax on board the monitor *Catskill* in Charleston harbor, 1865. The light colored paint on the turret was an identification mark. The 11-inch gun protrudes from the turret, not visible is the 15-inch gun. (U.S. Naval Historical Center, Norman Polmar Collection)

Fig 1.8: USS *Passaic*, laid up after war. The class namesake had an active war; notice dents in the turret from Confederate hits.

Catskill: SAtlBS 1863–65. Bombardment of Charleston forts, 7 Apr, off Fort Wagner, Charleston, 10–11 Jul and 18 Jul–8 Sep 1863. Hit by enemy fire, captain (G.W. Rodgers) killed, 17 Aug 1863. Decomm 26 Jul 1865. Renamed **Goliath**, 15 Jun 1869. Renamed **Catskill** 10 Aug 1869. N. Atlantic Sqn 1876–77.†

Ships captured: str *Prince Albert*, 9 Aug 1864; str *Celt* and str *Deer*, 18 Feb 1865.

Lehigh: NAtlBS 1863. Expedition up James River, Va., 6–20 Jul 1863. SAtlBS Aug 1863. Bombardment of Charleston forts, 1–8 Sep 1863, hit many times, and of Fort Sumter, 26 Oct–4 Nov 1863. Expedition up Stono River, SC, 5 Jul 1864 and up Stono and Folly rivers, 9–14 Feb 1865. James River Mar 1865. Decomm 9 Jun 1865. Practice ship, Naval Academy 1875–76. N. Atlantic Sqn 1876–79.†

Ship captured: str **Presto*. 2 Feb 1864.

Montauk: SAtlBS Jan 1863. Engaged battery at Fort McAllister, Ga., 27 Jan (hit 14 times) and 1 Feb (hit 48 times), 1863. Bombardment of Fort McAllister, damaged by torpedo during engagement with CSS *Nashville*, 28 Feb 1863. Bombardment of Charleston forts, 7 Apr and of Fort Wagner, Charleston, 10 Jul–4 Aug 1863. Expedition up Stono River, SC, 5 Jul 1864. Bombardment of Fort Anderson, Cape Fear River, 11–21 Feb 1865. Decomm 1865.†

Nahant: SAtlBS 1863. Bombardment of Fort McAllister, Ga., 3 Mar 1863. Bombardment of Charleston forts, 7 Apr 1863, hit 36 times, turret jammed. Engagement with CSS *Atlanta*, Wassaw Sound, Ga., 17 Jun 1863. Bombardment of Fort Wagner, Charleston, Jul–Aug 1863. Decomm 11 Aug 1865. Renamed **Atlas**, 15 Jun 1869. Renamed **Nahant**, 10 Aug 1869.†

Ship captured: str *Presto*. Feb 1865.

Nantucket: SAtlBS 1863. Bombardment of Charleston forts (hit 51 times), 7 Apr and of Fort Wagner, Charleston, 18 Jul–8 Sep 1863. Decomm 24 Jun 1865. Renamed **Medusa**, 15 Jun 1869. Renamed **Nantucket**, 10 Aug 1869. Recomm 1882 and 1884.†

Ship captured: str *Jupiter.*, 13 Sep 1863.

Passaic: NAtlBS 1863. Bombardment of Fort McAllister, Ga., 3 Mar 1863. Damaged during bombardment of Charleston forts, 7 Apr 1863. Bombardment of New Smyrna, Fla., 28 Jul 1863. Bombardment of Charleston forts, Aug–Sep 1863. Decomm 16 Jun 1865. Recomm 1876. Receiving ship, Washington, 1878–82, Annapolis 1883–92, and Boston NYd 1893–94.†

Ships captured: *Glide*,. 23 Feb 1863; str **Presto*, 2 Feb 1864

Patapsco: NAtlBS 1863. Bombardment of Fort McAllister, Ga., 3 Mar 1863. Bombardment of Charleston forts, 7 Apr and of Fort Wagner and Charleston forts, Jul–Oct 1863. Hit a torpedo (mine) and sank in Charleston River, 16 Jan 1865 (62 killed).

Ship captured: *Swift*, 9 Feb 1864

Sangamon: NAtlBS 1863. James River flotilla 1863. Expeditions up James River, 6–20 Jul and 4–7 Aug 1863. SAtlBS 1864. Decomm mid-1865. Renamed *Jason*, 15 Jun 1869.†

Weehawken: SAtlBS 1863. Bombardment of Charleston forts (hit 53 times), 7 Apr 1863. Engagement with CSS *Atlanta*, Wassaw Sound, Ga., 17 Jun 1863. Bombardment of Fort Wagner and Charleston forts, Jul–Oct 1863. Went aground under fire at Charleston, 8 Sep 1863. Foundered off Morris Island, Charleston, 6 Dec 1863 (31 lost).

Canonicus Class

Name	Builder	Keel Laid	Launched	Comm.
Canonicus	Boston, Mass. (City Point)	1862	1 Aug 1863	16 Apr 1864
Catawba	Cincinnati, Ohio (Swift)	1862	13 Apr 1864	10 Jun 1865*
Mahopac	Jersey City, N.J. (Secor)	1862	17 May 1864	22 Sep 1864
Manayunk	Pittsburgh, Pa. (Snowden & Mason)	1862	18 Dec 1864	27 Sep 1865*

Fig 1.9: The monitor *Tecumseh* ready for launching at the Secor yard in Jersey City. At right is her sister ship *Manhattan* launched the following month. This is the only known photograph of the *Tecumseh* which was sunk at Mobile Bay.

Fig 1.10: The monitor *Canonicus* with a schooner alongside. This class was more heavily armed than the *Passaic* class. Notice the stripe on the turret; monitors had markings of different colors to distinguish them. (U.S. Naval Historical Center)

Manhattan	Williamsburg, N.Y. (Perine)	1862	14 Oct 1863	6 Jun 1864
Oneota	Cincinnati, Ohio (Swift)	1862	21 May 1864	10 Jun 1865*
Saugus	Wilmington, Del. (Harlan)	1862	16 Dec 1863	7 Apr 1864
Tecumseh	Jersey City, N.J. (Secor)	1862	12 Sep 1863	19 Apr 1864
Tippecanoe	Cincinnati, Ohio (Greenwood)	22 Sep 1862	22 Dec 1864	15 Feb 1866*
Tonnage	2,100 tons D; 1,034 tons B.			
Dimensions	235′ (oa) × 43′8″ × 13′6″ (*Catawba, Oneota* 225′ × 43′3″; *Tippecanoe* 224′ × 43′ × 11′6″; *Mahopac, Manhattan, Tecumseh* 223′ × 43′4″).			
Machinery	1 screw, 2-cyl. Ericsson vibrating-lever engine (48″ × 2′). 4 boilers, IHP 320, 8 knots. (*Catawba, Oneota:* Niles; *Mahopac, Manhattan, Tecumseh,* Colwell, others bldr)			
Complement	85			
Armament	2–15″ SB guns *Canonicus* (1865) add 2–12 pdr			
Armor	10″ turret, 5″ sides, 1.5″ deck			

Notes: Enlarged Passaic class. *Catawba* and *Oneota* were never commissioned. *Canonicus* and *Wyandotte* rebuilt 1872–74. *Wyandotte, Ajax,* and *Manhattan* had hurricane decks added in 1870s.

Service records

Canonicus: James River flotilla 1864. Engagement at Howlett's, Trent's Reach, Va., 21 Jun, at Dutch Gap, Va., 16–18 Aug and at Howlett's Farm, Va., 5–6 Dec 1864. NAtlBS Dec 1864. Unsuccessful attack on Fort Fisher, N.C., 24–25 Dec 1864. Second attack on Fort Fisher, 13–15 Jan 1865, hit 36 times. SAtlBS Feb 1865 off Charleston. Decomm 30 Jun 1865. Renamed *Scylla*, 15 Jun 1869. Renamed *Canonicus*, 10 Aug 1869. Atlantic coast cruises, 1872–77. Decomm 1877. Steamer *Shannon* sank after colliding with *Canonicus* when anchored at New Orleans, 10 Mar 1878.†

Ship captured: str *Deer*, 18 Feb 1865.

Catawba: No active service. Sold to Peru, 2 Apr 1868.

Later history: Peruvian *Atahualpa*. Scuttled at Callao to prevent capture by Chile, 16 Jan 1880. Refloated and hulked. BU 1900s.

Mahopac: SAtlBS 1864–65. Engaged battery at Howlett's Farm, Va., 5–6 Dec 1864. Unsuccessful attack on Fort Fisher, N.C., 24–25 Dec 1864. Second attack on Fort Fisher, 13–15 Jan 1865. Advance on Richmond, Apr 1865. Decomm Jun 1865. Recomm 1866–72. Renamed *Castor*, 15 Jun 1869. Renamed *Mahopac*, 10 Aug 1869.†

Manayunk: Laid up at Mound City, Ill. until 1867, then New Orleans. La. Renamed *Ajax*, 15 Jun 1869. First comm 1 Jan 1871. N. Atlantic Sqn 1871, 1874–76.†

Manhattan: GulfBS 1864. Battle of Mobile Bay, 5 Aug 1864. Bombardment of Fort Morgan, Mobile Bay, 9–23 Aug 1864. Laid up Aug 1865. Renamed *Neptune*, 15 Jun 1869. Renamed *Manhattan*, 10 Aug 1869. Recomm 1873–77.†

Oneota: No active service. Sold to Peru, 2 Apr 1868.

Later history: Peruvian *Manco Capac*. Blown up at Arica to prevent capture by Chile, 7 Jun 1880.

Saugus: NAtlBS 1864. James River flotilla. Engagement at Howlett's, Trent's Reach, Va., 21 Jun, at Dutch Gap, Va., 13 Aug and at Howlett's Farm, Va., 5–6 Dec 1864. Unsuccessful attack on Fort Fisher, N.C., 24–25 Dec 1864. Damaged by bursting of 15-inch gun and several enemy hits at Second attack on Fort Fisher, 13–15 Jan 1865. Decomm 13 Jun 1865. Recomm 30 Apr 1869. Renamed *Centaur*, 15 Jun 1869. Renamed *Saugus*, 10 Aug 1869. Decomm 31 Dec 1870. Recomm 1872–76. Decomm 8 Oct 1877.†

Tecumseh: NAtlBS 1864. James River flotilla. Engagement at Howlett's, Trent's Reach, Va., 21 Jun 1864. WGulfBS Jul 1864. Struck a torpedo (mine) and sank during Battle of Mobile Bay, 5 Aug 1864 (93 killed).

Tippecanoe: Laid up at New Orleans. Renamed *Vesuvius*, 15 Jun 1869. Renamed *Wyandotte*, 10 Aug 1869. First comm 24 Jan 1876. N. Atlantic Sqn 1876–79. Station ship, Washington, D.C. 1879–85.†

*Delivered.

Fig 1.11: *Monadnock*, at Mare Island 1866 after an epic voyage around Cape Horn. She was the only one of her class to see active service during the war. Notice the built up bow and mast fitted for the ocean trip. (Dr. Francis J. Ducoin Collection)

Fig 1.12: Near sisters *Miantonomoh* and *Terror* at Portland, Maine, January 1870. Flags are at half-mast to honor the funeral fleet carrying the body of the noted merchant and philanthropist George M. Peabody who had died in England. (Peabody Essex Museum)

Monadnock Class

A four-ship class of double-turret monitors designed by Lenthall: *Agamenticus*, *Monadnock*, *Miantonomoh*, and *Tonawanda*.

Name	Builder	Keel Laid	Launched	Comm.
Agamenticus	Portsmouth NYd	1862	19 Mar 1863	5 May 1865
Monadnock	Boston NYd	1862	23 Mar 1864	4 Oct 1864

Tonnage	3,295 tons D; 1,564 tons B.
Dimensions	*Monadnock*: 250' (bp) × 52'6" × 12'3".
Agamenticus:	251' (bp) × 52' × d 15'6"
Machinery	2 screws, 2 2-cyl. Ericsson vibrating-lever engines (32" × 1'8"), 4 boilers, IHP 1400, 9 knots (Morris)
Complement	167
Armament	4–15" SB guns
Armor	11" turrets, 4.5" sides, 1.5" deck, 8" pilot house

Notes: Double turret monitors designed by Lenthall with wooden hulls that deteriorated rapidly; "rebuilt" 1874. *Agamenticus* had hurricane deck added between turrets prior to completion. Good sea boats. *Monadnock* had 3½' wood bulwark built on deck and a foremast for voyage to West Coast.

Service records

Agamenticus: Decomm 30 Sep 1865. Renamed *Terror*, 15 May 1869. Recomm. 27 May 1869. N. Atlantic fleet 1870–72. Decomm 10 Jun 1872. BU 1874. (Officially rebuilt as BM 4.)

Monadnock: NAtlBS 1864–65. Unsuccessful attack on Fort Fisher, N.C., 24–25 Dec 1864. Second attack on Fort Fisher, 13–15 Jan 1865. Supported final assault on Richmond, Apr 1865. Voyaged to Pacific coast, rounding Cape Horn, 1865–66. Decomm 30 Jun 1866. BU 1874. (Officially rebuilt as BM 3.)

Ship captured: str *Deer*, 18 Feb 1865.

Name	Builder	Keel Laid	Launched	Comm.
Miantonomoh	Brooklyn NYd	1862	15 Aug 1863	18 Sep 1865

Tonnage	3,401 tons D; 1,564 tons B.
Dimensions	250' (oa) × 53'8" × d16', 14'9"
Machinery	2 screws, 2 2-cyl. horizontal back-acting engines (30" × 2'3"), 4 boilers. NHP 800, 9 knots (*Novelty*)
Complement	150
Armament	4–15"SB guns
Armor	11" turrets, 4.5" sides, 1.5" deck, 8" pilot house.

Notes: Twin turret monitor, engines by Isherwood. Excellent sea boat.

Service record: N. Atlantic Sqn 1865. Cruise to European waters 1866–67. Recomm 15 Nov 1869. Sank schooner *Sarah* in collision at New York, 4 Dec 1869. Sank tug USS *Maria* in collision off Martha's Vineyard, 4 Jan 1870. Decomm 28 Jul 1870. BU 1874. (Officially rebuilt as BM 5.)

Name	Builder	Keel Laid	Launched	Comm.
Tonawanda	Philadelphia NYd	1863	6 May 1864	12 Oct 1865

Tonnage	3,400 tons D; 1,564 tons B.
Dimensions	259'6 (oa) 256' (bp) × 52'10" × d14', 13'5"
Machinery	2 screws, 4 inclined back-acting engines (30" × 1'9"). 4 boilers. (Merrick)
	150
Armament	4–15" SB guns
Armor	11" turrets, 4.5" sides, 1.5" deck, 8" pilot house.

Notes: Engines by Isherwood. Least successful of the class.

Service record: Training ship, Annapolis, 1866–72. Renamed *Amphitrite*, 15 May 1869. BU 1874 at Wilmington, Del. (Officially rebuilt as BM 2)

Dictator

Name	Builder	Keel Laid	Launched	Comm.
Dictator	New York, N.Y. (Delameter)	16 Aug 1862	26 Dec 1863	11 Nov 1864

Tonnage	4,438 tons D; 3,033 tons B.
Dimensions	312' (bp) × 50' × 20'6"

Fig 1.13: The twin turret *Tonawanda* moored at Annapolis in 1870. Her turrets were closer together than others of the class. (U.S. Naval Historical Center)

Fig 1.14: USS *Dictator* at anchor at an unidentified port about 1865. The tall structure aft is a ventilator. (Collection of the New-York Historical Society)

Machinery	1 screw, 2-cyl. Ericsson vibrating-lever engine (100″ × 4′), IHP 3,500, 9 knots (builder)
Complement	174
Armament	2–15″SB guns
Armor	15″ turret, 6″ sides, 1.5″ deck, 12″ pilot house

Notes: Single turret. Forward overhang of upper hull omitted. Supports for main shaft were inadequate, requiring new fittings before ship could go into active service. Excellent sea boat but had low speed and endurance. Designed by Ericsson as *Protector*. Launched on third attempt.

Service record: NAtlBS 1864-65. Decomm 5 Sep 1865. N. Atlantic Sqn 1869–71, 1874–77. Decomm 1 Jun 1877. Sold 27 Sep 1883 and BU.

Puritan

Name	Builder	Keel Laid	Launched	Comm.
Puritan	Greenpoint, N.Y. (Continental)	1863	2 Jul 1864	never

Tonnage	4,912 tons D; 3,265 tons B.
Dimensions	340′ (oa) × 50′ × 20′
Machinery	2 screws, 2-cyl. Ericsson vibrating-lever engine (100″ × 4′), 6 boilers, 15 knots (designed) (Allaire)
Armament	2-20″SB guns (designed)
Armor	15″ turret, 6″ sides, 12″ pilot house

Notes: The largest of Ericsson's monitors, a longer *Dictator*. Originally designed with two turrets, redesigned in 1865 with one. Never completed, armament was never mounted. Officially "rebuilt" after 1874 as a new ship (BM 1).

Service record: Construction suspended 1865.

Kalamazoo Class

Name	Builder	Keel Laid	Launched	Comm.
Kalamazoo	Brooklyn NYd	1863	never	never
Passaconaway	Portsmouth NYd	18 Nov 1863	never	never
Quinsigamond	Boston NYd	15 Apr 1864	never	never
Shackamaxon	Philadelphia NYd	1863	never	never

Tonnage	5,660 tons D; 3,200 tons B.
Dimensions	345′5″ (oa) 332′6″ (bp) × 56′8″ × 17′6″
Machinery	2 screws, 2 2-cyl. horizontal direct acting engines (46.5″ × 4′2″), 8 boilers, 10 knots (designed) (*Kalamazoo, Passaconaway:* Delamater, *Quinsigamond:* Atlantic, *Shackamaxon:* Pusey)
Armament	4-15″ SB guns
Armor	10″ turrets, 6″ sides, 3″ deck

Notes: Double-turret monitors, hull designed by Benjamin F. Delano, and machinery by John Baird, adapted for ocean cruising. None was ever launched; hulls built of poorly seasoned wood, which rotted on the stocks.

Service records

Kalamazoo: Construction suspended 17 Nov 1865. Renamed *Colossus*, 15 Jun 1869. BU on the stocks 1884.

Passaconaway: Construction suspended 17 Nov 1865. Renamed *Thunderer*, 15 Jun 1869. Renamed *Massachusetts*, 10 Aug 1869. BU on the stocks 1884.

Quinsigamond: Construction suspended 17 Nov 1865. Renamed *Hercules*, 15 Jun 1869. Renamed *Oregon*, 10 Aug 1869. BU on the stocks 1884.

Shackamaxon: Construction suspended 17 Nov 1865, with armor and machinery in place. Renamed *Hecla*, 15 Jun 1869. Renamed *Nebraska*, 10 Aug 1869. BU on the stocks 1874.

Casco Class

Name	Builder	Keel Laid	Launched	Comm.
Casco	Boston, Mass. (Atlantic)	1863	7 May 1864	4 Dec 1864
Chimo	Boston, Mass. (Adams)	1863	5 May 1864	20 Jan 1865
Cohoes	Greenpoint, N.Y. (Continental)	1863	31 May 1865	19 Jan 1866*
Etlah	St. Louis, Mo. (McCord)	1863	3 Jul 1865	12 Mar 1866*
Klamath	Cincinnati, Ohio (Swift)	1863	10 Apr 1865	6 May 1866*

Koka	Camden, N.J. (Wilcox)	1863	18 May 1865	18 Nov 1865*
Modoc	New York, N.Y. (Underhill)	1863	21 Mar 1865	23 Jun 1865**
Napa	Wilmington, Del. (Harlan)	1863	26 Nov 1864	4 May 1865**
Naubuc	Jersey City, N.J. (Perine)	1863	19 Oct 1864	17 Mar 1865
Nausett	Boston, Mass. (McKay)	1863	26 Apr 1865	10 Aug 1865
Shawnee	Boston, Mass. (Curtis & Tilden)	1863	13 Mar 1865	18 Aug 1865
Shiloh	St. Louis, Mo. (McCord)	1863	14 Jul 1865	12 Mar 1866*
Squando	Boston, Mass. (McKay)	1863	31 Dec 1864	6 Jun 1865
Suncook	Boston, Mass. (Globe)	1863	1 Feb 1865	17 Jul 1865
Tunxis	Chester, Pa. (Reaney)	1863	4 Jun 1864	12 Jul 1864
Umpqua	Pittsburgh, Pa. (Snowden & Mason)	1863	12 Dec 1864	7 May 1866**
Wassuc	Thomaston, Me. Maine (Lawrence)	1863	25 Jul 1865	28 Oct 1865**
Waxsaw	Baltimore, Md. (Denmead)	1863	4 May 1865	21 Oct 1865**
Yazoo	Philadelphia, Pa. (Cramp)	1863	8 May 1865	15 Dec 1865**
Yuma	Cincinnati, Ohio (Swift)	1863	30 May 1865	6 May 1866*

Tonnage	1,175 tons D; 614 tons B., except *Squando* 1,618 tons D; *Nausett* 1,487 tons D.
Dimensions	225′ × 45′ × d8′4″, except torpedo boats, 6′6″
Machinery	2 screws, 2 inclined direct-acting engines (22″ × 2′6″). 2 boilers, IHP 600, 9 knots. (*Cohoes*: Hews, *Klamath*: Moore, *Naubuc*: Dolan, *Yazoo*: Merrick, others: builder)
Complement	69
Armament	1–11″SB gun, except *Cohoes, Shawnee, Squando, Wassuc*, 2–11″SB; *Tunxis* 1–11″SB, 1–150 pdr MLR; *Casco, Napa, Naubuc* 1–11″SB, 1 spar torpedo; *Chimo* 1–150 pdr MLR, 1 spar torpedo; *Modoc*, 1 spar torpedo.
Armor	8″ turret, 3″ deck, 10″ pilot house

Notes: Single-turret monitors with turtleback deck, designed by Stimers with light draft to operate in shallow rivers. Design changes caused errors resulting in only 3″ of freeboard without turret and stores, and the deck was raised 22″ before completion. *Chimo* and *Tunxis* almost foundered on maiden voyage. Modifications caused delay in completion; most were delivered after war's end and laid up with no active service. *Casco, Chimo, Modoc, Napa*, and *Naubuc* were completed as torpedo boats armed with spar torpedoes without built-up deck or turrets. Those completed after the war were immediately laid up.

Service records

Casco: James River 1865. Decomm 10 Jun 1865. Renamed **Hero**, 15 Jun 1869. BU Apr 1875 at Washington.

Chimo: Station ship, Point Lookout, NC 1865. Decomm 24 Jun 1865. Renamed **Orion**, 15 Jun 1869. Renamed **Piscataqua**, 10 Aug 1869. Sold 1874 and BU.

Cohoes: Laid up 1867. Renamed **Charybdis**, 15 Jun 1869. Renamed **Cohoes**, 10 Aug 1869. Sold Jul 1874.

Etlah: Laid up 1866. Renamed **Hecate**, 15 Jun 1869. Renamed **Etlah**, 10 Aug 1869. Sold 12 Sep 1874.

Klamath: Laid up 1866. Renamed **Harpy**, 15 Jun 1869. Renamed **Klamath**, 10 Aug 1869. Sold 12 Sep 1874.

Koka: Construction suspended 17 Jun 1865 and laid up. Renamed **Argos**, 15 Jun 1869. Renamed **Koka**, 10 Aug 1869. BU Oct 1874.

Modoc: Laid up on completion. Renamed **Achilles**, 15 Jun 1869. Renamed **Modoc**, 10 Aug 1869. Sold and BU Aug 1875.

Napa: Laid up on completion 1865. Renamed **Nemesis**, 15 Jun 1869. Renamed **Napa**, 10 Aug 1869. BU 1875.

Naubuc: Decomm 27 Jun 1865. Renamed **Gorgon**, 15 Jun 1869. Renamed **Minnetonka**, 10 Aug 1869. BU 1875.

Nausett: Decomm 24 Aug 1865. Renamed **Aetna**, 15 Jun 1869. Renamed **Nausett**, 10 Aug 1869. BU Aug 1875.

Shawnee: Laid up Nov 1865. Renamed **Eolus**, 15 Jun 1869. Renamed **Shawnee**, 10 Aug 1869. Sold 9 Sep 1875 and BU.

Shiloh: Construction suspended 17 Jun 1865. Laid up 1866. Renamed **Iris**, 15 Jun 1869. In comm 1874. Sold 1874.

Squando: N. Atlantic Sqn 1865–66. Decomm 26 May 1866. Renamed **Erebus**, 15 Jun 1869. Renamed **Algoma**, 10 Aug 1869. Sold 1 Jul 1874 and BU.

Suncook: Laid up on completion. Renamed **Spitfire**, 15 Jun 1869. Renamed **Suncook**, 10 Aug 1869. Sold Jul 1874 and BU.

Tunxis: Rebuilt by Cramp 1864-66 and laid up 1866. Renamed **Hydra**, 15 Jun 1869. Renamed **Otsego**, 10 Aug 1869. BU 1874.

Umpqua: Laid up on completion. Renamed **Fury**, 15 Jun 1869. Renamed **Umpqua**, 10 Aug 1869. Sold 12 Sep 1874.

Wassuc: Laid up on completion. Renamed **Stromboli**, 15 Jun 1869. Renamed **Wassuc**, 10 Aug 1869. Sold 9 Sep 1875 and BU.

Waxsaw: Laid up on delivery. Renamed **Niobe**, 15 Jun 1869. Sold 25 Aug 1875 and BU.

Yazoo: Laid up on delivery. Renamed **Tartar**, 15 Jun 1869. Renamed **Yazoo**, 10 Aug 1869. Sold 5 Sep 1874.

Yuma: Laid up on delivery. Renamed **Tempest**, 15 Jun 1869, Renamed **Yuma**, 10 Aug 1869. Sold 12 Sep 1874.

*delivered
**completed

Fig 1.15: *Casco*-class monitors *Shawnee* and *Wassuc*, laid up at Charleston Navy Yard, 1871-72. (U.S. Naval Historical Center)

Fig 1.16: The torpedo boat *Casco* in the James River 1865, built as a monitor. The 11-inch gun is mounted without a turret and spar torpedo apparatus is on the bow. (U.S. Naval Historical Center)

Fig 1.17: The *New Ironsides* as she appeared during the war with masts and rigging removed and funnel lowered. She was even more difficult to handle at sea in this condition than with masts. Notice the pronounced tumblehome amidships. (Dr. Charles L. Peery Collection)

IRONCLADS

"Stevens Battery"

Name	Builder	Keel Laid	Launched	Comm.
(unnamed)	Hoboken, N.J. (Stevens)	1854	never	never
Tonnage	4,683 tons			
Dimensions	420' × 53' × 20'6"			
Machinery	2 screws, 8 vertical overhead beam engines, 10 boilers, IHP 8624 (Delamater)			
Armament	5–15" Rodman MLR, 2–10"MLR (proposed)			
Armor	6.75"			

Notes: Designed by Robert L. Stevens and laid down by him but never completed or named. Offer to complete vessel rejected by the Navy 1861. After the Civil War, title passed to others and the design was modified as a ram with an Ericsson turret, new machinery and boilers, but Congress refused to appropriate funds and the vessel was finally broken up on the stocks.
Service record: BU on stocks 1874–75.

New Ironsides

Name	Builder	Keel Laid	Launched	Comm.
New Ironsides	Philadelphia, Pa. (Cramp)	Nov 1861	10 May 1862	21 Aug 1862
Tonnage	4,120 tons D; 3,486 tons B.			
Dimensions	232' (oa) × 57'6" × 15'8"			
Machinery	1 screw, 2-cyl. horizontal direct-acting engine (50" × 2'6"), 4 boilers, HP 700, 6 knots (Merrick)			
Complement	460			
Armament	2–150pdr MLR, 2–50pdr MLR, 14–11"SB, 1–12pdr MLR, 1–12pdrSB. (Oct 1864) 2–50pdr MLR replaced by 2–60pdr MLR.			
Armor	3 to 4.5" sides, 1" deck, 10" conning tower			

Notes: One of three experimental ironclads ordered in 1861. Light draft wood-hull casemate ironclad with ram bow designed by B.H. Bartol for Merrick Co. Had unusually extreme length-to-beam ratio. Too slow for sea duty but was practically invulnerable to enemy fire. Originally had bark rig but masts were removed and replaced with light poles Jan 1863. Did not make designed speed of 9.5 knots.
Service record: SAtlBS Jan 1863. Bombardment of Charleston forts (hit 50 times), 7 Apr and of Fort.Wagner, Charleston, 18 Jul–8 Sep 1863. Slightly damaged by spar torpedo explosion of torpedo boat CSS *David*, 5 Oct 1863. Unsuccessful attack on Fort Fisher, N.C., 24–25 Dec 1864. Second attack on Fort Fisher, 13-15 Jan 1865. Decomm 6 Apr 1865. Destroyed by fire at League Island, 16 Dec 1866.

Galena

Name	Builder	Keel Laid	Launched	Comm.
Galena	Mystic, Conn. (Maxson Fish)	1861	14 Feb 1862	21 Apr 1862
Tonnage	950 tons D, 738 tons B.			
Dimensions	210' (oa) 180' (bp) × 36' × 11', d12'8"			
Machinery	1 screw, 2-cyl. Ericsson vibrating-lever engine (48" × 3'), 2 boilers, HP 800, 8 knots (Delamater)			
Complement	150			
Armament	2–100pdr MLR, 4–9"SB; (Apr 1864) 1–100pdr MLR, 1–30pdr MLR, 8–9"SB, 1–12pdrH.; (Apr 1865) 1–100pdr MLR replaced by 1–60pdr MLR.			
Armor	3.12" sides			

Notes: Third of three experimental ironclads authorized in 1861. Designed by S.H. Pook for C.S. Bushnell and Co. Ironclad wood corvette with tumblehome sides and armor of interlocking iron bars; two-mast schooner rig. Armor and engines installed at Greenpoint, NY. Armor was considered unsuccessful when ship was hit by plunging fire at almost right angles, and it was removed in 1863. Converted to unarmored screw sloop with three-mast ship rig.
Service record: NAtlBS 1862. Severely damaged during engagement at Drewry's Bluff, Va., 15 May 1862 (13 killed). Undergoing conversion 1863–64, recomm 15 Feb 1864. WGulfBS May 1864. Battle of Mobile Bay, 5 Aug 1864. Bomb of Fort Morgan, Mobile Bay, 9–23 Aug 1864. EGulfBS Apr–Nov 1864. NAtlBS Apr 1865. Decomm 17 Jun 1865. BU 1872. "Repaired" as new ship.

Fig 1.18: The ironclad steamer *Galena* as built as depicted by R.G. Skerrett. No photographs exist of the entire ship which was completely rebuilt in 1863 following her disastrous initial engagement. (U.S. Naval Historical Center)

Fig 1.19: The ironclad *Dunderberg* in service in the French Navy as *Rochambeau*. This view looking forward shows the casemate pierced with gunports. (Photomatic)

Dunderberg

Name	Builder	Keel Laid	Launched	Comm.
Dunderberg	New York (Webb)	4 Oct 1862	22 Jul 1865	never
Tonnage	7,060 tons D; 5,090 tons B.			
Dimensions	377′4″ (oa) 358′8″ (bp) × 72′9″ × 21′			
Machinery	1 screw, 2 horizontal back-acting engines (100″ × 3′9″), 6 boilers , IHP 4,500, 15 knots (Etna)			
Armament	4–15″SB, 8–11″SB guns (designed)			
Armor	3.5″ sides, 4.5″ casemates			

Notes: Seagoing ironclad frigate ram designed by Lenthall as a reproduction of CSS *Virginia* with sloping armored casemate sides and a 50-foot ram. Original plan included two turrets. Had double bottom and collision bulkheads. The longest wooden ship ever built. Not accepted by the Navy and returned to builder, Sep 1866. Purchased by France to prevent Prussia buying the vessel.

Later history: Sold to France, Jul 1867. Renamed ***Rochambeau***. Rebuilt and rearmed 1867. BU 1874.

Keokuk

Name	Builder	Keel Laid	Launched	Comm.
Keokuk ex-*Moodna*	New York, N.Y. (Underhill)	19 Apr 1862	6 Dec 1862	Mar 1863
Tonnage	677 tons B.			
Dimensions	159′6″ (oa) × 36′ × 9′3″			
Machinery	2 screws, 1 4-cyl. horizontal direct-acting condensing engine (23″ × 1′8″), 3 boilers, 9 knots (bldr)			
Complement	92			
Armament	2–11″SB.			
Armor	4″ hull			

Notes: Designed by Charles W. Whitney with guns mounted in two stationary cylindrical towers each with three gun ports. Turtleback hull. Armor of horizontal layers of timber and iron bars was unsuccessful.

Service record: SAtlBS 1863. Bombardment of Charleston forts (hit over 90 times), 7 Apr 1863. Foundered next day off Morris Island, 8 Apr 1863.

Note: Confederate ironclads *Atlanta* and *Tennessee* were commissioned after being captured and served actively during the war.

The spar torpedo boat *Stromboli* (later *Spuyten Duyvil*) was also armored (see p. 40.)

2
UNARMORED STEAM VESSELS

The first steam warships were driven by paddle wheels, but screw-propelled ships were much more efficient for naval purposes. In particular, the large paddle boxes interfered with the placement of the guns that were traditionally sited along the ship's broadside. Development of low-pressure and more powerful engines enabled propeller-driven ships to move faster. In addition, the engines could be placed below the waterline for better protection against enemy gunfire.

The Navy built several side-wheel warships, and among the earliest were the frigates *Missouri* and *Mississippi* of 1840. Although the *Missouri* was soon destroyed by fire, succeeding vessels, notably the *Susquehanna* and *Powhatan*, were especially successful and efficient ships. In 1847 the paddle wheeler *Saranac* and propeller *San Jacinto* were built as competitive sisters. In all tests between paddle wheel and propeller-driven ships, the propeller won and soon permanently displaced the earlier system.

In 1854 six large screw frigates were built: the five ships of the *Merrimack* class and the *Niagara*. On her first cruise to Europe, the *Merrimack* created a sensation in naval circles with battery and steaming endurance greater than contemporary European frigates. The *Hartford* class of steam sloops in 1858 again combined superior firepower with high endurance on a smaller hull.

A large number of sturdy steam sloops were built during the war. In addition smaller warships known as double-enders and 90-day gunboats were produced in large numbers and served throughout the war. Hastily built, they wore out quickly.

A series of new vessels was ordered toward the end of the war that sought to utilize the lessons learned during the war. Unfortunately, most of these were built with unseasoned timber, and the hulls deteriorated very quickly. These included the swift cruisers of the *Ammonoosuc* class, the frigates of the *Java* class, and the sloops of the *Contoocook* and *Algoma* classes. Only a few were actually completed, and all soon disappeared from the Navy List.

Of the cruisers designed for high speed, the *Wampanoag* attained a sustained speed of 17 knots on her trials, a speed unequalled by steam vessels until that time. Nevertheless the ships were never put into service and were the subject of some controversy. It was said the engines were too powerful for the frame, and fuel consumption was so great that the space required for coal left no room for sufficient ammunition.

The majority of the ships of these classes were broken up on the stocks, and those that were completed had very short careers.

Most of the ships of the *Swatara* and *Enterprise* classes were built under the guise of "repairing" older ships because this was the only way to obtain authorization of funds. Only the frigate *Trenton*, laid down in 1875, was built as a new ship.

Figure 2.1: A view of the New York Navy Yard probably taken during the summer of 1866. At left is the cruiser *Wampanoag* fitting out with a gunboat alongside, *Madawaska*, with *Susquehanna* outboard. The *Idaho* is at right with two gunboats inboard and the receiving ship *Vermont* behind. (U.S. Naval Historical Center)

SHIPS ON NAVY LIST, 1855

The following steamships acquired prior to 1855 were still on the Navy List at the outbreak of the Civil War. For full details, see *The Sailing Navy*.

Fig 2.2: The frigate *Saranac* anchored at an unidentified West Coast port. She was wrecked in 1875. (U.S. Naval Historical Center)

Fig 2.3: The paddle frigate *Powhatan* at anchor with a small tug alongside. (U.S. Naval Historical Center)

Side-Wheel Frigates

Mississippi

Launched:	5 May 1841
Armament:	(May 1861) 1–9″ SB, 10–8″/63, 1–12pdr; (Nov 1862) 1–10″ SB, 19–8″ SB/63, 1–20pdr MLR″

Service record: Blockading operations off Key West, Jun 1861. Passage past New Orleans forts and engagement with CSN vessels, 24 Apr 1862. Went aground during attempt to pass Port Hudson, was burned to prevent capture, later magazines blew up, 14 Mar 1863.

Ships captured: *Forest King*, 13 Jun 1861; *Empress*. 26 Nov 1861.

Saranac

Launched:	14 Nov 1848
Armament:	1862) 1–8″ SB, 8–8″/57, 2–20pdr MLR, 2–12pdr SB; (Jan 1864) 1–8″ SB replaced by 1–11″ SB; (Mar 1865) 1–11″ SB, 8–8″/55, 2–30pdr MLR, 2–12pdr.

Service record: Stationed on Pacific coast. Wrecked in Seymour Narrows off Vancouver Island, 18 Jun 1875.

Susquehanna

Launched:	5 Apr 1850
Armament:	(Jun 1863) 2–150pdr MLR, 12–9″ SB, 1–12pdr MLR; (1865) 2–100pdr MLR, 12–9″ SB, 1–30pdr MLR, 1–12pdr MLR

Service record: Mediterranean Sqn 1856–58, 1860–61. AtlBS 1861. Capture of Hatteras Inlet, 28–29 Aug 1861. Bombardment and occupation of Port Royal, SC, 7 Nov 1861. NAtlBS Apr 1862–63. Engagement with batteries at Sewells Point, Va., 8 May 1862. Out of commission, May 1863–Jul 1864. NAtlBS, 1864–65. Unsuccessful attack on Ft. Fisher, N.C., 24–25 Dec 1864. 150pdr rifle burst during second attack on Ft. Fisher, 13–15 Jan 1865. Decomm 14 Jan 1868. Sold 27 Sep 1883 and BU.

Ships captured: *Prince Alfred*, 9 Sep 1861; *Argonaut*, 13 Sep 1861; *San Juan*, 28 Sep 1861, *Baltimore*, 29 Sep 1861; *Coquette*, 3 Apr 1862, *Princeton*, 11 Jun 1862, str *Ann*, 29 Jun 1862; *Alabama*, 18 Apr 1863. Later USS *Fox*.

Powhatan

Launched:	14 Feb 1850
Armament:	(Nov 1861) 1–11″ SB, 10–9″ SB, 5–12pdr; (Oct 1863) 3–100pdr MLR, 1–11″ SB, 14–9″ SB; (Jan 1865) add 2–9″ SB, 4–12pdr SB.

Service record: Blockade of Mobile 1861. Operated off Charleston 1862–63. West Indies Sqn 1863–64. Unsuccessful attack on Ft. Fisher, N.C., 24–25 Dec 1864. Second attack on Ft. Fisher, 13–15 Jan 1865. South Pacific Sqn 1866–69. Home Sqn 1869–86.†

Ships captured: *Mary Clinton*, 29 May 1861; *Abby Bradford*, 13 Aug 1861; *C. Routereau*, 16 May 1862; *Major E. Willis*, 19 Apr 1863.

Side-Wheel Sloops

Allegheny

Launched:	22 Feb 1847

Service record: Receiving ship, Baltimore, 1856–68. Sold 15 May 1869.

Fulton

Launched:	30 Aug 1851

Service record: Paraguay Expedition 1858-59. Antislave trade patrol off Florida 1859 until stranded near Pensacola. While undergoing refit, captured by Confederates at Pensacola NYd, 12 Jan 1861, and destroyed by them, 10 May 1862.

Water Witch

Launched:	1852
Armament:	1862) 4–32pdr SB, 1–24pdr H.; (1864) 1–30pdr MLR, 1–12pdr MLR, 2–12pdr SB.

Service record: Paraguay Expedition, 1858-59. GulfBS May 1861. Engagement with CSN squadron near Head of Passes, Miss., 12 Oct 1861. EGulfBS 1862. SAtlBS Sep 1862. Joint expedition to St. Johns Bluff, Fla., 1–12 Oct and to Pocotaligo, S.C., 21–23 Oct 1862. Dispatch vessel. Assault on Jacksonville, Fla., 2–22 Feb–16 Apr 1864. Captured by Confederate boarders in Ossabaw Sound, Ga., 3 Jun 1864 and taken into service.

Ships captured: *Cornucopia*, 13 Nov 1861; *William Mallory*, 5 Mar 1862.

Fig 2.4: The side-wheel sloop *Water Witch* as she appeared during the Civil War. She was captured by Confederate boarders in 1864 and burned by them later in the year. (Peabody Essex Museum)

Side-Wheel Gunboat

Michigan

Launched: 5 Dec 1843

Service record: Lake Erie.†

Screw Frigate

San Jacinto

Launched: 16 Apr 1850

Armament: (1862) 1–11" SB, 10–9" SB, 1–12pdr MLR; (Dec 1863) 1–100pdr MLR, 10–9" SB, 1–20pdr MLR.

Service record: Africa Sqn 1859–60. In collision with French brig *Jules et Marie* off Cuba, 3 Nov 1861. Under command of Captain Charles Wilkes, stopped British str *Trent* east of Havana and removed Confederate envoys Mason and Slidell, 8 Nov 1861. NAtlBS Mar 1862. Engaged batteries at Sewell's Point, Va., 8 May 1862. EGulfBS Jun–Aug 1862. Search for CSS *Alabama*, Nov 1862–Jan 1863. Blockade off Mobile, Sep 1863. Search for CSS *Tallahassee* in N. Atlantic, Aug 1864. Wrecked on Grand Abaco Island, Bahamas, 1 Jan 1865.

Ships captured: Brig *Storm King* with 619 slaves off Congo River, 8 Aug 1860. *Buckshot*, 7 Aug 1863; str *Lizzie Davis*, 16 Sep 1863; *Roebuck*, 7 Jan 1864; *Lealtad*, 11 Mar 1864.

Screw Gunboat

Princeton

Launched: 29 Oct 1851

Armament: 4–8" SB, 6–32pdr SB.

Service record: Receiving ship, Philadelphia NYd, 1857–66. Sold 9 Oct 1866.

SCREW FRIGATES

Franklin

Name	Builder	Laid Down	Launched	Comm.
Franklin	Portsmouth NYd	May 1854	17 Sep 1864	3 Jun 1867
Tonnage	5,170 tons D; 3,173 tons B.			
Dimensions	265' (wl) × 53'8" × 24'3"			
Machinery	1 screw, 2-cyl. horizontal back-acting condensing engine (68" × 3'6"), 4 boilers, IHP 2,065, 10 knots (Atlantic)			
Complement	228			
Armament	4–100pdr MLR, 1–11" SB, 34–9" SB.			

Notes: Officially considered to be the rebuilt 74-gun ship-of-the-line of 1814, authorized 1853. Ship rig. Engines designed by Isherwood. Ordered 1863.

Service record: European Sqn 1867–71. N. Atlantic 1873. European Sqn 1874–76. Receiving Ship, Norfolk NYd 1877.†

Merrimack Class

Merrimack, *Wabash*, *Minnesota*, *Colorado* and *Roanoke* were sisters designed by Lenthall with differing machinery. These very fine warships were considered on completion to be superior to any warship in the world. They were good sailers, the engines being auxiliary only, but were too slow and had excessive draft.

Name	Builder	Laid Down	Launched	Comm.
Merrimack	Boston NYd	11 Jul 1854	15 Jun 1855	20 Feb 1856
Tonnage	4,636 tons D. 3,200 B			
Dimensions	300' (oa) 257'9" (bp) × 51'4" × 24'3"			
Machinery	1 screw, 2-cyl. horizontal double piston-rod back-acting engine (72" × 3'), 4 boilers, IHP 869, 6.1 knots (West Point)			
Complement	519			
Armament	14–8" SB/63, 2–10" SB, 24–9" SB			

Notes: Engines were too weak and unreliable and were being refitted in 1861.

Fig 2.5: The USS *Franklin* at Boston Navy Yard. Although started in 1854 she was not completed until after the Civil War and was in active service for only ten years. (U.S. Naval Historical Center)

Fig 2.6: The screw frigate *Merrimack*, a drawing by Clary Ray. No photographs exist of this famous ship. (U.S. Naval Historical Center, Norman Polmar Collection)

Service record: European cruise 1856–57. Pacific Sqn 1857–60. Burned to prevent capture while out of commission at Norfolk, NYd, 20 Apr 1861. Salved and rebuilt by CSN as ironclad *Virginia*. (See pg. 152)

Name	Builder	Laid Down	Launched	Comm.
Wabash	Philadelphia NYd	16 May 1854	24 Oct 1855	18 Aug 1856
Tonnage	4,650 tons D. 3,200 B.			
Dimensions	301'6" (oa) 262'6" (bp) × 51'4" × 23'			
Machinery	1 screw, 2-cyl. horizontal steeple condensing engine (72" × 3'), 4 boilers, IHP 950, 9 knots (Merrick)			
Complement	642			
Armament	(1862) 1-20" SB, 28-9" SB, 14-8"SB/63, 2-12pdrSB;			
	(Jul 1862) 8" replaced by 9" SB			
	(1863) 1-150pdr MLR, 2-100pdr MLR, 1-10" SB, 42-9" SB, 1-30pdr MLR, 1-12pdrH.			
	(1865) 1-150pdr MLR, 1-10" SB, 42-9" SB, 4-32pdr SB, 1-30pdr MLR.			

Notes: The only Navy ship with this type of engine.
Service record: Home Sqn 1856–58. Mediterranean Sqn 1858–59. AtlBS 1861. Capture of Hatteras Inlet, 28–29 Aug 1861. SAtlBS Oct 1861–Jan 1865. Occupation of Port Royal, SC, 7 Nov 1861. Blockade of Charleston. Attacked by torpedo boat CSS *David*, 18 Apr 1864. Unsuccessful attack on Ft. Fisher, N. C., 24–25 Dec 1864. Second attack on Ft. Fisher, 13–15 Jan 1865. Decomm 14 Feb 1865. Mediterranean Sqn 1871–74. Decomm 25 Apr 1874. Receiving ship, Boston, NYd and housed over, 1875.†

Ships captured: *Amelia*, 18 Jun 1861; *Hannah Balch*, Jul 1861; *Sarah Starr, Mary Alice*, 3 Aug 1861; *Wonder*, 15 May 1863.

Name	Builder	Laid Down	Launched	Comm.
Minnesota	Washington NYd	May 1854	1 Dec 1855	21 May 1857
Tonnage	4,833 tons D, 3,200 tons B.			
Dimensions	264'9" (wl) × 51'4" × 23'10"			
Machinery	1 screw, 2-cyl. horizontal trunk engine (79.5" × 3'), 4 boilers, IHP 973, 8.9 knots (bldr)			
Complement	646			
Armament	(May 1861) 1-10" SB, 28-9" SB, 14-8" SB/63, 2-24pdr SB, 2-12pdr SB.			
	(Dec 1862) 1-200pdr MLR, 1-11" SB, 4-100pdr MLR, 36-9" SB.			
	(Jul 1863) 1-150pdr MLR, 1-11" SB, 4-100pdr MLR, 38-9" SB, 2-12pdr MLRH, 2-12pdrH SB.			
	(Oct 1863) add 4-9" SB.			

Notes: Ship rig. Machinery designed by Daniel B. Martin.
Service record: East India Sqn 1857–59. AtlBS May 1861 (flagship). Capture of

Fig 2.7: The frigate *Minnesota* tied up at a Navy yard. She was damaged by her former sister *Merrimack* after running aground at Hampton Roads. (U.S. Naval Historical Center)

Fig 2.8: USS *Niagara* off Boston in 1863 after the modifications of 1862. Gunports for 11-inch guns were cut on the gun deck, but these were eliminated later in the year. (U.S. Naval Historical Center)

Hatteras Inlet, 28–29 Aug 1861. Battle of Hampton Roads, went aground and damaged by gunfire of CSS *Virginia*, 8–9 Mar 1862 (3 killed). NAtlBS 1862–65 (flagship). Not damaged when attacked by Confederate torpedo boat *Squib* while anchored off Newport News, 9 Apr 1864. Unsuccessful attack on Ft. Fisher, N.C., 24–25 Dec 1864. Second attack on Ft. Fisher, 13–15 Jan 1865 (15 killed). Decomm Jan 1868. Gunnery training ship, New York, 1875.†

Ships captured: *Mary Willis, North Carolina*, 14 May 1861; *J.H. Ethridge, William Henry, William & John, Mary, Industry, Bell Conway*, 15 May 1861; *Star, Crenshaw, Almira Ann*, 17 May 1861; *Hiawatha, Tropic Wind*, 10 May 1861; *Arcola*, 22 May 1861; *Pioneer*, 25 May 1861; *Iris, Catherine*, 27 May 1861; *Sally Magee*, 26 Jun 1861; *Sally Mears*, 1 Jul 1861; *Amy Warwick*, 10 Jul 1861; str *Vesta* and *Ranger*, 11 Jan 1864.

Name	Builder	Laid Down	Launched	Comm.
Colorado	Norfolk NYd	May 1854	19 Jun 1856	13 Mar 1858
Roanoke	Norfolk NYd	May 1854	13 Dec 1855	4 May 1857

Tonnage	4,772 tons D. 3,400 tons B.
Dimensions	262'10" (bp) 268'6" (wl) × 52'6" × 23'9"
Machinery	1 screw, 2-cyl. horizontal direct-acting trunk engine (79.5" × 3'), 4 boilers, IHP 997, 8.8 knots (Tredegar)
Complement	674
Armament	2–10" SB, 28–9" SB, 14–8"R/63 (*Roanoke* also 2–12pdr SB H).
	Colorado (1864) 1–150pdr MLR, 1–11" SB, 46–9" SB, 4–12pdrH. (1871) 2–100pdr MLR, 1–11" SB, 42–9" SB, 2–20pdrH, 6–12pdrH.

Notes: Ship rig. Hull similar to *Franklin*.

Service records

Colorado: GulfBS Jun 1861–Jun 1862. Boat party destroyed Confederate privateer *Judith* outfitting at Pensacola, 14 Sep 1861 (3 dead) WGulfBS Mar 1863–Feb 1864. NAtlBS Oct 1864–Jan 1865. Unsuccessful attack on Ft. Fisher, N.C., 24–25 Dec 1864. Second attack on Ft. Fisher, 13–15 Jan 1865 (3 killed). European Sqn 1865–67. Asiatic Stn 1870–73. Korean Expedition, 1871. North Atlantic Sqn 1873–75. Receiving Ship, New York, 1876–84. Sold 14 Feb 1885.

Ships captured: *Judith, 13 Sep 1861; str *Lewis Whitemore*, 6 May 1862.

Roanoke: Sank to bottom when launched; refloated. Home Sqn, 1858–60. N. Atlantic Sqn 1861. Present at Hampton Roads, 8 Mar 1862. Decomm 25 Mar 1862 for conversion to ironclad. (q.v.)

Ships captured: *Mary, 13 Jul 1861; *Albion*, 16 Aug 1861; *Alert*, 6 Oct 1861; *Thomas Watson.*, 15 Oct 1861.

Niagara

Name	Builder	Laid Down	Launched	Comm.
Niagara	Brooklyn NYd	Oct 1854	23 Feb 1856	6 Apr 1857

Tonnage	5,540 tons D. 4,580 tons B.
Dimensions	345' (oa) 328'10" (bp) × 55'3" × 24'8"
Machinery	1 screw, 3-cyl horizontal direct-acting engine (72" × 3'), 4 boilers, IHP 1955, 14.5 knots (Fulton)
Complement	657
Armament	4–32pdr guns.
	(Apr 1861), 12–9" SB.
	(Jun 1862), 1–80pdr MLR, 11–11" SB.
	(Oct 1863), 12–150pdr MLR, 20–11" SB, 1–24pdrH, 2–12pdr MLR.

Notes: A clipper-type hull designed by George Steers. The largest vessel built in the United States at the time; actually a large sloop with single gun deck. Ship rig with large sail area, two funnels. Refit 1862, new boilers, cutwater knee added and rearmed. Rearmed again 1863 but additional guns caused excessive weight resulting in removal of gun deck. Modifications started in 1870 canceled because of cost; was to receive new machinery, armor plating, and changes in gun and berth decks.

Service record: Laid first trans-Atlantic cable, 1857–58. Made cruise to Japan 1860–61. Blockade of Charleston May 1861. EGulfBS Jul 1861–62. Bombardment of defenses of Pensacola, Fla., 22–23 Nov 1861. Refitting Jun 1862–Oct 1863. European Sqn 1864–65. Unable to prevent escape of Confederate ironclad *Stonewall* from Ferrol, Spain, Mar 1865. Decomm 28 Sep 1865. Sold 6 May 1885.

Ships captured: *General Parkhill*, 12 May 1861; *Aid*, 5 Jun 1861; str *Georgia*, 15 Aug 1864.

Fig 2.9: USS *Delaware* at Shanghai, 1869, originally named *Piscataqua*. A frigate of the short-lived Java class she served only three years before being decommissioned. (U.S. Naval Historical Center)

Java Class

Name	Builder	Laid Down	Launched	Comm.
Antietam	Philadelphia NYd	1864	13 Nov 1875	1876
California	Portsmouth NYd	1864	3 Jul 1867	12 Dec 1870
ex-*Minnetonka*	(15 May 1869)			
Guerriere	Boston NYd	1864	9 Sep 1865	21 May 1867
Illinois	Portsmouth NYd	1864	never	never
Java	Brooklyn NYd	1864	never	never
New York	Brooklyn NYd	1864	never	never
ex-*Ontario*	(15 May 1869)			
Pennsylvania	Boston NYd	1864	never	never
ex-*Kewaydin*	(15 May 1869)			
Piscataqua	Portsmouth NYd	1864	11 Jun 1866	21 Oct 1867
Tonnage	3,954 tons D. 3,177 tons B.			
Dimensions	336'6" (oa) 312'6" (bp) × 46' × 21'5" (*Ontario*: 315' × 47')			
Machinery	1 screw, 2-cyl. horizontal back-acting engine (60" × 3'), 4 boilers (*Ontario* 6), IHP 1,780, 12 knots. *Antietam*, Morris Towne; *Guerriere*, Globe; *Illinois*, Corliss; *Java* and *New York*, Etna; *Pennsylvania*, Loring; *California* and *Piscataqua*, Woodruff.			
Complement	325			
Armament	2–100pdr MLR; 1–60pdr MLR; 2–20pdr MLR; 16–9" SB guns			

Notes: Hulls designed by Delano and engines by Isherwood. Built of unseasoned wood with diagonal iron bracing and decayed quickly. Construction of *Ontario* and others suspended 27 Nov 1865. Ship rig with two funnels.

Service records

Antietam: Machinery never installed, unarmed. Used as store hulk.†
California: Pacific Sqn (flagship) 1871–73. Decomm 3 Jul 1873. Sold May 1875.
Guerriere: S. Atlantic Sqn 1867–69. Went aground on Nantucket I., 29 Sep 1870. Mediterranean Sqn 1871–72. Badly damaged when stranded near Leghorn, 26 Jul 1871. Repaired for return to United States and decomm 22 Mar 1872. Sold 12 Dec 1872.
Illinois: BU on stocks, Feb 1872.
Java: BU on stocks, 1884.
New York: BU on stocks, 1888.
Pennsylvania: BU on stocks 1884.

Piscataqua: Asiatic Sqn 1867–70. Renamed **Delaware**, 15 May 1869. Decomm 5 Dec 1870. Foundered at wharf, New York, Feb 1877. Sold 1877 and BU

Hassalo Class

Name	Builder	Laid Down	Launched	Comm.
Hassalo	(unknown)	never	never	never
Watauga	(unknown)	never	never	never
Tonnage	3,365 tons			

Notes: Modified Java class. Projected, never built. Other details unknown, but probably were intended to have armor plating.

Trenton

Name	Builder	Laid Down	Launched	Comm.
Trenton	Brooklyn NYd	Dec 1873	1 Jan 1876	14 Feb 1877
Tonnage	3,900 tons D.			
Dimensions	271'6" (oa) 253' (bp) × 48' × 20'6"			
Machinery	1 screw, horizontal back-acting 3-cyl. compound engine; 8 boilers, IHP 3,500, 13 knots (Morgan)			
Complement	477			
Armament	11–8"R, 2–20pdr BLR			

Notes: Authorized 1873. An enlarged *Lancaster*. Wood hull. Ship rig with single funnel. 9.5-foot ram fitted to bow. First warship fitted with electric lighting 1883.

Service record: European Stn 1877–81. Asiatic Stn 1883–86.†

SCREW CRUISERS

These ships were fast cruisers designed to attack British shipping and ports in the event of war. Some armament was sacrificed for high speed. The hulls had an unusual length-to-beam ratio. *Wampanoag* and *Madawaska* were competitive sisters as to machinery, with similar hull and boilers. The machinery took up too much space, leaving inadequate room for crew and stores. The hull was too narrow forward to mount bow guns. These ships created great controversy in the Navy and were never used.

Ammonoosuc Class

Name	Builder	Laid Down	Launched	Comm.
Ammonoosuc	Boston NYd	1863	21 Jul 1864	15 Jun 1868
Neshaminy	Philadelphia NYd	1863	5 Oct 1865	never
Tonnage	3,850 tons D. 3,213 tons B.			
Dimensions	335' × 44'4" × 16'6"			
Machinery	1 screw, 2-cyl. horizontal geared direct-acting engines (100" × 4'), 8 boilers, *Neshaminy*, 12, IHP 4480, 17 knots; *Ammonoosuc*, Corliss; *Neshaminy*: Etna			
Armament	10–9" SB, 3–60pdr MLR, 2–24pdr SB			

Notes: Hulls designed by Delano; engines by Isherwood. *Ammonoosuc* never used although average speed on trials was 16.8 knots. *Neshaminy* not completed because hull was "twisted" 1869.

Service record:

Ammonoosuc: Completed at New York but laid up after trials. Renamed **Iowa**, 15 May 1869. Sold 27 Sep 1883.
Neshaminy: Renamed **Arizona**, 15 May 1869. Renamed **Nevada**, 10 Aug 1869. Sold incomplete Jun 1874 and BU.

Fig 2.10: The frigate *Trenton* shown reefing topsails was the first warship fitted with electric lighting. Completed in 1877 she was wrecked at Samoa in 1889. (U.S. Naval Historical Center, Norman Polmar Collection)

Wampanoag

Name	Builder	Laid Down	Launched	Comm.
Madawaska	Brooklyn NYd	1863	8 Jul 1865	27 Jun 1866
Wampanoag	Brooklyn NYd	3 Aug 1863	15 Dec 1864	17 Sep 1867

Tonnage	3,281 tons B. *Wampanoag*, 4,215 tons D; *Madawaska*, 4,170 tons D. (1871: 4,840 tons D.)
Dimensions	335' (bp) × 45'2" × 19'10"
Machinery	*Wampanoag*: 1 screw 2-cyl. horizontal-geared direct-acting engine (100" × 4'), 8 boilers, IHP 4,049, 17.5 knots (Novelty).
	Madawaska: 1 screw, 2-cyl. vibrating-lever engine (100' × 4'), 8 boilers, IHP 2,143, 11 knots (Allaire). (1871) 4-cyl. horizontal back-acting compound engine, 10 boilers, IHP 3,200, 10 knots.
Complement	375
Armament	10–9" SB, 3–60pdr MLR guns.
	Madawaska (1871) 2–100pdr MLR, 2–8"R, 18–9" SB; (1880) 2–11" SB, 16–9" SB, 2–100pdr MLR, 1–60pdr MLR.
	Wampanoag (1874) 2–100pdr MLR, 10–9" SB.

Notes: Near sisters, differing in machinery. Hulls designed by Delano, engines by Isherwood and Ericsson. *Wampanoag* exceeded designed speed on trials averaging 16.75 knots. The fastest ship afloat when completed. *Madawaska*'s engines were unsuitable, and the ship failed her designed speed on trials by 2 knots, making only 12.7 knots. Rebuilt 1869–71 with complete spar deck, four boilers, and two funnels removed, and reengined. Ship rig, masts restepped, bowsprit and cutwater knee added. Again failed contract speed.

Madawaska: Renamed ***Tennessee***, 15 May 1869. Flagship, Asiatic Sqn 1872. Flagship, N. Atlantic Sqn 1879.†

Wampanoag: N. Atlantic Fleet 1868. Decomm 5 May 1868. Renamed ***Florida***, 15 May 1869. Receiving ship, New London, 1874. Sold 27 Feb 1885 and BU.

Pompanoosuc

Name	Builder	Laid Down	Launched	Comm.
Pompanoosuc	Boston NYd	2 Jan 1864	never	never

Tonnage	4,446 tons D. 3,713 tons B.
Dimensions	335' × 48' × (U)
Machinery	1 screw, 2-cyl. horizontal-geared direct-acting engine (100" × 4'), 12 boilers (Corliss)
Armament	2–100pdr MLR, 2–60pdr MLR, 12–9" SB guns (projected)

Notes: Hull designed by Lenthall, engines by Isherwood.

Service record: Renamed ***Connecticut***, 15 May 1869. BU on stocks 1885.

Bon Homme Richard

Name	Builder	Laid Down	Launched	Comm.
Bon Homme Richard	(Unknown)	never	never	never

Tonnage	3,713 tons D.
Dimensions	(U)

20   Civil War Navies, 1855-1883

Fig 2.11: USS *Florida* laid up at Brooklyn Navy Yard in 1874. She is better known as the *Wampanoag*, which achieved over 17 knots on her trials but was immediately decommissioned. (U.S. Naval Historical Center)

Machinery	2 screws, 2-cyl. horizontal direct-acting engine (100″ × 4′). (Washington, NYd)
Armament	(U)

Note: Ship never built, engines built and put in storage.

Idaho

Name	Builder	Laid Down	Launched	Comm.
Idaho	Greenpoint, N.Y. (Steers)	1863	8 Oct 1864	2 Apr 1866

Tonnage	3,241 tons D. 2,638 tons B.
Dimensions	298′ (wl) × 44′6″ × 17′
Machinery	2 screws, 2 2-cyl. engines (type unknown) (30″ × 8′), HP 645, 8 knots (removed 1867) (Morgan)
Complement	400
Armament	6-32pdr, 1-30pdr, 1-12pdr H

Notes: Hull designed by Henry Steers; machinery by Dickerson. Failed trials and rejected by Navy. Forced by congressional resolution, in 1867 the Navy accepted the ship, which was completed as a sail storeship without engines. A fine and very fast sailing ship.

Service record: Rejected by the Navy, 25 May 1866. Converted to full-rigged sailing ship, comm 3 Oct 1867. Storeship for Asiatic Sqn. Dismasted and severely damaged in typhoon off Yokohama, 21 Sep 1869. Hulk sold at Yokohama 1874.

Chattanooga

Name	Builder	Laid Down	Launched	Comm.
Chattanooga	Philadelphia, Pa. (Cramp)	1863	13 Oct 1864	16 May 1866

Tonnage	3,043 tons D.
Dimensions	315′ (dk) × 46′ × 20′6″
Machinery	1 screw, 2-cyl. horizontal back-acting engine (84″ × 3′6″), 8 boilers, IHP 2,000, 13.5 knots (Merrick)
Complement	(U)
Armament	8–8″ SB, 3–60pdr MLR

Notes: Designed by builders. Ship rig, two funnels. Failed to meet contract speed.

Service record: Completed at Philadelphia, NYd. Decomm 3 Sep 1866. Sunk by floating ice at dock, League Island, Dec 1871.

SCREW SLOOPS

Hartford Class

Five ships authorized 3 Mar 1857: *Hartford, Brooklyn, Lancaster, Pensacola,* and *Richmond*. Designed by B.F. Delano.

Name	Builder	Laid Down	Launched	Comm.
Hartford	Boston NYd	1 Jan 1858	22 Nov 1858	27 May 1859

Tonnage	2,900 tons D; 1,900 tons B.
Dimensions	248′ (oa) 225′ (bp) × 44′ × 17′2″
Machinery	1 screw, 2-cyl. horizontal direct-acting engine (62″ × 2′10″), 2 boilers, IHP 1,024, 13.5 knots (Loring)
	(1880) horizontal back-acting engine (H. Loring)
	(1898) compound engine, IHP 2,000
Complement	310
Armament	16–9″ guns. (Jun 1862) 20–9″ SB, 2–20pdr MLR, 2–12pdr.
	(Jun 1863) 24–9″ SB, 1–45pdr MLR, 2–30pdr MLR.
	(Jun 1864) 2–100pdr MLR, 18–9″ SB, 1–30pdr MLR, 3–13pdrH.
	(1872) 2–11″ SB, 16–9″ SB, 2–20pdr MLR.

Notes: Ship rig. Rebuilt in 1870s with spar deck. Reengined 1880 with engines built for *Kewaydin*. Rerigged as bark 1887 for service as training ship. Reengined again 1898.

Service record: East India Sqn 1859–61. WGulfBS (flagship), 1861–65. Passage past New Orleans forts and engagement with CSN vessels, 24 Apr 1862 (3 killed). Made passage past batteries at Vicksburg, 28 Jun 1862. Engagement with CSS *Arkansas* above Vicksburg, 15 Jul 1862 (3 killed). Made passage past Port Hudson, La., 14 Mar, north past Grand Gulf, Miss. MS, 19 Mar (2 killed) and run south, 31 Mar 1863. Bombardment of Ft. Powell, Mobile Bay, 16–29 Feb 1864. Battle of Mobile Bay, 5 Aug 1864 (25 killed). Bombardment of Ft. Morgan, Mobile Bay, 9–23 Aug 1864. Repairing Dec 1864–Jul 1865. Asiatic Sqn 1865–68 and 1872–75.†

Ship captured: str *J.D. Clark,* 8 Apr 1863.

Name	Builder	Laid Down	Launched	Comm.
Brooklyn	New York, N.Y. (Westervelt)	1857	27 Jul 1858	26 Jan 1859

Tonnage	2,532 tons D; 2,070 tons B.

Fig 2.12: Admiral Farragut's flagship *Hartford* drying sails and laundry in the lower Mississippi during the war. (U.S. Naval Historical Center)

Fig 2.13: The *Brooklyn* after 1881, when an 8-inch muzzle-loader was installed on a pivot forward of the funnel. (U.S. Naval Historical Center)

Dimensions	247' (oa) 233' (wl) × 43' × 16'3"
Machinery	1 screw, 2-cyl. horizontal direct-acting cross-head engine (61" × 2'9"), 2 boilers, HP 1,116, 11 knots (Fulton)
Complement	335
Armament	1–10" SB, 20–9" SB guns.
	(1862) 24–9" SB, 2–12pdrH.
	(Jun 1863) 1–100pdr MLR, 22–9" SB, 1–30pdr MLR.
	(1864) 2–100pdr MLR, 2–60pdr MLR, 20–9" SB, 2–12pdrH.
	(1869) 2–11" SB, 18–9" SB.
	(1881) 1–8"R, 12–9" SB.

Notes: Ship rig. Rebuilt 1876–81 with spar deck, rearmed.

Service record: WGulfBS 1861–64. Passage past New Orleans forts and engagement with CSN vessels, 24 Apr 1862 (9 killed). Passage past batteries at Vicksburg, Miss., 28 Jun 1862. Bombardment of Grand Gulf, Miss. May 26, 1862. Passage past batteries at Vicksburg, 28 Jun 1862. Attack on Vicksburg, 22 Jul 1862. Bombarded Galveston, Tex., 10 Jan and 24 Feb 1863. Repairing Aug 1863–Apr 1864. WGulfBS 1864. Battle of Mobile Bay, struck 40 times, 5 Aug 1864 (11 killed). Bombardment of Ft. Morgan, Mobile Bay, 9–23 Aug 1864. NAtlBS Oct 1864–Jan 1865. Unsuccessful attack on Ft. Fisher, N.C., 24–25 Dec 1864. Second attack on Ft. Fisher, 13–15 Jan 1865. S. American stn 1865–67. Europe 1871–73. N. Atlantic 1874. S. America 1875 and 1881–84. Damaged in collision with British steamer *Mozart* at Montevideo, 1 May 1882.†

Ships captured: *H.E. Spearing*, 29 May 1861; *Pilgrim*, 7 Jun 1861; *Nahum Stetson*, 20 Jun 1861; *Macao*, 5 Sep 1861; str *Magnolia*,* 19 Feb 1862; *Blazer*, 27 May 1863; *Kate*, 28 May 1863; **Victoria & Star*, 30 May 1863.

Name	Builder	Laid Down	Launched	Comm.
Lancaster	Philadelphia NYd	Dec 1857	20 Oct 1858	12 May 1859
Tonnage	3,250 tons D; 2,362 tons B.			
Dimensions	235'8" (bp) × 46' × 18'6"			
Machinery	1 screw, 2-cyl. direct-acting double piston-rod engine (61" × 3'6"), 2 boilers, IHP 1,000, 10 knots (Reaney Neafie)			
	(1879) compound engine (60" × 3'), IHP 2,000, 12 knots.			
Complement	300			

* Later USS *Magnolia*.

Armament	2–11" SB, 20–9" SB.
	(May 1863) add 4–9" SB, 2–30pdr SB.
	(1878) 2–100pdr MLR, 16–9" SB.

Notes: Largest of the class, engines same as *Brooklyn*. Rebuilt 1879–81 at Portsmouth NYd, with new engines and boilers, ram bow. Recomm Aug 1881. Figurehead: eagle.

Service record: Pacific Sqn 1859–66. S. Atlantic Sqn 1870–75, 1885–88, 1895–97. European Sqn 1881–85, 1888–89.†

Name	Builder	Laid Down	Launched	Comm.
Pensacola	Pensacola NYd	Mar 1858	13 Aug 1859	16 Sep 1861
Tonnage	3,000 tons D; 2,158 tons B.			
Dimensions	230'8" (bp) × 44'5" × 18'7"			
Machinery	1 screw, Dickerson condensing engine (58" × 3'), IHP 1,165, 9.5 knots (Washington, NYd)			
	1865: 2-cyl. horizontal direct-acting engine (60" × 3') (Hazelhurst)			
Complement	269			
Armament	1–11" SB, 18–9" SB guns.			
	(Dec 1861) 1–42pdr MLR, 22–9" SB.			
	(Jul 1863) 1–100pdr MLR, 1–11" SB, 20–9" SB.			
	(1863) 1–11" SB replaced by 1–30pdr MLR.			
	(1868) 18–9" SB, 2–60pdr MLR.			

Notes: Hull designed by Lenthall and engines by Dickerson. Comm without engines 5 Dec 1859 and sailed to Washington, NYd for their installation. Engines completed Jan 1862 were so unreliable that ship was used mainly as a floating battery. Reengined in 1864–66 with machinery built for *Wanalosett*. Rebuilt in 1878 with spar deck and two funnels; engines from *Benicia* installed. Modified to single funnel, 1885.

Service record: WGulfBS Jan 1862. Passage past New Orleans forts and engagement with CSN vessels, 24 Apr 1862 (4 killed). Repaired 1864–66. Pacific Sqn 1866–83.†

Name	Builder	Laid Down	Launched	Comm.
Richmond	Norfolk NYd	1858	26 Jan 1860	Oct 1860
Tonnage	2,700 tons D; 1,929 tons B.			
Dimensions	225' (bp) × 42'6" × 17'5"			
Machinery	1 screw, 2-cyl. horizontal back-acting engine (58" × 3'), 3 boilers, IHP 1,078, 11 knots (Washington NYd)			
Complement	260			
Armament	14–9" SB.			
	(Feb 1862) 1–80pdr MLR, 20–9" SB, 1–30pdr MLR.			
	(Jun 1863) 1–100pdr MLR, 1–30pdr MLR, 20–9" SB, 2–12pdr SB, 1–24pdrH.			
	(Jun 1864) 1–100pdr MLR, 1–30pdr MLR, 18–9" SB.			
	(1886) 12–9" SB, 1–8"R, 1–60pdrBLR, 2–20pdrBLR.			

Notes: Ship rig. Engines designed by Archbold were not successful, replaced in 1866 by Isherwood engines (60' × 3').

Service record: Mediterranean 1860–61. Searched for CSS *Sumter* in Caribbean 1861. GulfBS Sep 1861. Rammed by CSS *Manassas* during engagement near Head of Passes, Miss., 12 Oct 1861. Damaged by gunfire during bombardment of Pensacola, Fla., 22–23 Nov 1861. Hit many times during passage past New Orleans forts and engagement with CSN vessels, 24 Apr 1862 (2 killed). Again hit during passage past batteries at Vicksburg, 28 Jun 1862 (2 killed). Engagement with CSS *Arkansas* above Vicksburg, 15 Jul 1862. Occupation of Baton Rouge, La., 17 Dec 1862. Damaged during attempt to pass Port Hudson, La., 14 Mar 1863 (3 killed). Battle of Mobile Bay, 5 Aug 1864. Bombardment of

Fig 2.14: The sloop *Richmond* in the lower Mississippi River during the war. (U.S. Naval Historical Center)

Ft. Morgan, Mobile Bay, 9–23 Aug 1864. Engagement with CSS *Webb* below New Orleans, 24 Apr 1865. European Sqn 1869–71. West Indies 1872–73. S. Pacific Sqn 1874–77. Asiatic Fleet (flagship) 1879–84.†

Mohican Class

Name	Builder	Laid Down	Launched	Comm.
Kearsarge	Portsmouth NYd	May 1861	5 Oct 1861	24 Jan 1862
Mohican	Portsmouth NYd	Aug 1858	15 Feb 1859	29 Nov 1859
Tonnage	*Kearsarge*: 1,550 tons D; 1,031 tons B. *Mohican*: 1,461 tons D; 994 tons B.
Dimensions	233′ (oa) 198′6″ (bp) × 33′10″ × 15′9″
Machinery	1 screw, 2-cyl. horizontal back-acting engine (54″ × 2′6″), 2 boilers, IHP 842, 11 knots (Woodruff)
Complement	160
Armament	2–11″ SB, 4–32pdr/42 guns.
	Kearsarge: (1864) add 1–30pdr MLR, 1–12pdr SB. (1873) 2–11″ SB, 4–9″ SB, 2–20pdr MLR.
	Mohican: (Apr 1864): 1–100pdr MLR, 4–9″ SB, 2–30pdr MLR, 2–32pdr/42, 1–12pdrH.
	(Nov 1864) 2–32pdr MLR replaced by 2–9″ SB.

Notes: Designed by William L. Hanscomb. Bark rig. *Kearsarge* built under 1861 emergency program. *Kearsarge* rebuilt in 1870s, sheer straightened and reengined 1887 with engines from *Nantasket*.

Service record

Kearsarge: European Sqn 1862–66. Sank CSS *Alabama* in engagement off Cherbourg, France, 19 Jun 1864. S. Pacific, 1868–70. Asiatic Stn, 1873–77. N. Atlantic Stn 1879–82.†

Mohican: African Sqn 1860–61. SAtlBS Oct 1861. Damaged during bombardment and occupation of Port Royal, S.C., 7 Nov 1861. Capture of Fernandina, Fla. and Brunswick, St. Simons, and Jekyl Islands, Ga., 2–12 Mar 1862. Search for CSS *Florida* and *Alabama*, Oct 1862–Apr 1864. NAtlBS Oct 1864–65. Unsuccessful attack on Ft. Fisher, N.C., 24–25 Dec 1864. Second attack on Ft. Fisher, 13–15 Jan 1865. SAtlBS Jan–Apr 1865. Pacific Sqn 1866–72. Cruise to Siberia 1869. Decomm 25 Jun 1872. Sank at her moorings at Mare Island 1872, and BU.

Ships captured: Ship *Erie* with 997 slaves off Congo River, 8 Aug 1860. *Arrow*, 25 Feb 1862. Mexican pirate *Forward* off Mexico, 17 Jun 1870.

Iroquois Class

Name	Builder	Laid Down	Launched	Comm.
Iroquois	Brooklyn NYd	Aug 1858	12 Apr 1859	24 Nov 1859
Oneida	Brooklyn NYd	Jun 1861	20 Nov 1861	28 Feb 1862
Wachusett	Boston NYd	Jun 1861	10 Oct 1861	3 Mar 1862
Tonnage	1,488 tons D; 1,016 tons B. (*Iroquois*), 1,032 tons B. (*Oneida*)
Dimensions	225′ (oa) 198′10″ (bp) × 33′10″ × 13′
Machinery	1 screw, 2-cyl. horizontal back-acting engine (54″ × 2′4″), except *Wachusett*: 2-cyl. horizontal steeple engine (50″ × 2′6″), 3 boilers (*Iroquois* 2), IHP 1202, 11.5 knots (*Wachusett* Morgan, others Fulton)
Complement	123
Armament	*Iroquois*: (1862) 2–11″ SB, 4–32pdr/42 SB.
	(Jan 1863) add 1–50pdr MLR, 1–12pdrH SB.
	(May 1864) 1–100pdr MLR, 1–60pdr MLR, 1–9″ SB, 4–32pdr/42.
	1886) 2–(11″ SB, 4–9″ SB, 1–60pdr MLR
	Oneida: (1862) 2–11″ SB, 4–32pdr/33, 3–30pdr MLR, 1–12pdrH.
	(1864) 2–11″ SB, 6–8″/63, 1–30pdr MLR, 2–24pdrH, 1–12pdrH.
	(1870) 1–11″ SB, 1–60pdr MLR, 6–32pdr SB.
	Wachusett: (1862) 2–11″ SB, 4–32pdr/27, 2–30pdr MLR, 1–20pdr MLR, 1–12pdr MLR.
	(1864) 3–100pdr MLR, 4–32pdr/42, 2–30pdr MLR, 1–12pdrH.
	(1878) 2–11″ SB, 4–8″ SB, 1–60pdr MLR.

Notes: Hulls designed by Lenthall. *Iroquois* built as barkentine and converted; others built with schooner rig. *Oneida* and *Wachusett* built under 1861 emergency program. *Wachusett* fitted with bilge keels 1863–65.

Service records

Iroquois: Mediterranean 1860–61. Search for CSS *Sumter* in Caribbean, 1861. WGulfBS 1862. Engagement with CSN vessels near Lucas Bend, Mo., Mississippi River, 11 Jan 1862. Bombardment of Fts. Jackson and St. Philip below New Orleans, Mississippi River, 18–28 Apr 1862 (6 killed). Occupation of Natchez, 13 May 1862. Bombardment of Grand Gulf, Miss., 9–10 Jun 1862. Passage past batteries at Vicksburg, 28 Jun 1862. Engagement with CSS *Arkansas* above Vicksburg, 15 Jul 1862. NAtlBS 1863–64. Mediterranean 1864. Search for CSS *Shenandoah* 1865. Asiatic Sqn 1867–70 and 1872–74. Decomm 1874. Pacific Stn 1882–92.†

Ship captured: str *Merrimac*,* 24 Jun 1863.

---

* Later USS *Merrimac*.

Fig 2.15: The sloop *Lancaster* in 1866 with her funnel retracted. (U.S. Naval Historical Center)

Oneida: WGulfBS 1862. Passage past New Orleans forts and engagement with CSN vessels, 24 Apr 1862. Occupation of Natchez, 13 May 1862. Bombardment of Grand Gulf, Miss., 9–10 Jun 1862. Made passage past batteries at Vicksburg, 28 Jun 1862. Engagement with CSS *Arkansas* above Vicksburg, 15 Jul 1862. Blockade of Mobile, Oct 1863–Aug 1864. Damaged during battle of Mobile Bay, 5 Aug 1864 (8 killed). Asiatic Sqn 1867–70. Sunk in collision when run down by British steamer *City of Bombay* in Yokohama Bay, 24 Jan 1870.

Wachusett: NAtlBS 1862. Supported operations in James River, 1862. Army operations at Gloucester and York, Va., 14–29 Apr and at Yorktown, Va., 4–7 May 1862. Search for CSS *Alabama* and *Florida* in Caribbean 1863. Repairing Jun 1863–Jan 1864. Protected commerce off Brazil 1864. Rammed and captured CSS *Florida* in neutral harbor of Bahia, Brazil, 7 Oct 1864. East Indies 1865–67. Mediterranean 1871–74. Gulf of Mexico 1879. S. Atlantic Stn 1879–80. Pacific Stn 1880–85.†

Ships captured: str *Virginia*,* 18 Jan 1863; str *Dolphin*, 25 Mar 1863.

Wyoming Class

Name	Builder	Laid Down	Launched	Comm.
Tuscarora	Philadelphia NYd	27 Jun 1861	24 Aug 1861	5 Dec 1861
Wyoming	Philadelphia NYd	Jul 1858	19 Jan 1859	Oct 1859
Tonnage	1,457 tons D; 997 tons B.			

* Later USS *Virginia*.

Dimensions: 222′ (oa) 198′6″ (bp) × 33′2″ × 14′10″

Machinery: 1 screw, 2-cyl. horizontal direct-acting engine (50″ × 2′6″), 3 boilers, IHP 793, 11 knots (Merrick)

Complement: 198

Armament: *Tuscarora*: 1–11″ SB, 2–32pdr.
(Dec 1861) 2–11″ SB, 4–32pdr/57, 2–32pdr/33, 1–30pdr MLR.
(Jul 1862) 1–100pdr MLR, 1–11″ SB, 4–8″/55, 2–30pdr MLR.
(Sep 1863) add 2–8″/55.
(1872) 2–11″ SB, 4–9″ SB.
Wyoming: 2–11″ SB, 4–32pdr.
(1863) 2–9″ SB, 4–32pdr SB.
(Sep 1865): 2–11″ SB, 1–60pdr MLR, 3–32pdr/57.
(1871) 1–11″, 4–9″, 2–20pdr MLR

Notes: Designed by Francis Grice. Bark rig. *Tuscarora* built under 1861 emergency program. Both rebuilt 1871 with ship rig.

Service records

Tuscarora: Search for Confederate raiders in European waters 1862–63. NAtlBS Oct 1863, storeship at Beaufort, N.C. Unsuccessful attack on Ft. Fisher, N.C., 24–25 Dec 1864. Second attack on Ft. Fisher, 13–15 Jan 1865 (3 killed). S. Pacific Sqn 1866–69. Caribbean 1870. S. Pacific Stn 1872–76. Landed marines at Honolulu to restore order Feb 1874. Decomm 31 May 1880. Sold 20 Nov 1883.

Wyoming: Stationed in California, 1860–62. Search for CSS *Alabama* in East Indies, 1862–64. Engaged batteries at Shimonoseki, Japan, and sank a steamer, 16 Jul 1863 (4 killed). Repaired at Philadelphia, N.Y.,d Jul 1864–Apr 1865. East Indies stn and Asiatic Sqn 1865–68. Punitive expedition to Formosa 1867. N. Atlantic Stn 1872–74. Receiving ship Washington N.Y.,d 1877–78. European Stn 1878–80. Practice ship, Naval Academy 1882–92.†

Dacotah

Name	Builder	Laid Down	Launched	Comm.
Dacotah	Norfolk NYd	1858	23 Mar 1859	1 May 1860

Tonnage	1,369 tons D; 996 tons B.
Dimensions	227′ (oa) 198′5″ (bp) × 32′9″ × 14′8″
Machinery	1 screw, 2-cyl. horizontal cross-head geared engine (63″ × 3′), 2 boilers, IHP 1000, 11 knots (Murray)
Complement	147
Armament	2–11″ SB, 4–32pdr.
	(1862) 1–100pdr MLR, 4–32pdr/41, 1–10″ SB, 2–12pdrH.
	(1863) add 1–30pdr MLR.

Notes: Bark rig. Engines removed 1870 and converted to sailing ship. Designed by S.T. Hartt.

Service record: East India Sqn 1860–61. NAtlBS Mar–Sep 1862. Engagement with batteries at Sewell's Point, 18–19 May 1862. Search for Confederate raiders in N. Atlantic 1862–63. NAtlBS Jan 1864–Aug 1864. Decomm at Mare Island 26 Jul 1869. Sold 30 May 1873.

Narragansett Class

Name	Builder	Laid Down	Launched	Comm.
Narragansett	Boston NYd	Jul 1858	15 Feb 1859	6 Nov 1859
Seminole	Pensacola NYd	Jul 1858	25 Jun 1859	25 Apr 1860

Tonnage	1,235 tons D; 804 tons B.
Dimensions	219′ (oa) 188′ (wl) × 30′2″ × 11′6″
Machinery	1 screw, 3 boilers. HP 250, 11 knots.
	Narragansett 2-cyl. horizontal direct-acting engine (48″ × 2′4″) (Boston Loco).
	Seminole 2-cyl. horizontal back-acting steeple engine (50′ × 2′6″) (Morgan).
Complement	120
Armament	1–11″ SB, 4–32pdr/42 SB *Seminole* (Jun 1863) 1–11″ SB, 1–30pdr MLR, 6–32pdr/43, 1–12pdr MLR.

Notes: Designed by E.H. Delano (*Narragansett*) and John L. Porter (*Seminole*).
Service record

Narraganset: Pacific coast 1861–65. Caribbean 1869. S. Pacific 1872–75. Decomm 1875. Sold 20 Nov 1883.

Seminole: Brazil Stn 1860–61. AtlBS 1861. Potomac Flotilla 1861. Bombardment at Freestone Point, Va., 25 Sep 1861. SAtlBS Nov 1861–Mar 1862. Occupation of Port Royal, S.C., 7 Nov 1861. Capture of Fernandina, Fla., and Brunswick, St. Simons, and Jekyl Islands, Ga., 2–12 Mar 1862. Engaged batteries at Sewell's Point, Va., 8 May 1862. WGulfBS Jul 1863. Battle of Mobile Bay, 5 Aug 1864. Bombardment of Ft. Morgan, Mobile Bay, 9–23 Aug 1864. Decomm 11 Aug 1865. Sold 20 Jul 1870.
Ships captured: *Albion*, 16 Aug 1861; *Lida*, 1 Dec 1861; str *Charleston*, 11 Jul 1863; *Sir William Peel*, 11 Sep 1863; *Josephine*, 14 Jan 1865; str *Denbigh*, 24 May 1865.
Later history: Merchant *Seminole*, rebuilt 1871. SE 1878.

Fig 2.16: The *Pawnee* during the war before her conversion to sail storeship. She differed from the other sloops by having her funnel aft of the mainmast. (U.S. Naval Historical Center)

Pawnee

Name	Builder	Laid Down	Launched	Comm.
Pawnee	Philadelphia NYd	Oct 1858	8 Oct 1859	11 Jun 1860

Tonnage	1,533 tons D; 1,289 tons B.
Dimensions	233′ (oa) 221′6″ (bp) × 47′ × 11′
Machinery	2 screws, 2-cyl. horizontal direct-acting geared engine (65″ × 3′), 3 boilers, IHP 590, 10 knots (Reaney Neafie)
Complement	151/181
Armament	4–11″ SB.
	(1860) 8–9″ SB, 2–12pdr SB.
	(May 1863) 1–100pdr MLR, 8–9″ SB, 1–50pdr MLR.
	(Jun 1864) add 2–9″ SB.
	(1865) add 2–9″ SB.

Notes: Designed by John W. Griffiths. Bark rig, clipper bow without bowsprit. Small draft with large battery. Engines removed 1870 and converted to storeship.
Service record: Home Sqn off Mexico 1860. Attempted relief of Ft. Sumter, Apr 1861. Potomac River 1861. Occupation of Alexandria, Va., 24 May 1861. Engaged batteries at Aquia Creek, Va., 29 May–1 Jun 1861. AtlBS Aug 1861–Jun 1862. Landings at Hatteras Inlet, 28–29 Aug 1861. Engagement with CSN squadron off Port Royal, S.C., 5 Nov 1861. Occupation of Port Royal, 7 Nov 1861. Bombardment of forts at St. Helena Sound, S.C., 25–28 Nov 1861. Capture of Fernandina, Fla. and Brunswick, St. Simons, and Jekyl Islands, Ga., 2–12 Mar 1862. SAtlBS Jan 1863–65. Engaged batteries in Stono River, S.C., 16 Jul (damaged) and 25 Dec 1863. Expedition up Stono River, 5 Jul and in Broad River, S.C., 27 Nov–30 Dec 1864. Engaged batteries in Togodo Creek, S. C., 9 Feb 1865. Expedition to Georgetown, S.C., 23 Feb 1865. Decomm 26 Jul 1865. Brazil Stn 1867–69. Converted to storeship 1870. Hospital and receiving ship, Key West, 1871–75 and Port Royal 1875–82. Sold 3 May 1884.
Ships captured: str *Thomas Collyer*, 25 May 1861; *Mary Wood, Ocean Wave, Harriet P. Ryan, Susan Jane*, 9 Sep 1861; *Darlington*,* 3 Mar 1862; *Rowena*, 9 Jun 1862.

Ossipee Class

Name	Builder	Laid Down	Launched	Comm.
Adirondack	Brooklyn NYd	1861	22 Feb 1862	30 Jun 1862
Housatonic	Boston NYd	1861	20 Nov 1861	29 Aug 1862
Juniata	Philadelphia NYd	Jun 1861	20 Mar 1862	4 Dec 1862
Ossipee	Portsmouth NYd	6 Jun 1861	16 Nov 1861	6 Nov 1862

---

* Later USS Darlington.

Fig 2.17: The sloop *Ossipee* off Honolulu in 1867, the crew manning the yards. (U.S. Naval Historical Center)

Fig 2.18: USS *Juniata* as she appeared in the 1880s. (Paul H. Silverstone Collection)

Tonnage	1,934 tons D; 1,240 tons B.
Dimensions	205′ (bp) × 38′ × 16′7″
Machinery	1 screw, 2-cyl. horizontal back-acting engine; *Juniata* 2-cyl. horizontal double-crosshead back-acting engine (42″ × 2′6″). 2 boilers, IHP 715, 12 knots. (*Adirondack*, Novelty; *Housatonic*, Globe; *Juniata*, Pusey; *Ossipee*: Reliance)
Complement	160
Armament	*Adirondack*: 2–11″ SB, 2–24pdr SB, 4–32pdr/57, 1–12pdr.
	Housatonic: 1–100pdr MLR, 3–30pdr MLR, 1–11″ SB, 2–32pdr/33, 2–24pdrH, 1–12pdrH.
	(1863) add 2–32pdr SB, 1–12pdrH.
	Juniata: 1–100pdr MLR, 1–11″ SB, 4–30pdr MLR, 1–12pdr, 4–24pdrH.
	(Jul 1864) 1–100pdr MLR, 2–30pdr MLR, 6–8″ SB, 1–12pdrH.
	(Oct 1864) add 2–8″ SB. 1878: 1–11″ SB, 6–9″ SB.
	Ossipee: 1–100pdr MLR, 1–11″ SB, 3–30pdr MLR, 6–32pdr/57, 1–12pdr SB, 1–12pdr MLR.
	(1873) 1–11″ SB, 6–9″ SB.

Notes: Hulls designed by Lenthall; machinery by Isherwood. Bark rig. *Juniata* had engine problems and was extensively repaired 1876–82.

Service records

Adirondack: SAtlBS 1862. Wrecked on Little Bahama Island, Bahamas, 23 Aug 1862.
   Ship captured: *Emma*, 23 Jul 1862.
Housatonic: SAtlBS 1862. Engagement with ironclads off Charleston, 31 Jan 1863. Sunk off Charleston by spar torpedo of submarine torpedo boat CSS *H.L. Hunley*, 17 Feb 1864 (5 dead).
   Ship captured: *Neptune*, 19 Apr 1863.
Juniata: NAtlBS 1863. West Indies 1863. Search for CSS *Tallahassee* off New York Aug 1864. NAtlBS 1864–65. Unsuccessful attack on Ft. Fisher, NC, 24–25 Dec 1864 (5 killed). Second attack on Fort Fisher, 13–15 Jan 1865 (5 killed). SAtlBS 1865. S. American Stn 1865–67. European Stn 1869–72. Search for survivors of *Polaris* west of Greenland 1873. European Stn 1874–76. Cruise around the world, 1882–85.†
   Ships captured: *Harvest*, 29 Apr 1863; str *Victor*, 28 May 1863; *Fashion*, 12 Jun 1863; *Elizabeth*, 14 Jun 1863; *Don Jose*, 2 Jul 1863.
Ossipee: NAtlBS 1862–63. WGulfBS May 1863–Jun 1865. Battle of Mobile Bay, 5 Aug 1864. Bombardment of Ft. Morgan, Mobile Bay, 9–23 Aug 1864. N. Pacific 1866–72. N. Atlantic 1873–78. Laid up 1878–83.†
   Ships captured: *Helena*, 30 Jun 1863; strs *James Battle* and *William Bagley*, 18 Jul 1863.

Sacramento Class

A class of six: *Sacramento*, *Canandaigua*, *Shenandoah*, *Lackawanna*, *Ticonderoga*, and *Monongahela*. All six were authorized in 1861, designed with no guns on the broadside, only pivots.

Name	Builder	Laid Down	Launched	Comm.
Sacramento	Portsmouth NYd	1861	28 Apr 1862	7 Jan 1863

Tonnage	2,100 tons D; 1,367 tons B.
Dimensions	229′6″ × 38′ × 8′10″
Machinery	1 screw, 2-cyl. horizontal back-acting condensing engine (42″ × 2′6″), 2 boilers, 12.5 knots (Taunton)
Complement	161
Armament	1–150pdr MLR, 2–11″ SB, 1–30pdr MLR, 2–24pdrH, 2–12pdr MLR, 2–12pdr SB.
	(Jun 1864) 3–100pdr MLR, 1–30pdr MLR, 6–8″ SB/63.
	(May 1865) 2–11″ SB, 2–9″ SB, 1–60pdr MLR, 2–24pdrH, 1–12pdr MLR, 1–12pdr SB.

Service record: SAtlBS 1863. European waters 1864–65. Blockaded CSS *Stonewall* at Ferrol, Spain, Mar 1865. Far East 1866–67. Went aground at mouth of the Godavari River, state of Madras, India, 19 Jun 1867 and became a loss.
Ship captured: *Wanderer*, 2 May 1863.

Name	Builder	Laid Down	Launched	Comm.
Canandaigua	Boston NYd	Dec 1861	28 Mar 1862	1 Aug 1862
Shenandoah	Philadelphia NYd	1861	8 Dec 1862	20 Jun 1863

Tonnage	2,030 tons D; (*Canandaigua*) 1,395 tons B, (*Shenandoah*) 1,378 tons B.
Dimensions	228′ (bp) × 38′9″ × 15′
Machinery	1 screw, 2-cyl. horizontal back-acting condensing engine (42″ × 2′6″), 2 boilers, IHP 1300, 12 knots (*Canandaigua*: Atlantic, *Shenandoah*: Merrick)
Complement	191
Armament	*Canandaigua*: 2–11″ SB, 1–8″ SB, 3–20pdr MLR (designed).
	(Aug 1862) 2–11″ SB, 1–150pdr MLR, 3–20pdr MLR, 2–12pdr MLR, 2–12pdr SB.
	(May 1865) 2–11″ SB, 2–9″ SB, 1–60pdr MLR, 2–24pdr, 1–12pdr MLR, 1–12pdr SB.
	(1878) 6–9″ SB, 2–8″R, 1–60pdr MLR.

Shenandoah: 2–11″ SB, 1–150pdr MLR, 1–30pdr MLR, 2–24pdrH, 2–12pdrH.

(May 1865) 2–11″ SB, 2–9″ SB, 1–60pdr MLR, 2–24pdrH, 2–12pdr MLR.

Notes: *Shenandoah* modified with clipper bow 1870.

Service records

Canandaigua: SAtlBS Aug 1862. Bombarded Charleston forts, 17 Aug 1863. European Stn 1865–69. Renamed **Detroit**, 15 May 1869. Renamed **Canandaigua**, 10 Aug 1869. West Indies and Gulf of Mexico 1872–75. Decomm 8 Nov 1875. BU 1884.

Ships captured: str *Thistle*,* 8 May 1863; *Secesh*, 15 May 1863; str *Raccoon, 19 Jul 1863.

Shenandoah: Search for Confederate raiders 1863. NAtlBS 1863–64. Unsuccessful attack on Ft. Fisher, NC, 24–25 Dec 1864. Second attack on Ft. Fisher, 13–15 Jan 1865. S. American Sqn 1865–66. Asiatic Sqn 1866–69. European Stn 1870–74. S. Atlantic Sqn 1879–82.†

Ship captured: str *Arabian, 15 Sep 1863.

Name	Builder	Laid Down	Launched	Comm.
Lackawanna	Brooklyn NYd	1862	9 Aug 1862	8 Jan 1863
Ticonderoga	Brooklyn NYd	1862	16 Oct 1862	12 May 1863

Tonnage	2,526 tons D; 1,533 tons B.
Dimensions	232′ (bp) × 38′2″ × 16′6″
Machinery	1 screw, 2-cyl. horizontal back-acting condensing engine (42″ × 2′6″), 2 boilers, IHP 1300, 11 knots (Allaire)
Complement	205
Armament	*Lackawanna:* 1–150pdr MLR, 2–11″ SB, 4–9″ SB, 1–50pdr MLR, 2–24pdr MLR, 2–12pdrH, 2–12pdr MLR.
	(1865) add 1–60pdr MLR.
	Ticonderoga: 1–150pdr MLR, 1–50pdr MLR, 6–9″ SB, 2–24pdrH, 2–12pdr MLR, 2–12pdr SB.
	(Sep 1863) 2–9″ SB replaced by 2–11″ SB.
	(Dec 1863) 1–100pdr MLR, 12–9″ SB, 1–30pdr MLR, 2–24pdrH.
	(Apr 1864) less 2–9″ SB.
	(May 1865) 2–11″ SB, 2–9″ SB, 1–60pdr MLR, 2–24pdrH, 2–12pdr MLR.

Notes: Hulls designed by Lenthall; machinery by Isherwood. *Ticonderoga* had bowsprit added 1865.

Service records

Lackawanna: WGulfBS 1863. Battle of Mobile Bay, 5 Aug 1864 (4 killed). Bombardment of Fort Morgan, Mobile Bay, 9-23 Aug 1864. Pacific 1866-71. Far East 1872-75.

Ships captured: str *Neptune***, 14 Jan 1863; str *Planter*, 15 Jun 1863.

Ticonderoga: West Indies Sqn Jun-Oct 1863. Search for Confederate raiders in N. Atlantic, 1864. Went aground near Maranham, 25 Aug 1864. NAtlBS 1864-65. Unsuccessful attack on Fort Fisher, NC, 24-25 Dec 1864. Damaged by explosion of 100-pdr Parrott rifle, 24 Dec 1864 (8 killed). Second attack on Fort Fisher, 13-15 Jan 1865 (2 killed). SAtlBS Jan-Mar 1865. European Sqn 1866-69. S.Atlantic Sqn 1871-73. N.Atlantic Sqn 1874. Cruise around the world 1877-80. Decomm 10 Sep 1882.†

Name	Builder	Laid Down	Launched	Comm.
Monongahela	Philadelphia NYd	Dec 1861	10 Jul 1862	15 Jan 1863

Tonnage	2,078 tons D; 1,378 tons B.
Dimensions	225′ (bp) × 38′ × 15′1″

* Later USS *Cherokee*.
** Later USS *Clyde*.

Fig 2.19: An interesting broadside of the sloop *Sacramento*, at Benguela, Angola, 7 March 1867. (U.S. Naval Historical Center)

Machinery	1 screw, 2-cyl. horizontal back-acting condensing engine (42″ × 2′6″), 3 boilers, IHP 532, 12 knots (Merrick)
Complement	176
Armament	1–200pdr MLR, 2–11″ SB, 2–24pdr MLR, 4–12pdr MLR.
	(Dec 1863) 1–200pdr MLR replaced by 1–150pdr MLR, add 5–32pdr/57.
	(May 1865) 2–11″ SB, 1–60pdr MLR, 1–24pdr, 1–12pdr MLR, 1–12pdr SB.
	(1878): 6–9″ SB, 1–60pdr MLR.

Notes: Barkentine rig. Armament had no direct forward fire. Engines removed 1883 and converted to sailing ship, bark rig. Full rigged ship 1890.

Service record: WGulfBS 1863. Went aground and was damaged by gunfire during attempt to pass Port Hudson, La., 14 Mar 1863 (6 killed). Bombardment below Donaldsonville, La., 7 Jul and at Whitehall Pt., La., 10 Jul 1863. Expedition to Brazos Santiago, Rio Grande, Tex., 27 Oct–3 Nov 1863. Damaged by ramming CSS *Tennessee* at Battle of Mobile Bay, 5 Aug 1864. Bombardment of Ft. Morgan, Mobile Bay, 9–23 Aug 1864. West Indies Sqn 1865–67. Cast aground by tidal wave during earthquake at St. Thomas, 18 Nov 1867; refloated 11 May 1868. S. Atlantic Stn, 1873–76. Far East 1877–79. Converted to supply ship 1883.†

Ships captured: *Matamoros, Volante, Dashing Wave, Science,* 5 Nov 1863.

Contoocook Class

Name	Builder	Laid Down	Launched	Comm.
Arapaho	(unknown)	never	never	never
Congress	Philadelphia NYd	1863	17 Jul 1868	4 Mar 1870
ex-*Cambridge* (10 Aug 1869) ex-*Pushmataha* (15 May 1869)				
Contoocook	Portsmouth NYd	1863	3 Dec 1864	14 Mar 1868
Keosauqua	(unknown)	never	never	never
Mondamin	(unknown)	never	never	never
Severn	Brooklyn NYd	Oct 1864	22 Dec 1867	27 Aug 1869
ex-*Mosholu* (15 May 1869)				
Tahgayuta	(unknown)	never	never	never
Wanalosett	(unknown)	never	never	never
Willamette	(unknown)	never	never	never
Worcester	Boston NYd	1863	25 Aug 1865	27 Feb 1871
ex-*Manitou* (15 May 1869)				

Tonnage	3,300 tons D; 2,348 tons B.

Fig 2.20: USS *Shenandoah* during the period 1865–69 after her bowsprit was fitted. (U.S. Naval Historical Center)

Dimensions	296'10" (dk) × 41' × 15'6"
Machinery	1 screw, 2-cyl. horizontal back-acting condensing engine (60" × 3'). 4 boilers, IHP 1220, 13 knots. (*Arapaho, Contoocook*, Providence; *Keosauqua*, Etna; *Worcester*, Woodruff; *Mondamin* and *Tahgayuta*, Washington IW; *Severn*, S.Brooklyn; *Congress*, Morris Towne; *Wanalosett*, Hazelhurst; *Willamette*: Poole)
Complement	250
Armament	Designed: 8–9" SB, 1–60pdr MLR.
	1878) 14–9" SB, 2–60pdr MLR.
	Contoocook 8–9" SB, 1–60pdr MLR, 4–24pdrH, 1–12pdrH, 1–12pdrHR

Notes: Smaller versions of *Wampanoag* with engines designed by Isherwood and hulls by Lenthall. Emphasis was on speed with leaner lines than previous vessels. Originally designed with a ram bow, abandoned at the end of the Civil War. Built of unseasoned timber and deteriorated quickly. Bark rig. Engines built for *Wanalosett* later used in *Pensacola*. *Worcester* received spar deck 1869.

Service records:

Arapaho: Canceled 1866.
Congress: S. Atlantic Sqn 1870–71. Mediterranean Sqn 1872–74. Decomm 26 Jul 1876. Sold 20 Sep 1883.
Contoocook: N. Atlantic Sqn 1868–69. Renamed **Albany**, 15 May 1869. Decomm 7 Jan 1870. Quarantine ship, New York 1870–72. Sold 12 Dec 1872.
Keosauqua: Canceled 1866.
Mondamin: Canceled 1866.
Severn: N. Atlantic Sqn 1869–71. Decomm 31 Dec 1871. Sold 2 Mar 1877 and BU.
Tahgayuta: Canceled 1866.
Wanalosett: Canceled 1866.
Willamette: Canceled 1866.
Worcester: Voyaged to France with war relief supplies 1871, boiler burst, 8 Mar 1871. (4 killed) N. Atlantic Sqn 1872–75. Receiving ship, Norfolk, NYd 1878. Sold 27 Sep 1883 and BU.

Algoma Class

Name	Builder	Laid Down	Launched	Comm.
Alaska	Boston NYd	1867	31 Oct 1868	8 Dec 1869
Benicia	Portsmouth NYd	May 1867	18 Aug 1868	1 Dec 1869
ex-*Algoma* (15 May 1869)				
Confiance	Boston NYd	never	never	never
Detroit	Brooklyn NYd	never	never	never
Kenosha	Brooklyn NYd	27 Jun 1867	8 Aug 1868	20 Jan 1869
Meredosia	(unknown)	never	never	never
Omaha	Philadelphia NYd	1867	10 Jun 1869	12 Sep 1871
ex-*Astoria* (10 Aug 1869) ex-*Omaha* (15 May 1869)				
Peacock	Brooklyn NYd	never	never	never
Serapis	Boston NYd	never	never	never
Taghkanic	(unknown)	never	never	never
Talladega	(unknown)	never	never	never

Tonnage	2,400 tons D.
Dimensions	250'6" (bp) × 38' × 16'6"

28 Civil War Navies, 1855-1883

Fig 2.21: The sloop *Ticonderoga* on 8 April 1864 as originally built before the modifications made after the war. (U.S. Naval Historical Center)

Machinery	1 screw, 2-cyl. horizontal back-acting engine (50″ × 3′6″), 4 boilers, IHP 800, 11.5 knots (*Benicia, Meredosia,* Boston, NYd; *Kenosha* Norfolk NYd; *Omaha,* Brooklyn NYd; others: bldr)
Complement	291
Armament	*Alaska,* 1–11″ SB, 6–8″ SB, 1–60pdr MLR
	Benicia, Omaha, Plymouth, 1–11″ SB, 10–9″ SB, 1–60pdr MLR, 2–20pdr MLR

Notes: Hulls designed by Lenthall and machinery by Isherwood. *Alaska, Algoma,* and *Omaha* ordered in 1867. Bark rig, two funnels. Engines of canceled ships used in *Swatara* class. Outdated when built.

Service records

Alaska: Asiatic Sqn 1870–73. Korean Expedition, May–Jun 1871. European Sqn 1873–76. Pacific Sqn 1878–82. Decomm 13 Feb 1883. Sold 20 Nov 1883.
Benicia: Asiatic Sqn 1870–72. Korean Expedition, May–Jun 1871. N. Pacific Sqn 1872–74. Decomm 29 Nov 1875.†
Confiance: Canceled 1866.
Detroit: Canceled 1866.
Kenosha: European Stn 1869–70. Renamed **Plymouth**, 15 May 1869. Mediterranean 1870–73. Decomm 17 May 1879. †
Meredosia: Canceled 1866.
Omaha: S. and N. Atlantic Sqns 1872–79.†
Peacock: Canceled 1866.
Serapis: Canceled 1866.
Taghkanic: Canceled 1866.
Talladega: Canceled 1866.

Swatara Class

Name	Builder	Laid Down	Launched	Comm.
Galena	Norfolk NYd	1872	13 Mar 1879	26 Aug 1880
Marion	Portsmouth NYd	1872	22 Dec 1873	12 Jan 1876
Mohican	Mare Id NYd	4 Sep 1872	19 Sep 1883	25 May 1885
Quinnebaug	Philadelphia NYd	1872	28 Sep 1875	2 Oct 1878
Swatara	Brooklyn NYd	1872	17 Sep 1873	11 May 1874
Vandalia	Boston NYd	1872	23 Oct 1874	10 Jan 1876

Tonnage	1,900 tons D (*Vandalia* 2,033 tons)
Dimensions	216′ (bp) × 37′ × 16′6″ (*Vandalia* 39′ × 17′3″)
Machinery	1 screw, compound engines, 10 boilers, IHP 1,200, 12 knots (*Marion,* Boston, NYd; *Quinnebaug,* Washington, NYd; others, bldr)
Complement	230

Fig 2.22: USS *Monongahela* was cast aground in a hurricane at St. Thomas, Virgin Islands, on 18 November 1867. This view was taken on 4 March 1868 during salvage operations. (Paul H. Silverstone Collection)

Armament	1–8″R, 6–9″ SB, 1–60pdr MLR, 2–20pdr MLR; *Marion* 1–11″, 6–9″, 1–60pdr MLR, 1–50pdr MLR.

Notes: *Marion, Quinnebaug, Swatara,* and *Vandalia* had rebuilt engines originally built for *Algoma* class vessels. They were officially considered as older vessels repaired. Bark rig.

Service records

Galena: European Stn 1881–82. S. America 1882–83.†
Marion: †
Mohican: †
Quinnebaug: European Stn 1879–89.†
Swatara: †
Vandalia: European Sqn 1876–79. In collision with Norwegian bark *Atlantic* in North Atlantic, 31 Oct 1876. N. Atlantic Sqn 1879–84.†

Fig 2.23: The sloop *Congress* at Venice about 1873. She was launched as *Pushmataha*. (U.S. Naval Historical Center)

SCREW GUNBOATS

Unadilla Class

Name	Builder	Laid down	Launched	Comm.
Aroostook	Kennebunk, Me. (Thompson)	1861	19 Oct 1861	20 Feb 1862
Cayuga	E. Haddam, Conn. (Gildersleeve)	1861	21 Oct 1861	21 Feb 1862
Chippewa	New York, N.Y. (Webb & Bell)	1861	14 Sep 1861	13 Dec 1861
Chocura	Boston, Mass. (Curtis & Tilden)	1861	5 Oct 1861	15 Feb 1862
Huron	Boston, Mass. (Curtis)	1861	21 Sep 1861	8 Jan 1862
Itasca	Philadelphia, Pa. (Hillman)	1861	1 Oct 1861	28 Nov 1861
Kanawha	E. Haddam, Conn. (Goodspeed)	1861	21 Oct 1861	21 Jan 1862
Katahdin	Bath, Me. (Larrabee)	1861	12 Oct 1861	17 Feb 1862
Kennebec	Thomaston, Me. (Lawrence)		5 Oct 1861	8 Feb 1862
Kineo	Portland, Me. (Dyer)	29 Jul 1861	9 Oct 1861	8 Feb 1862
Marblehead	Newburyport, Mass. (Jackman)	1861	16 Oct 1861	8 Mar 1862
Ottawa	New York, N.Y. (Westervelt)	1861	22 Aug 1861	7 Oct 1861
Owasco	Mystic, Conn. (Maxson Fish)	1861	5 Oct 1861	23 Jan 1862
Pembina	New York, N.Y. (Stack)	1861	28 Aug 1861	16 Oct 1861
Penobscot	Belfast, Me. (Carter)	1861	19 Nov 1861	16 Jan 1862
Pinola	Baltimore, Md. (Abrahams)	1861	1861	29 Jan 1862
Sagamore	Boston, Mass. (Sampson)	1861	18 Sep 1861	7 Dec 1861
Sciota	Philadelphia, Pa. (Birely)	1861	15 Oct 1861	15 Dec 1861
Seneca	New York, N.Y. (Simonson)	1861	27 Aug 1861	14 Oct 1861
Tahoma	Wilmington, Del. (Thatcher)	1861	2 Oct 1861	20 Dec 1861
Unadilla	New York, N.Y. (Englis)	3 Aug 1861	17 Aug 1861	30 Sep 1861
Winona	New York, N.Y. (Poillon)	1861	14 Sep 1861	11 Dec 1861
Wissahickon	Philadelphia, Pa. (Lynn)	1861	2 Oct 1861	25 Nov 1861

Tonnage	691 tons D; 507 tons B.
Dimensions	158'4" (wl) × 28' × 9'6"
Machinery	1 screw, 2-cyl. horizontal back-acting engine (30" × 1'6"), 2 boilers. 10 knots. (*Aroostook, Kennebec, Ottawa, Owasco, Pembina, Seneca,* and *Unadilla,* Novelty; *Cayuga,* Woodruff; *Chippewa, Katahdin, Kineo,* Morgan; *Chocura, Huron: Loring, Itasca, Sciota: Morris, Kanawha: Pacific, Marblehead:* Highland, *Penobscot, Winona,* Allaire; *Pinola:* Reeder, *Sagamore,* Atlantic; *Tahoma,* Reaney; *Wissahickon,* Merrick) 114
Armament	1–11" SB, 2–24pdr SB, 1–20pdr MLR, except: *Aroostook:* (Jun 1863) 1–24pdr SB replaced by 1–12pdr SB. (1864) add 1–12pdr SB. *Cayuga:* (Jun 1862) add 2–24pdr SB. (Jun 1863) add 1–30pdr MLR. *Chippewa:* (Oct 1864) add 2–24pdr SB. *Chocura:* (Apr 1865) 1–100pdr MLR, 1–30pdr MLR, 4–24pdr SB, 1–20pdr MLR. *Huron:* (Aug 1864) 1–11" SB, 1–30pdr MLR, 4–24pdrH. *Itasca:* (Dec 1861) 1–10" SB, 2–32pdr/27, 1–20pdr MLR. (Nov 1862) 1–11" SB, 2–32pdr/27, 1–20pdr MLR. *Kanawha:* (Dec 1863) add 1–9" SB until Jun 64. *Katahdin:* (Oct 1862) add 1–20pdr MLR.

Fig 2.24: The sloop *Alaska* of the *Algoma* class, completed in 1869. The funnels are retracted. (U.S. Naval Historical Center, Norman Polmar Collection)

Fig 2.25: The sloop *Plymouth* in 1877 during her Mississippi River cruise. She was completed as *Kenosha* but renamed shortly after. (U.S. Naval Historical Center)

Fig 2.26: USS *Omaha*, Algoma class, with her two funnels lowered.

Fig 2.27: The sloop *Quinnebaug* of the postwar Swatara class. (U.S. Naval Historical Center)

Kennebec: (Mar 1865) 1–11″ SB, 1–30pdr MLR, 1–24pdrH, 1–12pdr.

Kineo: (Dec 1862) add 2–32pdr/33.

Marblehead: (Jun 1863) add 2–24pdr. (Jun 1864) 2–8″/63 SB, 3–30pdr MLR, 2–24pdr.

Ottawa: (May 1863) 1–150pdr MLR, 1–30pdr MLR, 2–24pdrH, 1–12pdr. (Aug 1864) add 2–24pdrH.

Seneca: (Dec 1863) add 2-24pdrH. *Tahoma:* (1862): 1–10″ SB, 1–20pdr MLR, 4–24pdrH. (Jul 1863) 1–10″ replaced by 1–150pdr MLR.

Unadilla: (Oct 1862) add 2–24pdrH, 1–12pdr SB.

Winona (1863) add 2–32pdr/33. (1864) 1–11″ SB, 1–30pdr MLR, 1–12pdrH, 4–24pdrH.

Wissahickon (1863) 1–11″ SB replaced by 1–150pdr MLR.

Notes: Popularly known as "90-day gunboats." Ordered by Navy Department as an emergency measure and built rapidly of unseasoned timber. Designed by S. M. and S.H. Pook with engines by Isherwood. Two-mast schooner rig. Poor under sail, but made good steaming performances; rolled heavily.

Service records

Aroostook: NAtlBS Apr–Sep 1862. Engaged batteries at Drewrys Bluff, Va., 15 May 1862. WGulfBS Sep 1862–64. Asiatic Sqn 1867–69. 18 Sep 1869 decomm. Sold at Hong Kong, Oct 1869.
  Ships captured: **Josephine,* 5 Mar 1863; *Sea Lion,* 9 May 1863; *Eureka,* 22 Nov 1863; *Cosmopolite,* 23 Jan 1864; *Mary P. Burton,* 11 Mar 1864; *Marion,* 12 Mar 1864; **Matagorda.* 8 Jul 1864.
  Later history: FFU

Cayuga: WGulfBS 1862–65. Passage past New Orleans forts and engagement with CSN vessels, 24 Apr 1862. Bombardment of Baton Rouge, La. and engagement with CSS *Arkansas,* 5 Aug 1862. Occupation of Baton Rouge, 17 Dec 1862. Decomm 31 Jul 1865. Sold 25 Oct 1865.
  Ships captured: *Jessie J. Cox,* 25 Mar 1862; *Tampico,* 3 Apr 1863; *Blue Bell,* 2 Jul 1863; *J.T. Davis,* 10 Aug 1863; *Wave,* 22 Aug 1863; **Pushmataha,* 7 Oct 1863.
  Later history: Merchant *Veteran* 1865. Converted to bark 1869. SE 1885.

Chippewa: Blockade off North Carolina, 1862. Capture of Ft. Macon, N.C., 25–26 Apr 1862. Search in N. Atlantic for CSS *Florida,* 1862–63. SAtlBS 1863–Feb 65. Bombardment of Ft. Wagner, Charleston, 18 Jul 1863. Joint expedition up Ashepoo and S. Edisto Rivers, SC, 25–27 May 1864. Unsuccessful attack on Ft. Fisher, N.C., 24–25 Dec 1864. Second attack on Ft. Fisher, 13–15 Jan 1865 (2 killed). Bombardment of Ft. Anderson, 18 Feb and Fts. Strong and Lee, Cape Fear River 20–21 Feb 1865. James River, Mar–May 1865. Decomm 24 Jun 1865. Sold 30 Nov 1865.
  Ships captured: *Alliance,* 26 Apr 1862; *Napier,* 29 Jul 1862.
  Later history: FFU

Chocura: Army operations at Yorktown, Va., 4–7 May 1862. NAtlBS Nov 1862–Aug 1863. WGulfBS Nov 1863–65. Gulf Sqn 1866–67. Decomm 7 Jun 1867. Sold 13 Jul 1867.
  Ships captured: **Pearl,* 19 Nov 1862; *Pride,* 21 Jan 1863; *Frederick the Second* and *Agnes,* 3 May 1864; *Express,* 4 May 1864; *Louisa,* 12 Oct 1864; *Cora Smyser,* 28 Oct 1864; **Louisa,* 24 Nov 1864; *Lowood,* 4 Dec 1864; *Julia,* 5 Dec 1864; *Lady Hurley,* 6 Dec 1864; *Alabama,* 7 Dec 1864; **Delfina,* 22 Jan 1865.
  Later history: FFU

Huron: SAtlBS 1862. Capture of Fernandina, Fla. and Brunswick, St. Simons, and Jekyl Islands, Ga., 2–12 Mar 1862. Bombardment of Ft. McAllister, Ogeechee River, Ga., 29 Jul 1862. Engaged batteries in Stono River, S. C., 16 Jul 1863. NAtlBS 1864. Unsuccessful attack on Ft. Fisher, N.C., 24–25 Dec 1864. Second attack on Ft. Fisher, 13–15 Jan 1865. Bombardment of Ft. Anderson, 18 Feb and Fts. Strong and Lee, Cape Fear River 20–21 Feb 1865. S. America Stn 1865–68. Decomm 8 Oct 1868. Sold 14 Jun 1869.
  Ships captured: *Glide,* 19 Apr 1862; *Albert,* 1 May 1862; str *Cambria,* 26 May 1862; *Aquilla,* 4 Aug 1862; str **Stonewall Jackson,* 12 Apr 1863; str *Chatham,** 16 Dec 1863; **Sylvanus,* 2 Jan 1864.
  Later history: Merchant *D.H.Bills* 1869. SE 1876.

Itasca: GulfBS 1862. WGulfBS 1862. Severed chain across Mississippi River under heavy fire, 20 Apr 1862. Made passage past New Orleans forts and engagement with CSN vessels, 24 Apr 1862. Damaged during bombardment of Grand Gulf, Miss., 9–10 Jun 1862. Operations below Donaldsonville, La., 4 Oct 1862. Blockade of Galveston, 1863. Battle of Mobile Bay, 5 Aug 1864. Bombardment of Ft. Morgan, Mobile Bay, 9–23 Aug 1864. Sold 30 Nov 1865.
  Ships captured: *Lizzie Weston,* 19 Jan 1862; *Miriam,* 17 Jun 1863; *Sea Drift,* 22 Jun 1863; *Carrie Mair,* 30 Nov 1864; **Mary Ann,* 8 Dec 1864.
  ater history: Merchant *Aurora* 1865. Sold foreign 1867.

Kanawha: GulfBS 1862–65. Sold 13 Jun 1866.
  Ships captured: *Charlotte,*** *Cuba, Southern Independence, Victoria,* 10 Apr 1862; *R.C. Files,* 20 Apr 1862; *Annie,* 29 Apr 1862; str *Ann,* 19 Jun 1862; **Monticello,* 26 Jun 1862; **unidentified,* 17 Nov 1862; *Clara,* 25 Mar 1863; *Dart,* 1 May 1863; *Juniper,* 4 May 1863; *Comet,* 15 May 1863; *Hunter,* 17 May 1863; *Ripple,* 18 May 1863; *Wenona* (Albert), 29 Nov 1863; *Amanda,* 14 May 1864; str **Matagorda,* 8 Jul 1864; *Mary Ellen,* 8 Jan 1865.
  Later history: Merchant bark *Mariano* 1866. SE 1878.

Katahdin: WGulfBS 1862. Made passage past New Orleans forts and engagement with CSN vessels, 24 Apr 1862. Bombardment of Grand Gulf, Miss., 26 May and 9–10 Jun 1862. Made passage past batteries at

---

* Later USS *Chatham.*
** Later USS *Charlotte.*

Vicksburg, 28 Jun and at Baton Rouge, La., engagement with CSS *Arkansas*, 5 Aug 1862. Operations below Donaldsonville, La., 4 Oct 1862. Bombardment of Port Hudson, La., 13 Dec 1862. Occupation of Baton Rouge, La., 17 Dec 1862. Blockade of Galveston, Tex., 1863–64. Decomm 14 Jul 1865. Sold 30 Nov 1865.
Ships captured: *John Gilpin.* 25 Apr 1862; *Hanover*, 10 May 1863; *Excelsior*, 13 Jul 1863; *Albert Edward*, 31 Oct 1864.
Later history: Merchant *Juno* 1865. Renamed **Katahdin**?

Kennebec: WGulfBS 1862. Passage past New Orleans forts and engagement with CSN vessels, 24 Apr 1862. Made passage past batteries at Vick SBurg, 28 Jun 1862. Blockade duty, 1862–63. Battle of Mobile Bay, 5 Aug 1864. Blockade duty off Galveston 1864–65. Sold 30 Nov 1865.
Ships captured: *Ella*, 31 May 1862; *Juniper*, 4 May 1863; *Marshall J. Smith*, 9 Dec 1863; str *Grey Jacket*, 31 Dec 1863; *John Scott*, 8 Jan 1864.
Later history: Merchant *Kennebec* 1865. Converted to bark.

Kineo: WGulfBS, 1862. Hit during passage past New Orleans forts and engagement with CSN vessels, 24 Apr 1862. Bombarded Grand Gulf, Miss., 26 May 1862. Bombardment of batteries at Baton Rouge, La., and engagement with CSS *Arkansas*, 5 Aug 1862. Operations below Donaldsonville, La., 4 Oct 1862. Bombardment of Port Hudson, La., 13 Dec 1862. Ran aground during attempt to pass Port Hudson, 14 Mar 1863, towed Monongahela off under fire. Bombardment of Donaldsonville, 28 Jun and at Whitehall Pt., La., 10 Jul 1863. Repairing Aug 1863–64. WGulfBS Mar 1864. Blockade duty off Texas, 1864–65. Decomm 9 May 1865. Sold 9 Oct 1866.
Ship captured: *Stingray*, 22 May 1864
Later history: Merchant schooner *Lucy H. Gibson* 1866.

Marblehead: NAtlBS 1862. Army operations at Gloucester and York, Va., 14–29 Apr 1862. SAtlBS Aug 1862. Expedition to Pocotaligo, S.C., 21–23 Oct 1862. Engaged batteries in Stono River, S.C., 16 Jul 1863. Bombardment of Ft. Wagner, Morris I., Charleston, Aug 1863. Damaged while bombarding batteries in Stono River, 25 Dec 1863 (3 killed). Practice ship, Naval Academy, Jun 1864. N. Atlantic Sqn 1866–68. Decomm 4 Sep and sold 30 Sep 1868.
Ship captured: *Glide*, 23 Feb 1863.
Later history: Merchant bark *Marblehead* 1868. SE 1876.

Ottawa: SAtlBS 1861–65. Engaged CSN squadron off Port Royal, SC, 5 Nov 1861. Occupation of Port Royal, 7 Nov 1861. Army operations at Port Royal Ferry, 31 Dec 1861–2 Jan 1862. Engagement in Wilmington Narrows, N.C., 26–28 Jan 1862. Capture of Fernandina, Fla., and Brunswick, St. Simons, and Jekyl Islands, Ga., 2–12 Mar 1862. Operations in St. Johns River, Fla., 16 Apr–3 May 1862. Bombardment of Ft. Wagner, Charleston, 18 Jul–20 Aug 1863. Attack on Jacksonville, Fla., 2–22 Feb 1864. Expedition to Bulls Bay, SC, 12–17 Feb 1865. Decomm 12 Aug 1865. Sold 25 Oct 1865.
Ships captured: *Gen. C.C. Pinckney*, 6 May 1862; *Etiwan*,* 21 Jan 1863; str **Havelock*, 11 Jun 1863.
Later history: FFU

Owasco: WGulfBS 1862–65. Passage past New Orleans forts and engagement with CSN vessels, 24 Apr 1862. Capture of Galveston, Tex., 4 Oct 1862. Expedition to Brazos Santiago, Rio Grande, Tex., 27 Oct–3 Nov 1863. Decomm 12 Jul 1865. Sold 25 Oct 1865.
Ships captured: *Eugenia, President*, 16 Mar 1862; **Hanover*, 10 May 1863; *Active*, 21 Jun 1863; **Revenge*, 21 Jul 1863; *Dashing Wave, Science, Matamoros, Volante*, 4 Nov 1863; *Lily*, 17 Apr 1864; *Fanny*, 19 Apr 1864; *Laura*, 21 Apr 1864.
Later history: Merchant *Lulu* 1865, converted to sail 1869. SE 1885.

Pembina: SAtlBS 1861. Engaged CSN squadron off Port Royal, S.C., 5 Nov 1861. Occupation of Port Royal, 7 Nov and of Beaufort, S.C., 9 Nov 1861. Engaged forts in St. Helena Sound, S.C., 25–28 Nov and in Wassaw Sound, Ga., 5–6 Dec 1861. Army operations at Port Royal Ferry, 31 Dec 1861–2 Jan 1862. Capture of Fernandina, Fla., and Brunswick, St. Simons, and Jekyl Islands, Ga., 2–12 Mar 1862. GulfBS 1863–65. Battle of Mobile Bay, 5 Aug 1864. Decomm 22 Sep 1865. Sold 30 Nov 1865.

* Later USS *Percy Drayton*.

Ships captured: *Rowena*, 6 Jun 1862; *Elias Beckwith*, 23 Apr 1863; *Joe Flanner*, 24 Apr 1863; *Geziena Hilligonda*, 4 Dec 1864.
Later history: Merchant *Charles E. Gibson* 1865. Converted to schooner 1866. SE 1878.

Penobscot: NAtlBS 1862. Army operations at Gloucester and York, Va., 14–29 Apr 1862. WGulfBS Fall 1863. Bombarded batteries at San Bernard, Tex., 11–13 Jan 1863. Decomm 31 Jul 1865. Sold 19 Oct 1869.
Ships captured: *Sereta*, 8 Jun 1862; *Lizzie*, 1 Aug 1862; *Robert Burns*, 22 Oct 1862; **Pathfinder*, 2 Nov 1862; *Golden Eagle*, 13 Dec 1862; **Kate*, 12 Jul 1863; *Lily*, 28 Feb 1864; *Stingray, John Douglas*, 29 Feb 1864; *James Williams*, 12 Jul 1864; *Matilde*, 11 Feb 1865; **Mary Agnes, *Louisa*, 18 Feb 1865.
Later history: FFU

Pinola: WGulfBS 1862. Helped break chain across Mississippi River, 20 Apr and was damaged during passage past batteries below New Orleans, 24 Apr 1862 (3 killed). Made passage past batteries at Vicksburg, 28 Jun 1862 (2 killed). Blockade of Mobile 1863–64, and Texas 1864–65. Decomm 15 Jul 1865. Sold 30 Nov 1865.
Ships captured: *Cora*, 9 Mar 1862; *Ben Willis*, 2 Feb 1865; **Anna Dale*, 18 Feb 1865.
Later history: Merchant bark *Pinola* 1865.

Sagamore: EGulfBS 1862–65. Operations off Apalachicola, Fla., Apr 1862. Bombardment of New Smyrna, Fla., 28 Jul 1863. Decomm 1 Dec 1864. Sold 13 Jun 1865.
Ships captured: *Frances*, 23 Oct 1862; *Trier*, 28 Oct 1862; *Ellen, Agnes*, 24 Nov 1862; *By George*, 1 Dec 1862; *Alicia*, 10 Dec 1862; *Avenger*, 5 Jan 1863; *Julia*,** 8 Jan 1863; **Elizabeth*, 28 Jan 1863; **Florence Nightingale, Charm*, 23 Feb 1863; *unidentified schr, 2 Mar 1863; *Enterprise*, 8 Mar 1863; *New Year*, 26 Apr 1863; *Frolic*, 25 Jun 1863; *Clotilda*, 26 Jul 1863; *Shot, Ann, Southern Rights, Clara Louise*, 8 Aug 1863; *Meteor*, 30 Oct 1863; *Paul*, 7 Nov 1863.
Later history: Merchant *Kaga no Kami*, 1865. Renamed **Hijun** 1868. Became Japanese warship *Yoshun*, 1868. Merchant *Chinese Daimyo*.

Sciota: WGulfBS 1862–65. Passage past New Orleans forts and engagement with CSN vessels, 24 Apr 1862. Bombardment of Grand Gulf, Miss., 9–10 Jun 1862. Made passage past batteries at Vicksburg, 28 Jun 1862. Engaged CSS *Arkansas* above Vicksburg, 15 Jul 1862. Operations below Donaldsonville, La., 4 Oct 1862. Attack on Galveston, Tex., 10 Jan 1863. Burned three vessels off coast of Texas, 8–9 Jul 1863. Sank after collision with USS *Antona* in Mississippi River north of Quarantine, 14 Jul 1863. Raised in Aug and refitted at New Orleans. Unsuccessful landings at Matagorda peninsula, Texas, 31 Dec 1863. Struck a torpedo (mine) and sank in Mobile Bay, 14 Apr 1865, later salved. Sold 25 Oct 1865.
Ships captured: *Margaret*, 6 Feb 1862; *unidentified schr, 8 Jul 1863; *Mary Sorley*, 4 Apr 1864; *Pancha Larispa*, 27 Oct 1864; *Cora Smyser*, 28 Oct 1864.
Later history: Merchant *Poncas* 1865. Sold to Chile as a warship, renamed **Numble**. Sold 1868.

Seneca: SAtlBS, 1862–63. Engaged CSN sqn off Port Royal, S.C., 5 Nov 1861. Occupation of Port Royal, 7 Nov, Beaufort, S.C., 9 Nov and of Tybee Island, Ga. 24 Nov 1861. Engagement at Port Royal, 26 Nov 1861. Army operations at Port Royal Ferry, S.C., 31 Dec 1861–2 Jan 1862. Helped destroy Confederate privateer *Rattlesnake* in Ogeechee River, 28 Feb 1862. Capture of Fernandina, Fla., and Brunswick, St. Simons, and Jekyl Islands, Ga., 2–12 Mar 1862. Operations in St. Johns River, Fla., 16 Apr–3 May 1862. Engaged batteries at Ft. McAllister, Ga., 27 Jan–Feb 1863. Helped destroy Confederate privateer *Rattlesnake* in Ogeechee River, 28 Feb 1863. NAtlBS 1864. Bombardment of Ft. Wagner, Charleston, 18 Jul–8 Sep 1864. Repairing Jan–Oct 1864. Unsuccessful attack on Ft. Fisher, N.C., 24–25 Dec 1864. Second attack on Ft. Fisher, 13–15 Jan 1865. Bombardment of Ft. Anderson, Cape Fear River 11–21 Feb 1865. Decomm 24 Jun 1865. Sold 10 Sep 1868.
Ships captured: *Cheshire*, 6 Dec 1862; *Annie Dees*,*** 20 Nov 1862.

** Later USS *Julia*.
*** Later USS *Thunder*.

Later history: FFU

Tahoma : EGulfBS 1862–65. Raid on St. Marks, Fla., Jun 1862. Engaged batteries in Tampa Bay, Fla., 2–9 Apr and 16 Oct 1863. Repairing Jul 1864–Apr 1865. Gulf Sqn 1866–67. Decomm 27 Aug 1867. Sold 7 Oct 1867.

Ships captured: *unidentified, 26 Apr 1862; *Uncle Mose*, 7 Jul 1862; *Silas Henry*, 8 Jan 1863; *Margaret*, 2 Feb 1863; *Stonewall*,* 24 Feb 1863; *Crazy Jane*, 5 May 1863; *Statesman*, 6 Jun 1863; **Mary Jane*, *Harriet*, 18 Jun 1863; **Kate Dale*, str **Scottish Chief*, 16 Oct 1863.

Later history: FFU

Unadilla: SAtlBS 1861–65. Occupation of Port Royal, SC, 7 Nov 1861. Bombarded forts at St. Helena Sound, S.C., 25–28 Nov 1861. Bombardment of Ft. McAllister, Ogeechee River, Ga., 29 Jul 1862. Engaged ironclads off Charleston, 31 Jan 1863. Unsuccessful attack on Ft. Fisher, N.C., 24–25 Dec 1864. Second attack on Ft. Fisher, 13–15 Jan 1865. Bombardment of Ft. Anderson, Cape Fear River, 17–21 Feb 1865. James River Sqn 1865. Asiatic Sqn 1867–68. Sold Oct 1869 in Far East.

Ships captured: *Mary Teresa*, 20 May 1862; str *Lodona*,** 4 Aug 1862; str *Princess Royal*,*** 29 Jan 1863.

Later history: Merchant *Dang Wee* 1869. In collision with merchant *Delaware* in typhoon at Hong Kong, fall 1870.

Winona: GulfBS 1862. Snagged during passage past New Orleans forts and engagement with CSN vessels, 24 Apr 1862 (3 killed). Bombardment of Grand Gulf, Miss., 9–10 Jun 1862. Made passage past batteries at Vicksburg, 28 Jun 1862. Engaged CSS *Arkansas* above Vicksburg, 15 Jul 1862. Engaged CSS *Florida* off Mobile, 4 Sep 1862. Bombarded Port Hudson, La., 13 Dec 1862. Occupation of Baton Rouge, La., 17 Dec 1862. Bombarded Donaldsonville, La., 28 Jun 1863. SAtlBS Feb 1864–65. Expedition up Broad River, S.C., 27 Nov–30 Dec 1864 and to Bulls Bay, S.C., 12–17 Feb 1865. Decomm 9 Jun 1865. Sold 30 Nov 1865.

Ship captured: str *Little Ada*, 25 Mar 1864.

Later history: Merchant *C.L. Taylor* 1865. SE 1885.

Wissahickon: WGulfBS 1862. Reconnoitered forts in Mississippi River, 28 Mar 1862. Passage past New Orleans forts and engagement with CSN vessels, 24 Apr 1862. Bombardment of Grand Gulf, Miss., 9–10 Jun 1862. Made passage past batteries at Vicksburg, 28 Jun 1862. Engaged CSS *Arkansas* above Vicksburg, 15 Jul 1862. SAtlBS Oct 1862–65. Expedition to Pocotaligo, S.C., 21–23 Oct 1862. Engaged batteries at Ft. McAllister, Ogeechee River, Ga, 19 Nov 1862 and 27 Jan–28 Feb 1863. Helped destroy privateer *Rattlesnake* in Ogeechee River, 28 Feb 1863. Bombardment of Ft. Wagner, Charleston, 18 Jul–8 Sep 1863. Expedition in Broad River, S.C., 27 Nov–30 Dec 1864 and up Stono and Folly rivers, S.C., 9–14 Feb 1865. Decomm 1 Jul 1865. Sold 25 Oct 1865.

Ships captured: str **Georgiania*, 19 Mar 1863; str **Havelock*, 10 Jun 1863.

Later history: Merchant *Adele* 1865. SE 1885.

Kansas Class

Name	Builder	Laid down	Launched	Comm.
Kansas	Philadelphia NYd	1863	29 Sep 1863	21 Dec 1863
Maumee	Brooklyn NYd	1862	2 Jul 1863	29 Sep 1864
Nipsic	Portsmouth NYd	24 Dec 1862	15 Jun 1863	2 Sep 1863
Nyack	Brooklyn NYd	1862	6 Oct 1863	28 Sep 1864
Pequot	Boston NYd	1862	4 Jun 1863	15 Jan 1864
Saco	Boston NYd	1862	28 Aug 1863	11 Jul 1864
Shawmut	Portsmouth NYd	2 Feb 1863	17 Jun 1863	1 Nov 1864
Yantic	Philadelphia NYd	1862	19 Mar 1864	12 Aug 1864

Tonnage 836 tons D; 593 tons B.

---

* Later USS *Stonewall*.
** Later USS *Lodona*.
*** Later USS *Princess Royal*.

Dimensions 190′ () 179′6″ (bp) × 29′8″ × 12′ *Pequot*, *Maumee*, 171′6″(bp). 1872: *Yantic* 215′ (oa).

Machinery 1 screw, 2-cyl. horizontal back-acting engine (30″ × 1′9″), IHP 327, 11 knots (*Nipsic*, Woodruff; *Nyack*, S.Brooklyn; *Shawmut*, Corliss) except

Kansas, *Yantic*, 2-cyl. horizontal direct-acting engine (32″ × 1′6″) (*Yantic*, Merrick; *Kansas*, unknown)

Maumee, 2-cyl. horizontal vibrating-lever engine (40″ × 1″10″) (Stover)

Pequot, 2-cyl. segmental cylinder direct-acting engine (30″ × 1′9″) (Woodruff)

Saco, 2-cyl. horizontal vibrating-lever engine (28″ × 2′), 14 boilers. 7.5 knots (Corliss) (1866) 2-cyl. back-acting engines ; 4 boilers, 11 knots.

Yantic (1877) 2 compound engines, IHP 310, 11.5 knots

Complement 154

Armament 1–150pdr MLR, 2–9″ SB, 1–30pdr MLR, 2–20pdr MLR

Kansas: (Dec 1864) 1–150pdr MLR replaced by 1–100pdr MLR.

(Mar 1865) 1–100pdr MLR replaced by 1–11″ SB.

(Dec 1865) 2–9″ SB, 2–11″ SB, 3–12pdr MLR, 2–20pdr SB, 1–30pdr MLR.

(1870) 1–11″ SB, 2–9″ SB, 1–20pdr MLR.

Maumee (Oct 1864) 1–100pdr MLR, 1–30pdr MLR, 4–24pdrH, 1–12pdr MLR.

(Nov 1864) add 2–32pdr/57.

(Jun 1865) 1–100pdr MLR replaced by 1–11″ SB.

Nipsic: (1863) 1–150pdr MLR, 1–30pdr MLR, 2–9″ SB, 2–24pdr SB, 2–12pdr SB.

(Jun 1865) 1–100pdr MLR, 1–30pdr MLR, 2–8″ SB/63, 2–24pdrH SB, 2–12pdr MLR.

Nyack: (Sep 1864): 1–100pdr MLR, 2–9″ SB, 1–30pdr MLR, 2–24pdrH, 2–12pdrH.

Pequot: (Jan 1864): 1–150pdr MLR, 1–30pdr MLR, 6–32pdr/33, 2–24pdrH, 2–12pdrH.

Saco: (Jul 1864) 1–100pdr MLR, 1–30pdr MLR, 6–32pdr SB, 1–24pdrH, 1–12pdr MLR, 1–12pdr SB.

Shawmut: (Nov 1864) 1–100pdr MLR, 1–30pdr MLR, 2–9″ SB, 2–24pdrH,2–12pdrH

Fig. 2.28: The gunboat *Chocura* served most of her career in the Gulf of Mexico. (Dr. Charles Peery Collection)

Fig 2.29: USS *Aroostook*, a 90-day-gunboat, in Chinese waters, 1867–69. She was sold at Hong Kong. (U.S. Naval Historical Center)

Y*antic:* (Aug 1864) 1–100pdr MLR, 1–30pdr MLR, 2–9″ SB, 2–24pdrH, 2–12pdrH.

(Apr 1865) 1–100pdr R replaced by 2–9″ SB.

(1883) 3–8″R, 1–60pdr MLR.

Notes: Built for fast inshore cruising. Designed by Lenthall. *Pequot* and *Maumee* had different hull shape designed by William H. Webb. Two-mast topsail schooners with one large gun, straight stem. *Saco* had two funnels. *Nipsic, Nyack,* and *Shawmut* had engines designed by Isherwood, *Maumee* and *Saco* by John Ericsson, but those of *Saco* were replaced by Isherwood engines in 1865 after much engine trouble. *Kansas's* engines captured as cargo in blockade runner *Princess Royal.* Those remaining in 1869 were rerigged as ships and received cutwater knees. *Yantic* lengthened 1872 and reengined 1877.

Service records

Kansas: NAtlBS 1863–64. Engagement with CSS *Raleigh* off New Inlet, N.C., 6–7 May 1864. Unsuccessful attack on Ft. Fisher, N.C., 24–25 Dec 1864. Second attack on Ft. Fisher, 13–15 Jan 1865. James River 1865. S. Atlantic Stn, 1865–69. Central American canal survey expeditions 1870–71 and 1873. Decomm 10 Aug 1875. Sold 27 Sep 1883.
  Ships captured: str *Tristram Shandy,** 15 May 1864; str *Annie,* 31 Oct 1864; str **Stormy Petrel,* 7 Dec 1864.
Maumee: NAtlBS 1864. Unsuccessful attack on Ft. Fisher, N.C., 24–25 Dec 1864. Second attack on Ft. Fisher, 13–15 Jan 1865. Bombardment of Fts. Strong and Lee, Cape Fear River, 20–21 Feb 1865. Decomm 17 Jun 1865. Sold 15 Dec 1869.
Nipsic: SAtlBS 1863–65. Expedition to Murrells Inlet, S.C., 29 Dec 1863–1 Jan 1864 and to Georgetown, S.C., 23 Feb 1865. S. Atlantic Sqn, 1866–73. Decomm 1873 and BU.
  Ship captured: *Julia,* 27 Jun 1864.
Nyack: NAtlBS 1864–65. Unsuccessful attack on Ft. Fisher, N.C., 24–25 Dec 1864. Bombardment of Fts. Strong and Lee, Cape Fear River 18–21 Feb 1865. Served off west coast of S. America, 1866–1871. Decomm 15 Mar 1871. Sold 30 Nov 1883.
Pequot: NAtlBS Feb 1864. Operations at Malvern Hill, Va., 14–16 Jul 1864. SAtlBS 1864–65. Unsuccessful attack on Ft. Fisher, N.C., 24–25 Dec 1864. Second attack on Ft. Fisher, 13–15 Jan 1865 (3 killed). Bombardment of Ft. Anderson, Cape Fear River, 17–18 Feb 1865. Decomm 3 Jun 1865. Sold 1869.
  Ship captured: str *Don,*** 4 Mar 1864.
  Later history: Sold to Haiti 1869, renamed *Terreur.* "Worn out" 1875.

* Later USS *Tristram Shandy.*
** Later USS *Don.*

Saco: Search for Confederate raiders in N. Atlantic 1864. Decomm 17 Jan 1865. Caribbean 1866–67. Mediterranean 1870–71. Far East 1871–76. Decomm 13 Jul 1876. Sold 20 Nov 1883.
Shawmut: Towed to New York for installation of engines. NAtlBS 1865. Bombardment of Fts. Strong and Lee, Cape Fear River, 20–21 Feb 1865. Brazil Stn 1865–66. N. Atlantic Sqn 1867 and 1871–77. Decomm 22 Jan 1877. Sold 27 Sep 1883.
Yantic: Search for CSS *Tallahassee* in N. Atlantic, 1864. NAtlBS 1864–65. Unsuccessful attack on Ft. Fisher, N.C., 24–25 Dec 1864; 100pdr gun burst (6 killed). Second attack on Ft. Fisher, 13–15 Jan 1865 (2 killed). Bombardment of Fts. Strong and Lee, Cape Fear River 20–21 Feb 1865. Asiatic Stn 1873–77. Caribbean 1881.†

Resaca Class

Name	Builder	Laid down	Launched	Comm.
Alert	Washington NYd	1865	never	never
Epervier	Portsmouth NYd	1865	never	never
Nantasket	Boston NYd	1864	15 Aug 1867	22 Oct 1869
Quinnebaug	Brooklyn NYd	Oct 1864	31 Mar 1866	19 Jul 1867
Resaca	Portsmouth NYd	1864	18 Nov 1865	1866
Swatara	Philadelphia NYd	1864	23 May 1865	15 Nov 1865
Tonnage	1,129 tons D.			
Dimensions	230′ (oa) 216′ (bp) × 31′ × 12′10″ (*Quinnebaug, Swatara,* beam 30′)			
Machinery	1 screw, 2-cyl. horizontal back-acting engine (36″ × 3′), 3 boilers. IHP 750, 12 knots. *Alert* and *Nantasket,* Portsmouth, NYd; others, Washington, NYd). *Quinnebaug,* 2 screws, 2 2-cyl. horizontal direct-acting engines (38″ × 1′9″), 7 knots (Jackson).			
Complement	213			
Armament	1–60pdr MLR, 6–32pdr MLR, 3–20pdr MLR (*Swatara* and others)			

Notes: Engines designed by Isherwood. For comparison, *Quinnebaug* had British engines installed that proved inferior. Built of unseasoned timber that deteriorated rapidly. *Resaca* and *Nantasket* differed from others. Three-mast bark rig. *Epervier's* engines exhibited at Centennial Exposition 1876. *Nantasket* and *Swatara* modified to ship rig with bowsprits.

Service records

Alert: Canceled 1866.
Epervier: Canceled 1866.
Nantasket: N. Atlantic Sqn 1870–72, Santo Domingo. Decomm Jul 1872. Stricken 22 Jul 1875. Sold 1883.
Quinnebaug: S. American Stn 1867–70. Decomm 29 Jul 1870. BU 1871and replaced by a new ship.
Resaca: Pacific Stn 1866. Alaska 1867–69. Pacific 1869–72. Sold 18 Feb 1873.
  Later history: Merchant *Ventura* 1873. Wrecked off Santa Cruz, Cal., 20 Apr 1875.
Swatara: West Indies Sqn 1866. European Sqn 1866–69. N. Atlantic Sqn and Caribbean 1869–71. Decomm 20 Dec 1871. BU 1872 and replaced by a new ship.

Alert Class

Name	Builder	Laid down	Launched	Comm.
Alert	Roach	1873	18 Sep 1874	27 May 1875
Huron	Roach	1873	2 Sep 1874	15 Nov 1875
Ranger	Harlan	1873	10 May 1876	27 Nov 1876
Tonnage	1,020 tons D.			

34   Civil War Navies, 1855-1883

Fig 2.30: The Kansas-class gunboat *Shawmut* in the Potomac River (U.S. Naval Historical Center, Norman Polmar Collection)

Fig 2.31: The gunboat *Saco* was unique in having two tall funnels, later cut down. (U.S. Army Military History Institute, Donald L. Canney Collection)

Dimensions	199′9″ (oa) 177′4″ (bp) × 32′ × 13′
Machinery	1 screw, 2-cyl. horizontal compound engine, 5 boilers. IHP 560, 10 knots (*Ranger*, Harlan; others: bldr)
Complement	202
Armament	1–11″ SB, 2–9″ SB, 1–60pdr MLR *Alert*: also spar torpedo.

Notes: Iron hulls. *Huron* and *Ranger* schooner rig, *Alert* bark.

Service records
Alert: Asiatic Stn 1876–86. In collision with Japanese imperial yacht at Kobe, 18 Apr 1882.†
Huron: Caribbean and Gulf of Mexico 1876–77. Wrecked near Nag's Head, N. C., 24 Nov 1877 (104 dead).
Ranger: Asiatic Stn 1877–79. Surveying off Mexico and Pacific coast 1881–89.†

Enterprise Class

Name	Builder	Laid down	Launched	Comm.
Adams	Boston NYd	Feb 1874	24 Oct 1874	21 Jul 1876
Alliance ex-*Huron* (1876)	Norfolk NYd	1873	8 Mar 1875	8 Jan 1877
Enterprise	Portsmouth NYd	1873	13 Jun 1874	16 Mar 1877
Essex	Portsmouth NYd	1873	26 Oct 1874	3 Oct 1876
Nipsic	Washington NYd	1873	6 Jun 1878	11 Oct 1879

Tonnage	1,375 tons D.
Dimensions	185′ (bp) × 35′ × 16′4″
Machinery	1 screw, 2-cyl. vertical compound engine, 8 boilers, IHP 800, 11 knots (*Adams* and *Essex*, Atlantic; *Alliance*, Quintard; *Enterprise*, Woodruff IW; *Nipsic*, Wm.Wright)
Complement	190
Armament	1–11″ SB, 4–9″ SB, 1–60pdr MLR, except *Nipsic*, 6–9″ SB, 1–8″R, 1–60pdr MLR

Notes: Bark rigged, wood hulls. *Nipsic* officially a rebuilt older ship.

Service records
Adams: N. Atlantic Stn 1876–77. S. Atlantic Stn 1877–78. Pacific Stn 1878–89.†
Alliance: European Stn 1877–79. Search for polar steamer *Jeannette* 1881. N. Atlantic Sqn 1881–86.†
Enterprise: Surveying Mississippi River 1877 and Amazon River 1878. European Stn 1878–80. Hydrographic survey cruise around the world 1883–86.†
Essex: N. Atlantic Sqn 1877. Pacific Stn 1881–82. Asiatic Stn 1883–89.†
Nipsic: West Indies 1879–80. European Stn 1880–83. S. Atlantic Sqn 1883–86.†

SIDE-WHEEL SLOOP

Saginaw

Name	Builder	Laid Down	Launched	Comm.
Saginaw ex-*Toucey*	Mare Island NYd	16 Sep 1858	3 Mar 1859	5 Jan 1860

Tonnage	508 tons (U); 453 tons B.
Dimensions	163′ (oa) 155′ (bp) × 26′ × 4′5″ light
Machinery	Side wheels, 2-cyl. inclined oscillating engine (39″ × 4′), 9 knots (Union IW)
Complement	59
Armament	1–50pdr MLR, 1–32pdr/42, 2–24pdr MLR

Service record: East India Sqn 1860–62. Pacific Sqn 1863–66. Wrecked on Ocean Island, east of Midway, 29 Oct 1870.

SIDE-WHEEL GUNBOATS (DOUBLE-ENDERS)

Built for use in narrow and shallow coastal waters, the "double-enders" were designed to be able to proceed forward or backward and had a rudder at each end. They were very useful operating in rivers too narrow to permit turning around, but their shallow draft and flat bottoms made them generally poor sea boats. Hulls were designed by Lenthall and the engines by Isherwood.

Fig 2.32: The gunboat *Huron* shown with schooner rig was wrecked in 1877 after only two years in service. (U.S. Naval Historical Center)

Miami

Name	Builder	Laid down	Launched	Comm.
Miami	Philadelphia NYd	1861	16 Nov 1861	29 Jan 1862

Tonnage 730 tons B.
Dimensions 208′2″ (dk) × 33′2″ × 8′6″
Machinery Side wheels, 1 inclined direct-acting engine (44″ × 7′), 2 boilers. 8 knots (Merrick)
Complement 134
Armament 1–9′ SB, 1–80pdr MLR, 4–24pdr.
(1862) add 1–9″ SB.
(Apr 1863) 6–9″ SB, 1–100pdr MLR, 1–24pdr SB.

Service record: GulfBS 1862. Passage past New Orleans forts and engagement with CSN vessels, 24 Apr 1862. Bombardment of Vicksburg, 26–22 Jun 1862. NAtlBS Sep 1862–64. Expedition in Chowan River, N.C., 26–30 Jul 1863. Engagements with CSS *Albemarle* at Plymouth, N.C. (damaged, captain Lt. Cmdr C.W. Flusser killed), 19 Apr and in Albemarle Sound, 5 May 1864. James River sqn 1864–65. Decomm 22 May 1865. Sold 10 Aug 1865.
Later history: Merchant *Miami* 1865. RR 1869.

Maratanza

Name	Builder	Laid down	Launched	Comm.
Maratanza	Boston NYd	1861	26 Nov 1861	12 Apr 1862

Tonnage 786 tons B.
Dimensions 209′ × 32′11″ × 10′
Machinery Side wheels, 1 inclined direct-acting engine (44″ × 7′), 2 boilers, 10 knots (Loring)
Complement 111
Armament 1–100pdr MLR, 1–9″ SB, 4–24pdrH.
(May 1863) add 1–11″ SB, 1–9″ SB.
(1865) 1–11″ SB, 4–9″ SB, 2–24pdrH.

Service record: James River 1862. Army operations at Gloucester and York, Va., 14–29 Apr 1862. Captured CSS *Teaser** in James River, 4 Jul 1862. Blockade off

* Later USS *Teaser*.

Wilmington 1862. Engaged blockade runner *Kate* in Cape Fear River, 25 Sep 1862. Second attack on Ft. Fisher, N.C., 13–15 Jan 1865. Bombarded Cape Fear River forts, 18–21 Feb 1865. Decomm 21 Jun 1865. Sold 26 Aug 1868.
Ships captured: *Express*, 4 May 1863; *Ceres*, 7 Dec 1863; str **Georgiana McCaw*, 2 Jun 1864; strs *Stag*, *Charlotte*, 20 Jan 1865.
Later history: Merchant *Maratanza* 1868. Sold to Haiti as gunboat, renamed *Salnave*, 1868. Damaged in action with revolutionaries at Gonaives, 8 Aug 1869. Sunk at Cap Haitien, 13 Nov 1869, repaired, renamed *Union*.

Sebago Class

Name	Builder	Laid down	Launched	Comm.
Mahaska	Portsmouth NYd	1861	10 Dec 1861	5 May 1862
Sebago	Portsmouth NYd	May 1861	30 Nov 1861	26 Mar 1862

Tonnage 1,070 tons D; *Mahaska* 832 tons B., *Sebago* 852 tons B.
Dimensions 228′2″ (bp) × 33′10″ × 9′3″
Machinery Side wheels, 1 inclined direct-acting engine (44″ × 7′), 2 boilers, 11 knots [*Mahaska* (Morgan), *Sebago* (Novelty)]
Complement 148
Armament 1–9″ SB, 1–100pdr MLR, 4–24pdrH
Mahaska: (Nov 1862) 2–24pdrH replaced by 4–9″ SB.
(May 63) 6–9″ SB, 1–100pdr MLR, 2–12pdrH.
Sebago: (1864) 1–100pdr MLR, 5–9″ SB, 2–24pdrH, 2–12pdrH.

Service records:
Mahaska: Chesapeake Bay 1862. Expeditions to West Point, Va., Pamunkey River, 7–9 Jan and in James River, Va., 6–20 Jul 1863. NAtlBS 1863. Bombardment of Ft. Wagner, Charleston, 6 Aug–8 Sep 1863. Assault on Jacksonville, Fla., 2–22 Feb 1864. Expedition to St. Marks, Fla., 23 Feb–27 Mar 1865. Decomm 12 Sep 1868. Sold 20 Nov 1868.
Ships captured: *Gen. Taylor*, 20 Feb 1863; str **Little Magruder*, 8 Aug 1863; *Delia*, 17 Feb 1865.
Later history: Merchant *Jeannette* 1868. RR 1869
Sebago: NAtlBS Apr–Jun 1862. Army operations at Gloucester and York, Va., 14–29 Apr and at Yorktown, Va., 4–7 May 1862. Expedition up Pamunkey River, Va., 17 May 1862. SAtlBS 1862. Damaged by grounding in Wassaw Sound, 18 Jun 1863. WGulfBS 1864. Battle of Mobile Bay, 5 Aug 1864. Decomm 29 Jul 1865. Sold 19 Jan 1867.
Later history: FFU

Octorara

Name	Builder	Laid down	Launched	Comm.
Octorara	Brooklyn NYd	1861	7 Dec 1861	28 Feb 1862

Tonnage 981 tons D; 829 tons B.
Dimensions 205′ (bp) 193′2″ × 34′6″ × 4′10″
Machinery Side wheels, 1 inclined direct-acting engine (44″ × 7′), 2 boilers, 11 knots (Neptune)
Complement 118
Armament 1–80pdr MLR, 1–9″ SB, 4–24pdr.
(Jul 1863) 1–100pdr MLR, 3–9″ SB, 2–32pdr/33, 4–24pdrH.
(Jul 1865) 2–32pdr/33, 4–24pdr.

Service record: NAtlBS 1862. WGulfBS 1862. Helm jammed during passage past batteries at Vicksburg, Miss., 28 Jun 1862. WGulfBS Oct 1863–65. Made reconnaissance into Mobile Bay, 20 Jan 1864. Bombardment of Ft. Powell, Mobile Bay, 16–29 Feb 1864. Damaged during battle of Mobile Bay, 5 Aug 1864. Bombardment of Ft. Morgan, Mobile Bay, 9–23 Aug 1864. Attacked by submersible CSS *St. Patrick* off Mobile Bay, 28 Jan 1865. Capture of Mobile, 10–12 Apr 1865. Decomm 5 Aug 1865. Sold 9 Nov 1866.

Fig 2.33: The gunboat *Adams*, with *Ossipee* behind, probably taken during the 1870s at Boston.

Ships captured: str *Tubal Cain*, 24 Jul 1862; *Elias Reed*, 5 Nov 1862; *Mont Blanc*, 25 Dec 1862; *Rising Dawn*, 10 Jan 1863; *Brave*, 15 Jan 1863; *Florence Nightingale*, 13 Mar 1863; *Five Brothers, Rosalie*,* 16 Mar 1863; *John Williams*, 19 Mar 1863; *W.Y. Leitch*, 20 Apr 1863; *Handy*, 21 Apr 1863; str *Eagle*, 18 May 1863.

Later history: FFU

* Later USS *Rosalie*.

Paul Jones

Name	Builder	Laid down	Launched	Comm.
Paul Jones	Baltimore, Md. (Abrahams)	1861	17 Jan 1862	26 Apr 1862
Tonnage	1,210 tons D; 863 tons B.			
Dimensions	216′10″ (bp) × 35′4″ × 8′			

Fig 2.34: The side-wheel gunboat *Saginaw* was launched at Mare Island in 1859 and served only on the Pacific coast. (U.S. Naval Historical Center)

Machinery	Side wheels, 1 inclined direct-acting engine (48″ × 7′). 10 knots (Reaney)
Complement	148
Armament	1–100pdr MLR, 1–11″ SB, 2–9″ SB, 2–50pdr MLR, 2–24pdrH

Service record: SAtlBS 1862. Bombardment of Ft. McAllister, Ogeechee River, Ga., 29 Jul 1862. Bombardment at St. Johns Bluff, Fla., 17 Sep 1862. Joint expedition to St. Johns Bluff, 1–12 Oct and to Pocotaligo, S.C., 21–23 Oct 1862. Bombardment of Ft. Wagner, Charleston, 18–25 Jul 1863. Blockade off Charleston 1863–Aug 1864. EGulfBS Apr 1865. Sold 13 Jul 1867.

Later history: FFU

Port Royal

Name	Builder	Laid down	Launched	Comm.
Port Royal	New York, N.Y. (Stack)	1861	17 Jan 1862	26 Apr 1862

Tonnage	1,163 tons D; 805 tons B.
Dimensions	207′ (bp) × 34′4″ × 7′8″
Machinery	Side wheels, 1 inclined direct-acting engine (48″ × 7′), 9.5 knots (Novelty)
Complement	131
Armament	1–100pdr MLR, 1–10″ SB, 6–24pdrH.
	(Apr 1863) 1–100pdr MLR, 1–10″ SB, 2–9″ SB, 2–50pdr MLR, 2–24pdrH, 1–12pdr SB.

Service record: NAtlBS 1862–63. Engaged batteries at Sewells Point, Va., 8 May and at Drewrys Bluff, Va., 15 May 1862. Bombardment of Ft. Wagner, Charleston, 18 Jul 1863. EGulfBS 1864–65. Bombardment of Ft. Powell, Mobile Bay, 16–29 Feb 1864. Battle of Mobile Bay, 5 Aug 1864. Bombardment of Ft. Morgan, Mobile Bay, 9–23 Aug 1864. Decomm 23 May 1866. Sold 3 Oct 1866.

Ships captured: *Hortense*, 18 Feb 1863; *Fashion*, 22 May 1863.

Later history: Merchant *Port Royal*, 1866. RR 1886.

Cimarron

Name	Builder	Laid down	Launched	Comm.
Cimarron	Bordentown, N.J. (Mershon)	1861	16 Mar 1862	5 Jul 1862

Tonnage	993 tons D; 860 tons B.

Fig 2.35: The double-ender *Maratanza* at anchor in the James River in 1862. Notice the rounded stern.

Dimensions	205′ × 35′ × 9′
Machinery	Side wheels, 1 inclined direct-acting engine, 2 boilers, 10 knots (McKnight)
Complement	122
Armament	1–100pdr MLR, 1–9″ SB, 6–24pdrH.
	(1863) 2–24pdrH replaced by 2–9″ SB.
	(Jun 1864) 1–150pdr MLR, 3–9″ SB, 4–24pdrH SB, 4–12pdr H.

Notes: Name originally spelled *Cimerone*, changed prior to launch.

Service record: James River Jul–Sep 1862. SAtlBS Sep 1862–65. Bombardment at St. Johns Bluff, Fla., 17 Sep 1862. Bombardment of Ft. Wagner, Charleston, 18 Aug 1863. 100pdr gun exploded during bombardment near Legareville, S. C., 15 Feb 1864. Decomm 17 Aug 1865. Sold 6 Nov 1865.

Ships captured: *Evening Star*, 29 May 1863; str *Jupiter*, 13 Sep 1863.

Later history: FFU

Genesee Class

Name	Builder	Laid down	Launched	Comm.
Genesee	Boston NYd	1861	2 Apr 1862	3 Jul 1862
Tioga	Boston NYd	1861	18 Apr 1862	30 Jun 1862

Tonnage	1,120 tons D; 819 tons B.
Dimensions	209′ (bp) × 34′11″ × 10′6″
Machinery	Side wheels, 1 inclined direct-acting engine (48″ × 7′), 11.5 knots. (*Genesee*, Neptune; *Tioga*, Morgan)
Complement	113
Armament	1–100pdr MLR, 1–10″ SB, 6–24pdrH.
	Genesee: (May 1863) 4–24pdrH replaced by 4–9″ SB.
	(Sep 1863) 1–100pdr MLR, 5–9″ SB, 2–24pdrH.
	(Dec 1863) 2–100pdr MLR, 1–10″ SB, 4–9″ SB, 2–24pdrH.
	(Mar 64) less 1–100pdr MLR.
	Tioga: (Jul 1863): 4–32pdr/33 replaced 4–24pdrH.
	(Jun 1865) 1–10″ SB, 1–60pdr MLR, 6–32pdr/33, 2–24pdrH, 2–12pdr MLR.

Service records:

Genesee NAtlBS 1862. Blockade of Wilmington. WGulfBS Feb 1863. Damaged by 10-inch shell during attempt to pass Port Hudson, La., 14 Mar 1863. Blockade off Mobile Sep 1863. Bombardment at Grants Pass, Ala., 13 Sep 1863. Battle of Mobile Bay, 5 Aug 1864. Storeship 1864–65. Decomm 31 Jul 1865. Sold 3 Oct 1867.
  Ships captured: str *Fanny.* 12 Sep 1863.
  Later history: Merchant bark *Hattie C. Besse* 1867. SE 1870.
Tioga   NAtlBS 1862. James River Flotilla. West Indies Sqn Aug 1862. EGulfBS 1863. Decomm 29 Jun 1864–6 Jun 1865. Gulf Sqn 1865–66. Decomm 8 May 1866. Sold 15 Oct 1867.
  Ships captured: *Nonsuch,* 2 Dec 1862; str *Pearl,* 20 Jan 1863; *Avon,* 14 Feb 1863; *Florence Nightingale,* 13 Mar 1863; *Brothers,* 22 Mar 1863; str *Granite City,** 23 Apr; *Justina,* 23 Apr 1863; str *Victory,* 20 Jun 1863; *Julia,* 27 Jun 1863; str *Herald,* 25 Sep 1863; *Swallow,* 20 Mar 1864.
  Later history: FFU

Sonoma Class

Name	Builder	Laid down	Launched	Comm.
Conemaugh	Portsmouth NYd	1861	1 May 1862	16 Jul 1862
ex-*Cinemaugh* (24 Dec 1861)				
Sonoma	Portsmouth NYd	1861	15 Apr 1862	8 Jul 1862

Tonnage	1,105 tons D; 955 tons B.
Dimensions	233′9″ × 34′10″ × 8′7″
Machinery	Side wheels, 1 inclined direct-acting engine (48″ × 7′), 2 boilers, 11 knots (Novelty)
Complement	165
Armament	1–100pdr MLR, 1–11″ SB, 6–24pdrH, 1–12pdrH. *Conemaugh:* (May 1863) 4–24pdrH replaced by 4–9″ SB. (Jan 1864) 6–9″ SB, 1–100pdr MLR, 2–24pdrH, 1–12pdr. *Sonoma:* (Oct 1863) add 4–9″ SB. (Mar 1865) add 2–12pdr MLR.

Notes: *Sonoma* reengined 1863.
Service records:
Conemaugh: SAtlBS Aug 1862–Sep 1863. Expedition to Pocotaligo, S.C., 21–23 Oct 1862. WGulfBS Jan–Nov 1864. Battle of Mobile Bay, 5 Aug 1864. SAtlBS 1865. N. Atlantic Sqn 1867. Decomm 27 Jul 1867. Sold 1 Oct 1867.
  Ships captured: str **Queen of the Wave,* 25 Feb 1863; *unidentified, 10 May 1863; *Judson,* 30 Apr 1864.
  Later history: FFU
Sonoma: West Indies 1862 search for Confederate raiders. SAtlBS Oct 1863. Expedition in Broad River, S.C., 27 Nov–30 Dec 1864. Engaged batteries in Togodo Creek, S.C., 9 Feb 1865. Expedition to Bulls Bay, S. C., 12–17 Feb 1865. Decomm 13 Jun 1865. Sold 1 Oct 1867.
  Ships captured: str *Virginia***, 18 Jan 1863; *Springbok,* 3 Feb 1863; *Atlantic,* 15 Mar 1863; *Clyde,* 14 Apr 1863; str *Ida,* 8 Jul 1864.
  Later history: FFU

Sassacus Class

Name	Builder	Laid down	Launched	Comm.
Agawam	Thomaston, Me. (Lawrence)	Oct 1862	21 Apr 1863	9 Mar 1864
Algonquin	Brooklyn NYd	1863	21 Dec 1863	never
Ascutney	Newburyport, Mass. (Jackman)	1862	4 Apr 1863	28 Jul 1864

* Later USS *Granite City.*
** Later USS *Virginia.*

Chenango	New York, N.Y. (Simonson)	1862	19 Mar 1863	29 Feb 1864
Chicopee	Boston, Mass. (Curtis)	1862	4 Mar 1863	7 May 1864
Eutaw	Baltimore, Md. (Abrahams)	1862	Feb 1863	2 Jul 1863
Iosco	Bath, Me. (Larrabee)	Sep 1862	20 Mar 1863	26 Apr 1864
Lenapee	Brooklyn, N.Y. (Lupton)	1862	28 May 1863	30 Dec 1864
Mackinaw	Brooklyn NYd	1862	22 Apr 1863	23 Apr 1864
Massasoit	Boston, Mass. (Curtis & Tilden)	1862	8 Mar 1863	8 Mar 1864
Mattabesett	Boston, Mass. (Sampson)	1862	1863	7 Apr 1864
Mendota	Brooklyn, N.Y. (Tucker)	1862	13 Jan 1863	2 May 1864
Metacomet	New York, N.Y. (Stack)	1862	7 Mar 1863	4 Jan 1864
Mingoe	Bordentown, N.J. (Mershon)	1862	6 Aug 1863	29 Jul 1864
Osceola	Boston, Mass. (Curtis & Tilden)	1862	29 May 1863	10 Feb 1864
Otsego	New York, N.Y. (Westervelt)	1862	31 Mar 1863	Spring 1864
Pawtucket	Portsmouth NYd	3 Nov 1862	19 Mar 1863	26 Aug 1864
Peoria	Brooklyn NYd	1862	29 Oct 1863	26 Dec 1866
Pontiac	Philadelphia, N.Y. (Hillman)	1862	1863	7 Jul 1864
Pontoosuc	Thomaston, Me. (Lawrence)	Oct 1862	May 1863	10 May 1864
Sassacus	Portsmouth NYd	11 Sep 1862	23 Dec 1862	5 Oct 1863
Shamrock	Brooklyn NYd	1862	17 Mar 1863	13 Jun 1864
Tacony	Philadelphia NYd	1862	7 May 1863	12 Feb 1864
Tallahoma	Brooklyn NYd	1862	28 Nov 1863	27 Dec 1865*
Tallapoosa	Boston NYd	1862	17 Feb 1863	13 Sep 1864
Wateree	Chester, Pa. (Reaney)	1862	29 Aug 1863	20 Jan 1864
Winooski	Boston NYd	1862	30 Jul 1863	27 Jun 1865+
Wyalusing	Philadelphia, Pa.(Cramp)	1862	12 May 1863	8 Feb 1864

+*Completed at Brooklyn, NYd.*
**Delivered.*

Tonnage	1,173 tons D; 974 tons B.
Dimensions	236′ (bp) × 35′ × 9′6″, 12′ dpth
Machinery	Side wheels, inclined direct-acting engine (58″ × 8′9″) except *Algonquin* (48″ × 10′); 2 boilers. IHP 665, 13 knots, (*Agawam, Pontoosuc,* Portland; *Algonquin, Ascutney, Chenango,* Morgan; *Chicopee, Tallapoosa* Neptune; *Eutaw:* Vulcan; *Iosco, Massasoit,* Globe; *Mattabesett:* Allaire, *Mendota, Metacomet,* S.Brooklyn; *Mingoe, Wyalusing:* Pusey, *Osceola, Sassacus,* Atlantic; *Otsego,* Fulton; *Pawtucket, Winooski,* Providence; *Peoria,* Etna; *Pontiac,* Neafie; *Shamrock,* Poole; *Tacony,* Morris Towne; *Tallahoma,* Stover, others: bldr)
Complement	163/200

Armament   2-100 pdrMLR, 4-9"SB, 2-20pdrMLR, except

Algonquin and Peoria: none

Agawam (1864) 2-100pdrMLR, 4-9"SB, 2-24pdrSB, 1-12pdrMLR,1-12pdrSB.

Chenango, Chicopee, Eutaw, Lenapee, Otsego: (1864-5) add 2-24pdrH.

Iosco (Mar 1864) 2-100pdrMLR, 4-9"SB, 2-24pdrMLR, 2-12pdrH.

(Mar 1865) 1-100pdr MLR replaced by 1-11¢ SB.

Mackinaw: (Jan 1864) add 2-24pdrH. (May 1865): 1-15" SB, 6-9" SB, 2-24pdr, 2-12pdr.

Massasoit, Mattabessett, Metacomet: (Mar 1864) 2-100pdr MLR, 4-9" SB, 2-12pdr MLR, 2-24pdr.

Mendota: (Jul 1864) 1-20pdr replaced by 2-24pdrH.

Mingoe: (Aug 1864) add 2-24pdr, 2-12pdr MLR.

Osceola: (Jun 1864) add 1-12pdr SB, 1-12pdr MLR, 1-24pdr, less 2-20pdr MLR. (Mar 1865): 2-100pdr MLR, 1-11" SB, 1-12pdr SB, 1-24pdr.

Pawtucket: (1864) add 2-24pdrH. 1865: 1-100pdr MLR, 1-11" SB, 2-20pdr MLR.

Pontiac: (Jul 1864) add 4-24pdrH, 2-12pdr SB, 2-12pdr MLR.

Pontoosuc: (1864) add 2-24pdrH, 2-12pdr MLR. (Apr 1865) 1-100pdr MLR, 1-11" SB, 4-9" SB, 2-20pdr MLR, 2-24pdrH, 1-12pdr.

Sassacus (1864) 2-100pdr MLR, 4-9" SB, 2-20pdr MLR, 2-24pdrH, 2-12pdr MLR. (Feb 1865) 1-9" SB replaced by 1-100pdr MLR.

Shamrock (1864) add 2-24pdrH, 2-12pdr MLR. (Dec 1864) 2-100pdr MLR, 6-9" SB, 2-20pdr MLR, 2-12pdr SB. *Tacony* (Oct 1864) 2-11" SB, 3-9" SB, 1-24pdrH, 2-12pdr. (Sep 1865) 4-8" SB/63, 2-60pdr MLR, 2-24pdrH SB, 2-12pdr MLR, 2-12pdr SB.

Tallapoosa (Dec 1864) add 2-24pdrH. (1875) 1-11"BLR, 1-10"R. (1888) 1-8"R, 2-60pdr MLR.

Wateree (Jan 1864) add 4-24pdrH, 4-12pdr, less 2-20pdr.

Wyalusing (1864) 2-100pdr MLR, 4-9" SB, 4-24pdrH, 4-12pdrH

Notes: Wooden hulls, except *Wateree* which had an iron hull. Engines designed by Isherwood, except *Algonquin* by Dickerson. *Algonquin* engaged *Winooski* in a celebrated test of machinery in 1865–66, proving a complete failure and was never used. *Tallapoosa* rebuilt as single ender 1875. *Osceola* and *Shamrock* fitted with ram on bow 1864.

Service records:

Agawam: NAtlBS 1864–65. Engagement at Howlett's Bluff, Trents Reach, Va., 21 Jun 1864. Engaged batteries in Four Mile Creek, Va., Jul–Aug 1864 (3 killed). Decomm 31 Mar 1867. Sold 10 Oct 1867.
Later history: FFU

Algonquin: Failed trials and never commissioned. Sold 21 Oct 1869.
Later history: Merchant *Algonquin* 1869. S/F 1878.

Ascutney: NAtlBS Jul 1864. Search for CSS *Florida* in N. Atlantic, then blockade off Wilmington, N.C. Decomm 22 Sep 1864. Sold 28 Oct 1868.
Later history: FFU

Chenango: Damaged by explosion of port boiler while leaving New York, 15 Apr 1864 (33 dead). Recomm 1 Feb 1865. SAtlBS 1865. Decomm 1 Jul 1865. Sold 28 Oct 1868.
Ship captured: Elvira, 25 Feb 1865
Later history: FFU

Fig 2.36: USS *Conemaugh* had her paddle wheels further astern than most of the double enders. (U.S. Naval Historical Center)

Chicopee: NAtlBS Jun 1864–Dec 1865. Expedition to Plymouth, N.C., Roanoke River 28 Oct–2 Nov and up Roanoke River to Poplar Point, N.C., 9–28 Dec 1864. Decomm 19 Dec 1866. Sold 8 Oct 1867.
Later history: FFU

Eutaw: NAtlBS 1863. Operations in James River, from May 1864. Went aground in Hatteras Inlet, 11 Feb 1864. Decomm 8 May 1865. Sold 15 Oct 1867.
Later history: FFU

Iosco: Protected American shipping in Gulf of St. Lawrence 1864. NAtlBS Oct 1864. Unsuccessful attack on Ft. Fisher, N.C., 24–25 Dec 1864. Second attack on Ft. Fisher, 13–15 Jan 1865 (2 killed). Expedition up Roanoke River, N.C., 11–16 May 1865. Decomm 28 Jul 1865. Coal hulk New York, NYd Feb 1868. Bombardment of Ft. Anderson, Cape Fear River, 11–21 Feb 1865. Decomm 17 Oct 1867. Sold 26 Aug 1868.
Ships captured: *Sybil*, 21 Nov 1864; *Sarah M. Newhall*, 23 May 1865.
Lenapee: NAtlBS 1865.
Later history: FFU

Mackinaw: NAtlBS 1864, James River. Engagement at Dutch Gap, Va., 13 and 16–18 Aug 1864. Unsuccessful attack on Ft. Fisher, N.C., 24–25 Dec 1864. Second attack on Ft. Fisher, 13–15 Jan 1865. Bombardment of Ft. Anderson, Cape Fear River, 11–21 Feb 1865. Decomm May 1865. N. Atlantic Sqn and West Indies 1866–67. Decomm 4 May 1867. Sold 3 Oct 1867.
Ships captured: str *Matagorda*, 10 Sep 1864; *Mary*, 3 Dec 1864.
Later history: FFU

Massasoit: NAtlBS Oct 1864. Engagement at Trent's Reach, James River, Va., 24 Jan 1865. Decomm 27 Jun 1865. Sold 15 Oct 1867.
Later history: FFU

Mattabesett: NAtlBS 1864. Engagement with CSS *Albemarle*, Albemarle Sound, N.C., 5 May 1864 (2 killed). Decomm 31 May 1865. Sold 15 Oct 1867.
Ship captured: *Bombshell*, 5 May 1864.
Later history: FFU

Mendota: NAtlBS, James River 1864–65. Engaged battery near Four Mile Creek, Va., 16 Jul 1864 (1 killed). Decomm 12 May 1865. Sold 7 Dec 1867.

Metacomet: WGulfBS 1864. Forced steamer *Ivanhoe* ashore, 30 Jun 1864. Battle of Mobile Bay, damaged by CSS *Selma*, 5 Aug 1864. Bombardment of Ft. Morgan, Mobile Bay, 9–23 Aug 1864. Decomm 18 Aug 1865. Sold 28 Oct 1868.
Ships captured: str *Donegal*,* 6 Jun 1864; *Ivanhoe*, 30 Jun 1864; str *Susanna*, 27 Nov 1864; *Sea Witch*, 31 Dec 1864; *Lilly*, 6 Jan 1865.
Later history: FFU

Mingoe: SAtlBS 1864–65. Expeditions in Broad River, S.C., 27 Nov–30 Dec and to Georgetown, S.C., 23 Feb 1865. Sold 3 Oct 1867.
Later history: FFU

Osceola: NAtlBS, James River 1864. Engaged battery near Harrison's Landing, Va., 4 Aug 1864. Unsuccessful attack on Ft. Fisher, N.C., 24–25 Dec 1864. Damaged during second attack on Ft. Fisher, 13–15 Jan 1865.

---
* Later USS *Donegal*.

Bombardment of Ft. Anderson, Cape Fear River, 11–21 Feb 1865. Decomm 13 May 1865. Sold 1 Oct 1867.
Ships captured: str *Blenheim*, 25 Jan 1865.
Later history: Merchant *Eliza* 1868. Converted to schooner. Lost 1868?
Otsego: NAtlBS May 1864. Capture of Plymouth, N.C., Roanoke River, 29–31 Oct 1864. Sank in shallow water with decks above water after hitting two torpedoes (mines) in Roanoke River, 9 Dec 1864.
Pawtucket: NAtlBS Oct 1864–65. Unsuccessful attack on Ft. Fisher, N.C., 24–25 Dec 1864. Second attack on Ft. Fisher, 13–15 Jan 1865. Bombardment of Ft. Anderson, Cape Fear River, 11–21 Feb 1865. Decomm 15 Jun 1865. Sold 15 Oct 1867.
Later history: FFU
Peoria: N. Atlantic 1867, West Indies. Decomm 28 Jul 1867. Sold 26 Aug 1868.
Later history: FFU
Pontiac: SAtlBS 1864. Damaged during engagement with battery at Sullivan's Island, 7 Nov 1864. Expedition in Broad River, S.C., 27 Nov–30 Dec 1864. Decomm 21 Jun 1865. Sold 15 Oct 1867.
Ship captured: str *Amazon*, 2 Mar 1865.
Later history: FFU
Pontoosuc: Search for CSS *Tallahassee* in Gulf of St. Lawrence, 1864. SAtlBS 1864–65. Unsuccessful attack on Ft. Fisher, N.C., 24–25 Dec 1864. Second attack on Ft. Fisher, 13–15 Jan 1865. Bombardment of Ft. Anderson, Cape Fear River, 11–21 Feb 1865. Decomm 5 Jul 1865. Sold 3 Oct 1866.
Later history: FFU
Sassacus: NAtlBS 1864–65. Damaged in collision with CSS *Albemarle* during engagement in Albemarle Sound, N.C., 5 May 1864 (6 killed). Unsuccessful attack on Ft. Fisher, N.C., 24–25 Dec 1864. Second attack on Ft. Fisher, 13–15 Jan 1865 (2 killed). Bombardment of Ft. Anderson, Cape Fear River, 11–21 Feb 1865. Decomm 13 May 1865. Sold 15 Aug 1868.
Ships captured: str *Wild Dayrell, 1 Feb 1864; str *Nutfield, 5 Feb 1864.
Later history: FFU
Shamrock: NAtlBS 1864–Aug 1865. Capture of Plymouth, N.C., Roanoke River, 29–31 Oct 1864. West Indies Sqn Dec 1865. European Sqn 1866–68. Decomm 10 Aug 1868. Sold 1 Sep 1868.
Later history: FFU
Tacony: NAtlBS 1864. Capture of Plymouth, N.C., Roanoke River, 29–31 Oct 1864. Unsuccessful attack on Ft. Fisher, N.C., 24–25 Dec 1864. Second attack on Ft. Fisher, 13–15 Jan 1865 (2 killed). Decomm 7 Oct 1867. Sold 26 Aug 1868.
Later history: FFU
Tallahoma: No service. Sold 29 Aug 1868.
Later history: Merchant *Mary M. Roberts* 1868. SE 1870.
Tallapoosa: Search in N. Atlantic for Confederate raiders, 1864. EGulfBS 1865. Gulf Sqn 1866–67. Training ship, *Annapolis* 1872. Rebuilt 1876. †
Wateree: Pacific Sqn 1864. Driven ashore during earthquake and tidal wave at Arica, Peru, 13 Aug 1868. Hulk sold ashore 21 Nov 1868.
Winooski: Completed at Brooklyn NYd. N. Atlantic 1866. Caribbean 1867. Sold 25 Aug 1868.
Later history: FFU
Wyalusing: NAtlBS 1864. Engagement with CSS *Albemarle*, Albemarle Sound, N.C., 5 May 1864 (1 killed). Capture of Plymouth, N.C., Roanoke River, 29–31 Oct and up Roanoke River to Poplar Point, N.C., 9–28 Dec 1864. Decomm 10 Jun 1865. Sold 15 Oct 1867.
Ship captured: *Triumph*, 9 Jan 1865.
Later history: FFU

Mohongo Class

Name	Builder	Laid down	Launched	Comm.
Ashuelot	Boston, Mass. (McKay)	1864	22 Jul 1865	4 Apr 1866
Mohongo	Jersey City, N.J. (Secor)	1863	9 Jul 1864	23 May 1865
Monocacy	Baltimore, Md. (Denmead)	1863	14 Dec 1864	early 1866
Muscoota	Greenpoint, N.Y. (Continental)	1863	1864	5 Jan 1865
Shamokin	Chester, Pa. (Reaney)	1863	1864	31 Jul 1865*
Suwanee	Chester, Pa. (Reaney)	1863	13 Mar 1864	23 Jan 1865
Winnipec	Boston, Mass. (Loring)	1863	20 Aug 1864	1865

Tonnage	1,370 tons D; 1,030 tons B.
Dimensions	255′ (wl) × 35′ × 9′6″
Machinery	Side wheels, 1 inclined direct-acting engine (58″ × 8′9″), 2 boilers. 15 knots (*Mohongo*, Fulton; *Muscoota*, Morgan; others: bldr)
Complement	190
Armament	4–9″ SB, 2–100pdr MLR, 2–20pdr MLR, 2–24pdr, except *Ashuelot*, *Monocacy*, 4–8″ SB, 2–60pdr MLR, 2–20pdr MLR, 2–24pdrH.
	Monocacy (1889) 4–8″, 2–60pdrBLR

Notes: Iron hulls, schooner rig. Engines designed by Isherwood. Better sea boats than previous classes, but rolled heavily.

Service records:
Ashuelot Cruise to Europe with USS *Miantonomoh* 1866. Asiatic Stn 1866–83.†
Mohongo Pacific Sqn, S. America, 1865–67. Hawaii 1868. Decomm 29 May 1870. Sold 17 Nov 1870.
Later history: Merchant *Mohongo* 1870. SE 1878.
Monocacy Asiatic Stn 1866–1903. Korean Expedition 1871. †
Muscoota Sold 17 Jun 1869.
Later history: Merchant *Tennessee* 1869. Caught fire and beached near Little River, N.C., 29 Jun 1870.
Shamokin S. Atlantic Stn 1866–68. Decomm 24 Dec 1868. Sold 21 Oct 1869.
Later history: Merchant *Georgia* 1869. Conv to screw propeller and lengthened 1879. Wrecked in Gulf of Nicoya, Costa Rica, 30 Sep 1878.
Suwanee Pacific Sqn 1865–68. Wrecked in Queen Charlotte Sound, B.C., 9 Jul 1868.
Winnipec Practice ship, Naval Academy 1866–67. Sold 17 Jun 1869.
Later history: Merchant *South Carolina* 1869. Converted to screw and lengthened 1879. BU 1891.
*Delivered.

SPAR TORPEDO BOATS

Tugs *Alpha, Althea, Belle, Delta, Gamma, Hoyt, Martin, Rose,* and *Violet* were armed with spar torpedoes in 1864–65. In addition, *Fortune* and *Triana* were converted to experimental spar torpedo boats in 1871.

Spuyten Duyvil

Name	Builder	Keel Laid	Launched	Comm.
Stromboli	Fairhaven, Conn. (Pook)	1864	1864	Oct 1864

Tonnage	207 tons D; 116 tons B.
Dimensions	84′2″ (oa) 73′11″ (bp) × 20′8″ × 7′5″
Machinery	1 screw, 1 HP engine, 5 knots (Mystic)

Unarmored Steam Vessels 41

Fig 2.37: USS *Tallapoosa*, after rebuilding as a single-ended ship in 1876. (U.S. Naval Historical Center)

Complement	23
Armament	1 spar torpedo
Armor	5″ sides, 3″ deck, 5″ pilot house

Notes: Designed by William W. W. Wood. Wooden, low freeboard flush deck vessel with funnel and conning tower. Increase in draft used as protection. Retractable spar torpedo in bow.

Service record: Renamed *Spuyten Duyvil*, 19 Nov 1864. James River 1865. Engagement at Trent's Reach, James River, Va., 24 Jan 1865. Used as experimental vessel. Sold 1880.

Intrepid

Name	Builder	Keel Laid	Launched	Comm.
Intrepid	Boston NYd	1873	5 Mar 1874	31 Jul 1874
Tonnage	1,150 tons D. 438 tons B.			
Dimensions	170′3″ (wl) × 35′ × 12′			
Machinery	2 screws, 2 compound engines, 6 boilers. IHP 1,800, 10.6 knots (Morgan)			
Complement	(U)			
Armament	4–24pdr H, 5 spar torpedoes			

Notes: Designed by Isaiah Hanscom as an experimental torpedo ram. Conversion to light-draft gunboat 1882 for China service canceled 1889, planned armament 2–8″ guns. Too slow to be effective.

Service record:†

Alarm

Name	Builder	Keel Laid	Launched	Comm.
Alarm	Brooklyn NYd	1873	13 Nov 1873	1874
Tonnage	800 tons D.			
Dimensions	173′ (oa) 158′6″ (bp) × 28′ × 10′6″			
Machinery	Fowler wheel, 2 compound engines, 4 boilers. IHP 600, 10 knots (Morgan)			
Complement	25			
Armament	1–15″ SB, 3 spar torpedoes			
Armor	4½″ bow			

Fig 2.38: USS *Mohongo*, an iron-hulled double-ender gunboat completed after the war. (U.S. Naval Historical Center)

Notes: No rudder. Fowler feathering paddle wheel turning horizontally was used for both propulsion and steering, later replaced by a steering propeller. 32-foot ram bow with spar torpedoes on bow and on each beam.

Service record: Experimental vessel.†

HAND-PROPELLED SUBMARINE

Name	Builder	Keel Laid	Launched	Comm.
Alligator	Philadelphia, Pa. (Neafie)	1861	1 May 1862	Jun 1862
Dimensions	47′ × 4′6″ × d6′			
Complement	21			
Armament	2 spar torpedoes			

Note: At first propelled by oars, screw propeller installed later.

Service record: Disappeared at sea when cut adrift from tow in storm off North Carolina, 2 Apr 1863.

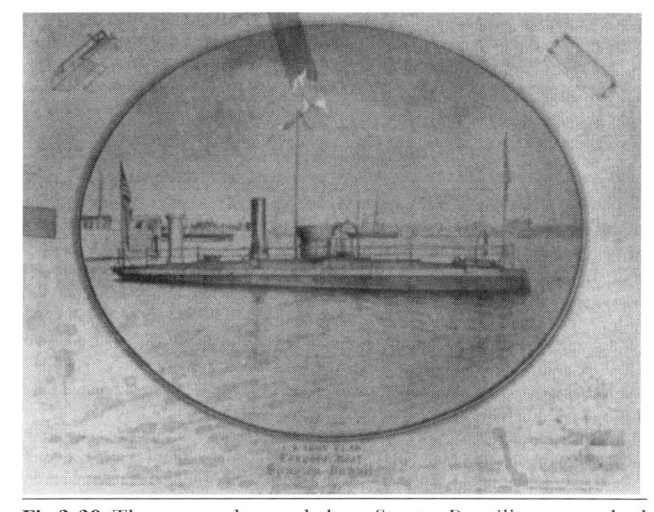

Fig 2.39: The armored torpedo boat *Spuyten Duyvil* in a retouched photo of this unusual vessel at Brooklyn Navy Yard following the war. The spar torpedo was retracted into the bow. (U.S. Naval Historical Center)

PICKET BOATS

Name	Builder
No. 1–3	New Brunswick N.J. (Lewis Hoagland)
No. 4–6	Boston, Mass. (Sylvanus Smith)
Dimensions	45' × 9'6",
Machinery	1 screw, double piston reciprocating Root engines; 7 to 8 knots,
Complement	7
Armament	1–12pdrH

Notes and service records:

No. 1: Delivered 22 Aug 1864. Sank CSS *Albemarle* in Roanoke River (under Lt. William B. Cushing) and sunk, 28 Oct 1864.

No. 2: Destroyed in Great Wicomico River, 18 Oct 1864.

No. 3: Cut adrift in Cape Fear River, 19 Feb 1865.

No. 4: Laid up 2 Jun 1865

3
ACQUIRED COMBATANT VESSELS

The requirements of the Navy's duties during the war were varied and great. Ships of all sizes were needed—larger ones for operations on the high seas and small shallow-draft vessels for inshore and riverine activities.

A number of big and fast vessels were chartered or purchased in the spring of 1861 for use as blockaders and to supplement the regular Navy ships. At a later date, some of these were used to protect American commercial vessels on sea lanes threatened by Confederate raiders, such as the valuable route from Panama to the East Coast connecting with the Pacific route from California.

Captured blockade runners were taken into service, being very fast and suitable for pursuing their former sisters as they attempted to reach or break out of the Confederate ports. After sighting a suspect, a chase would ensue, which might last many hours—sometimes resulting in an escape, often in capture or destruction of the vessel.

Medium-size vessels were used as gunboats in the rivers of Virginia and the Carolinas, and as close-in blockaders off Wilmington, Charleston, and other Southern ports. New York ferryboats were found to be very useful, with their capacity for steaming in either direction and with decks already strengthened for carrying heavy loads.

A host of small steamers and tugs were given flower names and were known to some as the "Navy's flower pots."

Most of these vessels were sold after the war. Their unstrengthened hulls and inadequate engines made them ill-suited for regular naval service, and they were disposed of in large batches within a few months after the end of the blockade.

PREWAR MERCHANT ACQUISITIONS

Name	Builder	Launched	Acquired	Comm.
Anacostia ex-*M. W. Chapin*	Philadelphia, Pa.	1856	17 Oct 1858	28 Jul 1859

Tonnage	217 tons B, 358 n/r
Dimensions	129' × 23' × 6', d5'
Machinery	1 screw, 1 vertical direct-acting engine (24" × 2'), 7.5 knots
Complement	67
Armament	(1861) 2–9" SB; (1864) add 1–30pdr MLR, 1–12pdr SB; (Apr 1865) 1–50pdr replaced by 1–30pdr MLR

Notes: Chartered for Paraguay Expedition 1858–59, purchased 1859 and renamed.

Service record: Paraguay Expedition 1858-59. Potomac Flotilla 1861–65. Engaged batteries at Aquia Creek, Va., 29 May–1 Jun, 1861, at Freestone Point., Va., 9 Dec 1861 and at Cockpit Point, Va., 1 Jan 1862. Army operations at Gloucester and York, Va., 14–29 Apr 1862. Engaged batteries at Port Royal, Va., 4 Dec 1862. Expedition to Northern Neck, Va., 12 Jan 1864. Decomm 12 Jun 1865. Sold 20 Jul 1865.

Ships captured: str *Eureka*,* 20 Apr 1862; *Monitor*, 6 Jun 1862; *Exchange*, 28 Dec 1862; *Emily*, 21 May 1863; *Flying Cloud*, 2 Jun 1863; *Buckskin*, 9 Nov 1864.

Later history: Merchant *Alexandria* 1865. Burned at City Point, Va., 22 Mar 1868.

Name	Builder	Launched	Acquired	Comm.
Crusader ex-*Southern Star*	Murfreesboro, N.C.	1858	Oct 1858	27 Oct 1858

Tonnage	545 tons B, 469 n/r
Dimensions	169' × 28' × 12'6"
Machinery	1 screw, 2 inclined direct-acting engines (23" × 2'2"), 1 boiler. 8 knots
Complement	79/92
Armament	(1861) 4–32pdr/33, 1–12pdr H; (Sep1862) add 2–20pdr MLR

Note: Three-mast bark, wood hull. Chartered for Paraguay Expedition 1858–59, purchased 1859 and renamed.

Service record: Paraguay Expedition 1858-59. Home Sqn 1859–61. SatlBS Jan–Jul 1862. NAtlBS Sep 1862, Chesapeake Bay, 1862–65. Decomm 13 Jun 1865. Sold 20 Jul 1865.

---
* Later USS *Eureka*.

44   Civil War Navies, 1855-1883

Fig 3.1: The USS *Crusader* was chartered for the expedition to Paraguay of 1859 and later purchased. (U.S. Naval Historical Center)

Ships captured: Slaver *Bogota*, 23 May 1860; slaver *William R. Kibby*, 23 Jul 1860. *Wanderer*, 14 May 1861; *Neptune*, 20 May 1861; *President Fillmore*, 22 Jun 1861; *General Taylor*, 20 Feb 1863; *A.P. Upshur*, 22 Feb 1863; **Henry A. Wise*, 9 Mar 1863; *Jemima, 14 Mar 1863; *Isaac L. Adkins*, 22 May 1864; *Catherine Coombs*, 27 Feb 1865.
Later history: Merchant *Kalorama*, 1865. Wrecked south of San Buenaventura, Calif., 25 Feb 1876.

Name	Builder	Launched	Acquired	Comm.
Despatch	Medford, Mass.	1852	20 Mar 1855	17 Jan 1856
ex-*City of Boston*				
Tonnage	775 tons D, 558 tons B. ; (1859:) 694 tons			
Dimensions	169′6″ (U) 154 (wl) × 30′6″ × 12′, d13′6″			
Machinery	1 screw, 2 vertical direct-acting engines, 2 boilers (Fulton)			
Complement	95/173			
Armament	(Jun 1863) 4–32pdr/57, 1–10″R, 1–20pdr MLR; (Nov 1863) 1–10″ MLR replaced by 1–100pdr MLR			

Notes: Reboilered 1857. Rebuilt 1859 at Norfolk NYd, as Second class sloop with new engines (Loring), recomm 19 Mar 1860.
Service Record: Antislavery patrol, 1858. Renamed *Pocahontas*, 27 Jan 1860. Evacuation of Ft. Sumter 1861. Potomac area patrol 1861. SAtlBS Oct 1861–62. Occupation of Port Royal, S.C., 7 Nov 1861. Occupation of Tybee Island, Ga., 24 Nov 1861. Engagement at Port Royal, 26 Nov 1861. Capture of Fernandina, Fla., and Brunswick, St. Simons, and Jekyl Islands, Ga., 2–12 Mar 1862 (3 killed). WGulfBS Oct 1862. Damaged in storm Aug 1863. Blockade of Texas 1864–65. Decomm 31 Jul 1865. Sold 30 Nov 1865.
Ships captured: str *James Guy*, 21 May 1861; *Cheshire*, 6 Dec 1861; str *Antona*,* 6 Jan 1863; *Morris*, 19 Dec 1864.
Later history: Merchant bark *Abby Bacon* 1865. RR 1898

Name	Builder	Launched	Comm.
John Hancock	Boston NYd	26 Oct 1850	19 Mar 1853
Tonnage	230 tons B; (1853) 382 tons B		
Dimensions	113′ (bp) × 22′ × 10′6″; (1853) 165′6″ × 22′ × 10′6″		
Machinery	1 screw, 2-cyl. oscillating HP engine (20″ × 1′9″), 9 knots. (Washington, N.Y.dNYd) (1853) 2 oscillating LP engines (20″ × 2′)		
Complement	20		
Armament	1–6pdr SB		

* Later USS *Antona*.

Fig 3.2: The USS *Pocahontas* was acquired by the Navy in 1856 as *Despatch* and renamed in 1860. It was rebuilt as a second class sloop at Norfolk Navy Yard in 1858. (Wilson Library, Univ. of North Carolina, Southern Historical Collection,)

Notes: Navy built, designed by Pook with original machinery by Copeland. Rebuilt, re-engined and lengthened 1853 with bark rig; relaunched 24 Feb 1853.
Service Record: North Pacific Survey Exp 1853–54. Decomm 23 Aug 1856. Receiving ship, San Francisco. Sold 17 Aug 1865.
Later history: Merchant *John Hancock* 1865. Converted to schooner 1869. Wrecked in Humboldt Bay about 1887.

Name	Builder	Launched	Acquired	Comm.
Mohawk	Philadelphia, Pa. (Teas)	11 Jun 1853	13 Sep 1858	19 Sep 1859
ex-*Caledonia* (14 Jun 59)				
Tonnage	459 tons B			
Dimensions	162′4″ × 24′4″ × 14′			
Machinery	1 screw, vertical direct-acting engine (30″ × 2′4″), 8 knots (Sutton)			
Complement	65/90			
Armament	1–30pdr MLR, 2–32pdr/33, 4–32pdr/27.			

Notes: Chartered for Paraguay Expedition as *Caledonia*, 1858–59. Purchased and renamed 1859. Three masts, one 1 funnel.
Service Record: Paraguay Expedition 1858-59. EGulfBS May 1861–Apr 1862. Blockade of Pensacola 1862. SAtlBS Jul 1862–63. Guardship, Port Royal, 1863–64. Sold 12 Jul 1864.
Ships captured: Slaver brig *Cygnet*, 18 Nov 1859; slaver *Wildfire* in Old Bahama Channel, 26 Apr 1860;. *George B. Sloat*, 5 Jul 1861.
Later history: Merchant *Alliance* 1865. Lost by stranding in Hatteras Inlet, N.C., 4 Mar 1869.

Name	Builder	Launched	Acquired	Comm.
Mystic	Philadelphia, Pa. (Cramp)	2 Apr 1853	26 May 1859	14 Jun 1859
ex-*Memphis* (14 Jun 1859), ex-*Mount Savage*				
Tonnage	452 tons B			
Dimensions	157′ × 24′7″ × 13′6″			
Machinery	1 screw, 1 vertical direct-acting engine (42″ × 4′), 1 boiler, 6 knots (Reaney Neafie)			
Complement	65/90			
Armament	(Oct 1861) 4–32pdr/27, 1–24pdr; (Aug 1862) add 1–24pdr H, 1–20pdr MLR			

Notes: Originally chartered for Paraguay Expedition 13 Sep 1858. three masts, one funnel.

Service record: Paraguay Expedition 1858-59. In collision with USS *State of Georgia*, 28 Sep 1862. Potomac Flotilla 1862–65. Expedition to West Point, Va., York R., 5–7 May 1863. Sold 24 Jun 1865.

Ships captured: Slaver *Thomas Achorn*, 27 Jun and slaver *Triton*, 16 Jul 1860 off Africa;. *Emily*, 26 Jan 1862; *Napier*, 29 Jul 1862; *Sunbeam*, 28 Sep 1862; *Emma D.*, 17 Nov 1863.

Later history: Merchant *General Custer* 1865. RR 1868

Pocahontas, see *Despatch*

Name	Builder	Launched	Acquired	Comm.
Pulaski	New York, N.Y. (Sneeden)	1854	1858	1858

ex-*Metacomet*

Tonnage	395 tons B
Dimensions	169'11" × 26' × d9'
Machinery	Side wheels, crosshead engine (Peas)
Complement	(U)
Armament	3–12pdr H

Note: Wood steamer. Operated out of Fall River, Mass. until chartered 1858 for Paraguay Expedition; purchased 1859.

Service record: Paraguay Expedition 1858-59. Brazil Station 1859–63. Decomm and sold at Montevideo, 22 Jan 1863.

Later history: Operated in River Plate until 1870.

Name	Builder	Launched	Acquired	Comm.
Sumter	Philadelphia, Pa. (Hillman)	19 Mar 1853	13 Sep 1858	1859

ex-*Atlanta* (26 May 1859), ex-*Parker Vein*

Tonnage	460 tons B
Dimensions	163' × 24'4" × 11'9"
Machinery	1 screw, 1 vertical back-acting engine (40" × 3'6") (Reaney Neafie)
Complement	64/90
Armament	4–32pdr/27, 1–12pdr MLR

Notes: Name also spelled *Sumpter*. Chartered for Paraguay Expedition 1858, purchased 26 May 1859 and renamed.

Service record: Paraguay Expedition 1858-59. SAtlBS Mar 1862. NAtlBS 1863. Sunk in collision with USAT *General Meigs* off Smith Island, N.C., 24 Jun 1863.

Ship captured: Slaver brig *Falmouth* off West Africa, 14 Jun 1861.

Name	Builder	Launched	Acquired	Comm.
Wyandotte	Philadelphia, Pa. (Birely Lynn)	26 Mar 1853	6 Jun 1859	14 Jun 1859

ex-*Western Port* (6 Jun 1859)

Tonnage	453 tons B
Dimensions	162'4" × 24'3" × 13'6"
Machinery	1 screw, vertical direct-acting condensing (Beard's) engine (40" × 3'6"), 7 knots (Reaney Neafie)
Complement	90
Armament	(Dec 1861) 4–32pdr/27, 1–24pdr H; (Dec 1862) add 1–20pdr MLR, 1–12pdr MLR

Notes: Chartered for Paraguay Expedition 1858. Purchased 1859 and renamed. Three masts, one funnel.

Service record: GulfBS 1861. SAtlBS Jan–May 1862. Potomac Flotilla Sep 1862–65. Guardship, Norfolk 1863–65. Decomm 3 Jun 1865. Sold 12 Jul 1865.

Ship captured: Bark *William* with 540 slaves off Cuba, 9 May 1860.

Later history: Merchant *Wyandotte* 1865. Wrecked off Duxbury, Mass., 26 Jan 1866.

ACQUIRED MERCHANT VESSELS LARGE SIDE-WHEEL COMBATANTS (SECOND AND THIRD RATE)

Ocean-going merchant vessels acquired as blockaders.

Name	Builder	Launched	Acquired	Comm.
Adela	Glasgow (Thomson)	1859	23 May 1863	Jun 1863

Tonnage	585 tons B
Dimensions	211' × 23'6" × 9'3", d12'
Machinery	Side wheels, 2-cyl. oscillating engine (52.5" × 4'6"), 4 boilers, 12 knots
Complement	58/70
Armament	2–20pdr MLR, 4–24pdr SB

Notes: Blockade runner, captured by USS *Quaker City* and *Huntsville* in the Bahama Islands, 7 Jul 1862. Brig rig, iron hull. Formerly yacht of the Earl of Eglinton.

Service record: EGulfBS, Aug 1863–Nov 1864. Engaged batteries at Tampa, Fla., 16 Oct 1863 (2 killed). Potomac Flotilla 1865. Sold 30 Nov 1865.

Ships captured: sloop *Laura*, 12 Oct 1863; *Maria*, 29 Mar 1864; *Badger*, 6 Nov 1864.

Later history: FFU.

Name	Builder	Launched	Acquired	Comm.
Advance	Greenock, Scotland (Caird)	3 Jul 1862	Sep 1864	28 Oct 1864

ex-*A.D. Vance*, ex-*Lord Clyde*

Tonnage	1,300 tons D, 808 tons B, 700 GRT
Dimensions	243' (U) 230' (U) × 26' × 11'8"
Machinery	Side wheels, 2-cyl. oscillating side-lever engines (63" × 6'6"), 6 boilers, 12 knots. (Caird)
Complement	98/107
Armament	1–20pdr MLR, 4–24pdr H

Notes: Blockade runner *Advance*, captured by USS *Santiago de Cuba*, 10 Sep 1864 off Wilmington. Iron hull, two funnels and two masts. Former Glasgow-to-Dublin packet steamer. Name sometimes written *A.D. Vance*.

Service record: NAtlBS 1864–65. Unsuccessful attack on Ft. Fisher, N.C., 24–25 Dec 1864. Second attack on Ft. Fisher, 13–15 Jan 1865. Renamed *Frolic*, 2 Jun 1865. Recomm 12 Jun 1865. European Squadron 1865–69. South Atlantic Station 1875–77. Decomm 31 Oct 1877. Sold 1 Oct 1883.

Name	Builder	Launched	Acquired	Comm.
Alabama	New York, N.Y. (Webb)	19 Jan 1850	1 Aug 1861	30 Sep 1861
Florida	New York, N.Y. (Webb)	Apr 1850	12 Aug 1861	5 Oct 1861

Tonnage	1,261 tons B
Dimensions	214'4" × 35'2" × 14'6", d22'
Machinery	Side wheels, 1 side-lever engine (75" × 8'), 13 knots (Novelty)
Complement	119/180
Armament	4–32pdr/57, 4–32pdr/42, 1–20pdr MLR
	Alabama: (Dec 1862) 1–9" SB, 2–30pdr MLR, 6–32pdr/57, 1–12pdr MLR.
	Florida: (Apr 1863) 4–9" SB, 1–100pdr MLR, 1–50pdr MLR, 1–12pdr MLR.

Notes: Fore-topsail schooner rig. Built for the New York and Savannah Steam Navigation Co. Wood hulls.

Service records:

Alabama: SAtlBS 1861–Jul1863. Capture of Fernandina, Fla., and Brunswick, St. Simons, and Jekyl Islands, Ga., 2–12 Mar 1862. Blockade off Houston 1863. NAtlBS May 1864–65. Unsuccessful attack on Ft. Fisher, N.C., 24–25 Dec 1864. Second attack on Ft. Fisher, 13–15 Jan 1865. Ordnance and despatch dispatch vessel, Hampton Roads, 1865. Decomm 14 Jul 1865. Sold 10 Aug 1865.

Ships captured: *Albion*, 25 Nov 1861; *Admiral*, 12 Dec 1861; *Catalina*, 20 Jun 1862; *Nellie*, 23 Sep 1861.

Later history: Merchant *Alabama* 1865. Converted to schooner 1872. Destroyed by fire 1878.

Florida: SAtlBS 1861–64. Occupation of Port Royal, S.C., 7 Nov 1861. Capture of Fernandina, Fla., and Brunswick, St. Simons, and Jekyl Islands, Ga., 2–12 Mar 1862. Gulf of Mexico Mar 1865. W. Indies 1866–67. Decomm 26 Apr 1867. Sold 5 Dec 1868.

Ships captured: *Ventura*, 19 Jun 1862; *Agnes.*, 25 Sep 1862; 11 Jun: str *Calypso*,* 11 Jun 1863; *Hattie*, 21 Jun 1863; str *Emily* and str *Fanny and Jenny*, 10 Feb 1864.

Later history: Merchant *Delphine* 1868. Sold to Haitian revolutionaries as gunboat, renamed *Republique* 1869. "Worn out" 1875.

Name	Builder	Launched	Acquired	Comm.
Arizona	Wilmington, Del. (Harlan)	1859	23 Jan 1863	9 Mar 1863

ex-CSS *Caroline*, ex-*Arizona*

Tonnage	950 tons B
Dimensions	201'6" (U) 200' (wl) × 34' × 8', d10'
Machinery	Side wheels, 1 vertical beam condensing engine (44" × 11'), 1 boiler. (bldr)
Complement	98
Armament	4–32pdr/42, 1–30pdr MLR, 1–12pdr MLR

Notes: Blockade runner *Caroline*, captured by USS *Montgomery* off Pensacola, 29 Oct 1862. Iron hull, two mast schooner.

Service record: WGulfBS 1863–65. Engagement with CSS *Queen of the West* in Berwick Bay, La., 14 Apr 1863. Engagement at Butte-a-la-Rose, La., and capture of Ft. Burton, 20 Apr 1863. Expedition up Red River, 3–13 May 1863. Attack on Sabine Pass, Tex., 8 Sep 1863. Blockade of Texas coast 1863–64. Destroyed by fire 38 miles below New Orleans, 27 Feb 1865 (4 dead).

Ship captured: *Aurelia*, 23 Mar 1863.

Name	Builder	Launched	Acquired	Comm.
Augusta	New York, N.Y. (Webb)	30 Sep 1852	1 Aug 1861	28 Sep 1861

Tonnage	1,310 tons B
Dimensions	220'8" × 35'4" × 14'3", d21'6"
Machinery	Side wheels, oscillating engine (85" × 8'), 2 boilers, 11 knots (Novelty)
Complement	157
Armament	4–32pdr/57, 4–32pdr/42, 1–12pdr MLR; (Aug 1862) add 1–20pdr MLR; (Feb 1863) 1–100pdr MLR, 2–30pdr MLR, 6–8" SB; (Jun 1864) 1–100pdr MLR, 2–30pdr MLR, 4–8" SB, 2–24pdr SB

Notes: Three-mast schooner rig, wood hull. Built for the New York and Savannah Steam Navigation Co. (Mitchell Line).

Service record: SAtlBS Oct 1861–65. Occupation of Port Royal, S.C., 7 Nov 1861. Occupation of Beaufort, S.C., 9 Nov 1861.

---

* Later USS Calypso.

Blockade off Charleston 1861–2 and 1863–65. Repairing at New York Jul 1863–May 1864. Repairing Jan 1865–Apr 1866 repairing. Cruised to Europe with Miantonomoh 1866–67. Sold 2 Dec 1868.

Ships captured: *Cheshire*, 6 Dec 1861; *Island Belle*, 31 Dec 1861.

Later history: Merchant *Magnolia* 1869. Foundered in storm off Cape Hatteras en route Savannah—New York, 30 Sep 1877.

Name	Builder	Launched	Acquired	Comm.
Banshee	Liverpool (Jones Quiggin)	22 Nov 1862	12 Mar 1864	Jun 1864

Tonnage	533 tons B, 325 GRT
Dimensions	220' × 20'4" × 10', d12'
Machinery	Side wheels, 2-cyl. oscillating engine (42" × 3'9"), 2 boilers, 12 knots (Laird)
Complement	60/89
Armament	1–30pdr MLR, 1–12pdr SB

Notes: Blockade runner, captured by USAT *Fulton* and USS *Grand Gulf* off Wilmington, 21 Nov 1863. Schooner rig, iron frame hull plated with steel, two pole masts. First steel vessel to cross the Atlantic. Engines were unreliable.

Service record: NAtlBS 1864–65. Unsuccessful attack on Ft. Fisher, N.C., 24–25 Dec 1864. Potomac Flotilla Jan 1865.

Sold 30 Nov 1865.

Later history: Merchant *J.L.Smallwood* 1865. British *Irene* 1867. SE 1895.

Name	Builder	Launched	Acquired	Comm.
Bat	Liverpool (Jones Quiggin)	21 Jun 1864	Nov 1864	13 Dec 1864

Tonnage	750 tons B, 505 n/r, 466 GRT
Dimensions	230' × 26' × 8', d12'
Machinery	Side wheels, 2-cyl. oscillating engines (52" × 4'), 2 boilers, 16 knots. (Watt)
Complement	82
Armament	1–30pdr MLR, 2–12pdr SB

Notes: Blockade runner, captured on first voyage by USS *Montgomery* off Wilmington, N.C., 10 Oct 1864. Steel hull, schooner rig, two funnels.

Service record: NAtlBS 1865–65. Decomm 17 May 1865. Sold 25 Oct 1865.

Later history: Merchant *Teazer* 1865. British *Miramichi* 1872. BU 1902.

Name	Builder	Launched	Acquired	Comm.
Bienville	Brooklyn, N.Y. (L & F)	1860	14 Aug 1861	23 Oct 1861
De Soto	Brooklyn, N.Y. (L & F)	25 Jun 1859	21 Aug 1861	1861

Tonnage	*Bienville*: 1,558 tons B, *DeSoto*: 1,675 tons B
Dimensions	253'3" × 38'6" × 16'2", d26'
Machinery	Side wheels, 1 vertical beam engine (68" × 11'), 2 boilers, HP 400, 11 knots (Morgan)
Complement	185
Armament	*Bienville*: 4–32pdr/42, 4–32pdr/57; (Jun 1863) 1–100pdr MLR, 1–12pdr SB, 1–30pdr MLR, 8–32pdr/57.
	De Soto: 8–32pdr/42, 1–30pdr MLR; (Dec 1862) 1–9" SB, 1–30pdr MLR, 6–32pdr/42, 2–12pdr SB

Notes: Wood hulls. Brig rig, one funnel Built for the New York–Mobile service of Livingston Crocheron and Co. *De Soto* reboilered 1864–65.

Fig 3.3: The former USS *Bat*, built in England to run the blockade, after the war as the merchant ship *Teazer*. The ship in the background is the former USS *Fahkee*.

Fig 3.4: The USS *De Soto* at Ponce, Puerto Rico, in 1868. With her sister *Bienville* she was built for the New York–Mobile run. (U.S. Naval Historical Center)

Service records:

Bienville: SAtlBS 1861–62. Occupation of Port Royal, S.C., 7 Nov 1861. Occupation of Beaufort, S.C., 9 Nov 1861. Capture off Fernandina, Fla. and Brunswick, St. Simons, and Jekyl Islands, Ga., 2–12 Mar 1862. WGulfBS 1863–65. Battle of Mobile Bay, 5 Aug 1864. Blockade of Galveston 1865. Decomm 1865. Sold 5 Oct 1865.
   Ships captured: *Sarah & Caroline*, 11 Dec 1861; *Arrow*, 25 Feb 1862; *Alert*, 26 Feb 1862; str *Stettin*,* 24 May 1862; str *Patras*, 27 May 1862; *La Criolla, Providence, Rebecca*, 29 May 1862; *Morning Star*, 27 Jun 1862; *Eliza*, 21 Aug 1862; *Louisa*, 23 Aug 1862; *Lightning*, 9 Mar 1863; *Annie Sophia, Pet*, 7 Feb 1865.
   Later history: Merchant *Bienville* 1867. Destroyed by fire off Eleuthera, Bahamas, 15 Aug 1872.

De Soto: WGulfBS, Dec 1861–65. NAtl Sqn, Sep 1865–67. Damaged during an earthquake at St. Thomas, 18 Nov 1867. Decomm 11 Sep and sold 30 Sep 1868.
   Ships captured: *Major Barbour*, 28 Jan 1862; *Star, Alphonsina*, 8 Feb 1862; *George Washington*, 28 Jun 1862; *William*, 1 Jul 1862; *Bright*, 23 Apr 1863; *Jane Adelie, Rapid, General Prim*, 24 Apr 1863; *Clarita*, 26 Apr 1863; *Sea Bird***⁵, 13 May 1863; str **Cuba*, 17 May 1863; *Mississippian*, 19 May 1863; *Lady Maria*, 6 Jul 1863; strs *James Battle, William Bagley*, 18 Jul 1863; str *Alice Vivian*, 16 Aug 1863; str *Nita*****⁶, 17 Aug 1863; str *Montgomery*, 13 Sep 1863; str *Leviathan*, 22 Sep 1863; str *Cumberland*, 5 Feb 1864.
   Later history: Merchant *De Soto* 1868. Burned below New Orleans, 7 Dec 1870.

Boxer, see *Tristram Shandy.*

Name	Builder	Launched	Acquired	Comm.
Britannia	Glasgow (Barclay Curle)	11 Apr 1862	29 Sep 1863	16 Sep 1863
Tonnage	495 tons B, 369 n/r, 594 GRT			
Dimensions	189′ × 26′ × 9′, d11′			

* Later USS *Stettin.*

** Later USS *Sea Bird.*

*** Later USS *Nita.*

Machinery	Side wheels, 2-cyl. steeple condensing engines (45″ × 4′10″), 2 boilers. 12.5 knots
Complement	75
Armament	(Sep 1864) 1–30pdr MLR, 2–12pdr MLR, 2–24pdr H; (Nov 1864) 1–30pdr MLR, 5–24pdr H.

Notes: Blockade runner, captured by USS *Santiago de Cuba* in the Bahamas, 25 Jun 1863. Iron hull.
Service record: NAtlBS Nov 1863–Jan 1865. Engagement with CSS *Raleigh* off New Inlet, N.C., 6–7 May 1864. Damaged in engagement with CSS *Tallahassee* off New Inlet, N.C., Aug 1864. Unsuccessful attack on Ft. Fisher, N.C., 24–25 Dec 1864. Second attack on Ft. Fisher, 13–15 Jan 1865. EGulfBS Jan 1865. Expedition to St. Marks, Fla., 23 Feb 1865. Sold 10 Aug 1865.
Later history: Merchant *Britannia* 1865. Sold foreign 1866. Stranded in Firth of Clyde, 30 Jan 1873.

Name	Builder	Launched	Acquired	Comm.
Clyde	Glasgow (Napier)	1861	25 Jul 1863	29 Jul 1863
ex-*Neptune*				
Tonnage	294 tons B			
Dimensions	200′6″ × 18′6″ × d8′			
Machinery	Side wheels, 2-cyl. inclined engines (42″ × 3′8″), 2 boilers, 9 knots			
Complement	67			
Armament	2–24pdr H; (Dec 1863) 2–12pdr MLR			

Notes: Blockade runner *Neptune*, captured by USS *Lackawanna*, 14 Jun 1863. Iron hull. Renamed 11 Aug 1863.
Service record: EGulfBS Sep 1863–65, W. Florida. Decomm 17 Aug 1865. Sold 25 Oct 1865.
Ship captured: *Amaranth, 27 Sep 1863.
Later history: Merchant *Indian River* 1865. Went ashore at mouth of Indian River, Fla., 3 Dec 1865.

Name	Builder	Launched	Acquired	Comm.
Connecticut	New York, N.Y. (Webb)	15 Jan 1861	18 Jul 1861	23 Aug 1861
ex-*Mississippi*				
Tonnage	1,725 tons, 2,150 n/r			
Dimensions	251′6″ × 38′2″ × 14′, d22′8″			

Machinery	Side wheels, 1 vertical beam engine (80″ × 11′), 10 knots (Morgan)
Complement	166
Armament	4–32pdr/42, 1–12pdr MLR; (Dec 1861) 10–32pdr/57, 1–50pdr MLR, 1–30pdr MLR; (Dec1863) 1–100pdr MLR, 2–30pdr MLR, 8–8″ SB

Notes: Brig rig, two masts. Built for the New York and Savannah Steam Navigation Co. but purchased by the Navy before entering service.

Service record: Transport and supply ship 1861–62. GulfBS 1862–63. Convoy ship off Aspinwall, Panama 1863. NAtlBS Aug 1863–Jul 1864. Damaged in collision with USS *Quaker City* in New Inlet, N.C., 22 Aug 1863. Decomm 11 Aug 1865. Sold 21 Sep 1865.

Ships captured: *Adeline*, 17 Nov 1861; *Emma*, 17 Jan 1862; *Rambler*, 9 Sep 1862; *Hermosa*, 30 Oct 1862; str *Juno*, 22 Sep 1863; str *Phantom*, 23 Sep 1863; str *Ceres*, 6 Dec 1863; *Sallie*, 20 Dec 1863; str *Scotia*, 1 Mar 1864; str *Minnie*, 9 May 1864; str *Greyhound*, 10 May 1864.

Later history: Merchant *South America*. BU 1879

Name	Builder	Launched	Acquired	Comm.
Cornubia	Hayle (Harvey)	27 Feb 1858	Nov 1863	17 Mar 1864

ex-*Lady Davis*, ex-*Cornubia*

Tonnage	589 tons B, 411 GRT
Dimensions	210′ (U) 196′ (bp) × 24′6″ × 10′, d13′3″
Machinery	Side wheels, 2-cyl. oscillating engine (50″ × 4′8″), 2 boilers. HP 230, 13 knots
Complement	76
Armament	1–20pdr MLR, 2–24pdr SB; (Jul 1864) 1–20pdr MLR replaced by 1–30pdr MLR; (Apr 1865) add 2–12pdr MLR

Notes: Blockade runner, captured on 23rd run by USS *Niphon* and *James Adger* off New Inlet, N.C., 8 Nov 1863. Iron hull, two masts.

Service record: WGulfBS Jul 1864–May 1865. Blockade of Texas. Decomm 9 Aug 1865. Sold 25 Oct 1865.

Ships captured: *Chaos*, 21 Apr 1865; str *Denbigh*, 24 May 1865; *Lecompte*, 25 May 1865.

Later history: Merchant *New England* 1865. Converted to barkentine 1871.

De Soto, see *Bienville*.

Name	Builder	Launched	Acquired	Comm.
Dumbarton	Renfrew, Scotland (Hill)	1863	20 Jul 1864	13 Aug 1864

ex-*Thistle*

Tonnage	636 tons B, 471 gross (Br)
Dimensions	204′ × 29′ × 10′, d11′
Machinery	Side wheels, 2-cyl. oscillating engines (57″ × 5′), 2 boilers, 10 knots (Inglis)
Complement	96
Armament	(1864) 2–32pdr/33, 2–12pdr H; (Mar1865) add 1–20pdr MLR.

Notes: Blockade runner *Thistle* (II), captured 4 Jun 1864 by USS *Fort Jackson* off North Carolina coast. Iron hull. Engines unreliable.

Service record: Search for CSS *Tallahassee*, 1864. NAtlBS Sep–Dec 1864. James River, Feb–Mar 1865. Decomm 27 Mar 1865. Sold 15 Oct 1867.

Later history: Merchant *City of Quebec*, British flag 1867. New engines, rerigged 1868. Sunk in collision with merchant ship *Germany* off Green Island, Saguenay River, 1 May 1870.

Fig 3.5: The USS *Connecticut* was built for the New York–Savannah run as *Mississippi* but purchased by the Navy in 1861. (U.S. Naval Historical Center)

Name	Builder	Launched	Acquired	Comm.
Emma Henry	Glasgow, Scotland (Thomson)	1864	13 Jan 1865	11 May 1865

Tonnage	521 tons B
Dimensions	212′ × 25′2″ × 6′, d10′
Machinery	Side wheels, 2-cyl. oscillating engine (44″ × 4′6″), 2 boilers. (U)
Complement	(U)
Armament	1–30pdr MLR, 2–24pdr H

Notes: Blockade runner, captured by USS *Cherokee* between Wilmington and Bermuda, 8 Dec 1864. Iron hull.

Service record: Search for CSS *Stonewall*, May 1865. Damaged in collision, 22 May 1865. Renamed *Wasp*, 13 Jun 1865. Brazil Sqn and South America 1865–76. Sold at Montevideo, 5 Jun 1876.

Later history: FFU.

Name	Builder	Launched	Acquired	Comm.
Eolus	Newburgh, N.Y. (Marvel)	1864	26 Jul 1864	12 Aug 1864

Tonnage	368 tons B
Dimensions	144′ (U) 140′ (U) × 25′ × 7′, d10′2″
Machinery	Side wheels, 1 vertical beam engine (40″ × 8′), NHP 285, 16 mph (Washington IW)
Complement	53
Armament	1–30pdr MLR, 2–24pdr H

Notes: Purchased on completion.

Service record: Search for CSS *Tallahassee* 1864. NAtlBS 1864–65. Unsuccessful attack on Ft. Fisher, N.C., 24–25 Dec 1864. Second attack on Ft. Fisher, 13–15 Jan 1865. Decomm 24 Jun 1865. Sold 1 Aug 1865.

Ships captured: str *Hope*, 22 Oct 1864; str *Lady Sterling*,* 28 Oct 1864.

Later history: Merchant *Eolus* 1865. BU 1894

Florida, see *Alabama*.

---

* Later USS *Lady Sterling*.

Name	Builder	Launched	Acquired	Comm.
Fort Donelson	Glasgow, Scotland (Thomson)	16 May 1860	Jan 1864	29 Jun 1864

ex-*Robert E. Lee*, ex-*Giraffe*

Tonnage	642 tons
Dimensions	283' (oa) 268' ( ) × 26' × 10', d13'8"
Machinery	Side wheels, 2-cyl. oscillating engine (56" × 3'), 6 boilers, 11 knots (Bldr)
Complement	137
Armament	2–30pdr MLR, 5–12pdr HR

Notes: Blockade runner *Robert E. Lee*, captured off Wilmington, N.C., on twenty-second trip by USS *Iron Age* and *James Adger*, 9 Nov 1863. Iron hull. Built as *Giraffe* for the Glasgow-Belfast service of the Burns Line.
Service record: NAtlBS 1864, North Carolina. Second bombardment of Ft. Fisher, N.C., 13–15 Jan 1865. Decomm 17 Aug 1865. Sold 25 Oct 1865.
Ship captured: str *Dacotah*, 15 Aug 1864.
Later history: Merchant *Isabella* 1865. Sold to Chile 1869 as naval vessel, renamed *Concepción*. Merchant 1869.

Name	Builder	Launched	Acquired	Comm.
Fort Jackson	New York, N.Y. (Simonson)	1862	22 Jul 1863	18 Aug 1863

ex-*Kentucky*, ex-*Union*

Tonnage	1,850 tons B, 2,085 n/r
Dimensions	250' × 38'6" × 18', d27'10"
Machinery	Side wheels, 1 vertical beam engine (80" × 12'), 4 boilers, 14 knots (Allaire)
Complement	194
Armament	1–100pdr MLR, 2–30pdr MLR, 8–9" SB

Notes: Hermaphrodite brig. Built for Vanderbilt's New York–Aspinwall service but purchased by the Navy on completion.
Service record: NAtlBS Jan 1864. Unsuccessful attack on Ft. Fisher, N.C., 24–25 Dec 1864. Second attack on Ft. Fisher, 13–15 Jan 1865. WGulfBS Feb 1865. Decomm 7 Aug 1865. Sold 27 Aug 1865.
Ships captured: str *Bendigo, 3 Jan 1864; str *Thistle,*, 4 Jun 1864; str *Boston*, 8 Jul 1864; str *Wando*,**, 21 Oct 1864; str *Lady Sterling*, 31 Oct 1864.
Later history: Merchant *North America* 1865. BU 1879 at Boston.

Frolic, see *Advance*.

Name	Builder	Launched	Acquired	Comm.
Gettysburg	Glasgow, Scotland (Napier)	28 May 1858	20 Nov 1863	2 May 1864

ex-*Margaret and Jessie*, ex-*Douglas*

Tonnage:	1100 tons D, 726 tons B
Dimensions	211' ( ) 205' ( ) × 26'3" × 10', d13'6"
Machinery	Side wheels, 2-cyl. oscillating engines (54" × 5'), 15 knots (bldr)
Complement	96
Armament	(May 1864) 1–30pdr MLR, 2–12pdr MLR, 4–24pdr H; (Dec1864) 2–12pdr MLR replaced by 2–32pdr/27

Notes: Blockade runner *Margaret and Jessie*, captured off Wilmington, N.C., by USS *Nansemond*, *Keystone State*, and *Howquah*, 5 Nov 1863. Former Isle of Man Packet, world's fastest steamer when built. Iron hull. Two funnels replaced by one, 1869.
Service record: NAtlBS 1864. Unsuccessful attack on Ft. Fisher, N.C., 24–25 Dec 1864. Second attack on Ft. Fisher, 13–15 Jan 1865. (6 killed) Went aground on Fishers I., N.Y., while towing monitor *Squando*, 11 Jun 1865. Decomm 23 Jun 1865. Recomm 3 Dec 1866. Caribbean, 1866–67, 1868–69. Mediterranean 1876–79. Sold 8 May 1879 at Genoa.
Ships captured: str *Little Ada*,***, 9 Jul 1864; str *Lilian*****, 24 Aug 1864; str *Armstrong*, 4 Dec 1864.
Later history: FFU.

Name	Builder	Launched	Acquired	Comm.
Harvest Moon	Portland, Me. (Dyer)	1862	16 Nov 1863	12 Feb 1864

Tonnage	546 tons B
Dimensions	193' × 29' × 8', d10'
Machinery	Side wheels, 1 vertical beam engine (41" × 10'), 9 knots/mph
Complement	72
Armament	1–20pdr MLR, 4–24pdr H, 1–12pdr H

Notes: Operated briefly between Maine and Boston.
Service record: SAtlBS 1864–65. Flagship of Admiral Dahlgren off Charleston, 1864–65. Expedition in Broad River, S.C., 27 Nov–30 Dec 1864. Expedition to Georgetown, S.C., 23 Feb 1865. Sunk by torpedo (mine) in Winyah Bay, S.C., 1 Mar 1865 (1 killed).

Name	Builder	Launched	Acquired	Comm.
Hatteras	Wilmington, Del. (Harlan)	1861	25 Sep 1861	Oct 1861

ex-*St. Mary's*

Tonnage	1,126 tons B
Dimensions	210' (bp) × 34' × d18'
Machinery	Side wheels, 1 condensing beam engine (50" × 11'), 1 boiler, HP 500
Complement	110
Armament	4–32pdr/27, 1–20pdr MLR

Notes: Iron hull. Three-mast schooner.
Service record: SAtlBS 1861. Destroyed seven schooners and installations during raid on Cedar Keys, Fla., 16 Jan 1862. GulfBS Jan 1862. Engaged CSS *Mobile* off Louisiana, 26 Jan 1862. Sunk in action with CSS *Alabama* off Galveston, 11 Jan 1863 (2 killed).
Ships captured: str *P.C. Wallis*, *Resolution*, 4 Apr 1862; *Magnolia*, 1 May 1862; str *Fashion*, str *Governor Mouton*, 6 May 1862; *Poody*, 17 May 1862; *Sarah*, 3 Jul 1862; *Elizabeth*, 5 Jul 1862; str *Indian No. 2*, 19 Jul 1862; *Josephine*, 28 Jul 1862.

Hornet, see *Lady Sterling*

Name	Builder	Launched	Acquired	Comm.
James Adger	New York, N.Y. (Webb)	10 Jan 1852	26 Jul 1861	20 Sep 1861

Tonnage	1,152 tons B, 1,085 n/r
Dimensions	215' (dk) × 33'6" × 12'6", d21'3"
Machinery	Side wheels, 1 side-lever engine (65" × 11'), 2 boilers, NHP 240, 12.5 knots (Allaire)
Complement	120

---

* Later USS *Dumbarton*.
** Later USS *Wando*.

*** Later USS *Little Ada*.
**** Later USS *Lilian*.

Armament   8–32pdr/42, 1–20pdr MLR; (May 1863) 1–9″ SB, 1–20pdr MLR, 6–32pdr/42, 1–12pdr H SB

Notes: Wood hull, three-mast schooner.

Service record: SAtlBS 1862. Capture of Fernandina, Fla., and Brunswick, St. Simons, and Jekyl Islands, Ga., 2–12 Mar 1862. Failed to capture blockade runner *Banshee* after 15-hour chase, Sep 1863. SAtlBS 1864–65. Caribbean 1866. Decomm 2 May 1866. Sold 9 Oct 1866.

Ships captured: str *Elizabeth*, 29 May 1862; str *Kate*, 1 Aug 1863; str *Cornubia*,*, 8 Nov 1863; str *Robert E. Lee*,**, 9 Nov 1863; str *Ella*, 26 Nov 1863.

Later history: Merchant *James Adger* 1866. BU 1878.

Name	Builder	Launched	Acquired	Comm.
Keystone State	Philadelphia, Pa. (Vaughan & Lynn)	1853	19 Apr 1861	19 Jul 1861
Tonnage	1,364 tons			
Dimensions	219′ × 35′6″ × 14′6″, d21′			
Machinery	Side wheels, 1 side-lever engine (56″ × 8′), 2 boilers. HP 300, 9.5 knots (Merrick)			
Complement	163			
Armament	4–12pdr; (Jun1863) 1–150pdr MLR, 6–8″ SB, 2–32pdr/57, 2–30pdr MLR; (Jun1864) 1–50pdr MLR, 2–8″ SB, 2–32pdr/57, 1–30pdr MLR			

Notes: Originally chartered by the Navy; later purchased and commissioned. Built for coastal service of the Ocean Steam Navigation Co., later chartered by Vanderbilt for service to Nicaragua. Wood hull, brig rig.

Service record: West Indies 1861. SAtlBS Jan 1862. Capture of Fernandina, Fla., and Brunswick, St. Simons, and Jekyl Islands, Ga., 2–12 Mar 1862. Damaged during engagement with Confederate rams off Charleston (40 killed dead), 31 Jan 1863. NAtlBS Oct 1863. Unsuccessful attack on Ft. Fisher, N.C., 24–25 Dec 1864. Bombardment of Masonboro Inlet, N.C., 11 Feb 1865. Decomm 25 Mar 1865. Sold 15 Sep 1865.

Ships captured: *Hiawatha*, 20 May 1861; *Mars*, 5 Feb 1862; **Liverpool*, 10 Apr 1862; *Success*, 15 Apr 1862; str *Elizabeth*, 28 May 1862; *Cora*, 31 May 1862; *Sarah*, 20 Jun 1862; *Fanny*., 22 Aug 1862; str *Margaret and Jessie*,***, 5 Nov 1863; str **Vesta*, 11 Jan 1864; str *Caledonia*, 30 May 1864; str *Siren*, 5 Jun 1864; str *Rouen*, 26 Jul 1864; str *Lilian*,****, 24 Aug 1864; *Elsie*, 5 Sep 1864.

Later history: Merchant *San Francisco* 1865. RR 1879

Name	Builder	Launched	Acquired	Comm.
Lady Sterling ex-*Lady Stirling*	Millwall (James.Ash)	18 Jun 1864	Nov 1864	24 Apr 1865
Tonnage	835 tons, 906 GRT, 614 n/r.			
Dimensions	242′ × 26′6″ × d13′3″			
Machinery	Side wheels, 2-cyl. oscillating engines (60″ × 5′), 4 boilers, 13 knots			
Armament	8 guns			

Notes: Blockade runner, captured off Wilmington, N.C., by USS *Eolus* and *Calypso*, 28 Oct 1864. Iron hull.

Service record: Renamed **Hornet**, 17 Jun 1865. Decomm 15 Dec 1865. Sold 26 Jun 1869.

Later history: Merchant *Hornet* 1869. Cuban filibuster 1869, gun runner to Haiti and Cuba 1871–72. Renamed *Marco Aurelia*, Spanish flag, 1872. BU about 1894.

---
* Later USS *Cornubia*.
** Later USS *Fort Donelson*.
*** Later USS *Gettysburg*.
**** Later USS *Lilian*.

Fig 3.6: The USS *Hornet* off Wilmington, N.C., in 1865. She was the blockade runner *Lady Stirling* captured in October 1864 and commissioned in the Navy as *Lady Sterling*. (U.S. Naval Historical Center)

Name	Builder	Launched	Acquired	Comm.
Lilian	Glasgow, Scotland (Thomson)	Mar 1864	6 Sep 1864	6 Oct 1864
Tonnage	630 tons B, 427 n/r			
Dimensions	225′6″ × 26′5″ × 8′2″, d10′			
Machinery	Side wheels, 2-cyl. oscillating engine (50″ × 4′4″), 4 boilers. 14 knots			
Complement	63			
Armament	1–30pdr MLR, 1–20pdr MLR			

Notes: Blockade runner, captured 24 Aug 1864 by USS *Keystone State* and *Gettysburg* off Cape Fear. Iron hull, three funnels.

Service record: NAtlBS 1864. Search for CSS *Olustee*, Nov 1864. Unsuccessful attack on Ft. Fisher, N.C., 24–25 Dec 1864. Second attack on Ft. Fisher, 13–15 Jan 1865. Decomm 5 Apr 1865. Sold 30 Nov 1865.

Later history: Merchant *Lillian* 1865. Spanish Navy corvette *Victoria de los Tunas*, 1870. Wrecked off Mariel, Cuba, Nov 1870.

Name	Builder	Launched	Acquired	Comm.
Magnolia	New York, N.Y. (Simonson)	22 Aug 1854	9 Apr 1862	22 Jul 1862
Tonnage	843 tons B, 1,067 n/r			
Dimensions	242′5 × 33′11″ × 5′, d11′3″			
Machinery	Side wheels, vertical beam engine (50″ × 12′), 2 boilers, 120 NHP, 12 knots (Allaire)			
Complement	95			
Armament	1–20pdr MLR, 2–24pdr; (Sep 1864) add 2–24pdr			

Notes: Blockade runner, captured 19 Feb 1862 by USS *Brooklyn* and *South Carolina* off Pass à l'Outre, La. Schooner rig.

Service record: EGulfBS 1862–65. Repairing Aug 1863–Apr 1864. Expedition to St. Marks, Fla., 23 Feb–27 Mar 1865. Decomm 10 Jun 1865. Sold 12 Jul 1865.

Ships captured: str *Memphis*,*****, 31 Jul 1862; *Flying Cloud*, 2 Dec 1862; *Carmita*,******, 27 Dec 1862; *Flying Fish*, 29 Dec 1862; str *Matagorda*, 10 Sep 1864.

Later history: Merchant *Magnolia*, 1865. RR 1866.

***** Later USS *Memphis*.
****** Later USS *Carmita*.

Name	Builder	Launched	Acquired	Comm.
Malvern	Wilmington, Del. (Harlan)	15 Oct 1860	1863	9 Feb 1864

ex-*Ella and Annie*, ex-*William G. Hewes*

Tonnage	1,477 tons B, 1,230 n/r
Dimensions	239'4" (dk) 234' (wl) × 33' × 9', d18'
Machinery	Side wheels, 1 vertical beam engine (50" × 11'), 1 boiler, HP 500 (Morgan)
Complement	68
Armament	4–20pdr MLR, 8–12pdr SB

Notes: Blockade runner *Ella and Annie*, captured 9 Nov 1863, by USS *Niphon* off New Inlet, N.C.. Iron hull. Built for Charles Morgan's Southern S.S. Co.

Service record: Provisionally commissioned to search for steamer *Chesapeake* seized by Confederates at sea, 10 Dec 1863. NAtlBS 1864. Unsuccessful attack on Ft. Fisher, N.C., 24–25 Dec 1864 (flagship of Adm. Porter). Second attack on Ft. Fisher, 13–15 Jan 1865 (3 killed). Bombardment of forts in Cape Fear River, 18–21 Feb 1865. Carried President Lincoln to Richmond, 2 Apr 1865. Decomm 1865. Sold 25 Oct 1865.

Ships captured: strs *Charlotte* and *Stag*, 20 Jan 1865.

Later history: Merchant *William G. Hewes* 1865. Wrecked in storm off Colorado Reef, Cuba, 20 Feb 1895.

Name	Builder	Launched	Acquired	Comm.
Merrimac	Great Britain	(U)	10 Mar 1864	1 May 1864

Tonnage	684 tons B
Dimensions	230' × 30' × 8'6", d11'
Machinery	Side wheels, 2-cyl. oscillating engines (U × 9'), 4 boilers, 11.5 knots
Complement	116
Armament	2–30pdr MLR, 4–24pdr, 2–12pdr (Sep1864) 1–30pdr MLR, 4–24pdr, 1–12pdr

Notes: Blockade runner, captured 24 Jul 1863 by USS *Iroquois* off Cape Fear, N.C.. Iron hull.

Service record: EGulfBS 1864–65. Foundered in gale off Florida, 15 Feb 1865.

Ship captured: *Henrietta*, 1 Jul 1864.

Mobile, see *Tennessee*.

Name	Builder	Launched	Acquired	Comm.
Quaker City	Philadelphia, Pa. (Vaughan and Lynn)	2 May 1854	25 Apr 1861	14 Dec 1861

Tonnage	1,428 tons B
Dimensions	244'9" (U) 227'3" (bp) × 36'6" × 13'8", d20'9"
Machinery	Side wheels, 1 side-lever engine (85" × 8'), 4 boilers. 13 knots (Merrick)
Complement	142
Armament	2–32pdr, 2–12pdr MLR; (Dec 1861) 8–32pdr/57, 1–20pdr MLR; (Aug 1863) 1–100pdr MLR, 1–30pdr MLR, 1–20pdr MLR, 6–8" SB; (Nov 1864) less 2–8" SB/63

Notes: Chartered 25 Apr 1861, purchased 12 Aug 1861. Wood hull, two funnels, two masts. Formerly operated by New York, Havana, and Mobile Line.

Service record: NAtlBS 1862. Search for Confederate raiders 1862–63. Went aground on North Edisto Island., S.C., 12 Oct 1862. Damaged in engagement with Confederate ironclads off Charleston, 31 Jan 1863. In collision with USS *Connecticut* in New Inlet, N.C., 22 Aug 1863. Unsuccessful attack on Ft. Fisher, N.C., 24–25 Dec 1864. GulfBS 1865. Decomm 18 May 1865. Sold 20 Jun 1865.

Ships captured: *North Carolina*, 14 May 1861; *Pioneer*, *Winifred*, 25 May 1861, *Lynchburg*, 30 May 1861; *General Green*, 4 Jun 1861; *Amy Warwick*, 10 Jun 1861; *Sally Magee*, 26 Jun 1861; *Sally Mears*, 1 Jul 1861; *Fairwind*, 29 Aug 1861; str *Elsie*, 4 Sep 1861; *Model*, 30 Jun 1862; *Lilla*, 3 Jul 1862; str *Adela*,*, 7 Jul 1862; *Orion*, 24 Jul 1862; *Mercury*, 4 Jan 1863; str *Douro*, 9 Mar 1863; str *Spunkie*, 9 Feb 1864; str *Elsie*, 4 Sep 1864; *R.H. Vermilyea*, 12 Mar 1864; *Telemaco*, 16 Mar 1864; *George Burkhart*, 17 Mar 1864; str *Cora*, 24 Mar 1864.

Later history: Merchant *Quaker City* 1865. The ship of Mark Twain's "Innocents Abroad," 1867. British *Columbia* 1869. Haitian gunboat *Mont Organisé* 1869. Sold Feb 1871, renamed *Republique*. Foundered at sea off Bermuda after boiler explosion, 25 Feb 1871.

Name	Builder	Launched	Acquired	Comm.
Rhode Island	New York, N.Y. (Westervelt)	6 Sep 1860	27 Jun 1861	29 Jul 1861

ex-*Eagle*, ex-*John P. King*

Tonnage	1,517 tons B
Dimensions	236'7" × 36'9" × 15', d18'5"
Machinery	Side wheels, 1 vertical beam engine (71" × 12'), 2 boilers. 13 knots (Allaire)
Complement	257
Armament	4–32pdr/42; (Dec 1861) add 1–30pdr MLR, 1–8"/55; (Jul 1863) 1–9", 1–30pdr MLR, 1–12pdr MLR, 1–12pdr SB; (Jan 1864) add 8–8"/63, 1–50pdr MLR; (Jan 1865) less 1–50pdr MLR

Notes: After first trial run, almost destroyed by fire at Hudson River pier and scuttled, 18 Dec 1860; salved and completed as *Eagle*.

Wood hull.

Service record: Supply ship. Gulf BS 1862. Recomm 11 Nov 1862. Towing USS *Monitor* south when that ship foundered off Cape Hatteras, 30 Dec 1862. Unsuccessful attack on Ft. Fisher, N.C., 24–25 Dec 1864. Second attack on Ft. Fisher, 13–15 Jan 1865. Decomm 1867. Sold 1 Oct 1867.

Ships captured: *Aristides*, 25 Nov 1861; *Phantom*, 8 Dec 1861; *Venus*, 26 Dec 1861; *Richard O'Bryan*, 4 Jul 1862; str **Margaret and Jessie*, 30 May 1863; str *Cronstadt*, 16 Aug 1863, str *Vixen*, 1 Dec 1863.

Later history: Merchant *Charleston* 1867. RR 1885.

---

* Later USS *Adela*.

Fig 3.7: The *Magnolia* was built in New York in 1854 and captured as a blockade runner in 1862. (Dr. Charles L. Peery Collection)

Name	Builder	Launched	Acquired	Comm.
Santiago de Cuba	New York, N.Y. (Simonson)	2 Apr 1861	6 Sep 1861	5 Nov 1861
Tonnage	1,567 tons B, 1,627 n/r			
Dimensions	238′ (dk) × 38′ × 16′2″, d19′6″			
Machinery	Side wheels, 1 vertical beam engine (66″ × 11′), 2 boilers, 14 knots (Neptune)			
Complement	143/179			
Armament	2–20pdr MLR, 8–32pdr/57; (Dec1864) 2–20pdr MLR, 5–32pdr/57, 1–30pdr MLR			

Notes: Wood hull, barkentine rig, one funnel, two masts. Built for New York to Cuba service.
Service record: Blockade off Havana 1861. Search for Confederate raiders, 1862–64. Unsuccessful attack on Ft. Fisher, N.C., 24–25 Dec 1864. Second attack on Ft. Fisher, 13–15 Jan 1865. Decomm 17 Jun 1865. Sold 21 Sep 1865.
Ships captured: *Victoria*, 3 Dec 1861; 8 Feb: **O.K.*, 8 Feb 1862; *unidentified str, 20 Mar 1862; *W.C. Bee*, 23 Apr 1862; str *Ella Warley*, 25 Apr 1862; *Mersey*, 26 Apr 1862; *Maria*, 30 Apr 1862; *Lucy C. Holmes*, 27 May 1862; str *Columbia*,* 3 Aug 1862; *Lavinia*, 27 Aug 1862; *Comet*, 25 Dec 1862; str *Victory*,** 21 Jun 1863; str *Britannia*,*** 25 Jun 1863; str *Lizzie*, 15 Jul 1863; str *A.D. Vance*,**** 10 Sep 1863; str *Lucy*, 2 Nov 1863.
Later history: Merchant *Santiago de Cuba* 1865. Re-engined and converted to screw 1877. Converted to schooner barge 1886, renamed *Marion*. RR 1899.

Name	Builder	Launched	Acquired	Comm.
State of Georgia	Philadelphia, Pa. (Vaughn & Lynn)	12 Feb 1852	25 Sep 1861	20 Nov 1861
Tonnage	1,204 tons B			
Dimensions	210′ (dk) 200′ (bp) × 33′ × 14′, d21′			
Machinery	Side wheels, 1 side-lever engine (72.5″ × 8′), 2 boilers, HP 400 (Merrick)			
Complement	113			
Armament	6–8″ SB/55, 2–32pdr/57, 1–30pdr MLR; (Apr1863) 1–100pdr MLR, 1–30pdr MLR, 6–9″ SB			

Notes: Built for Philadelphia and Savannah S.S. Co. Barkentine rig.
Service record: NAtlBS 1861–62. Bombardment and capture of Ft. Macon, N.C., 25–26 Apr 1862. Damaged in collision with USS *Mystic*, 28 Sep 1862. NAtlBS Nov 1863–Sep1864. SAtlBS 1865. Decomm 9 Sep 1865. Sold 25 Oct 1865.
Ships captured: *Constitution*, 22 May 1862; str *Nassau*, 28 May 1862; str *Sunbeam*, 28 Sep 1862; str *Annie*, 24 Feb 1863; *Mary Jane, 24 Mar 1863; *Rising Dawn*, 25 Mar 1863; *unidentified schr, 26 Sep 1863.
Later history: Merchant *Andrew Johnson*, 1866. Wrecked in hurricane off Currituck Inlet, N.C., 5 Oct 1866.

Name	Builder	Launched	Acquired	Comm.
Tennessee	Baltimore, Md. (Robb)	31 Aug 1853	25 Apr 1862	8 May 1862
Tonnage	1,275 tons B, 852 n/r			
Dimensions	210′ (dk) × 33′11″ × 12′, d19′			
Machinery	Side wheels, 1 vertical beam engine (72″ × 9′), 2 boilers (Reeder)			
Complement	217			

* Later USS *Columbia*.
** Later USS *Queen*.
*** Later USS *Britannia*.
**** Later USS *Advance*.

Armament	2–32pdr/33, 1–30pdr MLR, 1–12pdr MLR

Notes: One funnel, two masts. Built for James Hooper's West Indies & Venezuela S.S. Co. but later purchased by Charles Morgan for service to Nicaragua. Carried survivors of Walker's army from San Juan, then shifted to New York–New Orleans run. Captured at New Orleans, 25 Apr 1862.
Service record: WGulfBS 1862–64. Bombardment at Whitehall Point, La., 10 Jul 1863. Bombardment of Ft. Morgan, Mobile Bay, 9–23 Aug 1864. Renamed *Mobile*, 1 Sep 1864. Damaged in gale off Rio Grande, Oct 1864. Sold 30 Mar 1865.
Ships captured: *Friendship*, *Jane, 12 Oct 1863; *Annie Virdon*, 5 Oct 1864; *Emily, Louisa*, 19 Oct 1864.
Later history: Merchant *Republic* 1865. Foundered in hurricane off Savannah, 25 Oct 1865.

Name	Builder	Launched	Acquired	Comm.
Tristram Shandy	Greenock (Aitken Mansel)	13 Jan 1864	May 1864	12 Aug 1864
Tonnage	444 tons B, 636 GRT			
Dimensions	222′ × 23′6″ × 6′4″, d9′6″			
Machinery	Side wheels, 2-cyl. inclined direct-acting condensing engines (46″ × 2′6″), 2 boilers, 12 knots			
Complement	80			
Armament	1–20pdr MLR, 2–12pdr MLR			

Notes: Blockade runner, captured 15 May 1864 by USS *Kansas* off Wilmington, N.C.. Iron hull, schooner rig, two funnels.
Service record: NAtlBS 1864. Destroyed grounded blockade runner off Ft. Fisher, N.C., 3 Dec 1864. Unsuccessful attack on Ft. Fisher, N.C., 24–25 Dec 1864. Second attack on Ft. Fisher, 13–15 Jan 1865. EGulfBS Feb 1865. Renamed *Boxer*, 21 Jun 1865. Decomm Sep 1865. Sold 1 Sep 1868.
Ships captured: str *Blenheim*, 25 Jan 1865.
Later history: Merchant *Fire Fly* 1869. Wrecked off Havana 1874.

Name	Builder	Launched	Acquired	Comm.
Vanderbilt	New York, N.Y. (Simonson)	10 Dec 1855	17 Mar 1862	2 Sep 1862
Tonnage	3,360 tons B			
Dimensions	340′ (oa) 331′ (dk) × 47′6″ × 21′6″, d31′9″			
Machinery	Side wheels, 2 vertical beam engines (80″ × 12′), 4 boilers, IHP 2800, 14 knots (Allaire)			
Complement	209			
Armament	2–100pdr MLR, 12–9″ SB, 1–12pdr MLR; (Mar 1865) 1–100pdr MLR, 12–9″ SB, 2–30pdr MLR			

Notes: Two funnels, two masts, wood hull. Transatlantic passenger ship, maiden voyage 1857 for the Vanderbilt Line. Presented to the government by Commodore Vanderbilt in 1861 and transferred to Navy from War Dept 1862.
Service record: Search for CSS *Alabama* in N. and S. Atlantic, 1863–64. Flagship of Flying Sqn in West Indies, 1863. Unsuccessful attack on Ft. Fisher, N.C., 24–25 Dec 1864. Second attack on Ft. Fisher, 13–15 Jan 1865. Pacific Sqn. 1865–67. Decomm 24 May 1867. Sold 1 Apr 1873.
Ships captured: str *Peterhoff*,***** 25 Feb 1863; str *Gertrude*,****** 16 Apr 1863; *Saxon*, 30 Oct 1863.
Later history: Merchant *Three Brothers*, 1873; machinery removed and converted to full-rig ship. Anchor Line coal hulk at Gibraltar 1885. BU 1929 in Spain.

***** Later USS *Peterhoff*.
****** Later USS *Gertrude*.

Name	Builder	Launched	Acquired	Comm.
Wando ex-*Wando*, ex-*Let Her Rip*	Glasgow (Kirkpatrick)	25 Mar 1864	5 Nov 1864	22 Dec 1864

Tonnage	468 tons B
Dimensions	230' × 26' × 7', d11'5"
Machinery	Side wheels, 2-cyl. oscillating engines (54" × 4'), 4 boilers
Complement	86
Armament	1–30pdr MLR, 1–12pdr MLR, 1–12pdr SB

Notes: Blockade runner *Wando*, captured 21 Oct 1864 by USS *Fort Jackson* off Cape Romain, S.C.. Iron hull.

Service record: SAtlBS 1865. Blockade of Charleston. Expedition to Bulls Bay, S.C., 12–17 Feb 1865. Decomm 10 Aug 1865. Sold 30 Nov 1865.

Later history: Merchant *Wando* 1865. Foundered in gale south of Delaware Lightship, 3 Feb 1872.

Wasp, see *Emma Henry*.

LARGE SCREW COMBATANTS (SECOND AND THIRD RATE)

Ocean-going merchant vessels acquired as blockaders.

Name	Builder	Launched	Acquired	Comm.
Albatross	Mystic, Conn. (Greenman)	31 Oct 1858	23 May 1861	25 Jun 1861

Tonnage	378 tons B, 414 n/r
Dimensions	158' × 30' × 13', d10'
Machinery	1 screw, 2-cyl. vertical direct-acting engine (84" × 2'10"), 1 boiler, 11 knots (Corliss)
Complement	68/95
Armament	4–32pdr57, 1–12pdr MLR; (Jun 1863) add 1–30pdr MLR

Notes: Wood hull, three-mast schooner rig.

Service record: AtlBS 1861. Engaged CSS *Beaufort* at Bodies I., N.C., 21 Jul 1861. Occupation of Winyah Bay, S.C., 21 May 1862. WGulfBS 1862–Jun 1864. Made passage past Port Hudson, La., 14 Mar (1 killed dead) and Grand Gulf, Miss., 19 Mar 1863 (1 killed dead). Severely damaged during action against Ft. DeRussy, 4 May 1863 (2 killed). WGulfBS 1865. Decomm 11 Aug 1865. Sold 8 Sep 1865.

Ships captured: *Velasco*, 18 Jul 1861; *Enchantress*, 22 Jul 1861; *Elizabeth Ann*, 1 Aug 1861; *Alabama*, 14 Sep 1861; *Jane Campbell*, 14 Dec 1861; *York*, 16 Jan 1862; *Treaty*, *Louisa*, 20 Jun 1862; *Volante*, 2 Jul 1862; *Two Sisters*,*, 21 Sep 1862..

Later history: Merchant *Albatross* 1865. Converted to sail, 1888. SE 1895.

Name	Builder	Launched	Acquired	Comm.
Antona	Glasgow, Scotland (Neilson)	1859	28 Mar 1864	19 Mar 1863

Tonnage	549 tons GRT
Dimensions	166.9' ( ) 157'10" ( ) × 23.1' × 13'
Machinery	1 screw, 2 vertical direct-acting engines (26" × 2'6"), 1 boiler. 8 knots
Complement	56
Armament	(Dec 1863) 2–32pdr/33, 1–20pdr MLR, 2–24pdr; (Sep 1864) 2–32pdr/33, 2–12pdr, 2–24pdr

* Later USS *Two Sisters*.

Notes: Blockade runner, captured 6 Jan 1863 by USS *Pocahontas* off Mobile. Iron hull. Formally purchased after commissioning.

Service record: WGulfBS 1863–65. Sank USS *Sciota* in collision in Mississippi River, 14 Jul 1863. Decomm 12 Aug 1865. Sold 30 Nov 1865.

Ships captured: *Cecelia D.*, 16 Jul 1863; *Betsey*, 6 Aug 1863; *Mary Ann, 26 Nov 1863; *Exchange*, 20 Dec 1863; str **Will o'the Wisp*, 9 Feb 1865.

Later history: Merchant *Carlotta* 1867. RR 1874.

Name	Builder	Launched	Acquired	Comm.
Aries	Sunderland (Laing)	12 Feb 1862	20 May 1863	25 Jul 1863

Tonnage	820 tons B, 611 GRT
Dimensions	201' ( ) 198' (bp) × 27'10" × 16', d15.8'
Machinery	1 screw, 2-cyl. vertical inverted direct-acting condensing engine (42" × 2'), 2 boilers, 12 knots (Richardson)
Complement	90
Armament	4–8"/63, 1–30pdr MLR, 1–12pdr MLR; (1864) add 1–30pdr MLR

Notes: Blockade runner, captured by USS *Stettin* aground in Bulls Bay, S.C., 28 Mar 1863. Iron hull.

Service record: NAtlBS Nov 1863–Feb1865. Disabled in storm off Cape Lookout, N.C., 27 Aug 1863. Unsuccessful attack on Ft. Fisher, N.C., 24–25 Dec 1864. Second attack on Ft. Fisher, 13–15 Jan 1865. Bombardment of Masonboro Inlet, N.C., 11 Feb 1865. EGulfBS 1865. Decomm 14 Jun 1865. Sold 1 Aug 1865.

Ships captured: *Ceres*, 6 Dec 1863; str *The Dare, 7 Jan 1864; *Ranger, 11 Jan 1864.

Later history: Merchant *Aries* 1865. BU 1908.

Name	Builder	Launched	Acquired	Comm.
Augusta Dinsmore	Mystic, Conn. (Mallory)	1863	Jun 1863	17 Jul 1863

Tonnage	850 tons B, 653 new reg
Dimensions	169' × 32'6" × 12'6", d9'2"
Machinery	1 screw, 1 Ericsson double engine (40" × 2'2"), 1 boiler, 11 knots
Complement	(U)
Armament	2–12pdr MLR; (Dec1863) 1–20pdr MLR, 1–12pdr MLR, 2–24pdr SB

Notes: Wood, two-mast schooner.

Service record: SAtlBS 1863–64. Bombardment of Ft. Wagner, Charleston, Jul 1863. WGulfBS 1864, off Texas. Decomm 28 Aug 1865. Sold 5 Sep 1865.

Ships captured: *Scio*, 16 Feb 1864; *John*, 10 Sep 1864.

Later history: Merchant *Gulf City*, 1865. Wrecked on Cape Lookout, North Carolina, 11 Jan 1869.

Name	Builder	Launched	Acquired	Comm.
Calypso	Dumbarton (A. Denny)	15 Apr 1855	12 Oct 1863	24 Sep 1863

Tonnage	630 tons B, 487 n/r
Dimensions	190.3' (oa) 175'2" (bp) × 26'6" × 12', d14'5"
Machinery	1 screw, 2-cyl. geared steeple engine (44 1/2" × 3'6"), 2 boilers, 12 knots (Tulloch)
Complement	70
Armament	2–30pdr MLR, 4–24pdr; (Nov 1863) add 1–30pdr MLR; (Jul 1865) 1–30pdr MLR, 1–12pdr MLR, 4–24pdr

Fig 3.8: A drawing by Clary Ray depicting the USS *Vanderbilt*, one of the largest ships taken over by the Navy for the blockade.

Notes: Blockade runner, captured 11 Jun 1863 by USS *Florida* off Wilmington, N.C.. Iron hull, three-mast schooner of the Bristol Steam Nav. Co. for the Bristol–Dublin run.
Service record: NAtlBS 1863–65. Blockade off Wilmington, N.C.. Decomm 15 Aug 1865. Sold 30 Nov 1865.
Ships captured: *Herald*, 23 Oct 1863; str *Lady Stirling*,*, 28 Oct 1864.
Later history: Merchant *Winchester* 1866. BU 1886.

Name	Builder	Launched	Acquired	Comm.
Cambridge	Medford, Mass. (Curtis)	18 Nov 1859	30 Jul 1861	29 Aug 1861
Tonnage	858 tons B			
Dimensions	200′ × 32′ × 13′6″			
Machinery	1 screw, 1 vertical direct-acting engine (52″ × 3′2″), 1 boiler, 10.5 knots			
Complement	96			
Armament	2–8″/55, 1–12pdr H, 1–6pdr MLR; (Aug 1862) 4–8″/63, 1–30pdr MLR, 1–24pdr H; (Jul 1863) 4–8″/63, 4–30pdr MLR, 2–24pdr			

Notes: Two-mast square-rig, wood hull.
Service record: NAtlBS 1861–64. SAtlBS 1864–65. Sold 20 Jun 1865.
Ships captured: *Louisa Agnes*, *Revere*, 10 Sep 1861; *Julia*, 23 Sep 1861; **T.W. Riley*, 6 Nov 1861; **Kate*, 2 Apr 1862; str **Modern Greece*, 27 Jun 1862; **J.W. Pindar*, 17 Nov 1862; *Emma Tuttle*, *J.C. Roker*, 3 Dec 1862; *Time*, 23 Jan 1863; str **Dee*, 6 Feb 1864.
Later history: Merchant *Minnetonka* 1865. RR 1878.

---

* Later USS *Lady Sterling*.

Name	Builder	Launched	Acquired	Comm.
Cherokee ex-*Thistle*	Renfrew (Hill)	2 Jul 1859	13 Jan 1864	21 Apr 1864
Tonnage	606 tons B, 386 GRT			
Dimensions	194′6″ × 25′2″ × 11′6″, d12′11″			
Machinery	1 screw, 2-cyl. geared beam engines (44″ × 3′6″), 1 boiler, 13 knots (Inglis)			
Complement	92			
Armament	2–20pdr MLR, 4–24pdr SB			

Notes: Blockade runner *Thistle* (I) captured by USS *Canandaigua* off Charleston, 8 May 1863. Wood hull on iron frame. Former Glasgow-to-Londonderry packet steamer.
Service record: NAtlBS 1864. Unsuccessful attack on Ft. Fisher, N.C., 24–25 Dec 1864. Second attack on Ft. Fisher, 13–15 Jan 1865. EGulfBS Feb 1865. Decomm 23 Jun 1865. Sold 1 Aug 1865.
Ship captured: str *Emma Henry*,**, 8 Dec 1864.
Later history: Merchant *Cherokee*, 1866. Sold to Chile 1868 as naval vessel, renamed *Ancud*. Merchant 1878. Wrecked at Chiloe Island, off southwest Chile, 25 Aug 1889.

Name	Builder	Launched	Acquired	Comm.
Columbia	Dumbarton (A.Denny)	19 Jul 1862	4 Nov 1862	Dec 1862
Tonnage	503 tons B			
Dimensions	168′ × 25′ × d14′			

** Later USS *Emma Henry*.

Machinery   1 screw, 2-cyl. inverted engine (36″ × 2′6″), 1 boiler
Complement 100
Armament   6–24pdr SB, 1–30pdr MLR

Notes: Blockade runner, captured by USS *Santiago de Cuba* off Florida, 3 Aug 1862. Iron hull.

Service record: NAtlBS 1862–63. Wrecked off Masonboro Inlet, N.C., 14 Jan and burned to prevent capture, 17 Jan 1863. (Crew captured).

Name	Builder	Launched	Acquired	Comm.
Emma	Glasgow, Scotland (Barclay Curle)	24 Nov 1862	30 Sep 1863	4 Nov 1863
Gertrude	Glasgow, Scotland (Barclay Curle)	28 Nov 1862	4 Jun 1863	22 Jul 1863

Tonnage   350 tons B, 283 GRT
Dimensions   156′ × 21′ × 9′4″ (*Emma*) 10′6″ (*Gertrude*), d11′
Machinery   1 screw, 2-cyl. oscillating engine (32″ × 3′), 1 boiler, 8 to 12 knots
Complement   68
Armament   *Emma*: 6–24pdr H, 2–12pdr MLR; (Mar 1865) 4–24pdr H, 1–20pdr MLR, 1–12pdr MLR.
             Gertrude: 2–12pdr MLR, 6–24pdr H

Notes: Blockade runners. *Emma* captured 24 Jul 1863 by USAT *Arago*; *Gertrude* captured 16 Apr 1863 by USS *Vanderbilt* off Eleuthera. Iron hulls.

Service records:

Emma: NAtlBS 1863–65. Unsuccessful attack on Ft. Fisher, N.C., 24–25 Dec 1864. Second attack on Ft. Fisher, 13–15 Jan 1865. Bombardment of Masonboro Inlet, N.C., 11 Feb 1865. Decomm 30 Aug 1865. Sold 1 Nov 1865.
  Ship captured: str *Ella*, 3 Dec 1864.
  Later history: Merchant *Gaspe*, 1866. Wrecked at Langlois, Canada, 14 Jan 1872.
Gertrude: WGulfBS 1863, off Mobile, Texas, May 1864. Decomm 11 Aug 1865. Sold 30 Nov 1865.
  Ships captured: str *Warrior*, 16 Aug 1863; *Ellen*, 16 Jan 1864; *Echo*, 19 Feb 1865.
  Later history: Merchant *Gussie Telfair* 1865. RR 1878.

Name	Builder	Launched	Acquired	Comm.
Flag	Philadelphia, Pa. (Birely & Lynn)	Jun 1857	26 Apr 1861	28 May 1861

ex-*Phineas Sprague*

Tonnage   938 tons B, 637 new reg
Dimensions   195′3″ (bp) × 30′10″ × 15′, d10′9″
Machinery   1 screw, 1 vertical direct-acting engine (48″ × 3′10″), 1 boiler, HP 400, 12 knots (Merrick)
Complement   116
Armament   6–8″/55, 1–6pdr; (Jun 1863) 4–8″ SB, 1–10″ SB, 2–30pdr MLR

Notes: Three masts. Operated between Boston and Philadelphia.

Service record: SAtlBS 1861–65. Occupation of Tybee Island, Ga., 24 Nov 1861. Capture of Fernandina, Fla., and Brunswick, St. Simons, and Jekyl Islands, Ga., 2–12 Mar 1862. Decomm 25 Feb 1865. Sold 12 Jul 1865.

Ships captured: *Alert*, 6 Oct 1861; *Cheshire*, 6 Dec 1861; str *Emilie*, 7 Jul 1862; *Elmira Cornelius*, 11 Oct 1862; *David Crockett*, 13 Oct 1862; str *Anglia*, 27 Oct 1862; *Stonewall Jackson*, 12 Apr 1863; *Amelia*, 8 May 1863; *Cyclops*, 12 Jun 1864.

Later history: Merchant *Flag* 1865. BU 1876.

Name	Builder	Launched	Acquired	Comm.
Flambeau	Brooklyn, N.Y. (L & F)	1861	14 Nov 1861	27 Nov 1861

Tonnage   791 tons B, 766 n/r
Dimensions   185′ (dk) 173′6″ (bp) × 30′ × 11′, d18′
Machinery   1 screw, 1 vertical beam engine (50″ × 5′), 2 boilers, 12 knots (Esler)
Complement   92
Armament   1–30pdr MLR, 1–20pdr MLR; (Sep 1862) 2–24pdr H, 2–30pdr MLR, 1–20pdr MLR; (Feb 1865) 2–8″/55, 1–30pdr MLR; (Apr 1865) add 2–24pdr H

Notes: Built for China coastal trade. Brigantine rig. Wood hull.

Service record: SAtlBS 1861–65. Decomm 7 Jun 1865. Sold 12 Jul 1865.

Ships captured: *Active*, 26 Apr 1862; *Catalina*, 20 Jun 1862; *Bettie Cratzer*, 23 Jun 1863; *John Gilpin*, 28 Nov 1863.

Later history: Merchant *Flambeau* 1865. Stranded and lost off New Inlet Bar, N.C., 1 Mar 1867.

Name	Builder	Launched	Acquired	Comm.
Galatea	New York, N.Y. (Van Deusen)	1863	31 Jul 1863	29 Jan 1864
Glaucus	New York, N.Y. (Van Deusen)	1863	17 Jul 1863	18 Feb 1864
Neptune	New York, N.Y. (Van Deusen)	1863	17 Jul 1863	19 Dec 1863
Nereus	New York, N.Y. (Van Deusen)	21 Mar 1863	5 Oct 1863	19 Apr 1864
Proteus	New York, N.Y. (Van Deusen)	1863	30 Sep 1863	10 Mar 1864

Tonnage   1,244 tons
Dimensions   209′6″ (U) 203′6″ (U) × 35′6″ × 14′, d20′8″
Machinery   1 screw, 2-cyl. inverted direct-acting engine (44″ × 3′), 2 boilers, 11 knots (Esler)
Complement   164
Armament   *Glaucus*: 1–100pdr MLR, 2–30pdr MLR, 8–8″/55.
             Galatea, Neptune: (1864) 1–100pdr MLR, 8–32pdr/57, 2–30pdr MLR; (Mar 1865) less 2–32pdr/57. *Neptune*: 1–60pdr MLR, 2–30pdr MLR, 6–32pdr/57.
             Nereus, Proteus: (1864) 1–100pdr MLR, 2–30pdr MLR, 6–32pdr/57, 2–12pdr MLR; (Dec 1864) 1–60pdr MLR, 2–30pdr MLR, 6–32pdr/57, 2–12pdr.
             Proteus: (Apr 1865) 1–60pdr MLR, 1–30pdr MLR, 6–32pdr/57, 1–20pdr MLR

Notes: Wood hulls, schooner rig. Built for William P. Williams but purchased prior to completion.

Service records

Galatea: West India Sqn, based at Cap Haitien, 1864. Decomm 12 Jul 1865. Sold to Haiti, 15 Aug 1865.
  Later history: Haitian gunboat *Alexandre Petion*, 1865. Captured by revolutionaries at Cap Haitien, 15 Nov 1869. Blew up and sank off Haitian coast, 1893.
Glaucus: NAtlBS 1864–65. Transported Manuel Murillo, President of Colombia, to Cartagena, Mar 1864. Severely damaged by fire off Cape Fear while chasing a blockade runner, 28 May 1864. Went aground near Manassas Reef, Bahamas, 30 May 1865. Decomm 6 Jun 1865. Sold 12 Jul 1865.
  Later history: Merchant *Worcester* 1865. BU 1894 at Boston.
Neptune: West India Sqn 1864–65. Decomm 31 May 1865. Sold 12 Jul 1865.

Later history: Merchant *Allegany* 1865. Wrecked in fog off Long Island, N.Y., 5 Dec 1865.

Nereus: NAtlBS 1864. Blockade of Wilmington. Search for CSS *Tallahassee*, Sep 1864. Unsuccessful attack on Ft. Fisher, N.C., 24–25 Dec 1864. Second attack on Ft. Fisher, 13–15 Jan 1865 (3 killed). Search for CSS *Shenandoah* in Caribbean 1865. Decomm 15 May 1865. Sold 15 Jul 1865.
Later history: Merchant *Somerset* 1865. BU 1887.

Proteus: Blockade duty off Florida 1864–65. Expedition to St. Marks, Fla., Mar 1865. Sold 12 Jul 1865.
Ships captured: *R.S. Hood*, 9 Jun 1864; str *Jupiter*, 27 Jun 1864; *Ann Louisa*, 6 Sep 1864; str *Ruby*, 27 Feb 1865.
Later history: Merchant *Carroll* 1865. BU 1894.

Gertrude, see *Emma*.

Glaucus, see *Galatea*.

Name	Builder	Launched	Acquired	Comm.
Governor Buckingham	Mystic, Conn. (Mallory)	Apr 1863	29 Jul 1863	13 Nov 1863
Tonnage	886 tons B, 1,044 n/r			
Dimensions	177'6" × 32'2" × 13'6", d17'			
Machinery	1 screw, 1 vertical direct-acting engine. 1 boiler. 8 knots			
Complement	112			
Armament	1–100pdr MLR, 4–30pdr MLR, 1–20pdr MLR			

Notes: Hermaphrodite brig.
Service record: NAtlBS 1863–65. Unsuccessful attack on Ft. Fisher, N.C., 24–25 Dec 1864. Second attack on Ft. Fisher, 13–15 Jan 1865. Decomm 27 Mar 1865. Sold 12 Jul 1865.
Ships captured: str *Antonica, 20 Dec 1863; str *Lynx, 25 Sep 1864.
Later history: Merchant *Equator* 1865. Converted to barge, 1893.

Name	Builder	Launched	Acquired	Comm.
Grand Gulf ex-Onward	New York, N.Y. (Poillon)	28 Mar 1863	14 Sep 1863	28 Sep 1863
Tonnage	1,200 tons B			
Dimensions	216' × 34'6" × d17'9"			
Machinery	1 screw, 1 vertical direct-acting engine (50" × 4'6"), 2 boilers, 11 knots			
Complement	201			
Armament	1–100pdr MLR, 2–30pdr MLR, 3–8"/69, 5–8"/62			

Notes: Acquired new. Wood hull.
Service record: NAtlBS Nov 1863–Jul 1864. WGulfBS Apr 1865. Prison ship, New Orleans, 1865. Decomm 10 Nov and sold 30 Nov 1865.
Ships captured: str *Banshee,* 21 Nov 1863; *Mary Ann*, 6 Mar 1864; str *Young Republic*, 6 May 1864.
Later history: Merchant *General Grant* 1865. Burned and sank at New Orleans wharf, 19 Apr 1869.

Name	Builder	Launched	Acquired	Comm.
Hendrick Hudson ex-*Florida*	Greenpoint, N.Y. (Whitlock)	30 Jul 1859	20 Sep 1862	30 Dec 1862
Tonnage	460 tons B			
Dimensions	171' (dk) × 29'11" × d9'6"			

---

* Later USS *Banshee*.

Machinery	1 screw, 1 vertical direct-acting engine (36" × 3'6"), HP 100, 11 knots
Complement	88
Armament	2–20pdr MLR, 4–8"/63

Notes: Blockade runner *Florida*, captured 6 Apr 1862, by USS *Pursuit* at St. Andrews Bay, Fla. Wood two-mast schooner.
Service record: EGulfBS 1863. Rammed and sank blockade runner *Wild Pigeon* at sea, 21 Mar 1864. Expedition to St. Marks, Fla., 23 Feb–27 Mar 1865. Decomm 8 Aug 1865. Sold 12 Sep 1865.
Ships captured: *Margaret*, 1 Feb 1863; *Pacifique*, 27 Mar 1863; *Theresa*, 16 Apr 1863; *Wild Pigeon, 21 Mar 1864.
Later history: Merchant *Hendrick Hudson* 1865. Wrecked near Havana, 13 Nov 1867.

Name	Builder	Launched	Acquired	Comm.
Huntsville	New York, N.Y. (Westervelt)	10 Dec 1857	24 Apr 1861	9 May 1861
Montgomery	New York, N.Y. (Westervelt)	9 Jan 1858	2 May 1861	27 May 1861
Tonnage	*Huntsville*: 840 tons B, *Montgomery*: 787 tons B			
Dimensions	*Huntsville*: 196'4" (U) 175 (wl) × 29'8" × 14'4" *Montgomery*: 201'6" (U) × 28'7" × 15'6", d19'			
Machinery	1 screw, 1 inverted vertical direct-acting engine (52" × 3'6"), 1 boiler, 11 knots (Morgan)			
Complement	143			
Armament	*Huntsville*: 1–64pdr/106, 2–32pdr/33; (Jun 1862) 1–9" SB, 1–30pdr MLR, 2–32pdr/57.			
	Montgomery: 1–8", 4–32pdr/33; (Jul 1862) 1–10"/87, 1–30pdr MLR, 4–32pdr/33; (Jul 1863) 1–10"/106, 1–30pdr MLR, 4–8"/55			

Notes: Chartered May 1861, later purchased 18 Aug 1861. Three masts, schooner rig. Operated on New York–Savannah run for American Atlantic Screw S.S. Co.
Service records:
Huntsville: GulfBS 1861–65. Engaged CSS *Florida* off Mobile Bay, 24 Dec 1861. Refit Apr–Jun 1862. Decomm 19 Aug 1864. Recomm 29 Mar 1865. Transport duties. Decomm 28 Aug 1865. Sold 30 Nov 1865.
Ships captured: *Isabel*, 13 Aug 1861; *Zavala*, 1 Oct 1861; str *Adela*,** 7 Jul 1862; *Agnes*, 16 Jul 1862; str *Reliance*,*** 21 Jul 1862; *Ariel*,**** 11 Nov 1862; *Courier*, 22 Dec 1862; *Surprise*, 13 Mar 1863; *Minnie*, 6 Apr 1863; *Ascension*, 14 Apr 1863; *A.J. Hodge*, 13 May 1863; str *Union*, 19 May 1863.
Later history: Merchant *Huntsville* 1865. Destroyed by fire off Little Egg Harbor Light, N.J., 19 Dec 1877.

Montgomery: GulfBS 1861. Engaged CSS *Tallahassee* 8 Nov and CSS *Florida* and *Pamlico* off Horn Island Pass, Miss., 4 Dec 1861. EGulfBS Jan 1862. WGulfBS, 1862. NAtlBS 1863. Search for CSS *Tacony* off Nantucket and CSS *Florida* Jun–Jul 1863. Second attack on Ft. Fisher, N.C., 13–15 Jan 1865 (2 killed). Bombardment of Masonboro Inlet, N.C., 11 Feb 1865. Decomm 20 Jun 1865. Sold 10 Aug 1865.
Ships captured: *Finland*, 29 Aug 1861; *Isabel*, 1 Feb 1862; *Columbia*, 5 Apr 1862; *Will o' the Wisp*, 3 Jun 1862; str *Blanche*, 8 Oct 1862; str *Caroline*,***** 29 Oct 1862; *William E. Chester*, 20 Nov 1862; str *Dare*, 7 Jan 1864; str *Bendigo*, 13 Jan 1864; str *Pet*, 16 Feb 1864; str *Bat*,****** 10 Oct 1864.

** Later USS *Adela*.
*** Later USS *Hollyhock*.
**** Later USS *Ariel*.
***** Later USS *Arizona*.
****** Later USS *Bat*.

Fig 3.9: The USS *Proteus* was one of five sister ships taken over by the Navy while under construction and served in the blockade. (Dr. Charles L. Peery Collection)

Fig 3.10: The USS *Hendrick Hudson* was captured as a blockade runner off the Gulf Coast of Florida. (Dr. Charles L. Peery Collection)

Later history: Merchant *Montgomery* 1866. Sunk in collision with steamer *Seminole* off Cape Hatteras, 7 Jan 1877.

Name	Builder	Launched	Acquired	Comm.
Iron Age	Kennebunk, Me. (Thompson)	Nov 1862	28 Apr 1863	25 Jun 1863
Tonnage	424 tons B			
Dimensions	144′ × 25′ × d12′6″			
Machinery	1 screw			
Complement	107			
Armament	3–30pdr MLR, 6–8″ SB			

Service record: NAtlBS 1863–64. Went aground in Lockwood's Folly Inlet near Wilmington, N.C., 11 Jan 1864 and destroyed to prevent capture.
Ships captured: *unidentified, 15 Sep 1863; str *Venus*, 21 Oct 1863; str *Robert E. Lee*,* 9 Nov 1863.

Name	Builder	Launched	Acquired	Comm.
Iuka	Fairhaven, Conn. (Pook)	1863	8 Mar 1864	23 May 1864
ex-*Commodore*				
Tonnage	944 tons B			
Dimensions	200′ × 31′6″ × 20′			
Machinery	1 screw, 2 horizontal direct-acting engines (40″ × 2′), 1 boiler, 10 knots (Delamater)			
Complement	116			
Armament	(Jun 1864) 1–100pdr MLR, 2–8″/55, 2–30pdr MLR, 2–24pdr; (Apr 1865) 1–100pdr MLR, 2–8″/55, 1–30pdr MLR, 1–20pdr MLR			

Notes: Wood hull, acquired on completion.
Service record: EGulfBS 1864. Blockade in Gulf of Mexico. Expedition to St. Marks, Fla., 23 Feb–27 Mar 1865. Decomm 22 Jun 1865. Sold 1 Aug 1865.
Ship captured: *Comus*, 31 Mar 1865.
Later history: Merchant *Andalusia* 1865. Burned and sank off Cape Hatteras, 3 Mar 1867.

---

* Later USS Fort *Donelson*.

Name	Builder	Launched	Acquired	Comm.
Lodona	Hull, England (Samuelson)	Jan 1862	20 Sep 1862	5 Jan 1863
Tonnage	861 tons B, 688 GRT			
Dimensions	210′ × 27′6″ × 11′6″, d16′6″			
Machinery	1 screw, 2 vertical direct-acting engines (34″ × 2′8″), 1 boiler, 7 knots			
Complement	97			
Armament	1–100pdr MLR, 1–30pdr MLR, 1–9″ SB, 4–24pdr H			

Notes: Blockade runner, captured 4 Aug 1862 by USS *Unadilla* in Ossabaw Sound, S.C. Iron hull, bark rig.
Service record: SAtlBS 1863. Bombardment of Fts. Wagner and Gregg, Charleston, Aug 1863. Decomm 11 May 1865. Sold 20 Jun 1865.
Ships captured: *Minnie*, 20 Apr 1863; *Arctic*, 15 Nov 1863; *Hope*, 10 Jul 1864.
Later history: Merchant *Lodona* 1865. Lost (cause unknown), 31 May 1879.

Name	Builder	Launched	Acquired	Comm.
Massachusetts	Boston, Mass. (Loring)	1860	3 May 1861	24 May 1861
South Carolina	Boston, Mass. (Loring)	1860	3 May 1861	22 May 1861
Tonnage	1,165 tons B, 1,215 n/r (*Massachusetts*: 1,155 tons B)			
Dimensions	*Massachusetts*: 219′10″ × 33′2″ × 13′8″, d18′ *South Carolina*: 217′11″ × 33′6″ × 14′6″			
Machinery	1 screw, 1 vertical direct-acting engine (62″ × 3′8″), 2 boilers, HP 600, 11 knots (bldr)			
Complement	112			
Armament	*Massachusetts*: 1–32pdr/42, 4–8″/63; (Apr 1865) 1–30pdr MLR, 4–8″/63, 2–24pdr.			
	South Carolina: 4–8″/63, 1–32pdr/42; (May 1863) 2–8″/63, 2–32pdr/42, 1–30pdr MLR, 1–24pdr H; (Jun 1863) add 2–8″.			

Note: Iron hull, one funnel. Built for service between Boston, Norfolk, Charleston, and Savannah. *Massachusetts* used as supply ship.
Service records:
Massachusetts: GulfBS Jun 1861–Jan 1862. Damaged by gunfire of CSS *Florida* off Ship Island, Miss., 21 Oct 1861. Recomm as transport and supply

vessel, 16 Apr 1862. SAtlBS 1863. Struck a torpedo (mine) which failed to explode at Charleston, 19 Mar 1865. Decomm 22 Sep 1865. Sold 1 Oct 1867.

Ships captured: *Perthshire*, 9 Jun 1861; *Achilles*, 17 Jun 1861; *Nahum Stetson*, 19 Jun 1861; *Brilliant, Trois Freres, Olive Branch, Fanny, Basile*, 23 Jun 1861; *Charles Henry*, 7 Aug 1861; *Persis*, 12 Mar 1864; str *Caledonia*, 30 May 1864.

Later history: Merchant *Crescent City* 1868. Lengthened 1873. RR 1892

South Carolina: GulfBS 1861–62. SAtlBS Jun 1862–65. Converted to storeship, 1865. Decomm 17 Aug 1866. Sold 5 Oct 1866.

Ships captured: *Shark*,* *Louisa, Dart*,** *McCanfield, Venus, Ann Ryan*, 4 Jul 1861; *Falcon, Caroline*, 5 Jul 1861; *George G. Baker*, 6 Jul 1861; *Sam Houston*,*** 7 Jul 1861; **Tom Hicks*, 9 Jul 1861; *T.J.Chambers*, 12 Jul 1861; *Anna Taylor*, 11 Sep 1861; *Isilda*,**** *Joseph H. Toone*, 4 Oct 1861; *Edward Barnard*, 16 Oct 1861; *Florida*, 11 Dec 1861; str *Magnolia*,***** 19 Feb 1862; **Patriot*, 27 Aug 1862; *Nellie*, 29 Mar 1863; **Arletta*, 3 Mar 1864; str *Alliance*, 12 Apr 1864.

Later history: Merchant *Juniata* 1866. Converted to schooner barge, 1893. Foundered in tow in snowstorm, 17 Feb 1902.

Name	Builder	Launched	Acquired	Comm.
Memphis	Dumbarton (Denny)	3 Apr 1862	4 Sep 1862	4 Oct 1862
Tonnage	1,780 tons D, 791 tons B, 1,010 GRT			
Dimensions	227′ × 30′1″ × 15′6″			
Machinery	1 screw, 2 inverted direct-acting engines (46″ × 3′), 2 boilers. 705 hp, 14 knots			
Complement	100			
Armament	4–24pdr SB, 2–12pdr MLR, 1–30pdr MLR; (Jun 1864) add 4–20pdr MLR			

Notes: Blockade runner, captured by USS *Magnolia* off Charleston, 31 Jul 1862. Iron hull, brig rig.

Service record: SAtlBS 1862. Engagement with ironclads off Charleston, 31 Jan 1863. Attacked by torpedo boat *David* but torpedo did not explode, in N. Edisto River, 6 Mar 1864. Decomm 6 May 1867. Sold 8 May 1869.

Ships captured: str *Ouachita*, 14 Oct 1862; *Mercury*, 4 Jan 1863; *Antelope*, 31 Mar 1863; str **Havelock*, 11 Jun 1863.

Later history: Merchant *Mississippi* 1869. Destroyed by fire at Seattle, 13 May 1883.

Name	Builder	Launched	Acquired	Comm.
Mercedita	Brooklyn, N.Y. (Lupton)	20 Apr 1861	31 Jul 1861	3 Dec 1861
Tonnage	840 tons B, 776 n/r			
Dimensions	195′ (dk) 183′6″ (wl) × 30′3″ × 12′9″. d18′10″			
Machinery	1 screw, 2 inverted direct-acting engines (30″ × 2′8″), 2 boilers, HP 300,14 knots (Murphy)			
Complement	121			
Armament	8–32pdr/57, 1–20pdr MLR; (May1863) 1–100pdr MLR, 2–20pdr MLR, 4–32pdr/57, 2–24pdr			

Notes: Wood hull. Three-mast schooner rig. One funnel.

Service record: GulfBS Jan 1862. Engaged batteries at St. Vincent, Fla., 3 Apr 1862. Sank British schr *Ellen* in collision off Nassau, 1 Aug 1862. SAtlBS Sep 1862. Engagement with ironclads off Charleston, 31 Jan 1863, rammed and damaged by CSS *Palmetto State* (2 killed). West India Sqn Apr 1863, then NAtlBS Jun 1863. WGulfBS Mar 1865. Protection of American interests, Santo Domingo, Aug 1865. Decomm 14 Oct and sold 25 Oct 1865.

Ships captured: **Julia*, 24 Jan 1862; str *Bermuda*,****** 27 Apr 1862; *Victoria and Ida*, 12 Jul 1862; *William*, 21 Oct 1863.

Later history: Merchant *Mercedita*, 1865. Rig changed to barkentine 1879 and to schooner 1886. Mercantile barge 1900, lost 1901.

Montgomery, see *Huntsville*.

Name	Builder	Launched	Acquired	Comm.
Monticello	Greenpoint, N.Y. (Williams)	1859	12 May 1861	May 1861
Tonnage	655 tons B, 525 n/r			
Dimensions	180′ × 29′ × 12′10″, d16′10″			
Machinery	1 screw, 1 vertical direct-acting engine (40″ × 2′2″), 1 boiler. HP 220, 11.5 knots			
Complement	137			
Armament	1–10″ SB, 2–32pdr/33; (Sep 1861) add 2–32pdr/42; (Aug 1862) 1–10″ SB, 2–30pdr MLR, 2–32pdr/42, 2–32pdr/33; (Dec 1862) 1–10″ SB replaced by 1–100pdr MLR; (Feb 1864) 1–100pdr MLR, 3–30pdr MLR, 2–9″ SB			

Notes: Wood hull. Chartered, then purchased 12 Sep 1861.

Service record: NAtlBS, blockade in James River May 1861. Renamed *Star*, 3 May 1861. Engaged batteries at Sewell's Point, Va., 18–19 May 1861. Renamed *Monticello*, 23 May 1861. Capture of Hatteras Inlet, 28–29 Aug 1861. Blockade of Wilmington, Mar 1862–64. Sank USS *Peterhoff* in collision, 6 Mar 1864. Unsuccessful attack on Ft. Fisher, N.C., 24–25 Dec 1864. Second attack on Ft. Fisher, 13–15 Jan 1865 (4 killed). Decomm 24 Jul 1865. Sold 1 Nov 1865.

Ships captured: *Tropic Wind.*, 21 May 1861; *Revere*, 11 Oct 1862; **Ariel*, **Ann Maria*, 18 Nov 1862; *Sue*, 30 Mar 1863; *Odd Fellow*, 15 Apr 1863; **Golden Liner*, 27 Apr 1863; *unidentified str, 27 Dec 1864.

Later history: Merchant *Monticello* 1865. Foundered off Newfoundland, 19 Apr 1872.

Name	Builder	Launched	Acquired	Comm.
Mount Vernon	New York (Sneeden)	10 Jul 1859	23 Apr 1861	May 1861
Tonnage	625 tons B, 617 n/r			
Dimensions	173′6″ × 28′8″ × 12′, d16′			
Machinery	1 screw, vertical direct-acting engine, HP 220, 11.5 knots			
Complement	50			
Armament	1–32pdr/57, 2–32pdr/33; (Apr 1863) 1–100pdr MLR, 2–32pdr/42, 2–32pdr/33; (Nov 1863) 1–100pdr MLR, 2–20pdr MLR, 2–9″ SB			

Notes: Wood hull, topsail schooner.

Service record: Blockade off North Carolina. Engagement with CSS *Raleigh* off New Inlet, N.C., 6–7 May 1864. Decomm 27 Jun 1865. Sold 12 Jul 1865.

Ships captured: *East*, May 1861; *Wild Pigeon*, 19 Jul 1861; *British Queen*, 1 Mar 1862; **Kate*, 2 Apr 1862; *Constitution*, 22 May 1862; **Emily*, 26 Jun 1862; *Napier*, 29 Jul 1862; **Sophia*, 4 Nov 1862; *Levi Rowe*, 26 Nov 1862; **Emma Tuttle*, 3 Dec 1862; **Industry*, 1 Feb 1863; *Mary Jane*, 24 Mar 1863; *Rising Dawn*, 25 Mar 1863; *St. George*, 22 Apr 1863.

Later history: Merchant *Mount Vernon* 1865. Sold foreign, 1869.

---

* Later USS *Shark*.
** Later USS *Dart*.
*** Later USS Sam *Houston*.
**** Later USS *Isilda*.
***** Later USS *Magnolia*.

****** Later USS *Bermuda*.

Name	Builder	Launched	Acquired	Comm.
Niphon	Boston, Mass. (S. Smith)	Feb 1863	22 Apr 1863	24 Apr 1863
Tonnage	475 tons B			
Dimensions	157'6" (oa) 153'2" (bp) × 25'6" × 10'6"			
Machinery	1 screw, 2 vertical inverted direct-acting engines (26" × 2'2"), 1 boiler, 10 knots (Atlantic)			
Complement	70/100			
Armament	1–20pdr MLR, 2–12pdr MLR, 4–32pdr/42; (Nov 1864) add 2–32pdr/33			

Notes: Composite hull, barkentine rig. Built for China coast trade.

Service record: NAtlBS 1863–64. Decomm 1 Dec 1864. Sold 17 Apr 1865.

Ships captured: str *Banshee*, 29 Jul 1863; str **Hebe*, 23 Aug 1863; str *Cornubia*,* 23 Aug 1863; str *Ella and Annie*,** 9 Nov 1863; str **Lynx*, 25 Sep 1864; str **Night Hawk*, 29 Sep 1864; str **Condor*, 1 Oct 1864; str *Annie*,*** 31 Oct 1864.

Later history: Merchant *Tejuca* 1865. Sold foreign 1867. FFU.

Neptune, see *Galatea*.

Nereus, see *Galatea*.

Name	Builder	Launched	Acquired	Comm.
Penguin	Mystic, Conn. (Mallory)	26 Nov 1859	23 May 1861	25 Jun 1861
Tonnage	389 tons B, 514 n/r			
Dimensions	155' × 30'5" × 12', d10'8"			
Machinery	1 screw, Ericsson vibrating-lever engine (48" × 2'), 10 knots (Delamater)			
Complement	69			
Armament	1–12pdr MLR, 4–32pdr/57; (Apr 1863) add 2–20pdr MLR			

Notes: Three-mast schooner.

Service record: NAtlBS Aug 1861. Potomac Flotilla. SAtlBS Oct 1861. Occupation of Port Royal, S.C., 7 Nov 1861. Capture of Fernandina, Fla., and Brunswick, St. Simons, and Jekyl Islands, Ga., 2–12 Mar 1862. WGulfBS 1863–65. Decomm 24 Aug 1865. Sold 18 Sep 1865.

Ships captured: **Louisa*, 11 Aug 1861; *Albion*, 25 Nov 1861; str **Matagorda*, 8 Jul 1864; str **Granite City*, 21 Jan 1865.

Later history: Merchant *Florida* 1865. Converted to schooner, 1884. Abandoned 1903.

Name	Builder	Launched	Acquired	Comm.
Peterhoff	Sunderland, England (Oswald)	25 Jul 1861	Feb 1863	Feb 1864
Tonnage	800 tons B, 819 GRT			
Dimensions	220' (U) × 29' × 17'			
Machinery	1 screw, vertical direct-acting engine			
Complement	(U)			
Armament	5–32pdr, 1–30pdr MLR, 1–12pdr H			

Notes: Blockade runner, captured by USS *Vanderbilt* off St. Thomas, 25 Feb 1863. Laid up in New York one year pending decision of prize court. Iron steamer.

Service record: NAtlBS 1864. Sunk in collision with USS *Monticello* off New Inlet, N.C., 6 Mar 1864.

* Later USS *Cornubia*.
** Later USS *Malvern*.
*** Later USS *Preston*.

Fig 3.11: The USS *Memphis* was a blockade runner built in England and captured in 1862.

Name	Builder	Launched	Acquired	Comm.
Preston	London, England (Dudgeon)	1863	31 Oct 1864	6 Feb 1865
ex-*Annie*, ex-*Pallas*				
Tonnage	428 tons B			
Dimensions	179' × 23'1" × 10', d13'4", also reported as 175'6" × 23'4" × d12'5"			
Machinery	2 screws, 2 2-cyl. direct-acting engines (26" × 1'8"), IHP 600, 14 knots (Sun Engine)			
Complement	(U)			
Armament	1–30pdr MLR, 2–24pdr SB			

Notes: Blockade runner *Annie*, captured off New Inlet, N.C., by USS *Wilderness* and *Niphon*, 31 Oct 1864. Iron hull, schooner rig.

Service record: WGulfBS 1865, off Texas. Decomm 8 Aug 1865. Sold 30 Nov 1865.

Later history: Merchant *Rover* 1865. Sold foreign 1868.

Name	Builder	Launched	Acquired	Comm.
Princess Royal	Glasgow, Scotland (Tod)	20 Jun 1861	18 Mar 1863	29 May 1863
Tonnage	619 tons B, 774 GRT, 973 n/r			
Dimensions	196'9" × 27'3" × 11', d16'			
Machinery	1 screw, 2-cyl. horizontal geared engine (49" × 3'3"), 2 boilers, 11 knots. (Bldr)			
Complement	90			
Armament	2–30pdr MLR, 1–9" SB, 4–24pdr H			

Notes: Blockade runner, captured by USS *Unadilla* off Charleston, 29 Jan 1863, with cargo of marine engines. Built for service in Irish Sea. Iron hull.

Service record: WGulfBS 1863–65. Bombardment of Donaldsonville, La., 28 Jun 1863. Decomm 21 Jul 1865. Sold 17 Aug 1865.

Ships captured: *Atlantic*, 10 Aug 1863; *Flying Scud*, 12 Aug 1863; *Flash*, 27 Nov 1863; *Cora*, 19 Dec 1863; *Neptune*, 19 Nov 1864; **Alabama*, 6 Dec 1864; *Anna Sophia*, 7 Feb 1865; str **Will o'the Wisp*, 10 Feb 1865; **Le Compt*, 24 May 1865.

Later history: Merchant *General Sherman* 1865. Foundered off Cape Fear, N.C., 10 Jan 1874.

Name	Builder	Launched	Acquired	Comm.
R.R. Cuyler	New York, N.Y. (Sneeden)	20 Aug 1859	28 Aug 1861	23 May 1862
Tonnage	1,202 tons B			
Dimensions	237′ × 33′3″ × d16′			
Machinery	1 screw, 1 vertical direct-acting engine (70″ × 4′), 2 boilers, 14 knots (Allaire)			
Complement	116/154			
Armament	2–32pdr/57, 6–32pdr/33; (Jul 1862) 1–30pdr MLR, 8–32pdr/57, 1–12pdr SB; (Jun 1863) 1–30pdr, 10–32pdr/57; (Oct 1864) add 1–30pdr MLR			

Notes: Chartered May 1861. Wood hull, two funnels. In service between New York, Havana, and New Orleans.

Service record: Blockade off Florida 1861–64. Second attack on Ft. Fisher, N. C., 13–15 Jan 1865. Decomm 1 Jul 1865. Sold 15 Aug 1865.

Ships captured: *Finland, 19 Aug 1861; A.J. Vein, str Anna, str Henry Lewis, 22 Nov 1861; J.W. Wilder,* 20 Jan 1862; Grace E. Baker, 29 Mar 1862; Jane, 3 May 1862; Anna Sophia, 27 Aug 1862; str Eugenie,** 6 May 1863; *Isabel, 18 May 1863; str Kate Dale, 14 Jul 1863; str Armstrong, 4 Dec 1864.

Later history: Merchant R.R. Cuyler 1865. Sold to government of Colombia as warship, Dec 1866, renamed El Rayo. Rejected by new government, remained at Cartagena. Wrecked on reef in storm at Cartagena, 12 Sep 1867.

Name	Builder	Launched	Acquired	Comm.
Stars and Stripes	Mystic, Conn. (Mallory)	May 1861	27 Jul 1861	19 Sep 1861
Tonnage	407 tons B			
Dimensions	150′6″ (dk) 124′3″ (U) × 34′6″ × 9′, d16′4″			
Machinery	1 screw, 2 vertical direct-acting engines (29″ × 2′2″), 1 boiler. 10.5 knots (Delamater)			
Complement	94			
Armament	4–8″/55, 1–20pdr MLR, 1–12pdr			

Notes: Purchased new. Three-mast schooner.

Service record: AtlBS 1861. Landings at Roanoke Island, N.C., 7–8 Feb 1862. Capture of New Berne, N.C., 13–14 Mar 1862. EGulfBS Oct 1862–65. Expedition to St. Marks, Fla., 23 Feb–27 Mar 1865. Decomm 30 Jun 1865. Sold 10 Aug 1865.

Ships captured: *Charity, 15 Dec 1861; str *Modern Greece, 27 Jun 1862; Mary Elizabeth, 24 Aug 1862; Pacifique, 25 Mar 1863; Florida, 3 Jun 1863; *Caroline Gertrude, 29 Dec 1863; str Laura, 18 Jan 1864.

Later history: Merchant Stars and Stripes 1865. Lengthened and renamed Metropolis 1871. Went aground and lost off Currituck Beach, N.C., 31 Jan 1878.

Name	Builder	Launched	Acquired	Comm.
Stettin	Sunderland (Pile)	19 Sep 1861	4 Sep 1862	12 Nov 1862
Tonnage	502 tons B, 480 tons net			
Dimensions	171′ (bp) × 28′ × 12′, d16′6″			
Machinery	1 screw, 2 inverted engines (36″ × 2′4″), 2 boilers, 6 knots			
Complement	72			
Armament	1–30pdr MLR, 4–24pdr H			

Notes: Blockade runner, captured off Charleston by USS Bienville, 24 May 1862. Iron hull, brig rig.

---

* Later USS J.W.Wilder.
** Later USS Glasgow.

Service record: AtlBS 1862–65. Blockade of Charleston. Decomm 6 Apr 1865. Sold 22 Jun 1865.

Ships captured: str Aries,*** 28 Mar 1863; str St. John's, 18 Apr 1863; str *Havelock, 11 Jun 1863; str Diamond, 23 Sep 1863.

Later history: Merchant Sheridan, 1865. Stranded on Bodie Island, 24 Sep 1866.

Name	Builder	Launched	Acquired	Comm.
Varuna	Mystic, Conn. (Mallory)	Sep 1861	31 Dec 1861	Feb 1862
Tonnage	1,247 tons B			
Dimensions	218′ × 34′8″ × 12′			
Machinery	1 screw			
Complement	157			
Armament	6–8″/63, 2–8″/55, 2–30pdr MLR			

Notes: Purchased prior to completion.

Service record: WGulfBS 1862. Rammed and sunk by CSS Governor Moore and Stonewall Jackson during passage past New Orleans forts, 24 Apr 1862 (3 killed).

Name	Builder	Launched	Acquired	Comm.
Vicksburg	Mystic, Conn. (Maxson Fish)	Aug 1863	20 Oct 1863	2 Dec 1863
Tonnage	886 tons B, 522 n/r			
Dimensions	185′ (oa) 171′ (U) × 33′ × 13′8″, d17′6″			
Machinery	1 screw, vertical direct-acting condensing engine (36″ × 3′), 1 boiler. IHP 200, 9 knots (Mystic Iron Works)			
Complement	122			
Armament	1–100pdr MLR, 4–30pdr MLR, 1–20pdr MLR, 1–12pdr SB			

Notes: Wood hull, brigantine rig.

Service record: NAtlBS 1864. Blockade of Wilmington 1864. Bombardment of Masonboro Inlet, N.C., 11 Feb 1865. Decomm 29 Apr 1865. Sold 12 Jul 1865.

Ship captured: Indian, 30 Apr 1864.

Later history: Merchant Vicksburg 1865. Lost on Fire Island, N.Y., Mar 1875.

Name	Builder	Launched	Acquired	Comm.
Virginia	Dumbarton, Scotland (Denny)	1861	1 Sep 1863	12 Jun 1863

ex-Virginia, ex-Pet

Tonnage	581 tons B, 442 n/r
Dimensions	181′6″ (oa) 175′6″ (bp) × 26′ × 8, d14′
Machinery	1 screw, 2 vertical direct-acting engines (38″ × 2′), 1 boiler, 9 knots
Complement	61
Armament	1–30pdr MLR, 5–24pdr H, 1–12pdr MLR

Notes: Blockade runner Virginia, captured off Mujeres Island, Mexico, by USS Wachusett and Sonoma, 18 Jan 1863. Iron hull, bark rig.

Service record: WGulfBS Jun 1863. Blockade of Texas. Expedition to Brazos Santiago, Rio Grande, Tex., 27 Oct–3 Nov 1863. Sold 30 Nov 1865.

Ships captured: Jenny, 6 Oct 1863; str Matamoras, 4 Nov 1863; Science, Volante, Dashing Wave, 5 Nov 1863; Mary Douglas, 15 Feb 1864; Henry Colthirst, 22 Feb 1864; Camilla, *Catherine Holt, 29 Feb 1864; Randall, 8 Mar 1864; Sylphide, 10 Mar 1864; *Juanita, 11 Apr 1864; *Rosina, 15 Apr 1864; Alma, 19 Apr 1864; *Experiment, 3 May 1864; Belle, 27 Dec 1864.

Later history: Merchant Virginia 1865. Converted to barge 1885.

*** Later USS Aries.

Name	Builder	Launched	Acquired	Comm.
Young Rover	Medford, Mass. (Curtis)	1860	27 Jul 1861	10 Sep 1861
Tonnage	418 tons B
Dimensions	141′ × 28′2″ × 11′, d17′
Machinery	1 screw. 1 engine (18″ × 2′), HP 75, 7 knots
Complement	48
Armament	1–12pdr MLR, 4–32pdr/42

Notes: Wood hull, bark rig.

Service record: AtlBS 1861. NAtlBS 1862. EGulfBS Jun 1862. Blockade off Florida. Guardship, Hampton Roads 1863. Sold 22 Jun 1865.

Later history: Merchant *Young Rover* 1865. Converted to bark 1865. Wrecked near Zanzibar, 29 Jun 1866.

COASTAL SIDE WHEEL COMBATANTS (FOURTH RATE)

Merchant vessels acquired for coastal and riverine use.

Name	Builder	Launched	Acquired	Comm.
Calhoun ex-*Cuba*	New York, N.Y. (Sneeden)	1851	19 Mar 1862	1862
Tonnage	508 tons B
Dimensions	174′4″ × 27′6″ × d11′
Machinery	Side wheels, 1 vertical beam engine (44″ × 10′)
Complement	68
Armament	1–30pdr MLR, 2–32pdr/33

Notes: Former Confederate privateer, captured as blockade runner by USS *Samuel Rotan* off Southwest Pass, La, 23 Jan 1862. Wood hull. Originally served out of Charleston, later purchased by Charles Morgan at New Orleans. As a warship, one funnel, one mast.

Service record: WGulfBS 1862. Engagement off Brashear City, Berwick Bay, La., 1–3 Nov 1862. Engagement and attack at Bayou Teche, La., 14 Jan 1863 (3 killed including captain). Engagement with CSS *Queen of the West* in Berwick Bay, La., 14 Apr 1863. Engagement at Butte-a-la-Rose, La. and capture of Ft. Burton, 20 Apr 1863. Bombardment at Grants Pass, Ala., 13 Sep 1863. Bombardment of Ft. Powell, Mobile Bay (flagship), 16–29 Feb 1864. Decomm 6 May 1864.

Ships captured: *Charles Henry*, 4 May 1862; *Rover*, 5 May 1862; str *Lewis Whiteman*, 6 May 1862; *Corypheus*,* 13 May 1862; *Venice (Venus)*, 14 May 1862; str *Fox*, 12 Sep 1863.

Later history: Transferred to U.S. Army, 4 Jun 1864; renamed *General Sedgwick*. Sold 17 Nov 1865. Merchant *Calhoun* 1866. BU 1883.

Name	Builder	Launched	Acquired	Comm.
Ceres	Keyport, N.J. (Terry)	1856	11 Sep 1861	Sep 1861
Tonnage	144 tons B
Dimensions	108′4″ × 22′4″ × 6′3″, d7′7″
Machinery	Side wheels, 1 beam engine (30″ × 6′8″), 1 boiler. 9 knots
Complement	45
Armament	1–30pdr MLR, 1–32pdr/33; (Apr 1863) 2–30pdr MLR, 2–24pdr SB

Service record: Potomac Flotilla 1861. NAtlBS 1861–65. Landings at Roanoke Island, N.C., 7–8 Feb 1862. Engagement with enemy vessels, capture of Elizabeth City, N.C. and expedition to Edenton, N.C., 10–12 Feb 1862.

* Later USS *Corypheus*.

Expedition to Hamilton, N.C., Roanoke River, 9 Jul 1862. Engagements with CSS *Albemarle*, at Plymouth, N.C., 19 Apr (2 killed) and 5 May 1864. Expedition to Pungo River, N.C., 16–21 Jun 1864. Decomm 14 Jul 1865. Sold 25 Oct 1865.

Ships captured: *Actor, 6 Mar 1862; str *Alice*, 14 May 1862; str *Wilson*, 9 Jun 1862; *Ann C. Davenport.*, 12 May 1864.

Later history: Merchant *Ceres* 1865. RR 1887.

Name	Builder	Launched	Acquired	Comm.
Coeur de Lion	Coxsackie, N.Y.	1853 Apr 1861	Apr 1861 2 Oct 1861	2 Oct 1861

ex-USLHS *Coeur de Lion*, ex-*Alfred van Santvoord*

Tonnage	110 tons B
Dimensions	100′ × 20′6″ × 4′6″
Machinery	Side wheels, 1 HP donkey engine, 1 boiler
Complement	29
Armament	1–30pdr MLR, 1–12pdr MLR, 1–12pdr H

Notes: Acquired from Lighthouse Board. Wood hull.

Service record: Potomac and James River sqns 1861–65. Engaged batteries at Port Royal, Va., 4 Dec 1862. Operations in Nansemond River, Va., 11 Apr–4 May 1863; disabled 18 Apr. Returned to Lighthouse Board 3 Jun 1865.

Ships captured: *Emily Murray*, 9 Feb 1863; *Odd Fellow, Sarah Margaret*, 11 Jun 1863; *Robert Knowles*, 16 Sep 1863.

Later history: Lighthouse steamer *Coeur de Lion* 1865. Sold 1867, merchant *Alice*. RR 1873.

Name	Builder	Launched	Acquired	Comm.
Commodore	New Orleans, La.	1863	31 Jul 1863	1863
Tonnage	80 tons B
Dimensions	100′ × 20.4′ × 4.3′
Machinery	Side wheels
Complement	56
Armament	(Oct 1864) 1–20pdr MLR, 2–12pdr MLR, 1–24pdr

Service record: WGulfBS. Patrolled Lake Pontchartrain 1863–65. Renamed *Fort Gaines*, 1 Sep 1864. Sold 12 Aug 1865.

Ship captured: *Locadie*, 8 Dec 1864.

Later history: Merchant *Fort Gaines* 1865. RR 1870.

Name	Builder	Launched	Acquired	Comm.
Cowslip ex-*Meteor*	Newburgh, N.Y.	1863	21 Dec 1863	27 Jan 1864
Tonnage	220 tons B
Dimensions	123′ × 24′ × 7′, d8′
Machinery	Side wheels, 1 beam engine (34″ × 8′), 1 boiler
Complement	36
Armament	1–20pdr MLR, 2–24pdr SB

Service record: *Cowslip*. WGulfBS 1864. Raid into Biloxi Bay, 31 May 1864. Mobile Bay, Aug 1864. Sold 28 Aug 1866.

Ship captured: *Last Push*, 29 May 1864.

Later history: Merchant *Harry Wright* 1865. Destroyed by fire at New Orleans, 27 Jul 1886.

Name	Builder	Launched	Acquired	Comm.
Delaware	Wilmington, Del. (Harlan)	1861	14 Oct 1861	1861

ex-*Delaware*, ex-*Virginia Dare*

| Tonnage | 357 tons B |

Fig 3.12: USS *Calhoun*, a former Confederate blockade runner used by the Navy for two years in the Gulf of Mexico area.

Dimensions	161' × 27' × 6', d8'3"
Machinery	Side wheels, 1 beam condensing engine (38" × 10'), 13 knots
Complement	57/65
Armament	2–32pdr/57, 2–32pdr/27, 1–12pdr MLR; (Jan 1862) 1–9" SB, 1–32pdr/57, 1–12pdr MLR

Note: Iron hull, schooner rig.

Service record: NAtlBS 1861. Landings at Roanoke Island., N.C., 7–8 Feb 1862. Engagement with enemy vessels, capture of Elizabeth City, N.C. and expedition to Edenton, N.C., 10–12 Feb 1862. Reconnaissance to Winton, N.C., Chowan River, 18–20 Feb 1862. Capture of New Berne, N.C., 13–14 Mar 1862. Reconnaissance in Neuse River, N.C., 12–16 Dec 1862. Engagements at Dutch Gap, Va., 13 and 18 Aug 1864. Decomm 5 Aug 1865.

Ships captured: *Lynnhaven*, 10 Feb 1862; *Zenith*, 3 Mar 1862; *unidentified str, 21 Mar 1862; *Albemarle*,* *Lion*, 26 Mar 1862.

Later history: Revenue Cutter Service, 30 Aug 1865. Renamed **Louis McLane**, 1873. Sold 1903, merchant *Louis Dolive*. RR 1919.

Name	Builder	Launched	Acquired	Comm.
Granite City	Dumbarton, Scotland (A. Denny)	11 Nov 1862	16 Apr 1863	16 Apr 1863

ex-*City of Dunedin*

Tonnage	315 tons B
Dimensions	160' × 23' × 5'6", d9'2"
Machinery	Side wheels, 2-cyl. inclined engines (38' × 4'6"), 2 boilers
Complement	69
Armament	1–12pdr MLR, 6–24pdr H; (Jan 1864) add 1–20pdr MLR

Notes: Blockade runner *Granite City*, captured by USS *Tioga* in Bahamas Islands, 22 Mar 1863. Iron hull.

Service record: WGulfBS Aug 1863–64. Attack on Sabine Pass, Tex., 8 Sep 1863. Unsuccessful landing on Matagorda peninsula, Texas, 31 Dec 1863.

---

* Later USS *Albemarle*.

Captured with USS *Wave* by Confederate batteries at Calcasieu Pass, La., 28 Apr 1864.

Ships captured: **Concordia*, 5 Oct 1863; *Anita*, 27 Oct 1863; *Teresita*, *Amelia Ann*, 18 Nov 1863.

Later history: Ran aground as Confederate blockade runner near Velasco, Tex., 21 Jan 1865.

Name	Builder	Launched	Acquired	Comm.
Harriet Lane	New York (Webb)	20 Nov 1857	17 Sep 1861	

ex-USRC *Harriet Lane*

Tonnage	750 tons, 639 tons B
Dimensions	180' (dk), 177'6" (wl) × 30' × 5', d12'6"
Machinery	Side wheels, inclined direct-acting engine (42" × 7'), 2 boilers, 12 knots (Allaire)
Complement	100
Armament	2–32pdr/33; (Aug 1861) 1–8" SB, 4–32pdr MLR; (Feb 1862) 3–9" SB, 1–30pdr MLR, 1–12pdr MLR

Notes: Two-mast brigantine. Only steam vessel in service in Revenue Cutter Service 1861, transferred to USN, 30 Mar 1861.

Service record: Served with Navy in Paraguayan expedition 1858–59. Attempted relief of Ft. Sumter, Charleston harbor; fired first shot by USN ship, 12 Apr 1861. Capture of Hatteras Inlet, ran aground, 28–29 Aug 1861. Engaged batteries at Freestone Pt., Va., 9 Dec 1861. Mortar Flotilla 1862. Bombardment of Fts. Jackson, and St. Philip below New Orleans, 18–28 Apr 1862. Passage past New Orleans forts, engagement with CSN vessels, 24 Apr 1862. Occupation of forts at Pensacola, May 1862. Covered operations at Vicksburg, Jun–Jul 1862. Bombardment, capture of Galveston, Tex., 4 Oct 1862. Captured by Confederate vessels during reoccupation of Galveston, 1 Jan 1863.

Ships captured: *Catherine*, *Iris*, 26 May 1861; *Union*, 5 Jun 1861; *Henry C. Brooks*, 9 Sep 1861; *Joanna Ward*, 23 Feb 1862.

Later history: Converted to blockade runner, renamed *Lavinia*. Interned at Havana, 1865. Converted to merchant bark, renamed *Elliot Richie*, 1865. Foundered off Pernambuco, Brazil, 13 May 1884.

Name	Builder	Launched	Acquired	Comm.
Hetzel	Baltimore	1845	21 Aug 1861	1861
Tonnage	301 tons B, 200 tons			
Dimensions	150′ × 22′ × 6′6″, d8′			
Machinery	Side wheels, crosshead condensing engine. 1 boiler			
Complement	69			
Armament	(1861) 1–9″ SB, 1–80pdr MLR; (Apr 1863) 1–9″ SB, 1–32pdr/57; (Jul 1865) 2–12pdr MLR, 2–24pdr			

Notes: Acquired by U.S. Coast Survey 1849, transferred to Navy 1861. Two masts, one funnel.

Service record: NAtlBS Nov 1861, off North Carolina. Engagement with CSS *Patrick Henry* near Newport News, 2 Dec 1861. Landings at Roanoke Island, N.C., 7–8 Feb 1862. Engagement with enemy vessels, capture of Elizabeth City, N.C., expedition to Edenton, N.C., 10–12 Feb 1862. Capture of New Berne, N.C., 13–14 Mar 1862. Expedition to Plymouth, N.C., 31 Oct–7 Nov 1862. Returned to U.S. Coast Survey, Oct 1865.

Later history: U.S. Coast Survey Ship *Hetzel*. Sank at moorings in Edenton Bay, N.C., 1873. Refitted, hulked.

Name	Builder	Launched	Acquired	Comm.
Isaac N. Seymour	Keyport, N.J. (Terry)	1860	26 Oct 1861	Nov 1861
Tonnage	133 tons B			
Dimensions	100′ × 19′8″ × 6′6″			
Machinery	Side wheels, 1 beam engine (30″ × 6′), 11 knots			
Complement	30			
Armament	1–30pdr MLR, 1–20pdr MLR; (Jan 1862) 1–30pdr MLR, 1–12pdr MLR			

Service record: NAtlBS 1861–65. Engagement with CSS *Patrick Henry* near Newport News, 2 Dec 1861. Landings at Roanoke Island., N.C., 7–8 Feb 1862. Engagement with enemy vessels, capture of Elizabeth City, N.C., expedition to Edenton, N.C., 10–12 Feb 1862. Sank after hitting submerged object in Hatteras Inlet, 20 Feb 1862; raised and repaired. Struck a bank, sank in Neuse River, 24 Aug 1862; again raised and repaired. Expedition to Hamilton, N.C., 31 Oct–7 Nov 1862. Reconnaissance in Neuse River, 12–16 Dec 1862. Expedition in James River, 6–20 Jul 1863. Engagement with CSS *Albemarle*, Albemarle Sound, N.C., 5 May 1864. Blockade of North Carolina 1864–65. Decomm 16 May 1865.

Later history: To U.S. Lighthouse Board 20 Jun 1865. USLHS *Tulip* 1865. Merchant *Magnolia*, 1882. Sold to the Canadian flag, 1888. Burned at Sydney, NS, 15 Jan 1897.

Name	Builder	Launched	Acquired	Comm.
Isonomia	New York, N.Y. (Stack)	1864	16 Jul 1864	16 Aug 1864
ex-*Shamrock*				
Tonnage	593 tons B, 896 n/r			
Dimensions	215′3″ (U) 212′ (dk) × 29′6″ × 7′			
Machinery	Side wheels, 1 vertical beam engine (45″ × 12′), 1 boiler, 12 knots (Murphy)			
Complement	63			
Armament	1–30pdr MLR, 2–24pdr H			

Notes: Purchased on completion.

Service record: NAtlBS 1864. Coastal blockade, Florida. Expedition to St. Marks, Fla., 23 Feb–27 Mar 1865. Decomm 28 Jun 1865. Sold 12 Jul 1865.

Ship captured: *George Douthwaite*, 8 May 1865.

Later history: Merchant *City of Providence* 1865. Sold foreign, 1867.

Fig 3.13: The little *Coeur de Lion* was taken over from the Lighthouse Service and operated in Virginia waters. (Mariners Museum, Newport News, Va.)

Name	Builder	Launched	Acquired	Comm.
Jacob Bell	New York, N.Y. (Brown, Bell)	1842	22 Aug 1861	22 Aug 1861
Tonnage	229 tons B			
Dimensions	141′3″ × 21′ × d8′1″			
Machinery	Side wheels			
Complement	49			
Armament	1–8″ SB, 1–32pdr/32; (Apr1863) add 1–50pdr MLR, 2–12pdr SB			

Notes: Wood hull.

Service record: Potomac Flotilla 1861–62. Engaged batteries at Potomac Creek, Va., 23 Aug 1861. Bombardment at Freestone Point, Va., 25 Sep, 9 Dec 1861. Expedition in Rappahannock River, Tappahannock, Va., 13–15 Apr 1862. NAtlBS 1862. Engaged batteries at Port Royal, Va., 4 Dec 1862. Expeditions to Northern Neck, Va., 12 Jan, in Rappahannock River, 16–19 May, to Northern Neck, 11–21 Jun 1864. Decomm 13 May 1865. Foundered at sea while under tow of USS *Banshee* to New York, 6 Nov 1865.

Ships captured: *Chapel Point*, 20 Sep 1862; *Robert Wilbur, 4 Nov 1862; *Gold Leaf*, 23 Aug 1863.

Name	Builder	Launched	Acquired	Comm.
John L. Lockwood	Athens, N.Y.	1854	1 Sep 1861	21 Sep 1861
Tonnage	180 tons B			
Dimensions	114′ × 24′ × 6′6″, d7′3″			
Machinery	Side wheels, beam engine (32″ × 7′8″), 1 boiler, 11 knots			
Complement	30			
Armament	(1861) 1–80pdr MLR, 1–12pdr MLR, 1–12pdr H SB; (Apr1863) 1–32pdr/42, 1–12pdr MLR, 1–12pdr H SB			

Notes: Wood hull.

Service record: NAtlBS 1861–65. Landings at Roanoke Island, N.C., 7–8 Feb 1862. Engagement with enemy vessels, capture of Elizabeth City, N.C., expedition to Edenton, N.C., 10–12 Feb 1862. Capture of New Berne, N.C., 13–14 Mar 1862. Expedition to block Chesapeake, Albemarle Canal, 23 Apr 1862. Reconnaissance in Neuse River, N.C., 12–16 Dec 1862. Decomm 23 May 1865. Sold 15 Sep 1865.

Ships captured: str *Alice*, 14 May 1862; *Twilight*, 1 Jan 1865.

Later history: Merchant *Henry Smith* 1865. War Dept *Chester A. Arthur* 1876. Merchant *Victor* 1892. BU 1927.

Name	Builder	Launched	Acquired	Comm.
Mercury	Greenpoint, N.Y. (W. Collyer)	15 Jun 1854	17 Aug 1861	3 Oct 1861
Tonnage	187 tons B			
Dimensions	128′ × 22′10″ × 5′6″, d8′			
Machinery	Side wheels, 1 engine (36″ × 8′), 1 boiler			
Complement	56			
Armament	1–20pdr, 1–30pdr MLR			

Service record: James River 1864. Expedition to Milford Haven, Va., 24 Sep 1864. Army operations in Great Wicomico River, Va., 17 Oct 1864. Sold 29 Aug 1873.

Later history: FFU.

Name	Builder	Launched	Acquired	Comm.
Mount Washington ex-*Mount Vernon*	Philadelphia, Pa. (Birely)	11 Apr 1846	22 Apr 1861	May 1861
Tonnage	359 tons B			
Dimensions	200′ × 24′ × 6′6″, d9′			
Machinery	Side wheels, 1 LP vertical beam engine (44″ × 11′), 12 knots (Reaney Neafie)			
Complement	40			
Armament	(May 1863) 1–32pdr/47			

Notes: Wood hull. Renamed 4 Nov 1861. Operated on James River until purchased by War Department in 1861, then transferred to Navy.

Service record: Operated in Potomac area 1861. Operations in Nansemond River, Va. 11 Apr–4 May 1863. Disabled by enemy fire at Western Branch, 6 May, damaged at Hatt's Point, 12 May 1863. Engagement at Dutch Gap, Va., 16–18 Aug 1864. NAtlBS Feb 1865. Sold 21 Jun 1865.

Later history: Merchant *Mount Washington* 1865. BU 1885.

Name	Builder	Launched	Acquired	Comm.
Nansemond ex-*James F. Freeborn*	Brooklyn, N.Y. (L & F)	1862	13 Aug 1863	19 Aug 1863
Tonnage	335 tons B			
Dimensions	155′ (dk) 146′ (U) × 26′ × 8′3″, d9′6″			
Machinery	Side wheels, 1 vertical beam engine (40″ × 9′), 1 boiler, 15 knots (Fletcher)			
Complement	55/63			
Armament	(Sep 1864) 1–30pdr MLR, 2–24pdr			

Notes: Wood hull.

Service record: NAtlBS 1863. Engagement with CSS *Raleigh* off New Inlet, N.C., 6–7 May 1864. Unsuccessful attack on Ft. Fisher, N.C., 24–25 Dec 1864. Second attack on Ft. Fisher, 13–15 Jan 1865. Decomm 8 Aug 1865.

Ships captured: str *Douro, 11 Oct 1863; str *Venus, 21 Oct 1863; str *Margaret & Jessie*,* 5 Nov 1863.

Later history: To U.S. Revenue Cutter Service, 22 Aug 1865. Renamed **William H. Crawford**, 20 Nov 1873. Sold 24 Apr 1897. Merchant *General J.A.Dumont*, 1900. Burned at Severn Side, Md., 22 Dec 1914.

---

* Later USS *Gettysburg*.

Fig 3.14: The *Harriet Lane* as depicted by artist Clary Ray. Named after the niece of President Buchanan, she was the only steamship in the Revenue Cutter Service in 1861 and was taken over by the Navy. (U.S. Naval Historical Center)

Name	Builder	Launched	Acquired	Comm.
Nita ex-*Crescent*	Mobile, Ala.	1856	10 Sep 1863	8 Jan 1864
Tonnage	210 tons B			
Dimensions	146′ × 22′4″ × 5′, d7′			
Machinery	Side wheels, 1 vertical beam condensing engine (28″ × 6′), 1 boiler			
Complement	46			
Armament	1–12pdr HR, 2–12pdr H SB, 1–24pdr H SB; (Mar 1864) 1–12pdr HR, 3–24pdr H SB			

Notes: Captured 17 Aug 1863, by USS *De Soto* en route Havana–Mobile. Wood hull.

Service record: EGulfBS 1864, off west coast of Florida. Decomm 3 May and sold 25 May 1865.

Ships captured: str *Nan Nan, 24 Feb 1864; *Three Brothers*, 11 Apr 1864; *Unknown*, 24 Oct 1864.

Later history: FFU.

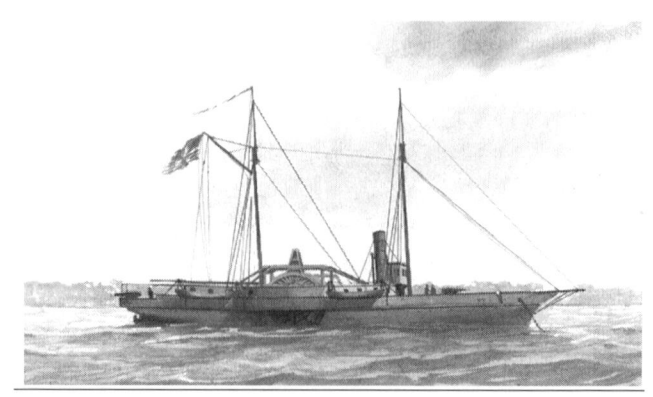

Fig 3.15: The *Hetzel*, depicted in a drawing by Clary Ray, was acquired from the Coast Survey. (U.S. Naval Historical Center)

Name	Builder	Launched	Acquired	Comm.
Philippi ex-*Ella*	Great Britain?	1863	23 Feb 1864	Apr 1864
Tonnage	311 tons B			
Dimensions	140′ × 24′ × d9′10″			
Machinery	Side wheels			
Complement	41			
Armament	1–20pdr MLR, 1–24pdr H, 2–12pdr MLR			

Notes: Blockade runner *Ella*, captured by USS *Howquah* off Ft. Fisher, N.C., 10 Nov 1863.

Service record: WGulfBS 1864. Went aground in Mobile Bay near Ft. Morgan, set on fire and sunk by Confederate batteries, 5 Aug 1864.

Name	Builder	Launched	Acquired	Comm.
Planter	Charleston, S.C.	1860	May 1862	May 1862
Tonnage	313 tons B			
Dimensions	147′ × 30′ × 3′9″, d7′10″			
Machinery	Side wheels, 2-cyl. HP engine (18″ × 6′), 2 boilers			
Complement	(U)			
Armament	1–32pdr, 1–24pdr H			

Notes: Delivered to federal vessels off Charleston by her pilot, Negro slave Robert Smalls, 13 May 1862.

Service record: SAtlBS 1862. Expedition to Pocotaligo, S.C., 21–23 Oct 1862. Transferred to War Dept, 10 Sep 1862.

Later history: Merchant *Planter*, 1866. Lost off Cape Romain, S.C., 1 Jul 1876.

Name	Builder	Launched	Acquired	Comm.
Selma ex-CSS *Selma*, ex-*Florida*	Mobile, Ala.	1856	5 Aug 1864	5 Aug 1864
Tonnage	320 tons B			
Dimensions	252′ × 30′ × 6′			
Machinery	Side wheels, 1 inclined direct-acting condensing engine. 9 knots			
Complement	99			
Armament	2–9″R, 1–8″R, 1–6″R			

Notes: Captured in Mobile Bay, 5 Aug 1864. Wood hull.

Service record: Bombardment of Ft. Morgan, Mobile Bay, 9–23 Aug 1864. Decomm 15 Jul 1865; sold Aug 1865.

Later history: Merchant *Selma* 1865. Foundered off mouth of Brazos River, Tex., 24 Jun 1868.

Name	Builder	Launched	Acquired	Comm.
Shawsheen ex-*Young America*	Greenpoint, N.Y. (Sneeden Whitlock)	8 Aug 1854	23 Sep 1861	1861
Tonnage	126 tons B			
Dimensions	118′ × 22′6″ × 7′3″			
Machinery	Side wheels			
Complement	40			
Armament	(1861) 2–20pdr MLR; (Apr 1863) 1–30pdr MLR, 1–20pdr MLR, 1–12pdr H R			

Notes: Former New York City tug.

Service record: Hampton Roads area 1861, arrived in damaged condition. Engagement with CSS *Patrick Henry* near Newport News, 2 Dec 1861. Landings at Roanoke Island, N.C., 7–8 Feb 1862. Engagement with enemy vessels, capture of Elizabeth City, N.C., expedition to Edenton, N.C., 10–12 Feb 1862. Expedition to block Chesapeake & Albemarle Canal, 23 Apr 1862. Expedition to Hamilton, N.C., Roanoke River, 9 Jul 1862. Reconnaissance in Neuse River, N.C., 12–16 Dec 1862. James River 1863–64. Disabled by Confederate artillery in James River and blown up to prevent capture, 7 May 1864 (3 killed).

Ships captured: *James Norcom*, 28 Mar 1862; *Henry Clay*, 22 Jun 1863; *Dolphin, Elizabeth, Helen Jane, James Brice, Sally*, 20 Jul 1863; *Telegraph*, 29 Jul 1863.

Name	Builder	Launched	Acquired	Comm.
Thomas Freeborn	Brooklyn, N.Y. (L & F)	17 Nov 1860	7 May 1861	May 1861
Tonnage	345 tons D, 269 tons B			
Dimensions	143′4″ ( ) 140′ (wl) × 25′6″ × 6′6″, d8′6″			
Machinery	Side wheels, 1 vertical beam engine (40″ × 8′) (Allaire)			
Complement	67			
Armament	1–32pdr/60, 1–32pdr/27; (Apr 1863) 1–8″/55, 1–32pdr/27, 1–12pdr MLR			

Notes: Steam tug. Wood hull.

Service record: Potomac Flotilla 1861–65. Engaged batteries at Sewell's Pt, 18–19 May, at Aquia Creek, Va., 29 May–1 Jun 1861. Decomm 17 Jun 1865. Sold 20 Jul 1865.

Ships captured: *Bachelor*, 17 Jun 1861; *A.B. Leon*, 16 Jul 1861; *Jane Wright*, 2 Aug 1861; *Pocahontas, Mary Grey*, 4 Aug 1861; *Christiana Lee*, str *Mail*, 1 Aug 1862; *Thomas W. Reilly*, 1 Oct 1862; *William Smith*, 3 Mar 1865.

Later history: Merchant *Philip*, 1865. RR 1887.

Name	Builder	Launched	Acquired	Comm.
Tritonia ex-*Sarah S.B. Cay*	East Haddam, Conn.	1863	1 Dec 1863	23 Apr 1864
Tonnage	202 tons B			
Dimensions	178′ × 22′4″ × d7′6″			
Machinery	Side wheels			
Complement	26			
Armament	2–12pdr; (Dec 1864) 1–30pdr MLR, 1–12pdr, 1–24pdr			

Notes: Wood hull.

Service record: James River Division 1864. WGulfBS Jul 1864. Recovered str *Belfast*, taken by guerrillas, in Tombigbee River, Ala., 29 Jan 1866. Sold 5 Oct 1866.

Later history Merchant *Belle Brown* **1866. Lost 1880.**

Name	Builder	Launched	Acquired	Comm.
Underwriter	Brooklyn, N.Y.	1852	23 Aug 1861	23 Aug 1861
Tonnage	341 tons B			
Dimensions	185′ (U) 170′ (U) × 23′7″ × 8′1″			
Machinery	Side wheels, oscillating engines			
Complement	69			
Armament	1–80pdr MLR, 1–8″/63; (Oct 1861) add 2–12pdr; (Apr 1863) 2–8″/55, 1–12pdr MLR, 1–12pdr SB			

Service record: Potomac Flotilla 1861. NAtlBS Oct 1861. Landings at Roanoke Island, N.C., 7–8 Feb 1862. Engagement with enemy vessels, capture of Elizabeth City, N.C., expedition to Edenton, N.C., 10–12 Feb 1862. Capture of New Berne, N.C., 13–14 Mar 1862. Captured by enemy boat crew while lying at anchor in Neuse River, N.C., destroyed by them, 2 Feb 1864 (3 killed).

Name	Builder	Launched	Acquired	Comm.
Vixen	New York, N.Y. (Brown & Bell)	1845	26 Aug 1861	31 Jul 1862

ex-US.C.S, ex-USS *Vixen*

Tonnage	300 tons
Dimensions	118′ (dk) × 22′6″ × 7′10″, d12′
Machinery	Side wheels, 1 half beam horizontal engine (36″ × 6′)
Complement	41
Armament	(Aug 1862) 2–20pdr MLR; (Dec 1862) 2–32pldr/27

Notes: Acquired from U.S. Coast Survey as reconnaissance vessel. Originally built for Mexican government, seized by United States at start of Mexican War; served in USN 1845–55. Two-mast schooner rig. Sister ship *Spitfire* sold by USN 1848.

Service record: Conducted surveys at Port Royal, S.C., 1861. Bombardment of forts at St. Helena Sound, S.C., 25–28 Nov 1861. SAtlBS 1862. Expedition to Pocotaligo, S.C., 21–23 Oct 1862. Returned to Coast Survey, 8 Nov 1862. Conducted surveys, patrols along coast of Florida 1863–64. Joint expedition up Ashepoo, S.Edisto Rivers, S.C., 25–27 May 1864.

Later history: Coast Survey *Vixen* 1862.

Name	Builder	Launched	Acquired	Comm.
Wilderness	Brooklyn, N.Y.	1864	30 May 1864	20 Jul 1864

ex-*B.N. Crary* (or *Creary*)

Tonnage	390 tons B
Dimensions	137′ × 25′ × 6′
Machinery	Side wheels, beam engine (40″ × 8′), 13 knots
Complement	41
Armament	(Oct 1864) 4–24pdr

Notes: Wood hull. Converted to gunboat Oct 1864.

Service record: NAtlBS 1864. Unsuccessful attack on Ft. Fisher, N.C., 24–25 Dec 1864. Second attack on Ft. Fisher, 13–15 Jan 1865. Decomm 10 Jun 1865.

Ship captured: str *Annie*,* 31 Oct 1864.

Later history: To U.S. Revenue Cutter Service, 7 Sep 1865. Renamed *John A. Dix*, 11 Jun 1873. Sold 18 May 1891. Merchant *Governor John A. Dix*, 1891.

Name	Builder	Launched	Acquired	Comm.
William G. Putnam	Brooklyn, N.Y.	1857	24 Jul 1861	Sep 1861

Tonnage	149 tons B
Dimensions	103′6″ × 22′ × 7′6″
Machinery	Side wheels, single direct-acting engine (32″ × 6′), 7 knots
Complement	32/62
Armament	(Oct 1861) 4–32pdr/51, 2–32pdr/33, 1–24pdr H; (Jun 1863) 1–20pdr MLR, 4–32pdr/51, 2–32pdr/33, 1–12pdr MLR; (Mar 1864) 1–30pdr MLR, 4–32pdr/51, 2–32pdr/33, 2–12pdr MLR

Notes: Wood tug, sometimes known as ***General Putnam***. Reboilered 1863.

Service record: NAtlBS 1861. Landings at Roanoke Island, N.C., 7–8 Feb 1862. Engagement with enemy vessels, capture of Elizabeth City, N.C., expedition to Edenton, N.C., 10–12 Feb 1862. Expedition to block Chesapeake and Albemarle Canal, 23 Apr 1862. Expedition up Pamunkey River, Va., 8–13 Mar 1864. Operated in Virginia waters 1863–64. Decomm 2 Jun 1865.

Ships captured: *Lonely Bell*, 21 Mar 1862; *Scuppernong*, 9 Jun 1862.

Later history: To U.S. Lighthouse Board, 2 Jun 1865. USLS *Putnam* 1865. Merchant *Putnam* 1893. RR 1896.

---

* Later USS *Preston*.

COASTAL SIDE-WHEEL COMBATANTS (EX-FERRYBOATS, FOURTH RATE)

Most of these ships were New York and Brooklyn ferryboats, useful in narrow waters because of their ability to move equally well in either direction. They also had decks strengthened to carry heavy loads suitable for conversion to gunboats.

Name	Builder	Launched	Acquired	Comm.
Clifton	New York, N.Y. (Simonson)	1861	2 Dec 1861	early 1862

Tonnage	892 tons B
Dimensions	210′ (oa) 185′ (dk) × 40′ × d13′4″
Machinery	Side wheels, vertical beam engine (50″ × 10′) (Allaire)
Complement	121
Armament	2–9″ SB, 4–32pdr/57; (Jun 1862) add 1–9″ SB, 1–30pdr MLR; (1863) 2–9″ SB, 4–32pdr SB, 2–30pdr MLR

Notes: Iron-strapped wood hull.

Service record: WGulfBS 1862–63. Damaged in collision with USS *R.B. Forbes*, Feb 1862. Passage past New Orleans forts, engagement with CSN vessels, 24 Apr 1862. Bombardment of Vicksburg, 26–22 Jun 1862. Damaged at Vicksburg, 28 Jun 1862 (7 killed). Bombardment and capture of Galveston, Tex., 4–9 Oct 1862. Bombardment at Lavaca, Tex., 31 Oct–1 Nov 1862. Engagement at Butte-a-la-Rose, La., capture of Ft. Burton, 20 Apr 1863. Disabled by Confederate batteries, captured at Sabine Pass, Tex., 8 Sep 1863.

Ship captured: *H. McGuin*, 18 Jul 1863.

Later history: Comm as CSS *Clifton* (q.v.)

Name	Builder	Launched	Acquired	Comm.
Commodore Barney	New York, N.Y. (Stack)	1859	2 Oct 1861	1861

ex-*Ethan Allen*

Name	Builder	Launched	Acquired	Comm.
Commodore Perry	New York, N.Y. (Stack)	1859	2 Oct 1861	Oct 1861

Tonnage	512 tons B
Dimensions	144′6″ (bp) × 33′ × 9′, d12′
Machinery	Side wheels, 1 vertical beam engine (38.5″ × 9′), IHP 500, 11 knots (Novelty)
Complement	68/108
Armament	*Barney*: (1862) 3–9″ SB, 1–100pdr MLR; (Aug 1862) add 1–9″ SB, 2–12pdr H; (Sep 1863) 5–9″ SB, 100pdr MLR, 1–12pdr SB.
	Perry: (Jan 1863) 2–9″ SB, 2–32pdr/47, 1–12pdr SB H; (Jul 1864) 1–100pdr MLR, 4–9″ SB, 1–12pdr SB

Notes: Former New York ferryboats.

Service records:

Commodore Barney: Damaged in storm off Virginia, Oct 1861. NAtlBS 1862–65. Landings at Roanoke Island, N.C., 7–8 Feb 1862. Reconnaissance to Winton, N.C., Chowan River, 18–20 Feb 1862. Capture of New Berne, N.C., 13–14 Mar 1862. Operations in Nansemond River, Va., Apr–May 1863 (3 killed). Expeditions to White House, Va., York and Pamunkey Rivers, 23–30 Jun, up James River, 4–7 Aug 1863; damaged by mine explosion, 5 Aug (2 killed). Expedition up Nansemond River, 13–14 Apr 1864. Sold 20 Jul 1865.

  Later history: Merchant *Commodore Barney*, 1865. Foundered at wharf at Jacksonville, Fla., 22 Sep 1901.

Commodore Perry: NAtlBS Jan 1862–65. Landings at Roanoke Island., N.C., 7–8 Feb 1862. Engagement with enemy vessels, capture of Elizabeth City, N.C., expedition to Edenton, N.C., 10–12 Feb 1862. Reconnaissance to

Winton, N.C., Chowan River, 18–20 Feb 1862. Capture of New Berne, N.C., 13–14 Mar 1862. Expedition to Hamilton, N.C., Roanoke River, 9 Jul 1862. Operations at Franklin, Va., 3 Oct 1862 (2 killed). Expeditions to Plymouth, N.C., 31 Oct–7 Nov 1862, in Chowan River, 26–30 Jul 1863, up Nansemond River, Va., 13–14 Apr 1864. Decomm 26 Jun 1865. Sold 12 Jul 1865.

Ships captured: *Lynnhaven*, 10 Feb 1862; *John, Nathaniel Taylor*, 8 Apr 1862; *America, Comet, J.J. Crittenden*, 10 Apr 1862; str *Alice*, 14 May 1862; str *Wilson*, 9 Jun 1862.

Later history: Merchant *Commodore Perry* 1865. RR 1907.

Name	Builder	Launched	Acquired	Comm.
Commodore Hull ex-*Nuestra Senora de Regla*	Brooklyn, N.Y.	1861	1 Sep 1862	27 Nov 1862
Tonnage	376 tons B
Dimensions	131′ × 28′4″ × 9′, d11′
Machinery	Side wheels, 1 inclined engine (36″ × 9′), 1 boiler, 10 knots
Complement	68
Armament	2–30pdr MLR, 4–24pdr SB; (Sep1864) 1–30pdr MLR replaced by 1–32pdr MLR

Notes: Built as ferry for Havana harbor. Seized by United States at Port Royal, S.C., en route to Cuba, Dec 1861, a seizure later ruled illegal.

Service record: NAtlBS 1862–65. Engagement with CSS *Albemarle*, Albemarle Sound, N.C., 5 May 1864. Damaged by batteries in Roanoke River during capture of Plymouth, N.C., 29–31 Oct 1864 (4 killed). Decomm 8 Jun 1865. Sold 27 Sep 1865.

Later history: Merchant *Waccamaw* 1865. Lost before 1885 (cause unknown).

Name	Builder	Launched	Acquired	Comm.
Commodore Jones	New York, N.Y. ?	1863	12 May 1863	21 May 1863
Tonnage	542 tons B
Dimensions	154′ × 32′6″ × d11′8″
Machinery	Side wheels, 12 knots
Complement	88/103
Armament	1–9″ SB, 1–5.1″R, 4–24pdr SB; (Jul 1863) 1–9″ SB, 1–50pdr MLR, 2–30pdr MLR, 4–24pdr SB

Notes: Built as New York ferryboat, acquired while under construction.

Service record: NAtlBS 1863–64. Evacuation of West Point, Va., 31 May 1863. Army operations in Mattaponi River, 3–7 Jun and Chickahominy River, 10–13 Jun 1863. Expedition in James River, 6–20 Jul 1863. Sunk by an electric torpedo (mine) in James River, 6 May 1864 (about 40 killed).

Name	Builder	Launched	Acquired	Comm.
Commodore McDonough	New York, N.Y. ?	1862	5 Aug 1862	24 Nov 1862
Commodore Morris	New York, N.Y.	1862	5 Aug 1862	19 Nov 1862
Tonnage	532 tons B
Dimensions	154′ × 32′6″ × 8′6″, d12′
Machinery	Side wheels, 1 inclined engine (38″ × 10′), 8 knots
Complement	75
Armament	*McDonough:* 1–9″ SB, 1–20pdr MLR, 4–24pdr H; (Jun 1863) 1–9″ SB, 1–100pdr MLR, 2–50pdr MLR, 2–24pdr H. *Morris:* 1–9″ SB, 1–100pdr MLR, 4–24pdr H; (May 1863) 2–24pdr H replaced by 2–30pdr MLR.

Notes: Built as New York ferryboats; acquired while under construction.

Service records

Commodore McDonough: SAtlBS 1862–65, South Carolina. Engaged batteries in Stono River, 30 Jan, at James I., S.C., 17 Apr 1863. Operations in S. Edisto River, 25–27 May 1864. Army operations in Stono and Folly Rivers, S.C., Feb 1865. Foundered while in tow en route from Port Royal to New York, 23 Aug 1865.

Commodore Morris: NAtlBS 1862–65. Expeditions to West Point, Va., Pamunkey River, 7–9 Jan, 1863, to West Point, Va., York River, 5–7 May 1863, to White House, Va., York and Pamunkey Rivers, 23–30 Jun 1863. Expedition up Nansemond River, Va., 13–14 Apr 1864. Decomm 24 Jun 1865. Sold 12 Jul 1865.

Ships captured: *John C. Calhoun, Harriet, Music*, 22 Jan 1863.

Later history: Merchant *Clinton* 1865. To U.S. Army, renamed *General John Simpson* 1917–1920. BU 1931.

Name	Builder	Launched	Acquired	Comm.
Commodore Read ex-*Atlantic*	Brooklyn, N.Y.	1857	19 Aug 1863	8 Sep 1863
Tonnage	650 tons B
Dimensions	179′ × 33′6″ × 6′3″, d13′2″
Machinery	Side wheels, 1 vertical beam engine (45″ × 11′)
Complement	84
Armament	2–100pdr MLR, 4–24pdr H; (Oct 1864) 2–100pdr MLR, 4–9″ SB

Note: Former New York ferryboat.

Service record: Potomac Flotilla 1863–65. Expedition up Rappahannock River, 18–22 Apr 1864. Sold 20 Jul 1865.

Later history: Merchant *State of Maryland*. Wrecked in Chesapeake Bay, 31 Mar 1876.

Name	Builder	Launched	Acquired	Comm.
Ellen	Greenpoint, N.Y. (E.Webb)	1 Feb 1853	10 Oct 1861	16 Oct 1861
Tonnage	341 tons B
Dimensions	125′6″ × 28′6″ × 8′, d10′6″
Machinery	Side wheels, 1 Copeland's inclined engine (36″ × 8′), 12 knots (Novelty)
Complement	50
Armament	2–32pdr/33, 2–30pdr MLR

Service record: SAtlBS Nov 1861. Army operations at Port Royal Ferry, S.C., 31 Dec 1861–2 Jan 1862. Engagement in Wassaw Sound, Ga., 26–28 Jan 1862. Capture of Fernandina, Fla., Brunswick, St. Simons, and Jekyl Islands, Ga., 2–12 Mar 1862. Operations in St. Johns River, Fla., 16 Apr–3 May 1862. Decomm 30 Oct 1862. Used as carpenter shop at Port Royal. Sold 2 Sep 1865.

Later history: Probably BU 1865.

Name	Builder	Launched	Acquired	Comm.
Fort Henry	New York, N.Y.	1862	25 Mar 1862	3 Apr 1862
Tonnage	519 tons B
Dimensions	150′6″ × 32′ × d11′9″
Machinery	Side wheels
Complement	120
Armament	2–9″ SB, 4–32pdr/57

Service record: EGulfBS 1862–65, West Florida. Expedition to St. Marks, Fla., Mar 1865. Decomm 8 Jul 1865. Sold 15 Aug 1865.

Ships captured: *G.L. Brockenborough*,* 15 Oct 1862; *Anna*,** 26 Feb 1863; *Ranger, Bangor*, 25 Mar 1863; *Isabella*, 22 May 1863; *Anna Maria*, 28 Jun 1863; *Emma*, 3 Jul 1863; *Southern Star*, 6 Aug 1863.

Later history: Merchant *Huntington* 1865. Burned at Hunter's Point, N.Y., 21 Feb 1868.

Name	Builder	Launched	Acquired	Comm.
Hunchback	New York, N.Y. (Simonson)	1852	16 Dec 1861	3 Jan 1862
Tonnage	517 tons B			
Dimensions	179'5" × 29'3" × 9', d11'7"			
Machinery	Side wheels, 1 vertical beam engine (40" × 8'), 12 knots			
Complement	99			
Armament	3–9" SB, 1–100pdr MLR; (Apr 1863) 4–9" SB, 1–200pdr MLR, 1–12pdr MLR, 1–12pdr H; (Mar 1865) 5–9" SB, 1–100pdr MLR, 1–12pdr MLR, 1–12pdr H			

Notes: Former New York ferryboat.

Service record: NAtlBS 1862. Landings at Roanoke Island, N.C., 7–8 Feb 1862. Reconnaissance to Winton, N.C., Chowan River, 18–20 Feb 1862. Capture of New Berne, N.C., 13–14 Mar 1862. Operations at Franklin, Va., 3 Oct 1862 (2 killed). Expedition to Hamilton, N.C., 31 Oct–7 Nov 1862. Engagement at Trent's Reach, James River, 24 Jan 1865. Decomm 12 Jun 1865. Sold 12 Jul 1865.

Ships captured: *G.H. Smoot*, 18 May 1862; *Eugenia*, 20 May 1862; *Winter Shrub*., 21 May 1862.

Later history: Merchant *General Grant* 1865. BU 1880.

Name	Builder	Launched	Acquired	Comm.
John P. Jackson	Brooklyn, N.Y. (Burtis)	2 Aug 1860	6 Nov 1861	14 Feb 1862
Tonnage	750 tons B			
Dimensions	192' × 36'6" × d12'			
Machinery	Side wheels, 1 vertical beam engine (45" × 11'), 8 knots (Fulton)			
Complement	99			
Armament	(Jun 1863) 4–32pdr/57, 1–9" SB, 1–6" MLR; (Jul 1864) 1–6"R replaced by 1–100pdr MLR			

Notes: Jersey City, N.J., ferry.

Service record: WGulfBS, Mortar Flotilla, 1862. Engagement at Pass Christian, Miss., 4 Apr 1862. Passage past New Orleans forts, engagement with CSN vessels, 24 Apr 1862. Disabled by enemy fire at Warrenton, Miss., 25 Jun 1862. Damaged by fire off New Orleans, 8 Oct 1862. Bombardment of Ft. Powell, Mobile Bay, 16–29 Feb 1864. Battle of Mobile Bay, 5 Aug 1864. Decomm 5 Sep 1865; sold 27 Sep 1865.

Ships captured: *Cuba, Belle of Mobile*, 22 Oct 1862; *Le Caddie, Union*, 12 Jan 1863; str *P.C. Wallis*, 4 Apr 1863; str *Fox*.12 Sep 1863; *Syrena*, 21 Oct 1863; *Medora*, 8 Dec 1864.

Later history: Merchant *J.P. Jackson* 1865. RR 1871.

Name	Builder	Launched	Acquired	Comm.
Morse ex-*Marion*	New York (Roosevelt)	1859	7 Nov 1861	9 Nov 1861
Tonnage	513 tons B			

* Later USS *G.L. Brockenborough*.
** Later USS *Anna*.

Dimensions	142'6" (bp) × 33' × 8'6", d12'4"
Machinery	Side wheels, 1 vertical beam engine (38" × 9'), HP 500, 11 knots (Novelty)
Complement	78/96
Armament	2–9"; (Feb 1863) 2–9", 2–100pdr MLR, 2–24pdr

Notes: Brooklyn ferry.

Service record: NAtlBS 1861–64. Landings at Roanoke Island, N.C., 7–8 Feb 1862. Engagement with enemy vessels, capture of Elizabeth City, N.C., expedition to Edenton, N.C., 10–12 Feb 1862. Reconnaissance to Winton, N.C., Chowan River, 18–20 Feb 1862. Capture of New Berne, N.C., 13–14 Mar 1862. Expeditions to West Point, Va., York River, 5–7 May, to White House, Va., York and Pamunkey Rivers, 23–30 Jun 1863, up Pamunkey River, 8–13 Mar 1864. Rappahannock River, 1865. Decomm 21 May 1865. Sold 20 Jul 1865.

Later history: Merchant *Lincoln* 1865. RR 1885.

Name	Builder	Launched	Acquired	Comm.
Satellite	New York, N.Y.	1854	24 Jul 1861	27 Sep 1861
Tonnage	217 tons B			
Dimensions	120'7" × 22'9" × 8'6"			
Machinery	Side wheels			
Complement	43			
Armament	1–8"/55, 1–30pdr MLR			

Notes: Former New York ferryboat.

Service record: Potomac Flotilla 1861. Expedition in Rappahannock River, Tappahannock, Va., 13–15 Apr 1862. Supported submarine *Alligator*, Jun 1862. With USS *Reliance*, captured by Confederate boarders in Rappahannock River, 23 Aug 1863. Operated briefly with Confederate crew at mouth of Rappahannock River, but destroyed to prevent recapture, 28 Aug 1863.

Ships captured: *Emily*, 21 May 1863; *Sarah, *Arctic, 28 May 1863; *Three Brothers*, 17 Aug 1863.

Name	Builder	Launched	Acquired	Comm.
Shokokon	New York (Simonson)	1862	3 Apr 1863	18 May 1863
ex-*Clifton*				
Tonnage	709 tons B			
Dimensions	185' (dk) 181'7" ( ) × 32' × 8'6", d13'6"			
Machinery	Side wheels, 1 vertical beam engine (43" × 10'), 1 boiler. IHP 570, 10 knots (Allaire)			

Fig 3.16: The former ferryboat *Commodore Perry* as a gunboat. (U.S. Naval Historical Center)

Complement   120

Armament   1–30pdr MLR, 4–24pdr; (Mar 1864) 1–24pdr replaced by 1–30pdr MLR; (Mar 1865) 2–9″ SB, 2–30pdr MLR, 4–24pdr

Notes: Wood hull. New York ferry.

Service record: NAtlBS 1863. Expedition in James River, 6–20 Jul 1863. Blockade off Wilmington 1863. Damaged in hurricane, Aug 1863. Expedition up Pamunkey River, Va., 8–13 Mar 1864. Blockade of Wilmington, Sep 1864. Sold 25 Oct 1865.

Ships captured: str *Hebe*, 18 Aug 1863; *Alexander Cooper*, 23 Aug 1863.

Later history: Merchant *Lone Star* 1865. RR 1886.

Name	Builder	Launched	Acquired	Comm.
Somerset	Brooklyn, N.Y.	1862	4 Mar 1862	3 Apr 1862

Tonnage   521 tons B
Dimensions   151′ × 32′4″ × d11′3″
Machinery   Side wheels, 1 engine (36″ × 9′)
Complement   110
Armament   2–9″ SB, 4–32pdr/57

Notes: Wood hull.

Service record: EGulfBS 1862–65, Florida coast. Sold 12 July 1865.

Ships captured: str *Circassian*,* 4 May 1862; *Curlew*, 16 Jun 1862; *Hortense*, 18 Feb 1863.

Later history: Merchant *Somerset*, 1866. RR 1914.

Name	Builder	Launched	Acquired	Comm.
Southfield	New York, N.Y. (Englis)	1857	16 Dec 1861	Dec 1861

Tonnage   751 tons B
Dimensions   200′ × 34′ × 6′6″, d11′8″
Machinery   Side wheels, 1 vertical beam engine, 12 knots
Complement   61
Armament   1–100pdr MLR, 3–9″ SB; (Apr 1863) add 2–9″ SB

Notes: Wood hull. Staten Island Ferry.

Service record: NAtlBS 1862–64. Landings at Roanoke Island., N.C., 7–8 Feb 1862. Capture of New Bern, N.C., 13–14 Mar 1862. Damaged while supporting Army troops at Plymouth, N.C., 10 Dec 1862. Expedition in Chowan River, S. C., 1–2 Mar 1864. Rammed and sunk by CSS *Albemarle* at Plymouth, N.C., 19 Apr 1864 (32 were killed or lost and 23 died as prisoners of war).

Name	Builder	Launched	Acquired	Comm.
Stepping Stones	New York, N.Y.	1861	30 Sep 1861	Oct 1862

Tonnage   226 tons B
Dimensions   110′ × 24′ × 4′6″, d8′
Machinery   Side wheels, beam engine (30″ × 6′)
Complement   21
Armament   (May 1863) 1–20pdr MLR, 3–12pdr MLR, 2–12pdr SB; (Mar 1865) 3–12pdr MLR, 3–12pdr SB

Notes: Former New York ferryboat.

Service record: Potomac Flotilla, dispatch boat 1861. Operations in Nansemond River, Va., 11 Apr–4 May 1863. Expedition up Nansemond River, Va., 13–14 Apr 1864. Decomm 23 Jun 1865. Sold 12 Jul 1865.

Ships captured: *Little Elmer*, *Reliance*, 9 Nov 1864.

Later history: Merchant *Cambridge* 1865. Converted to barge 1871. FFU.

* Later USS *Circassian*.

Name	Builder	Launched	Acquired	Comm.
Westfield	New York (Simonson)	1861	22 Nov 1861	Jan 1862

Tonnage   891 tons B
Dimensions   215′ × 35′ × d13′6″
Machinery   Side wheels. 1 vertical beam engine (50″ × 10′) (Morgan)
Complement   116
Armament   1–100pdr MLR, 1–9″ SB, 4–8″/55

Service record: Passage past New Orleans forts, engagement with CSN vessels, 24 Apr 1862. Bombardment of Vicksburg, 26–22 Jun 1862. Bombardment, capture of Galveston, Tex., 4 Oct 1862. Burst gun during bombardment of Lavaca, Tex., 31 Oct–1 Nov 1862. Blown up to prevent capture when Confederates recaptured Galveston, 1 Jan 1863 (14 killed).

Name	Builder	Launched	Acquired	Comm.
Whitehall	Brooklyn, N.Y. (Burtis)	1850	10 Oct 1861	Oct 1861

Tonnage   326 tons B
Dimensions   126′ (keel) × 28′2″ × 8′, d10′
Machinery   Side wheels, inclined engine (36″ × 8′)
Complement   (U)
Armament   2–30pdr MLR, 2–32pdr/33

Notes: Wood hull.

Service record: SAtlBS 1861. Unable to reach station because of poor condition. Engaged CSS *Sea Bird* in Hampton Roads, 29 Dec 1861. Damaged during Battle of Hampton Roads, 8 Mar 1862 (3 killed). Destroyed by fire off Ft. Monroe, 10 Mar 1862.

COASTAL COMBATANTS (RIVERBOATS, FOURTH RATE)

Name	Builder	Launched	Acquired	Comm.
Antelope	Parkersburg, Va.	1861	31 Aug 1864	Sep 1864

ex-*Lavinia Logan*

Tonnage   145 tons
Dimensions   (U)
Machinery   Stern wheel
Armament   2–30pdr R, 4–24pdr SB

Service record: WGulfBS 1862–64. Struck snag and sank in Mississippi River, 23 Sep 1864.

Name	Builder	Launched	Acquired	Comm.
Barataria	New Orleans, La.	1857	1 Jan 1863	1863

ex-CSS *Barataria*

Tonnage   400 or 52 tons
Dimensions   125′ × (U) × 3′6″
Machinery   Stern wheel
Armament   3 guns

Notes: Ironclad gunboat, captured at New Orleans, April 1862. 1-inch armor plating. Little known about this vessel. Also spelled *Barrataria*.

Service record: WGulfBS 1863. Struck a snag in Lake Maurepas, La., burned to prevent capture, 7 Apr 1863.

Name	Builder	Launched	Acquired	Comm.
Bloomer	New Albany, Ind.	1856	1 Jan 1863	24 Jan 1863
Tonnage	130 or 95 tons			
Dimensions	(U)			
Machinery	Stern wheel, HP engine			
Complement	49			
Armament	(Feb 1864) 1–32pdr/57, 1–12pdr MLR			

Notes: Captured by USS *Charlotte* in Choctawatchie River, Fla., 24 Dec 1862.
Service record: EGulfBS 1863–65. Operations in St. Andrews Bay, Fla., 10–18 Dec 1863. Wrecked on coast of Florida, Jun 1865; salved. Sold 22 Sep 1865.
Later history: Merchant *Emma* 1865. Sold foreign 1868.

Name	Builder	Launched	Acquired	Comm.
Diana	Brownsville, Pa.	1858	Nov 1862	1 Jan 1863
Tonnage	239 tons			
Dimensions	(U)			
Machinery	Side wheels			
Armament	(U)			

Notes: Merchant steamer captured at New Orleans, 27 Apr 1862. Used by Army as transport.
Service record: Engagement off Brashear City, Berwick Bay, La., 1–3 Nov 1862. Engagement at Bayou Teche, La., 14 Jan 1863. Captured by Confederate troops in Grand Lake, La., 28 Mar 1863 (6 killed). Burned by U.S. forces, 12 Apr 1863.

Name	Builder	Launched	Acquired	Comm.
Kinsman	Elizabeth, Pa.	1854	1 Jan 1863	Oct 1862
ex-*Colonel Kinsman*, ex-*Gray Cloud*				
Tonnage	245 tons			
Dimensions	(U)			
Machinery	Side wheels			
Armament	(U)			

Notes: Steamer commandeered for the Army at New Orleans, May 1862. Transferred to the Navy, 1 Jan 1863.
Service record: Damaged in engagement with CSS *J.A. Cotton* off Brashear City, Berwick Bay, La., 3 Nov 1862. Engagement at Bayou Teche, La., 14 Jan 1863. Struck a snag and sank in Berwick Bay, La., near Brashear City, 23 Feb 1863.
Ships captured: str *A.B. Seger*, 4 Nov 1862; str **Osprey, J.P. Smith*, 9 Nov 1862.

COASTAL SCREW COMBATANTS (FOURTH RATE)

Name	Builder	Launched	Acquired	Comm.
Acacia	East Boston, Mass.	Sep 1863	28 Oct 1863	Dec 1863
ex-*Vicksburg*				
Tonnage	300 tons B			
Dimensions	125' × 23'2" × 11'6"			
Machinery	1 screw, 1 condensing engine (36" × 3'), 1 boiler, 12 knots			
Complement	58			
Armament	2–30pdr MLR, 1–12pdr MLR, 1–12pdr SB			

Notes: Schooner rig.
Service record: SAtlBS 1864–65. Decomm 12 May 1865. Sold 20 Jun 1865.
Ship captured: str *Julia*, 23 Dec 1864.
Later history: Merchant *Wabash* 1865. RR 1881.

Name	Builder	Launched	Acquired	Comm.
Curlew	Williamsburg, N.Y.	1853	15 Sep 1861	Fall 1861
Tonnage	392 tons B			
Dimensions	126'2" × 32'8" × 8', d12'8"			
Machinery	1 screw, vertical direct-acting engine			
Complement	88			
Armament	6–32pdr/57, 1–20pdr MLR; (Feb 1863) 8–24pdr H			

Service record: Operations at Port Royal, Beaumont, S.C., 5–9 Nov 1861. Transferred to War Dept, 16 Jan 1862.
Later history: Merchant *South Side* 1866. RR 1912.

Name	Builder	Launched	Acquired	Comm.
Currituck	New York, N.Y.	1843	20 Sep 1861	27 Feb 1862
ex-*Seneca*				
Tonnage	193 tons B			
Dimensions	120' × 23' × d7'6"			
Machinery	1 screw, 1 direct-acting engine (22" × 2')			
Complement	52			
Armament	1–32pdr/57, 1–20pdr MLR; (May 1864) add 3–32pdr/57			

Notes: Wood hull, schooner rig.
Service record: Towed *Monitor* from New York to Hampton Roads, Mar 1862. Potomac Flotilla 1862–65. Army operations at Yorktown, Va., 4–7 May 1862. Expedition up Pamunkey River, Va., 17 May 1862. Engaged batteries at Port Royal, Va., 4 Dec 1862. Decomm 7 Aug 1865. Sold 15 Sep 1865.
Ships captured: *Director*, 4 May 1862; *Water Witch*, 5 May 1862; *American Coaster, Planter*, 7 May 1862; *Potter*, 3 Jan 1863; *Hampton*, 13 Jan 1863; *Queen of the Fleet*, 25 Jan 1863; *Ladies Delight*, 14 May 1863; *Emily*, 21 May 1863; *Three Brothers*, 21 Oct 1863.
Later history: Merchant *Arlington* 1865. Burned at Mobile, Ala., 23 Nov 1870.

Name	Builder	Launched	Acquired	Comm.
Dai Ching	Brooklyn, N.Y. (Jewett)	1862	21 Apr 1863	11 Jun 1863
Tonnage	520 tons B			
Dimensions	175'2" () 170'6" ( ) × 29'4" × 9'6", d11'			
Machinery	1 screw, 2 LP direct-acting engines (32" × 2'2"), 2 boilers, 6 knots. (McLeod)			
Complement	83			
Armament	1–100pdr MLR, 4–24pdr H SB, 2–20pdr MLR			

Notes: Ordered for F.T. Ward's Chinese Navy. Wood hull.
Service record: SAtlBS 1863–65. Bombardment of Ft. Wagner, Charleston, 24 Jul–23 Aug 1863. Assault on Jacksonville, Fla., 2–22 Feb 1864. Joint expedition up Ashepoo and S. Edisto Rivers, S.C., 25–27 May 1864. Went aground in Combahee River, S.C., burned to prevent capture, 26 Jan 1865.
Ships captured: *George Chisholm*, 14 Nov 1863; *Coquette*, 26 Jan 1865.

Name	Builder	Launched	Acquired	Comm.
Dawn	New York, N.Y. (Sneeden)	1857	26 Apr 1861	9 May 1861
Tonnage	399 tons B			
Dimensions	154' × 28'10" × 12', d9'8"			
Machinery	1 screw, 1 vertical direct-acting (rotary) engine (40" × 2'), 11 knots (Delamater)			
Complement	34/60			
Armament	2–32pdr/57; (1862) add 1–20pdr MLR; (May 1863) 1–100pdr MLR, 2–32pdr/57, 1–30pdr MLR, 1–12pdr			

Acquired Combatant Vessels 71

Notes: Wood hull. One funnel aft, three masts. New boiler 1862.
Service record: Potomac Flotilla 1861. SAtlBS May 1862–Jul 1863. Engaged batteries at Ft. McAllister, Ogeechee River, Ga., 19 Nov 1862, 27 Jan–28 Feb 1863. Engaged CSS *Nashville* at Genesis Point, Ga., 28 Feb 1863. NAtlBS, Jan 1864–65. Decomm 17 Jun 1865. Sold 1 Nov 1865.
Ships captured: *General Knox, Georgiana*, 24 May 1861; *Josephus*, 24 Jul 1861.
Later history: Merchant *Eutaw* 1865, rebuilt. Wrecked at Pecks Beach, NJ, 27 Dec 1869.

Name	Builder	Launched	Acquired	Comm.
Daylight	New York, N.Y. (Sneeden)	1860	10 May 1861	7 Jun 1861
Tonnage	682 tons B			
Dimensions	170′ × 30′6″ × 13′, d11′			
Machinery	1 screw, Ericsson double-trunk (rotary) engines (44″ × 2′), 5 knots (Delamater)			
Complement	57			
Armament	4–32pdr/57; (May1863) 6–32pdr/57, 1–30pdr MLR, 1–12pdr MLR			

Notes: Improved version of *Dawn*, funnel aft.
Service record: Blockade duty 1861–Aug 1863. Damaged during bombardment, capture of Ft. Macon, N.C., 25–26 Apr 1862. NAtlBS Sep 1863–Oct 1864. James River 1864–65. Decomm 24 May 1865. Sold 25 Oct 1865.
Ships captured: *John Hamilton*, 5 Jul 1861; *Monticello*, 25 Aug 1861; *Extra, Good Egg*, 29 Aug 1861; *Alliance*, 26 Apr 1862; *Racer*, 30 Oct 1862; *Sophia*, 4 Nov 1862; *unidentified brig, 17 Nov 1862; *Brilliant*, 3 Dec 1862; *Coquette*, 8 Dec 1862; *Gondar*, 26 Dec 1862; *unidentified, 21 Jan 1863.
Later history: Merchant *Santee* 1865. Converted to barge 1886. RR 1907.

Name	Builder	Launched	Acquired	Comm.
Don ex-*Diana*	London (Dudgeon)	1863	21 Apr 1864	May 1864
Tonnage	390 tons B			
Dimensions	162′ × 23′ × 6′, d12′3″			
Machinery	2 screws, 2 horizontal engines (26″ × 1′9″), 4 boilers, 600 IHP, 14 knots			
Complement	94			
Armament	2–20pdr MLR, 6–24pdr SB			

Notes: Blockade runner *Don*, captured by USS *Pequot* off Beaufort, N.C., 4 Mar 1864. Iron hull. Mounted experimental 15-inch gun, Jan 1866.
Service record: Potomac Flotilla 1864–65. NAtl Sqn 1866–68. Decomm 18 May 1868. Sold 29 Aug 1868.
Later history: Merchant *Don*, 1868. Spanish *Cantabria* 1871. SE 1884.

Name	Builder	Launched	Acquired	Comm.
Dragon	Buffalo, N.Y.	1861	Dec 1861	1862
Tonnage	118 tons B			
Dimensions	92′ × 17′ × d9′6″			
Machinery	1 screw			
Complement	42			
Armament	1–30pdr MLR, 1–24pdr SB			

Notes: Wood hull.
Service record: NAtlBS 1862. Damaged by shell from CSS *Virginia* at battle of Hampton Roads, 8 Mar 1862. James River Flotilla 1862. Potomac Flotilla Aug 1862–65. Engaged batteries near Ft. Lowry, Va., 21 Feb 1863. Decomm 13 May 1865. Sold 29 Jul 1865.
Ship captured: *Samuel First,* 6 May 1863.
Later history: Merchant *Brandt* 1865. RR 1880.

Name	Builder	Launched	Acquired	Comm.
E.B. Hale ex-*Edmund B. Hale*	Sleightsburg, N.Y.	1861	27 Jul 1861	4 Sep 1861
Tonnage	220 tons B			
Dimensions	117′ × 28′ × 8′6″			
Machinery	1 screw, 1 vertical engine (26″ × 2′2″), 8 knots			
Complement	50			
Armament	4–32pdr/42; (Feb 1863) add 1–20pdr MLR; (May 1863) 1–30pdr MLR, 4–32pdr/42.			

Service record: Potomac Flotilla 1861. SAtlBS 1862. Army operations at Port Royal Ferry, S.C., 31 Dec 1861–2 Jan 1862. Bombardment at St. Johns Bluff, Fla., 17 Sep 1862. Expeditions to St. Johns Bluff, Fla., 1–3 Oct 1862, up Ashepoo, S. Edisto Rivers, S.C., 25–27 May 1864. Decomm 11 May 1865. Sold 20 Jun 1865.
Ships captured: str *Governor Milton*, 9 Oct 1862; *Pilot*, 21 Oct 1862; *Wave*, 4 Nov 1862.
Later history: Merchant *E.B. Hale*. RR 1867.

Name	Builder	Launched	Acquired	Comm.
Estrella	London, England	1853	1862	1862
Tonnage	438 tons B, 566 GRT			
Dimensions	178′ × 26′ × 6′, d8′			
Machinery	1 screw, oscillating engine (52″ × 3′)			
Complement	57			
Armament	1–30pdr MLR, 2–32pdr/33, 2–24pdr H; (Jun 1865) 1–30pdr MLR, 2–12pdr H			

Notes: Blockade runner, captured Jul 1862, transferred from Army. Iron hull.
Service record: WGulfBS Nov 1862–67. Engagement off Brashear City, Berwick Bay, La., 1–3 Nov 1862. Engagement at Bayou Teche, La., 14 Jan 1863. Engagement with CSS *Queen of the West* in Berwick Bay, 14 Apr 1863. Engagement at Butte-a-la-Rose, La., capture of Ft. Burton, 20 Apr 1863. Expedition up Red River, 3–13 May 1863. Battle of Mobile Bay, 5 Aug 1864. Decomm 16 Jul 1867. Sold 9 Oct 1867.
Ships captured: str *Hart*, Apr 1863; *Julia A. Hodges*, 6 Apr 1864.
Later history: Merchant *Estrella* 1867. Converted to side wheel. Lost (cause unknown), 1870.

Name	Builder	Launched	Acquired	Comm.
Eureka	Georgetown, D.C.	1861	22 Aug 1862	1862
Tonnage	32 tons			
Dimensions	85′ × 12′8″ × d3′6″			
Machinery	1 screw			
Complement	19			
Armament	2–12pdr			

Notes: Captured 20 Apr 1862 in Rappahannock River by USS *Anacostia*.
Service record: Potomac Flotilla 1862–65. Expeditions up Nansemond River, Va., 13–14 Apr, to Northern Neck, Va., 11–21 Jun 1864. Went aground in Nomini Creek, Va., 20 Dec 1864. Sold 15 Sep 1865.
Later history: FFU.

Name	Builder	Launched	Acquired	Comm.
Fuchsia ex-*Kiang Soo*	Brooklyn, N.Y. (Jewett)	1862	16 Jun 1863	Aug 1863
Tulip ex-*Chi Kiang*	Brooklyn, N.Y. (Jewett)	1862	16 Jun 1863	1863

Fig 3.17: USS *Fuchsia*, a unit of the Potomac Flotilla, was ordered as a lighthouse tender for F.T. Ward's Chinese Navy. (U.S. Naval Historical Center)

Tonnage	240 tons B
Dimensions	101′4″ () 97′3″ ( ) × 21′9″ × 8′, d11′5″
Machinery	1 screw, 2 horizontal direct-acting engines (20″ × 2′) (McLeod)
Complement	43/57
Armament	1–20pdr MLR, 2–24pdr H
	Fuchsia: (Mar 1864) 1–20pdr MLR, 4–24pdr H, 1–12pdr MLR
	Tulip: (Sep 1864) add 1–12pdr SB

Note: Lighthouse tenders built for F.T. Ward's Chinese Navy. Wood hulls.
Service records:
Fuchsia: Potomac Flotilla 1863–64. Expeditions in Machodoc Creek, Va., 13 Apr, in Rappahannock River, Va., 16–19 May, to Northern Neck, Va., 11–21 Jun 1864. Decomm 5 Aug 1865. Sold 23 Sep 1865.
  Ship captured: *Three Brothers*, 21 Oct 1862.
  Later history: Merchant *Donald* 1865. RR 1889.
Tulip: Potomac Flotilla Aug 1863–64. Expedition to Northern Neck, Va., 12 Jan 1864. Sunk by boiler explosion off Ragged Point, Va., 11 Nov 1864 (49 killed).

Name	Builder	Launched	Acquired	Comm.
Henry Andrew	New York, N.Y.	1847	10 Sep 1861	Oct 1861

Tonnage	177 tons B
Dimensions	150′ × 26′ × d7′6″
Machinery	1 screw (Swiftsure propeller)
Complement	49
Armament	2–32pdr/33, 1–20pdr MLR

Notes: Built as sailing brig, converted to steam, 1859.
Service record: SAtlBS 1861. Expedition up Wright's and Mud Rivers, S.C., Jan–Feb 1862. Engaged enemy in Mosquito Inlet, Fla., 21–22 Mar 1862. Wrecked in storm south of Cape Henry, Va., 24 Aug 1862.

Name	Builder	Launched	Acquired	Comm.
Henry Brinker	Brooklyn, N.Y.	1861	29 Oct 1861	15 Dec 1861

Tonnage	108 tons B
Dimensions	82′ × 26′7″ × 7′
Machinery	1 screw, 2 vertical engines (18″ × 1′8″), 1 boiler, 5 knots
Complement	18
Armament	1–30pdr MLR; (Sep 1864) add 2–12pdr

Service record: NAtlBS Jan 1862–Nov 1863. Engagement with enemy vessels, capture of Elizabeth City, N.C., expedition to Edenton, N.C., 10–12 Feb 1862. Landings at Roanoke Island, N.C. 7–8 Feb 1862. Capture of New Bern, N.C., 13–14 Mar 1862. Inactive at Newport News 1864–65. Decomm 29 Jun 1865. Sold 20 Jul 1865.
Later history: Possibly merchant *Relief*. BU 1867.

Name	Builder	Launched	Acquired	Comm.
Hibiscus	Fairhaven, Conn. (Pook)	1864	16 Nov 1864	29 Dec 1864
Spirea	Fairhaven, Conn. (Pook)	1864	30 Dec 1864	9 Jan 1865

Tonnage	406 tons B
Dimensions	175′ × 30′ × 7′, d10′ (as merchant 1868)
Machinery	2 screws, 2 Wright's segmental engines (30″ × 2′1″), 2 boilers, 9 knots
Complement	65/86
Armament	2–30pdr MLR, 4–24pdr H

Notes: Wood hulls.
Service records:
Hibiscus: EGulfBS 1865. Expedition to St. Marks, Fla. 23 Feb–27 Mar 1865. Decomm 19 Aug 1865. Sold 5 Oct 1866.
Later history: Merchant *Francis Wright* 1866. Renamed *Hibiscus*, 1870. Lost at sea (cause unknown), 1 May 1873.
Spirea: EGulfBS 1865. Expedition to St. Marks, Fla., 23 Feb–27 Mar 1865. Decomm 23 Aug 1865. Sold 5 Oct 1866.
Later history: Merchant *Sappho* 1867. Abandoned off Cape Hatteras, 14 Dec 1867.

Name	Builder	Launched	Acquired	Comm.
Howquah	East Boston, Mass.	1863	17 Jun 1863	1 Sep 1863

Tonnage	397 tons B
Dimensions	120′7″ × 22′10″ × 12′
Machinery	1 screw, 1 vertical engine (36″ × 3′), 10 knots
Complement	55
Armament	2–30pdr MLR, 2–12pdr MLR; (Apr 1864) 3–30pdr MLR, 1–12pdr MLR, 1–12pdr H SB

Notes: Wood hull. Schooner rig.
Service record: NAtlBS 1863–65. Engagement with CSS *Raleigh* off New Inlet, N.C., 6–7 May 1864. Unsuccessful attack on Ft. Fisher, N.C., 24–25 Dec 1864. Second attack on Ft. Fisher, 13–15 Jan 1865. Bombardment of Masonboro Inlet, N.C., 11 Feb 1865. EGulfBS 1865. Decomm 22 Jun 1865. Sold 10 Aug 1865.
Ships captured: str *Margaret & Jessie*,* 5 Nov 1863; str *Ella*,** 10 Nov 1863; str **Lynx*, 25 Sep 1864.
Later history: Merchant *Equator* 1865. RR 1883.

Name	Builder	Launched	Acquired	Comm.
Isaac Smith	Brooklyn, N.Y. (L & F)	1861	9 Sep 1861	16 Oct 1861

Tonnage	453 tons B, 382 n/r
Dimensions	171′6″ × 31′4″ × 7′, d9′
Machinery	1 screw (Swiftsure propeller), beam engine
Complement	96/119
Armament	1–30pdr MLR, 8–8″ SB/63

Notes: Wood hull.

---

* Later USS *Gettysburg*.
** Later USS *Philippi*.

Service record: SAtlBS 1861–63. Engagement with CSN squadron off Port Royal, S.C., 5 Nov 1861. Bombardment and occupation of Port Royal, 7 Nov 1861. Engagement in Wassaw Sound, Ga., 26–28 Jan 1862. Capture of Fernandina, Fla., Brunswick, St. Simons, and Jekyl Islands, Ga., 2–12 Mar 1862. Disabled by Confederate batteries in Stono River, 30 Jan 1863, surrendered.

Ship captured: *British Empire,* 3 Apr 1862.

Later history: Renamed CSS *Stono.* Wrecked near Ft. Moultrie, S.C., 5 Jun 1863.

Name	Builder	Launched	Acquired	Comm.
Little Ada	Renfrew, Scotland (Simons)	22 Dec 1863	18 Aug 1864	5 Oct 1864
Tonnage	150 tons B, 236 GRT			
Dimensions	112′ × 18′6″ × 8′, d10′			
Machinery	1 screw, 2-cyl. direct-acting engine (22″ × 1′8″), 1 boiler, IHP 100, 10 knots			
Complement	27/53			
Armament	2–20pdr MLR			

Notes: Blockade runner, captured by USS *Gettysburg* in South Santee River, 9 Jul 1864. Iron hull, schooner rig.

Service record: NAtlBS 1864–65. Unsuccessful attack on Ft. Fisher, N.C., 24–25 Dec 1864. Second attack on Ft. Fisher, 13–15 Jan 1865. Bombardment of Ft. Anderson, Cape Fear River, 18 Feb 1865. Potomac Flotilla 1865. Decomm 24 Jun 1865. Transferred to War Dept 12 Aug 1865.

Later history: War Dept *Ada* 1865. Transferred to Coast Survey. Merchant *Peter Smith* 1878. Canadian, renamed *Little Ada,* 1909. Renamed *Buxton* ,1921. Renamed *Betty Jane Hearn,* 1923. Renamed *Poling Bros. No.2* 1928. Sunk in ice off Great Captains Island, Conn., 2 Jun 1940.

Name	Builder	Launched	Acquired	Comm.
Louisiana	Wilmington, Del. (Harlan)	1860	10 Jul 1861	Aug 1861
Tonnage	438 tons D, 295 tons B			
Dimensions	143′2″ × 27′3″ × 8′6″			
Machinery	1 screw, 1 inverted direct-acting condensing engine (32″ × 2′2″), 1 boiler (Bldr)			
Complement	85			
Armament	1–8″ SB, 2–32pdr/57, 1–32pdr/33, 1–12pdr MLR			

Note: Three-mast schooner, two funnels, iron hull.

Service record: NAtlBS 1861. Landings at Roanoke Island, N.C., 7–8 Feb 1862. Engagement with enemy vessels, capture of Elizabeth City, N.C., expedition to Edenton, N.C., 10–12 Feb 1862. Reconnaissance to Winton, N.C., Chowan River, 18–20 Feb 1862. Capture of New Berne, N.C., 13–14 Mar 1862. Expedition to Washington, N.C., 21 Mar 1862. Expedition to Pungo River, N. C., 16–21 Jun 1864. Used as an explosion ship at Ft. Fisher, N.C., 24 Dec 1864 but exploded without effect.

Ships captured: *S.T.Garrison,* 7 Sep 1861; *Alice L. Webb,* 5 Nov 1862; *R.T. Renshaw,* 20 May 1863.

Name	Builder	Launched	Acquired	Comm.
Madgie	Philadelphia, Pa.	1858	15 Oct 1861	1862
Tonnage	220 tons B			
Dimensions	122′6″ × 22′7″ × d8′5″			
Machinery	1 screw, direct-acting engine			
Complement	45			
Armament	1–8″/63, 1–30pdr MLR; (Mar 1862) 1–30pdr MLR, 1–20pdr MLR; (May 1863) add 2–24pdr H, 1–12pdr SB			

Notes: Wood hull.

Service record: SAtlBS 1862–63. Bombardment of Ft. McAllister, Ogeechee River, Ga., 29 Jul 1862. Foundered in tow off Frying Pan Shoals, N.C., 11 Oct 1863.

Ship captured: *Southern Belle,* 20 Jun 1862.

Name	Builder	Launched	Acquired	Comm.
Naugatuck	New York, N.Y. (Dunham)	1844	1862 (U)	

ex-USRC *E.A. Stevens,* ex-*Naugatuck*

Tonnage	192 tons B
Dimensions	110′ (U) 101′ (bp) × 21′6″ × 6′
Machinery	2 screws, 2 inclined engines, 1 boiler
Complement	22
Armament	1–100pdr MLR, 2–12pdr MLR, 2–12pdr H; (Nov 1862) 1–6pdr MLR, 1–42pdr MLR

Notes: Loaned to government by John Stevens, taken into Revenue Service, and loaned to the Navy. Originally built with single screw, used by Stevens as experimental vessel. Fitted out as twin-screw ironclad to demonstrate plans for "Stevens Battery," including a plan of protection in which the forward and aft compartments were flooded to submerge the hull partially, increasing draft to 9′10″. As a result of the gun explosion, 15 May 1862 the protection plan was never tested. 12-inch gun was loaded by depressing barrel, loading from below.

Service record: NAtlBS 1862. Engaged batteries at Sewell's Point., Va., 8 May 1862, at Drewry's Bluff, Va., 15 May 1862 (gun exploded). Returned to USRCS.

Later history: USRC *E.A. Stevens* 1862 (q.v.).

Name	Builder	Launched	Acquired	Comm.
New London	Mystic, Conn. (Greenman)	5 Oct 1859	26 Aug 1861	29 Oct 1861
Tonnage	221 tons B			
Dimensions	135′ (U) 125′ (U) × 26′ × 9′6″, d7′8″			
Machinery	1 screw, 1 vertical direct-acting engine (34″ × 2′6″), 1 boiler, 9.5 knots (Delamater)			
Complement	47			
Armament	1–20pdr MLR, 4–32pdr/57; (Apr 1862) 1–32pdr/57 replaced by 1–42pdr MLR; (Dec 1863) 1–20pdr MLR, 1–8″ SB, 3–32pdr/57			

Notes: Wood hull, three mast schooner rig.

Fig 3.18: The *Norwich* was a small screw steamer acquired by the Navy in 1861.

Service record: GulfBS 1861–65. Engagement at Pass Christian, Miss., 25 Mar, 4 Apr 1862. Bombardment below Donaldsonville, La., 7 Jul, and at Whitehall Point, La. (disabled), 10 Jul 1863. Decomm 3 Aug 1865. Sold 8 Sep 1865.

Ships captured: *Olive*, 21 Nov 1861; str *Anna*, 22 Nov 1861; *A.J. View*, str *Henry Lewis*, 28 Nov 1861; *Advocate*, 1 Dec 1861; *Delight, Osceola, Express*, 9 Dec 1861; *Gypsy*, 28 Dec 1861; *Capt. Spedden*, 31 Dec 1861; *Zulima, 12 Apr 1862; *Tampico*, 2 Apr 1863; *Raton Del Nilo*, 3 Dec 1863.

Later history: Merchant *Acushnet* 1865. RR 1910.

Name	Builder	Launched	Acquired	Comm.
Norwich	Norwich, Conn.	1861	26 Sep 1861	28 Dec 1861
Tonnage	431 tons B, 329 n/r			
Dimensions	132′5″ × 24′6″ × 10′, d16′5″			
Machinery	1 screw, 1 vertical direct-acting engine (34″ × 2′6″), 1 boiler, 6 knots			
Complement	80			
Armament	(1862) 1–30pdr MLR, 4–8″/55			

Notes: Wood hull.

Service record: SAtlBS 1862, blockade of Savannah. Assault on Jacksonville, Fla., 2–22 Feb 1864. Decomm 30 Jun 1865. Sold 10 Aug 1865.

Ships captured: str *Wild Dayrell, 1 Feb 1864; str **St. Mary's*, 7 Feb 1864.

Later history: Merchant *Norwich* 1865. Foundered at sea, 17 Feb 1873.

Name	Builder	Launched	Acquired	Comm.
Patroon	Philadelphia, Pa.	1859	28 Oct 1861	18 Mar 1862
Tonnage	183 tons B			
Dimensions	113′ × 22′5″ × 7′			
Machinery	1 screw			
Complement	49			
Armament	1–20pdr MLR, 4–32pdr/33			

Notes: Wood hull. Hull in poor condition when purchased.

Service record: SAtlBS 1862. Bombardment at St. Johns Bluff, Fla., 17 Sep 1862. Expedition to Pocotaligo, S.C., 21–23 Oct 1862. Decomm 18 Nov 1862. Sold 30 Dec 1862.

Later history: Purchased by War Dept, 8 Dec 1863. Sunk at Brazos, Tex., 10 Nov 1865.

Name	Builder	Launched	Acquired	Comm.
Potomska	Hoboken, N.J. (Capes)	1854	25 Sep 1861	20 Dec 1861
Tonnage	287 tons B			
Dimensions	140′ (dk) 134′6″ (U) × 27′ × 11′, d8′8″			
Machinery	1 screw, 1 vertical direct-acting engine (34″ × 2′6″), 1 boiler, 9 knots (Delamater)			
Complement	77/95			
Armament	4–32pdr/57, 1–20pdr MLR			

Notes: Wood hull, three-mast schooner.

Service record: SAtlBS 1862–65. Engagement in Wassaw Sound, Ga., 26–28 Jan 1862. Capture of Fernandina, Fla., Brunswick, St. Simons, and Jekyl Islands, Ga., 2–12 Mar 1862. Expedition to Bulls Bay, S.C., 12–17 Feb 1865. Decomm 16 Jun 1865. Sold 10 Aug 1865.

Ship captured: *Belle*, 23 Feb 1863.

Later history: Merchant *Potomska* 1865. Wrecked at Saluda, Tex., 15 Jul 1866.

Name	Builder	Launched	Acquired	Comm.
Sachem	New York, N.Y.	1844	20 Sep 1861	1861
Tonnage	197 tons B			
Dimensions	121′ × 23′6″ × d7′6″			
Machinery	1 screw			
Complement	52			
Armament	1–20pdr MLR, 4–32pdr/57			

Service record: Survey ship for attack on New Orleans forts, Mar–Apr 1862. Engaged enemy while blockading Aransas Pass, Tex., Jun 1862. Damaged while defending Galveston against enemy attack, 31 Dec 1862. Disabled by enemy batteries during attack on Sabine Pass, Tex. and captured, 8 Sep 1863.

Later history: CSS *Sachem* (q.v.).

Spirea, see *Hibiscus*.

Name	Builder	Launched	Acquired	Comm.
Sunflower	East Boston, Mass.	1863	2 May 1863	29 Apr 1863
Tonnage	294 tons			
Dimensions	104′5″ × 20′9″ × 12′			
Machinery	1 screw, 1 vertical direct-acting engine (36″ × 3′), 10.5 knots			
Complement	52			
Armament	2–30pdr MLR			

Service record: EGulfBS May 1863–65. Occupation of Tampa, Fla., 4–7 May 1864. Decomm 3 Jun 1865. Sold 10 Aug 1865.

Ships captured: *Echo*, 31 May 1863; *Pushmataha*, 12 Jun 1863; *General Worth*, 27 Aug 1863; *Last Trial*, 6 Oct 1863; *Hancock*, 24 Dec 1863; *Josephine*, 24 Mar 1864; *Neptune*, 6 May 1864; *Pickwick*, 6 Dec 1864.

Later history: Merchant *Sunflower* 1865. Sunk in collision with *Juniata* in Southwest Pass, La., 29 Jan 1870.

Name	Builder	Launched	Acquired	Comm.
Teaser	Philadelphia, Pa.	1855?	4 Jul 1862	1862

ex-CSS *Teaser*, (may be) ex-*Wide Awake*?

Tonnage	64 tons
Dimensions	80′ × 18′ × d7′
Machinery	1 screw, 1 engine (20″ × 1′8″), 1 boiler
Complement	25
Armament	(1862) 1–32pdr MLR; (Jan 1864) 1–50pdr MLR, 1–24pdr H; (Dec 1864) 1–50pdr MLR replaced by 1–30pdr MLR

Notes: Captured in James River by USS *Maratanza* after being disabled in action, 4 Jul 1862. Wood hull tug.

Service record: Potomac Flotilla Sep 1862. Bombardment of Brandywine Hill, Rappahannock River, Va., 10 Dec 1862. Operations in Nansemond River, Va., 11 Apr–4 May 1863. Expedition in Machodoc Creek, Va., 13 Apr 1864. Decomm 2 Jun 1865. Sold 25 Jun 1865.

Ship captured: *Grapeshot*, 6 Nov 1862.

Later history: Merchant *York River* 1865. RR 1873.

Tulip, see *Fuchsia*.

Name	Builder	Launched	Acquired	Comm.
Uncas	New York, N.Y.	1843	20 Sep 1861	14 Oct 1861
Tonnage	192 tons B			
Dimensions	118'6" × 23'4" × 7'6"			
Machinery	1 screw, 1 vertical engine (24" × 1'10"), 11.5 knots			
Complement	62/82			
Armament	1–20pdr MLR, 2–32pdr/57; (Apr 1863) add 2–32pdr/57			

Notes: Purchased for Coast Survey. Machinery unreliable.
Service record: WGulfBS Apr 1862. Surveyed Mississippi River for attack on New Orleans, Apr 1862. SAtlBS Apr 1862. Expedition to St. Johns Bluff, Fla., 1–12 Oct, to Pocotaligo, S.C., 21–23 Oct 1862. Decomm, sold 21 Aug 1863.
Ship captured: *Belle*, 26 Apr 1862.
Later history: Merchant *Claymont* 1863. RR 1886.

Name	Builder	Launched	Acquired	Comm.
Valley City	Philadelphia, Pa. (Birely)	1859	26 Jul 1861	13 Sep 1861
Tonnage	190 tons B, 318 n/r			
Dimensions	133' (U) 127'6" (U) × 21'10" × 8'4"			
Machinery	1 screw, 1 vertical engine (24" × 2'), 1 boiler, 10 knots			
Complement	48/82			
Armament	4–32pdr/42; (Dec 1864) 4–32pdr/42, 2–20pdr MLR, 1–12pdr.			

Notes: Wood hull.
Service record: Potomac Flotilla 1861. Bombardment at Freestone Point, Va. 25 Sep 1861. NAtlBS 1862. Landings at Roanoke Island, N.C., 7–8 Feb 1862. Engagement with enemy vessels, capture of Elizabeth City, N.C. and expedition to Edenton, N.C., 10–12 Feb 1862. Damaged during capture of New Berne, N.C., 13–14 Mar 1862. Expedition to Hamilton, N.C., 31 Oct–7 Nov 1862, in Chowan River, N.C., 26–30 Jul 1863. Damaged in collision with transport *Vidette*, 21 Sep 1863. Expedition to Pungo River, N.C., 16–21 Jun 1864. Capture of Plymouth, N.C., Roanoke River, 29–31 Oct 1864. Expedition to Poplar Point, N.C., 9–28 Dec 1864 (3 killed). Sold 15 Aug 1865.
Ships captured: *M. O'Neill*, 5 May 1864; str *Philadelphia*, 10 Jan 1865.
Later history: Merchant *Valley City*, 1865. Foundered off Cape San Blas, Fla., 30 Jan 1882.

Name	Builder	Launched	Acquired	Comm.
Victoria	Philadelphia, Pa.	1855	26 Dec 1861	13 Mar 1862
Tonnage	254 tons B			
Dimensions	119'9" ( ) 113' ( ) × 23' × 12', d9'3"			
Machinery	1 screw, 1 vertical direct-acting engine (28" × 2'6"), 1 boiler. 6 knots			
Complement	44			
Armament	1–30pdr MLR, 2–8"/63			

Notes: Wood hull, in yard for repairs many times because of poor condition of hull.
Service record: NAtlBS 1862–64. Blockade of Wilmington. Damaged in collision with USS *Cherokee*, summer 1864. Decomm 4 May 1865. Sold 30 Nov 1865.
Ships captured: str *Nassau*, 28 May 1862; *Emily*, 26 Jun 1862; *Minna*, 18 Feb 1863; str *Nicolai I*, 21 Mar 1863; str *Georgianna McCaw*, 2 Jun 1864.
Later history: Merchant *Victoria* 1866. RR 1871

Name	Builder	Launched	Acquired	Comm.
Wamsutta	Hoboken, N.J. (Capes)	13 Aug 1853	20 Sep 1861	14 Mar 1862
Tonnage	270 tons B			
Dimensions	129'3" × 26'8" × 11', d8'6"			
Machinery	1 screw, 1 vertical engine, 1 boiler, 9 knots (Delamater)			
Complement	57			
Armament	1–20pdr MLR, 4–32pdr/57			

Service record: SAtlBS 1862–65. In collision with steamer *Mayflower*, Nov 1862. Decomm 29 Jun 1865. Sold 20 Jul 1865.
Ships captured: *Amelia*, 8 May 1863; str *Rose*, 2 Jun 1864; str *Flora*, 22 Oct 1864; 4 Feb: *unidentified str, 4 Feb 1865.
Later history: Merchant *Wamsutta* 1865. Converted to barge 1879.

Name	Builder	Launched	Acquired	Comm.
Western World	Greenpoint, N.Y. (W.Collyer)	1856	21 Sep 1861	3 Jan 1862
Tonnage	441 tons B			
Dimensions	178' × 34'3" × 8'6"			
Machinery	1 screw, 1 vertical direct-acting engine (34" × 2'10"), 7 knots (Allaire)			
Complement	86			
Armament	(1862) 1–30pdr MLR, 2–32pdr/57; (Feb 1863) add 2–32pdr/47			

Service record: SAtlBS 1862. Engagement in Wilmington Narrows, N.C., 26–28 Jan 1862. NAtlBS Mar 1863. Operated off Virginia coast and Chesapeake Bay. Expedition to White House, Va., Pamunkey River, 23–30 Jun 1863. Potomac Flotilla Feb 1864. NAtlBS Nov 1864–May 1865. Decomm 26 May 1865. Sold 24 Jun 1865.
Ships captured: *Volante*, 2 Jul 1862; *A.Carson, Martha Ann*, 24 Dec 1863.
Later history: Merchant *Petersburg* 1865. Converted to barge 1880.

Name	Builder	Launched	Acquired	Comm.
Whitehead	New Brunswick, N.J.	1861	17 Oct 1861	19 Nov 1861
Tonnage	132 tons D			
Dimensions	93' × 19'9" × 8'			
Machinery	1 screw, 2 inclined engines, 1 boiler			
Complement	45			
Armament	(Jan 1862) 1–9" SB; (May 1863) 1–100pdr MLR, 3–24pdr H			

Service record: NAtlBS 1861–62. Engagement with CSS *Patrick Henry* near Newport News, 2 Dec 1861. Landings at Roanoke Island, N.C., 7–8 Feb 1862. Engagement with enemy vessels, capture of Elizabeth City, N.C. and expedition to Edenton, N.C., 10–12 Feb 1862. Reconnaissance to Winton, N.C., Chowan River, 18–20 Feb 1862. Expedition to block Chesapeake and Albemarle Canal, 23 Apr 1862. Operations at Franklin, Va., 3 Oct 1862. Expeditions in Chowan River, 26–30 Jul 1863 and 1–2 Mar 1864. Engagement with CSS *Albemarle* at Plymouth, N.C., 5 May 1864. Capture of Plymouth, Roanoke River, 29–31 Oct 1864. Decomm 29 Jun 1865. Sold 10 Aug 1865.
Ships captured: *America, Comet, J.J.Crittenden*, 10 Apr 1862; *Eugenia*, 20 May 1862; *Ella D.*, 22 May 1862; str *Arrow*, 28 Jul 1864.
Later history: Merchant *Nevada* 1865. Destroyed by fire at New London, Conn., 1 Sep 1872.

4
SERVICE VESSELS

SIDE-WHEEL AUXILIARIES (FOURTH RATE)

Name	Builder	Launched	Acquired	Comm.
Baltimore	Philadelphia, Pa.	1848	22 Apr 1861	Apr 1861
Tonnage	500 tons B			
Dimensions	200' × 26'8" × d10'			
Machinery	Side wheels			
Complement	18			
Armament	1–32pdr/42			

Note: Captured as Confederate steamer in Potomac River, 21 Apr 1861. Wood hull.
Service record: Ordnance vessel, Washington NYd NYd. Transported President Lincoln and party to Norfolk, 9 May 1862. Sold 24 Jun 1865.
Later history: Merchant *Baltimore* 1865. Lost 1866. RR 1868.

Name	Builder	Launched	Acquired	Comm.
Cactus	Brooklyn, N.Y.	1863	9 Dec 1863	4 May 1864
ex-*Polar Star*				
Tonnage	176 tons B			
Dimensions	110' × 22'6" × 7'			
Machinery	Side wheels, 1 LP engine (31" × 7'), 8 knots			
Complement	39			
Armament	1–30pdrMLR MLR, 1–12pdrMLR MLR, 1–12pdrSB SB			

Service record: NAtlBS 1864. Supply ship. Decomm 8 Jun 1865.
Later history: To U.S. Lighthouse Board, 20 Jun 1865, sold 1910. Merchant *Prospect* 1910. RR 1921

Name	Builder	Launched	Acquired	Comm.
Chatham	Fayetteville, N.C.	1852	Dec 1863	22 Jun 1864
Tonnage	198 tons B			
Dimensions	120' × 26' × 7'7"			
Machinery	Side wheels			
Complement	26			
Armament	None			

Notes: Confederate vessel, captured in Doboy Sound by USS *Huron*, 16 Dec 1863. Probably the iron hull ship built by Laird in England 1836 and reassembled in Savannah.
Service record: SAtlBS 1864. Transport, store vessel, Port Royal. Decomm Apr 1865. Sold 2 Sep 1865.
Later history: Merchant *Chatham* 1865. RR 1868.

Name	Builder	Launched	Acquired	Comm.
Darlington	Charleston, S.C.	1849	3 Mar 1862	Mar 1862
Tonnage	298 tons			
Dimensions	132'6" × 30' × d8'4"			
Machinery	Side wheels, 1 horizontal crosshead HP engine			
Complement	23			
Armament	2–24pdr H			

Notes: Captured in Cumberland Sound, Ga., by USS *Pawnee*, 3 Mar 1862. Wood hull.
Service record: Expedition to St. Johns Bluff, Fla., 1–12 Oct, and to Pocotaligo, S.C., 21–23 Oct 1962. Transferred to War Dept, Sep 1862.
Later history: Merchant *Darlington* 1866. BU 1874.

Name	Builder	Launched	Acquired	Comm.
Donegal	Wilmington, Del. (Harlan)	1860	1864	3 Sep 1864
ex-*Donegal*, ex-*Austin*				
Tonnage	1,150 tons B, 951 n/r			
Dimensions	206' × 36' × 8', d10'6"			
Machinery	Side wheels, 1 vertical beam engine (44" × 11'), 1 boiler, 10 knots (Bldr)			
Complement	80/130			
Armament	2–20pdr MLR, 2–12pdr SB			

Notes: Blockade runner, captured off Mobile by USS *Metacomet*, 6 Jun 1864. Iron hull, two masts, one funnel. Built for Charles Morgan's New Orleans–Galveston service.
Service record: Supply ship, SAtlBS 1864. Blockade duty 1865. Decomm 8 Sep, sold 27 Sep 1865.

Later history: Merchant *Austin* 1865. Struck a wreck in Mississippi River below New Orleans and sank, 6 Jun 1876.

Name	Builder	Launched	Acquired	Comm.
Ella	New York, N.Y.	1859	30 Jul 1862	10 Aug 1862
Tonnage	230 tons B			
Dimensions	150′ × 23′ × d8′6″			
Machinery	Side wheels, 1-cyl. engine (36″ × 8′), 8 knots			
Complement	39			
Armament	(1862) 2-24pdr H ; (May 1863) 1-12 pdrSB H, 1-12 pdrH R			

Notes: Wood hull.
Service record: Potomac Flotilla, picket, dispatch boat, 1862-65. Decomm 4 Aug 1865. Sold 15 Sep 1865.
Later history: Merchant *Ella*, 1865. RR 1875.

Name	Builder	Launched	Acquired	Comm.
Eugenie	Hull, England (Samuelson)	9 Jul 1861	1863	9 Jul 1863
Tonnage	252 tons B, 428 GRT			
Dimensions	235;′ x 24;3″ x 6′0″, d11′9″			
Machinery	Side wheels, 2 oscillating engines, 9.5 knots			
Complement	(U)			
Armament	1-12pdr H, 1-12pdr MLR; (Feb 1863) none; (Dec 1865) 1-20pdr MLR, 1-12pdr			

Notes: Blockade runner captured by USS *R.R. Cuyler* off Mobile Bay, 6 May 1863. South Eastern Railway cross-channel steamer. Renamed *Glasgow* 21 Jan 1864.
Service record: WGulfBS, dispatch, supply ship, 1863. Sank after hitting a submerged obstruction off Mobile, 8 May 1865; raised 19 Jun. Store ship, 1866-68. Decomm 17 Oct 1868. Sold 4 Jun 1869.
Later history: British merchant *Hilda*, 1869. BU 1889.

Name	Builder	Launched	Acquired	Comm.
Honduras	New York, N.Y. (Collyer)	22 May 1861	31 Jul 1863	8 Sep 1863
Tonnage	376 tons B			
Dimensions	150′ (dk) × 27′ × 9′, d10′2″			
Machinery	Side wheels, 1 vertical beam engine (38″ × 8′), 1 boiler, 7 knots (Neptune)			
Complement	57			
Armament	1–20Pdr MLR, 2–24pdr H, 2–12pdr MLR			

Notes: Wood, two masts. Schooner rig.
Service record: EGulfBS 1863. Supply ship, dispatch boat. Occupation of Tampa, Fla., 4–7 May 1864. Expedition to St. Marks, Fla., 23 Feb–27 Mar 1865. Sold 5 Sep 1865.
Ship captured: str *Mail*, 15 Oct 1863.
Later history: Merchant *Governor Marvin* 1865. Wrecked off Key West, Fla., 1870.

Name	Builder	Launched	Acquired	Comm.
Ice Boat	Kensington, Pa.	1837	23 Apr 1861	23 Apr 1861
ex-*Philadelphia Ice Boat*				
Tonnage	526 tons			
Dimensions	(U)			
Machinery	Side wheels			
Complement	50			
Armament	4–32pdr			

Fig 4.1: The USS *Honduras* was used principally as a supply ship for the East Gulf Blockading Squadron. (U.S. Naval Historical Center)

Notes: Icebreaker. Loaned by City of Philadelphia.
Service record: Served in area of Washington, D.C., Chesapeake Bay, 1861. Returned to Philadelphia, Nov 1861.

Name	Builder	Launched	Acquired	Comm.
King Philip	Baltimore, Md. (Robinson)	1845	21 Apr 1861	28 Apr 1861
ex-*Powhatan*				
Tonnage	309 tons B			
Dimensions	204′ × 22′11″ × d8′			
Machinery	Side wheels			
Complement	14			
Armament	1 gun			

Note: Renamed 4 Nov 1861.
Service record: Dispatch vessel in Potomac and Rappahannock Rivers, 1861–65. Sold 15 Sep 1865.
Later history: FFU

Name	Builder	Launched	Acquired	Comm.
Philadelphia	Chester, Pa. (Reaney Neafie)	25 Oct 1859	22 Apr 1861	Apr 1861
Tonnage	504 tons B			
Dimensions	200′ × 30′ × 7′6″, d10′			
Machinery	Side wheels, 1 vertical beam engine (45″ × 11′), 1 boiler. 8 knots (bldr)			
Complement	24			
Armament	2–12pdr MLR			

Note: Iron hull. Built for service between Norfolk and Baltimore.
Service record: Operated in Potomac area as transport ferry. NAtlBS Oct 1861–62. Capture of New Berne, N.C., 13–14 Mar 1862. SAtlBS Aug 1863–65 (flagship). Decomm 31 Aug 1865. Sold 15 Sep 1865.
Later history: Merchant *Philadelphia* 1865; renamed *Ironsides*, 1869. Stranded at Hog Island, Va., 29 Aug 1873.

Name	Builder	Launched	Acquired	Comm.
Phlox	Boston, Mass.	1864	2 Aug 1864	14 Sep 1864
ex-*F.W. Lincoln*				

Tonnage	317 tons B
Dimensions	145' × 24' × 6', d9
Machinery	Side wheels, 1 overhead beam engine (28" × 7'6"), 1 boiler. 12 knots
Complement	32
Armament	(U)

Notes: Wood hull.
Service record: NAtlBS 1864. Used as dispatch vessel. Decomm 28 Jul 1865. Practice ship, Naval Academy.†

Name	Builder	Launched	Acquired	Comm.
Wyandank	New York, N.Y. (Simonson)	1847	12 Sep 1861	1861

Tonnage	399 tons D
Dimensions	132'5" × 31'5" × d10'10"
Machinery	Side wheels
Complement	45
Armament	(1861) 2–12pdr SB; (Jul 1865) 1–20pdr MLR, 1–12pd SB

Notes: Wood hull ferry. Storeship.
Service record: *Wyandank*: Potomac flotilla storeship, 1861–65. Floating barracks, Annapolis. BU 1879.
Ships captured: *Rising Sun*, 5 Sep 1862; *Southerner*, 22 Sep 1862; *Thomas C. Worrell*, 24 Feb 1863; *A.W.Thompson*, *Vista*, 28 Feb 1863; *Champanero*, 14 Mar 1865.

SCREW AUXILIARIES (FOURTH RATE)

Name	Builder	Launched	Acquired	Comm.
Admiral	Fairhaven, Conn. (Pook)	1863	8 Jan 1864	5 Feb 1864

Tonnage	1,248 tons B
Dimensions	220' (U) 209' (U) × 34'6" × 14', d10'6"
Machinery	1 screw, 2 vertical direct-acting engines (36" × 3'), 1 boiler
Complement	(U)
Armament	1–30pdr MLR, 1–12pdr MLR, 2–24pdr H

Notes: Wood hull, one funnel, two masts.
Service record: Storeship, GulfBS 1864–65. Renamed **Fort Morgan**, 1 Sep 1864. Decomm 22 Aug 1865. Sold 5 Sep 1865.
Ships captured: str *Ysabel*, 28 May 1864; *John A. Hazard*, 5 Nov 1864; *Lone*, 5 Nov 1864.
Later history: Merchant *Cuba* 1865. Reported fitting out as a Fenian privateer 1866. Converted to schooner 1879. RR 1892.

Name	Builder	Launched	Acquired	Comm.
Arethusa	Philadelphia, Pa.	1864	1 Jul 1864	29 Jul 1864
ex-*Wabash*				

Tonnage	195 tons B
Dimensions	110' × 22' × 8'8"
Machinery	1 screw, 1 direct-acting engine (34" × 2'6") (Neafie)
Complement	32
Armament	2–12pdr SB; (Dec 1864) add 1–20pdrR

Service record: SAtlBS 1864. Collier, Port Royal, S.C. Decomm, sold 3 Jan 1866.
Later history: FFU

Name	Builder	Launched	Acquired	Comm.
Arkansas	Philadelphia, Pa. (Cramp)	1863	27 Jun 1863	29 Jun 1863
ex-*Tonawanda*				

Tonnage	752 tons B
Dimensions	191' ( ) 176' (bp) × 29'6" × 14', d19'
Machinery	1 screw, 1 vertical direct-acting engine (40" × 2'6"), 15 knots
Complement	88
Armament	4–32pdr/33, 1–12pdr MLR; (Oct 1863) add 1–20pdr MLR

Note: Transport, tug. Barkentine rig, wood hull.
Service record: WGulfBS 1863–65. Decomm 30 Jun 1865. Sold 20 Jul 1865.
Ship captured: *Watchful*, 27 Sep 1864.
Later history: Merchant *Tonawanda* 1865. Wrecked off Grecian Shoals, Florida, 28 Mar 1866.

Name	Builder	Launched	Acquired	Comm.
Bermuda	Stockton, England (Pearse)	9 Jul 1861	14 Oct 1862	13 May 1863

Tonnage	1,238 tons B, 1,003 tons GRT
Dimensions	211' × 30'3" × 16'8", d21'2"
Machinery	1 screw, 2-cyl. vertical direct-acting engine (45" × 2'6"), 2 boilers, 11 knots. (Frossick)
Complement	(U)
Armament	1–9" SB, 2–30pdr MLR

Notes: Supply ship. Blockade runner, captured off Grand Abaco Island by USS *Mercedita*, 27 Apr 1862. Iron hull.
Service record: WGulfBS 1863–65. Sold 21 Sep 1865.
Ships captured: *Carmita*, 14 Aug 1863; *Artist*, 15 Aug 1863; *Florrie*, 2 Oct 1863; *Mary Campbell*, 14 Nov 1863; *Fortunate, 30 May 1864.
Later history: Merchant *General Meade* 1865; renamed *Bahamas* 1878 Foundered in hurricane 500 miles southeast of New York, 10 Feb 1882.

Name	Builder	Launched	Acquired	Comm.
Circassian	Belfast, Ireland (Hickson)	18 Jul 1856	8 Nov 1862	12 Dec 1862

Tonnage	1,750 tons B, 1,457 n/r, 1,387 GRT
Dimensions	255' (Br) 241' (bp) × 39' × 18', d23'6"
Machinery	1 screw, geared beam engine (60" × 4'), 2 boilers, NHP 350, 10 knots. (Elder)
Complement	142
Armament	4–9" SB, 1–100pdr MLR, 1–12pdr MLR; (Jan 1864) add 1–30pdr MLR

Notes: Blockade runner, captured off Cuba by USS *Somerset*, 4 May 1862. Iron hull, three masts, funnel aft of mainmast. Too slow. Built for North Atlantic Steam Nav. Co. (Galway Line), used as a transport during the Sepoy Mutiny, 1857.
Service record: EandWGulfBS 1863–65, supply ship. Decomm 26 Apr 1865. Sold 22 Jun 1865.
Ships captured: *John Wesley*, 16 Jan 1863; str *Minna*, 9 Dec 1863.
Later history: Merchant *Circassian* 1865. Converted to full-rigged ship 1873. Wrecked in gale at Bridgehampton, Long Island, 11 Dec 1876.

Name	Builder	Launched	Acquired	Comm.
Fahkee	Greenpoint, N.Y. (Williams)	4 Nov 1862	15 Jul 1863	24 Sep 1863

Tonnage	660 tons B, 601 n/r
Dimensions	175' (dk) 163' (U) × 29'6" × 13'3", d18'

Machinery   1 screw, 1 vertical direct-acting engine (36″ × 4′), 1 boiler. 7 knots (Pusey)
Complement   73
Armament   2-24pdr H, 1-10pdr MLR. (Feb1864) add 2-24pdr H

Note: Built for China trade. Wood hull, hermaphrodite brig, 1 one funnel.

Service record: NAtlBS 1863–65, Supply ship. SAtlBS Apr 1865. Decomm 28 Jun 1865. Sold 10 Aug 1865.

Ship captured: str *Bendigo*, 3 Jan 1864.

Later history: Merchant *Fahkee*. Canadian *Pictou* 1872. Probably burned and sank off Magdalen Island, Quebec, 18 Nov 1873.

Name	Builder	Launched	Acquired	Comm.
Home	Brooklyn, N.Y. (Tucker)	1862	14 Aug 1863	21 Aug 1863

ex-*Key West*

Tonnage   725 tons B, 618 n/r
Dimensions   168′10″ (dk) × 29′9″ × 13′6″ or 10′
Machinery   1 screw, 2-cyl. horizontal direct-acting engine (32″ × 2′2″), 2 boilers, 6 knots (McLeod)
Complement   88
Armament   2-24pdr H, 1-12pdr HR

Notes: Wood hull.

Service record: SAtlBS 1863. Accommodation ship for monitors, Charleston. Decomm 24 Aug 1865. Sold Sep 16 Sep 1865.

Later history: Merchant *Key West* 1865. Wrecked off Cape Hatteras, N.C., 12 Oct 1870.

Name	Builder	Launched	Acquired	Comm.
Kensington	Philadelphia, Pa. (Lynn)	1858	27 Jan 1862	15 Feb 1862

Tonnage   1,052 tons B, 1,003 n/r
Dimensions   195′ × 31′10″ × 18′
Machinery   1 screw, 1 vertical direct-acting engine (56″ × 3′8″), 1 boiler, 10 knots. (Merrick)
Complement   72
Armament   2-32pdr/42, 1-30pdr MLR

Note: Wood hull. Operated between Philadelphia and Boston.

Service record: WGulfBS 1862–63. Supply, water vessel. Bombardment of Sabine Pass, 24–25 Sep 1863. NAtlBS Aug–Nov 1864, supply ship. Decomm 5 May 1865. Sold 12 Jul 1865.

Ships captured: *Troy*, 13 Aug 1862; *Velocity*,* 30 Sep 1862; *Adventure*, 1 Oct 1862; *Dart*, 6 Oct 1862; *Conchita*, *Mary Ann*, *Eliza*, str *Dan*, Oct 1862; *Course*, 11 Nov 1862; *Maria*, 12 Nov 1862.

Later history: Merchant *Kensington* 1865. Sunk in collision with Argentine bark *Templar* off Carolina coast, 27 Jan 1871.

Name	Builder	Launched	Acquired	Comm.
Mary Sanford	Mystic, Conn. (Mallory)	1862	13 Jul 1863	20 Aug 1863

Tonnage   757 tons B, 442 n/r
Dimensions   162′ × 31′6″ × 12′6″, d16′9″
Machinery   1 screw, 2-cyl. direct-acting engine (26″ × 2′6″), 1 boiler, 9 knots (Reliance)
Complement   60

---

* Later USS *Velocity*.

Armament   2-24pdr; (Mar 1864) 2-12pdr MLR, 3-24pdr

Notes: Wood hull.

Service record: SAtlBS 1863–65. Transport, freight ship. Expedition to Murrells Inlet, S.C., 29 Dec 1863–1 Jan 1864. Blockade of Charleston 1864. Decomm 21 Jun 1865. Sold 13 Jul 1865.

Later history: Merchant *Mary Sanford* 1865. Wrecked off Cape Hatteras, 13 Nov 1871.

Name	Builder	Launched	Acquired	Comm.
New Berne	New York, N.Y. (Poillon)	1 Jul 1862	27 Jun 1863	15 Aug 1863

ex-*United States*

Tonnage   978 tons B
Dimensions   202′ (dk) 195′ (U) × 32′ × 13′6″
Machinery   1 screw, 2-cyl. vertical inverted direct-acting engine (36″ × 3′), 1 boiler, 13 knots (Delamater)
Complement   92
Armament   2-24pdr, 2-12pdr MLR; (Aug 1863) 1-30pdr MLR, 4-24pdr, 1-12pdr MLR; (Jul 1864) less 1-30pdr MLR

Notes: Iron strapped hull, brigantine rig.

Service record: NAtlBS 1863, supply ship. Decomm 29 Mar 1868. Transferred to War Dept, 1 Dec 1868.

Ships captured: str *Pevensey*, 9 Jun 1864; *G.O. Bigelow*, 16 Dec 1864.

Later history: Merchant *Newbern*. Wrecked north of San Pedro, Cal., 14 Oct 1894.

Name	Builder	Launched	Acquired	Comm.
Queen	New York, N.Y. (Novelty)	1861	29 Sep 1863	15 Aug 1863

ex-*Victory*, ex-*T.D. Wagner*, ex-*Julie Usher*, ex-*Annie Childs*, ex-*North Carolina*

Tonnage   618 tons B, 554 n/r
Dimensions   172′ (dk) 168′8″ (wl) × 28′4″ × 9′11″, d13′6″
Machinery   1 screw, 1 vertical inverted direct-acting engine (42″ × 3′6″), 1 boiler (bldr)
Complement   83
Armament   3-32pdr/51, 1-12pdr MLR; (Dec 1863) 4-32pdr/51, 1-20pdr MLR, 2-12pdr

Notes: Blockade runner *Victory*, captured off Eleuthera Island by USS *Santiago de Cuba*, 21 Jun 1863. Iron hull, two-mast schooner. Operated between New York and Wilmington, seized there in 1861.

Service record: Transport, supply ship. Decomm 21 Jun 1865. Sold 16 Oct 1865.

Ship captured: *Louisa*, 11 Feb 1864.

Later history: Merchant *Gulf Stream* 1865. Lengthened 1874. Wrecked in gale and fog near Hartford Inlet, N.J., 30 Jan 1903.

Name	Builder	Launched	Acquired	Comm.
Trefoil	Boston, Mass. (McKay)	1864	4 Feb 1865	1 Mar 1865
Yucca	Boston, Mass. (McKay)	1864	25 Feb 1865	3 Apr 1865

Tonnage   373 tons B
Dimensions   145′7″ × 23′7″ × 11′3″
Machinery   1 screw, 2 engines, 2 boilers
Complement   44
Armament   1-30pdr MLR, 1-12pdr SB

Notes: Wood hull steamers acquired new.

Service records

Trefoil: WGulfBS 1865, dispatch boat. Decomm 30 Aug 1865. Sold 28 May 1867.

Later history: Merchant *Gen. H.E. Paine* 1867. Stranded at Grand Haven, Mich. in storm, 19 Nov 1879.

Yucca: Gulf Stn 1865–68. Sold 26 Aug 1868.

Later history: Merchant *Yucca* 1868. Mexican *Union* 1870.

Name	Builder	Launched	Acquired	Comm.
Union	Mystic, Conn. (Mallory)	9 Aug 1862	24 Apr 1861	16 May 1861
Tonnage	1,114 tons B			
Dimensions	219'6" (dk) × 34' × 16', d23'			
Machinery	1 screw, 2 vertical direct-acting engines (36" × 3'), 2 boilers, 13.5 knots (Delamater)			
Complement	75			
Armament	1–12pdr MLR; (Nov 1863) 1–20pdr MLR			

Notes: Brigantine rig. Chartered, then purchased after commissioning. Wood hull.

Service record: AtlBS 1861. Damaged in collision with Spanish ship *Plus Ultra*, 2 Jul 1861. Forced Confederate privateer *York* aground off Cape Hatteras, 9 Aug 1861. Potomac Flotilla Aug 1861. Out of commission 1862. Dispatch, supply vessel to Gulf of Mexico 1863. Decomm 29 Sep 1865. Sold 25 Oct 1865.

Ships captured: *F.W. Johnson*, 1 Jan 1861; *Hallie Jackson*, 10 Jun 1861; *Amelia*, 18 Jun 1861; *B.F. Martin*, 28 Jul 1861; *Linnet*, 21 May 1863; str *Spaulding*, 11 Oct 1863; str *Mayflower*, 14 Jan 1864; *O.K.*, 27 Apr 1864; *Caroline*, 10 Jun 1864..

Later history: Merchant *Missouri* 1865. Burned and sank northeast of Abaco Island, Bahamas, 22 Oct 1872.

Yucca, see *Trefoil*.

TUGS

Navy-Built Steam Tugs

Fortune Class

Name	Builder	Launched	Comm.
Fortune	Boston, Mass. (Tetlow)	23 Mar 1865	19 May 1871
Leyden	Boston, Mass. (Tetlow)	1865	1865
Mayflower	Boston, Mass. (Tetlow)	1865	Feb 1866
Nina	Chester, Pa. (Reaney)	27 May 1865	30 Sep 1865
Palos	Boston, Mass. (Tetlow)	1864	11 Jun 1870
Pinta	Chester, Pa. (Reaney)	29 Oct 1864	Oct 1865
Speedwell	Boston, Mass. (Tetlow)	1865	13 Nov 1865
Standish	Boston, Mass. (Tetlow)	26 Oct 1864	1865
Triana	Williamsburg, N.Y. (Perine)	29 Apr 1865	25 Oct 1865
Tonnage	420 tons D. 350 tons B		
Dimensions	137' (oa) × 26' × 9'6"		
Machinery	1 screw, vertical compound engines, 10 knots (*Nina*, *Pinta*: bldr)		
Complement	52		
Armament	2–3pdr		

Notes: *Palos* converted to gunboat for service in China, 1870 and was first U.S. warship to transit the Suez Canal. *Fortune* and *Triana* fitted as experimental torpedo boats. Iron hulls.

Service records

Fortune: Various duties on East Coast 1871–91. Converted to spar torpedo boat 1871.†

Leyden: Yard tug Boston 1866–79, Portsmouth 1879–97 and Newport 1897.†

Mayflower: Survey expedition to Tehuantepec, Mexico 1870. Dispatch boat, Portsmouth 1872. Training ship Annapolis 1876.†

Nina: Yard tug Washington ,NYd 1866–71. Yard 1883.†

Palos: Yard tug Boston 1866–69. First U.S. naval vessel to run on oil fuel, May–Jun 1867. Converted to gunboat 1870. First USN ship to transit Suez Canal, Aug 1870. Asiatic Station 1871–93. Fired upon by a Korean fort, 1 Jun 1871. Korean Expedition 1871.†

Pinta: Yard tug Philadelphia.†

Speedwell: Yard tug Portsmouth 1866–76, and Washington, then Norfolk.†

Standish: Yard tug Norfolk 1871–79, then Newport. Practice ship and station tug, Annapolis until 1921.†

Triana: Yard tug Washington 1867. Converted to spar torpedo boat 1871.†

Maria Class

Name	Builder	Launched	Comm.
Maria	Williamsburg, N.Y. (Perine)	1864	11 Apr 1865
Pilgrim	Wilmington, Del. (Pusey)	1 Nov 1864	2 Mar 1865
Tonnage	170 tons		
Dimensions	(U) × (U) × 6'		
Machinery	1 screw, vertical inverted engine, 12 knots		

Notes: Iron hulls

Service record

Maria: Sunk in collision with monitor *Miantonomoh* off Martha's Vineyard, 4 Jan 1870.

Pilgrim:†

Blue Light Class

Name	Builder	Launched
Blue Light	Portsmouth NYd	27 Feb 1864
Port Fire	Portsmouth NYd	8 Mar 1864
Tonnage	103 tons	
Machinery	1 vertical inverted engine, 1 screw	

Notes: Powder tugs.

Service record

Blue Light: Boston NYd 1864–70. Washington NYd 1871–73. New London 1874–75. Sold 27 Sep 1883.

Port Fire: Sold Jan 1878 and BU.

ACQUIRED SIDE-WHEEL TUGS

Name	Builder	Launched	Acquired	Comm.
Columbine	New York, N.Y.	1850	12 Dec 1862	1862
ex-*A.H. Schultz*				
Tonnage	133 tons B			
Dimensions	117' × 20'7" × d6'2"			
Machinery	Side wheels			

Fig 4.2: USS *Pinta* in Juneau harbor, 1889. Built as a tug, she was converted for service in Alaska in 1881. (U.S. Naval Historical Center)

Complement 25
Armament 2–20pdr MLR

Notes: Former identity of this ship questionable. (See CSS *Schultz*, p 185)

Service record: SAtlBS 1863–64. Assault on Jacksonville, Fla., 2–22 Feb 1864. EGulfBS 1864–65. Expedition up St. Johns River, 9–12 Mar 1864. Ran aground and captured in St. Johns River, 23 May 1864.

Name	Builder	Launched	Acquired	Comm.
Daffodil	Keyport, N.J. (Terry)	1862	17 Nov 1862	Nov 1862

ex-*Jonas Smith*

Tonnage	173 tons B
Dimensions	110′6″ × 22′6″ × 5′6″
Machinery	Side wheels, 1 beam engine (30″ × 6′), 1 boiler. 8 knots
Complement	28/35
Armament	2–20pdr MLR

Service record: SAtlBS 1862. Port Royal, S.C. 1862–65. Expedition to Murrells Inlet, S.C., 29 Dec 1863–1 Jan 1864 and in Broad River, S.C., 27 Nov–30 Dec 1864. Engaged batteries in Togodo Creek, S.C., 9 Feb 1865. NAtlSqn 1865. Sold 13 Mar 1867.

Ships captured: *Wonder*, 13 May 1863; str *General Sumter*, 12 Mar 1864; str *Hattie Brock*, 14 Mar 1864.

Later history: Merchant *Aaron Wilbur* 1867. U.S. Lighthouse Board 1871, renamed *Arbutus*. Merchant *Cora* 1875. RR 1880.

Name	Builder	Launched	Acquired	Comm.
Ellis	Wilmington, Del.	1860	19 May 1862	Apr 1862

ex-CSS *Ellis*, ex-*Fairfield*

Tonnage	100 tons
Dimensions	(U) × (U) × 6′
Machinery	Side wheels
Complement	28
Armament	2 guns

Notes: Confederate armed tug, captured by the Army at Elizabeth City, N.C., 10 Feb 1862.

Service record: NAtlBS 1862. Capture of Ft. Macon, N.C., 25–26 Apr 1862. Expedition to Swansboro, N.C., 15–19 Aug 1862. Ran aground in New River Inlet during attack on Jacksonville, N.C., and destroyed to prevent capture, 25 Nov 1862.

Ship captured: *Adelaide, 22 Oct 1862.

Name	Builder	Launched	Acquired	Comm.
Geranium	Newburgh, N.Y.	1863	5 Sep 1863	15 Oct 1863

ex-*John A. Dix*

Tonnage	224 tons B
Dimensions	128′6″ × 23′3″ × 5′, d8′
Machinery	Side wheels, 1 beam engine (34″ × 8′), 1 boiler, 10 knots
Complement	39/45
Armament	1–20pdr MLR, 2–12pdr MLR; (Mar 1865) 2–20pdr MLR, 1–24pdr H, 1–12pdr MLR

Service record: SAtlBS 1863. Expedition up Stono and Folly Rivers, S.C., 9–14 Feb 1865. Operations at Bull's Bay, S.C., February 1865. Decomm 15 Jul 1865.

Later history: To U.S. Lighthouse Board, 18 Oct 1865. Sold 1910.

Name	Builder	Launched	Acquired	Comm.
Heliotrope	(U)	(U)	16 Dec 1863	24 Apr 1864

ex-*Maggie Baker*

Tonnage	238 tons B
Dimensions	134′ × 24′6″ × 5′

Machinery   Side wheels, 1 inclined engine (28" × 4'), 6 knots
Complement 24/66
Armament   1-12pdr H; (Apr 1865) 1-30pdr MLR, 2-12pdr MLR

Notes: Wood hull.
Service record: NAtlBS 1864, tug and ordnance boat. Expedition up Rappahannock River, 6–8 Mar 1865, and up Mattox Creek, Va., 16–18 Mar 1865.
Later history: To U.S. Lighthouse Board, 17 Jun 1865. Merchant barge *John Bolgiano*. SE 1893.

Name	Builder	Launched	Acquired	Comm.
Hollyhock ex-*Reliance*	(U)	(U)	5 Mar 1863	Mar 1863

Tonnage   352 tons B
Dimensions 135' × 26'9" × 7', d11'
Machinery   Side wheels, 2-cyl. engine, 14 knots
Complement 42
Armament   1-20pdr MLR, 2-12pdr H

Notes: Captured by USS *Huntsville* in Bahama Channel, 21 Jul 1862. Renamed Jul 1863.
Service record: Tender and supply ship at New Orleans, 1863–65. Sold 5 Oct 1865.
Later history: Merchant *Hollyhock* 1865. RR 1868.

Name	Builder	Launched	Acquired	Comm.
Ida	Gretna, La.	1860	3 Feb 1863	1863

Tonnage   104 tons B
Dimensions (U)
Machinery   Side wheels
Armament   1 gun

Service record: Mortar Flotilla, Mississippi River 1863. Supported operations in Mobile Bay 1865. Sunk by torpedo (mine) in Blakely River, Ala., 13 Apr 1865. Raised and sold, 23 Sep 1865.

Name	Builder	Launched	Acquired	Comm.
Island Belle	Keyport, N.J. (Terry)	1855	4 Sep 1861	Sep 1861

Tonnage   123 tons B
Dimensions 100' × 20'4" × d6'7"
Machinery   Side wheels
Complement 24
Armament   1-32pdr/27, 1-12pdr MLR

Note: Tug and dispatch boat.
Service record: Potomac Flotilla 1861–62. Tug and dispatch boat. Bombardment at Mathias Point, Va., 12 Oct 1861. Expedition in Rappahannock River, Tappahannock, Va., 13–15 Apr 1862. NAtlBS 1862. Burned to prevent capture after it ran aground in Appomattox River, 27 Jun 1862.

Name	Builder	Launched	Acquired	Comm.
O.M. Pettit	Williamsburg, N.Y.	1857	17 Aug 1861	4 Oct 1861

Tonnage   165 tons B
Dimensions 106' × 24'4" × 6'
Machinery   Side wheels, 8 knots
Complement 30
Armament   1-30pdr MLR, 1-20pdr MLR

Service record: SAtlBS 1862–65. Sold 2 Sep 1865.
Later history: Merchant *Oliver M. Pettit*, 1865. RR 1879.

Name	Builder	Launched	Acquired	Comm.
Oleander	Keyport, N.J. (Terry)	10 Jan 1863	28 Mar 1863	Apr 1863

Tonnage   263 tons B
Dimensions 144'10" × 22'6" × 6'
Machinery   Side wheels, 1 vertical beam engine (36" × 7'), 1 boiler, 11 knots
Complement 35
Armament   2-20pdr MLR

Notes: Purchased prior to completion.
Service record: SAtlBS 1863–65. Bombardment of New Smyrna, Fla., 28 Jul 1863. Assault on Jacksonville, Fla., 2–22 Feb 1864. Decomm 18 Aug 1865. Sold 5 Sep 1865.
Later history: Merchant *Annie*, 1865. Burned at Point Clear, Ala., 19 Apr 1881.

Name	Builder	Launched	Acquired	Comm.
Yankee	New York, N.Y.	1860	1 Jun 1861	Apr 1861

Tonnage   329 tons B
Dimensions 146' × 25'7" × d9'7"
Machinery   Side wheels
Complement 48
Armament   2-32pdr/33; (Apr 1863) 1-50pdr MLR, 1-8"/55, 1-24pdr H, 1-12pdr SB

Notes: Tug chartered Apr 1861 and acquired later.
Service record: Relief of Ft. Sumter, Apr 1861. Potomac Flotilla 1861–65. Engaged batteries at Cockpit Point, Va., 1 Jan 1862. NAtlBS 1862. Operations in Nansemond River, Va., 11 Apr–4 May 1863. Decomm 16 May 1865. Sold 15 Sep 1865.
Ships captured: *Favorite*, 18 Jul 1861; **T.W. Riley* and **Jane Wright*, 16 Aug 1861; *Remittance.*, 28 Aug 1861; *J.W. Sturges*, 27 Jul 1862; *Cassandra*, 11 Jul 1863; *Nanjemoy*, 15 Jul 1863; *Clara Ann*, 1 Aug 1863.
Later history: Merchant *Yankee* 1865. Sold foreign, 1871.

ACQUIRED SCREW TUGS

Name	Builder	Launched	Acquired	Comm.
A.C. Powell	Syracuse, N.Y.	1861	3 Oct 1861	1861

Tonnage   90 tons B
Dimensions 62' × 17' × 6'5"
Machinery   1 screw, single engine (15" × 1'3"), 1 boiler, 4.5 knots
Complement 18
Armament   1-24pdr SB

Notes: Wood hull.
Service record: Potomac Flotilla 1861. James River Flotilla, Jul 1862. Renamed *Alert*, Aug 1862. Operations in Nansemond River, Va., 11 Apr–4 May 1863. Burned and sank at Norfolk NYd, 31 May 1863; salved. NAtlBS Oct 1863. James River Flotilla, May 1864. Renamed *Watch*, 2 Feb 1865. Potomac Flotilla, Apr 1865. Decomm 26 May 1865. Sold 5 Jul 1865.
Later history: Merchant *Watch* 1865. RR 1886.

Name	Builder	Launched	Acquired	Comm.
Alpha ex-*Fred Wheeler*	Philadelphia, Pa.	1863	3 Jun 1864	3 Jun 1864

Tonnage   55 tons B
Dimensions 72' × 16'6" × 7"
Machinery   1 screw, 1 vertical HP engine (18" × 1'6"), 9 knots
Complement 13
Armament   Spar torpedo

Notes: Outfitted as spar torpedo boat, 1864.

Service record: Designated *Tug No.1* or *Picket Boat No.1*. Renamed **Alpha**, Dec 1864. James River Flotilla. Sold 23 Sep 1865.
Later history: Merchant *Alpha* 1865. Burned (cause unknown), 5 Jun 1886.

Name	Builder	Launched	Acquired	Comm.
Althea	New Brunswick, N.J.	1863	9 Dec 1863	1864
ex-*Alfred A. Wotkyns*				
Tonnage	72 tons B			
Dimensions	70′ × 16′4″ × d7′			
Machinery	1 screw. 9 knots			
Complement	15			
Armament	1–12pdr SB			

Notes: Converted by Secor & Co. Fitted for spar torpedoes 1864.
Service record: NAtlBS 1864. James River. WGulfBS 1864. Sunk by torpedo (mine) in Blakely River, Ala., 12 Mar 1865 (2 dead); salved and recomm 7 Nov 1865. Decomm 25 Apr 1866. Sold 8 Dec 1866.
Later history: Merchant *Martin Kalbfleisch*, 1868. RR 1896.

Name	Builder	Launched	Acquired	Comm.
Amaranthus	Wilmington, Del. (Bishop)	1864	1 Jul 1864	12 Jul 1864
ex-*Christiana*				
Tonnage	182 tons B			
Dimensions	117′ × 21′ × d9′			
Machinery	1 screw, 1 vertical LP engine (30″ × 2′6″), 1 boiler, 9.5 knots			
Armament	3–24pdr SB			

Service record: SAtlBS 1864–65. Storeship and tug. Decomm 19 Aug 1865. Sold 5 Sep 1865.
Later history: Merchant *Christiana* 1865. RR 1900

Name	Builder	Launched	Acquired	Comm.
Anemone	Philadelphia, Pa.	1864	13 Aug 1864	14 Sep 1864
ex-*Wicaco*				
Tonnage	156 tons B			
Dimensions	99′ × 20′5″ × 11′			
Machinery	1 screw, 1 vertical LP engine (30″ × 2′2″), 1 boiler, 11 knots			
Complement	30			
Armament	2–24pdr SB, 2–12pdr SB			

Fig 4.3: The side-wheel tug *Yankee*. (Mariners Museum, Newport News, Va.)

Service record: NAtlBS 1864–65. Unsuccessful attack on Ft. Fisher, N.C., 24–25 Dec 1864. Sold 25 Oct 1865.
Later history: Merchant *Wicaco* 1865. RR 1896.

Name	Builder	Launched	Acquired	Comm.
Aster	Wilmington, Del. or Philadelphia, Pa.?	1864	25 Jul 1864	12 Aug 1864
ex-*Alice*				
Tonnage	285 tons B			
Dimensions	122′6″ × 23′ × 10′			
Machinery	1 screw, 1 vertical LP engine (40″ × 3′6″), 1 boiler			
Complement	30			
Armament	1–30pdr MLR, 2–12pdr SB			

Notes: Purchased new. Wood hull.
Service record: Ran aground at Ft. Fisher while chasing blockade runner *Annie* and destroyed to prevent capture, 8 Oct 1864.
Ship captured: str *Annie*, 7 Oct 1864.

Name	Builder	Launched	Acquired	Comm.
Azalea	Boston, Mass. (McKay)	1864	31 Mar 1864	7 Jun 1864
Tonnage	176 tons B			
Dimensions	110′ × 21′6″ × 10′			
Machinery	1 screw, 1 vertical engine (30″ × 2′8″), 9 knots			
Complement	42			
Armament	(Jun 1864) 1–30pdr MLR, 1–20pdr MLR.; (Oct 1864) 1–30pdr MLR, 1–24pdr SB			

Notes: Acquired from builder.
Service record: SAtlBS 1864–65. Blockade of Charleston and Savannah. Sold 10 Aug 1865.
Ships captured: *Pocahontas*, 8 Jul 1864; *Sarah M. Newhall*, 23 May 1865.
Later history: Merchant *Tecumseh* 1865. RR 1890.

Name	Builder	Launched	Acquired	Comm.
Belle	Philadelphia, Pa.	1864	2 Jun 1864	Jun 1864
Unit	Philadelphia, Pa.	1862	2 Jun 1864	1864
ex-*Union*				
Tonnage	56 tons			
Dimensions	62′2″ × 15′2″ × 8′			
Machinery	1 screw, HP engine, 7.5 knots			
Complement	19/24			
Armament	*Belle*: 1–12pdr MLR, 1–24pdr SB			

Note: *Belle* used as spar torpedo boat.
Service record
Belle: NAtlBS. Despatch vessel. Capture of Plymouth, N.C., 29–31 Oct 1864. Expedition up Roanoke River to Poplar Point, N.C., 9–28 Dec 1864. Sold 12 Jul 1865.
Later history: Merchant *Belle* 1865. RR 1891.
Unit: NAtlBS 1864. Hampton Roads. Sold 12 Jul 1865.
Later history: Merchant *Unit* 1865. RR 1902.

Name	Builder	Launched	Acquired	Comm.
Berberry	Philadelphia, Pa.	1864	13 Aug 1864	12 Sep 1864
ex-*Columbia*				
Tonnage	160 tons B			

Service Vessels 85

Dimensions	99'6" × 26'3" × 8'3"
Machinery	1 screw, 1 vertical direct-acting condensing engine (30" × 2'2"), 1 boiler, 5 knots
Complement	31
Armament	2–24pdr SB, 2–12pdr SB

Service record: NAtlBS 1864–65, off North Carolina. Sold 12 Jul 1865.
Later history: Merchant *Rescue* 1865. Sold foreign 1902.

Name	Builder	Launched	Acquired	Comm.
Beta	Gloucester, N.J.	1863	3 Jun 1864	1864
ex-*J.E. Bazely*				

Tonnage	50 tons
Dimensions	70' × 16' × 7'
Machinery	1 screw, 1 vertical HP engine (18" × 1'6"), 10 knots
Complement	14
Armament	(U)

Notes: Also known as *Tug No.2*.
Service record: James River. New Berne, N.C. 1864. Capture of Plymouth, N.C., Roanoke River, 29–31 Oct 1864. Sunk by torpedo (mine) in Roanoke River, 10 Dec 1864 (2 killed).

Name	Builder	Launched	Acquired	Comm.
Bignonia	Cleveland, Ohio	1863	20 Jul 1864	14 Sep 1864
ex-*Mary Grandy*				

Tonnage	321 tons B
Dimensions	130'10" × 21'2" × 10'8", d12'
Machinery	1 screw, 1 overhead LP engine (30" × 2'6"), 1 boiler, 10 knots
Complement	41/50
Armament	1–30pdr MLR, 2–12pdr SB

Service record: NAtlBS 1864–65. Sold 12 Jul 1865.
Later history: Merchant *Balize* 1865. Sold foreign 1903.

Name	Builder	Launched	Acquired	Comm.
Buckthorn	East Haddam, Conn.	1863	22 Dec 1863	7 Apr 1864
ex-*Signal*				

Tonnage	128 tons B
Dimensions	87' × 22' × d7'7"
Machinery	1 screw, 8.5 knots
Complement	(U)
Armament	1–30pdr MLR, 2–12pdr SB

Notes: One mast, could be used as a derrick.
Service record: WGulfBS 1864. Tender and dispatch vessel. Battle of Mobile Bay, 5 Aug 1864. Laid up 1868. Sold 7 Sep 1869.
Later history: Merchant *Buckthorn* 1869. RR 1900.

Name	Builder	Launched	Acquired	Comm.
Camelia	Buffalo, N.Y.	1862	17 Sep 1863	28 Nov 1863
ex-*Governor*				

Tonnage	195 tons B
Dimensions	111' × 19'10" × d11'
Machinery	1 screw, 1 overhead HP engine (30" × 2'6"), 1 boiler, 10 knots
Complement	40
Armament	2–20pdr MLR

Service record: SAtlBS 1864–65 off Charleston. Sold 15 Aug 1865.
Later history: Merchant *Camelia*, 1865. RR 1905.

Name	Builder	Launched	Acquired	Comm.
Carnation	Philadelphia, Pa. (Neafie)	1863	17 Aug 1863	20 Oct 1863
ex-*Ajax*				

Tonnage	82 tons B
Dimensions	73'6" × 17'6" × 7'6"
Machinery	1 screw, 1 overhead engine (20" × 1'8"), 1 boiler, 10 knots
Complement	19
Armament	1–20pdr MLR, 1–12pdr MLR; (Feb 1865) 1–24pdr SB, 1–12pdr MLR

Service record: SAtlBS 1863–65, South Carolina. Decomm 8 Jul 1865. Sold 10 Aug 1865.
Later history: Merchant *Edward W. Gorgas* 1865. RR 1880.

Name	Builder	Launched	Acquired	Comm.
Catalpa	Brooklyn, N.Y.	1864	29 Jun 1864	12 Jul 1864
ex-*Conqueror*				

Tonnage	191 tons B
Dimensions	105'3" × 22'2" × 9'
Machinery	1 screw, 1 vertical direct-acting condensing engine (34" × 2'6"), 1 boiler, 10 knots
Complement	37
Armament	2–24pdr, 1–12pdr SB.; (Dec 1864) add 1–12pdr MLR

Service record: SAtlBS 1864. Decomm 1 Sep 1865. Yard tug, New York.†

Name	Builder	Launched	Acquired	Comm.
Clematis	Cleveland, Ohio	1863	30 Jul 1864	14 Sep 1864
ex-*Maria Love*				

Tonnage	296 tons B
Dimensions	127' × 22' × 10'
Machinery	1 screw, 1 overhead HP engine (32" × 2'6"), 1 boiler, 12 knots
Complement	46
Armament	1–30pdr MLR, 2–12pdr SB

Service record: James River area 1864–65. Gulf Sqn 1865–66. Decomm 6 Jun 1866. Sold 26 Nov 1866.
Later history: Merchant *Clematis* 1866. Converted to schooner 1879.

Name	Builder	Launched	Acquired	Comm.
Clinton	Wilmington, Del.	1863	14 Jun 1864	1864
ex-*Lena Clinton*				

Tonnage	50 tons
Dimensions	61' ( ) 58'8" (bp) × 15'10" × 7"
Machinery	1 screw, 1 vertical engine, 1 boiler, 11 knots
Complement	16

Service record: NAtlBS 1864–65, picket boat in James River and Norfolk NYd. New York NYd 1865–70. Sold 3 Aug 1870.
Later history: Merchant *Mary Lewis,* 1870. Renamed *Milburn,* 1909. RR 1933.

Name	Builder	Launched	Acquired	Comm.
Clover	Philadelphia, Pa.	1863	11 Nov 1863	28 Nov 1863
ex-*Daisy*				

Tonnage	129 tons
Dimensions	92' × 19' × 9'
Machinery	1 screw, 1 vertical condensing engine (26" × 2'2"), 7 knots

Complement 19
Armament 1–12pdr MLR, 1–12pdr SB

Service record: SAtlBS 1864. Beaufort, N.C.. Decomm 27 Jul 1865. Sold 21 Sep 1865.
Ship captured: *Coquette*, 26 Jan 1865.
Later history: Merchant *Clover* 1865. Sold foreign 1878.

Name	Builder	Launched	Acquired	Comm.
Cohasset	Philadelphia, Pa. (Neafie)	1860	13 Sep 1861	Oct 1861

ex-*Narragansett*, ex-*E.D.Fogg*

Tonnage	100 tons
Dimensions	82′ × 18′10″ × 9′
Machinery	1 screw, 1 inverted vertical HP engine (16″ × 6′). 8 knots (Bldr)
Complement	12
Armament	1–20pdr MLR, 2–24pdr H

Service record: AtlBS 1861. Operations in Nansemond River, Va., 11 Apr–4 May 1863. Expedition up James River, 4–7 Aug 1863. Beaufort, N.C. 1864. Yard tug Boston, NYd, 1865–82 and Newport, R.I., 1882–92.†

Name	Builder	Launched	Acquired	Comm.
Crocus	Mystic, Conn	1863	31 Jul 1863	1863

ex-*Solomon Thomas*

Tonnage	122 tons
Dimensions	79′ × 18′6″ × 7′6″, d9′3″
Machinery	1 screw, LP engine, 7.5 knots
Armament	2 guns

Service record: Wrecked on Bodie's Island, N.C., 17 Aug 1863 (all saved).

Name	Builder	Launched	Acquired	Comm.
Dandelion	Philadelphia, Pa. (Winson)	1862	21 Nov 1862	Dec 1862

ex-*Antietam*

Tonnage	111 tons
Dimensions	85′9″ × 19′6″ × 7′9″
Machinery	1 screw, 1 direct-acting LP engine (27″ × 2′), 1 boiler, 9 knots
Complement	21
Armament	2–12pdr

Service record: SAtlBS 1863–65. Bombardment of Ft. McAllister, Ga., 3 Mar 1863. Bombardment of Ft. Wagner, Charleston, July–August 1863. Assault on Jacksonville, Fla., 2–22 Feb 1864. Decomm 14 Jul 1865. Sold 15 Aug 1865.
Later history: Merchant *Dandelion* 1865. Sold foreign, 1866.

Name	Builder	Launched	Acquired	Comm.
Delta	Philadelphia, Pa.	1863	3 Jun 1864	1864

ex-*Linda*

Tonnage	44 tons
Dimensions	66′ × 14′ × 7′8″
Machinery	1 screw, 1 engine (16″ × 1′4″), 1 boiler, 9 knots
Complement	4
Armament	Spar torpedo

Notes: Also known as *Tug No.4*. Renamed 27 Nov 1864. Converted to torpedo tug.

Service record: James River 1864. North Carolina coast 1865. Sold 5 Sep 1865.
Later history: Merchant *Delta* 1865. RR 1924.

Name	Builder	Launched	Acquired
Emerald	Philadelphia, Pa. (Neafie)	(U)	3 Aug 1864

ex-*Fairy*

Tonnage	50 tons
Dimensions	58′ × 14′ × d6′
Machinery	1 screw, 12.5 knots

Notes: Yacht. Not comm.
Service record: Ferry at Portsmouth, NYd 1864–83. Sold 1883.

Name	Builder	Launched	Acquired	Comm.
Epsilon	Philadelphia, Pa.	1864	3 Jun 1864	1864

ex-*Harry Bumm*

Tonnage	51 tons
Dimensions	66′ × 15′ × 7′6″
Machinery	1 screw, 1 HP direct-acting engine (17″ × 1′5″), 1 boiler, 3 knots
Complement	10
Armament	None

Notes: Also known as *Tug No.5*. Renamed Nov 1864.
Service record: James River, 1864–65. Sold 12 Jul 1865.
Later history: Merchant *Epsilon* 1865. Exploded and sank at New York, 27 May 1872.

Name	Builder	Launched	Acquired	Comm.
Gamma	Philadelphia, Pa.	1863	3 Jun 1864	1864

ex-*R.F. Loper*

Tonnage	36 tons
Dimensions	65′ (oa) 56′5″ (bp) × 14′3″ × d5′4
Machinery	1 screw, 1 engine (16″ × 1′4″), 1 boiler, 12 knots
Armament	(U)

Note: Also known as *Tug No.3*.
Service record: James River, picket boat. New Berne, N.C., 1865. Sold 25 Oct 1865.
Later history: Merchant *Peter Smith* 1865. Burned at New York, 9 May 1893.

Name	Builder	Launched	Acquired	Comm.
Gladiolus	Philadelphia, Pa	1864	2 Jun 1864	15 Jun 1864

ex-*Sallie Bishop*

Dimensions	88′ × 18′6″ × 8′
Machinery	1 screw, 1 vertical LP engine (30″ × 2′4″), 1 boiler
Complement	25
Armament	2–12pdr MLR, 1–24pdr H

Service record: SAtlBS 1864. Blockade of Charleston. Decomm 30 Aug 1865. Sold 15 Sep 1865.
Ship captured: str *Syren*, 18 Feb 1865.
Later history: Merchant *Gladiolus* 1865. Lost 1887.

Name	Builder	Launched	Acquired	Comm.
Glance	Chester, Pa. (Reaney)	1863	2 Jun 1864	Jul 1864

ex-*Glide*

Tonnage	80 tons

Dimensions	75' × 17' × 8'
Machinery	1 screw, 1 vertical HP engine (20" × 2'), 1 boiler, 8 knots (bldr)
Complement	14
Armament	None

Service record: Hampton Roads, Va., yard tug 1864–65, and Philadelphia, NYd, 1865–83. Sold 27 Sep 1883.

Name	Builder	Launched	Acquired	Comm.
Harcourt	Buffalo, N.Y.	1863	14 Jun 1864	1864
ex-*J.W. Harcourt*				

Tonnage	68 tons
Dimensions	66' × 16'3" × 7'9"
Machinery	1 screw, 1 HP engine, 1 boiler. 9 knots
Armament	None

Service record: NAtlBS 1864. James River 1865. Decomm 20 Nov 1865. Sold 16 Apr 1867.
Later history: Merchant *Isaac R. Staples* 1867. Renamed *Gertrude* 1883. RR 1889.

Name	Builder	Launched	Acquired	Comm.
Honeysuckle	Buffalo, N.Y.	1862	19 Aug 1863	3 Dec 1863
ex-*William G. Fargo*				

Tonnage	241 tons
Dimensions	123' ( ) 121'6" ( ) × 20'2" × 10'
Machinery	1 screw, 1 HP overhead engine (30" × 2'6"), 1 boiler, 12 knots
Complement	39
Armament	2–20pdr MLR

Service record: EGulfBS 1864–65. Dispatch and supply vessel 1864. Blockade off Florida 1865. Decomm 30 Jun 1865. Sold 15 Aug 1865.
Ships captured: *Fly*, 11 Jan 1864; *Florida*, 20 Mar 1864; *Miriam*, 29 Apr 1864; *Augusta*, 17 Jan 1865; *Sort*, 28 Feb 1865; *Phantom*, 3 Mar 1865.
Later history: Merchant *Honeysuckle* 1865. RR 1900.

Name	Builder	Launched	Acquired	Comm.
Hoyt	Philadelphia, Pa.	1863	1 Jul 1864	1864
ex-*Luke Hoyt*				

Tonnage	20 tons
Dimensions	45' × 10'5" × 6'
Machinery	1 screw, 1 vertical HP engine, 2 knots
Complement	6
Armament	1 spar torpedo

Notes: Spar torpedo boat. Designed as weapon to oppose Confederate rams in Roanoke River but was never used in combat.
Service record: New Berne, N.C. 1864. Sold 10 Aug 1865.
Later history: Merchant *Luke Hoyt* 1865. RR 1914.

Name	Builder	Launched	Acquired	Comm.
Hydrangea	Buffalo, N.Y	1862	16 Oct 1863	18 Apr 1864
ex-*Hippodrome*				

Tonnage	215 tons
Dimensions	120' × 20'3" × d7'
Machinery	1 screw, 1 overhead LP engine (30" × 2'6"), 1 boiler, 11 knots
Complement	29
Armament	1–20pdr MLR, 1–12pdr H

Service record: NAtlBS 1864. SAtlBS 1864. Decomm 1 Sep 1865. Sold 25 Oct 1865.
Later history: Merchant *Norman* 1865. Wrecked off Cape May, N.J., 17 Nov 1886.

Name	Builder	Launched	Acquired	Comm.
Innis	Philadelphia, Pa.	1863	5 Oct 1863	1863

Tonnage	112 tons B
Dimensions	85' × 19'6" × 8',
Machinery	1 screw, 1 overhead engine, 1 boiler 12 knots
Armament	(U)

Service record: NAtlBS 1864. Renamed *Kalmia*, 24 Apr 1864. Sold 25 Oct 1865.
Later history: Merchant *Francis B. Thurber* 1865. Renamed *James Hughes* 1898. Destroyed by fire at Bartletts Point, N.Y.,15 Jun 1905.

Name	Builder	Launched	Acquired	Comm.
Iris	Brooklyn, N.Y	1863	16 Oct 1863	1863
ex-*Willet Rowe*				

Tonnage	158 tons
Dimensions	87' × 19' × 9'
Machinery	1 screw, 1 overhead LP engine (28" × 2'4"), 1 boiler, 12 mph
Complement	34
Armament	2–20pdr MLR

Service record: SAtlBS 1863. Blockade of Charleston. Expedition to Bull's Bay, S.C., Feb 1865. Decomm 15 Jul 1865.
Later history: To U.S. Lighthouse Board, 18 Oct 1865.

Name	Builder	Launched	Acquired	Comm.
Jasmine	Brooklyn, N.Y.	1862	29 May 1863	17 Jun 1863
ex-*Peter B. Van Hutten*				

Tonnage	122 tons
Dimensions	79' × 18' × 7'6", d9'2"
Machinery	1 screw, 1 LP engine (26" × 2'2"), 2 boilers
Complement	19
Armament	1–20pdr MLR, 1–12pdr H

Service record: WGulfBS 1863. Decomm 12 May 1865.
Ship captured: *Relampago*, 14 Jul 1863.
Later history: To U.S. Lighthouse Board, 13 Jun 1866. To U.S. Revenue Cutter Service 1873, renamed ***William E. Chandler***. Sold 1903.

Name	Builder	Launched	Acquired	Comm.
Jean Sands	Brooklyn, N.Y.	1863	18 Oct 1864	1864

Tonnage	139 tons
Dimensions	102' × 22'8" × d6'2"
Machinery	1 screw, vertical inverted engine
Armament	None

Notes: Salvage tug.
Service record: Norfolk NYd, tug and salvage vessel 1864–92.†

Name	Builder	Launched	Acquired	Comm.
Jonquil	Wilmington, Del.	1862	21 Oct 1863	28 Oct 1863
ex-*J.K. Kirkman*				

Tonnage	90 tons D
Dimensions	69'4" × 17'6" × 7'
Machinery	1 screw, 1 vertical condensing engine (20" × 1'8"), 8 knots
Complement	15

Armament   1–12pdr MLR, 1–12pdr SB.; (Aug 1864) 2–12pdr H
Service record: SAtlBS 1863. Blockade of Charleston. Decomm 2 Aug 1865. Sold 21 Oct 1865.
Later history: Merchant *B. Bramell* 1865. Renamed *Sophie* 1883. RR 1921.

Name	Builder	Launched	Acquired	Comm.
Juniper ex-*Uno*	Camden, N.J.	1864	30 May 1864	11 Jul 1864

Tonnage   116 tons B
Dimensions   79'6" × 18'4" × 9'
Machinery   1 screw, 1 overhead condensing engine (24" × 1'8"), 1 boiler, 10 knots
Complement   26
Armament   1–20pdr MLR, 1–12pdr MLR
Service record: Potomac Flotilla 1864–65. Decomm 26 May 1865.
Later history: To U.S. Lighthouse Board, 19 Jun 1865. To U.S. Revenue Cutter Service 1873, renamed ***Peter G. Washington***. Sold 1906.

Kalmia, see *Innis*.

Name	Builder	Launched	Acquired	Comm.
Laburnum ex-*Lion*	Philadelphia, Pa.	1864	24 Jun 1864	7 Jul 1864

Tonnage   181 tons B
Dimensions   110' × 22' × 9'
Machinery   1 screw, vertical direct-acting engine, 10 knots
Complement   29
Armament   2–20pdr MLR, 2–24pdr H
Service record: SAtlBS 1864. Blockade of Charleston. Decomm 24 Jan 1866. Sold 16 Mar 1866.
Later history: Merchant *D.P. Ingraham*, 1866. Sold foreign 1878.

Name	Builder	Launched	Acquired	Comm.
Larkspur ex-*Pontiac*	Wilmington, Del.	1863	6 Oct 1863	16 Oct 1863

Tonnage   125 tons B
Dimensions   90'9" × 19'2" × 9'
Machinery   1 screw, 1 vertical direct-acting engine (26" × 2'4"), 9 knots
Complement   26
Armament   1–12pdr H, 1–12pdr MLR; (Feb 1865) add 1–24pdr H
Service record: SAtlBS 1863–65. Blockade of Charleston. Decomm 8 Jul 1865. Sold 10 Aug 1865.
Later history: Merchant *Larkspur* 1865. Renamed *M. Vandercook* 1885. Renamed *Somerville* 1898. RR 1905.

Name	Builder	Launched	Acquired	Comm.
Lavender ex-*May Flower*	Philadelphia, Pa.	1864	25 May 1864	1864

Tonnage   173 tons
Dimensions   112' × 22' × d7'6"
Machinery   1 screw, 1 vertical direct-acting LP engine (30" × 2'6"), 1 boiler
Complement   23
Armament   2–12pdr MLR, 2–24pdr H
Service record: SAtlBS 1864. Wrecked in squall off North Carolina coast, 12 Jun 1864 (9 dead).

Name	Builder	Launched	Acquired	Comm.
Leslie	(U)	(U)	1861	1861

Tonnage   100 tons
Dimensions   (U)
Machinery   1 screw
Complement   10
Armament   2 guns
Notes: Transferred from War Department.
Service record: Washington NYd 1861. Potomac Flotilla, tender. Returned to War Department, 2 Jun 1865.

Name	Builder	Launched	Acquired	Comm.
Lilac	Philadelphia, Pa.	1863	15 Apr 1863	18 Apr 1863

Tonnage   129 tons B
Dimensions   92' () 85'7" ( ) × 19'1" × 8'
Machinery   1 screw, 1 vertical direct-acting condensing engine, 9 knots
Complement   17
Armament   1–12pdr SB, 1–12pdr MLR
Service record: NAtlBS 1863. James River, Beaufort, N.C., 1864. Decomm 16 Jun and sold 12 Jul 1865.
Ship captured: Confederate War Department tug *Seaboard*, 4 Apr 1865.
Later history: Merchant *Eutaw* 1865. RR 1888.

Name	Builder	Launched	Acquired	Comm.
Lupin ex-*C. Vanderbilt*	Philadelphia, Pa.	1861	19 Nov 1863	1863

Tonnage   68 tons
Dimensions   69' × 16'2" × d6'6"
Machinery   1 screw, 1 HP engine (20" × 1'8"), 1 boiler
Armament   (U)
Service record: Sold 25 Oct 1865.
Later history: Merchant *C. Vanderbilt* 1865. Renamed *Lewis S. Wandell* 1883. Sold foreign 1884.

Name	Builder	Launched	Acquired	Comm.
Marigold	Philadelphia, Pa.	1863	13 Jun 1863	13 Jun 1863

Tonnage   115 tons B
Dimensions   84'7" × 18'9" × 7'
Machinery   1 screw, 1 vertical direct-acting condensing engine (26" × 2'2"), 1 boiler
Complement   17
Armament   2–12pdr MLR
Service record: EGulfBS 1863–65. Sold 6 Oct 1866.
Ships captured: *Last Trial*, 6 Oct 1863; *Salvadora*, 25 Feb 1865.
Later history: Merchant *William A. Hennessey* 1866. Destroyed by fire at New York, 30 Nov 1875.

Name	Builder	Launched	Acquired	Comm.
Martin ex-*James McMartin*	Albany, N.Y.	1864	16 Jun 1864	Jun 1864

Tonnage   25 tons
Dimensions   45'3" × 11'3" × 5'9"

Machinery	1 screw, 1 vertical HP engine (13 1/2" × 1'3"), 6 knots
Complement	9
Armament	Spar torpedo

Notes: Iron hull. Spar torpedo boat.
Service record: NAtlBS 1864. North Carolina waters 1864. Capture of Plymouth, N.C., 29–31 Oct 1864. Sold 10 Aug 1865.
Later history: Merchant *Martin* 1865. Renamed *John Laughlin Jr.* 1882. RR 1894.

Name	Builder	Launched	Acquired	Comm.
Moccasin	Philadelphia, Pa.	1864	11 Jul 1864	14 Jul 1864
ex-*Hero*				

Tonnage	192 tons B
Dimensions	104'5" × 22'3" × 9'
Machinery	1 screw, vertical direct-acting engine (32" × 2'10"), 1 boiler, 10 knots
Complement	31
Armament	3–12pdr MLR

Notes: Renamed 25 Jul 1864.
Service record: NAtlBS 1864. Search for CSS *Tallahassee*, Aug 1864. Unsuccessful attack on Ft. Fisher, N.C., 24–25 Dec 1864. Potomac Flotilla Mar 1865. Decomm 12 Aug 1865.
Later history: To U.S. Revenue Cutter Service, 18 Sep 1865. Renamed *George M. Bibb* 1881. Sold 1891. Merchant *Pentagoet* 1891. Foundered at sea, 27 Nov 1898.

Name	Builder	Launched	Acquired	Comm.
Monterey	San Francisco, Cal.	1862	20 Apr 1863	18 May 1863
ex-*Monitor*				

Tonnage	87 tons
Dimensions	75' × 18' × 7'
Machinery	1 screw, 1 HP engine

Service record: Mare Island NYd 1863–92.†

Name	Builder	Launched	Acquired	Comm.
Narcissus	East Albany, N.Y.	Jul 1863	23 Sep 1863	2 Feb 1864
ex-*Mary Cook*				

Tonnage	115 tons B
Dimensions	81'6" × 18'9" × 6'
Machinery	1 screw, 1 overhead cylinder engine (20" × 1'10"), 1 boiler, 14 knots
Complement	19/32
Armament	1–20pdr MLR, 1–12pdr SB

Notes: Purchased before completion.
Service record: WGulfBS Feb 1864. Struck a torpedo (mine) and sank off Mobile, 7 Dec 1864; salved and repaired. Wrecked at Egmont Key, Fla., 4 Jan 1866 (no survivors).
Ship captured: *Oregon*, 24 Aug 1864.

Name	Builder	Launched	Acquired	Comm.
Peony	Philadelphia, Pa.	1864	7 Dec 1864	Jan 1865
		ex-*Republic*		

Tonnage	180 tons
Dimensions	104'6" × 20'6" × 8'6"
Machinery	1 screw, 1 vertical direct-acting condensing engine (34" × 2'8"), 1 boiler, 9 knots
Armament	1–24pdr SB

Service record: NAtlBS 1865. Second attack on Ft. Fisher, N.C., 13–15 Jan 1865. Sold 1 Aug 1865.
Later history: Merchant *Republic* 1865. RR 1894.

Name	Builder	Launched	Acquired	Comm.
Periwinkle	Philadelphia, Pa. (Neafie)	1864	9 Dec 1864	Jan 1865
ex-*America*				

Tonnage	387 tons B
Dimensions	140' × 28' × 10'6"
Machinery	1 screw, 1 vertical condensing engine (40" × 3'), 1 boiler (Bldr)
Complement	37
Armament	2–24pdr

Notes: Two-mast schooner rig.
Service record: Potomac Flotilla Jan–Jun 1865. Decomm 1867. Hall Scientific Expedition to the Arctic 1871. Renamed **Polaris**, 25 Apr 1871. Reached farthest point north by a vessel, 81'11'N, 1872. Crushed after being caught in ice in Baffin Bay, 24 Oct 1872.

Name	Builder	Launched	Acquired	Comm.
Pink	Newburgh, N.Y.	1863	14 Dec 1863	6 Feb 1864
ex-*Zouave*				

Tonnage	184 tons B
Dimensions	110'4" × 24'6" × d7'
Machinery	1 screw
Complement	24
Armament	1–30pdr MLR, 2–12pdr SB

Service record: NAtlBS 1864. WGulfBS Aug 1864. Ran aground on Dauphin Island, Ala. and lost, 22 Sep 1865.

Polaris, see *Periwinkle*.

Name	Builder	Launched	Acquired	Comm.
Poppy	Philadelphia, Pa.	1862	31 Oct 1863	10 Nov 1863
ex-*Addie Douglas*				

Tonnage	93 tons
Dimensions	88' × 19' × 7'3"
Machinery	1 screw, 1 vertical LP engine (24" × 2'), 1 boiler, 8 knots
Complement	20
Armament	1–12pdr SB, 1–12pdr MLR

Service record: NAtlBS 1863–65. Hampton Roads and James River. Sold 30 Nov 1865.
Later history: Merchant *Isaac M. North* 1865. RR 1893.

Name	Builder	Launched	Acquired	Comm.
Primrose	Whitehall, N.Y.	1862	14 Jan 1863	26 Feb 1863
ex-*Nellie B. Vaughan*				

Tonnage	94 tons
Dimensions	83' × 17'6" × 7'
Machinery	1 screw, 1 vertical inverted HP engine (20" × 1'8")

Complement 26

Armament 1–30pdr MLR, 1–24pdr H

Service record: Potomac Flotilla. Operations in Nansemond River, Va., 11 Apr–4 May 1863. Washington NYd 1865–71. Sold 17 Mar 1871.

Ships captured: *Sarah Lavinia*, 8 May 1863; *Flying Cloud and *Richard Vaux*, 2 Jun 1863.

Name	Builder	Launched	Acquired	Comm.
R.B. Forbes	Boston, Mass. (Tufts)	1845	17 Aug 1861	Aug 1861

Tonnage	329 tons B
Dimensions	121′ × 25′6″ × 12′3″
Machinery	2 screws, 2 inclined condensing engines (36″ × 3′), 1 boiler, 11 knots
Complement	(U)
Armament	2–32pdr/47; (Jan 1862) 1–30pdr MLR, 1–32pdr/57

Notes: Iron hull wrecking tug. In service before actual acquisition, 20 Sep 1861.

Service record: SAtlBS Oct–Dec 1861. Occupation of Port Royal, S.C., 7 Nov 1861. Driven ashore in gale and wrecked south of Currituck Inlet, Va., 25 Feb 1862.

Name	Builder	Launched	Acquired	Comm.
Reliance	Keyport, N.J. (Terry)	4 Jun 1860	7 May 1861	13 May 1861
Resolute	Keyport, N.J. (Terry)	4 Jun 1860	7 May 1861	12 May 1861

Tonnage	90 tons B
Dimensions	93′ (U) 88′2″ (U) × 17′ × 8′, d7′5″
Machinery	1 screw, vertical direct-acting engine (17″ × 1′5″), 1 boiler
Complement	(Cobb & Fields) 17
Armament	1–24pdr H, 1–12pdr H

Service records:

Reliance: Potomac Flotilla 1861. Engaged batteries at Aquia Creek, Va., 29 May–1 Jun 1861. Expedition up Rappahannock River to Tappahannock, Va., 13–15 Apr 1862. Captured with *Satellite* by Confederate boarders in Rappahannock River, 23 Aug 1863. Sunk at Port Royal, 28 Aug 1863.
Ships captured: *Blossom*, 12 Aug 1862; *Pointer*, 31 Oct 1862; *E. Waterman*, 20 Mar 1863.
Later history: Raised and sold 1865. Merchant *Reliance* 1865. Lost (cause unknown), 26 Apr 1883.

Resolute: Potomac Flotilla 1861–65. Engaged batteries at Aquia Creek, Va., 29 May–1 Jun 1861. Decomm 26 May 1865. Sold 24 Jun 1865.
Ships captured: *unknown, 28 May 1861; *Somerset, 8 Jun 1861; *Buena Vista*, 17 Jul 1861; *Ocean Wave*, 18 Jul 1861; *Eagle*, 21 Aug 1861; *S.S. Jones*, 10 Aug 1862; *Capitola*, 8 Nov 1862.
Later history: Merchant *Resolute* 1865. RR 1899.

Name	Builder	Launched	Acquired	Comm.
Rescue	Wilmington, Del. (Harlan)	1861	21 Aug 1861	Sep 1861

Tonnage	111 tons B
Dimensions	80′ × 18′ × 8′
Machinery	1 screw, inverted vertical engine (26″ × 2′), 6 knots (bldr)
Complement	20
Armament	1–20pdr MLR, 1–12pdr MLR; (Oct 1864) less 1–12pdr MLR

Notes: Iron hull. Purchased prior to completion.

Service record: Potomac Flotilla 1861. NAtlBS Nov 1861. Blockade of Charleston Nov 1862–Jun 1864. Potomac Flotilla Sep 1864–65. Washington NYd 1865–89. †

Ships captured: *Harford*, 18 Sep 1861; *Martha Washington*, 11 Oct 1861; *Ada, 5 Nov 1861; *Urbana*, 8 Nov 1861.

Later history: Merchant *Hercules* 1891.

Name	Builder	Launched	Acquired	Comm.
Rocket ex-*J.D. Billard*	Mystic, Conn.	1862	12 Oct 1863	(U)

Tonnage	127 tons
Dimensions	85′8″ × 18′10″ × 7′
Machinery	1 screw, 1 vertical inverted HP engine (25″ × U), 8.5 knots

Notes: Reboilered 1884.

Service record: New York, NYd, ordnance tug 1863–84.†

Name	Builder	Launched	Acquired	Comm.
Rose ex-*A.I. Fitch*	New Brunswick, N.J.	1863	12 Dec 1863	8 Feb 1864

Tonnage	96 tons
Dimensions	84′ × 18′2″ × 7′3″
Machinery	1 screw, 8.5 knots
Complement	17
Armament	(Aug 1864) 1–20pdr MLR, 1–12pdr SB

Note: Fitted for spar torpedo 1864.

Service record: Potomac Flotilla 1864. WGulfBS Aug 1864–65. Pensacola NYd 1865–83. Stricken 3 Mar 1883. Sold 20 Sep 1883.

Name	Builder	Launched	Acquired	Comm.
Saffron ex-*John T. Jenkins*	New Brunswick, N.J.	1863	8 Dec 1864	17 Dec 1864

Tonnage	73 tons
Dimensions	66 × 17′1 × 8′
Machinery	1 screw, 1 vertical HP engine, 1 boiler
Complement	16
Armament	1 gun

Note: May also have been known as *Theta*. Wood hull.

Service record: NAtlBS 1865. Sold 25 Oct 1865.

Later history: Merchant *Clifton* 1865. Lost (cause unknown), 1885.

Name	Builder	Launched	Acquired	Comm.
Snowdrop ex-*Albert DeGroot*	Buffalo, N.Y.	1863	16 Oct 1863	(U)

Tonnage	125 tons B
Dimensions	91′ × 17′6″ × 8′
Machinery	1 screw, 1 overhead cylinder engine (24″ × 2′), 1 boiler, 12 mph
Complement	14
Armament	2 guns

Service record: NAtlBS 1864. Hampton Roads area. Norfolk NYd 1865–83. Sold and BU 1884.

Name	Builder	Launched	Acquired	Comm.
Sorrel ex-*Gen. W.S. Hancock*	Philadelphia, Pa.	1864	1 Aug 1864	1864

Tonnage	68 tons
Dimensions	77′ × 16′6″ × 6′6″
Machinery	1 screw, 1 vertical HP engine (18″ × 1′6″), 1 boiler

Service record: Philadelphia NYd 1864–83. Sold 27 Sep 1883.

Later history: FFU.

Name	Builder	Launched	Acquired	Comm.
Sweet Brier	Buffalo, N.Y.	1862	22 Sep 1863	25 Jan 1864
ex-*Dictator*				
Tonnage	243 tons			
Dimensions	120' × 21'3" × 9'6"			
Machinery	1 screw, 1 vertical direct-acting engine (30" × 2'6"), 1 boiler, 9 knots			
Complement	37			
Armament	1–12pdr SB, 1–20pdr MLR; (Aug 1864) 1–20pdr MLR, 2–24pdr SB			

Service record: SAtlBS 1864–65. Blockade of Charleston. Decomm 13 Jul 1865. Sold 25 Oct 1865.

Ship captured: *Pocahontas,* 8 Jul 1864.

Later history: Merchant *Conqueror* 1865. RR 1900.

Name	Builder	Launched	Acquired	Comm.
Tigress	(U)	Aug 1861	Aug 1861	Aug 1861
Tonnage	(U)			
Dimensions	(U)			
Machinery	1 screw, 1 HP engine, 1 boiler			

Service record: Potomac Flotilla. Sunk in collision with merchant vessel *State of Maine* off Indian Head, Md., 10 Sep 1861. Wreck raised and sold.

Unit, see *Belle.*

Name	Builder	Launched	Acquired	Comm.
Verbena	Brooklyn, N.Y.	1864	7 Jun 1864	11 Jul 1864
ex-*Ino*				
Tonnage	104 tons B			
Dimensions	78'4" × 17'6" × 8'			
Machinery	1 screw, 1 overhead cylinder engine (24" × 1'8"), 1 boiler, 12 mph			
Complement	20			
Armament	1–20pdr MLR, 1–12pdr SB			

Service record: Potomac Flotilla 1864. Decomm 13 Jun 1865. Sold 20 Jul 1865.

Later history: Merchant *Game Cock* 1865. Renamed *Edward G. Burgess,* 1885. RR 1900

Name	Builder	Launched	Acquired	Comm.
Violet	Brooklyn, N.Y.	1862	30 Dec 1862	29 Jan 1863
ex-*Martha*				
Tonnage	146 tons B			
Dimensions	85' × 19'9" × d11'			
Machinery	1 screw, 1 inverted direct-acting engine (30" × 2'4"), 1 boiler			
Complement	20			
Armament	1–12pdr SB, 1–12pdr MLR; (Feb 1864) 2–12pdr MLR, 1–24pdr			

Service record: NAtlBS Feb 1863. Helped capture and refloat grounded blockade runner *Ceres* at mouth of Cape Fear River, 11 Apr 1863. Ran aground off Cape Fear, N.C., while attempting to refloat steamer *Antonica,* 20 Dec 1863; refloated and repaired. Fitted with spar torpedo 1864. Ran aground off Cape Fear River, 7 Aug 1864 and destroyed to prevent capture.

Name	Builder	Launched	Acquired	Comm.
Young America	New York	1857	Apr 1861	1861
Tonnage	173 tons			
Dimensions	87'1" × 20'2" × 10'6"			
Machinery	1 screw			
Complement	13			
Armament	1–30pdr MLR, 1–32pdr/33, 1–12pdr MLR; (Apr 1863) 1–30pdr MLR, 1–31pdr/27; (Nov 1863) 1–30pdr MLR, 1–24pdr H			

Notes: Confederate tug captured in Hampton Roads by USS *Cumberland,* 24 Apr 1861.

Service record: Potomac Flotilla 1861–62. Decomm 9 Jun 1865. Sold 12 Jul 1865.

Later history: Merchant *Young America* 1865. RR 1901.

Name	Builder	Launched	Acquired	Comm.
Zeta	Philadelphia, Pa.	1864	3 Jun 1864	8 Jun 1864
ex-*J.G. Loane*				
Tonnage	34 tons			
Dimensions	58' × 13' × 7'6"			
Machinery	1 screw, 1 engine (15" × 1'3"), 1 boiler, 8 knots			
Complement	10			
Armament	None			

Notes: Also known as *Tug No. 6.* Renamed Nov 1864.

Service record: Torpedo tug in James River, 1865. Sold 24 Jun 1865.

Later history: Merchant *Zeta* 1865. Renamed *W.H. Mohler* 1892. Burned off Dundalk, Md., 8 Nov 1921.

Name	Builder	Launched	Acquired	Comm.
Zouave	Albany, N.Y.	1861	20 Dec 1861	1 Feb 1862
Tonnage	127 tons			
Dimensions	95 × 20'10" × 9'			
Machinery	1 screw, 2 HP-direct-acting engines, 10 knots			
Complement	25			
Armament	2–30pdr MLR			

Service record: NAtlBS 1862. Battle of Hampton Roads, 8 Mar 1862. Operations in Nansemond River, Va., 11 Apr–4 May 1863. Decomm 14 Jun 1865. Sold 12 Jul 1865.

Ship captured: *J.C.McCabe.,* 18 Jan 1863.

Later history: Merchant *Zouave* 1865. Renamed *Three Brothers* 1914. RR 1918.

5
SAILING SHIPS

SHIPS ON THE NAVY LIST BEFORE 1855

The following ships acquired prior to 1855 were still on the Navy List at the outbreak of the Civil War. For full details see *The Sailing Navy*.

Ships of the Line

Name	Rate	Launched
Alabama	74	23 Jan 1864
Armament	(Jun 1864) 4–100pdr MLR, 6–9″; (Jun 1865) add 2–24pdr	

Service record: Renamed *New Hampshire*, 28 Oct 1863. Completed as a storeship. Depot ship, Port Royal, S.C., SatlBS 1864–65. Receiving ship, Norfolk NYd 1866–76, also Port Royal, Norfolk, and Newport, finally at New London, 1891–92.†

Name	Rate	Launched
Columbus	74	1 Mar 1819

Service record: In ordinary from 1848. Burned to prevent capture at Norfolk NYd, 20 Apr 1861.

Name	Rate	Launched
Delaware	74	21 Oct 1820

Service record: In ordinary from 1844. Burned to prevent capture at Norfolk NYd, 20 Apr 1861

New Hampshire, see *Alabama*.

Name	Rate	Launched
New York	74	Never

Service record: Burned on the stocks to prevent capture at Norfolk NYd, 20 Apr 1861.

Name	Rate	Launched
North Carolina	74	7 Sep 1820
Armament	(Apr 1862) 1–30pdr MLR, 4–9″ SB	

Service record: Receiving ship New York 1839–66. Sold 1 Oct 1867.

Name	Rate	Launched
Ohio	74	30 May 1820
Armament	(1863) 1–8″ MLR, 4–100pdr MLR, 12–32pdr	

Service record: Receiving ship Boston d 1850–75. Sold 27 Sep 1883.

Name	Rate	Launched
Pennsylvania	120	18 Jul 1837
Armament	(1850) 16–8″ MLR, 104–32pdr	

Service record: Receiving ship Norfolk NYd 1842–61. Burned to prevent capture at Norfolk NYd, 20 Apr 1861.

Name	Rate	Launched
Vermont	74	15 Sep 1848
Armament	(Feb 1862) 4–8″/63, 20–32pdr/57; (Apr 1863) 10–8″/63, 6–32pdr/57, 2–32pdr/42	

Service record: Laid down 1818. In ordinary after launching. Completed for use as storeship. Badly damaged in storm while under tow to Port Royal, S.C., 24 Feb 1862. Ordnance and depot ship Port Royal 1862–64. Receiving ship New York 1864–1901.†

Name	Rate	Launched
Virginia	74	Never

Service record: Laid down 1822. Never launched and broken up on stocks 1884.

Note: *New Orleans*, 120 guns, laid down 1815 at Sackets Harbor, N.Y. on Lake Ontario, remained on the stocks until broken up in 1883.

Frigates

Name	Rate	Launched
Brandywine	44	16 Jun 1825

Service record: Storeship, NAtlBS, Hampton Roads, 1861, later Norfolk NYd. Destroyed by fire at Norfolk, 3 Sep 1864.

Name	Rate	Launched
Columbia	44	9 Mar 1836
Armament	(1853) 10–8″ MLR, 40–32pdr	

Service record: In ordinary from 1855. Scuttled and burned to prevent capture at Norfolk NYd, 20 Apr 1861.

94 Civil War Navies, 1855-1883

Name	Rate	Launched
Congress	44	16 Aug 1841
Armament	(Mar 1862) 10–8″ SB, 40–32pdr	

Service record: AtlBS 1861. Damaged by gunfire of CSS *Virginia* in Hampton Roads, Va., and destroyed by fire, 8 Mar 1862 (120 killed).

Name	Rate	Launched
Constitution	44	21 Oct 1797
Armament	(Sep 1861) 6–32pdr/42, 10–32pdr/33	

Service record: Training ship, Naval Academy 1860–82. Rebuilt at Philadelphia NYd 1871.†]

Name	Rate	Launched
Independence (razee)	54	22 Jun 1814
Armament	(1854) 10–8″ MLR, 46–32pdr	

Service record: Built as ship of the line, razeed to frigate 1837. Receiving ship, Mare Island 1857–1912.†

Name	Rate	Launched
Potomac	44	22 Mar 1822
Armament	(May 1861) 10–8″/63, 24–32pdr/57, 16–32pdr/33, 2–12pdr SB; (Jul 1864) 4–8″/63, 19–32pdr/57, 1–32pdr/33, 10–30pdr MLR, 1–20pdr MLR	

Service record: WGulfBS 1861. Receiving ship, Pensacola NYd 1861–67 and Philadelphia NYd 1867–77. Decomm 13 Jan 1877. Sold 24 May 1877.
Ships captured: str *Bloomer*, 24 Dec 1862; *Champion*, 14 Jan 1864.

Name	Rate	Launched
Raritan	44	13 Jun 1843
Armament	(1848) 8–8″ MLR, 42–32pdr	

Service record: In ordinary from 1852. Scuttled to prevent capture at Norfolk NYd, 20 Apr 1861.

Name	Rate	Launched
Sabine	44	3 Feb 1855
Armament	(Aug 1861) 2–10″ SB, 10–8″/63, 18–32pdr/57, 18–32pdr/33; (Sep 1861) 2–10″ SB replaced by 2–8″/64; (Sep 1863) 2–100pdr MLR, 2–20pdr MLR, 10–9″ SB, 18–32pdr/57, 16–32pdr/33, 2–12pdr H; (Jul 1864) 2–100pdr MLR, 10–9″ SB, 14–32pdr/57, 8–32pdr/33, 2–12pdr MLR	

Service record: Paraguay Expedition 1858-59. NAtlBS 1861–64. Training ship Norfolk NYd 1864. Receiving ship Portsmouth NYd 1872–76. Laid up 1877. Sold 23 Sep 1883.

Name	Rate	Launched
St. Lawrence	44	25 Mar 1847
Armament	(Jul 1861) 10–8″/63, 24–32pdr/57, 16–32pdr/33, 2–12pdr SB; (May 1863) less 6–32pdr/33, add 2–50pdr MLR; (Sep 1863) 8–9″ SB, 2–32pdr/57, 2–12pdr SB; (Oct 1864) add 1–30pdr MLR	

Service record: Paraguay Expedition 1858-59. AtlBS 1861. Damaged by gunfire of CSS *Virginia* at Hampton Roads, 8 Mar 1862. EGulfBS Mar 1862–May 1863.

Fig 5.1: The Federal blockading fleet off Hampton Roads in Dec 1864, with the ironclad *New Ironsides* with masts in center and the two-turret monitor *Monadnock* to the left.

NAtlBS Aug 1864, Ordnance ship. Barracks ship, Norfolk NYd, 1867–75. Sold 31 Dec 1875.
Ships captured: *Herald*, 16 Jul 1861; privateer **Petrel*, 28 Jul 1861; *Fanny Lee*, 6 Nov 1861.

Name	Rate	Launched
Santee	44	16 Feb 1855
Armament	(May 1861) 2–64pdr/106, 10–8″/63, 20–32pdr/57, 16–32pdr/33, 2–12pdr; (Oct 1862) 1–11″ SB, 1–100pdr MLR, 10–32pdr/33.	

Service record: WGulfBS 1861–62. School ship, Naval Academy, Newport, later Annapolis, 1862–1912.†
Ships captured: *C.P. Knapp*, 8 Aug 1861; *Delta*, 27 Oct 1861; **Royal Yacht*, 7 Nov 1861; *Garonne*, 30 Dec 1861.

Name	Rate	Launched
Savannah	44	5 May 1842
Armament	(Jan 1861) 2–10″ SB, 8–8″/63, 14–32pdr/57; (Feb 1862) 1–10″ SB, 6–8″/63, 12–32pdr/57; (Sep 1862) 1–11″ SB, 2–9″ SB (Dec 1862) add 4–32pdr/57.	

Service record: Blockade of Georgia, 1861. Naval academy practice ship 1862–70. Sold 27 Sep 1883.
Ships captured: *E.Waterman*, 30 Nov 1861; *Cheshire*, 6 Dec 1861.

Name	Rate	Launched
United States	44	10 May 1797

Service record: In ordinary from 1849. Seized by Confederates at Norfolk NYd, 20 Apr 1861. Renamed **Confederate States**. Broken up 1865 after being recovered at Norfolk in 1862.

Sloops

Name	Rate	Launched
Constellation	24	28 Aug 1854
Armament	(Mar 1862) 16–8″/63, 4–32pdr/57, 1–30pdr MLR, 1–20pdr MLR, 2–12pdr SB; (1871) 1–100pdr MLR, 10–10″.	

Service record: African Sqn 1859–61. Captured slaver *Triton* off West coast of Africa, 21 Jun 1861. Mediterranean 1862–64. Receiving ship 1865–1933 at Norfolk NYd, Philadelphia NYd, Annapolis, and Newport. †
Ship captured: Slaver *Delicia* off Cabinda, Africa, 21 Dec 1859; Slaver *Triton* off West coast of Africa, 21 Jun 1861.

Name	Rate	Launched
Cumberland (ze)	22	24 May 1842
Armament	(Mar 1862) 22–9″ SB, 1–10″ SB, 1–70pdr MLR	

Service record: Razee sloop 1855–56. Towed out of Norfolk NYd, 20 Apr 1861. NatlBS 1861–62. Capture of Hatteras Inlet, 28–29 Aug 1861. Rammed and sunk by CSS *Virginia* in Hampton Roads, Va., 8 Mar 1862 (121 killed and wounded).
Ships captured: *Cambria*, 23 Apr 1861; tug *Young America** and *George M. Smith*, 24 Apr 1861; *Sarah & Mary*, 1 May 1861; *Carrie*, 2 May 1861; *A.J. Russell*, 3 May 1861; *Elite*, 4 May 1861; *Dorothy Haines*, 11 May 1861.

* Later USS *Young America*.

Name	Rate	Launched
Cyane	22	2 Aug 1837
Armament	(May 1865) 14–32pdr, 4–68pdr, 1–12pdr H	

Service record: Pacific Squadron 1858–71. Decomm 20 Sep 1871.†
Ship captured: *J.M. Chapman*, 15 Mar 1863.

Name	Rate	Launched
Dale	16	8 Nov 1839
Armament	(Jul 1861) 12–32pdr/27, 2–32pdr/33, 1–12pdr H; (Feb 1863) 2–32pdr/33, 1–30pdr MLR	

Service record: SAtlBS 1861. Store and guard ship, Port Royal, S.C. Store ship, Key West 1863–65. Training ship, Naval Academy 1867.†
Ships captured: *Specie*, 12 Oct 1861; *Mabel*, 15 Nov 1861.

Name	Rate	Launched
Decatur	16	9 Apr 1839
Armament	(Apr 1863) 4–8″, 4–32pdr/42; (Dec 1865) 12–32pdr/27, 4–32pdr/33	

Service record: In ordinary from 1859. Harbor battery, San Francisco 1863. Sold 17 Aug 1865.

Name	Rate	Launched
Falmouth	18	3 Nov 1827
Armament	(Aug 1861) 2–32pdr/33	

Service record: Paraguay Expedition 1858-59. Stationary storeship Aspinwall, Panama 1860. Sold 7 Nov 1863.

Name	Rate	Launched
Germantown	20	21 Aug 1846
Armament	(1857) 8–8″ SB, 12–32pdr SB	

Service record: In ordinary 1860. Burned to prevent capture at Norfolk NYd, 20 Apr 1861. Hulk raised again 22 Apr 1863 and sold.

Name	Rate	Launched
Jamestown	20	16 Sep 1844
Armament	(May 1861) 6–8″/55, 14–32pdr/42	

Service record: AtlBS 1861. Pacific Squadron 1862–65. Converted to transport and store ship 1866. N. Pacific Sqn 1867–68. Pacific Sqn 1869–71. School ship, Hawaii, 1876–79. Training ship, Atlantic, 1882–88. 1889–92.†
Ships captured: **Alvarado*, 5 Aug 1861; *Aigburth*, 31 Aug 1861; **Colonel Long*, 4 Sep 1861; *Havelock*, 15 Dec 1861; *Intended*, 1 May 1862.

Name	Rate	Launched
John Adams	18	17 Nov 1830
Armament	(May 1862) 2–30pdr MLR, 2–8″/55, 4–32pdr/33; (Dec 1864) add 2–20pdr MLR	

Service record: Pacific and Far East 1853–62. Training ship, Naval Academy 1862–63. SAtlBS 1863–65. Decomm Sep 1867. Sold 5 Oct 1867.

Name	Rate	Launched
Levant	22	28 Dec 1837

Service record: Disappeared en route from Hawaii to Panama after 18 Sep 1860.

Name	Rate	Launched
Lexington	18	9 Mar 1826

Service record: Sold 1860.

Name	Rate	Launched
Macedonian (razee)	20	1 Nov 1836
Armament	\multicolumn{2}{l}{(1861) 2–10″ SB, 16–8″ SB, 4–32pdr; (Nov 1862) 1–10″/87, 4–8″/55, 1–12pdr; (May 1863) 2–100pdr MLR, 8–8″/63, 4–32pdr/42, 2–12pdr; (May 1864) 2–12pdr replaced by 2–9″ SB; (Sep 1864) 2–100pdr MLR, 2–9″ SB, 8–8″/63, 2–32pdr/42, 4–12pdr}

Service record: Frigate razeed to sloop 1852–53. Gulf and Caribbean 1861. West India Sqn 1862–63. Practice ship, Naval Academy 1864–70. Decomm 1871. Sold 31 Dec 1875.

Name	Rate	Launched
Marion	16	24 Apr 1839
Armament	\multicolumn{2}{l}{(Jun 1861) 12–32pdr/27, 2–32pdr/33, 1–12pdr H; (1862) 10–32pdr, 1–20pdr MLR; (Jul 1862) 4–32pdr/27, 2–32pdr/33, 1–20pdr MLR, 1–12pdr H}

Service record: In ordinary from 1860. GulfBS 1861. Practice ship, Naval Academy 1862–70. Decomm and BU 1871.

Ships captured: Slaver *Brothers* off southeast coast of Africa, 8 Sep 1858; slaver *Orion* off Congo River, 21 Apr 1859; slaver *Ardennes* off Congo River, 25 Jun 1859..

Name	Rate	Launched
Plymouth	20	11 Oct 1843
Armament	\multicolumn{2}{l}{(1859) 2–8″ SB, 6–32pdr SB}

Service record: Under repair at Norfolk NYd 1860–61. Seized by Confederates at Norfolk NYd. 20 Apr 1861.

Name	Rate	Launched
Portsmouth	20	23 Oct 1843
Armament	\multicolumn{2}{l}{(Sep 1861) 16–8″/63, 1–12pdr; (Jul 1863) 16–8″/63, 2–8″/55, 1–20pdr MLR, 1–12pdr; (Jun 1864) add 1–100pdr MLR}

Service record: Africa Sqn 1859–61. Captured slaver *Virginian* off Congo River, 6 Feb 1860. Captured brig *Falmouth* off Porto Praya, 5 Jun 1860. GulfBS 1862. Passage past New Orleans forts and engagement with CSN vessels, 24 Apr 1862. Station ship New Orleans, 1862–65. Training ship 1878–1911.†

Ships captured: Slaver *Emily* off Loango, Africa, 21 Sep 1859; Slaver *Virginian* off Congo River, 6 Feb 1860; Slaver brig *Falmouth* off Porto Praya, Cape Verde, 5 Jun 1860; str *Labuan* and *Wave*, 18 Feb 1862; *Pioneer*, 20 Feb 1862.

Name	Rate	Launched
Preble	16	13 Jun 1839
Armament	\multicolumn{2}{l}{(Jan 1861) 10–32pdr/33; (Jul 1861) 2–8″/63, 1–32pdr/43, 6–32pdr/33, 1–12pdr; (Jun 1864) 4–8″/63, 12–32pdr/33, 2–20pdr MLR}

Service record: Paraguayan Expedition 1859. GulfBS 1861–63. Engagement with CSS *Ivy*, 9 Oct and with CSN squadron, near Head of Passes, Miss., 12 Oct 1861. Guard ship Pensacola 1862–63. Destroyed by accidental fire at Pensacola, Fla., 27 Apr 1863.

Name	Rate	Launched
St. Louis	18	18 Aug 1828
Armament	\multicolumn{2}{l}{(Oct 1861) 4–8″/63, 14–32pdr/33; (Feb 1862) 4–8″/55, 12–32pdr/33, 2–20pdr MLR, 1–12pdr SB}

Service record: Home Sqn 1858–61. Patrolled trans-Atlantic area 1862–64. SAtlBS Nov 1864. Decomm 12 May 1865. Receiving ship, League Island 1866–94.†

Ship captured: *Macao*, 5 Sep 1861.

Name	Rate	Launched
St. Mary's	20	24 Nov 1844
Armament	\multicolumn{2}{l}{(Dec 1862) 6–8″/55, 16–32pdr/42}

Service record: Pacific Sqn 1860–66, 1870–72. School ship, New York, 1875–1908.†

Name	Rate	Launched
Saratoga	20	26 Jul 1842
Armament	\multicolumn{2}{l}{(Jun 1863) 6–8″/55, 12–32pdr/42, 1–30pdr MLR, 2–12pdr MLR, 1–12pdr SB}

Service record: Africa station 1861. Guard ship off Delaware Capes, 1863. SAtlBS Jan 1864. Decomm 28 Apr 1865. Gunnery ship, Annapolis 1875. Training ship 1877–88.†

Ship captured: Slaver *Nightingale** off Kabinda, Angola, 21 Apr 1861

Name	Rate	Launched
Vandalia	18	26 Aug 1828
Armament	\multicolumn{2}{l}{(Nov 1863) 1–30pdr MLR, 4–8″/55, 16–32pdr/33}

Service record: SAtlBS May 1861. Bombardment and occupation of Port Royal, S.C., 7 Nov 1861. Receiving ship Portsmouth NYd 1863–70. Broken up 1870–72.

Ships captured: *Solferino*, 26 Jun 1861; *Henry Middleton*, 21 Aug 1861; *Ariel*, 6 Oct 1861; *Thomas Watson*, 15 Nov 1861.

Name	Rate	Launched
Vincennes	18	27 Apr 1826
Armament	\multicolumn{2}{l}{(May 1861) 4–8″/55, 14–32pdr/33; (Nov 1861) 4–8″/55, 2–9″ SB}

Service record: GulfBS 1861. Engagement with CSS *Ivy* at Head of Passes, 9 Oct and with CSN squadron near Head of Passes, Miss., 12 Oct 1861. Guard ship Ship Island, Miss. 1862–65. Decomm 28 Aug 1865. Sold 5 Oct 1867.

Ships captured: *Empress*, 27 Nov 1861; *H.McGuin*, 18 Jul 1863.

Name	Rate	Launched
Warren	18	29 Nov 1826

Service record: Store ship 1846–62. Sold at Panama 1 Jan 1863.

Later history: Used as coal hulk as late as 1874.

Brigs

Name	Rate	Launched
Bainbridge	12	26 Apr 1842
Armament	\multicolumn{2}{l}{(Jan 1861) 6–32pdr/27}

Service record: Paraguayan Expedition 1859–60. GulfSqn May 1861–Jun 1862. EGulfBS Aug 1862. Damaged in storm at Aspinwall, Panama, 24 Nov 1862. Capsized off Cape Hatteras, 21 Aug 1863 (1 survivor).

Ships captured: *New Castle*, 11 May 1862; str *Swan*, 24 May 1862; *Baigorry*, 9 Jun 1862.

---

* Later USS Nightingale

Name	Rate	Launched
Dolphin	10	17 Jun 1836
Armament	(1859) 3–11" SB, 1–9" SB	

Service record: Paraguay Expedition 1858-59. In ordinary 1861. Burned to prevent capture at Norfolk NYd, 20 Apr 1861.

Ship captured: Slaver *Echo* off north coast of Cuba, 21 Aug 1858.

Name	Rate	Launched
Perry	10	9 May 1843
Armament	(Apr 1861) 6–32pdr/27, 1–12pdr; (Apr 1862) 2–20pdr MLR, 6–32pdr/27, 1–12pdr	

Service record: Paraguay Expedition 1858-59. AtlBS 1861. Panama, May–Nov 1862. NAtlBS Mar–Aug 1863. SAtlBS Nov 1863–May 1865. Decomm 29 Apr 1865. Sold 10 Aug 1865.

Ships captured: *Hannah M. Johnson*, 31 May 1861; privateer *Savannah*, 3 Jun 1861; *Ellen Jane* and *Blooming Youth*, 18 Dec 1861; *Sue*, 31 Mar 1863; *Alma*, 2 May 1863.

Storeships

Name	Rate	Launched
Relief	2	14 Sep 1836
Armament	(Jul 1862) 1–30pdr MLR, 2–32pdr/33; (Oct 1864) 1–32pdr/33	

Service record: Expedition to Pocotaligo, S.C., 21–23 Oct 1862. Pacific 1864–66. Receiving ship Washington 1871–77. Sold 27 Sep 1883.

Name	Rate	Launched
Fredonia	4	1845

Service record: Storeship Pacific Sqn. Valparaiso 1853–62, and Callao 1862–68. Lost in earthquake and tidal wave at Arica, Peru, 13 Aug 1868 (27 dead).

Name	Rate	Launched
Supply	4	1846
Armament	(Jul 1861) 4 32pdr/27; (Aug 1862) add 1–12pdr R; (May 1863) 4 20pdr MLR, 2–24pdr H	

Service record: Storeship, Paraguay Expedition 1859. Decomm 23 Apr 1879. Sold 3 May 1884.

Ship captured: 29 Jan 1862: *Stephen Hart*, 29 Jan 1862..

Name	Rate	Launched
Release	2	1853
Armament	(1861) 2–32pdr/27; (Feb 1863) add 1 30pdr R, 1 12pdr R	

Service record: Paraguay Expedition 1858-59. SAtlBS Jan 1862–Jan 1863. EGulfBS Jun 1863 off Florida. Operations in St. Andrews Bay, Fla., 10–18 Dec 1863. Sold 21 Sep 1865.

Ships captured: *Edisto, *Elizabeth, *Wando*, and *Theodore Stoney*; 14 Feb 1862; *George Washington*, *Mary Louise*, and *Julia Worden*; 27 Mar 1862; *Lydia & Mary*; 29 Mar 1862; *Flash*; 2 May 1862; *John Thompson*; 2 Sep 1862; *Elmira Cornelius*; 12 Oct 1862; str *Scotia*; 24 Oct 1862; *Susan McPherson*; 31 Oct 1862; *Ann*, 8 Jul 1863; *Erniti*, 19 Aug 1863; *William A. Kain*,. 22 Jan 1864.

Later history: Merchant *Restless* 1865. SE 1870.

WARTIME ACQUISITIONS

Mortar Schooners

Name	Builder	Launched	Acquired	Comm.
Adolph Hugel	Philadelphia, Pa.	1860	21 Sep 1861	11 Jan 1862
Tonnage	269 tons			
Dimensions	114' × 29'6" × 9'			
Complement	34			
Armament	1–13"M, 2–32pdr/57			

Service record: Mortar Flotilla, Mississippi Sqn, 1862. Bombardment of Fts. Jackson and St. Philip below New Orleans, Mississippi River, 18–28 Apr 1862. Bombardment of Vicksburg, 26 Jun–22 Jul 1862. Potomac Flotilla, 1862–65. Decomm 17 Jun 1865. Sold 20 Jul 1865.

Ships captured: *Kate*, 24 Feb 1863; *Chatham*, 27 Feb 1863; *Music*, 17 Sep 1863; *F. U.Johnson.*, 1 Dec 1863; *Coquette*, 26 Oct 1864; *James Landry*, 28 Oct 1864; *Zion*, 2 Nov 1864.

Name	Builder	Launched	Acquired	Comm.
Arletta	Mystic, Conn.	1860	7 Sep 1861	30 Jan 1862
Tonnage	199 tons			
Dimensions	103' × 27' × 10'6"			
Complement	21/39			
Armament	(Feb 1862) 1–13"M, 2–32pdr/57, 2–12pdr SB; (1863) less 1–13"M			

Service record: Mortar Flotilla, WGulfBS 1862. Bombardment of Fts. Jackson and St. Philip below New Orleans, 18–28 Apr 1862 (1 killed). Bombardment of Vicksburg, 26 Jun–22 Jul 1862. NAtlBS 1862–65. Ordnance store vessel, Beaufort, N.C., 1863. Decomm 28 Sep 1865. Sold 30 Nov 1865.

Later history: Merchant *Arletta* 1865. FFU.

Name	Builder	Launched	Acquired	Comm.
C.P. Williams	Hoboken, N.J. (Capes)	1851	2 Sep 1861	21 Jan 1862
Tonnage	210 tons			
Dimensions	103'8" × 28'3" × 9'			
Complement	35/48.			

Fig 5.2: One of the mortar schooners used by Admiral Porter at New Orleans. (Peabody Essex Museum)

Armament (1862) 1–13″M, 2–32pdr/57, 2–12pdr SB; (May 1863) add 1–20pdr MLR; (Dec 1864) add 2–24pdr SB

Service record: Mortar Flotilla, Mississippi Sqn., 1862. Bombardment of Fts. Jackson and St. Philip below New Orleans, 18–28 Apr 1862. Bombardment of Vicksburg, 26 Jun–22 Jul 1862. SAtlBS, Nov 1862. Engaged batteries at Ft. McAllister, Ogeechee River, Ga., 19 Nov 1862 and 27 Jan–3 Mar 1863. Engaged batteries in Stono River, S.C., 25 Dec 1863. Expedition up Stono and Folly Rivers, 9–14 Feb 1865. Decomm 27 Jun 1865. Sold 10 Aug 1865.

Later history: Merchant *Sarah Purves* 1866. SE 1885.

Name	Builder	Launched	Acquired	Comm.
Dan Smith	Fairhaven, Conn.	1859	7 Sep 1861	30 Jan 1862
Tonnage	149 tons			
Dimensions	87′9″ × 25′2″ × 10′			
Complement	32			
Armament	(Feb 1862) 1–13″M, 2–12pdr SB			

Service record: Mortar Flotilla, Mississippi Sqn. Bombardment of Fts. Jackson and St. Philip below New Orleans, 18–28 Apr 1862. Bombardment of Vicksburg, 26 Jun–22 Jul 1862. Potomac Flotilla, Oct 1862. SAtlBS Jul 1863. Bombardment of forts in Charleston harbor, 13–15 Aug 1863. Expedition up Stono and Folly Rivers, S.C., 9–14 Feb 1865. Decomm 28 Jun 1865. Sold 10 Aug 1865.

Ship captured: *Sophia*, 3 Mar 1864.

Later history: Merchant *Volant* 1866. (British) SE 1870.

Name	Builder	Launched	Acquired	Comm.
George Mangham	Philadelphia, Pa.	1854	21 Sep 1861	11 Jan 1862
Tonnage	274 tons			
Dimensions	110′ × 28′ × 10′			
Complement	26			
Battery	(1862) 1–13″M, 2–32pdr/57; (Dec 1864) 6–32pdr/57, 1–12pdr MLR			

Service record: Mortar Flotilla, Mississippi Sqn. Bombardment of Fts. Jackson and St. Philip below New Orleans, 18–28 Apr 1862. Bombardment of Vicksburg, 26 Jun–22 Jul 1862. Potomac Flotilla, Dec 1862–Jul 1863. Antiraider patrol off Prince Edward Island, Aug–Nov 1863. SAtlBS 1864. Decomm 9 Sep and sold 27 Sep 1865.

Later history: FFU.

Name	Builder	Launched	Acquired	Comm.
Henry Janes	Pt. Jefferson, N.Y. (Bayles)	1854	27 Sep 1861	30 Jan 1862
Tonnage	261 tons			
Dimensions	109′9″ × 29′8″ × 9′			
Complement	35			
Armament	(Feb 1862) 1–13″M, 2–32pdr/57; (May 1864) less 1–13″M			

Service record: Mortar Flotilla, Mississippi Sqn. Bombardment of Fts. Jackson and St. Philip below New Orleans, 18–28 Apr 1862. Bombardment of Vicksburg, 26 Jun–22 Jul 1862. Engagement with CSS *Arkansas* above Vicksburg, 15 Jul 1862. Bombardment and capture of Galveston, Tex., 4 Oct 1862. Bombardment of Port Hudson, La., 8 May–9 Jul 1863. Bombardment of Ft. Powell, Mobile Bay, 16–29 Feb 1864. NAtlBS Aug 1864. Decomm 12 Jul and sold 20 Jul 1865.

Ships captured: *Eliza*, Oct 1862; *Matilda*, Jan 1863.

Later history: FFU.

Name	Builder	Launched	Acquired	Comm.
Horace Beals	New York, N.Y. (Roosevelt)	1856	19 Sep 1861	5 Feb 1862
Tonnage	296 tons			
Dimensions	121′6″ × 30′8″ × d11′8″			
Complement	39			
Armament	2–32pdr/33, 1–30pdr MLR; (Jan 1863) 1–32pdr/33.; (Jan 1864) 2–32pdr/33			

Service record: Mortar Flotilla, Mississippi Sqn. Bombardment of Fts. Jackson and St. Philip below New Orleans, 18–28 Apr 1862. Bombardment of Vicksburg, 26 Jun–22 Jul 1862. Engagement with CSS *Arkansas* above Vicksburg, 15 Jul 1862. Decomm 13 May and sold 30 May 1865.

Later history: Merchant *Horace Beals* 1865. Later Swedish *Britannia*, SE 1885.

Name	Builder	Launched	Acquired	Comm.
John Griffith	New York, N.Y.	1854	16 Sep 1861	20 Jan 1862
Tonnage	246 tons			
Dimensions	113′8″ × (U)			
Complement	39			
Armament	(Jan 1862) 1–13″M, 2–32pdr/57; 2–12pdr H			

Service record: Mortar Flotilla, Mississippi Sqn. Bombardment of Fts. Jackson and St. Philip below New Orleans, 18–28 Apr 1862. Bombardment of Vicksburg, 26 Jun–22 Jul 1862. Engagement with CSS *Arkansas* above Vicksburg, 15 Jul 1862. WGulfBS 1862–64. Bombardment of Port Hudson, La., 8 May–9 Jul 1863. Bombardment of Ft. Powell, Mobile Bay, 16–29 Feb 1864. SAtlBS 1864. Decomm 21 Aug and sold 8 Sep 1865.

Later history: FFU.

Name	Builder	Launched	Acquired	Comm.
Maria A. Wood	Philadelphia, Pa.	1860	21 Sep 1861	19 Nov 1861
Tonnage	344 tons			
Dimensions	1 25′ × 29′6″ × 9′			
Complement	25			
Armament	(Dec 1861) 2–32pdr/57			

Service record: WGulfBS 1861–62. Occupation of Pensacola, 10 May 1862. WGulfBS 1864–65. Decomm 22 Aug 1866. Sold 6 Sep 1866.

Later history: FFU.

Name	Builder	Launched	Acquired	Comm.
Maria J. Carlton	Saybrook, Conn. (Dennison)	(U)	15 Oct 1861	29 Jan 1862
Tonnage	178 tons			
Dimensions	98′ × 27′ × (U)			
Complement	28			
Armament	(Feb 1862) 1–13″M, 2–12pdr MLR			

Service record: Mortar Flotilla, Mississippi Sqn. Bombardment of Fts. Jackson and St. Philip below New Orleans, 18–19 Apr and sunk by Confederate gunfire, 19 Apr 1862 (none killed).

Name	Builder	Launched	Acquired	Comm.
Matthew Vassar ex-*Matthew Vassar Jr.*	Poughkeepsie, N.Y. (French)	1855	Sep 1861	25 Jan 1862
Tonnage	216 tons			
Dimensions	93′7″ × 27′2″ × 8′6″			

Complement   29

Armament   (Jan 1862) 1–13″M, 2–32pdr; (Feb 1862) add 2–12pdr; (May 1863) 1–30pdr MLR, 2–32pdr/42

Service record: Mortar Flotilla, Mississippi Sqn. Bombardment of Fts. Jackson and St. Philip below New Orleans, 18–28 Apr 1862. Bombardment of Vicksburg, 26 Jun–22 Jul 1862. NAtlBS 1863–64. EGulfBS Nov 1864–65. Decomm 10 Jul 1865. Sold 10 Aug 1865.

Ships captured: *New Eagle* and *Sarah*, 15 May 1862; *Florida*, 11 Jan 1863; *Golden Liner*, 27 Apr 1863; *John Hale*, 3 Feb 1865.

Later history: FFU.

Name	Builder	Launched	Acquired	Comm.
Norfolk Packet	E. Haddam, Conn. (Goodspeed)	1851	10 Sep 1861	7 Feb 1862

Tonnage   349 tons

Dimensions   109′6″ × 28′2″ × 11′

Complement   51

Armament   (Feb 1862) 1–13″M, 2–32pdr/57, 2–12pdr H; (May 1863) 2–20pdr MLR, 2–32pdr/57, 1–12pdr MLR

Service record: Mortar Flotilla, Mississippi Sqn. Bombardment of Fts. Jackson and St. Philip below New Orleans, 18–28 Apr 1862. Bombardment of Vicksburg, 26 Jun–22 Jul 1862. SAtlBS Nov 1862–Jun 1865. Bombardment of Ft. McAllister, Ga., 3 Mar 1863. Decomm 12 Jul 1865. Sold 10 Aug 1865.

Ships captured: *Ocean Bird*, 23 Oct 1863; *Linda*, 11 Mar 1864; *Sarah Mary*, 26 Jun 1864.

Later history: FFU.

Name	Builder	Launched	Acquired	Comm.
Oliver H. Lee	Hoboken, N.J. (Capes)	1851	27 Aug 1861	4 Feb 1862

Tonnage   199 tons

Dimensions   100′9″ × 28′4″ × 8′

Complement   37

Armament   (Feb 1862) 1–13″M, 2–32pdr/57, 2–12pdr SB; (Jun 1863) less 2–12pdr SB; (Dec 1864) 4–32pdr/57, 2–12pdr MLR

Service record: Mortar Flotilla, Mississippi Sqn. Bombardment of Fts. Jackson and St. Philip below New Orleans, 18–28 Apr 1862. Bombardment of Vicksburg, 26 Jun–22 Jul 1862. Engagement with CSS *Arkansas* above Vicksburg, 15 Jul 1862. Bombardment of Port Hudson, La., 8 May–9 Jul 1863. WGulfBS Aug 1863–65. Expeditions up Broad River, S.C., 27 Nov–30 Dec 1864 and to St. Marks, Fla., 23 Feb–27 Mar 1865. Decomm 10 Jul 1865. Sold 19 Aug 1865.

Ship captured: str *Sorts*, 10 Dec 1864.

Later history: Merchant *William S. Doughton* 1865. SE 1895.

Name	Builder	Launched	Acquired	Comm.
Orvetta	Northport, N.Y. (Carl)	1858	1 Oct 1861	27 Jan 1862

Tonnage   171 tons

Dimensions   93′ × 27′2″ × 7′

Complement   43

Armament   (Feb 1862) 1–13″M, 2–32pdr/57; (Dec 1864) 2–32pdr/33

Service record: Mortar Flotilla, Mississippi Sqn. Bombardment of Fts. Jackson and St. Philip below New Orleans, 18–28 Apr 1862. Bombardment of Vicksburg, 26 Jun–22 Jul 1862. Engagement with CSS *Arkansas* above Vicksburg, 15 Jul 1862. Bombardment of Port Hudson, La., 8 May–9 Jul 1863. WGulfBS 1863. Bombardment of Ft. Powell, Mobile Bay, 16–29 Feb 1864. Decomm 3 Jul and sold 15 Aug 1865.

Later history: Merchant *Orvetta* 1865. SE 1870.

Name	Builder	Launched	Acquired	Comm.
Para	Wilmington, Del.	1860	9 Sep 1861	4 Feb 1861

Tonnage   190 tons

Dimensions   98′ × 24′ × 9′

Complement   35

Armament   (Feb 1862) 1–13″M, 2–32pdr/57; (Mar 1864) 1–12pdr MLR, 2–20pdr MLR, 2–32pdr/57

Service record: Mortar Flotilla, Mississippi Sqn. Bombardment of Fts. Jackson and St. Philip below New Orleans, 18–28 Apr 1862. Bombardment of Vicksburg, 26 Jun–22 Jul 1862. SAtlBS 1863. Bombardment of Ft. McAllister, Ga., 3 Mar 1863. Expedition up Stono River, S.C., 5 Jul 1864. Decomm 5 Aug and sold 8 Sep 1865.

Ships captured: *Emma*, 19 Jun 1863; str *Hard Times*, 21 Feb 1864.

Later history: FFU.

Name	Builder	Launched	Acquired	Comm.
Racer	Hoboken N.J. (Capes)	1852	29 Aug 1861	21 Jan 1862

Tonnage   252 tons

Dimensions   105′ × 28′10″ × 9′10″

Complement   35

Armament   (Oct 1861) 4–32pdr/57; (Jan 1862) 1–13″M, 2–32pdr/57

Service record: Mortar Flotilla, Mississippi Sqn. Bombardment of Fts. Jackson and St. Philip below New Orleans, 18–28 Apr 1862. Bombardment of Vicksburg, 26 Jun–22 Jul 1862. Potomac Flotilla Sep 1862–63. SAtlBS Sep 1863. Bombardment of Ft. Wagner, Charleston, 13–15 Aug 1863. Expedition up Stono River, S.C., 5 Jul 1864. Decomm 2 Sep and sold 27 Sep 1865.

Later history: FFU.

Name	Builder	Launched	Acquired	Comm.
Sarah Bruen	Brookhaven, N.Y.	3 Sep 1854	3 Sep Feb 1854 1862	3 Feb 1862

Tonnage   233 tons

Dimensions   105′6″ × 26′7″ × 9′6″

Complement   35

Armament   (Feb 1862) 1–13″M, 2–32pdr/57; (Jul 1864) less 1–13″M

Service record: Mortar Flotilla, Mississippi Sqn. Bombardment of Fts. Jackson and St. Philip below New Orleans, 18–28 Apr 1862. Bombardment of Vicksburg, 26 Jun–22 Jul 1862. Engagement with CSS *Arkansas* above Vicksburg, 15 Jul 1862. WGulfBS 1862–64. Bombardment of Port Hudson, La., 8 May–9 Jul 1863. Bombardment of Ft. Powell, Mobile Bay, 16–29 Feb 1864. Blockade of Charleston, Jul 1864–65. Decomm 6 Jul and sold 15 Aug 1865.

Later history: Merchant *Sarah Bruen* 1865. Later British *Mollie A. Read*, SE 1885.

Name	Builder	Launched	Acquired	Comm.
Sea Foam	Falmouth, Mass.	1855	14 Sep 1861	27 Jan 1862

Tonnage   264 tons B

Dimensions   112′6″ × 26′ × d9′3″

Complement   35

Armament   (Feb 1862) 1–13″M, 2–32pdr/57; (Aug 1864) 2–32pdr/33

Service record: Mortar Flotilla, Mississippi Sqn. Bombardment of Fts. Jackson and St. Philip below New Orleans, 18–28 Apr 1862. Ran aground below New Orleans, Jun 1862. Bombardment of Port Hudson, La., 8 May–9 Jul 1863. WGulfBS 1863. SAtlBS 1864. Store ship, Port Royal, S.C., 1864–65. Bombardment of Ft. Powell, Mobile Bay, 16–29 Feb 1864. NAtlBS 1865. Decomm 16 May 1865. Sold 12 Jun 1865.

Ships captured: *New Eagle* and *Sarah*, 15 May 1862.

Later history: FFU.

Name	Builder	Launched	Acquired	Comm.
Sidney C. Jones	E.Haddam, Conn. (Goodspeed)	Apr 1856	7 Oct 1861	29 Jan 1862

Tonnage	245 tons
Dimensions	98′ × 27′ × 7′8″
Complement	36.
Armament	(Nov 1861) 2–32pdr/57; (Feb 1862) 1–13″M, 2–32pdr/57, 2–12pdr SB

Service record: Mortar Flotilla, Mississippi Sqn. Bombardment of Fts. Jackson and St. Philip below New Orleans, 18–28 Apr 1862. Bombardment of Vicksburg, 26 Jun–15 Jul 1862. Engagement with CSS *Arkansas* above Vicksburg, ran aground and was burned to prevent capture, 15 Jul 1862.

Name	Builder	Launched	Acquired	Comm.
Sophronia	New York, N.Y.	1854	3 Sep 1861	25 Jan 1862

Tonnage	217 tons
Dimensions	104′6″ × 28′4″ × 8′4″
Complement	32
Armament	(Feb 1862) 1–13″M, 2–32pdr/57, 2–12pdr SB

Service record: Mortar Flotilla, Mississippi Sqn. Bombardment of Fts. Jackson and St. Philip below New Orleans, 18–28 Apr 1862. Bombardment of Vicksburg, 26 Jun– 22 Jul 1862. Potomac Flotilla Aug 1862. Decomm 21 Aug 1865. Sold 8 Sep 1865.

Ship captured: *Mignonette*, 19 May 1863.

Later history: FFU.

Name	Builder	Launched	Acquired	Comm.
T.A. Ward	New York, N.Y.	1853	9 Oct 1861	17 Jan 1862

Tonnage	284 tons
Dimensions	114′6″ × 28′2″ × 10′6″
Complement	38
Armament	(Jan 1862) 1–13″M, 2–32pdr/57; (Feb 1862) add 2–12pdr SB; (Apr 1863) 4–32pdr/57, 1–12pdr SB

Service record: Mortar Flotilla, Mississippi Sqn. Bombardment of Fts. Jackson and St. Philip below New Orleans, 18–28 Apr 1862. Bombardment of Vicksburg, 26 Jun–22 Jul 1862. Potomac Flotilla, Aug 1862–63. NAtlBS Jul 1863. SAtlBS Sep 1863. Decomm 22 Jul 1865. Sold 25 Sep 1865.

Ships captured: *G.W. Green*, 16 Nov 1862; *Rover, 17 Oct 1863; str *Alliance*, 12 Apr 1864.

Later history: Merchant *T.A. Ward* 1865. SE 1870.

Name	Builder	Launched	Acquired	Comm.
William Bacon	Brookhaven, N.Y.	1852	6 Sep 1861	3 Feb 1862

Tonnage	183 tons
Dimensions	95′ × 26′ × 8′10″
Complement	36
Armament	(Feb 1862) 1–13″M, 2–32pdr/57, 2–12pdr SB; (May 1863) 1–30pdr MLR, 2–32pdr/57; (Sep 1863) 4–32pdr/57

Service record: Mortar Flotilla, Mississippi Sqn. Bombardment of Fts. Jackson and St. Philip below New Orleans, 18–28 Apr 1862. Potomac Flotilla 1862. NAtlBS Dec 1862. Blockade of Wilmington. Decomm 17 Jun 1865. Sold 20 Jul 1865.

Ships captured: *Ann Squires*, 1 Oct 1862; str *Nicolai I*, 21 Mar 1863.

Later history: Merchant *Elizabeth White*. SE 1870.

Ships

Name	Builder	Launched	Acquired	Comm.
Ben Morgan ex-*Mediator*	Philadelphia, Pa.	1826	27 May 1861	1861

Tonnage	407 tons
Dimensions	114′6″ × 29′6″ × d14′3″
Complement	35

Service record: Ordnance store ship, Hampton Roads, 1861–65. Sold 30 Nov 1865.

Later history: FFU.

Name	Builder	Launched	Acquired	Comm.
Charles Phelps	Westerly, R.I.	1842	24 Jun 1861	1861

Tonnage	362 tons
Dimensions	110′ × 27′4″ × 18′
Complement	23
Armament	(Jul 61) 1–32pdr/33 SB; (Feb 1864) none

Note: Also reported built 1848 at New London.

Service record: NAtlBS 1861–65, coal supply ship, Hampton Roads. Sold 25 Oct 1865.

Later history: Merchant *Progress* 1866.

Name	Builder	Launched	Acquired	Comm.
Courier	Newburyport, Mass. (Currier)	1855	7 Sep 1861	17 Sep 1861

Tonnage	556 tons
Dimensions	135′ × 30′ × d15′
Complement	82
Armament	2–31pdr

Service record: Storeship. Wrecked on Abaco Island, Bahamas, 14 Jun 1864.

Ships captured: *Emeline* and *Angelina*, 16 May 1863; *Maria Bishop*, 17 May 1863.

Later history: FFU.

Name	Builder	Launched	Acquired	Comm.
Fearnot	Newburyport, Mass. (Jackman)	1859	20 Jul 1861	28 Aug 1861

Tonnage	1,012 tons
Dimensions	178′ × 35′ × d23′6″
Complement	45
Armament	(Aug 1861) 6–32pdr/33; (Sep 1863) 1–8″ SB

Service record: WGulfBS 1861. Coal and supply ship, Key West, Fla. Decomm 18 Jul 1866. Sold 3 Oct 1866.

Later history: Merchant *Nevada* 1866. SE 1870.

Guard, see *National Guard*.

Name	Builder	Launched	Acquired	Comm.
Ino	Williamsburg, N.Y. (Perine)	1 Apr 1851	30 Aug 1861	23 Sep 1861

Tonnage	895 tons
Dimensions	160′6″ × 34′11″ × 18′9″
Armament	(Sep 1861) 6–32pdr/57, 2–32pdr/42; (Feb 1862) add 1–20pdr MLR; (Mar 1863) 6–32pdr/57, 2–100pdr MLR, 2–30pdr MLR; (May 1864) add 1–30pdr MLR

Service record: Storeship. Decomm 13 Feb 1866. Sold 19 Mar 1867.

Ship captured: *La Manche*, 23 Aug 1862.

Later history: Merchant *Ino* 1867. Renamed *Shooting Star III* and *Ellen*.

Sailing Ships 101

Name	Builder	Launched	Acquired	Comm.
Morning Light	Philadelphia, Pa. (Cramp)	15 Aug 1853	2 Sep 1861	21 Nov 1861
Tonnage	937 tons			
Dimensions	172' × 34'3" × 19'			
Complement	120			
Armament	(Nov 1861) 8–32pdr/57			

Service record: WGulfBS 1862. Captured and burned at Sabine Pass, Tex., 23 Jan 1863.
Ships captured: *Jorgen Lorentzen,*. 26 Dec 1861; *Venture*, 19 Jun 1862.

Name	Builder	Launched	Acquired	Comm.
National Guard	E. Haddam, Conn. (Gildersleeve)	1857	6 Jul 1861	23 Dec 1862
Tonnage	1,046 tons			
Dimensions	160' × 38' × 20'7"			
Armament	(Dec 1861) 4–32pdr/33; (Jan 1864) 1–30pdr MLR; (May 1865) 1–30pdr MLR, 4–32pdr/57			

Service record: West India Sqn, supply ship. 1862–65. Renamed **Guard**, 2 Jun 1866. European Sqn supply ship, 1866–69. Darien Expedition 1870. Decomm 15 Dec 1878. Sold 27 Sep 1883.

Name	Builder	Launched	Acquired	Comm.
Nightingale	Portsmouth, N.H. (Hanscombe)	16 Jun 1851	6 Jul 1861	18 Aug 1861
Tonnage	1,066 tons B			
Dimensions	177'10" × 36' × d20'			
Complement	51/186			
Armament	(Aug 1861) 4–32pdr/33; (Jun 1864) 4–8"			

Note: A famous clipper ship named after Jenny Lind. Captured as a slaver near mouth of Congo River by USS *Saratoga*, 20 Apr 1861.
Service record: Coal and store ship 1861. EGulfBS 1862. Ordnance ship, Pensacola, Fla., 1863–64. Decomm 20 Jun 1864. Sold 11 Feb 1865.
Later history: Merchant *Nightingale* 1865. Foundered in North Atlantic, 27 Apr 1893.

Name	Builder	Launched	Acquired	Comm.
Onward	Medford, Mass. (Curtis)	3 Jul 1852	9 Sep 1861	11 Jan 1862
Tonnage	874 tons			
Dimensions	167' (bp) × 34'8" × 20'			
Complement	103			
Armament	(Jan 1862) 8–32pdr/57; (Oct 1862) 1–30pdr MLR, 8–32pdr/57			

Service record: SAtlBS 1862–63. With *Mohican* blockaded Confederate tenders *Agrippina* and *Castor* at Bahia, Brazil, May 1863. Storeship, Callao, Peru 1866–84. Sold 14 Nov 1884.
Ships captured: *Chase, 26 Apr 1862; *Sarah, 1 May 1862; *Magicienne*, 28 Jan 1863.

Name	Builder	Launched	Acquired	Comm.
Pampero	Mystic, Conn. (Mallory)	18 Aug 1853	7 Jul 1861	Aug 1861
Tonnage	1,375 tons			
Dimensions	202'3" × 38'2" × 20'			
Complement	50			
Armament	(Aug 1861) 2–32pdr/33; (Aug 1863) 4–32pdr/33, 1–20pdr MLR, 1–24pdr H; (Aug 1865) 1–24pdr H replaced by 1–30pdr MLR			

Service record: GulfBS 1861. WGulf BS, Storeship and collier. Decomm 20 Jul 1866. Sold 1 Oct 1867.
Later history: FFU.

Name	Builder	Launched	Acquired	Comm.
Roman	New Bedford, Mass.	1835	18 May 1861	1861
Tonnage	350 tons			
Dimensions	112' × 26'3" × 18'			
Complement	19			
Armament	(Jun 1861) 1–32pdr/33; (Feb 1864) 1–32pdr/27			

Notes: Whaler
Service record: NAtlBS 1861, coal and ordnance storeship, Hampton Roads. Sold 30 Nov 1865.
Later history: Merchant *Roman* 1865. Crushed in ice in Bering Strait, 7 Sep 1871.

Name	Builder	Launched	Acquired	Comm.
Shepherd Knapp	New York, N.Y. (Westervelt)	23 Feb 1856	28 Aug 1861	1861
Tonnage	838 tons			
Dimensions	160'10" × 33'8" × 13'			
Complement	93			

Service record: W. Indies 1861–62. Wrecked on reef at Cap Haitien, Haiti, 18 May 1863.
Ship captured: *Fannie Laurie*, 4 Sep 1862.

Name	Builder	Launched	Acquired	Comm.
William Badger	(U)	(U)	18 May 1861	1862
Tonnage	334 tons			
Dimensions	106' × 26' × d13'3"			
Armament	(Jun 1861) 1–32pdr/33.			

Service record: Stationary supply ship, Hampton Roads, 1862. Supply hulk, Beaufort, N.C., 1863–65. Sold 17 Oct 1865.
Later history: FFU.

Barks

Name	Builder	Launched	Acquired	Comm.
A. Houghton	Robbinston, Me. (Rideout)	1852	12 Oct 1861	19 Feb 1862
Tonnage	326 tons			
Dimensions	113'4" × 25'3" × 12'			
Complement	27			
Armament	(Mar 1862) 2–32pdr/51' (Aug 1864) 4–32pdr/42, 2–20pdr MLR			

Service record: Mortar Flotilla, ordnance vessel 1862. Storeship, Pensacola, Aug 1862–Mar 1863. Ordnance vessel, Hampton Roads, Apr–Oct 1863. Storeship, Port Royal, S.C., Oct 1863–May 1865. Decomm 3 Jun 1865. Sold 10 Aug 1865.
Later history: Merchant bark *A. Houghton* 1865. SE 1870.

Name	Builder	Launched	Acquired	Comm.
Amanda	New York	1858	6 Aug 1861	1861
Tonnage	368 tons			

Dimensions 117'6" × 27'9" × d12'6"
Complement 71
Armament (Oct 1861) 6-32pdr/42; (May 1863) 6-32pdr/42, 1-20pdr MLR, 1-12pdr H

Service record: NAtlBS Nov 1861–62. EGulfBS Mar 1862–May 1863. Went aground in St. George's Sound, Fla. and burned to prevent capture, 29 May 1863.
Ships captured: str *Swan*, 24 May 1862; unidentified bark, 17 Jun 1862.

Name	Builder	Launched	Acquired	Comm.
Arthur	Amesbury, Mass.	1855	1 Aug 1861	11 Dec 1861

Tonnage 554 tons
Dimensions 133' × 31'2" × 14'1"
Complement 31/86

Service record: GulfBS Jan 1862. Blockade off Texas. Damaged in collision with merchant ship off Rio Grande, 28 Mar 1863. Guard ship, Pensacola, Oct 1863–Aug 1865. Sold 27 Sep 1865.
Ships captured: *J.J.McNeil*, 25 Jan 1862; *Reindeer*, 9 Jul 1862; *Monte Cristo and *Belle Italia, 19 Jul 1862; *Hannah, *Elma, *Breaker, and str **A. Bee*, 12 Aug 1862; *Water Witch*, 24 Aug 1862.
Later history: FFU.

Name	Builder	Launched	Acquired	Comm.
Avenger	(U)	(U)	1 Aug 1861	11 Dec 1861

Tonnage 554 tons
Dimensions 133' × 31'2" × 14'1"
Armament (Aug 1861) 6-32pdr/42

Service record: Sold 27 Sep 1865.
Later history: FFU.

Name	Builder	Launched	Acquired	Comm.
Braziliera	Baltimore, Md. (Abrahams)	1856	30 Jul 1861	27 Oct 1861

Tonnage 540 tons
Dimensions 135'8" × 28'7" × 10'
Armament (Aug 1861) 6-32pdr/42; (Feb 1864) 6-32pdr/42, 1-12pdr SB, 1-24pdr SB

Service record: NAtlBS 1862. Damaged in collision with USS *Amanda* in Hampton Roads, 3 Mar 1862. SAtlBS Jun 1862. Engagement with CSS *North Carolina* in Cape Fear River, May 1864. Sold 2 Jun 1865.
Ships captured: *Chance*, 28 Jun 1862; *Defiance*, 7 Sep 1862; *Mary*, 13 Oct 1863; *Antoinette, 8 Dec 1863; *Buffalo, 1 Feb 1864.
Later history: FFU.

Name	Builder	Launched	Acquired	Comm.
Ethan Allen	E. Boston, Mass. (Gardner)	Mar 1859	23 Aug 1861	3 Oct 1861

Tonnage 556 tons
Dimensions 153'6" × 35'1" × 13'
Complement 87
Armament (Oct 1861) 4-32pdr/51, 2-32pdr/33; (Dec 1861) add 1-12pdr; (Apr 1863) add 1-20pdr MLR

Service record: GulfBS 1861–63. SAtlBS Nov 1863. Expedition to Murrells Inlet, S.C., 29 Dec 1863–1 Jan 1864. Decomm 26 Jun 1865. Sold 20 Jul 1865.
Ships captured: *Fashion*, 29 Nov 1861; *Olive Branch*, 21 Jan 1862; *Atlanta, *Spitfire, and *Caroline, 18 Feb 1862; *Gypsy*, 19 Mar 1863.
Later history: FFU.

Fig 5.3: The bark USS *Ethan Allen*, an active blockader, at Charlestown Navy Yard, Boston. At right is the ship-of-the-line *Ohio*. (Peabody Essex Museum)

Name	Builder	Launched	Acquired	Comm.
Farallones ex-*Massachusetts* (Jan 1863)	Boston, Mass. (Hall)	23 Jul 1845	Jan 1862	17 Jun 1863

Tonnage 750 tons B
Dimensions 178' or 156'6" (bp) 161' × 32'2" × 15'6"
Armament 2-9pdr SB; (Jul 1863) 6-32pdr/33

Notes: Former trans-Atlantic steamer acquired by War Dept as a transport in Mexican War and transferred to Navy 1 Aug 1849. Transferred to War Dept, May 1859, and returned Jan 1862. Ericsson lifting screw, 2 inclined direct-acting engines, 2 boilers, HP 170, 8 knots. Removed and converted to sail, 1862.
Service record: Converted to bark at Mare Island 1862 and renamed. Storeship, Pacific Sqn, 1863–67. Sold 15 May 1867.
Later history: Merchant *Alaska* 1867. Wrecked at Callao, Peru, 24 Jul 1871.

Name	Builder	Launched	Acquired	Comm.
Fernandina ex-*Florida*	Eastport, Me.	1850	29 Jul 1861	16 Nov 1861

Tonnage 297 tons
Dimensions 115' × 29' × 10'
Complement 86
Armament (Aug 1861) 6-32pdr/42; (Jun 1863) 6-32pdr/42, 1-24pdr H, 1-20pdr MLR

Service record: NAtlBS Dec 1861–Jun 1862. SAtlBS Jun 1862–63. Decomm 29 Apr and sold 2 Jun 1865.
Ships captured: *William H. Northrup*, 25 Dec 1861; *Kate, 2 Apr 1862; *Annie Thompson*, 16 Jan 1864.
Later history: FFU.

Name	Builder	Launched	Acquired	Comm.
Gem of the Sea	Warren, R.I. (Chase Davis)	1853	3 Aug 1861	15 Oct 1861

Tonnage 371 tons

Sailing Ships 103

Dimensions 116' × 26'3" × d13'4"
Complement 65
Armament (Aug 1861) 6–32pdr/42; (Oct 1861) 4–32pdr/42; (Jun 1863) 4–32pdr/42, 1–20pdr MLR

Service record: SAtlBS 1861–62. EGulfBS Dec 1862. Decomm 24 Feb 1865. Sold 6 May 1865.

Ships captured: *Prince of Wales*, 24 Dec 1861; *Fair Play*, 12 Mar 1862; *Mary Stewart*, 3 Jun 1862; *Seabrook*, 12 Jun 1862; *Volante*, 2 Jul 1862; **Ann*, 30 Dec 1862; *Charm*, 23 Feb 1863; **Petee*, 10 Mar 1863; *Maggie Fulton*, 8 Apr 1863; **Inez*, 18 Apr 1863; *George*, 29 Jul 1863; *Richard*, 31 Aug 1863; **Director*, 30 Sep 1863; *Matilda*, 21 Oct 1863.

Later history: FFU.

Name	Builder	Launched	Acquired	Comm.
Gemsbok	E. Boston, Mass. (R.E. Jackson)	1857	7 Sep 1861	30 Aug 1861
Tonnage	622 tons			
Dimensions	141'7" × 30'3" × d17'			
Complement	103			
Armament	(Sep 1861) 4–8"/63, 2–32pdr/33; (Apr 1865) add 1–20pdr MLR			

Service record: SAtlBS 1861–62. Capture of Ft. Macon, N.C., 25–26 Apr 1862. West Indies Sqn, storeship, Feb–Jul 1863. SAtlBS 1865. Sold 12 Jul 1865

Ships captured: *Harmony*, 19 Sep 1861; *Mary E. Pindar*, 22 Sep 1861; *Beverly*, 3 Oct 1861; *Ariel*, 18 Oct 1862; *Gondar* and *Glenn*, 26 Apr 1862.

Later history: Merchant bark *Gemsbok* 1865. SE 1870.

Name	Builder	Launched	Acquired	Comm.
Ironsides Jr.	(U)	(U)	Aug 1863	1863
Tonnage	200 tons.			

Service record: Storeship, Port Royal, 1863–64.

Name	Builder	Launched	Acquired	Comm.
J.C. Kuhn	E. Haddam, Conn. (Gildersleeve)	1859	6 Jul 1861	23 Aug 1861
Tonnage	888 tons			
Dimensions	153' × 35' × 13'5"			
Complement	61			
Armament	(Apr 1861) 2–32pdr/33; (Jan 1864) 6–32pdr/38			

Service record: GulfBS 1861. Supply and coal vessel. Vicksburg, Jun 1862. Storeship, Pensacola 1864. Renamed *Purveyor*, 10 Apr 1866. Sold 7 Jul 1869.

Later history: Merchant *J.C. Kuhn* 1869. Renamed *C.E. Jayne*, Norwegian *Jason*, 1877. RR 1910.

Name	Builder	Launched	Acquired	Comm.
James L. Davis	Pt. Jefferson, N.Y. (Darling)	1857	29 Sep 1861	30 Dec 1861
Tonnage	461 tons			
Dimensions	133' × 30'7" × 12'			
Complement	75.			
Armament	(Feb 1862) 4–8"/55.			

Service record: WGulfBS 1862. EGulfBS 1862. Occupation of Tampa, Fla., 4–7 May 1864. Sold 20 Jun 1865.

Ships captured: *Florida*, 10 Mar 1862; *Isabel*, 23 Sep 1862.

Later history: Merchant *Gen. G.G. Meade*. SE 1868.

Name	Builder	Launched	Acquired	Comm.
Kingfisher	Fairhaven, Me. (Fish)	1857	2 Aug 1861	3 Oct 1861
Tonnage	451 tons			
Dimensions	121'4" × 28'8" × 16'6"			
Complement	97			
Armament	(Oct 1861) 4–8" SB; (May 1863) 4–8" SB, 1–20pdr MLR, 1–12pdr			

Service record: EGulfBS 1861–62. SAtlBS Dec 1862. Went aground and lost in St. Helena Sound, S.C., 28 Mar 1864

Ships captured: *Olive Branch*, 21 Jan 1862; *Teresita*, 30 Jan 1862; *Lion*, 25 Feb 1862.

Name	Builder	Launched	Acquired	Comm.
Midnight	New York, N.Y. (Collyer)			
ex-Dawn		8 Jul 1857	31 Jul 1861	19 Oct 1861
Tonnage	386 tons			
Dimensions	126' × 27'10" × 11'			
Complement	70			
Armament	(Oct 1861) 4–32pdr/42; (May 1863) 1–20pdr MLR, 4–32pdr/42, 2–32pdr/57; (Mar 1864) 2–32pdr/57, 4–32pdr/42, 1–20pdr MLR, 1–12pdr MLR			

Service record: GulfBS 1861–62 off Texas. SAtlBS Oct 1862–63. EGulfBS Oct 1864–65. Sold 1 Nov 1865.

Ship captured: *Defy*, 3 Feb 1864.

Later history: FFU.

Name	Builder	Launched	Acquired	Comm.
Pursuit	Baltimore, Md.	1857	3 Sep 1861	17 Dec 1861
Tonnage	603 tons			
Dimensions	144' × 34'10" × d15'			
Complement	92			
Armament	(Dec 1861) 6–32pdr/57; (May 1863) add 1–20pdr MLR			

Service record: EGulfBS 1862–65. Decomm 5 Jun 1865. Sold 12 Jul 1865.

Ships captured: *Anna Belle*, 6 Mar 1862; **Lafayette*, 4 Apr 1862; str *Florida*,* 6 Apr 1862; *Andromeda*. 26 May 1862; *Kate*, 23 Jun 1863; *Peep O'Day*, 4 Dec 1864; *Mary*, 16 Mar 1865.

Later history: Merchant *Pursuit* 1865. SE 1870.

Purveyor, see *J.C. Kuhn*.

Name	Builder	Launched	Acquired	Comm.
Restless	Madison, Conn.	1854	26 Aug 1861	24 Dec 1861
Tonnage	265 tons			
Dimensions	108'8" × 27'8" × 10'			
Complement	66			
Armament	(Dec 1861) 4–32pdr/51; (Jun 1863) 1–20pdr MLR, 4–32pdr/51, 2–12pdr SB			

Service record: SAtlBS Jan 1862–Jan 1863. EGulfBS Jun 1863 off Florida. Operations in St. Andrews Bay, Fla., 10–18 Dec 1863. Sold 21 Sep 1865.

Ships captured: **Edisto*, **Elizabeth*, **Wando*, and **Theodore Stoney*, 14 Feb 1862; **George Washington*, **Mary Louise*, and *Julia Worden*, 27 Mar 1862; *Lydia & Mary*, 29 Mar 1862; *Flash*, 2 May 1862; *John Thompson*, 2 Sep 1862; *Elmira Cornelius*, 12 Oct 1862; str *Scotia*, 24 Oct 1862; *Susan McPherson*, 31 Oct 1862; *Ann*, 8 Jul 1863; *Erniti*, 19 Aug 1863; *William A. Kain*, 22 Jan 1864.

* Later USS *Hendrick Hudson*.

104 Civil War Navies, 1855-1883

Later history: Merchant *Restless* 1865. SE 1870.

Name	Builder	Launched	Acquired	Comm.
Roebuck	New York, N.Y. (Collyer)	6 May 1856	21 Jul 1861	8 Nov 1861
Tonnage	455 tons			
Dimensions	135' × 27' × 14'6"			
Complement	69			
Armament	(Aug 1861) 6–32pdr; (Oct 1861) 4–32pdr/42; (Aug 1862) 1–20pdr MLR, 4–32pdr/42.			

Service record: SAtlBS 1861–62. EGulfBS Sep 1862–Jul 1864. Decomm 17 Oct 1864. Sold 20 Jul 1865.
Ships captured: *Kate*, 27 Dec 1862; *Emma Amelia*, 2 May 1863; *Ringdove*, 17 Dec 1863; *Maria Louise*, 10 Jan 1864; *Susan*, 11 Jan 1864; *Young Racer, 14 Jan 1864; *Caroline*, 18 Jan 1864; *Eliza & Mary*, 19 Jan 1864; *Two Brothers*, 25 Feb 1864; **Rebel & Nina*, 27 Feb 1864; *Lauretta*, 1 Mar 1864; *Last Resort*, 30 Jun 1864; *Terrapin*, 10 Jul 1864.
Later history: Merchant *Roebuck* 1865. SE 1870.

Name	Builder	Launched	Acquired	Comm.
William G.Anderson	E. Boston, Mass. (Gardner)	1 Sep 1859	23 Aug 1861	2 Oct 1861
Tonnage	593 tons			
Dimensions	149'7" × 30'1"			
Armament	(Oct 1861) 2–32pdr/33, 4–32pdr/51, 1–24pdr H; (Jun 1863) 1–20pdr MLR, 2–32pdr/33, 4–32pdr/51, 1–12pdr MLR			

Service record: WGulfBS 1861. Captured Confederate privateer *Beauregard* in Bahama Channel, 12 Nov 1861. Blockade of Galveston, Jun 1862–65. Decomm 21 Jul 1866. Sold 28 Aug 1866.
Ships captured: *Montebello*, 11 Jun 1862; *Lily*, 31 Aug 1862; *Theresa*, 4 Sep 1862; *Reindeer*, 17 Sep 1862; *Royal Yacht*, 15 Apr 1863; *Nymph*, 17 Apr 1863; *Mack Canfield*, 25 Aug 1863; *America, 27 Aug 1863.
Later history: Merchant *Yokohama* 1866. SE 1870.

Brigs

Name	Builder	Launched	Acquired	Comm.
Bohio	Williamsburg, N.Y.	1856	9 Sep 1861	30 Dec 1861
Tonnage	197 tons			
Dimensions	100' × 24'9" × d9'4"			
Complement	34			
Armament	(Jan 1862) 2–32pdr/57; (Jul 1863) 2–32pdr/57,2–32pdr/33, 1–12pdr MLR, 1–12pdr SB			

Service record: WGulfBS Jan 1862–Mar 1864. Converted to coal vessel 1864. Decomm 25 Jul 1865. Sold 27 Sep 1865.
Ships captured: *Eugenie Smith*,* 7 Feb 1862; *Henry Travers*, 8 Mar 1862; *Deer Island, 13 May 1862; *L. Rebecca*, 21 Jun 1862; *Wave*, 27 Jun 1862.
Later history: Merchant brig *Bohio* 1865. SE 1870.

Name	Builder	Launched	Acquired	Comm.
Valparaiso	Baltimore, Md.	1836	22 Nov 1861	1861
Tonnage	402 tons			
Dimensions	117'6" × 27'6"			
Complement	36			

* Later USS *Eugenie*.

| Armament | No guns |

Service record: SAtlBS 1861. Storeship, Port Royal, S.C.. Sold 2 Sep 1865.
Later history: FFU.

Schooners

Name	Builder	Launched	Acquired	In service
Albemarle	(U)	(U)	9 May 1863	1862
Tonnage	200 tons			
Dimensions	85' × 25'6" × d7'7"			
Complement	22			

Notes: Captured by USS *Delaware* off Pantego Creek, N.C., 26 Mar 1862.
Service record: Ordnance supply vessel, NatlBS 1863–65. Sold 19 Oct 1865.

Name	Builder	Launched	Acquired	In service
Dana	(U)	(U)	10 Jun 1861	1861
ex-*US Coast Survey*				
Armament	(Oct 1861) 2–32pdr/33; (Sep 1862) 2–32pdr/33, 2–24pdr SB, 1–12pdr MLR			

Service record: Potomac Flotilla, guard ship, and coal depot. Stricken Jul 1862.
Ships captured: *Teaser*, 5 Jul 1861; *T.J. Evans*, 1 Sep 1861.

Name	Builder	Launched	Acquired	Comm.
Eugenie	Lewistown, Me.	1844	22 Apr 1862	1862
ex-*Eugenie Smith*				
Tonnage	150 tons			
Complement	36			
Armament	1 gun			

Note: Captured by USS *Bohio* off Mississippi River, 7 Feb 1862.
Service record: Guard ship, Key West. Sold Nov 1864.
Ship captured: str *Alabama*, 12 Sep 1863.
Later history: FFU.

Name	Builder	Launched	Acquired	Comm.
G.W. Blunt	E. Boston, Mass.	1861	23 Nov 1861	4 Dec 1861
Tonnage	121 tons			
Dimensions	76'6" × 20'6" × 9'			
Complement	16			
Armament	(Jul 1863) 2–12pdr MLR			

Service record: SatlBS 1862–64. Mail and dispatch boat. Salvage ship 1864. Decomm 16 Aug 1865. Sold 20 Oct 1865.
Ship captured: *Wave*, 19 Apr 1862.
Later history: FFU.

Name	Builder	Launched	Acquired	Comm.
Hope	(U)	(U)	29 Nov 1861	14 Dec 1861
Tonnage	134 tons			
Dimensions	86'6" × 21'3" × 9'6"			
Armament	(Mar 1864) 1–20pdr MLR			

Service record: SAtlBS 1862. Salvage ship 1865. Decomm 6 Sep 1865. Sold 25 Oct 1865.
Ships captured: *Emma Tuttle*, 27 Jan 1863; *Racer*, 1 Aug 1863.
Later history: FFU.

Name	Builder	Launched	Acquired	Comm.
James S. Chambers	(U)	(U)	4 Sep 1861	16 Dec 1861
Tonnage	401 tons			
Dimensions	124′6″ × 29′3″			
Complement	62			
Armament	(Jun 1862) 4–32pdr/57; (Apr 1863) add 1–20pdr MLR, 1–12pdr H			

Service record: GulfBS 1862–64. SAtlBS 1865. Expedition to Bulls Bay, S.C., 12–17 Feb 1865. Decomm 31 Aug 1865. Sold 27 Sep 1865.
Ships captured: *Corelia*, 23 Aug 1862; str *Union*, 25 Aug 1862; *Ida and *Relampago*, 4 Mar 1863; *Rebekah*, 18 Jun 1863.
Later history: FFU.

Name	Builder	Launched	Acquired	Comm.
Kittatinny ex-*Stars and Stripes*	(U)	(U)	21 Sep 1861	9 Dec 1861
Tonnage	421 tons			
Dimensions	129′ × 29′ × d11′6″			
Complement	66			
Armament	(Dec 1861) 4–32pdr/57; (Jul 1863) 4–32pdr/57, 1–30pdr MLR, 1–12pdr MLR			

Service record: GulfBS 1862–63. WGulfBS Sep 1863, Texas. Decomm 14 Sep 1865. Sold 27 Sep 1865.
Ships captured: *Julia*, 11 May 1862; *Emma*, 26 Sep 1862; *Matilda*, 25 Nov 1862; *Diana*, 25 Nov 1862; 12 Mar: *D. Sargent*, 1863; 25 Oct: *Reserve*, 25 Oct 1863.
Later history: FFU.

Name	Builder	Launched	Acquired	Comm.
Rachel Seaman	Philadelphia, Pa.	1861	21 Sep 1861	16 Nov 1861
Tonnage	303 tons			
Dimensions	115′ × 30′ × d9′			
Complement	13			
Armament	(Oct 1861) 2–32pdr/57; (Feb 1864) 1–32pdr/33, 1–12pdr MLR; (Sep 1864) 2–12pdr MLR.			

Service record: GulfBS Nov 1861–May 1864. Blockade of Texas. Bombarded Sabine Pass forts, 25 Sep 1862. Decomm 22 May 1865. Sold 30 May 1865
Ships captured: *Velocity*,* 25 Sep 1862; str *Dart*, 6 Oct 1862; *Maria* and *Cora*, 11 Nov 1862; *Nymph*, 21 Apr 1863; *Maria Alfred*, 13 Apr 1864.
Later history: FFU.

Name	Builder	Launched	Acquired	Comm.
Samuel Rotan	Tuckahoe, N.J.	1858	21 Sep 1861	12 Nov 1861
Tonnage	212 tons			
Dimensions	110′ × 28′6″ × 9′			
Complement	29			
Armament	(Oct 1861) 2–2pdr/57; (Dec 1861) add 1–24pdr H; (Feb 1863) 1–30pdr MLR, 2–32pdr/57; (Dec 1863) add 1–24pdr H; (Dec 1864) 2–30pdr MLR, 2–32pdr/57, 1–24pdr H			

Service record: GulfBS 1861. EGulfBS 1862. NAtlBS 1863. Decomm 10 Jun 1865. Sold 15 Aug 1865.
Ships captured: Privateer str *Calhoun*,** 23 Jan 1862; *Martha Ann*, 24 Apr 1863; *Champion*, 1 Jul 1863.
Later history: FFU.

Name	Builder	Launched	Acquired	Comm.
Wanderer	Setauket, N.Y. (J.Rowland)	1857	May 1861	
Tonnage	300 tons			
Dimensions	106′ × 25′6″ × 9′6″			
Complement	26			
Armament	(May 1863) 1–20pdr MLR, 2–24pdr H; (Jan 1865) 1–20pdr MLR			

Note: Sometime slaver seized at Key West May 1861.
Service record: EGulfBS 1861–65. Sold 28 Jun 1865.
Ships captured: *Belle*, 15 Jul 1861; *Ranger*, 25 Mar 1863; *Annie B.*, 17 Apr 1863.
Later history: Merchant *Wanderer*, 1865. Lost off Cape Maisi, Cuba, 21 Jan 1871.

---

* Later USS Velocity.
** Later USS Calhoun.

106 Civil War Navies, 1855-1883

Small Schooners and Sloops

Name	Builder	Built	Acquired	Dimensions	Tons	Type	Armament
America	New York, N.Y. (Wm.H.Brown)	1851	19 May 1862	111 × 25	100	Yacht	1–12pdr MLR, 2–24pdr SB
ex-*Memphis*, ex-*Camilla*, ex-*America*							
Anna		1857	11 Mar 1863	46 × 14	27	schr	1–12pdr R
ex-*La Criolla*, ex-*Nora* (?)							
Ariel		24 Jul 1863	24 Jul 1863		20	schr	1–12pdr SB
Beauregard	Charleston	1850	24 Feb 1862		101	schr	1–30pdr MLR, 2–12pdr H SB
ex-*Priscilla C. Ferguson*							
Carmita			10 Mar 1863	65 × 20	61	schr	
Charlotte			6 Nov 1862	56 × 17	70	schr	
Chotank							
ex-*Savannah*	Richmond, Me.	1842	2 Jul 1861	56 × 17	53	schr	2–9" SB, 1–11"R
Corypheus	Brookhaven, N.Y.	1859	12 Jun 1862		82	schr	1–30pdr MLR, 1–24pdr H
Dart			4 Jul 1861		94	schr	
Fox	Baltimore	1859	6 May 1863		80	schr	2–12pdr MLR
ex-*Alabama*, ex-*Fox*							
G.L. Brockenborough			15 Nov 1862			sloop	
George W. Rodgers, see *Shark*							
Granite			19 Jan 1862		75	sloop	1–32pdr/57
Howell Cobb			10 Jun 1861			schr	
Isilda			1 Nov 1861			schr	
ex-*Isilda* (British)							
Julia			15 Feb 1863		10	sloop	None
J.W. Wilder			19 May 1863			schr	
Lightning			9 Mar 1865			schr	
Percy Drayton			12 Nov 1863			sloop	
ex-*Hettiwan*							
Renshaw		1862	28 Oct 1862	68 × 20	80	schr	
Rosalie			6 May 1863	45 × 17	28	sloop	1–12pdr SB
Sam Houston	Baltimore, Md.	1859	1861		66	schr	1–12pdr SB
Sea Bird			12 Jul 1863	59 × 18	58	schr	1–12pdr H R
Shark	Portsmouth, N.H.	1860	5 Sep 1863	76 × 22	87	schr	2–20pdr MLR
Stonewall			24 Jul 1863		30	schr	1–12pdr SB
Susan A. Howard			19 May 1863	50 × 17		schr	
Thunder			9 Dec 1863			sloop	
ex-*Annie Dees*							
Two Sisters	Baltimore, Md.	1856	21 Sep 1862		54	schr	1–12pdr SB
Velocity			30 Sep 1862		87	schr	
Wildcat		1862			30	schr	

Notes: *America* was the namesake of the America's Cup. *Anna* was also spelled *Annie*, and *Isilda* was also spelled *Ezilda*. *Granite* was an ex U.S. Lighthouse Board vessel. *Howell Cobb* was an ex-U.S. Coast Survey vessel.

Service records:

America: Found sunk in St. Johns River, Fla., Mar 1862. Raised and refitted. SAtlBS 1862–63. School ship, Naval Academy. Sold 20 Jun 1873.
   Ship captured: *David Crockett*, 13 Oct 1862.
   Later history: Reacquired 1 Oct 1921. Laid up 1941 and disintegrated.

Anna: Captured by USS *Fort Henry* in Suwanee River, 26 Feb 1863. Tender to USS *Dale*, west coast of Florida. Wrecked by an explosion off Cape Roman, Fla., Jan 1865.

Ariel: Captured as blockade runner by USS *Huntsville* in Gulf of Mexico, 14 Nov 1862. EGulfBS 1862–65. Tender. Operation at Bayport, Fla., 10 Jul 1864. Sold 28 Jun 1865.
   Ships captured: *Good Luck*, 6 Jan 1863; *Magnolia*, 16 Dec 1863; *General Finegan, 28 May 1864.

Beauregard: Captured as privateer by USS *William G. Anderson* in Bahama Channel, 12 Nov 1861. EGulfBS Apr 1862–Jun 1865. Engaged batteries

at Tampa Bay, Fla., 2–9 Apr 1863. Bombardment of New Smyrna, Fla., 28 Jul 1863. Sold 28 Jun 1865.
  Ships captured: *Lucy,* 20 Jun 1862; *Phoebe,* 26 Aug 1863; *Last Trial,* 6 Oct 1863; *Volante,* 5 Nov 1863; *Minnie,* 15 Jan 1864; *Racer,* 28 Jan 1864; *Hannah, Linda,* 11 Mar 1864; *Spunky,* 7 Apr 1864; *Oramoneta,* 18 Apr 1864; *Resolute,* 12 May 1864.
  Later history: FFU.
Carmita: Captured by USS *Magnolia* off Marquesas Key, 27 Dec 1862. EGulfBS 1863, lighter and storeship. Sold 1866.
Charlotte: Captured as blockade runner by USS *Kanawha* off Mobile, 10 Apr 1862. WGulfBS 1862. Sold 27 Apr 1867.
  Ship captured: str *Bloomer,** 24 Dec 1862.
Chotank: Captured as privateer *Savannah* by USS *Perry,* 3 Jun 1861. Potomac Flotilla 1862. Laid up 1863–65. Sold 15 Aug 1865.
Corypheus: Captured by USS *Calhoun* in Bayou Bonfuca, La., 13 May 1862. WGulfBS 1862–64. Battle of Sabine Pass, 1 Jan 1863. Sold 15 Sep 1865.
  Ship captured: *Water Witch,* 23 Aug 1862.
Dart: Captured by USS *South Carolina* off Galveston, Tex, 4 Jul 1861. BU 21 Oct 1861.
  Ships captured: *Cecilia,* 24 Sep 1861; **Reindeer,* Sep 1861.
Fox: Captured as blockade runner by USS *Susquehanna,* 18 Apr 1863. EGulfBS 1863–65. Sold 28 Jun 1865.
  Ships captured: *Edward,* 20 Dec 1863; **Powerful,* 24 Dec 1863; **Good Hope,* 18 Apr 1864; *Oscar,* 1 May 1864; *Fannie McRae,* 23 Jan 1865; **Rob Roy,* 2 Mar 1865.
G.L. Brookenborough: Captured by USS *Fort Henry* scuttled in Apalachicola River, 15 Oct 1862 and raised. EGulfBS 1862. Wrecked in gale in St. George's Sound, Fla., 27 May 1863.
Granite: NAtlBS 1862. Landings at Roanoke I., N.C., 7–8 Feb 1862. Returned to U.S. Lighthouse Board, 29 Jun 1865.
Howell Cobb: Potomac River, 1861–62. Went aground off Cape Ann, 22 Dec 1861. Returned to U.S. Coast Survey Jul 1862.
Isilda: Captured as blockade runner by USS *South Carolina* off Timbalier, La., 4 Oct 1861. GulfBS 1862. Sold 1863.
  Ship captured: str **Havana,* 5 Jun 1862.
Julia: British sloop captured by USS *Sagamore* off Jupiter Inlet, Fla., 8 Jan 1863. SAtlBS 1864. BU at Key West 1865.
  Ship captured: *Stonewall*, 20 Feb 1863..
J. W. Wilder: Captured by USS *R.R. Cuyler* off Mobile Bay, 20 Jan 1862. WGulfBS 1863, tender. Coal hulk. Sold ?.
Lightning: Captured at Port Royal, S.C., 9 Mar 1865. Sold 5 Aug 1865.
Percy Drayton: Captured as blockade runner by USS *Ottawa* off Charleston, 21 Jan 1863. SAtlBS, Tender. Sold 2 Sep 1865.
Renshaw: Captured new and unrigged in Tar River, N.C., 20 May 1862. Ordnance hulk. NAtlBS. Sold 12 Aug 1865.
Rosalie: Captured as blockade runner by USS *Octorara* off Charleston, 16 Mar 1863. Tender, Charlotte, Fla. 1863. Sold 28 Jun 1865.
  Ships captured: *Ann,* 8 Jul 1863; *Georgie,* 26 Jul 1863; *Director,* 30 Sep 1863; str *Emma,* 9 Jun 1864.
Sam Houston: Captured by USS *South Carolina* off Galveston, 7 Jul 1861. WgulfBS 1861–65, dispatch vessel. Sold 25 Apr 1866.
Sea Bird: Captured by USS *De Soto* off Pensacola, 14 May 1863. WGulfBS 1863–65. Operation at Bayport, Fla., 10 Jul 1864. Sold 28 Jun 1865.
  Ships captured: *Lucy,* 21 Oct 1864; *Annie and **Florida,* 11 Apr 1865.
Shark: Captured off Galveston by USS *South Carolina,* 4 Jul 1861. Chartered as dispatch boat 1862–64. Renamed **George W. Rodgers**, 17 Jan 1865. SAtlBS 1865. Decomm 16 Aug 1865. Sold 8 Sep 1865.
Stonewall: Pilot boat, captured by USS *Tahoma* at Point Rosa, Fla., 24 Feb 1863. Tender, Key West. Sold 28 Jun 1865.
  Ship captured: *Josephine,* 24 Mar 1864.
Susan A. Howard: Ordnance boat, off North Carolina. Sold 15 Sep 1865.
Thunder: Captured as blockade runner off Charleston by USS *Seneca,* 20 Nov 1862. SAtlBS, 1863, tender. Sold 8 Aug 1865.

* Later USS *Bloomer.*

Fig 5.4:. The famous yacht *America* at Annapolis about 1870. The namesake of the America Cup, she was used as a training ship for the Naval Academy. (U.S. Naval Historical Center)

Two Sisters: Captured by USS *Albatross* off Rio Grande River, 21 Sep 1862. EGulfBS 1863. Expedition to St. Marks, Fla., 23 Feb–27 Mar 1865. Sold 28 Jun 1865.
  Ships captured: *Richards,* 1 Feb 1863; *Agnes,* 31 Mar 1863; *Oliver S. Breese,* 16 May 1863; *Frolic,* 25 Jun 1863; *Maria Alberta,* 27 Nov 1863; *William,* 13 Jan 1864.
Velocity: Blockade runner captured by USS *Kensington* and *Rachel Seaman* at Sabine, Tex., 25 Sep 1862. Recaptured at Sabine Pass, 23 Jan 1863.
  Ship captured: *Corse,* 11 Nov 1862.
Wildcat: Captured 1862. Operated in South Carolina waters 1862–65. Sold 28 Jul 1865.

6
THE MISSISSIPPI RIVER FLEET

With the secession of the Southern states, it was immediately apparent that whoever controlled the Mississippi River would control the continent. The great river was the north–south highway of the United States, a principal artery of commerce and communication. In addition, the multiplicity of rivers snaking through the region formed a network of waterways into the heart of the South, and they all led to the Mississippi. Control of the river would split the Confederacy, preventing goods and supplies from flowing from the west to the eastern heartland, as well as reopen commerce for the Union Midwestern states.

In 1861 it was the U.S. Army that acquired and later built the first armed vessels. These were the "timberclads," three lightly protected river steamers converted at Louisville, Ky. The *Conestoga*, *Lexington*, and *Tyler* were soon joined by better-protected armored boats built by James B. Eads and several boats converted by him and others.

Although operated by the Army, the Western Gunboat Flotilla steamers were commanded by specially attached Navy officers. It was not until 1 October 1862, following the failure of the first attack on Vicksburg, that most of these Army vessels were transferred to the Navy as commissioned naval vessels.

Another group of ships taken up by the Army was known as Ellet rams, named after their progenitor, Colonel Charles Ellet. This officer acquired several river boats and outfitted them as lightly armed rams, which he personally led into battle.

Many flat-bottomed river steamers with their characteristic tall smoke pipes, both side wheelers and stern wheelers, were acquired and lightly armored. They were known as "tinclads" and, uniquely among Civil War naval vessels, bore identifying numbers on their pilot houses.

Larger heavily armored vessels soon appeared on the rivers: *Choctaw*, *Lafayette*, and *Eastport*. Powerfully armed ships, their experimental armor included rubber, which was quite useless. Meanwhile the Navy was building monitors designed specially for river operations. The *Ozark*, *Neosho*, and *Osage* and the four vessels of the *Milwaukee* class arrived in time to join in the fighting. The later *Marietta* and *Sandusky* were completed only after the end of combat operations.

To wrest control of the Mississippi, the federal forces attacked at both its northern and southern ends in a two-prong drive that aimed to meet midway and split the Confederacy. Farragut's deep-sea Navy gathered strength in the South, finally capturing the major port of New Orleans in May 1862. In the north, supporting the Army, the makeshift armed river steamers setting forth from their base at Cairo, Ill., joined battle at Fts. Henry and Donelson, Island No. 10, and Memphis, overcoming Confederate defenses and eliminating most of their opponents' river defense fleet.

Several attempts were made to turn the enemy lines at Vicksburg by expeditions up and around the Yazoo River, culminating in success in April 1863. After almost a year of frustrating disappointments, Vicksburg fell on 4 July 1863, finally giving the Union full control of the vital Mississippi along its entire length.

Union gunboats proceeded far up the Cumberland and Tennessee Rivers through Kentucky and Tennessee even into Alabama. In 1864 the river fleet penetrated up the Red River in Louisiana and Arkansas, only to become trapped by the rapidly falling water level of the river. Only by an ingenious arrangement of manmade dams and waterfalls were the heavy ironclads able to escape downriver.

On 14 August 1865, the Mississippi Squadron was disbanded, and within a few years the Navy closed its stations on the inland rivers.

ARMORED VESSELS

River Monitors

Neosho Class

Name	Builder	Laid down	Launched	Comm.
Neosho	Carondelet, Mo. (Carondelet)	1862	18 Feb 1863	13 May 1863
Osage	Carondelet, Mo. (Carondelet)	1862	13 Jan 1863	10 Jul 1863
Tonnage	523 tons B.			

Fig 6.1: Monitors laid up after the end of the war at Mound City, Ill. The sternwheeler *Neosho* is in center looking aft. The flatness and low draft of these ships is apparent. At left and behind are five monitors of the *Casco* class, *Yuma*, *Shiloh*, and *Klamath* and two others (probably *Etlah* and *Umpqua*). In rear right is one of the *Marietta* class with two funnels abreast and her sister alongside. (Public Library of Cincinnati, Hamilton County Collection)

Dimensions	180′ (oa) × 45′ × 4′6″
Machinery	Stern wheel, 2-cyl. horizontal HP engine (22″ × 6′), 4 boilers, IHP 400, 12 mph. (Fulton)
Complement	100
Armament	2–11″ SB guns; (1864) add 1–12pdr MLR.
Armor	6″ turret, 2.5″ sides, 1.25″ deck

Notes: Single-turret monitors designed by Eads. Wood hulls, with "turtleback" design and very shallow draft. The only stern-wheel monitors.

Service records

Neosho: Red River Expedition, 12 Mar–16 May 1864. Attacked battery near Simmsport, La., 8 Jun 1864. Operations in Cumberland River, Dec 1864. Decomm 23 Jul 1865. Renamed ***Vixen***, 15 Jun 1869. Renamed ***Osceola***, 10 Aug 1869. Sold 17 Aug 1873.

Osage: Expedition up Black and Ouachita Rivers, La., 1–5 Mar 1864. Red River Expedition, 12 Mar–16 May 1864. WGulfBS 1865. Sunk by a torpedo (mine) in Blakely River, Ala., 29 Mar 1865. Raised and hulk sold 22 Nov 1867.

Later history: Merchant *Osage* 1867. Possibly sunk in Sodo Lake near Shreveport, La. 1870. RR 1870.

Ozark

Name	Builder	Laid down	Launched	Comm.
Ozark	Peoria, Ill. (Collier)	1862	18 Feb 1863	18 Feb 1864

Tonnage	578 tons B.
Dimensions	180′ (oa) × 50′ × 5′
Machinery	4 screws, 2 2 2-cyl. engines (type unknown) (15″ × 2′), 6 boilers, 9 mph (3 rudders) (McCord)
Complement	120
Armament	2–11″ SB, 1–10″ SB, 3–9″ SB
Armor	6″ turret, 2.5″ sides, 1.25″ deck.

Notes: Combination single turret and four guns in casemate. Underpowered, unwieldy.

Fig 6.2: USS *Osage*, a single-turret monitor designed for river warfare with sternwheels. (U.S. Naval Historical Center)

Service record: Red River Expedition, 12 Mar–16 May 1864. Decomm 24 Jul 1865. Sold 29 Nov 1865.

Milwaukee Class

Name	Builder	Laid down	Launched	Comm.
Chickasaw	St. Louis, Mo. (Gaylord)	1862	10 Feb 1864	14 May 1864
Kickapoo	St. Louis, Mo. (Allen)	1862	12 Mar 1864	8 Jul 1864
Milwaukee	Carondelet, Mo. (Carondelet)	27 May 1862	8 Feb 1864	27 Aug 1864
Winnebago	Carondelet, Mo. (Carondelet) 1862	1862	4 Jul 1863	27 Apr 1864
Tonnage	970 B.			
Dimensions	229′ (oa) × 56′ × 6′			
Machinery	4 screws, 2 2-cyl. horizontal HP engines (type unknown) (26′ × 2′), 7 boilers, 9 knots (Fulton IW)			
Complement	138			
Armament	4–11″ SB.			
Armor	8″ turrets, 1.5″ deck			

Notes: Double-turret monitors designed by Eads with one Ericsson turret and one Eads turret.

Service records:

Chickasaw: WGulfBS 1864. Battle of Mobile Bay, 5 Aug 1864 (hit 11 times). Bombardment of Ft. Morgan, Mobile Bay, 9–23 Aug 1864. Decomm 6 Jul 1865. Renamed **Samson**, 15 Jun 1869. Renamed **Chickasaw**, 10 Aug 1869. Sold 12 Sep 1874.

Later history: Merchant *Chickasaw* 1875. Railroad ferry. Converted to side wheels 1881, renamed *Gouldsboro* 1882. BU 1944.

Kickapoo: WGulfBS 1864–65. Decomm 29 Jul 1865. Renamed **Cyclops**, 15 Jun 1869. Renamed **Kewaydin**, 10 Aug 1869. Sold 12 Sep 1874.

Milwaukee: WGulfBS 1864-65. Struck a torpedo (mine) and sank in Blakely River, 18 Mar 1865 (none lost).

Winnebago: Mississippi Sqn 1864. WGulfBS Jul 1864. Battle of Mobile Bay, 5 Aug 1864 (hit 19 times). Bombardment of Ft. Morgan, Mobile Bay, 9–23 Aug 1864. Decomm 27 Sep 1865. Renamed **Tornado**, 15 Jun 1869. Renamed **Winnebago**, 10 Aug 1869. Sold 12 Sep 1874.

Fig 6.3: USS *Ozark*, unique in having both turret and casemate guns. Notice the 9-inch guns on deck aft. The structure at the stern is a water closet. (Paul H. Silverstone Collection)

Fig 6.4: One of the *Milwaukee* class showing the layout of the deck with the Ericsson turret aft and Eads type forward. (West Point Library, Orlando Poe Collection)

Marietta Class

Name	Builder	Laid down	Launched	Completed
Marietta	Pittsburgh, Pa. (Tomlinson)	1862	4 Jan 1865	16 Dec 1865
Sandusky	Pittsburgh, Pa. (Tomlinson)	1862	20 Jan 1865	26 Dec 1865

Tonnage	479 tons B.
Dimensions	173'11" (oa) × 52' × 5'
Machinery	4 screws, 2 2-cyl. engines (type unknown) (15" × 2'). 6 boilers. 7 mph (Bldr)
Complement	100
Armament	2–11" SB guns
Armor	6" turret, 1.25" sides

Notes: Light-draft, single single-turret, flat-bottomed river boats. Two funnels abreast, iron hull. Completed after the end of the war and never commissioned.

Service records

Marietta: Laid up at Mound City on delivery. Renamed *Circe*, 15 Jun 1869. Renamed *Marietta*, 10 Aug 1869. Sold 12 Apr 1873.

Sandusky: Laid up at Mound City on delivery. Renamed *Minerva*, 15 Jun 1869. Renamed *Sandusky*, 10 Aug 1869. Sold 12 Apr 1873.

River Ironclads

Cairo Class

Name	Builder	Laid down	Launched	Comm.
Cairo	Mound City, Ill. (Eads)	1861	Oct 1861	25 Jan 1862
Carondelet	St. Louis, Mo. (Eads)	1861	22 Oct 1861	15 Jan 1862
Cincinnati	Mound City, Ill. (Eads)	1861	1861	16 Jan 1862
Louisville	St. Louis, Mo. (Eads)	1861	1861	16 Jan 1862
Mound City	Mound City, Ill. (Eads)	1861	1861	16 Jan 1862
Pittsburg	St. Louis, Mo. (Eads)	1861	1861	16 Jan 1862
St. Louis	St. Louis, Mo. (Eads)	27 Sep 1861	12 Oct 1861	31 Jan 1862

Tonnage	512 tons
Dimensions	175' (oa) × 51'2" × 6'
Machinery	Center wheel, 2-cyl. horizontal HP engines (22" × 6'), 5 boilers, 9 mph (5.5 knots)
Complement	251
Armament	3–8" SB, 4–42pdr MLR, 6–32pdr MLR, 1–12pdr MLR except *Cairo:* (as built) also 2–42pdr MLR; (Apr 1862) add 1–42pdr MLR; (Nov 1862) 3–8"/63, 3–42pdr/80, 6–32pdr/43, 1–30pdr MLR, 1–12pdr SB. *Carondelet:* (Nov 1862) 4–8"/63, 1–42pdr/80, 6–32pdr/42, 1–50pdr MLR, 1–30pdr MLR, 1–12pdr SB; (May 1863) add 3–9" SB, less 5–32pdr/43.; (Jan 1864) 2–100pdr MLR, 1–50pdr MLR, 1–30pdr MLR, 3–9" SB, 4–8" SB/63; (Dec 1864) less 4–8" SB. *Cincinnati:* (Sep 1862) 2–42pdr replaced by 2–30pdr MLR; (1865) 2–100pdr MLR, 3–9" SB, 2–30pdr MLR, 6–24pdr SB. *Louisville:* (Sep 1862) 2–42pdr replaced by 2–30pdr MLR; (Nov 1862) add 3–9" SB, less 1–8" SB; (1864) 1–100pdr MLR, 4–9" SB, 2–30pdr MLR, 6–32pdr/42 *Mound City:* (1863) add 1–30pdr MLR, 1–50pdr MLR, less 2–42pdr; (Jun 1863) 3–9" SB, 3–8"/63, 2–7"/84, 3–32pdr/42, 2–30pdr MLR; (1864) 1–100pdr MLR, 4–9" SB, 3–8" SB, 1–50pdr MLR, 3–32pdr, 1–30pdr MLR; (1864) 1–32pdr replaced by 1–100pdr MLR. *Pittsburg:* (Sep 1862) 2–30pdr MLR, 3–8" SB, 2–42pdr MLR/80, 6–32pdr/42, 1–12pdr SB; (May 1863) 2–32pdr/42 replaced by 2–9" SB; (Dec 1863) 1–100pdr MLR, 4–9" SB, 2–8" SB, 4–32pr/42, 2–30pdr MLR, 1–12pdr SB. (Sep 1864) less 2–32pdr. *St. Louis:* (Oct 1862) 2–42pdr/80 replaced by 2–30pdr MLR; (Dec 1862) add 2–10" SB; (1863) 1–10" SB, 2–8"/63, 2–9" SB, 6–32pdr/42, 2–30pdr MLR.
Armor	2.5" casemates, 1.25" pilot house

Notes: Built by Army to naval specifications. Designed by Lenthall as modified by Pook and Eads. Known as "Pook Turtles." Had rectangular casemate with sloped armored sides and a paddle wheel amidships near the stern. All completed within three months. WGF. Transferred to the Navy 1 Oct 1862. Distinguished by colored bands on funnels. *Louisville, Pittsburgh,* and *Mound City* had taller funnels.

Service records

Cairo: WGF. Occupation of Clarksville, Tenn., 19 Feb 1862. Bombardment of Ft. Pillow, Tenn., 13 Apr 1862. Engagement with enemy vessels and batteries at Ft. Pillow, 10 May 1862. Battle of Memphis, 6 Jun 1862. Expedition up Yazoo River, 21 Nov–11 Dec 1862. Struck a torpedo (mine) and sank in Yazoo River, 12 Dec 1862. Wreck raised 1965. On display in museum at Vicksburg, Miss.

Carondelet: WGF. Capture of Ft. Henry, Tenn., 6 Feb 1862. Attack on Ft. Donelson, Tennessee River, 14 Feb 1862 (4 killed). Siege of Island No.10, 15 Mar–7 Apr 1862. Bombardment of Ft. Pillow, Tenn., 13 Apr 1862. Engagement with enemy vessels and batteries at Ft. Pillow, 10 May 1862. Battle of Memphis, 6 Jun 1862. Bombardment of St. Charles, Ark., and expedition up White River, 17 Jun 1862. Severely damaged and run aground in engagement with CSS *Arkansas* above Vicksburg, 15 Jul 1862 (4 killed). Expedition up Yazoo River, 21 Nov–11 Dec 1862. Expedition to Steele's Bayou, Miss., 14–26 Mar 1863. Ran past batteries at Vicksburg, 16 Apr 1863. Bombardment of Grand Gulf, Miss., 29 Apr 1863. Bombardment of Vicksburg, 18–22 May and 27 May 1863. Red River Expedition, 12 Mar–16 May 1864. Engaged batteries at Bell's Mill, Cumberland River, Tenn., 3–4 Dec 1864. Decomm 20 Jun 1865. Sold 29 Nov 1865.

Later history: Hull became wharf boat at Gallipolis, Ohio. Engines used in towboat *Quaker*.

Cincinnati: WGF. Capture of Ft. Henry, Tenn., 6 Feb 1862. Siege of Island No.10, 15 Mar–7 Apr 1862. Bombardment of Ft. Pillow, Tenn., 13 Apr 1862. Rammed and sunk during engagement at Ft. Pillow, 10 May 1862. Raised and refitted. Expedition up Yazoo River, 21 Nov–11 Dec 1862. Bombardment of Drumgoulds Bluff, Yazoo River, 28 Dec 1862. Expedition up White River, bombardment and capture of Ft. Hindman, Ark., 10–11 Jan 1863. Expedition to Steele's Bayou, Miss., 14–26 Mar 1863. Sunk by enemy batteries during bombardment of Vicksburg, 27 May 1863 (1 killed). Raised, Aug 1863 and refitted. WGulfBS Feb 1865. Took surrender of CSS *Nashville* and *Morgan* in Tombigbee River, 10 May 1865. Decomm 4 Aug 1865. Sold 28 Mar 1866.

Later history: Sank at moorings in Cache River, 1866.

Louisville: WGF. Attack on Ft. Donelson, Tennessee River, 14 Feb 1862 (4 killed). Siege of Island No.10, 15 Mar–7 Apr 1862. Battle of Memphis, 6 Jun 1862. Engagement with CSS *Arkansas* above Vicksburg, 15 Jul 1862. Bombardment of Drumgoulds Bluff, Yazoo River, 28 Dec 1862. Expedition up White River, capture of Ft. Hindman, Ark., 10–11 Jan 1863. Expedition to Steele's Bayou, Miss., 14–26 Mar 1863. Ran past batteries at Vicksburg, 16 Apr 1863. Bombardment of Grand Gulf, Miss., 29 Apr 1863. Red River Expedition, 12 Mar–16 May 1864. Decomm 21 Jul 1865. Sold 29 Nov 1865.

Mound City: WGF. Action at Columbus, Ky., 23 Feb 1862. Siege of Island No.10, 15 Mar–7 Apr 1862. Bombardment of Ft. Pillow, Tenn., 13 Apr 1862. Rammed by CSS *General Price* during engagement off Ft. Pillow, 10 May and by CSS *General Van Dorn*, 11 May 1862 and went aground. Expedition up White River, disabled during bombardment of St. Charles, Ark., 17 Jun 1862 (103 killed). Expeditions up Yazoo River, Greenville, Miss., 16–22 Aug 1862 and to Steele's Bayou, Miss., 14–26 Mar 1863. Ran past batteries at Vicksburg, 16 Apr 1863. Bombardment of Grand Gulf, Miss., 29 Apr 1863. Bombardment of Vicksburg, 18–22 May, 27 May (5 killed) and 20 Jun 1863. Red River Expedition, 12 Mar–16 May 1864. Sold 9 Nov 1865. BU 1866.

Ships captured: str *Red Rover*,* 7 Apr 1862; *Clara Dolsen*,† 14 Jun 1862.

Pittsburg: WGF. Attack on Ft. Donelson, Tennessee River, 14 Feb 1862. Siege of Island No.10, 15 Mar–7 Apr 1862. Bombardment of Ft. Pillow, Tenn., 13 Apr 1862. Engagement with enemy squadron and batteries at Ft. Pillow, 10 May 1862. Expeditions up Yazoo River, 21 Nov/11 Dec 1862 and to Steele's Bayou, Miss., 14–26 Mar 1863. Ran past batteries at Vicksburg, 16 Apr 1863. Severely damaged by gunfire at bombardment of Grand Gulf, Miss., 29 Apr 1863 (6 killed). Bombardment of Ft. Beauregard, Harrisonburg, La., 10–11 May and expedition up Red River, 3–13 May 1863. Red River Expedition, 12 Mar–16 May 1864. Sold 29 Nov 1865. Abandoned Jun 1870.

St. Louis: WGF. Engagement with CSN vessels near Lucas Bend, Mo., Mississippi River, 11 Jan 1862. Bombardment and capture of Ft. Henry, Tenn., 6 Feb 1862. Disabled (hit 59 times) during attack on Ft. Donelson, Tennessee River, 14 Feb 1862. Action at Columbus, Ky., 23 Feb 1862. Siege of Island No.10, 15 Mar–7 Apr 1862 (2 killed). Bombardment of Ft. Pillow, Tenn., 13 Apr 1862. Engaged enemy vessels and batteries at Ft. Pillow, 10 May 1862. Battle of Memphis, 6 Jun 1862. Expedition up White River, bombardment of St. Charles, Ark., 17 Jun 1862. Renamed ***Baron de Kalb***, 8 Sep 1862. Expedition up Yazoo River, 21 Nov–11 Dec 1862. Bombardment of Drumgoulds Bluff, Yazoo River, 28 Dec 1862. Expedition up White River, capture of Ft. Hindman, Ark., 10–11 Jan 1863 (2 killed). Yazoo Pass expedition, attack on Ft. Pemberton, Tallahatchie River, 11–23 Mar 1863 (2 killed). Bombardment and feigned attack, Haynes' Bluff, Miss., 29 Apr–2 May 1863. Capture of Haynes' Bluff, Yazoo River, 18 May 1863. Destruction of Yazoo City NYd, 20–23 May 1863. Expedition up Yazoo River, 24–31 May 1863. Sunk by a torpedo (mine) one mile below Yazoo City, 13 Jul 1863.

Ships captured: str *Lottie*, 5 Dec 1862; *Alonzo Child*, 19 May 1863

---

* Later USS *Red Rover* (hospital ship).

† Later USS *Clara Dolsen*.

Fig 6.5: *Baron de Kalb*, off Cairo, Ill., with *Cincinnati* and *Mound City*, 1863. The ships of this class differed in many ways. (U.S. Naval Historical Center, Paul H. Silverstone Collection)

Chillicothe

Name	Builder	Laid down	Launched	Comm.
Chillicothe	Cincinnati, Ohio (Brown)	1862	1862	5 Sep 1862

Tonnage	395 tons D (?), 203 tons B.
Dimensions	162′ × 50′ × 4′ (also given as 159′ × 46.5′ × 6′10″)
Machinery	Side wheels and 2 screws, 2 engines (type unknown) (20″ × 8′), 3 boilers, 7 knots (Junger)
Complement	(U)
Armament	2–11″ SB; (Oct 1863) add 1–12pdr SB.
Armor	2″ sides, 1″ deck, 3″ pilot house

Notes: Designed by Samuel Hartt. Converted at New Albany, Ind. Weak hull, tendency to hog.

Service record: Expedition up White River, capture of Ft. Hindman, Ark., 10–11 Jan 1863. Yazoo Pass expedition, damaged by gunfire (11th and 13th) (4 killed) during attack on Ft. Pemberton, Tallahatchie River, 11–23 Mar 1863. Red River Expedition, 12 Mar–16 May 1864 (captain killed). Sold 29 Nov 1865.

Later history: Destroyed by burning at Cairo, Ill., Sep 1872.

Indianola

Name	Builder	Laid down	Launched	Comm.
Indianola	Cincinnati, Ohio (Brown)	1862	4 Sep 1862	14 Jan 1863

Tonnage	442 tons B., 511 tons (U).

Fig 6.6: The city-class gunboat *Louisville* had very tall funnels.

114 Civil War Navies, 1855-1883

Dimensions	175′ × 52′ × 5″
Machinery	Side wheels and 2 screws, 4 engines (types unknown) (22″ × 6′6″ and 18″ × 1′8″), 5 boilers, 6 knots (Junger)
Complement	144
Armament	2–11″ SB (forward), 2–9″ SB (aft) guns
Armor	3″ casemate, 1″ deck

Notes: Designed by Joseph Brown for the Army and transferred to the Navy 12 Jan 1863. Reported comm 27 Sep 1862 and ready for service but actually completed later. Similar to *Chillicothe*.

Service record: Ran past Vicksburg batteries, 19 Feb 1863. Blockaded mouth of Red River, 19–21 Feb 1863. Rammed by Confederate vessels during engagement near New Carthage, Miss., below Vicksburg, run aground and surrendered, 24 Feb 1863. Destroyed by Confederates to prevent recapture, 4 Mar 1863. Hulk refloated 5 Jan 1865. Sold 29 Nov 1865 and BU.

Tuscumbia

Name	Builder	Laid down	Launched	Comm.
Tuscumbia	New Albany, Ind.	1862	12 Dec 1862	12 Mar 1863

Tonnage	575 tons B., 915 tons (U)
Dimensions	178′ × 75′ × 7′
Machinery	Side wheels and 2 screws, 4 engines (types unknown) (30″ × 7′ and 20″ × 2′), 6 boilers, 10 mph. (McCord)
Complement	(U)
Armament	3–11″ SB (forward), 2–9″ SB guns (aft)
Armor	6″ casemates

Notes: Designed by Joseph Brown as a casemate ironclad; poorly built. Tendency to hogging.

Service record: Recapture of Ft. Heiman in Tennessee River, 12–14 Mar 1863. Ran past batteries at Vicksburg, 16 Apr 1863. Hit 81 times during bombardment of Grand Gulf, Miss., 29 Apr 1863 (5 killed). Bombardment of Vicksburg, 18–22 May 1863. Repairing Aug 1863–May 1864. Decomm Feb 1865. Sold 29 Nov 1865. Stripped 1867; hulk beached at Cache River and burned Oct 1870.

Converted River Ironclads

Benton

Name	Builder	Launched	Acquired	Comm.
Benton	St. Louis, Mo. (Eads)	1861	Nov 1861	24 Feb 1862

ex-*Submarine No. 7*, ex-*Benton*

Tonnage	633 tons
Dimensions	202′ × 72′ × 9′
Machinery	Center wheel, 2 inclined engines (28″ × 7′), 5.5 knots
Complement	176
Armament	2–9″ SB, 7–42pdr MLR, 7–32pdr/43; (Aug 1862) 2–9″/90, 4–42pdr/80, 8–32pdr/42, 2–50pdr MLR, 1–12pdr HS; (Jan 1863) 2–32pdr replaced by 2–9″ SB; (Dec 1863) 2–100pdr MLR, 8–9″ SB, 4–32pdr/42, 2–50pdr MLR
Armor	2.5″ casemates, 2.5″ pilot house

Notes: Converted from a catamaran snag boat to a design by James B. Eads. Had a rectangular wooden casemate with sloping sides. Transferred from War Dept 1 Oct 1862. The most powerful of the early river ironclads.

Service record: WGF. Flagship, Mississippi Sqn 1862–63. Siege of Island No. 10, 15 Mar–7 Apr 1862. Bombardment of Ft. Pillow, Tenn., 13 Apr 1862. Engagement with squadron and batteries at Ft. Pillow, 10 May 1862. Battle of Memphis, 6 Jun 1862. Engagement with CSS *Arkansas* above Vicksburg, 15 Jul 1862. Expedition up Yazoo River, Greenville, Miss., 16-22 Aug 1862. Expedition in Yazoo River, dragging for torpedoes and bombardments at Haynes Bluff (damaged) (2 killed including captain, Lt. Cdr. W. Gwin) and Drumgoulds Bluff, 23–26 Dec 1862. Ran past batteries at Vicksburg, 16 Apr 1863. Bombardment of Grand Gulf, Miss., 29 Apr 1863 (7 killed). Expedition up Red River, 3–13 May 1863. Bombardment of Vicksburg, 18–22 May, 27 May, and 20 Jun 1863. Red River Expedition, 12 Mar–16 May 1864. Expedition up Red River and capture of CSS *Missouri*, 1–6 Jun 1865. Decomm 20 Jul 1865. Sold 29 Nov 1865 and BU.

Ships captured: str *Sovereign*, 5 Jun 1862; *Fairplay*, 18 Aug 1862.

Fig 6.7: A bow view of the *Tuscumbia* showing the three gun ports in the bow. Notice the enormous width of the ship. (U.S. Naval Historical Center)

Essex

Name	Builder	Launched	Acquired	Comm.
Essex	New Albany, Ind. (Page & Bacon)	1856	1861	Oct 1861

ex-*New Era* (Dec 1861)

Tonnage	355 tons 1862: 1,000 tons.
Dimensions	159′ × 47′6″ × 6′; (1862) 198.5′ × 58′ × 6.8′
Machinery	Center wheel, 2 2-cyl. engines (type unknown) (18″ × 6′), 4 boilers, 5.5 knots (Gaty)
Complement	134

Fig 6.8: USS *Benton*, with the tug *Fern* astern. The casemate had five gun ports on each side, four forward and two aft.

Fig 6.9: The USS *Essex* at Baton Rouge in 1862. The dome on the housing is the armored pilot house.

Armament	5–9″ SB; (Jan 1862) 1–10″ SB, 3–9″ SB, 1–32pdr/43, 1–12pdr BH; (Aug 1862) add 2–50pdr MLR; (Jun 1863) 1–100pdr MLR, 4–9″ SB, 1–32pdr SB, 2–50pdr MLR, 4–12pdr SB; (1864) 2–100pdr MLR, 6–9″ SB, 1–12pdr MLR, 3–12pdr SB.
Armor	3″ casemates

Notes: Converted from a merchant river ferry to a timberclad with casemate and one funnel. Armor added, hull lengthened and renamed Dec 1861, and further rebuilt by W.D. Porter, Feb–Jun 1862. Transferred from the Army, 1 Oct 1862.

Service record: WGF. Cumberland River expedition, Nov 1861. Engagement with CSN vessels near Lucas Bend, Mo., Mississippi River, 11 Jan 1862. Boiler burst when struck by shell during attack on Ft. Henry, Tenn., 6 Feb 1862 (6 killed). Attack on CSS *Arkansas* at Vicksburg, 22 Jul, and again at Baton Rouge, La., 5 Aug 1862. Bombardment of Port Hudson, La., 13 Dec 1862. Occupation of Baton Rouge, 17 Dec 1862. Bombardment of Port Hudson, 8 May–9 Jul 1863. Bombardment at Whitehall Point, La., 10 Jul 1863. Red River Expedition, 12 Mar–16 May 1864. Decomm 20 Jul 1865. Sold 29 Nov 1865.

Later history: Merchant *New Era* 1865. Hull burned for scrap Dec 1870.

Eastport

Name	Builder	Launched	Acquired	Comm.
Eastport	New Albany, Ind.	1852	Aug 1862	9 Jan 1863

Tonnage	570 tons
Dimensions	280′ × 43′ or 32′ × 6′3″
Machinery	Side wheels, 2 HP engines (26″ × 9′), 5 boilers
Complement	(U)
Armament	6–9″ SB, 2–100pdr MLR; (Jul 1863) 4–9″ SB, 2–100pdr MLR, 2–50pdr MLR.
Armor	(U)

Notes: Ironclad ram, captured while conversion incomplete at Cerro Gordo, Tenn., 7 Feb 1862. Completed at Mound City.

Service record: WGF. Damaged by grounding near Vicksburg, 2 Feb 1863. Red River Expedition, 12 Mar–16 May 1864. Capture of Ft. de Russy, Ark., Mar 1864. Damaged by torpedo (mine) explosion below Grand Ecore, La., in Red River, 15 Apr and destroyed to prevent capture, 26 Apr 1864.

Lafayette

Name	Builder	Launched	Acquired	Comm.
Lafayette	Louisville, Ky.	1848	14 Sep 1862	27 Feb 1863

ex-*Fort Henry* (USA), ex-*Aleck Scott*

Tonnage	1,193 tons
Dimensions	292′ (oa) × 44′ (60′oa) × 8′
Machinery	Side wheels, 2 engines (type unknown) (26″ × 8′), 6 boilers, 4 knots (upstream)
Complement	210
Armament	2–11″ SB, 4–9″ SB, 2–100pdr MLR; (Apr 1863) add 4–24pdr H; (May 1863) 2–11″ SB, 2–9″ SB, 2–100pdr MLR, 2–24pdr H, 2–12pdr H.
Armor	2.5″ + 2″ rubber casemate

Fig 6.10: The USS *Eastport* was captured while under conversion and completed for the U.S. Navy; the only ironclad not commenced by the North. (Arkansas History Commission)

Notes: Purchased as an Army Quartermaster vessel 1861 and converted by Eads at St. Louis to a design of William D. Porter. Superstructure replaced by single casemate; ram bow. Rubber armor useless.

Service record: Ran past batteries at Vicksburg, 16 Apr 1863. Bombardment of Grand Gulf, Miss., 21 and 29 Apr 1863. Expedition up Red River, 3–13 May 1863. Red River Expedition, 12 Mar–16 May 1864. Expedition up Red River, capture of CSS *Missouri*, 1–6 Jun 1865. Decomm 23 Jul 1865. Sold 28 Mar 1866 and BU.

Choctaw

Name	Builder	Launched	Acquired	Comm.
Choctaw	New Albany, Ind.	1856	27 Sep 1862	23 Mar 1863

Tonnage	1,004 tons
Dimensions	270′ (oa) × 45′ (69′oa) × 8′
Machinery	Side wheels, 2 engines (type unknown) (24″ × 8′), 6 boilers, 2 knots (upstream)
Complement	106
Armament	1–100pdr MLR, 1–9″ SB, 2–30pdr MLR; (May 1863) add 2–24pdr SB; (Sep 1863) 1–100pdr MLR, 2–30pdr MLR, 3–9″ SB, 2–12pdr MLR

Fig 6.11: The powerful USS *Choctaw* with a tug aft. This and other converted ironclads show how the superstructure was cut down to leave only a casemate for the guns. (U.S. Naval Historical Center)

Fig 6.12: The ironclad *Lafayette*, one of the most heavily armed ships on the river. She is easily distinguished from the *Choctaw* by the higher continuous casemate. (U.S. Naval Historical Center)

Armor	1″ + 1″ rubber casemate (forward)

Notes: Converted from a merchant steamer to plans by William D. Porter. Armor and armament were too heavy for the hull. Rubber armor was useless. Transferred from War Dept 1 Oct 1862.

Service record: Bombardment and feigned attack (hit 53 times), Haynes' Bluff, Miss., 29 Apr–2 May 1863. Capture of Haynes' Bluff, Yazoo River, 18 May 1863. Destruction of Yazoo City NYd, 20–23 May 1863. Red River Expedition, 12 Mar–16 May 1864. Decomm 22 Jul 1865. Sold 28 Mar 1866.

UNARMORED VESSELS

Timberclads

All of the following timberclads were acquired from the War Department. They were originally converted at Louisville, Ky., in 1861.

Conestoga

Name	Builder	Launched	Acquired	Comm.
Conestoga	Brownsville, Pa.	1859	3 Jun 1861	1861

Tonnage	572 tons
Dimensions	(U)
Machinery	Side wheels, 2 HP engines (24″ × 7′), 12 mph
Complement	(U)
Armament	4–32pdr/43; (Sep 1862) 1–12pdr MLR, 4–32pdr/43; (Jan 1864) 3–32pdr/42, 3–30pdr MLR, 1–12pdr SB.

Notes: Converted side-wheel towboat.

Service record: WGF. Engaged CSS *Jackson* off Lucas Bend, Ky., 10 Sep 1861. Broke up enemy force at Eddyville, Ky., 27 Oct 1861. Capture of Ft. Henry, Tenn., 6 Feb 1862. Expedition to Florence, Ala., Tennessee River, 6–11 Feb 1862. Attack on Ft. Donelson, Tennessee River, 14 Feb 1862. Action at Columbus, Ky., 23 Feb 1862. Expedition up White River, bombardment of St. Charles, Ark., 17 Jun 1862. Expedition to burn Palmyra, Tenn., 3 Apr 1863. Expedition to Trinity, La., Red River, 10 Jul 1863. Expedition up Black and Ouachita Rivers, La., 1–5 Mar 1864. Sunk in collision with USS *General Price* below Grand Gulf, Mississippi River, 8 Mar 1864 (2 lost).

Fig 6.13: The timberclad gunboat *Conestoga* can be distinguished from *Tyler* by the position of the horizontal bands on the paddlewheel box. (The Public Library of Cincinnati, Hamilton County Collection)

Ships captured: strs *V.R. Stephenson* and *Gazelle*, 16 Sep 1862; strs *Muscle* and *Sallie Wood*,* 8 Feb 1862; strs *Evansville* and *Rose Hambleton*, 12 Feb 1863; strs *Lillie Martin* and *Sweden*, 24 Oct 1863.

Lexington

Name	Builder	Launched	Acquired	Comm.
Lexington	Belle Vernon, Pa.	1860	5 Jun 1861	12 Aug 1861
Tonnage	362 tons D, 448 tons			
Dimensions	177'7" × 36'10" × 6'			
Machinery	Side wheels, 2 HP engines (20" × 6'), 3 boilers, 7 knots			
Complement	(U)			
Armament	2–32pdr/43, 4–8" SB; (Sep 1862) 4–8" SB, 1–32pdr/42, 2–30pdr MLR, 1–12pdr H; (Feb 1864) less 2–8" SB; (Sep 1864) 6–8" SB, 1–32pdr/42, 2–30pdr MLR, 1–12pdr MLR.			

Notes: Built by L.M.Speer.

Service record: WGF. Engagements with CSS *Jackson* off Hickman, Ky., 4 Sep and 8 and 10 Oct 1861. Engagement with gunboats at Lucas Bend, Mississippi River, 13 Oct 1861. Supported army at Iron Bank, Ky., 7 Nov 1861. Engaged battery at Columbus, Ky., 7 Jan 1862. Capture of Ft. Henry, Tenn., 6 Feb 1862. Expedition to Florence, Ala., Tennessee River, 6–11 Feb 1862. Engaged battery at Chickasaw, Ala., 12 Mar 1862. Siege of Island No.10, 15 Mar–7 Apr 1862. Supported Army at Pittsburg Landing (Shiloh), Tenn., 6–7 Apr 1862. Expedition up White River and bombardment of St. Charles, Ark, 17 Jun 1862. Expedition up Yazoo River, 21 Nov–11 Dec 1862. Expedition in Yazoo River, dragging for torpedoes, bombardments at Haynes Bluff, and Drumgoulds Bluff, 23–26 Dec 1862. Expedition up White River, capture of Ft. Hindman, Ark., 10–11 Jan 1863. Defense of Ft. Donelson, Tenn., 3 Feb 1863. Expedition to burn Palmyra, Tenn., 3 Apr 1863. Reconnaissance up White River, Ark., 12–15 Aug 1863. Expedition up Black and Ouachita Rivers, La., 1–5 Mar 1864. Red River Expedition, 12 Mar–16 May 1864. Repulsed attack on White River Station, Ark., June 22, 1864. Decomm 2 Jul 1865. Sold 17 Aug 1865.

* Later USS *Sallie Wood*.

Fig 6.14: The USS *Lexington* is easily distinguished from the other timberclads by the forward position of her funnels. (U.S. Naval Historical Center)

Tyler

Name	Builder	Launched	Acquired	Comm.
Tyler	Cincinnati, Ohio	1857	5 Jun 1861	Aug 1861
ex-*A.O. Tyler*				
Tonnage	420 tons D. 575 tons			
Dimensions	180' × 45'4" × 6'			
Machinery	Side wheels, 2-cyl. HP engine (22" × 8'), 4 boilers, 8 knots			
Complement	67			
Armament	6–8"/63, 1–32pdr/43; (Sep 1862) 6–8"/63, 3–30pdr MLR, 1–12pdr SB; (Mar 1864) add 4–24pdr.			

Notes: Sank 27 Jan 1860, salved.

Service record: WGF. Engaged CSS *Jackson* off Hickman, Ky., 4 Sep 1861. Engagement with gunboats at Lucas Bend, Mississippi River, 13 Oct 1861. Supported army at Iron Bank, Ky., 7 Nov 1861. Engaged battery at Columbus, Ky., 7 Jan 1862. Capture of Ft. Henry, Tenn., 6 Feb 1862. Expedition to Florence, Ala., Tennessee River, 6–11 Feb 1862. Attack on Ft. Donelson, Tennessee River, 14 Feb 1862. Supported Army at Pittsburg Landing (Shiloh), Tenn., 6–7 Apr 1862. Damaged during engagement with CSS *Arkansas* above Vicksburg, 15 Jul 1862 (8 killed). Expedition up Yazoo River, 21 Nov–11 Dec 1862. Expedition up Yazoo River, dragging for torpedoes and bombardments at Haynes Bluff and Drumgoulds Bluff, 23–26 Dec 1862. Bombardment and feigned attack, Haynes Bluff, Miss., 29 Apr–2 May 1863. Engaged battery at Clarendon, Ark., 24 Jun 1864. Sold 17 Aug 1865.

Ships captured: str *Alfred Robb*,† 21 Apr 1862; str *Lady Walton*, 6 Jun 1863; str *Gillum*, 25 Feb 1864.

Ellet Rams (War Department)

These were river steamers purchased by the Army Quartermaster Department and hurriedly converted into rams by Col. Charles Ellet, Jr. Their hulls were reinforced, and their bows filled with timber. They originally carried no armament. The "Ellet rams" formed an independent command that was never incorporated into the Navy, although it operated under naval orders.

Name	Builder	Launched	Acquired	Comm.
Lancaster	Cincinnati, Ohio	1855	Apr 1862	May 1862
ex-*Kosciusko*, ex-*Lancaster No.3*				
Tonnage	257 tons			

† Later USS *Alfred Robb*.

118   Civil War Navies, 1855-1883

Fig 6.15: The timberclad gunboat *Tyler*. (The Public Library of Cincinnati, Hamilton County Collection)

Dimensions	176′ × 30′ × 5.5′
Machinery	Side wheels
Complement	(U)
Armament	(U)

Notes: Wood hull. Converted at Cincinnati.
Service record: WGF. Battle of Memphis, 6 Jun 1862. Damaged in engagement with CSS *Arkansas* above Vicksburg, 15 Jul 1862. Sunk by Confederate batteries while passing Vicksburg, 25 Mar 1863.

Name	Builder	Launched	Acquired	Comm.
Lioness	Brownsville, Pa.	1859	22 Apr 1862	May 1862
Tonnage	198 tons			
Dimensions	160′ × 31′			
Machinery	Stern wheel, (22″ × 7′), 4 boilers			
Complement	(U)			
Armament	(U)			

Note: Converted at Pittsburgh.
Service record: WGF. Battle of Memphis, 6 Jun 1862. Expedition up Yazoo River, Greenville, Miss., 16–22 Aug 1862. Expedition in Yazoo River, dragging for torpedoes and bombardment at Haynes Bluff and Drumgoulds Bluff, 23–26 Dec 1862. Yazoo Pass expedition, attack on Ft. Pemberton, Tallahatchie River, 11–23 Mar 1863. Laid up after Jul 1863. Sold 5 Sep 1865.
Later history: Merchant *Lioness* 1865. RR 1869.

Fig 6.16: An Ellet ram. Notice the sharp ram bow; originally these rams were unarmed, relying solely on the ram as a weapon. This picture was erroneously identified as the *General Price*.

Name	Builder	Launched	Acquired	Comm.
Mingo	California, Pa.	1859	8 Apr 1862	1862
Tonnage	228 tons			
Dimensions	170′ × 29′			
Machinery	Stern wheel. 12 knots			
Complement	(U)			
Armament	none			

Note: Converted at Pittsburgh.
Service record: WGF. Battle of Memphis, arrived after the action, 6 Jun 1862. Sank accidentally at Cape Girardeau, Mo., Nov 1862.

Name	Builder	Launched	Acquired	Comm.
Monarch	Fulton, Ohio	1853	23 Apr 1862	1862
Tonnage	406 tons			
Dimensions	(U)			
Machinery	Side wheels.			
Complement	(U)			
Armament	(U)			

Notes: Sank at Louisville, 5 Mar 1861, salved. Converted at Madison, Ind.
Service record: WGF. Expedition to Craigheads Point, Miss., 3 Jun 1862. Battle of Memphis, 6 Jun 1862, rammed CSS *General Price* and ran CSS *Little Rebel* aground. Pursued enemy ships up Yazoo River, 26 Jun 1862. Expedition up White River, bombardment and capture of Ft. Hindman, Ark., 10–11 Jan 1863. Laid up after Jul 1863. Sunk by ice while laid up below St. Louis, Dec 1864 and BU.

Name	Builder	Launched	Acquired	Comm.
Queen of the West	Cincinnati, Ohio	1854	May 1862	1862
Tonnage	406 tons			
Dimensions	181′ × 36′ × 6′			
Machinery	Side wheels, 3 boilers			
Complement	120			
Armament	1–30pdr, 3–12pdr H			

Note: Converted at Cincinnati.
Service record: WGF. Rammed at Battle of Memphis and run aground, 6 Jun 1862; sank CSS *General Lovell* and captured *General Price*. Engagement with CSS *Arkansas* above Vicksburg, 15 and 22 Jul 1862. Expedition up Yazoo River, 21 Nov–11 Dec 1862. Expedition in Yazoo River, dragging for torpedoes and bombardments at Haynes Bluff and Drumgoulds Bluff, 23–26 Dec 1862. Damaged and rammed CSS *City of Vicksburg* off Vicksburg, 2 Feb 1863. Ran aground while attempting to evade Confederate batteries at Ft. de Russy, La., and captured, 14 Feb 1863.
Ships captured: strs **Berwick Bay*, **A.W. Baker*, and **Moro*, 3 Feb 1863; str *Era No. 5*, 14 Feb 1863.
Later history: Taken into service by Confederate Navy. (q.v.)

Name	Builder	Launched	Acquired	Comm.
Switzerland	Cincinnati, Ohio	1854	18 May 1862	1862
Tonnage	413 tons			
Dimensions	178.4′ × 36.8′ × 8.1′			
Machinery	Side wheels			
Complement	(U)			
Armament	(U)			

Note: Converted at New Albany, Ind.
Service record: WGF. Battle of Memphis, 6 Jun 1862. Expedition up Yazoo River, Greenville, Miss., 16–22 Aug 1862. Damaged by gunfire while passing

Fig 6.17: The Ellet ram *Switzerland*, later in the war, notice the guns on the upper deck.

batteries at Vicksburg, March 25, 1863. Ran past batteries at Grand Gulf, Miss., 31 Mar 1863. Expedition up Red River and bombardment of Harrisonburg, La., 3–13 May 1863. Sold 21 Oct 1865.

Later history: Merchant *Switzerland* 1865. RR 1870

Name	Builder	Launched	Acquired	Comm.
T.D. Horner	Brownsville, Pa.	1859	18 May 1862	Never
Tonnage	123 tons			
Dimensions	(U)			
Machinry	Stern wheel			
Complement	(U)			
Armament	2–12pdr MLR			

Notes: Tug. Never acquired by Navy.

Service record: WGF. Sold 17 Aug 1865.

Later history: Merchant *T.D. Horner* 1865. Damaged beyond repair by hitting a bridge at Louisville, 1 Jan 1868.

Name	Builder	Launched	Acquired	Comm.
Dick Fulton	McKeesport, Pa.	1860	May 1862	
ex-*Dick Fulton No.2*				
Tonnage	98 tons			
Machinery	Stern wheel			

Notes: Sold 3 Jan 1866.

Later history: Merchant *Baltic*. Exploded and sank at New Orleans, 20 Feb 1866.

Rams

Name	Builder	Launched	Acquired	Comm.
Avenger	New Albany, Ind. (Hill & Payneau)	1863	1863	29 Feb 1864
ex-*Balize*				
Vindicator	New Albany, Ind. (Hill & Payneau)	1863	7 Dec 1863	24 May 1864
Tonnage	410 or 389 tons			
Dimensions	210′ or 181′ × 41.5′ × 6′			
Machinery	Side wheels, 2 engines (28″ × 7′6″), 4 boilers, 11 mph			
Complement	(U)			
Armament	*Avenger*: (Sep 1863) 1–100pdr MLR, 4–24pdr SB, 1–12pdr MLR; (Dec 1864) 1–100pdr MLR, 5–24pdr SB, 1–10pdr MLR; (Apr 1865) 1–100pdr MLR, 11–24pdr SB, 1–12pdr MLR. *Vindicator*: (May 1864) 1–100pdr MLR, 2–24pdr H, 2–12pdr MLR; (Dec 1864) 1–12pdr MLR replaced by 1–30pdr MLR			

Notes: Built for the War Dept and transferred on completion. Near sisters.

Service records

Avenger: Damaged in collision with merchant vessel south of Cairo, 12 Mar 1864. Landed party at Bruinsburg, Miss., 22 Nov 1864. Decomm 1 Aug 1865. Sold 29 Nov 1865.

Later history: Merchant *Balize* 1865. RR 1871

Vindicator: Expedition up Yazoo River, Nov 1864. Engaged ram CSS *Webb* off mouth of Red River, 23–24 Apr 1865. Decomm Jul 1865. Sold 29 Nov 1865.

Later history: Merchant *New Orleans* 1865. RR 1869

River Gunboats

Name	Builder	Launched	Acquired	Comm.
General Bragg	New York, N.Y. (Westervelt)	1850	Jun 1862	9 Jul 1862
ex-CSS *General Bragg*, ex-*Mexico*				
Tonnage	1,043 tons			
Dimensions	208′ × 32′8″ × 12′, d15′			
Machinery	Side wheels, 1 beam LP engine (56″ × 10′), 1 boiler, 10 knots (Morgan)			
Complement	(U)			
Armament	1–30pdr MLR, 1–32pdr/42, 1–12pdr MLR			

Notes: Confederate cottonclad captured following engagement near Memphis, Tenn., 6 Jun 1862.

Fig 6.18: The ram *Vindicator* built in 1863.

120   Civil War Navies, 1855-1883

Fig 6.19: The gunboat *General Bragg* with a tug alongside. Her appearance is not that of a usual river boat, having been built in New York. In the stream at right is the transport *Maria Denning*. (Paul H. Silverstone Collection)

Service record: WGF. Patrolled Mississippi from Helena to Yazoo River. Expedition up Yazoo River, Greenville, Miss., 16–22 Aug 1862. Disabled while engaging battery at Tunica Bend, La., 15 Jun 1864. Decomm 24 Jul 1865. Sold 1 Sep 1865.
Later history: Merchant *Mexico* 1865. Sold foreign 1870.

Name	Builder	Launched	Acquired	Comm.
General Price	Cincinnati, Ohio	1856	Jun 1862	11 Mar 1863

ex-CSS *General Sterling Price*, ex-*Laurent Millaudon*

Tonnage	483 tons
Dimensions	182′ × 30′ × 13′
Machinery	Side wheels. (24″ × 8′), 4 boilers, 12 mph.
Complement	77
Armament	(Mar 1863) 4–9″ SB; (Oct 1864) 2–9″ SB, 1–12pdr MLR, 1–12pdr SB.

Notes: Former side-wheel towboat converted to ram. Sunk at Battle of Memphis, 6 Jun 1862; captured and salved. Repaired at Cairo, Ill. Also known as *General Sterling Price*.
Service record: WGF. Expedition to Steele's Bayou, Miss., 14–26 Mar 1863. Ran past batteries at Vicksburg, 16 Apr 1863. Expedition up Red River, 3–13 May, bombardment of Ft. Beauregard, Harrisonburg, La., 10–11 May 1863. Bombardment of Vicksburg, 27 May and 20 Jun 1863. Sank USS *Conestoga* in accidental collision below Grand Gulf, 8 Mar 1864. Red River Expedition, 12 Mar–6 Apr 1864. Decomm 24 Jul 1865. Sold 3 Oct 1865.
Later history: FFU

Name	Builder	Launched	Acquired	Comm.
Sumter	Algiers, La.	1853	1862	1862

ex-CSS *General Sumter*, ex-*Junius Beebe*

Tonnage	524 tons
Dimensions	182′ × 28′4″
Machinery	Side wheels, 1 LP engine
Complement	(U)
Armament	(U)

Notes: Cottonclad captured after Battle of Memphis, 6 Jun 1862.
Service record: Went aground off Bayou Sara, La., Aug 1862 and abandoned.

Fig 6.20: The gunboat *General Price* was a Confederate ram captured at Memphis in June 1862, originally known as the *General Sterling Price*. (U.S. Naval Historical Center)

Large Tinclads

Name	Builder	Launched	Acquired	Comm.
Black Hawk	New Albany, Ind.	1857	24 Nov 1862	6 Dec 1862

ex-*New Uncle Sam*

Tonnage	902 tons
Dimensions	260′ × 45′6″ × 6′; also reported as 285′ × 38′ × 6.5′
Machinery	Side wheels, (28″ × 10′), 6 boilers
Complement	141
Armament	(1862) 2–32pdr/33, 2–30pdr MLR, 1–12pdr SB, 1–12pdr MLR; (Feb 1864) 2–30pdr MLR, 8–24pdr SB, 3–12pdr MLR.

Notes: Renamed 13 Dec 1862. Used by Army, Grant's headquarters before attack on Fts. Henry and Donelson.
Service record: Mississippi Sqn (flagship of Porter and S.P.Lee). Operations around Vicksburg, Dec 1862. Expedition up White River, capture of Ft. Hindman, Ark., 10–11 Jan 1863. Bombardment and feigned attack, Haynes' Bluff, Miss., 29 Apr–2 May 1863. Siege of Vicksburg, May–Jul 1863. Red River Expedition, 12 Mar–16 May 1864. Destroyed by fire and sank near Cairo, Ill, 22 Apr 1865.
Ships captured: str *Fulton, Argus*, 7 Oct 1863.

Name	Builder	Launched	Acquired	Comm.
Ouachita	New Albany, Ind.	1861	29 Sep 1863	18 Jan 1864

ex-*Louisville*

Tonnage	572 tons
Dimensions	227′6″ × 38′ × 7′

Fig 6.21: The large tinclad *Black Hawk* was Admiral Porter's flagship on the Mississippi throughout the war. Her striped sides were unique.

Machinery	Side wheels, 2 engines (26" × 7'6"), 5 boilers, 8 mph (upstream)
Complement	(U)
Armament	5–30pdr MLR, 18–24pdr, 15–12pdr SB, 1–12pdr.

Notes: Confederate Army cargo ship *Louisville* captured in Little Red River by USS *Manitou* and *Rattler*, 13 Jul 1863. Converted to heavily armed gunboat.

Service record: Mississippi Sqn. Expedition up Black and Ouachita Rivers, La., 1–5 Mar 1864. Red River Expedition, 12 Mar–16 May 1864. Expedition up Red River, capture of CSS *Missouri*, 1–6 Jun 1865. Decomm 3 Jul 1865. Sold 25 Sep 1865.

Later history: Merchant *Vicksburg* 1865. Destroyed by fire at Cairo, Ill., 6 Jul 1869.

Tinclads

The tinclads were the only Civil War naval vessels to carry identifying numbers, which were painted on their pilothouses:

1.	*Rattler, Tempest*	33.	*Victory*
2.	*Marmora*	34.	*Victory*
3.	*Romeo*	35.	*Reindeer*
4.	*Juliet*	36.	*Peosta*
5.	*Petrel*	37.	*Naumkeag*
6.	*Cricket*	38.	*Exchange*
7.	*New Era*	39.	*Tensas*
8.	*Signal, Grosbeak*	40.	*Alexandria*
9.	*Forest Rose*	41.	*Nyanza*
10.	*Linden, Ibex*	42.	*Stockdale*
11.	*Prairie Bird*	43.	*Glide (II)*
12.	*Curlew*	44.	*Meteor*
13.	*Fort Hindman*	45.	*Wave*
14.	*Kenwood*	46.	*Tallahatchie*
15.	*Hastings*	47.	*Elk*
16.	*Little Rebel*	48.	*Rodolph*
17.	*Fairplay*	49.	*Carrabasset*
18.	*Brilliant*	50.	*Gazelle*
19.	*St. Clair*	51.	*Fairy*
20.	*General Pillow*	52.	*Elfin, Oriole*
21.	*Alfred Robb*	53.	*Naiad*
22.	*Springfield*	54.	*Nymph*
23.	*Silver Lake*	55.	*Undine, Kate*
24.	*Champion*	56	*Siren*
25.	*Covington, Colossus*	57.	*Peri*
26.	*Queen City, Mist*	58.	*Huntress*
28.	*Silver Cloud*	59.	*Sibyl*
29.	*Tawah, Collier*	60.	*Gamage, General Sherman*
30.	*Fawn*	61.	*General Thomas*
31.	*Paw Paw*	62	*General Grant*
32.	*Key West, Abeona*	63.	*General Burnside*

Sidewheelers

No.	Name	Builder	Launched	Acquired	Comm.
32	*Abeona*	Cincinnati, Ohio	1864	21 Dec 1864	10 Apr 1865

Fig 6.22: The large tinclad *Ouachita*, photographed toward the end of the war at Baton Rouge. There are gun ports on both lower and upper decks, and circular pillboxes forward and aft. (U.S. Naval Historical Center)

Tonnage	206 tons
Dimensions	157' × 31'6" × d4'6"
Machinery	#Side wheels (14" × 5')
Armament	2–30pdr MLR, 2–24pdr SB, 1–12pdr MLR

Service record: Mississippi Sqn, patrol and guard vessel. Decomm 4 Aug 1865. Sold 17 Aug 1865.

Later history: Merchant *Abeona* 1865. Destroyed by fire at Cincinnati, 7 Mar 1872.

No.	Name	Builder	Launched	Acquired	Comm.
40	*Alexandria*	Plaquemine, La.	1862	Jul 1863	Dec 1863

ex-CSS *St. Mary*

Tonnage	60 tons
Dimensions	89'9" × 15' × 4'
Machinery	Side wheels, 1 engine (10" × 3'6"), 1 boiler, 4 mph
Armament	1–24pdr SB, 1–12pdr

Notes: Confederate cottonclad steamer *St. Mary* captured at Yazoo City, Miss., 13 Jul 1863. Name *Yazoo* not approved.

Service record: Mississippi Sqn, 1863–65. Sold 17 Aug 1865.

Later history: Merchant *Alexandria* 1865. Sank on Amite River, La., 5 Oct 1867.

No.	Name	Builder	Launched	Acquired	Comm.
49	*Carrabasset*	Louisville, Ky.	1863	23 Jan 1864	12 May 1864

Tonnage	202 tons
Dimensions	155' × 31'7" × d4'7"
Machinery	Side wheels
Complement	45
Armament	2–32pdr/42, 4–24pdr SB

Service record: WGulfBS 1864–65. Expedition in Berwick Bay, La., 21 Mar 1865. Decomm 25 Jul 1865. Sold 12 Aug 1865.

Later history: Merchant *Annie Wagley*. Snagged and lost at Labadieville, La., 1 May 1870.

122 Civil War Navies, 1855-1883

No.	Name	Builder	Launched	Acquired	Comm.
24	*Champion*	Cincinnati, Ohio	1860	14 Mar 1863	26 Apr 1863

ex-*Champion No. 4*

Tonnage	115 tons
Dimensions	145'8" × 26'5" × 3'6"
Machinery	Side wheels, 2 engines (15" × 6'), 2 boilers, 4 mph
Armament	2–30pdr MLR, 1–24pdr SB H, 2–12pdr SB H; (Dec 1864) 2–30pdr MLR, 2–24pdr SB, 4–12pdr MLR.

Service record: Mississippi Sqn. Decomm 1 Jul 1865. Sold 29 Nov 1865.
Later history: Merchant *Champion No.4* 1865. RR 1868.

No.	Name	Builder	Launched	Acquired	Comm.
25	*Covington*	Cincinnati, Ohio	1862	13 Feb 1863	1863

ex-*Covington No.2*

Tonnage	224 tons
Dimensions	126' × 37' × d6'6"
Machinery	Side wheels
Complement	76
Armament	4–24pdr SB, 2–30pdr MLR, 2–50pdr MLR.

Notes: Converted ferry.
Service record: Tennessee River 1863. Badly damaged by Confederate troops in Red River south of Alexandria, La., abandoned and burned, 5 May 1864.
Ships captured: str *Eureka*, 2 Jul 1863; str *Gillum*, 25 Feb 1864.

No.	Name	Builder	Launched	Acquired	Comm.
47	*Elk*	Cincinnati, Ohio	1863	8 Dec 1863	6 May 1864

ex-*Countess*

Tonnage	162 tons
Dimensions	156' × 29' × d3'10"
Machinery	Side wheels
Complement	65
Armament	2–32pdr/42, 4–24pdr SB

Notes: Renamed 26 Jan 1864.
Service record: WGulfBS 1864. Lower Mississippi River 1864–65. Expedition in Lake Pontchartrain, La., 13–15 Oct 1864. Sold 24 Aug 1865.
Ship captured: *Yankee Doodle*, 10 Jun 1864.
Later history: Merchant *Countess* 1865. Sunk 1868.

No.	Name	Builder	Launched	Acquired	Comm.
17	*Fairplay*	New Albany, Ind.	1859	6 Sep 1862	1862

Tonnage	162 tons
Dimensions	138.8' × 27' × 4.9'
Machinery	Side wheels, 2 engines (16" × 5'), 2 boilers. 5 mph
Armament	2–12pdr H, 2–12pdr MLR SB; (May 1863) 1–32pdr/33, 2–12pdr H, 4–12pdr MLR; (Oct 1863) 1–30pdr MLR, 4–12pdr MLR, 2–12pdr H SB; (Mar 1864) add 1–30pdr MLR.

Notes: Captured as Confederate transport at Milliken's Bend in Mississippi River, 18 Aug 1862.
Service record: WGF. Defense of Ft. Donelson, Tenn., 3 Feb 1863. Pursuit of Morgan's Raiders up Ohio River, Jul 1863. Engaged battery at Bell's Mill, Cumberland River, Tenn., 3–4 Dec 1864. Decomm 9 Aug and sold 17 Aug 1865.
Later history: Merchant *Cotile* 1865. BU 1871

Fort Hindman, see *James Thompson*

Fig 6.23: Tinclad number 17, the *Fairplay*, showing the arrangement of gun ports on these ships. (U.S. Naval Historical Center)

No.	Name	Builder	Launched	Acquired	Comm.
50	*Gazelle*	Madison, Ind.	1863	21 Nov 1863	Feb 1864

ex-*Emma Brown*

Tonnage	117 tons
Dimensions	135' × 23' × 5'
Machinery	Side wheels, 2 engines (16" × 5'), 2 boilers, 4 mph
Armament	6–12pdr MLR; (Sep 1864) 6–24pdr MLR.

Service record: Red River Expedition, 12 Mar–16 May 1864. Decomm 7 Jul 1865. Sold 17 Aug 1865.
Later history: Merchant *Plain City* 1865. BU 1869.

No.	Name	Builder	Launched	Comm.
63	*General Burnside*	Chattanooga, Tenn.	1864	8 Aug 1864
62	*General Grant*	Chattanooga, Tenn.	1864	20 Jul 1864
60	*General Sherman*	Chattanooga, Tenn.	1864	27 Jul 1864
61	*General Thomas*	Chattanooga, Tenn.	1864	8 Aug 1864

Tonnage	201 tons (*General Grant*: 204, *General Sherman*: 187, *General Thomas*: 184)
Dimensions	171' × 26' × 4.8' (*General Sherman*: 168', *General Thomas*: 165')
Machinery	Side wheels (16" × 5.5')
Armament	2–20pdr MLR, 3–24pdr H, except *General Grant* 2–30pdr MLR, 3–24pdr H.

Note: Built for War Department.
Service records

General Burnside: Tennessee River Fleet (flagship) 1864. Supported Army at Decatur, Ala., 12 Dec 1864. Returned to War Department, 1 Jun 1865.
General Grant: Patrolled upper Tennessee River. Supported Army at Decatur, Ala., 12 Dec 1864. Destruction of Guntersville, Ala., 11–15 Jan 1865. Returned to War Department, 2 Jun 1865.
General Sherman: Mississippi Sqn. Upper Tennessee River. Supported Army at Decatur, Ala., 12 Dec 1864. Returned to War Department, 3 Jun 1865.
General Thomas: Completed Jun 1864. Tennessee River. Engaged enemy force near Whitesburg, Tenn., 28–30 Oct 1864. Supported Army at Decatur, Ala., 22–24 Dec 1864. Returned to War Department, 3 Jun 1865.
   Later history: Sold 1866, Merchant *Ingomar*. Sank after running on to a sunken barge at Tomlinson's Run, Ohio River, 24 Mar 1868. Raised and sold. Hit a snag and sank above Wheeling, W.Va., 31 Dec 1868.

The Mississippi River Fleet 123

No.	Name	Builder	Launched	Acquired	Comm.
20	*General Pillow*	(U)	(U)	Jun 1862	Aug 1862
ex-CSS *B.M.Moore*					

Tonnage	38 tons
Dimensions	81'5" × 17'1" × 3'
Machinery	Side wheels, 2 engines (10" × 3'6"), 2 boilers
Armament	2–12pdr H SB

Notes: Confederate steamer captured on Hatchee River by USS *Pittsburg*, 9 Jun 1862. Transferred from Army 30 Sep 1862.
Service record: WGF. Mississippi Sqn. Tennessee and Cumberland Rivers. Decomm Jul 1865. Sold 26 Nov 1865.
Later history: FFU

No.	Name	Builder	Launched	Acquired	Comm.
8	*Grossbeak*	Cincinnati, Ohio	1864	3 Feb 1865	24 Feb 1865
ex-*Fanny*					

Tonnage	196 tons
Dimensions	163'8" × 28'4" × d4'6"; also reported as 179' × 27' × 5.5'
Machinery	Side wheels, 2 boilers
Armament	2–20pdr MLR, 2–30pdr MLR, 1–12pdr SB, 2–24pdr SB

Service record: Mississippi Sqn. Rescued survivors from burning steamer *Sultana* off Memphis, 27 Apr 1865. Sold 17 Aug 1865.
Later history: Merchant *Mollie Hambleton* 1865. Foundered at Galveston, Tex., 9 Jun 1871.

No.	Name	Builder	Launched	Acquired	Comm.
15	*Hastings*	Monongahela, Pa.	1860	24 Mar 1863	Apr 1863
ex-*Emma Duncan*					

Tonnage	293 tons
Dimensions	173' × 34'2" × d5'4"
Machinery	Side wheels, (20' × 6'), 3 boilers.
Armament	2–30pdr MLR, 2–32pdr/42, 4–24pdr

Notes: Renamed 7 Apr 1863.
Service record: Tennessee River 1863–64. Defense of Ft. Pillow, Tenn., 12 Apr 1864. Operations in White River, Jun 1864. Engaged enemy above St. Charles, Ark., 4 Jul 1864. Decomm 7 Jul 1865. Sold 17 Aug 1865.
Later history: Merchant *Dora* 1865. RR 1872.

No.	Name	Builder	Launched	Acquired	Comm.
10	*Ibex*	Harmer, Ohio	1863	10 Dec 1864	4 Apr 1865
ex-*Ohio Valley*					

Tonnage	235 tons
Dimensions	157'× 33' × d4'6"
Machinery	#Side wheels, 3 boilers.
Armament	2–30pdr MLR, 1–12pdr MLR, 4–24pdr H

Notes: Reported built by Knox, Marietta, Ohio.
Service record: Mississippi Sqn. Decomm 5 Aug and sold 17 Aug 1865.
Later history: Merchant *Harry Dean* 1865. Destroyed by boiler explosion near Gallipolis, Ohio, 3 Jan 1868.

No.	Name	Builder	Launched	Acquired	Comm.
13	*James Thompson*	Jeffersonville, Ind.	1 Nov 1862	14 Mar 1863	Apr 1863

Tonnage	280 tons
Dimensions	150' × 37' × 2'4"
Machinery	Side wheels, 1 direct-acting engine (16" × 5'), 2 boilers
Armament	2–8"/55 SB, 4–8"/63; (Jun 1864) add 1–100pdr MLR; (Mar 1865) 1–100pdr MLR, 4–8"/63, 2–8"/55, 1–12pdr MLR.

Notes: Ferry. Built by Howard.
Service record: Mississippi Sqn. Renamed ***Manitou***, 2 Jun 1863. Expedition to Trinity, La., Red River, 10 Jul 1863. Expedition up Black, Tensas, and Ouachita Rivers, 13–20 Jul, captured CSS *Louisville* at Little Red River, 13 Jul 1863. Renamed ***Fort Hindman***, 5 Nov 1863. Expedition up Black and Ouachita Rivers, La., 1–5 Mar 1864. Red River Expedition, 12 Mar–16 May 1864 (3 killed). Expedition up Red River, capture of CSS *Missouri*, 1–6 Jun 1865. Decomm 3 Aug and sold 17 Aug 1865.
Ships captured: str *Louisville*,* 13 Jul 1863; str *Volunteer*,† 25 Nov 1863; str *John L. Roe*, 27 Jan 1864.
Later history: Merchant *James Thompson* 1865. RR 1874.

No.	Name	Builder	Launched	Acquired	Comm.
41	*Nyanza*	Belle Vernon, Pa.	1863	4 Nov 1863	21 Dec 1863

Tonnage	203 tons
Dimensions	(U)
Machinery	#Side wheels
Armament	(Dec 1863) 6–24pdr H; (Jun 1864) add 2–20pdr MLR.

Service record: Mississippi Sqn. Decomm 21 Jul and sold 15 Aug 1865.
Ships captured: *J.W.Wilder*, 15 Mar 1864; *Mandoline*, 13 Apr 1864.
Later history: Merchant *Nyanza* 1865. RR 1873.

No.	Name	Builder	Launched	Acquired	Comm.
36	*Peosta*	Cincinnati, Ohio	1857	13 Jun 1863	2 Oct 1863

Tonnage	204 tons
Dimensions	151'2" × 34'3" × 6'
Machinery	Side wheels, 2 engines (18" × 5'6"), 2 boilers, 5 mph
Armament	3–30pdr MLR, 3–32pdr/42, 6–24pdr H, 2–12pdr SB

Service record: Mississippi Sqn, Tennessee River. Engaged enemy troops at Paducah, Ky., 25 Mar 1864. Decomm 7 Aug and sold 17 Aug 1865.
Later history: Merchant *Peosta* 1865. Destroyed by fire at Memphis, 25 Dec 1870.

No.	Name	Builder	Launched	Acquired	Comm.
26	*Queen City*	Cincinnati, Ohio	1863	13 Feb 1863	1 Apr 1863

Tonnage	210 tons
Dimensions	(U)
Machinery	Side wheels
Armament	2–30pdr MLR, 2–32pdr/42, 4–24pdr H.

Note: Former ferry.
Service record: Mississippi Sqn, Tennessee River. Expedition to Helena, Ark., 13 Oct 1863. Disabled in action with Confederate Army at Clarendon, Ark. and captured, 24 Jun 1864, later blown up.

No.	Name	Builder	Launched	Acquired	Comm.
22	*Springfield*	Cincinnati, Ohio	1862	20 Nov 1862	12 Jan 1863
ex-*W.A. Healy*					

Tonnage	146 tons

---

* Later USS *Ouachita*.
† Later USS *Volunteer*.

Dimensions 134′9″ × 26′11″ × 4′
Machinery #Side wheels, 2 engines (10″ × 3′6″), 2 boilers, 5 mph
Armament 6–24pdr H

Service record: Mississippi Sqn. Expedition to burn Palmyra, Tenn., 4 Apr 1863. Pursuit of Morgan's Raiders up Ohio River, Jul 1863. Decomm 30 Jun 1865. Sold 17 Aug 1865.

Later history: Merchant *Jennie D.* 1865. RR 1875

No.	Name	Builder	Launched	Acquired	Comm.
29	*Tawah*	Brownsville, Pa.	1859	19 Jun 1863	Oct 1863
ex-*Ebenezer*					

Tonnage	108 tons
Dimensions	114′ × 33′ × d3′9″
Machinery	Side wheels
Armament	4–24pdr, 2–30pdr MLR, 2–24pdr H, 2–12pdr

Notes: Former ferry.

Service record: Mississippi Sqn. Engaged Confederate force on Tennessee River and recaptured USS *Venus*, 2 Nov 1864. Damaged in action with shore batteries at Johnsonville, Tenn., and burned to prevent capture, 4 Nov 1864.

No.	Name	Builder	Launched	Acquired	Comm.
39	*Tensas*	Cincinnati, Ohio	1860	29 Sep 1863	1 Jan 1864
ex-*Tom Sugg*					

Tonnage	62 tons
Dimensions	91′8″ × 22′5″ × 4′
Machinery	Side wheels, 2 engines (11″ × 3′), 2 boilers, 4 mph
Armament	2–24pdr H.

Notes: Confederate cottonclad *Tom Sugg* captured in Little Red River at Searcy's Landing, Ark. by USS *Cricket*, 14 Aug 1863, and converted.

Service record: Mississippi Sqn. Decomm 7 Aug and sold 17 Aug 1865.

Later history: Merchant *Teche* 1865. Wrecked in Bayou Teche, La., 1868.

No.	Name	Builder	Launched	Acquired	Comm.
33	*Victory*	Cincinnati, Ohio	1863	May 1863	8 Jul 1863
ex-*Banker*					

Tonnage	160 tons
Dimensions	157′ × 30′3″ × 4′2″
Machinery	#Side wheels, 2 engines (13″ × 4′6″), 2 boilers, 5 mph
Armament	6–24pdr H

Service record: Mississippi Sqn. Pursuit of Morgan's Raiders up Ohio River, Jul 1863. Repulsed raid on Paducah, Ky., 4 Nov 1864. Decomm 30 Jun 1865. Sold 17 Aug 1865.

Later history: Merchant *Lizzie Tate* 1865. Snagged and sank near Grand Bayou, La., 8 Feb 1866. Converted to barge 1867.

Sternwheelers

No.	Name	Builder	Launched	Acquired	Comm.
21	*Alfred Robb*	Pittsburgh, Pa.	1860	Jun 1862	1 May 1863

Tonnage	86 tons
Dimensions	114′9″ × 20′ × 4′6″
Machinery	Stern wheel, 2 engines (16″ × 5′), 3 boilers, 9.5 knots
Armament	2–12pdr MLR, 2–12pdr SB

Notes: Confederate transport captured at Florence, Ala., by USS *Tyler*, 21 Apr 1862. Also known as **Lady Foote**. Converted at Cairo, Ill

Service record: WGF. Mississippi Sqn. Defense of Ft. Donelson, Tenn., 3 Feb 1863. Expedition to burn Palmyra, Tenn., 3 Apr 1863. Engaged enemy force at Cerro Gordo, Tenn., 19 Jun 1863. Decomm 9 Aug and sold 17 Aug 1865.

Later history: Merchant *Robb* 1865. BU 1873

No.	Name	Builder	Launched	Acquired	Comm.
27	*Argosy*	Monongahela, Pa.	1862	24 Mar 1863	29 Mar 1863

Tonnage	219 tons
Dimensions	156′4″ × 33′ × 4′6″
Machinery	Stern wheel, 2 engines (15″ × 5′), 3 boilers, 5 mph
Complement	71
Armament	(Mar 1863) 6–24pdr, 2–12pdr MLR; (Jan 1864) 6–24pdr, 2–12pdr SB, 1–12pdr MLR; (Feb 1864) 2–32pdr/42, 4–24pdr; (Jan 1865) as Jan 1864.

Service record: Mississippi Sqn, Tennessee and Cumberland Rivers. Decomm 11 Aug and sold 17 Aug 1865.

Ship captured: str *Ben Franklin*, 12 Dec 1863.

Later history: Merchant *Argosy* 1865. Destroyed by fire at Cincinnati, 7 Mar 1872.

No.	Name	Builder	Launched	Acquired	Comm.
18	*Brilliant*	Brownsville, Pa.	1862	13 Aug 1862	1862

Tonnage	227 tons
Dimensions	154′8″ × 33′6″ × 5′
Machinery	Stern wheel, 2 engines (16 3/8″ × 4′6″), 3 boilers, 6 mph
Armament	2–12pdr MLR, 2–12pdr SB; (Dec 1864) add 2–24pdr SB.

Notes: Purchased by War Department.

Service record: Mississippi Sqn 1862. Defense of Ft. Donelson, Tenn., 3 Feb 1863. Expedition to burn Palmyra, Tenn., 3 Apr 1863. Supported attack on Nashville, 3–16 Dec 1864. Sold 17 Aug 1865.

Later history: Merchant *John S. McCune* 1865. Burned at Prairie Landing, Ark., 6 Dec 1867.

No.	Name	Builder	Launched	Acquired	Comm.
29	*Collier*	Cincinnati, Ohio	1864	7 Dec 1864	18 Mar 1865
ex-*Allen Collier*					

Tonnage	176 tons
Dimensions	158′ × 30′ × d4′
Machinery	#Stern wheel (15″ × 4.5′)
Armament	2–20pdr MLR, 1–12pdr MLR, 6–24pdr H.

Service record: Mississippi Sqn. Expedition up Red River, and capture of CSS *Missouri*, 1–6 Jun 1865. Decomm 29 Jul 1865. Sold 17 Aug 1865.

Later history: Merchant *Imperial* 1865. RR 1867.

No.	Name	Builder	Launched	Acquired	Comm.
25	*Colossus*	Freedom, Pa.	1863	6 Dec 1864	24 Feb 1865

Tonnage	183 tons
Dimensions	155′2″ × 31′9″ × 4′
Machinery	Stern wheel, 2 engines (13 ½″ × 4′6″), 2 boilers, 5 mph
Armament	2–30pdr MLR, 4–24pdr SB, 1–12pdr SB

Service record: Mississippi Sqn. Decomm 3 Jul 1865. Sold 17 Aug 1865.

Later history: Merchant *Memphis* 1865. Snagged and lost at Pine Bluff, Ark., 17 Dec 1866.

No.	Name	Builder	Launched	Acquired	Comm.
6	Cricket	Pittsburgh, Pa.	1860	18 Nov 1862	19 Jan 1863
ex-Cricket No.2					

Tonnage	178 tons
Dimensions	154'1" × 28'2" × 4'
Machinery	Stern wheel, 2 engines (13" × 4'6"), 2 boilers, 6 knots
Armament	(Jan 1863) 6–24pdr H; (Aug 1864) 2–20pdr MLR, 1–12pdr, 4–24pdr H.

Service record: Engaged battery above Greenville, Miss., 2 and 4 May 1863. Reconnaissance up White River, Ark., 12–15 Aug 1863. Expedition up Black and Ouachita Rivers, La., 1–5 Mar 1864. Red River Expedition, 12 Mar–16 May 1864. Fought off Confederate boarders and damaged by artillery, 26 Apr 1864 (25 casualties). Decomm 30 Jun 1865. Sold 17 Aug 1865.

Ships captured: strs *Kaskaskia* and *Tom Sugg*,* 14 Aug 1863.

Later history: Merchant *Cricket No.2* 1865. BU 1867

No.	Name	Builder	Launched	Acquired	Comm.
12	Curlew	Elizabeth, Pa.	1861	17 Dec 1862	16 Feb 1863
ex-Florence					

Tonnage	196 tons
Dimensions	159' × 32'1" × 4'
Machinery	Stern wheel, 2 engines (15½" × 4'6"), 2 boilers, 4 mph
Armament	6–32pdr/57, 1–20pdr MLR; (Feb 1863) 8–24pdr H.

Service record: Expedition up Red, Black, Tensas, and Ouachita Rivers, Jul 1863. Engaged battery at Gaines Landing, Ark., 24 May 1864. Decomm 5 Jul 1865. Sold 17 Aug 1865.

Later history: FFU

No.	Name	Builder	Launched	Acquired	Comm.
52	Elfin	Cincinnati, Ohio	1863	23 Feb 1864	1864
ex-W.C. Mann					

Tonnage	192 tons
Dimensions	155' × 31' × d4'4"
Machinery	Stern wheel
Complement	50
Armament	8–24pdr H

Service record: Mississippi Sqn. After engaging enemy batteries, burned to prevent capture at Johnsonville, Tenn., 4 Nov 1864.

No.	Name	Builder	Launched	Acquired	Comm.
38	Exchange	Brownsville, Pa. (Cox & Williams)	1862	6 Apr 1863	Jun 1863

Tonnage	211 tons
Dimensions	155'3" × 33'5" × 5'
Machinery	Stern wheel, 2 engines (16" × 4'6"), 3 boilers, 6 mph
Complement	81
Armament	2–32pdr/42, 4–24pdr H

Notes: Built by Cox & Williams.

Service record: Tennessee River 1863. Expedition up Yazoo River, 2 Feb–22 Apr 1864. Damaged by gunfire of enemy battery at Columbia, Ark., 1 Jun 1864 (1 killed). Decomm 6 Aug and sold 17 Aug 1865.

Later history: Merchant *Tennessee* 1865. Snagged and lost near Decatur, Neb., 25 Apr 1869.

---

* Later USS *Tensas*.

No.	Name	Builder	Launched	Acquired	Comm.
51	Fairy	Cincinnati, Ohio	1863	10 Feb 1864	Mar 1864
ex-Maria					

Tonnage	173 tons
Dimensions	157' × 31'6" × 5'
Machinery	Stern wheel, 2 engines (14" × 5'), 2 boilers, 5.5 mph
Armament	8–24pdr H; (Jul 1864) 2–30pdr MLR, 6–24pdr H

Service record: Mississippi Sqn. Tennessee River. Decomm 8 Aug and sold 17 Aug 1865.

Later history: FFU

No.	Name	Builder	Launched	Acquired	Comm.
30	Fawn	Cincinnati, Ohio	1863	13 May 1863	11 May 1863
ex-Fanny Barker					

Tonnage	174 tons
Dimensions	158'8" × 30'5" × 3'6"
Machinery	Stern wheel, 2 engines (12" × 4'), 2 boilers, 4 mph
Armament	(May 1863) 6–24pdr H; (Mar 1864) add 1–12pdr MLR; (Jan 1865) add 1–24pdr H.

Notes: Renamed 19 Jun 1863.

Service record: Served in White River. Engaged battery at Clarendon, Ark., 24 Jun 1864. Decomm 30 Jun 1865. Sold 17 Aug 1865.

Later history: Merchant *Fanny Barker* 1865. Wrecked near St. Joseph, Mo., 24 Mar 1873.

No.	Name	Builder	Launched	Acquired	Comm.
9	Forest Rose	Freedom, Pa.	1862	15 Nov 1862	3 Dec 1862

Tonnage	260 tons
Dimensions	155' × 32'3" × 5'
Machinery	Stern wheel, 2 engines (16" × 5'), 3 boilers, 6 mph
Armament	2–30pdr MLR, 4–24pdr; (Aug 1863) add 2–32pdr/42.

Service record: Mississippi Sqn. Bombardment of Drumgoulds Bluff, Yazoo River, 28 Dec 1862. Expedition up White River, capture of Ft. Hindman, Ark., 10–11 Jan 1863. Yazoo Pass expedition, attack on Ft. Pemberton, Tallahatchie River, 11–23 Mar 1863. Capture of Haynes' Bluff, Yazoo River, 18 May 1863. Destruction of Yazoo City NYd, 20–23 May 1863. Expedition up Yazoo River, 24–31 May 1863. Expedition to Trinity, La., Red River, 10 Jul 1863. Red River Expedition, May 5–15, 1864. Decomm 7 Aug and sold 17 Aug 1865.

Ships captured: str *Chippewa Valley*, 14 Feb 1863; str *Elmira*, 13 Jul 1863.

Later history: Merchant *Anna White* 1865. Destroyed by ice at St. Louis, Mo., 4 Feb 1868.

No.	Name	Builder	Launched	Acquired	Comm.
60	Gamage	Cincinnati, Ohio	1864	22 Dec 1864	23 Mar 1865
ex-Willie Gamage					

Tonnage	187 tons
Dimensions	148'6" × 30'3" × d4'6"
Machinery	#Stern wheel
Armament	6–24pdr H, 2–20pdr MLR, 1–12pdr MLR

Service record: Mississippi Sqn. Expedition up Red River, capture of CSS *Missouri*, 1–6 Jun 1865. Decomm 29 Jul 1865. Sold 17 Aug 1865.

Later history: Merchant *Southern Belle* 1865. Burned at Plaquemine, La., 11 Oct 1876.

126 Civil War Navies, 1855-1883

Fig 6.24: Tinclad number 30, the *Fawn*, underway. (Mariners Museum, Newport News)

No.	Name	Builder	Launched	Acquired	Comm.
	Glide (I)	Shousetown, Pa.	1862	17 Nov 1862	3 Dec 1862
Tonnage	137 tons
Dimensions	(U)
Machinery	Stern wheel
Armament	6–24pdr H

Service record: Mississippi Sqn. Bombardment and capture of Ft. Hindman, Ark., expedition up White River, 10–11 Jan 1863. Destroyed by fire while refitting at Cairo, Ill., 7 Feb 1863.

No.	Name	Builder	Launched	Acquired	Comm.
43	*Glide* (II)	Murraysville, Va.	1863	30 Nov 1863	1864
Tonnage	232 tons
Dimensions	160.4′ × 33′ × 5.1′
Machinery	#Stern wheel
Armament	2–32pdr/42, 4–24pdr H

Service record: WGulfBS 1864. Blockade in Berwick Bay, La., 1864–65. Decomm 1 Aug and sold 12 Aug 1865.

Ship captured: *Malta*, 3 Mar 1865.

Later history: Merchant *Glide*. Destroyed by boiler explosion 59 miles above New Orleans, 13 Jan 1869.

No.	Name	Builder	Launched	Acquired	Comm.
58	*Huntress*	New Albany, Ind.	1862	May 1864	10 Jun 1864
Tonnage	211 tons
Dimensions	131′8″ × 31′3″ × 5′

Fig 6.25: The sternwheel tinclad *Forest Rose*, Number 9, with two fuel barges alongside. (U.S. Naval Historical Center)

Machinery	Stern wheel, 2 engines (12½" × 4'), 2 boilers, 6 mph
Armament	2–30pdr, 4–24pdr H

Service record: Mississippi Sqn. Patrolled river between Memphis and Columbus, Ky. Decomm 10 Aug and sold 17 Aug 1865.

Later history: Merchant *Huntress* 1865. Snagged and lost near Alexandria, La., 30 Dec 1865.

No.	Name	Builder	Launched	Acquired	Comm.
4	*Juliet*	Brownsville, Pa.	1862	1 Nov 1862	14 Dec 1862

Tonnage	157 tons
Dimensions	155'6" × 30'2" × 5'
Machinery	Stern wheel, 2 engines (13" × 3'6"), 2 boilers
Armament	6–24pdr H

Service record: Mississippi Sqn. Expedition in Yazoo River, dragging for torpedoes, 23–26 Dec 1862. Expedition up White River, bombardment and capture of Ft. Hindman, Ark., 10–11 Jan 1863. Red River Expedition, 12 Mar–16 May 1864. Damaged by batteries, 26–27 Apr 1864. Decomm 30 Jun 1865. Sold 17 Aug 1865.

Ship captured: str *Fred Nolte*, 15 Jun 1863.

Later history: Merchant *Goldena* 1865. Wrecked in White River Cutoff, Ark., 31 Dec 1865.

No.	Name	Builder	Launched	Acquired	Comm.
55	*Kate*	Belle Vernon, Pa.	1864	23 Dec 1864	2 Apr 1865

ex-*Kate B. Porter*

Tonnage	241 tons
Dimensions	160' × 31' × 4.1'
Machinery	Stern wheel, 2 engines (15" × 4'6"), 2 boilers
Armament	2–20pdr MLR, 6–24pdr H, 2–12pdr H

Notes: Built by L.M.Spear.

Service record: Mississippi Sqn. Decomm 25 Mar and sold 29 Mar 1866.

Later history: Merchant *James H. Trover* 1866. Stranded 300 miles below Ft. Benton, Mont., 21 Jun 1867.

No.	Name	Builder	Launched	Acquired	Comm.
14	*Kenwood*	Cincinnati, Ohio	3 Apr 1863	15 Jul 1863	24 May 1863

Tonnage	232 tons
Dimensions	154' × 33' × 5'6"
Machinery	Stern wheel, 2 engines (16" × 5'), 3 boilers, 7 mph
Complement	40
Armament	(May 1863) 2–32pdr/42, 4–24pdr H; (Dec 1863) 2–30pdr MLR, 4–24pdr H, 1–12pdr; (Jun 1864) add 2–12pdr H (Dec 1864) 2–32pdr/42, 6–24pdr SB

Notes: Built by H.A. Jones.

Service record: Mississippi Sqn. Arkansas River. Expedition to capture Yazoo City and destroy ships, 13 Jul 1863. Operated off Port Hudson, La., 1863–65. Expedition up Red River, capture of CSS *Missouri*, 1–6 Jun 1865. Decomm 7 Aug and sold 17 Aug 1865.

Ship captured: str *Black Hawk*, 3 Nov 1863.

Later history: Merchant *Cumberland* 1865. Exploded and sank at Shawneetown Ill., 14 Aug 1869.

No.	Name	Builder	Launched	Acquired	Comm.
32	*Key West*	California, Pa.	1862	16 Apr 1863	26 May 1863

ex-*Key West No.3*

Tonnage	207 tons
Dimensions	156' × 32' × 4.5'
Machinery	Stern wheel
Armament	6–24pdr H; (Jun 1863) add 1–12pdr MLR, 2–24pdr SB.

Service record: Mississippi Sqn, Tennessee River. Expedition to Eastport, Miss., 8–14 Oct 1864. Helped recapture transport *Venus*, 2 Nov, then burned to prevent capture at Johnsonville, Tenn., 4 Nov 1864.

No.	Name	Builder	Launched	Acquired	Comm.
10	*Linden*	Belle Vernon, Pa.	1860	20 Nov 1862	3 Jan 1863

Tonnage	177 tons
Dimensions	154' × 31' × d4'
Machinery	#Stern wheel
Armament	6–24pdr H

Service record: Mississippi Sqn. Bombardment and feigned attack, Haynes' Bluff, Miss., 29 Apr–2 May 1863. Capture of Haynes' Bluff, Yazoo River, 18 May 1863. Destruction of Yazoo City NYd, Miss., 20–23 May 1863. Expedition up Yazoo River, 24–31 May 1863. Struck a snag and sank in Arkansas River, 22 Feb 1864.

No.	Name	Builder	Launched	Acquired	Comm.
2	*Marmora*	Monongahela, Pa. (W. Latta)	1862	17 Sep 1862	21 Oct 1862

ex-*Marmora No.2*

Tonnage	207 tons
Dimensions	155' × 33'5" × 4'6"
Machinery	Stern wheel, 2 engines (15–1/4" × 5'6"), 2 boilers, 6.9 knots
Armament	(Oct 1862) 2–24pdr, 2–12pdr MLR; (Jun 1864) add 4–24pdr; (Mar1865) 2–12pdr MLR, 6–24pdr.

Notes: Built by W. Latta.

Service record: Mississippi Sqn. Expedition up Yazoo River, 21 Nov–11 Dec 1862. Expedition in Yazoo River, dragging for torpedoes and bombardment of Haynes' Bluff and Drumgoulds Bluff, 23–26 Dec 1862. Expedition up White River, bombardment and capture of Ft. Hindman, Ark., 10–11 Jan 1863. Yazoo Pass expedition, attack on Ft. Pemberton, Tallahatchie River, 11–23 Mar 1863. Reconnaissance up White and Little Red Rivers, Ark., 12–15 Aug 1863. Expedition up Yazoo River, 2 Feb–22 Apr 1864. Decomm 7 Jul 1865. Sold 17 Aug 1865.

Later history: FFU

No.	Name	Builder	Launched	Acquired	Comm.
44	*Meteor*	Portsmouth, Ohio	1863	10 Nov 1863	8 Mar 1864

ex-*Scioto*

Tonnage	221 tons
Dimensions	156' × 33'6" × 4'3"
Machinery	#Stern wheel
Armament	2–32pdr/42, 4–24pdr; (Oct 1864) 2–30pdr MLR, 4–24pdr.

Service record: WGulfBS 1864. Guard vessel at Head of Passes, Mar 1864–Feb 1865. Operations against Mobile, Mar–Apr 1865. Decomm 12 Sep 1865. Sold 5 Oct 1865.

Later history: Merchant *De Soto* 1865. RR 1869

No.	Name	Builder	Launched	Acquired	Comm.
26	*Mist*	Allegheny, Pa.	1864	23 Dec 1864	3 Mar 1865

Tonnage	232 tons
Dimensions	157'3" × 30'4" × d4'4"

Machinery	Stern wheel, 2 engines (12″ × 5′), 2 boilers, 5.5 knots
Armament	2–20pdr MLR, 4–24pdr, 1–12pdr

Service record: Mississippi Sqn. Decomm 4 Aug and sold 17 Aug 1865.
Later history: Merchant *Mist* 1865. RR 1874

No.	Name	Builder	Launched	Acquired	Comm.
34	*Moose*	Cincinnati, Ohio	1863	20 May 1863	May 1863
ex-*Florence Miller No.2*					

Tonnage	189 tons
Dimensions	154′8″ × 32′2″ × 5′
Machinery	Stern wheel, 2 engines (14″ × 4′6″), 2 boilers, 6 knots
Armament	2–20pdr, 2–12pdr, 6–24pdr

Service record: Mississippi Sqn. Destroyed Confederate guerrilla force at Brandenburg, Ky., on Ohio River, 9–11 Jul 1863. Pursuit of Morgan's raiders up Ohio River, Jul 1863. Defense of Ft. Pillow, Tenn., 12 Apr 1864. Engaged battery at Bell's Mill, Cumberland River, 3–4 Dec 1864. Attacked guerrillas at Centre Furnace, Tenn., 29 Apr 1865. Decomm 12 Apr 1865. Sold 17 Aug 1865.
Later history: Merchant *Little Rock* 1865. Destroyed by fire at Clarendon, Ark., 29 Dec 1867.

No.	Name	Builder	Launched	Acquired	Comm.
53	*Naiad*	Freedom, Pa.	1863	3 Mar 1864	3 Apr 1864
ex-*Princess*					

Tonnage	185 tons
Dimensions	156′10″ × 30′4″ × 4′5″
Machinery	Stern wheel, 2 engines (13″ × 3′6″), 3 boilers, 6 mph
Armament	8–24pdr; (Dec 1864) 2–30pdr MLR, 6–24pdr; (Jun 1865) 4–30pdr MLR, 6–24pdr.

Service record: Mississippi Sqn. Damaged engaging battery at Ratliff's Landing, La., 15–16 Jun 1864. Engaged battery near Rowe's Landing, La., 2 Sep 1864. Decomm 30 Jun 1865. Sold 17 Aug 1865.
Later history: Merchant *Princess* 1865. Snagged and lost at Napoleon, Missouri, 1 Jun 1868.

No.	Name	Builder	Launched	Acquired	Comm.
37	*Naumkeag*	Cincinnati, Ohio	1863	14 Apr 1863	16 Apr 1863

Tonnage	148 tons
Dimensions	154′4″ × 30′5″ × 5′6″
Machinery	Stern wheel, 2 engines (14 1/4″ × 3′6″), 2 boilers, 6 mph
Armament	(Apr 1863) 2–30pdr MLR, 4–24pdr.

Service record: Mississippi Sqn. Destroyed Confederate guerrilla force at Brandenburg, Ky. on Ohio River, 9–11 Jul 1863. Pursuit of Morgan's Raiders up Ohio River, 19 Jul 1863. Engaged battery at Clarendon, Ark., 24 Jun 1864. Decomm 11 Aug and sold 17 Aug 1865.
Later history: Merchant *Montgomery* 1865. Destroyed by fire at Erie, Ala., 19 Jan 1867.

No.	Name	Builder	Launched	Acquired	Comm.
7	*New Era*	Wellsville, Ohio	1862	27 Oct 1862	Dec 1862

Tonnage	157 tons
Dimensions	137′1″ × 29′6″ × 4′
Machinery	Stern wheel, 2 engines (14″ × 4′6″), 2 boilers
Armament	6–24pdr H

Service record: Mississippi Sqn. Expedition up White River, bombardment and capture of Ft. Hindman, Ark., 10–11 Jan 1863. Defense of Ft. Pillow, Tenn., 12–14 Apr 1864. Decomm 28 Jun 1865. Sold 17 Aug 1865.
Ships captured: *W.A. Knapp, Rowena, White Cloud, Curlew,* Feb 1863.
Later history: Merchant *Goldfinch* 1865. Destroyed by fire at Evansville, Ind., 3 Jun 1868.

No.	Name	Builder	Launched	Acquired	Comm.
54	*Nymph*	Cincinnati, Ohio	1863	8 Mar 1864	11 Apr 1864
ex-*Cricket No.3*					

Tonnage	171 tons
Dimensions	161′2″ × 30′4″ × 5′
Machinery	Stern wheel, 2 engines (14″ × 4′), 2 boilers, 4 mph
Armament	8–24pdr SB, 4–24pdr

Service record: Mississippi Sqn. Decomm 28 Jun and sold 17 Aug 1865.
Later history: Merchant *Cricket No.3*, 1865. FFU

No.	Name	Builder	Launched	Acquired	Comm.
52	*Oriole*	Cincinnati, Ohio	1864	7 Dec 1864	22 Mar 1865
ex-*Florence Miller No.3*					

Tonnage	236 tons
Dimensions	125′ × 26′5″ × 6′3″; also reported as 160′ × 33.5′ × 5′
Machinery	Stern wheel (14″ × 5′)
Armament	2–30pdr MLR, 1–12pdr MLR, 6–24pdr SB

Service record: Mississippi Sqn. Decomm 4 Aug and sold 17 Aug 1865.
Later history: Merchant *Agnes* 1865. Snagged and sunk at Warrenton, Miss., 3 Mar 1869.

No.	Name	Builder	Launched	Acquired	Comm.
57	*Peri*	Cincinnati, Ohio	1863	30 Apr 1864	20 Jun 1864
ex-*Reindeer*					

Tonnage	155 tons
Dimensions	147′6″ × 28′2″ × 5′6″
Machinery	Stern wheel, 2 engines (13 1/4″ × 4′), 2 boilers, 6 mph
Armament	(Jun 64) 1–30pdr MLR, 6–24pdr H; (Dec 64) add 1–30pdr MLR.

Service record: Sold 17 Aug 1865.
Later history: Merchant *Marietta* 1865. Sunk at Omaha, Neb., 8 Jan 1868.

No.	Name	Builder	Launched	Acquired	Comm.
5	*Petrel*	Brownsville, Pa.	1862	22 Dec 1862	1863
ex-*Duchess*					

Tonnage	226 tons
Dimensions	(U)
Machinery	Stern wheel
Armament	8–24pdr H

Service record: Mississippi Sqn. Bombardment and feigned attack, Haynes' Bluff, Miss., 29 Apr–2 May 1863. Capture of Haynes' Bluff, Yazoo River, 18 May 1863. Destruction of Yazoo City NYd, 20–23 May 1863. Expeditions up Yazoo River, 24–31 May, to Trinity, La., Red River, 10 Jul 1863 and up Yazoo River, 2 Feb–22 Apr 1864. Disabled in action and captured in Yazoo River, 22 Apr 1864, then burned.

Ship captured: str *Elmira*, 13 Jul 1863.

Fig 6.26: The tinclad *Rattler*, Number 1, was lost in December 1864. A later acquired tinclad was given her number. (U.S. Naval Historical Center)

No.	Name	Builder	Launched	Acquired	Comm.
11	*Prairie Bird*	Millersport, Ohio	1862	19 Dec 1862	Jan 1863
ex-*Mary Miller*					

Tonnage	171 tons
Dimensions	159'10" × 29'3" × 5'
Machinery	Stern wheel, 2 engines (14" × 4'), 2 boilers, 6 knots
Armament	8–24pdr H

Service record: Mississippi Sqn. Bombardment of Eunice, Miss., 14–15 Jun 1863. Expedition up Yazoo River, 21–22 Apr 1864. Damaged engaging batteries at Gaines Landing, Ark., 11 Aug 1864. Sold 17 Aug 1865.
Ship captured: str *Union*, 21 Jul 1864.
Later history: FFU

No.	Name	Builder	Launched	Acquired	Comm.
1	*Rattler*	Cincinnati, Ohio	1862	11 Nov 1862	19 Dec 1862
ex-*Florence Miller*					

Tonnage	165 tons
Dimensions	(U)
Machinery	Stern wheel
Armament	2–30pdr MLR, 4–24pdr; (Dec 1863) add 2–24pdr.

Notes: Renamed 5 Dec 1862.
Service record: Mississippi Sqn. Expedition up White River, bombardment and capture of Ft. Hindman, Ark., 10–11 Jan 1863. Yazoo Pass expedition, attack on Ft. Pemberton, Tallahatchie River, 11–23 Mar 1863. Raids up Red, Tensas, and Ouachita Rivers, Jul 1863. Driven ashore in a gale, struck a snag and sank near Grand Gulf, Miss., 30 Dec 1864.
Ship captured: str *Louisville*,* 13 Jul 1863

No.	Name	Builder	Launched	Acquired	Comm.
35	*Reindeer*	Cincinnati, Ohio	1863	25 May 1863	25 Jul 1863
ex-*Rachael Miller*					

Tonnage	212 tons
Dimensions	154' × 32'9" × 6'

* Later USS *Ouachita*.

Machinery	Stern wheel, 2 engines (16" × 5'), 3 boilers, 8 mph
Armament	6–24pdr H; (Mar 1865) 2–30pdr MLR, 6–24pdr H.

Notes: Placed in service before commissioning.
Service record: Mississippi Sqn. Destroyed Confederate guerrilla force at Brandenburg, Ky., on Ohio River, 9–11 Jul 1863. Pursuit of Morgan's Raiders up Ohio River, 19 Jul 1863. Engaged battery at Bell's Mill, Cumberland River, Tenn., 3–4 Dec 1864. Dispatch vessel 1865. Decomm 7 Aug and sold 17 Aug 1865.
Later history: Merchant *Mariner* 1865. Stranded in Missouri River near Decatur, Neb., 9 May 1867.

No.	Name	Builder	Launched	Acquired	Comm.
48	*Rodolph*	Cincinnati, Ohio	1863	31 Dec 1863	18 May 1864

Tonnage	217 tons
Dimensions	(U)
Machinery	#Stern wheel
Complement	60
Armament	2–32pdr/42, 4–24pdr H; (Aug 1864) 2–32pdr replaced by 2–30pdr MLR.

Service record: WGulfBS 1864. Operations in Mobile Bay, Aug 1864. Expedition to Bon Secours, Ala., 8–11 Sep 1864. Sunk by torpedo (mine) in Blakely River, 1 Apr 1865 (4 killed).

No.	Name	Builder	Launched	Acquired	Comm.
3	*Romeo*	Brownsville, Pa.	1862	31 Oct 1862	11 Dec 1862

Tonnage	175 tons
Dimensions	154'2" × 31'2" × 4'6"
Machinery	Stern wheel, 2 engines (12" × 4'), 2 boilers
Armament	6–24pdr H; (Jul 1864) 8–24pdr H; (Sep 1864) 6–24pdr H.

Service record: Mississippi Sqn. Expedition in Yazoo River, dragging for torpedoes, 23–26 Dec 1862. Expedition up White River, bombardment and capture of Ft. Hindman, Ark., 10–11 Jan 1863. Yazoo Pass expedition, attack on Ft. Pemberton, Tallahatchie River, 11–23 Mar 1863. Bombardment and feigned attack, Haynes' Bluff, Miss., 29 Apr–2 May 1863. Bombardment of Haynes' Bluff, Yazoo River, 18 May 1863. Expedition up Yazoo River, 2 Feb–22 Apr 1864. Decomm 30 Jun 1865. Sold 17 Aug 1865.
Later history: Merchant *Romeo* 1865. Converted to sidewheel. RR 1870

No.	Name	Builder	Launched	Acquired	Comm.
19	*St. Clair*	Belle Vernon, Pa.	1862	13 Aug 1862	24 Sep 1862

Tonnage	203 tons
Dimensions	156' × 32' × 2'4"
Machinery	Stern wheel, (15 1/2" × 5'), 2 boilers
Complement	66
Armament	2–12pdr SB, 2–12pdr MLR; (May 1863) 2–24pdr H, 1–12pdr MLR, 2–12pdr SB; (Dec 1864) 2–50pdr MLR, 4–24pdr H, 2–12pdr MLR; (Mar 1865) 2–50pdr MLR replaced by 2–30pdr MLR.

Service record: Mississippi Sqn. Defense of Ft. Donelson, Tenn., 3 Feb 1863. Disabled by enemy troops at Palmyra, Tenn., 3 Apr 1863. Sank Army steamer *Hope* in collision in Mississippi River, 16 Feb 1864. Red River Expedition, 12 Mar–16 May 1864. Engaged enemy forces below Alexandria, La., 21 Apr 1864. Decomm 12 Jul 1865. Sold 17 Aug 1865.
Later history: Merchant *St. Clair* 1865. RR 1869

No.	Name	Builder	Launched	Acquired	Comm.
59	*Sibyl*	Cincinnati, Ohio	1863	27 Apr 1864	16 Jun 1864
ex-*Hartford*					

Tonnage	176 tons	
Dimensions	150.5' × 29.4' × 5.4'	
Machinery	#Stern wheel (16" × 6')	
Armament	2–30pdr MLR, 2–24pdr.	

Service record: Mississippi Sqn, dispatch boat. Decomm 31 Jul 1865. Sold 17 Aug 1865.

Later history: Merchant *Comet* 1865. RR 1876

No.	Name	Builder	Launched	Acquired	Comm.
8	*Signal*	Wheeling, Va.	1862	22 Sep 1862	Oct 1862

Tonnage	190 tons
Dimensions	157' × 30' × 1'10"
Machinery	Stern wheel
Armament	(Oct 1862) 2–30pdr MLR, 4–24pdr H, 1–12pdr MLR; (May 1863) 4–24pdr H, 2–12pdr MLR H; (Feb 1964) add 2–32pdr/42.

Service record: Mississippi Sqn. Expedition up Yazoo River, 21 Nov–11 Dec 1862. Expedition in Yazoo River, dragging for torpedoes, 23–26 Dec 1862. Expedition up White River, bombardment and capture of Ft. Hindman, Ark., 10–11 Jan 1863. Yazoo Pass expedition, attack on Ft. Pemberton, Tallahatchie River, 11–23 Mar 1863. Bombardment and feigned attack, Haynes' Bluff, Miss., 29 Apr–2 May 1863. Expedition up Yazoo River, 24–31 May 1863. Expedition to capture Yazoo City and destruction of ships, 13 Jul 1863. Disabled in Red River while engaging enemy batteries near Alexandria, La. and run aground, 5 May 1864; set afire to prevent capture.

No.	Name	Builder	Launched	Acquired	Comm.
28	*Silver Cloud*	Brownsville, Pa.	1862	1 Apr 1863	4 May 1863

Tonnage	236 tons
Dimensions	155'1" × 33'2" × 6'
Machinery	Stern wheel, 2 engines (16" × 5'), 3 boilers, 7 mph
Armamennt	6–24pdr H; (Sep 1864) add 1–24pdr MLR.

Service record: Mississippi Sqn. Expedition to Eastport, Miss., May 1863. Defense of Ft. Donelson, Tenn., 3 Feb 1863. Expedition to burn Palmyra, Tenn., 3 Apr 1863. Defense of Ft. Pillow, 12–14 Apr 1864. Engaged battery at Bell's Mill, Tenn., Cumberland River, 3–4 Dec 1864. Decomm 13 Jul 1865. Sold 15 Aug 1865.

Later history: Merchant *Silver Cloud* 1865. Converted to side wheel. Snagged and lost in Buffalo Bayou, Tex., 2 Oct 1866.

Nto.	Name	Builder	Launched	Acquired	Comm.
23	*Silver Lake*	California, Pa.	1862	15 Nov 1862	24 Dec 1862
ex-*Silver Lake No.3*					

Tonnage	236 tons
Dimensions	155'1" × 32'2" × 6'
Machinery	Stern wheel, 2 engines (15" × 5'), 2 boilers, 6 knots
Armament	6–24pdr H; (May 1865) 2–20pdr MLR, 3–24pdr H, 3–12pdr SB; (Jul 1865) 1–12pdr SB replaced by 1–24pdr H.

Service record: Mississippi Sqn. Defense of Ft. Donelson, Tenn., 3 Feb 1863. Bombarded Florence, Ala., 31 Mar, and Palmyra, Tenn., 4 Apr 1863. Pursuit of Morgan's Raiders up Ohio River, Jul 1864. Engaged battery at Bell's Mill, Tenn., Cumberland River, 3–4 Dec 1864. Decomm 11 Aug and sold 17 Aug 1865.

Later history: Merchant *Mary Hein* 1865. Converted to side wheel. Destroyed by fire in Red River, La., 28 Feb 1866.

No.	Name	Builder	Launched	Acquired	Comm.
56	*Siren*	Parkersburg, Va.	1862	11 Mar 1864	30 Aug 1864
ex-*White Rose*					

Tonnage	232 tons
Dimensions	154'7" × 32'3" × 5'
Machinery	Stern wheel, 2 engines (16 1/2" × 4'), 2 boilers, 7 mph
Armament	2–30pdr MLR, 6–24pdr H

Service record: Receiving ship, Mound City, Ill., Mar–Aug 1864. Mississippi Sqn. Decomm 12 Aug and sold 17 Aug 1865.

Later history: Merchant *White Rose* 1865. RR 1867

No.	Name	Builder	Launched	Acquired	Comm.
42	*Stockdale*	W. Brownsville, Pa.	1863	13 Nov 1863	26 Dec 1863
ex-*J. T. Stockdale*					

Tonnage	188 tons
Dimensions	(U)
Machinery	#Stern wheel
Complement	63
Armament	2–30pdr MLR, 4–24pdr H

Service record: WGulfBS 1864. Engaged enemy party in Tchefuncta River, La., 16 May 1864. Battle of Mobile Bay, 5 Aug 1864. Expedition to Bon Secours River, Miss., 8–11 Sep 1864. Decomm and sold 24 Aug 1865.

Ship captured: *Medora*, 8 Dec 1864.

Later history: Merchant *Caddo* 1865. RR 1871

No.	Name	Builder	Launched	Acquired	Comm.
46	*Tallahatchie*	Cincinnati, Ohio	1863	23 Jan 1864	19 Apr 1864
ex-*Cricket No.4*					

Tonnage	171 tons
Dimensions	(U)
Machinery	#Stern wheel
Complement	51
Armament	2–32pdr, 4–24pdr

Service record: Mississippi Sqn. Red River Expedition, 12 Mar–16 May 1864. WGulfBS Jun 1864–65. Decomm 21 Jul 1865. Sold 12 Aug 1865.

Later history: Merchant *Coosa* 1865. Destroyed by fire at Licking River, Ky., 7 Sep 1869.

No.	Name	Builder	Launched	Acquired	Comm.
1	*Tempest*	Louisville, Ky.	1862	30 Dec 1864	26 Apr 1865

Tonnage	161 tons
Dimensions	162' × 32.8' × 5.8'
Machinery	#Stern wheel
Armament	2–30pdr MLR, 2–20pdr MLR, 2–24pdr H, 2–12pdr.

Service record: Mississippi Sqn. Decomm and sold 29 Nov 1865.

Later history: Merchant *Tempest* 1865. Destroyed by fire at Tattoo Landing in Ouachita River, Ark., 27 Dec 1869.

No.	Name	Builder	Launched	Acquired	Comm.
55	*Undine*	Cincinnati, Ohio	1863	7 Mar 1864	Apr 1864
ex-*Ben Gaylord*					

Tonnage	179 tons
Dimensions	(U)
Machinery	Stern wheel, 2 boilers,

| Armament | 8–24pdr H |

Service record: Mississippi Sqn. Struck a snag and almost sank in Tennessee River off Clifton, Tenn., 25 Jul 1864, raised 31 Jul. Expedition to Eastport, Miss., 8–14 Oct 1864. Disabled during engagement in Tennessee River near Paris Landing, Tenn., and captured, 30 Oct 1864. Burned by Confederates to prevent recapture, 4 Nov 1864.

No.	Name	Builder	Launched	Acquired	Comm.
45	Wave	Monongahela, Pa.	1863	14 Nov 1863	

ex-*Argosy No.2*

Tonnage	229 tons
Dimensions	154′ × 31′ × 4.5′
Machinery	#Stern wheel (15″ × 4′)
Armament	6 guns

Service record: WGulfBS 1864. Captured with *Granite City* by Confederate batteries at Calcasieu Pass, La., 6 May 1864.

Other Tinclads

No.	Name	Builder	Launched	Acquired	Comm.
16	Little Rebel	Belle Vernon, Pa.	1859	9 Jan 1863	1863

ex-CSS *Little Rebel*, ex-*R. & J. Watson*

Tonnage	161 tons
Dimensions	112′ × 22′ (estimated) × 12′
Machinery	1 screw, 1 engine (18″ × 2′), 2 boilers, 10 knots
Armament	3–12pdr MLR; (Mar 1863) 2–24pdr H, 2–12pdr MLR.

Notes: Confederate cottonclad ram, captured at Battle of Memphis, 6 Jun 1862. Converted to gunboat at Cairo, Ill.

Service record: WGF. Mississippi Sqn, with Ellet's ram sqn. Expedition up Red River, capture of CSS *Missouri*, 1–6 Jun 1865. Decomm 24 Jul 1865. Sold 29 Nov 1865.

Later history: Merchant *Spy* 1865. RR 1874.

No.	Name	Builder	Launched	Acquired	Comm.
31	Paw Paw	St. Louis, Mo.	1862	9 Apr 1863	25 Jul 1863

ex-*Fanny*, (12 May 1863), ex-*St. Charles*

Tonnage	175 tons
Dimensions	120′ × 34′ × 6′
Machinery	Center wheel, 2 engines (20″ × 6′), 2 boilers, 4 mph
Armament	2–30pdr MLR, 6–24pdr H

Notes: Renamed 12 May 1863.

Service record: Mississippi Sqn. Struck a snag and sank in Walnut Bend, 6 Aug 1863; salved and repaired. Supported army on the Tennessee River, Oct–Dec 1863. Engaged enemy troops at Paducah, Ky., 25 Mar 1864. Decomm 1 Jul 1865. Sold 17 Aug 1865. BU 1865.

RIVER SERVICE CRAFT

Name	Builder	Launched	Acquired	In service
Abraham	Elizabeth, Pa.	1858	30 Sep 1862	Jun 1862

ex-*Victoria*

Tonnage	405 tons
Dimensions	222′ × 32′ × 5′10″
Machinery	Side wheels. (22″ × 7′), 4 boilers
Armament	(U)

Notes: Storeship. Confederate transport *Victoria*, captured at Memphis, 6 Jun 1862. Renamed 15 Oct 1862.

Service record: Mississippi Sqn, storeship. Blockade of Vicksburg. Wharf and inspection boat, Cairo and Mound City, Ill. Sold 30 Sep 1865.

Later history: Merchant *Lexington* 1865. Rebuilt. Destroyed by fire at Algiers, La., 3 Feb 1869.

Name	Builder	Launched	Acquired	Comm.
Benefit	Metropolis, Ill.	1863	1863	May 1864

Tonnage	213 tons
Dimensions	(U)
Machinery	Side wheels
Armament	(U)

Notes: Chartered 1863.

Service record: Red River expedition. Returned to owner, 1865.

Later history: Merchant *Benefit*. Burned at Starke Landing, Ala., 6 Apr 1867.

Name	Builder	Launched	Acquired	In service
Clara Dolsen	Cincinnati, Ohio	1861	1862	1862

Tonnage	939 tons
Dimensions	268′ × 42′ × d8′9″
Machinery	Side wheels. 5 boilers
Armament	1–32pdr/33

Notes: Confederate steamer, captured on White River by USS *Mound City* and tug *Spitfire*, 14 Jun 1862. One of the largest and finest steamers on the river.

Service record: WGF. Mississippi Sqn. Expedition to Henderson, Ky., 19–24 Jul 1862. Receiving ship, Cairo, Ill. 1862–64. Returned to owner May 1864.

Later history: Merchant *Clara Dolsen*. Destroyed by fire at St. Louis, Mo., 4 Feb 1868.

Name	Builder	Launched	Acquired	Comm.
General Lyon	New Albany, Ind.	1860	30 Sep 1862	Apr 1862

ex-CSS *De Soto*

Tonnage	390 tons
Dimensions	180′ × 35′ × 7′
Machinery	Side wheels (23″ × 7′)
Armament	2–12pdr MLR; (Feb 1864) add 1–32pdr/42.

Notes: Confederate gunboat *De Soto* captured at Island No.10, 7 Apr 1862. Transferred from War Dept. Renamed 24 Oct 1862.

Service record: WGF. Mississippi Sqn, Ordnance, stores, and dispatch ship. Decomm 3 Aug and sold 17 Aug 1865.

Later history: Merchant *Alabama* 1865. Destroyed by fire at Grand View, La, 1 Apr 1867.

Name	Builder	Launched	Acquired	Comm.
Grampus	(U)	(U)	22 Jul 1863	1863

ex-*Ion*

Tonnage	230 tons
Dimensions	180′ × 27′ × d5′
Machinery	Side wheels
Armament	None

Service record: Mississippi Sqn. Receiving ship, Cincinnati, Ohio. Sold 1 Sep 1868.

Later history: FFU

Name	Builder	Launched	Acquired	Comm.
Great Western	Cincinnati, Ohio	1857	10 Feb 1862	1862

| Tonnage | 429 tons |
| Dimensions | 178′ × 45′ × 8′ |

Machinery   Side wheels (22.5″ × 8′)
Armament   1–12pdr, 1–32pdr/57, 1–6pdr MLR

Notes: Purchased by War Department.

Service record: WGF. Western Flotilla Ordnance boat. Siege of Vicksburg. Receiving ship, Cairo, Ill., Jul 1864, and Mound City, Ill., Mar 1865. Sold 29 Nov 1865.

Later history: FFU

Name	Builder	Launched	Acquired	Comm.
Judge Torrence	Cincinnati, Ohio	1857	10 Feb 1862	25 Dec 1862
Tonnage	419 tons			
Dimensions	179′1″ × 45′6″ × 9′			
Machinery	Side wheels, 2 engines (20″ × 8′), 3 boilers, 6 knots.			
Armament	2–24pdr H SB; (Oct 1864) 2–24pdr H SB, 1–6pdr MLR, 1–12pdr H.			

Notes: Purchased by War Dept. Transferred to USN, 30 Sep 1862.

Service record: WGF. Mississippi Sqn. Ordnance boat. Decomm 1 Aug and 17 Aug 1865.

Later history: Merchant *Amazon*. Snagged and sunk off Napoleon, Ark., 19 Feb 1868.

Kentucky, captured at Memphis, 6 Jun 1862. WGF. No further information.

Name	Builder	Launched	Acquired	Comm.
Lavinia Logan	Parkersburg, Va.	1861	31 Aug 1864	1864
Tonnage	145 tons			
Dimensions	(U)			
Machinery	Stern wheel			
Armament	(U)			

Notes: Purchased by War Dept as transport and powder boat. Acquired by USN, 31 Aug 1864.

Service record: Sunk in Mississippi River, 23 Sep 1864.

Name	Builder	Launched	Acquired	Comm.
Maria Denning	Cincinnati, Ohio	1858	1861	Nov 1861
Tonnage	870 tons			
Dimensions	275′ × 41′ × 8′			
Machinery	Side wheels. (26″ × 9′), 5 boilers			
Armament	(U)			

Service record: Receiving ship, Cairo, Ill. Nov 1861–Apr 1862. Transferred to War Dept. Dec 1862.

Later history: Stranded in Cumberland River, Mar 1864. Burned at Algiers, La, 11 May 1866.

Name	Builder	Launched	Acquired	Comm.
New National ex-*Lewis Whiteman* ?	Cincinnati, Ohio	1851	6 Jun 1862	Jun 1862
Tonnage	317 tons ?			
Dimensions	178′ × 29′ × 6.5′			
Machinery	Side wheels			
Armament	1–12pdr MLR; (Dec 1863) 2–32pdr/42, 2–12pdr MLR.			

Notes: Confederate transport captured at Memphis, 6 Jun 1862. Transferred to Navy, 30 Sep 1862. Mail and supply boat. Former identity presumed (details for *Lewis Whiteman*)

Service record: WGF. Mississippi Sqn, mail and supply boat and receiving ship. Returned to owner, 21 Mar 1863 and chartered by Navy. Expedition to capture Yazoo City, 13 Jul 1863. Decomm 12 Apr 1865.

Later history: Merchant *New National* 1865.

Name	Builder	Launched	Acquired	Comm.
Red Rover	Cape Girardeau, Mo.	1859	Apr 1862	10 Jun 1862
Tonnage	625 tons			
Dimensions	256′ × 40.9′ × 7.5′			
Machinery	Side wheels, 2 engines (28″ × 8′), 5 boilers, 8 knots			
Complement	47 + 30 medical staff			
Armament	1–32pdr/33			

Notes: Confederate steamer, captured by USS *Mound City* at Island No.10, 7 Apr 1862. First hospital ship of USN.

Service record: WGF. Mississippi Sqn, hospital boat. Damaged by fire off Vicksburg, summer 1862. Decomm 17 Nov and sold 29 Nov 1865.

Later history: FFU

Name	Builder	Launched	Acquired	Comm.
Sallie Wood	Paducah, Ky.	1860	1862	1862
Tonnage	256 tons			
Dimensions	160′ × 31′			
Machinery	Stern wheel (14″ × 5′)			
Armament	(U)			

Note: Captured on Tennessee River at Chickasaw, Ala., 8 Feb 1862.

Service record: Transport, Western Flotilla. Damaged by artillery and run aground at Argyle Landing, 30 Jul 1862.

Name	Builder	Launched	Acquired	Comm.
Samson	California, Pa.	1860	30 Sep 1862	1862
Tonnage	230 tons			
Dimensions	169′ × 29′			
Machinery	Stern wheel. (22″ × 7.5′), 4 boilers,			
Armament	(U)			

Notes: Transferred from War Dept. Floating machine shop.

Fig 6.27: The Navy's first hospital ship, the *Red Rover*. Notice the words "USN Hospital" on the paddle wheel box. (U.S. Naval Historical Center)

Service record: WGF. Ellet Ram fleet 1862. Mississippi Sqn 1862–65. Sold 17 Aug 1865
Later history: Merchant *Samson* 1865. BU 1869

Name	Builder	Launched	Acquired	Comm.
Sovereign	Shousetown, Pa.	1855	9 Jan 1863	1863
Tonnage	336 tons			
Dimensions	228.6′ × 37′ × 6.4′			
Machinery	Side wheels (24″ × 6.5′)			
Armament	(U)			

Notes: Confederate transport, captured near Island No.37 by *Spitfire*, 5 Jun 1862.
Service record: WGF, Commissary boat in Yazoo River. Accommodation ship at Cairo, Ill., 1863–65. Sold 29 Nov 1865.
Later history: FFU

Name	Builder	Launched	Acquired	Comm.
Volunteer	Monongahela, Pa.	1862	29 Feb 1864	1864
Tonnage	209 tons			
Dimensions	125.1′ × 33′ × 4.5′			
Machinery	Stern wheel, 2 engines (15″ × 5′), 2 boilers, 6 mph			
Armament	1–12pdr SB			

Notes: Confederate steamer captured off Natchez Island, Miss., by USS *Fort Hindman*, 25 Nov 1863.
Service record: Mississippi Sqn. Defense of Ft. Pillow, Tenn., 12 Apr 1864. Decomm Aug 1865. Sold 29 Nov 1865.
Later history: Merchant *Talisman* 1865. Rebuilt 1866. RR 1872.

Name	Builder	Launched	Acquired	Comm.
William H. Brown	Monongahela, Pa.	1860	13 Jun 1861	1861
Tonnage	200 tons			
Dimensions	230′ × 26′			
Machinery	Stern wheel (20″ × 7′)			
Armament	2–12pdr			

Notes: Dispatch vessel. Transferred from War Dept 30 Sep 1862. Also known as *Brown*.
Service record: WGF. Mississippi Sqn, dispatch vessel and transport. Disabled during engagement with batteries in Red River, 13 Apr 1864. Decomm 12 Aug and sold 17 Aug 1865.
Later history: Merchant *W. H. Brown*, 1865. BU 1875

Note: All transferred from War Dept.
Service records (see Tugs, p 134)

Dahlia: WGF. Mississippi Sqn. Sold 17 Aug 1865.
    Later history: Merchant *Dahlia* 1865. RR 1872.

Daisy: WGF. Mississippi Sqn. Sold 17 Aug 1865.
    Later history: Merchant *Little Queen* 1865. RR 1871.

Fern: WGF. Mississippi Sqn. Expedition up Red River to capture CSS *Missouri*, 1–6 Jun 1865. Sold 12 Aug 1865.
    Later history: Merchant *Fern* 1865. SE 1882.

Hyacinth: WGF. Mississippi Sqn. Sold 17 Aug 1865.
    Ships captured: *Sovereign*,* 5 Jun 1862; *Clara Dolsen*,† 14 Jun 1862.
    Later history: Merchant *Rolla* 1865. RR 1884.

Ivy: WGF. Mississippi Sqn 1862. Expedition up White River, capture of Ft. Hindman, Ark. and 10–11 Jan 63. Ran past batteries at Vicksburg, 16 Apr 63. Expedition up Red River, 3–13 May 63. Sold 17 Aug 1865.
    Later history: Merchant *Ivy* 1865. RR 1874

Laurel: WGF. Mississippi Sqn. Expedition up Yazoo River, 21 Nov–11 Dec 1862. Decomm 12 Aug and sold 17 Aug 1865.
    Later history: Merchant *Laurel* 1865. BU 1903.

Lily: WGF. Mississippi Sqn. Sunk in collision with ironclad USS *Choctaw* in Yazoo River, 28 May 1863.

Mignonette: WGF. Mississippi Sqn. Station tug, Cairo, Ill. 1862–65. Sold 18 Apr 1873.

Mistletoe: WGF. Cairo, Ill., tug 1862–63. Mississippi Sqn. Sold 20 Nov 1865.
    Later history: Merchant *Ella Wood* 1866. RR 1871

Myrtle: WGF. Mississippi Sqn. Cairo, Ill. Sold 17 Aug 1865.
    Later history: Destroyed by boiler explosion on Lower Mississippi, 28 Jan 1897.

Nettle: WGF. Mississippi Sqn. Sunk in collision with an ironclad warship in Mississippi River, 20 Oct 1865.

Pansy: WGF. Mississippi Sqn. Sold 1 Sep 1868
    Later history: FFU

Thistle: WGF. Mississippi Sqn. Expedition up White River, capture of Ft. Hindman, Ark., 10–11 Jan 63. Expedition to Steele's Bayou, Miss., 14–26 Mar 63. Decomm 12 Aug and sold 17 Aug 1865.
    Later history: FFU.

---

* Later USS *Sovereign*.
† Later USS *Clara Dolsen*.

TUGS

Name	Built at	Launched	Date Acquired	Tons	Dimensions	Machinery
Dahlia	St. Louis, Mo.	1861	30 Sep 1862	54		Sgl cyl. (18″ × 1′8″), 1 boiler, 10 mph
ex-*Firefly* (24 Oct 1862)						
Daisy	Oswego, N.Y.	1854	30 Sep 1862	54	73′4″ × 13′10″	1 engine (22″ × 1′10″) 1 boiler, 10 mph
ex-*Mulford* (24 Oct 1862), ex-*J.E. Mulford*						
Fern	St. Louis, Mo.	1861	30 Sep 1862	45	62′6″ × 14′4″	1 screw, (16″ × 1′8″), 1 boiler, 10 knots
ex-*Intrepid* (19 Oct 1862)						
Hyacinth	St. Louis, Mo.	1862	30 Sep 1862	50		1 engine (18″ × 1′8″), 1 boiler, 8 knots
ex-*Spitfire* (19 Oct 1862)						
Ivy	St. Louis, Mo.	1861	30 Sep 1862	47		1 engine (16″ × 1′6″), 1 boiler, 10 knots
ex-*Terror*						
Laurel	St. Louis, Mo.	1862	30 Aug 1862	35	60′ × 14′	1 engine (18″ × 1′8″), 1 boiler, 5 knots
ex-*Erebus* (19 Oct 1862)						
Lily	(U)	1862	5 May 1862	50		1 screw
ex-*Jessie Benton* (19 Oct 1862)						
Mignonette	St. Louis, Mo. (U)	(U)	30 Sep 1862	50		Side wheels
ex-*Dauntless* (19 Oct 1862)						
Mistletoe	St. Louis, Mo.	1861	30 Sep 1862	38	61′5″ × 14′4″	1 screw
ex-*Restless*						
Myrtle	Keyport, N.J	(U)	30 Sep 1862	60	75′4″ × 16′3″	2 screw, 2 engine (15″ × 1′4″), 2 boilers
ex-*Resolute* (15 Oct 1862)						
Nettle	St. Louis, Mo. (U)	(U)	30 Sep 1862	50		Screw
ex-*Wonder* (19 Oct 1862)						
Pansy	New Haven, Mo.	1861	30 Sep 1862	46		1 screw
ex-*Sampson* (24 Oct 1862)						
Thistle	St. Louis, Mo.	(U)	30 Sep 1862	50		Side wheels
ex-*Spiteful*						

Fig 6.28: The tug *Daisy* at Mound City, Ill., during the war. The large building on shore is the hospital. (U.S. Naval Historical Center)

7
UNITED STATES REVENUE CUTTER SERVICE

Established on 4 August 1790, the Revenue Cutter Service had only twenty-eight vessels available at the outbreak of the Civil War. Six had been seized by the rebels, and four were on the Pacific coast. Five cutters on the Great Lakes were ordered to the Atlantic, and several ships were loaned from other government agencies, such as the Lighthouse Board and the Coast Survey.

Although the Revenue Marine, as it was commonly known, had experimented with steamers in the 1840s, only the *Harriet Lane* remained in service by 1861, together with a number of schooners. She was transferred to the Navy, but several other steamers were acquired.

One of those acquired was the *E.A. Stevens* or *Naugatuck*. This curious ship was converted to demonstrate the theories of construction of the never-completed *Stevens Battery*. In July 1863, the cutter *Caleb Cushing* was seized by rebels at Portland, Maine, and destroyed by them when recapture at sea was certain.

In 1863 the six cutters *Mahoning*, *Ashuelot*, *Wayanda*, *Kankakee*, *Kewanee*, and *Pawtuxet* were built. At the end of the war, the Navy ships *Delaware*, *Jasmine*, *Juniper*, *Moccasin*, *Nansemond*, and *Wilderness* were among surplus ships transferred for permanent service with the Revenue Marine, while other new construction was already in hand.

STEAMERS

Name	Builder	Launched	Comm.
Harriet Lane	New York, N.Y. (Webb)	20 Nov 1857	28 Feb 1858
Tonnage	639 tons B		
Dimensions	180' × 30' × 10'		
Machinery	Side wheels, inclined direct-acting engine (42" × 7'), 12 knots (Allaire)		

Service record: Paraguay Expedition 1858-59. Served in USN from 30 Mar 1861; permanently transferred, 10 Sep 1861 (see p. 62).

Bibb, loaned from Coast Survey (q.v.) 31 May 1861, returned Nov 1861.

Corwin, loaned from Coast Survey (q.v.) 31 May 1861, returned 17 Sep 1861.

Name	Builder	Launched	Acquired	Comm.
Hercules	Baltimore, Md. (Patapsco)	1850	10 Aug 1861	11 Sep 1861
Reliance	Baltimore, Md. (Patapsco)	1850	10 Aug 1861	1861
Tiger	Baltimore, Md. (Patapsco)	1850	10 Aug 1861	11 Sep 1861
Tonnage	123 tons			
Dimensions	100' × 17' 6" × 9' 4"			
Machinery	Side wheels, 1 direct-acting engine (25" × 2' 2")			

Service records:

Hercules: Rappahannock River. Sold 18 May 1864.

Later history: Merchant *Hercules*, RR 1865.

Reliance: Chesapeake Bay. Attacked by enemy on Wicomico River, 12 Aug 1864 (1 killed). Sold Dec 1865. RR 1866.

Tiger: Chesapeake Bay. Sold 27 Jul 1865.

Later history:Later history: Sold foreign 1870.

Name	Builder	Launched	Acquired	Comm.
Shubrick	Philadelphia NYd	8 Aug 1857	23 Aug 1861	Oct 1861
Tonnage	305 tons			
Dimensions	140' 8" × 29' × 9'			
Machinery	Side wheels, 1 steeple engine (50" × 4')			
Armament	4–12pdr, 1–24pdr, 1–30pdrR.			

Service record: Acquired from U.S. Lighthouse Board; returned 24 Dec 1866. Served on Pacific coast. Transferred to USN on 15 Feb 1865 for 90 days for surveying the Bering Sea. Sold 1886.

Name	Builder	Launched	Acquired	Comm.
Nemaha ex-*Flora* (13 Jan 1864)	Keyport, N.J. (Terry)	1854	24 Feb 1862	5 Mar 1862
Tonnage	281 tons			
Dimensions	162' × 24' × 8' 6"			
Machinery	Side wheels			

Armament 1–20pdrR

Service record: Carolina Coast. Burned at mouth of Wicomico River, 7 Feb 1868 (2 killed).

Name	Builder	Launched	Acquired	Comm.
E.A.Stevens	New York, N.Y. (Dunham)	1844	12 Mar 1862	13 Mar 1862

ex-USS *Naugatuck*, ex-*E.A. Stevens*, ex-*Naugatuck*

Tonnage	120 tons
Dimensions	101′ × 21′ 6″ × 6′
Machinery	2 screws , 2-cyl engine.

Service record: Served in USN, 1862 (see USS *Naugatuck*, p. 73). Rebuilt 1871. Sold 24 Apr 1890.

Later history: Merchant *Argus* SE 1896.

Name	Builder	Launched	Acquired	Comm.
Miami	Glasgow, Scotland	1853	28 Jan 1862	14 Mar 1862

ex-*Lady Le Marchant*

Tonnage	213 tons
Dimensions	115′ (length)
Machinery	1 screw, 2 oscillating engines.
Armament	1–24pdr, 1–12pdr.

Service record: Sold 19 Apr 1871.

Name	Builder	Launched	Acquired	Comm.
Cuyahoga	New York, N.Y. (Westervelt)	1854	Apr 1863	Apr 1863

ex-*General Santa Anna* (Mexican)

Tonnage	308 tons
Dimensions	152′ (oa) 139′ (bp) × 27.7′ × 13.1′
Machinery	1 screw, 2-cyl. oscillating engine (36″ × 2′ 8″), 2 boilers (Faron)

Service record: Damaged in collision off Cape Henlopen, 13 Mar 1864. Sold 27 Jul 1867.

Later history: Japanese *Settsu*, training ship 1872.

Name	Builder	Launched	Comm.
Ashuelot	New York, N.Y. (Englis)	8 Jul 1863	May 1864
Kankakee	New York, N.Y. (Westervelt)	15 Sep 1863	Dec 1864
Kewanee	Baltimore, Md. (Robb)	23 Sep 1863	Jun 1864
Mahoning	Philadelphia, Pa. (Lynn)	29 Jul 1863	Feb 1864
Pawtuxet	New York, N.Y. (Stark)	7 Jul 1863	Jul 1864
Wayanda	Baltimore, Md. (Fardy)	1 Sep 1863	Apr 1864

Ashuelot: Tonnage: 323 tons; Dimensions: 138′ × 29′ × 6′ 8″; Machinery: side wheels, oscillating engines. (Novelty)
  Later history: Sold 20 Jun 1867. To Japan Mar 1868, renamed *Takao*, later renamed *Kaiten No.2*. Destroyed by Imperial ships, 1869.

Kankakee: Tonnage: 313 tons; Dimensions: 137′ × 26′ 6″ × 4′ 9″; Machinery: 1 screw, 2 LP oscillating engines (36″ × 3′) (Gray). Armament: 1–30pdrR, 6–24pdrH
  Later history: Sold 28 May 1867. Japanese *Kawachi*, Feb 1869, later BU.

Kewanee: Tonnage: 236 tons; Dimensions: 141′ × 27.2′ × 11.2′ , Machinery: 1 screw
  Later history: Sold 10 Jul 1867. Japanese *Musashi*, 1868. Blew up in Yokohama harbor Apr 1869, salved.

Mahoning: Tonnage: 375 tons; Dimensions: 130′ × 27′ × 5′ 4″; Machinery: side wheels, Complement: 40
  Later history: Rebuilt as screw steamer, 1868, 330 tons, 146′ 6″(oa) × 28′ 6″ × 11′ 4″, oscillating engines (36″ × 3′). Renamed **Levi Woodbury**, 5 Jun 1873.†

Pawtuxet: Tonnage: 230 tons; Dimensions: 143′ × 26′ 6″ × 11′ 6″, Machinery: 1 screw, 2-cyl. oscillating engine.
  Later history: Sold 9 Aug 1867. Merchant *Pawtuxet* RR

Wayanda: Tonnage: 450 tons; Dimensions: 170′ (bp) × 27′ × d11′
  Later history: Rebuilt about 1868, Sold 18 Nov 1873. Merchant *Los Angeles* RR 1896.

Name	Builder	Launched	Acquired	Comm.
Bronx	Brooklyn, N.Y.	1863	1863	Jan 1864

ex-*Addison F. Andrews*

Tonnage	220 tons
Dimensions	119′ × 22′ × 5′ 6″, d9′
Machinery	Side wheels, beam engine.

Service record: Foundered after striking rock in Long Island Sound, 4 Apr 1873.

Name	Builder	Launched	Comm.
William H. Seward	Wilmington, Del.	1864	Oct 1864

Tonnage	254 tons
Dimensions	137′ × 22′ × 5′ 6″
Machinery	Side wheels (28′ × 6′)
Complement	30

Service record: †

Name	Builder	Launched	Acquired	Comm.
Northerner	Newburgh, N.Y.	1864	18 Apr 1864	Aug 1864

Tonnage	319 tons
Dimensions	142′ × 42′ × 9′
Machinery	Side wheels (40″ × 8′)
complement	37

Service record: Renamed **Thomas Ewing**, 19 Nov 1874.†

Name	Builder	Launched	Acquired	Comm.
Commodore Perry	Buffalo, N.Y. (Wright)	Oct 1864 1864	20 Mar 1865	20 Mar 1865

Tonnage	403 tons
Dimensions	166′ (oa) × 23′ 6″ × 6′ 6″
Machinery	2 screws, 4 HP engines, 4-cyl. (18″ × 1′ 10″), 2 boilers
Complement	37

Service record: Great Lakes. Sold 3 Oct 1883.

Later history: Merchant *Periwinkle* 1884. Burned at Toledo, Ohio, 1897.

Fig 7.1: The revenue cutter *Levi Woodbury* after 1873 when she was rebuilt as a screw steamer. She was originally built as the side wheeler *Mahoning* in 1863. (U.S. Naval Historical Center)

Name	Builder	Launched	Comm.
William Pitt Fessenden	Cleveland, Ohio (Peck)	1865	1865
John Sherman	Cleveland, Ohio (Peck)	1865	May 1866
Salmon P. Chase	New York, N.Y. (Murphy)	1865	8 Oct 1865
Hugh McCulloch	Baltimore, Md. (Fardy)	1865	28 Jul 1865
Andrew Johnson	Buffalo, N.Y. (Gray)	1865	Oct 1865

Fessenden: Tonnage: 476 tons, Dimensions: 180′ × 29′ × d11′ ; Machinery: side wheels, vertical beam engine (48″ × 9′) (Fletcher); Complement: 37.
  Service record: Great Lakes. Sold 29 Mar 1883.†
Sherman: Tonnage: 476 tons, Dimensions: 180′ × 29′ × d11′ ; Machinery: side wheels, vertical beam engine (48″ × 9′) (Fletcher); Complement: 37
  Service record: Sold 25 Jun 1872. Converted to schooner, RR 1893.
Chase: Tonnage: 287 tons; Dimensions: 176′ × 27′ × d11′ ; Machinery: side wheels
  Service record: Sold 15 Jun 1875.
  Later history: Merchant *Admiral*. Sold foreign s/f 1883.
McCulloch: Tonnage: 904 tons; Dimensions: 178′ × 27′ 11″ × 8′ ; Machinery: side wheels
  Service record: Sold 20 Mar 1876.

Later history: Merchant *John H. Starin* RR 1911.
Johnson: Tonnage: 499 tons, Dimensions: 175′ × 26′ 4″ × 8′ ; Machinery: side wheels, vertical beam engine, (Gray), Complement 37: 3 guns.
  Service record: Great Lakes.†

Name	Builder	Launched	Acquired	Comm.
Uno	Camden, N.J.	1864	29 Jun 1865	1865

ex-USS *Juniper* (27 Jul 1865), ex-*Uno*

Tonnage	111 tons
Dimensions	79′ 6″ × 18′ 4″ × 9′
Machinery	1 screw, overhead engine (24″ × 1′ 8″)
Complement	12

Service record: Rebuilt 1873. Renamed *Peter G. Washington*, 25 Nov 1873.†

Name	Builder	Launched	Comm.
John A. Dix	Newburgh, N.Y. (Murphy)	28 Jul 1865	1865

Tonnage	290 tons
Dimensions	144′ (oa) × 26′ × 11′
Machinery	Side wheels, beam engine (40″ × 8′)

Service record: Great Lakes. Sold 27 Jun 1872.

138   Civil War Navies, 1855-1883

Fig 7.2: The revenue cutter *Salmon P. Chase*, at Oswego, N.Y., was built in 1865. (U.S. Naval Historical Center, Paul H. Silverstone Collection)

Name	Builder	Launched	Comm.
Lincoln	Baltimore, Md. (Fardy)	May 1864	1 Sep 1865

Tonnage	546 tons
Dimensions	165' × 26' × 10'
Machinery	Oscillating engine (36" × 2' 6")

Service record: Served in Alaska. Sold 14 Apr 1874.

Later history: Merchant *San Luis*, sunk off San Francisco 15 Feb 87.

Name	Builder	Launched	Acquired	Comm.
Wilderness	Brooklyn, N.Y.	1864	7 Sep 1865	Sep 1865

ex-USS *Wilderness*, ex-*B.N.Crary*

Tonnage	390 tons
Dimensions	137' × 25' × 6'
Machinery	Side wheels, beam engine (40" × 8')
Complement	33

Service record: Renamed ***John A. Dix***, 11 Nov 1873.†

Name	Builder	Launched	Acquired	Comm.
Nansemond	Brooklyn, N.Y. (L & F)	1862	22 Aug 1865	Oct 1865

ex-USS *Nansemond*, ex-*James F. Freeborn*

Tonnage	325 tons B.

Fig 7.3: The revenue cutter *Andrew Johnson* was built in Buffalo in 1865. (Langsdale Library, University of Baltimore, Steamship Historical Society of America Collection)

Dimensions	146' × 26' × 8' 3"
Machinery	Side wheels, vertical beam engine (40" × 9')

Service record: Renamed ***William H. Crawford***, 1873.†

Name	Builder	Launched	Acquired	Comm.
Delaware	Wilmington, Del. (Harlan)	1861	30 Aug 1865	Nov 1865

ex-USS *Delaware*, ex-*Virginia Dare*

Tonnage	357 tons
Dimensions	161' × 27' × 6'
Machinery	Side wheels, 1 beam engine (38" × 10')
Complement	33
Armament	2 guns

Service record: Renamed ***Louis McLane***, Jun 1873.†

Name	Builder	Launched	Acquired	Comm.
Moccasin	Philadelphia, Pa.	1864	18 Sep 1865	Dec 1865

ex-USS *Moccasin*, ex-*Hero*

Tonnage	192 tons
Dimensions	104' 5 × 22' 3" × 9'
Machinery	1 screw, vertical direct-acting engine (34" × 2' 8")
Complement	26

Service record: Renamed ***George M. Bibb***, 16 Dec 1881. Lengthened at New York (128'), recomm. 10 Apr 1882.†

Name	Builder	Launched	Acquired	Comm.
Jasmine	Brooklyn, N.Y.	1862	2 Jun 1866	1866

ex-USS *Jasmine*

Tonnage	117 tons
Dimensions	79' × 18' × 7' 6"
Machinery	1 screw, LP engine (26" × 2' 2")

Service record: Refits, 1870 and 1873. Renamed ***William D. Chandler***, 18 Dec 1873.†

Name	Builder	Launched	Acquired	Comm.
Hannibal Hamlin	Wilmington, Del.	1864	12 Dec 1866	1867

ex-*D.A. Mills* (11 Jan 1867)

Tonnage	96 tons
Dimensions	85' × 18' × 7'
Machinery	screw (22" × 1' 8")
Complement	10
Armament	1 gun

Service record: Rebuilt 1874.†

Name	Builder	Launched	Acquired	Comm.
Mosswood	Baltimore, Md.	1863	14 Dec 1866	Apr 1867

Tonnage	143 tons
Dimensions	107' (oa) 97' (wl) × 20' × 8'
Machinery	1 screw (30" × 2' 6")
Complement	26

Note: ex-U.S. Army.

Service record: Damaged by fire at shipyard, 27 Jan 1867. Renamed *Hugh McCulloch*, 15 Oct 1877.†

Name	Builder	Launched	Acquired	Comm.
James Guthrie	Baltimore, Md.	1864	29 Aug 1868	Oct 1868

ex-*George J. Loane*

Tonnage	113 tons
Dimensions	85' (oa) × 17' × 8' 7"
Machinery	1 screw (20" × 1' 8")
Complement	10
Armament	1 gun

Service record: Sold 3 Apr 1882.

Later history: Merchant *Joseph Cummings* RR 1894.

Name	Builder	Launched	Completed
U.S. Grant	Wilmington, Del. (Pusey)	1871	1871

Tonnage	263 tons
Dimensions	163' × 25' × 9' 6"
Machinery	screw (36" × 3'); 10 knots
Complement	45

Notes: Iron hull, bark rig.
Service record:†

Name	Builder	Launched	Completed
Albert Gallatin	Buffalo, N.Y. (Bell)	1871	1871
Alexander Hamilton	Buffalo, N.Y. (Bell)	1871	18 Oct 1871

Tonnage	223 tons
Dimensions	144' (oa) 136' (bp) × 23' 6" × 9' 6"
Machinery	Fowler screw, horizontal direct-acting (28" × 2' 4"); (1872) *Gallatin*: 1 screw, (34" × 2' 6"); *Hamilton*: 1 screw, compound engines
Complement	38

Notes: Fowler screw a failure, rebuilt 1872.
Service records
Gallatin: Recomm 1874.†
Hamilton:†

Name	Builder	Launched	Comm.
Schuyler Colfax	Camden, N.J. (Dialogue)	1871	4 Nov 1871

Tonnage	486 tons
Dimensions	179' 6" (oa) × 25' × 8' 4"
Machinery	sidewheels, (34" × 9')
Complement	40.

Note: Rebuilt by Pusey & Jones, 1878.†

Name	Builder	Launched	Comm.
Manhattan	Philadelphia, Pa. (Weidner)	May 1873	May 1873

Tonnage	145 tons
Dimensions	102' (oa) × 20' 6" × 8' 6"
Machinery	1 screw, compound, HP 210

Notes: Iron hull tug
Service record: Great Lakes 1875–83.†

Name	Builder	Comm.
Oliver Wolcott	San Francisco, Calif. (Risdon)	30 Jul 1873

Tonnage	199 tons
Dimensions	155' × 22' × 9' 7"
Machinery	1 screw, vertical (34" × 2' 10")
Complement	35.

Notes: Wood hull.
Service record:†

Name	Builder	Comm.
George S. Boutwell	Buffalo, N.Y. (Bell)	29 Oct 1873

Tonnage	326 tons D; 152 tons
Dimensions	138' (oa) × 23' × 7' 10"
Machinery	2 screws, compound
Complement	37

Service record: Driven ashore in a hurricane in Savannah River, 27 Aug 1881.†

Name	Builder	Comm.
Samuel Dexter	Boston, Mass. (Atlantic)	18 Jun 1874
Richard Rush	Boston, Mass. (Atlantic)	7 Jul 1874

Tonnage	188 tons
Dimensions	143' 6" (oa) 129' (wl) × 22' 9" × 9' 6"
Machinery	1 screw, inverted compound (26" × 3'); HP 400 (bldr)

Service records: *Dexter*:† *Rush*:†

Name	Builder	Comm.
Alexander J. Dallas	Portland, Me. (Fessenden)	28 Jul 1874

Tonnage	179 tons
Dimensions	140' (oa) 129' 6" (bp) × 21' 6" × 10' 6"

Machinery	1 screw, inverted compound (34: × 3′); HP 300 , 10 kts (bldr)

Notes: Wood hull.†

Name	Builder	Comm.
John F. Hartley	San Francisco , Calif. (Risdon)	9 Aug 1875
Tonnage	65 tons	
Dimensions	64′ 6″ × 11′ × 6′	
Machinery	1 screw (15″ × 1′)	
Complement	10.	

Service record:†

Name	Builder	Launched	Comm.
Tench Coxe	Baltimore, Md. (Malster)	7 Jun 1876	23 Oct 1876
Tonnage	46 tons		
Dimensions	71′ (oa) × 15′ × 7′		
Machinery	1 screw, vertical inverted (20″ × 1′ 8″)		

Service record: Harbor vessel, Philadelphia.†

Name	Builder	Launched	Comm.
Thomas Corwin	Portland, Ore. (Oregon)	1876	17 Jul 1877
Tonnage:	213 tons		
Dimensions	145' (oa) 137′ 6″ (bp × 24′ × 11′ 3″		
Machinery	1 screw, inverted (34″ × 2′ 10″)		
Complement	38		

Notes: Wood hull. Served mainly in Alaska.†

Name	Builder	Launched	Comm.
Salmon P. Chase	Philadelphia, Pa. (T. Brown)	1878	Aug 1878

Tonnage	142 tons
Dimensions	115′ 5″ (oa) × 25′ 7″ × 11′ 6″
Complement	35

Notes: Bark, wood hull.

Service record:†

Name	Builder	Launched	Comm.
James Guthrie	Baltimore, Md. (H.A. Ramsey)	13 May 1882	1 Jun 1882
Tonnage	126 tons		
Dimensions	85′ × 17′ × 8′ 7″		
Machinery	1 screw, vertical (20″ × 1′ 8″)		
Complement	11		

Service record: Tug, Baltimore.†

Name	Builder	Launched	Comm.
Walter Forward	Wilmington, Del. (Pusey)	17 Jul 1882	23 Sep 1882
Tonnage	257 tons		
Dimensions	153′ 6″ (oa) × 25′ × 9′ 9″		
Machinery	2 screws, 2-cyl. (24″ × 2′ 4″)		

Notes: Iron hull.

Service record:†

Name	Builder	Launched	Comm.
William P. Fessenden	Buffalo, N.Y. (Union DD)	26 Apr 1883	Sep 1883
Tonnage	330 tons		
Dimensions	191′ 8″ (oa) 177′ (bp) × 28′ × 10′		
Machinery	Iron side wheel, vertical beam engines (48″ × 9′) from old *Fessenden*		

Service record:†

SMALL SCHOONERS

Name	Length	Builder	Launch/Acquired.	Fate
Andrew Jackson	73'	Washington, D.C.	1832	Sold 31 Oct 1865
Washington (brig)	91'	Baltimore, Md. (McCully)	Aug 1837	Seized by rebels at New Orleans, 31 Jan 1861
Walter B. Forward	90'	Washington, D.C. (Easby)	23 Apr 1842	Sold 30 Nov 1865
William J. Duane	102'	Philadelphia, Pa. (Tees)	1849	Seized by rebels at Norfolk, 18 Apr 1861.
Morris	102'	Baltimore, Md. (Brown)	26 Apr 1849	Sold 10 Dec 1868
Joseph Lane ex-*Campbell* (11 Mar 1855)	(U)	Portsmouth, Va. (Graves & Fenbie)	30 Jul 1849	Sold 20 Jul 1869
William L. Marcy	94'	Bristol, R.I. (Hood)	1853	To USCS, 5 Mar 1862
Jefferson Davis	94'	Bristol, R.I. (Hood)	Jun 1853	Hospital boat, Washington Terr.,1862
Robert McClelland	100'	Somerset, Mass. (Hood)	11 Jul 1853	Seized by rebels in Louisiana, 1861, renamed *Pickens*
James C. Dobbin	100'	Somerset, Mass. (Hood)	13 Jul 1853	Sold 6 Apr 1881
James Campbell	100'	Somerset, Mass. (Hood)	9 Jul 1853	Sold 8 Jul 1875+
Caleb Cushing	100'	Somerset, Mass. (Hood)	12 Jul 1853	Captured by Confederate privateers 1862 sunk, 29 Jul 1863
William Aiken ex-*Eclipse*	(U)	(U)	1855	Seized by rebels at Charleston, renamed **Petrel**
Henry Dodge	80'	Portsmouth, Va. (Page & Allen)	1856	Seized by rebels in Texas, 2 Mar 1861
Lewis Cass	80'	Portsmouth, Va. (Page & Allen)	1856	Seized by rebels in Alabama, 30 Jan 1861
Philip Allen	80'	Portsmouth, Va. (Page & Allen)	1856	Sold 9 Dec 1865
Isaac Toucey	63'	Milan, Ohio (Merry & Gay)	Aug 1857	Sold 22 Jun 1869
John B. Floyd[5]	63'	Milan, Ohio (Merry & Gay)	1857	Sold 16 May 1864
Jacob Thompson[5]	63'	Milan, Ohio (Merry & Gay)	1857	Sold 12 Oct 1870
Aaron V. Brown	63'	Milan, Ohio (Merry & Gay)	1857	Sold 23 Aug 1864
Howell Cobb[5]	63'	Milan, Ohio (Merry & Gay)	1857	Wrecked off Cape Ann, 27 Dec 1861.
Jeremiah S. Black[5]	63'	Milan, Ohio (Merry & Gay)	1857	Sold 1868
John Appleton	(U)	Portsmouth, Va. (Page & Allen)	1857	To USN 1861
Agassiz	58'	Baltimore, Md.	31 May 1861[4]	Returned to USCS, 29 Dec 1865
Arago[7]	(U)	(U)	31 May 1861[4]	Returned to USCS, 1861
Varina[7]	31'	(U)	May 1861[4]	Returned to USCS 22 Nov 1865
William H. Crawford[7]	102'	Philadelphia, Pa.	31 May 1861[4]	Sold 21 Jun 1869
Petrel	85'	Williamsburg, N.Y. (Hathorn)	1867	Sold 21 Oct 1873
Racer	85'	Williamsburg, N.Y. (Hathorn)	1866	Sold 30 Jul 1873
Active	90'	Philadelphia, Pa. (Lynn)	May 1867	Sold 13 May 1875
Antietam	(U)	Baltimore, Md. (Fardy)	1 Mar 1864[4]	Sold Jan 1871
Reliance	110'	Baltimore, Md. (Fardy)	Jun 1867	Sold 5 Jan 1875
Vigilant	110'	Baltimore, Md. (Fardy)	1867	Discarded 1870
Relief	92'	Philadelphia, Pa. (Birely Lynn)	1867	Discarded 1870
Rescue	92'	Philadelphia, Pa. (Birely Lynn)	1867	Sold 23 Jun 1874
Resolute	90'	Philadelphia, Pa. (Lynn)	Jun 1867	Sold 10 Feb 1872
Saville	15'	Mystic, Conn.	1872	Sold 16 Oct 1884

[1] Commissioned.
[2] Merchant *Pedro Varela*, 1876.
[3] Merchant *John L. Thomas*, 1881.
[4] Acquired.
[5] Transferred from Great Lakes via Quebec Dec 1861.
[6] Merchant *A.V. Brown*, 1864.
[7] Ex-US Coast Survey vessel.
[8] Sunk near Pass a l'Outre, 18 Jan 1870.
[9] Merchant *Addie L. Bird*, 1875, renamed *Annie Thatcher*, 1896.
[10] Merchant *Leo*, 1875. s/e 1896.

LAUNCHES

Name	Length	Builder	Launch/Acq.	Fate
Discover	38'	New York, N.Y.	1869	Sold 19 Mar 1896
Search	38'	New York, N.Y.	1869	Sold 11 Jul 1896
Vanderbilt	30'	(U)	1875	Sold 1 Aug 1891
Alert	40'	New York, N.Y.	1876	Sold 8 Jul 1896

8
UNITED STATES COAST SURVEY

STEAMERS

Name	Builder	Launched
Bibb	Pittsburgh, Pa. (Knapp)	1845
Tonnage	409 tons B.	
Dimensions	161' (oa) 143' (bp) × 23' × 10'	
Machinery	Side wheels, side lever engine	
Complement	35	

Service record: Built for Revenue Marine as *Tyler* with Hunter's Wheel propulsion, transferred to USCS 9 Jan 1847. Converted to side wheels 1862. Loaned to Revenue Cutter Service, 31 May 1861, returned 1861. Slightly damaged by torpedo (mine) explosion in Charleston harbor, 17 Mar 1865.

Name	Builder	Launched
Walker	Pittsburgh, Pa. (Tomlinson)	1845
Tonnage	305 tons B.	
Dimensions	132 (pp) × 24'6" × 9'8"	
Machinery	Side wheels, 2 horizontal half beam engines	

Service record: Built for Revenue Marine, transferred 1852. Rebuilt 1862. Sunk in collision off Abscon, N.J., 21 Jun 1860.

Name	Builder	Launched
Corwin[†]	Philadelphia, Pa. (Vaughan Lynn)	1852
Tonnage	(U)	
Dimensions	125' × 24' × d10'	
Machinery	Side wheels, 1 steeple engine, (Merrick)	

Service record: Served with Revenue Cutter Service 31 May to 17 Sep 1861.
Ships captured: *Director*, 4 May 1862; *Waterwitch*, 5 May 1862.

Hetzel[‡] (see USN p. 62)
Vixen[‡] (see USN p. 45)

SAILING VESSELS

Brig: *Fauntleroy* (78 tons, 1852)
Schooners: *Agassiz*,[†] *Arago*,[†] *Bailey*, *Bancroft*, *Bowditch*, *Caswell*, *Crawford*, *Dana*,[‡] *Gerdes*, *G.M. Bache*, *Guthrie*, *Hassler*, *Howell Cobb*,[‡] *Humboldt*, *James Hall*, *John Y. Mason*, *Joseph Henry*, *Marcy*, *Meredith*, *Peirce*, *Petrel*,§ *Torrey*, *Twilight*, *Varina*[†]
Tender: *Fire Fly*.§

[†]Loaned to Revenue Marine.
[‡]Loaned to U.S. Navy.
§Seized by Confederates.

PART II
Confederate States Navy

INTRODUCTION TO PART II

When South Carolina seceded from the Union on 20 December 1860, followed by the other Southern states, the entity of the Confederate States of America did not automatically come into existence. For a brief period, these were separate independent states, and the ships they seized or armed were not part of a common navy.

Efforts to bring a Confederate Navy into being were fraught with difficulties. By judicious strategy, the Union seized points along the long coast, which effectively kept the Southern states' "navies" apart. Even after being officially incorporated into the Confederate Navy, each state's navy fought its own war. Because of the geographical situation, there were no occasions when ships of the different states joined to fight the common foe.

Aside from the few ships they were able to seize in southern ports, the Confederacy had little hope of building a navy. The industrial revolution had lagged far behind in the South, and the few factories capable of making arms, engines, or armor were already in great demand by the army, which by the geography of the war had first priority.

Ingenuity was not to be denied, however, and some memorable naval designs and weapons were produced, a few of which have made their mark on history. Southern engineers devised the casemate ironclad rams, most of similar shape and design, of which the most notable was the *Virginia*, converted from the USS *Merrimack*. Her appearance at Hampton Roads in the midst of the Union fleet caused consternation as she roamed freely among the wooden warships, wreaking havoc. It was only the timely arrival of the *Monitor* that stopped her and showed up her defects; the *Virginia's* formidable aspect, like that of her near sisters, was belied by defective machinery and jerry-built armor.

Submarines of primitive design were produced, and, despite several disasters, attained the first sinking of a warship by a submarine. Mines (then called "torpedoes") were used with great success against Union ships.

A most effective weapon against the South was the blockade of the Southern ports. Because of the lack of industrial capacity, it was absolutely necessary for the South to import manufactured goods, especially war materiel; to pay for these goods, cotton had to be exported.

A large trade began, with ships running out of the main southern ports, such as Wilmington, Charleston, Savannah, Mobile, New Orleans, and Galveston, as well as many other points on the Florida and Texas coasts. The "runners" had only to go to nearby neutral ports where they could leave their cotton and pick up goods destined for the South. Bermuda, Nassau, and Havana became the most widely used exchange points, requiring a comparatively short voyage.

To cope with this situation, the Union Navy was required to add many ships to patrol the seas, it being a settled principle of international law that a blockade, to be legal, had to be effective.

A number of blockade runners were owned by the Confederate government or by state governments, but the majority was privately owned. They were mostly of British register, many having been specially built for the occasion. They were very fast, low in the water, and cheaply built. Some became very successful, making many voyages; others were captured on their first run. A number of these fast ships were taken into the Union Navy to join the blockaders.

The Confederate Navy also took to the high seas in the form of commerce raiders. Ships were outfitted or built in Britain until the British government, severely taken to task by the American minister in London, halted the practice. To evade neutrality laws, these ships sailed out as merchant ships, and were armed and commissioned at sea. They were quite successful and tied up a substantial number of U.S. warships searching for them and guarding American flag merchant ships. *Alabama*, *Florida*, and *Shenandoah* are names that became legendary.

After the war the British government paid reparations in the "Alabama Claims" treaty, admitting it was wrong for a neutral country to permit a belligerent to build ships of war in its yards. This foresight paid off in later years when the British fought nonmaritime powers, particularly during the Boer War.

Modern and more powerful fighting vessels were also ordered abroad. Small armored ocean-going turret ships were contracted for in Britain by the industrious Captain James Bulloch, and some other vessels were contracted for in France. Of all these ships only the *Stonewall* put to sea under the Confederate flag, the others being halted by government decree. They eventually ended up in various foreign navies.

The Mississippi River was the backbone of the Confederacy. It and its major tributaries were highways of commerce and constituted the best line of logistical support for the armies. The Union needed to control these rivers for its own sake and to deny them to the South. Union control of the Mississippi split the South.

On the Mississippi River and its major tributaries—the Ohio, the Cumberland, the Tennessee, and the Red—the South responded to the threat by arming river steamers and building casemate ironclads. But the strength of the Union thrust swept aside these weak forces. Although plans for many vessels were put in hand, most were destroyed or captured incomplete, and only a very few got into action. With the capture of Vicksburg in 1863, the river war moved to lesser streams.

VESSELS IN COMMISSION, JANUARY 10, 1863

James River: ironclad *Richmond*; gunboats *Hampton, Nansemond, Beaufort,* and *Raleigh*; schoolship *Patrick Henry;* tender *Drewry;* and steamer *Torpedo.*
Cape Fear River: ironclad *North Carolina;* and floating battery *Arctic.*
Charleston: ironclads *Chicora, Charleston,* and *Palmetto State;* and tender *Juno.*
Savannah: ironclad *Savannah;* floating battery *Georgia;* gunboat *Isondiga;* and steamer *Sampson.*
Mobile: gunboats *Morgan, Gaines,* and *Selma;* floating batteries *Tuscaloosa* and *Huntsville,* ram *Baltic;* and receiving ship *Dalman.*
Red River: ironclad *Missouri.*
At sea: sloops *Alabama, Florida,* and *Georgia.*

VESSELS IN COMMISSION, APRIL 30, 1864

James River: ironclads *Virginia, Fredericksburg,* and *Richmond*; gunboats *Hampton, Nansemond, Roanoke, Beaufort, Drewry,* and *Torpedo,* and steam sloop *Patrick Henry.*
North Carolina (inland waters): ironclads *Albemarle* and *Neuse.*
Cape Fear River: ironclads *North Carolina* and *Raleigh;* floating battery *Arctic;* and gunboat *Yadkin.*
Charleston: ironclads *Chicora, Charleston,* and *Palmetto State.*
Savannah: ironclads *Savannah* and *Georgia;* gunboat *Isondiga;* and steamer *Sampson.*
Mobile: ironclad *Tennessee,* gunboats *Morgan, Gaines,* and *Selma;* floating batteries *Tuscaloosa* and *Huntsville,* and ram *Baltic.*
Red River: ironclad *Missouri.*
St. Marks River, Fla.: gunboat *Spray.*
At sea: sloops *Alabama, Florida,* and *Georgia.*
In France: sloop *Rappahannock.*

9
ARMORED VESSELS

SEAGOING ARMORED SHIPS

North Carolina Class

Name	Builder	Laid down	Launched	Comm.
Mississippi	Birkenhead, England (Laird)	Apr 1862	29 Aug 1863	—
North Carolina	Birkenhead, England (Laird)	Apr 1862	4 Jul 1863	—

Tonnage	2,750 tons D.
Dimensions	224′6″ (bp) × 42′6″ × 17
Machinery	1 screw, horizontal direct-acting engines (56″ × 2′9″), 4 boilers, IHP 1,450, 10 knots. (Bldr)
Complement	153
Armament	4–9″ MLR (Royal Navy)
Armor	5″ turrets with 10″ faces, 3″ to 4.5″ sides

Notes: First seagoing turret warships superior to any federal warship. Three-mast bark rig, hinged bulwarks, telescopic funnels. Contracted by Cdr. James D. Bulloch. The famous "Laird Rams" embargoed by the British government and taken over for the Royal Navy. Built under code names *El Monassir* and *El Tousson* supposedly for the Egyptian government. Seized by the British government Oct 1863 while anchored under guard in the Mersey River and purchased Feb 1864 for the Royal Navy.

Later history

Mississippi: Completed as HMS *Wivern*, 10 Oct 1865. Coast defense ship at Hong Kong 1880. Floating workshop and depot ship 1904. BU 1922.
North Carolina: Completed as HMS *Scorpion*, 10 Oct 1865. Coast defense ship at Bermuda 1869. Sunk as a target at Bermuda 1901.

Santa Maria

Name	Builder	Laid down	Launched	Comm.
"Santa Maria"	Glasgow, Scotland (Thomson)	1863	23 Feb 1864	Never

Tonnage	4,770 tons D., 3,200 tons B?
Dimensions	270′8″ (bp) × 49′6″ × 18′4″
Machinery	1 screw, horizontal direct-acting engine, 4 boilers, IHP 1,000, 8.5 knots
Complement	500
Armament	20–60pdr MLR, 8–18pdr
Armor	Battery and belt 4.5″–5.5″

Notes: Contracted by Lt. James H. North and canceled Dec 1863. Never named by the CSN, this vessel was known variously as *Santa Maria*, *Glasgow*, and *Frigate No.61*.

Later history: Sold by builders to Denmark, Dec 1863, not delivered until Dec 1864 because of war with Prussia and Austria. Danish *Danmark*, 1864. BU 1907.

Fig 9.1: The *Mississippi* was begun in 1862 by Laird of Birkenhead for the Confederate Navy. One of the famous "Laird Rams," which were seized by the British government in 1863 as a violation of British neutrality, she is seen here as HMS *Wivern* in the Hamoaze River at Plymouth in 1865. Her bulwarks are down exposing the turrets. (U.S. Naval Historical Center)

150 Civil War Navies, 1855-1883

Stonewall Class

Name	Builder	Laid down	Launched	Comm.
Stonewall	Bordeaux, France (Arman)	1863	21 Jun 1864	Jan 1865
(Unnamed)	Bordeaux, France (Arman)	1863	Jun 1864	Never

Tonnage	1,390 tons
Dimensions	186'9" (oa) 165'9" (wl) 157'6" (bp) × 32'6" × 14'3"
Machinery	2 screws, horizontal direct-acting engines, 2 boilers. IHP 1,200 = 10.8 knots (Mazeline)
Complement	135
Armament	1–11"/300 R, 2–5"/70 R
Armor	Belt 4.5", c/t 5.5"

Notes: Ironclad rams contracted by Bulloch and built in France under code names *Sphinx* and *Cheops*, respectively. Embargoed by the French government, Feb 1864. Twin rudders and twin keels. Designed to operate in shallow waters.

Service record:

Stonewall (Sphinx): Sold to Denmark, renamed *Staerkodder* but refused by Danish government and returned as *Olinde*. Comm by CSN at sea. Left Ferrol, Spain, 24 Mar 1865. At Havana at end of the war and turned over to United States.
   Later history: Sold to Japan, renamed *Kotetsu*, arrived at Yokohama, 24 Apr 1868. Transferred to Imperial government, renamed *Azuma*, 1871. BU 1908.

Unnamed (Cheops): Sold by builder to Prussia.
   Later history: Prussian *Prinz Adalbert*, 29 Oct 1865, rearmed and completed, 1866. BU 1878.

Casemate Ironclads

Manassas

Name	Builder	Launched	Acquired	Comm.
Manassas	Medford, Mass. (Curtis)	1855	12 Sep 1861	Dec 1861
ex-*Enoch Train*				

Tonnage	387 tons B.
Dimensions	143' × 33' × 17' (as merchant vessel: 128' × 26' × d12'6")
Machinery	1 screw, 1 inclined engine (36" × 2'6"), 4 knots (Loring)
Complement	35
Armament	1–64 pdr; (later) 1–32pdr.
Armor	1.5" over 12" wood.

Notes: Towboat, acquired 1861 and converted at Algiers, La., to an ironclad ram. Comm as a privateer; taken over by CSN in Oct 1861. Hull was plated over with a convex shape, which caused cannon shot to glance off, projecting only 2'6" above the water. Purchased by Confederate government, Dec 1861.

Service record: Lower Mississippi River. Attacked Federal squadron at Head of Passes, La., 12 Oct 1861, ramming USS *Richmond*, but damaged during the action. Engaged Federal squadron below New Orleans, 24 Apr 1862, ramming several vessels; run aground and burned in the Mississippi River.

Virginia (I)

Name	Builder	Launched	Acquired	Comm.
Virginia	Boston NYd	14 Jun 1855	17 Feb 1862	Mar 1862
ex-USS *Merrimack*				

Tonnage	3,200 tons B.

Fig 9.2: The ironclad *Stonewall* after being turned over to the United States. Notice the single turret aft of the mainmast, and the long ram on the bow. (Paul H. Silverstone Collection)

Dimensions	263' (bp) × 51'4 × 22'
Machinery	1 screw, 2-cyl. horizontal double piston-rod back-acting engines (72" × 3'), 4 boilers, IHP 1,200, 9 knots (West Point)
Complement	320
Armament	2–7" MLR, 6–9" SB, 2–6"/32 MLR
Armor	2" + 24" wood

Notes: USN frigate *Merrimack*, burned to the waterline at Norfolk NYd to prevent capture, 20 Apr 1861; hulk raised and rebuilt as an ironclad ram, starting Jul 1861. Cut down to the waterline and reconstructed with sloping armored sides pierced for guns and a 4-foot ram bow. Designed by Cdr. John M. Brooke and John L. Porter. Engines were weak, steering poor.

Service record: Battle of Hampton Roads, 8 Mar 1862. Damaged by gunfire, sank U.S. sloop *Cumberland* by gunfire and ramming, then frigate *Congress* by gunfire. Engaged U.S. ironclad *Monitor*, 9 Mar, in inconclusive battle, the first between powered ironclad vessels. Sortied into Hampton Roads and captured three transports, 11 Apr 1862. Run ashore and burned by crew to prevent capture near Craney Island in James River, 11 May 1862; her deep draft prevented her from going upstream to Richmond.

Arkansas Class

Name	Builder	Laid down	Launched	Comm.
Arkansas	Memphis, Tenn. (Shirley)	Oct 1861	25 Apr 1862	26 May 1862
Tennessee	Memphis, Tenn. (Shirley)	Oct 1861	Never	Never

Tonnage	(U)
Dimensions	165' (bp) × 35' × 11'6"
Machinery	2 screws, low-pressure engines (24" × 7'), IHP 900, 8 mph/7 knots
Complement	200
Armament	2–9" SB, 2–8"/64, 2–6" MLR, 2–32pdr SB
Armor	18" iron and wood

Notes: Casemate ironclad with ram bow and sloping sides on long flat hull. Hurriedly built with poor engines.

Service records

Arkansas: Taken to Yazoo City, Miss., for completion before Federal troops occupied Memphis, May 1862. Engaged Federal ironclads in Yazoo

Fig 9.3: The ironclad ram *Arkansas*, which caused havoc and consternation by running through the Federal fleet off Memphis, July 1862, shown in a drawing by R.G. Skerrett.

Fig 9.4: The ironclad ram *Tennessee* after being captured at the Battle of Mobile Bay. She was then commissioned in the U.S. Navy. (U.S. Naval Historical Center)

River, 15 Jul 1862; damaged running past Federal fleet to Vicksburg. Attacked at Vicksburg by ram *Queen of the West*, 22 Jul 1862. Attacked by US ironclad *Essex* above Baton Rouge, drifted ashore and burned to prevent capture, 6 Aug 1862.

Tennessee: Burned to prevent capture on the stocks at Memphis, 5 Jun 1862.

Mississippi

Name	Builder	Laid down	Launched	Comm.
Mississippi	Jefferson City, La. (Tift)	14 Oct 1861	19 Apr 1862	Never

Tonnage	1,400 tons
Dimensions	260' × 58' × 12'6"
Machinery	3 screws, 3 engines (36" × 2'6"), 14 knots (Patterson Iron Works)
Complement	(U)
Armament	2–7" MLR, 18 other guns (see Notes)
Armor	3.75"

Notes: Ironclad steamer, never completed. Ten gun ports on each side and two each forward and aft; armament never mounted. Designed by Asa and Nelson Tift.

Service record: Burned to prevent capture prior to completion during fall of New Orleans, 25 Apr 1862.

Louisiana

Name	Builder	Laid down	Launched	Comm.
Louisiana	Jefferson City, La. (Murray)	15 Oct 1861	6 Feb 1862	Never

Tonnage	1,400 tons
Dimensions	264', 246'(oa) × 62' × 7'
Machinery	2 screws and 2 paddle wheels, 4 engines, 6 boilers (Patterson Iron Works)
Complement	250
Armament	2–7" MLR, 3–9", 4–8", 7–32pdr MLR
Armor	4"

Notes: One of the largest of the casemate ironclads. Designed by E.C. Murray with two paddle wheels in a center well, one behind the other, and twin rudders. Five gun ports on each side and three each forward and aft. Engines taken from steamer *Ingomar*.

Service record: Towed while incomplete to Ft. St. Philip below New Orleans as a floating battery, 20 Apr 1862. Burned to prevent capture and blew up, 28 Apr 1862.

Atlanta

Name	Builder	Launched	Acquired	Comm.
Atlanta	Glasgow, Scotland (Thomson)	9 May 1861	Spring 1862	22 Nov 1862

ex-*Fingal*

Tonnage	1,006 tons
Dimensions	204' (oa) × 41' × 15'9"
Machinery	3 screws, 2 vertical direct-acting engines (39" × 2'6"), 1 boiler, 6 knots (J & G Thomas)
Complement	145
Armament	2–7" MLR, 2–6.4" MLR, spar torpedo
Armor	4" casemate, 1/2" deck

Notes: Converted at Savannah by N. & A. Tift from iron-hulled blockade runner *Fingal*, which broke the blockade under Captain Bulloch. Cut down to waterline; the armored deck projected 6 feet beyond the hull with a casemate on top. Purchased by Confederate Army, 1861.

Service record: Savannah station. Captured in Wassaw Sound, Ga., by U.S. monitors *Nahant* and *Weehawken* after being damaged by gunfire and run aground, 17 Jun 1863 (1 killed). Comm in USN as USS *Atlanta*, 2 Feb 1864. SAtlBS and NatlBS, James River, 1864–65. Sold 4 May 1869.

Later history: Sold to Haiti; renamed *Triumph*. Sailed from Philadelphia for Haiti, 8 Dec 1869 and disappeared at sea.

Eastport

Name	Builder	Launched	Acquired	Comm.
Eastport	New Albany, Ind.	1852	31 Oct 1861	Never

Notes: Converted to ironclad at Cerro Gordo, Tenn. May have been the former *C.E. Hillman*.

Service record: Captured by Union gunboats while undergoing conversion at Cerro Gordo, 7 Feb 1862. Taken to Cairo, Ill. and completed as USS *Eastport*. (q.v.)

Fig 9.5: The ironclad ram *Atlanta* as a U.S. warship in the James River, 1865. (U.S. Naval Historical Center)

Richmond Class

Name	Builder	Laid down	Launched	Comm.
Chicora	Charleston, S.C. (Eason)	25 Apr 1862	23 Aug 1862	Nov 1862
North Carolina	Wilmington, N.C. (Berry)	Spring 1862	Oct 1863	Dec 1863
Palmetto State	Charleston, S.C. (Cameron)	Jan 1862	11 Oct 1862	Sep 1862
Raleigh	Wilmington, N.C. (Cassidy)	Spring 1862	Fall 1864	30 Apr 1864
Richmond	Norfolk NYd	Feb 1862	6 May 1862	Jul 1862
Savannah	Savannah, Ga. (Willink)	Apr 1862	4 Feb 1863	30 Jun 1863

Tonnage	(U)
Dimensions	172'6" (oa) 150' (bp) × 34' × 12', d14'
Machinery	1 screw, 6 knots
Complement	180
Armament	*Chicora:* 2–9"SB, 4–6" 32pdr MLR
	North Carolina: 4 guns
	Palmetto State: 10–7" MLR
	Raleigh: 4–6"R
	Richmond: 1–7" MLR, 1–10" SB, 2–6.4"MLR, spar torpedo
	Savannah: 2–7" MLR, 2–6.4" MLR
Armor	4" + 22" wood

Notes: Ironclad rams built to a basic design of John L. Porter. Completion was delayed by shortage of equipment and strikes. *Richmond* was sometimes referred to as *Virginia II* and *Young Virginia*. *North Carolina* fitted with engine from gunboat *Uncle Ben*; hull was structurally weak, could not cross Wilmington bar. They were underpowered, slow, top-heavy, and difficult to steer.

Service records

Chicora: Defense of Charleston. Attacked Federal blockading fleet, 31 Jan 1863. Defense of Charleston forts, 7 Apr 1863. Sunk to prevent capture prior to fall of Charleston, 18 Feb 1865.

North Carolina: Defense of Wilmington, N.C. Foundered at Smithville, N.C., as result of worm damage, 27 Sep 1864.

Palmetto State: Defense of Charleston. Attacked Federal blockading fleet and rammed USS *Mercedita*, 31 Jan 1863. Defense of Charleston forts, 7 Apr 1863. Sunk to prevent capture prior to fall of Charleston, 18 Feb 1865.

Raleigh: Defense of Wilmington, N.C. Engaged Federal blockading vessels off New Inlet, N.C., 6 May but went aground and was wrecked on Wilmington Bar the following day, 7 May 1864.

Richmond: Towed to Richmond after launching and completed there. James River. Engagements at Dutch Gap, 13 Aug, Ft. Harrison, 29–31 Sep, and Chapin's Bluff, 22 Oct 1864. Attacked while aground at Trent's Reach, Va., 23–24 Jan 1865. Sunk to prevent capture in James River prior to fall of Richmond, 3 Apr 1865.

Savannah: Defense of Savannah. Burned to prevent capture at Savannah, 21 Dec 1864.

Fig 9.6: The ironclad *Chicora*, built for the defense of Charleston, S.C.

Albemarle Class

Name	Builder	Laid down	Launched	Comm.
Albemarle	Whitehall, N.C. (Elliot)	Apr 1863	1 Jul 1863	17 Apr 1864
Neuse	Whitehall, N.C.	1863	Nov 1863	Apr 1864
(Unnamed)	Edwards Ferry, N.C. (Elliot)	Late 1864	Never	Never

Tonnage	376 tons (*Neuse*).
Dimensions	152′ (oa) 139′ (bp) × 34′ × 9′
Machinery	2 screws, 2 horizontal noncondensing engines (18″ × 1′7″), 2 boilers, IHP 400, 4 knots
Complement	150
Armament	2–6.4″/100 MLR
Armor	6″

Notes: Octagonal casemate on a flat hull, designed by Cdr. James W. Cooke for shallow North Carolina waters.

Service records

Albemarle: Damaged at launch and taken to Halifax, N.C., for completion. Attacked Union forces at Plymouth, N.C., sinking USS *Southfield*, 19 Apr 1864. Attacked Federal squadron below Plymouth, damaged, 5 May 1864 (1 killed). Sunk in Roanoke River by Lt. William B. Cushing in spar torpedo boat *Picket Boat No. 1*, 28 Oct 1864. Raised by Union forces and taken to Norfolk NYd, Apr 1865. Sold 15 Oct 1867. BU 1867.

Neuse: North Carolina waters. Taken to Kinston, N.C., for completion. Ran aground off Kinston, May 1864. Remained there until sunk to prevent capture, Mar 1865.

Unnamed unit: Destroyed on stocks to prevent capture, Apr 1865.

Missouri

Name	Builder	Laid down	Launched	Comm.
Missouri	Shreveport, La.	Dec 1862	14 Apr 1863	12 Sep 1863

Tonnage	(U)
Dimensions	183′ (oa) × 53′8″ × 8′6″, d10′3″
Machinery	Center wheel, 2 engines (24″ × 7′6″), 6 mph/5.3 knots
Complement	(U)
Armament	1–11″, 1–9″, 2–32pdr.
Armor	4 1/2″ rails

Notes: Two ships planned; second ship canceled in 1863. Engines taken from *Grand Era*.

Service record: Served in Red River. Lower water level in Red River prevented ship from moving from Shreveport. Surrendered at Shreveport, 3 Jun 1865. Sold by USN at Mound City, Ill, 29 Nov 1865.

Charleston

Name	Builder	Laid down	Launched	Comm.
Charleston	Charleston, S.C. (Eason)	Dec 1862	1863	Sep 1863

Tonnage	(U)
Dimensions	189′ (oa) 167′ (bp) × 34′ × 14′d
Machinery	6 knots
Complement	150
Armament	2–9″SB, 4 R
Armor	(U)

Notes: Ironclad ram. Known as the "Ladies Gunboat."

Service record: Defense of Charleston. Burned to prevent capture at Charleston, S.C., 18 Feb 1865.

Huntsville Class

Name	Builder	Laid down	Launched	Comm.
Huntsville	Selma, Ala. (Bassett)	1862	7 Feb 1863	1863
Tuscaloosa	Selma, Ala. (Bassett)	1862	7 Feb 1863	1863

Tonnage	(U)
Dimensions	152′ (oa) × 34′ × 7′
Machinery	1 screw, high pressure engines, 3 knots
Complement	(U)
Armament	3–32pdr, 1–6.4″R
Armor	4″

Notes: Improved *Albemarle* type, only partially armored. Engines defective; vessels could be used only as floating batteries. Two others of similar type (160′ × 41′ × 10′6″) were under construction at Oven Bluff, Ala., on the Tombigbee River, but were not completed.

Service record: Defense of Mobile. Taken to Mobile for completion. Sunk as block ships in Mobile River, 12 Apr 1865.

Jackson

Name	Builder	Laid down	Launched	Comm.
Jackson	Columbus (Ga.) NYd	1862	22 Dec 1864	Never

Tonnage	1,250 tons
Dimensions	223′6″ (oa) 208′6″ (bp) × 59′ × 8′
Machinery	2 screws, 2 horizontal direct-acting HP engines (28″ × 2′)
Complement	(U)
Armament	4–7″R, 2–6.4″R
Armor	4″ casemate

Notes: Also known as *Muscogee*. Designed with center-wheel machinery but drew too much water after first launch; lengthened and rebuilt early in 1864 as a modified *Albemarle* type with twin screws.

Service record: Destroyed by Union cavalry before completion, Apr 1865.

Milledgeville Class

Name	Builder	Laid down	Launched	Comm.
Milledgeville	Savannah, Ga. (Willink)	Feb 1863	Oct 1864	Never
(Unnamed)	Savannah, Ga. (Kenston & Hawks)	(U)	Never	Never
(Unnamed)	Charleston, S.C.	(U)	Oct 1864	Never
(Unnamed)	Charleston, S.C.	(U)	Never	Never
Tonnage	650 tons			
Dimensions	175' (bp) × 35'3" × 9', 12'dpth			
Machinery	2 screws			
Complement	(U)			
Armament	6 guns			
Armor	6" casemate			

Notes: Shallow draft ships similar to the *Richmond* class. The two being built at Charleston were similar.

Service record: All destroyed incomplete to prevent capture, Dec 1864.

Wilmington

Name	Builder	Laid down	Launched	Comm.
Wilmington	Wilmington, N.C.	1863	Never	Never
Tonnage	(U)			
Dimensions	224' long			
Machinery	2 screws			
Complement	(U)			
Armament	2 guns			
Armor	(U)			

Notes: Two short casemates with one pivot gun in each. Machinery built at Columbus, Ga.

Service record: Destroyed on the stocks, Jan 1865.

Columbia Class

Name	Builder	Laid down	Launched	Comm.
Columbia	Charleston, S.C. (Jones & Eason)	(U)	10 Mar 1864	1864
Texas	Richmond NYd	(U)	Jan 1865	Never
Tonnage	1,520 tons D			
Dimensions	*Columbia*: 213' (oa) 189' (bp) × 51'4" × 13'6"			
	Texas: 217' (oa) × 48'6" × 13'6"			
Machinery	*Columbia*: 1 screw, 2 horizontal direct-acting HP engines (36" × 2'), 5 boilers.			
	Texas: 2 screws, 4 horizontal direct-acting condensing engines (26" × 1'8").			
Complement	50			
Armament	6 guns			
Armor	6"			

Notes: Similar vessels built to same basic design, with shorter casemate on *Texas*. Three gun ports on each side, and two facing forward and aft. Designed by William A. Graves.

Service records

Columbia: Defense of Charleston. Ran onto a sunken wreck near Ft. Moultrie, 12 Jan 1865. Salvaged by USN and towed to Norfolk, 25 May 1865. Sold by USN 10 Oct 1867.

Texas: Seized incomplete at Richmond by USN, 4 Apr 1865. Sold 15 Oct 1867 and BU.

Tennessee (II)

Name	Builder	Laid down	Launched	Comm.
Tennessee	Selma, Ala. (Bassett)	Oct 1862	Feb 1863	16 Feb 1864
Tonnage	1,273 tons			
Dimensions	209' (oa) 189' (bp) × 48' × 14'			
Machinery	2 screws and side wheels, 2 HP engines (24" × 7'), 4 boilers, 6 knots.			
Complement	133			
Armament	2–7"MLR, 4–6.4"MLR			
Armor	5" casemates, 6" forward, 2" deck			

Notes: Modified *Columbia* type. Engines taken from a riverboat steamer.

Service record: Defense of Mobile. Battle of Mobile Bay, 5 Aug 1864 (flagship); disabled and captured (2 killed). Comm in USN as USS *Tennessee*, 19 Aug 1864. Assault on Ft. Morgan, 23 Aug 1864. Decomm 19 Aug 1865. Sold 27 Nov 1867 and BU.

Fredericksburg

Name	Builder	Laid down	Launched	Comm.
Fredericksburg	Richmond NYd	1863	30 Nov 1863	Mar 1864
Tonnage	c. 700 tons			
Dimensions	188' (oa) 170' (bp) × 40'3" × 9'6", d10'10"			
Machinery	2 screws			
Complement	150			
Armament	1–11"SB, 1–8"MLR, 2–6.4"MLR			
Armor	(U)			

Notes: Ironclad ram. Improved *Albemarle*. Did not receive armament until Mar 1864.

Service record: James River flotilla. Action at Trent's Reach, 21 Jun 1864. Blown up to prevent capture in James River following fall of Richmond, 4 Apr 1865.

Virginia (II)

Name	Builder	Laid down	Launched	Comm.
Virginia	Richmond NYd	1863	Jun 1864	Jun 1864
Displacement	(U)			
Dimensions	197' (oa) 180' (bp) × 47'6" × 9'6"			
Machinery	1 screw, 10 knots.			
Complement	150			
Armament	1–11"SB, 1–8"MLR, 2–6.4"MLR			
Armor	5"sides, 6"forward			

Notes: Casemate ironclad similar to the *Charleston*.

Service record: James River flotilla. Action at Trent's Reach, 21 Jun 1864. Engagements at Dutch Gap, 13 Aug and 22 Oct 1864. Damaged during second action at Trent's Reach, 23–24 Jan 1865. Blown up to prevent capture in James River following fall of Richmond, 3 Apr 1865.

Nashville Class

Name	Builder	Laid down	Launched	Comm.
Nashville	Montgomery, Ala.	(U)	Mid-1863	Never
(Unnamed)	Selma, Ala. (Shirley)	(U)	Mar 1863	Never
Tonnage	1,100 tons			
Dimensions	271' (oa) 250' (bp) × 62'6" × 10'9"			
Machinery	Sidewheels, 2 engines (30" × 9')			
Complement	(U)			
Armament	3–7"MLR, 1–24 pdr H.			

Armor   6" casemate, 2" forward and pilot house.

Notes: Armor for *Nashville* taken from *Baltic*. A third side-wheel ironclad was started at Oven Bluff, Ala.

Service records

Nashville: Taken to Mobile for completion, Jun 1863. Surrendered incomplete in Tombigbee River, Ala., 10 May 1865. Sold by USN, 22 Nov 1867 and BU.
Unnamed unit: Irreparably damaged when launched; BU Apr 1864.

(Unnamed)

Name	Builder	Laid down	Launched	Comm.
(Unnamed)	Richmond, Va.	1865	Never	Never

Tonnage	(U)
Dimensions	220' × 27' × 11'6"
Machinery	4 screws
Complement	(U)
Armament	(U)
Armor	(U)

Notes: Designed by Graves. Double-ended ship with two rudders and a ram on each end. Engines to be built in England.

(Unnamed)

Name	Builder	Laid down	Launched	Comm.
(Unnamed)	Columbus, Ga.	(U)	Never	Never

Tonnage	(U)
Dimensions	175' × 45' × 9'
Machinery	(U)
Complement	(U)
Armament	2–11"SB
Armor	12" turret

Notes: A monitor-type ironclad with turret; never completed.

In addition the following vessels were under construction during the war. Few details are known:

Unnamed vessel, being built at Elizabeth City, N.C. No work done.
Unnamed vessel, being built by Eliot at Edwards Ferry, N.C. Set adrift at Hamilton, N.C., Mar 1865 and sunk by Confederate mine.
Unnamed side-wheel ram being built at Oven Bluff, Ala. Destroyed on stocks.
Unnamed twin screw side-wheel ram being built at Yazoo City, Miss.: Destroyed prior to completion, 21 May 1863. Dimensions: 310' × 70'; 4–4.5" armor.
Unnamed ironclad being built at Pensacola: Destroyed Mar 1862.

10
UNARMORED STEAM VESSELS

CRUISERS

Alabama

Name	Builder	Laid down	Launched	Comm.
Alabama	Birkenhead, England (Laird)	1861	14 May 1862	24 Aug 1862
ex-*Enrica*				

Tonnage	1,050 tons
Dimensions	220' (oa) 211'6" (wl) × 31'9" × 14'
Machinery	1 screw, 2 horizontal direct-acting condensing engines (56" × 2'3"), 4 boilers, IHP 600, 13 knots (Bldr)
Complement	148
Armament	6–32pdr/55 SB, 1–110pdr MLR (7"), 1–68pdr SB (8")

Notes: Bark rigged sloop-of-war known as "Hull 290." Ordered 1 Aug 1861 by Capt. James Bulloch. Made rendezvous with *Agrippina* and *Bahama*, and commissioned under Capt. Raphael Semmes at sea off the Azores. Took 60 prizes.

Service record: Cruised in North Atlantic, captured and sank over twenty ships, 1862. West Indies, sank USS *Hatteras* off Galveston, 11 Jan 1863. Cruised in East Indies, 1863, stopping at Capetown and Singapore. Arrived at Cherbourg, France, 11 Jun 1864. Sunk in action with USS *Kearsarge* off Cherbourg, 19 Jun 1864 (about 28 killed).

Ships captured: **Ocmulgee*, 5 Sep 1862; **Starlight*, 7 Sep 1862; **Ocean Rover*, 8 Sep 1862; **Alert*, **Weather Gauge*, 9 Sep 1862; **Altamaha*, 13 Sep 1862; **Benjamin Tucker*, 14 Sep 1862; **Courser*, 16 Sep 1862; **Virginia*, 17 Sep 1862; **Elisha Dunbar*, 18 Sep 1862; **Brilliant*, 3 Oct 1862; **Wave Crest*, **Dunkirk*, 7 Oct 1862; *Tonawanda*, 9 Oct 1862; **Manchester*, 11 Oct 1862; **Lamplighter*, 15 Oct 1862; **Lafayette*, 23 Oct 1862; **Crenshaw*, 26 Oct 1862; **Lauraetta*, 28 Oct 1862; *Baron de Custine*, 29 Oct 1862; **Levi Starbuck*, 2 Nov 1862; **Thomas B. Wales*, 8 Nov 1862; **Clara L. Sparks*, 21 Nov 1862; **Parker Cook*, 30 Nov 1862; *Nina*, *Union*, 5 Dec 1862; str *Ariel*, 7 Dec 1862; **Golden Rule*, 26 Jan 1863; **Chastelaine*, 27 Jan 1863; **Palmetto*, 3 Feb 1863; **Golden Eagle*, **Olive Jane*, 21 Feb 1863; *Washington*, 27 Feb 1863; *Bethia Thayer*, 1 Mar 1863; **John A. Parks*, 2 Mar 1863; *Punjab*, 15 Mar 1863; *Morning Star*, **Kingfisher*, 23 Mar 1863; *Charles Hill*, **Nora*, 25 Mar 1863; **Louisa Hatch*, 4 Apr 1863; **Kate Cory*, **Lafayette*, 15 Apr 1863; **Nye*, 24 Apr 1863; str **Dorcas Prince*, 26 Apr 1863; **Sea Lark*, **Union Jack*, 3 May 1863; *Justina*, *Gildersleeve*, 25 May 1863; **Jabez Snow*, 29 May 1863; **Amazonian*, 2 Jun 1863; **Talisman*, 5 Jun 1863; *Conrad*, 20 Jun 1863; **Anna F. Schmidt*, 2 Jul 1863; **Express*, 6 Jul 1863; *Sea Bride*, 5 Aug 1863; *Martha Wenzell*, 9 Aug 1863; **Amanda*, 6 Nov 1863; **Winged Racer*, 10 Nov 1863; **Contest*, 1 Nov 1863; **Harriet Spalding*, 18 Nov 1863; *Texas Star*, 24 Dec 1863; **Highlander*, **Sonora*, 26 Dec 1863; **Emma Jane*, 14 Jan 1864; **Rockingham*, 23 Apr 1863; **Tycoon*, 27 Apr 1864.

Alexandra

Name	Builder	Launched	Comm.
Alexandra	Liverpool, England (Miller)	7 Mar 1863	never

Tonnage	124 tons (300 tons?)
Dimension	230' × (U), also reported as 125' × 22' × 9'
Machinery	1 screw, 10 knots (Fawcett)
Complement	(U)
Armament	None

Notes: Bark rigged wooden steamer. Seized by British government in Apr 1863 and not released until May 1864. Sailed as merchant *Mary* but detained at Nassau until the end of the war.

Chickamauga

Name	Builder	Launched	Comm.
Chickamauga	London, England (Dudgeon)	1863	Sep 1864
ex-*Edith*			

Tonnage	585 tons (U), 370 GRT
Dimensions	175' × 25' × 7'9", d15'
Machinery	2 screws, 2 2-cyl. engines (34" × 1'9"), IHP 894, 13.4 knots
Armament	1–84pdr, 2–32pdr, 2–24pdr

Notes: Former blockade runner *Edith* (nine successful runs) purchased at Wilmington 1864. Unsuitable as a raider. Iron hull, two funnels, two masts.

Service record: Cruised in North Atlantic, Oct–Nov 1864, taking several prizes. Burned to prevent capture at Fayetteville, N.C., 25 Feb 1865.

Ships captured: *Albion Lincoln*, 29 Oct 1864; *M.L. Potter*, 30 Oct 1864; **Emily L. Hall*, **Shooting Star*, 31 Oct 1864; **Goodspeed*, **Otter Rock*, 1 Nov 1864; *Speedwell*, 2 Nov 1864.

Fig 10.1: The celebrated Confederate raider *Alabama* at Singapore in December 1863. This is the first photograph of this famous ship to have been discovered. (Tennessee State Library and Archives)

Florida

Name	Builder	Launched	Comm.
Florida	Liverpool, England (Miller)	Jan 1862	17 Aug 1862
ex-*Oreto*			
Tonnage	410 GRT		
Dimensions	191′ × 27′3″ × 13′		
Machinery	1 screw, 2 horizontal direct-acting engines (42″ × 2′), 9.5 knots (12 under sail) (Fawcett)		
Complement	(U)		
Armament	6–6″ MLR, 2–7″ MLR, 1–12pdrH		

Notes: Sloop rig, two funnels. Designed after British gunboats. Contracted by Bulloch. Supposedly built for Italy. Commissioned in the Bahamas. Intended name *Manassas*. Took 37 prizes.

Service record: Comm at Green Cay, Bahamas. Made celebrated dash through Federal blockade to Mobile, 4 Sep 1862, sailed 16 Jan 1863. Cruised North Atlantic, 1863. Laid up at Brest, France, Aug 1863–Feb 1864. Attacked by USS *Wachusett* and taken as prize while anchored at Bahia, Brazil, 7 Oct 1864, and towed out to sea—a breach of Brazilian neutrality. Sunk in collision with transport *Alliance* at Newport News, Va., 28 Nov 1864.

Ships captured: **Estelle*, 19 Jan 1863; **Corris Ann*, **Windward*, 22 Jan 1863; **Jacob Bell*, 12 Feb 1863; **Star of Peace*, 6 Mar 1863; **Aldebaran*, 13 Mar 1863; *Lapwing*, 28 Mar 1863; **M.J. Colcord*, 30 Mar 1863; **Commonwealth*, 17 Apr 1863; **Henrietta*, 23 Apr 1863; **Oneida*, 24 Apr 1863; *Clarence*, 6 May 1863; **Crown Point*, 13 May 1863; **Southern Cross*, 6 Jun 1863; *Red Gauntlet*, 14 Jun 1863; **B.F. Hoxie*, 16 Jun 1863; *Varnum H. Hill*, 27 Jun 1863; *Sunrise*, 7 Jul 1863; **Wm. B. Nash*, **Rienzi*, 8 Jul 1863; *Francis B. Cutting*, 6 Aug 1863; **Anglo-Saxon*, 21 Aug 1863; **Avon*, 29 Mar 1864; **George Latimer*, 18 May 1864; *Zelinda*, 10 Jun 1864; **W.C. Clark*, 17 Jun 1864; **Harriet Stevens*, 1 Jul 1864; **Golconda*, 8 Jul 1864; **Margaret Y. Davis*, **Greenland*, 9 Jul 1864, **Gen. Berry*, **Zelinda*, str **Electric Spark*, 10 Jul 1864; **Mondamin*, 26 Sep 1864.

Fig 10.2: The cruiser *Florida* seen at Brest, France, was one of the Confederate raiders built in England. She destroyed many Yankee ships at sea until her capture in the harbor of Bahia, Brazil, by Cdr. Napoleon Collins in USS *Wachusett*, October 7, 1864. (U.S. Naval Historical Center)

Georgia

Name	Builder	Launched	Comm.
Georgia	Dumbarton, Scotland (W. Denny)	9 Jan 1863	9 Apr 1863

ex-*Japan*, ex-*Virginian*

Tonnage	690 tons, 1150 tons D, 648 GRT
Dimensions	212' × 27' × 13'9", also reported as 206.2' × 27.2' × 14.7'
Machinery	1 screw, 2 steeple condensing engines (49" × 3'9"), IHP 900, 13 knots
Complement	(U)
Armament	2–100pdr MLR, 2–24pdr SB, 1–32pdr MLR

Notes: Wood hull on iron frame, single funnel, brig rig. Purchased Mar 1863.
Service record: Met steamer *Alar* off Ushant to take on guns and stores, Apr 1863. Comm at sea 9 Apr 1863. Captured nine prizes in Atlantic, 1863. Arrived at Cherbourg, France, 28 Oct 1863 and decomm. Sold 1 Jun 1864 at Liverpool as commercial vessel. Taken at sea by USS *Niagara* off Portugal, 15 Aug 1864 and condemned as a prize.
Ships captured: *Dictator*, 25 Apr 1863; *George Griswold*, 8 Jun 1863; *Good Hope*, 12 Jun 1863; *J.W. Seaver*, 14 Jun 1863; *Constitution*, 25 Jun 1863; *City of Bath*, 28 Jun 1863; *Prince of Wales*, 16 Jul 1863; *John Watts*, 30 Aug 1863; *Bold Hunter* 9 Oct 1863.
Later history: Merchant *Georgia* 1865. Sold to the Canadian flag, 1870. Stranded off Tenant's Harbor, Me., 14 Jan 1875.

Georgiana

Name	Builder	Launched	Comm.
Georgiana	Glasgow, Scotland (Lawrie)	1 Dec 1862	(see below)

Tonnage	519 tons GRT
Dimensions	205'6" × 25'3" × 14'9"
Machinery	1 screw, IHP 120
Complement	140
Armament	(U)

Notes: Brig rig, iron hull. Clipper bow, two masts.
Service record: Sailed to Charleston for outfitting as a cruiser. Damaged by gunfire of USS *Wissahickon*; beached and abandoned on fire off Charleston, 19 Mar 1863.

Nashville

Name	Builder	Launched	Comm.
Nashville	New York, N.Y. (Collyer)	22 Sep 1853	1 Oct 1861

Tonnage	1,221 tons
Dimensions	215'6" × 34'6" × d21'9"
Machinery	Side wheels, 1 side lever engine (85" × 8'), 2 boilers (Novelty)
Armament	2–12pdr

Notes: Brig rigged passenger steamer, seized at Charleston and fitted as a cruiser 1861. One funnel, two masts.
Service record: Cruised to British waters, Nov 1861–Feb 1862, taking two prizes. Escaped from Beaufort, N.C., 17 Mar 1862. Sold as a blockade runner 1862, renamed *Thomas L. Wragg*. Comm 5 Nov 1862 as privateer **Rattlesnake**. Destroyed in Ogeechee River by USS *Montauk*, 28 Feb 1863.
Ships captured: *Harvey Birch*, 19 Nov 1861; *Robert Gilfillan*, 26 Feb 1862.

Rappahannock

Name	Builder	Launched	Comm.
Rappahannock	London, England (Mare)	24 Nov 1855	Nov 1863

ex-HMS *Victor*

Tonnage	1,042 tons
Dimensions	201' (bp) × 30'3" × 14'6"
Machinery	1 screw, 2 reciprocating engines, NHP 350, IHP 1000, 11 knots
Complement	100
Armament	2–9" MLR

Notes: Former British corvette, purchased Nov 1863 in Great Britain as a replacement for *Georgia*. Three-mast schooner rig, two funnels. Cover name *Scylla*. Escaped to Calais for repairs but detained there by the French government, Feb 1864. Decomm Aug 1864.

Shenandoah

Name	Builder	Launched	Comm.
Shenandoah	Glasgow, Scotland (Stephen)	17 Aug 1863	19 Oct 1864

ex-*Sea King*

Tonnage	1,160 tons (1018 GRT)
Dimensions	230' × 32' × 20'6"; also reported as 220' × 36' × 20'
Machinery	1 screw, direct-acting engines (33" × 4'), 2 boilers, 9 knots
Complement	73
Armament	4–8" SB, 2–32pdr MLR, 2–12pdr SB

Notes: Composite auxiliary screw steamship, first in the world, designed for transporting troops to East India. Purchased Sep 1864, comm at sea under Lt.

Fig 10.3: The cruiser *Shenandoah* hauled out at Williamstown Dockyard, Sydney, Australia, in February 1865. Under Maffitt she destroyed the American whaling fleet off Alaska. (U.S. Naval Historical Center)

Cdr. James L. Maffitt. Took 38 prizes mostly after the close of hostilities, in the Bering Sea.

Service record: Comm off Funchal, Madeira Is., after meeting steamer *Laurel* and receiving crew, guns, and ammunition, Oct 1864. Captured six prizes in South Atlantic, 1864. Arrived Melbourne, Australia, 25 Jan 1865. Cruised whaling grounds in Pacific and off Alaska, 1865, taking 21 prizes. Learned of war's end in Aug 1865 and surrendered to the British at Liverpool, 5 Nov 1865.

Ships captured: *Alina*, 30 Oct 1864; *Charter Oak*, 5 Nov 1864; *D. Godfrey*, 8 Nov 1864; *Susan*, 10 Nov 1864; Kate Prince, Adelaide, 12 Nov 1864; *Lizzie M. Stacey*, 13 Nov 1864; *Edward*, 4 Dec 1864; *Delphine*, 29 Dec 1864; *Edward Cary*, *Harvest*, *Hector*, *Pearl*, 1 Apr 1865; *Abigail*, 27 May 1865; *Euphrates*, *William Thompson*, Milo, 22 Jun 1865; *Jerah Swift*, *Sophia Thornton*, *Susan Abigail*, 24 Jun 1865; *General Williams*, 23 Jun 1865; *Catharine*, Gen. Pike, *William C. Nye*, *Gipsey*, *Isabella*, *Nimrod*, 26 Jun 1865; *Brunswick*, *Congress*, *Covington*, *Favorite*, *Hillman*, *Isaac Howland*, James Murray, *Martha*, *Nassau*, Nile, *Waverly*, 28 Jun 1865.

Later history: Sold 1866 to Sultan of Zanzibar, renamed *El Majidi*. Lost in hurricane off Zanzibar, 15 Apr 1872.

Sumter

Name	Builder	Launched	Comm.
Sumter	Philadelphia, Pa. (Vaughn & Lynn)	12 Dec 1857	Jun 1861

ex-*Habana*

Tonnage	437 tons
Dimensions	184' × 30' × 12'
Machinery	1 screw, 1 vertical direct-acting engine (34" × 1'9"), 10 knots (Merrick)
Complement	(U)
Armament	1–8", 4–32pdr

Notes: Bark rig. Purchased Apr 1861 and converted to a cruiser at New Orleans. Operated out of New Orleans before the war.

Service record: Cruised West Indies (under Captain Semmes), captured 18 prizes, 1861. Laid up and disarmed at Gibraltar. Sold Dec 1862.

Ships captured: *Golden Rocket*, 3 Jul 1861; Cuba, Machias, 4 Jul 1861; Albert

Adams, Ben Dunning, 5 Jul 1861; *Lewis Kilham, Naiad, West Wind,* 6 Jul 1861; *Abbie Bradford,* 25 Jul 1861; *Joseph Maxwell,* 27 Jul 1861; **Joseph Park,* 25 Sep 1861; **Daniel Trowbridge,* 27 Oct 1861; *Montmorency,* 25 Nov 1861; **Arcade,* 26 Nov 1861; **Vigilant,* 3 Dec 1861; **Ebenezer Dodge.,* 8 Dec 1861; *Investigator, *Neapolitan.,* 18 Jan 1862.

Later history: Blockade runner *Gibraltar* 1863. Last known at Liverpool Jul 1864.

Tallahassee

Name	Builder	Launched	Comm.
Tallahassee	London, England (Dudgeon)	1863	Jul 1864
ex-*Atalanta*			
Tonnage	546 tons D, 418 GRT		
Dimensions	250' × 23'6" × 13'4"		
Machinery	2 screws, 2 2-cyl. engines (34" × 1'9"), IHP 1220, 14 knots		
Complement	120		
Armament	1–84pdr, 2–24pdr, 2–32pdr		

Notes: Fast cross-Channel steamer *Atalanta* used as a blockade runner; purchased 1864. Iron hull.

Service record: Sailed from Wilmington, N.C., cruised in North Atlantic, Aug 1864. Renamed **Olustee**. Damaged while running Federal blockade, 29 Oct 1864. Disarmed and renamed **Chameleon**, again ran blockade, 24 Dec 1864. Unable to return to Confederate port, sailed to Liverpool, Apr 1865 and was sold.

Ships captured: **A. Richards, *Bay State, *Carrie Estelle, Carroll, *James Funk, *Sarah A. Boyce, *William Bell,* 11 Aug 1864; **Adriatic, *Atlantic, Billow, Goodspeed, *Suliote, *Spokane,* 12 Aug 1864; **Lamont Dupont, *Glenavon,* 13 Aug 1864; **James Littlefield, J.H. Hoven,* 14 Aug 1864; **Floral Wreath, *Etta Caroline, *Howard, *Mary A. Howes, Sarah B. Harris,* 15 Aug 1864; **P.C. Alexander, *Leopard, *Magnolia, *Pearl, *Sarah Louise,* 16 Aug 1864; **Josiah Achorn, Neva, *North America,* 17 Aug 1864; *Rowan,* 20 Aug 1864; *Restless,* 23 Aug 1864. As **Olustee**: **Empress Theresa,* 1 Nov 1864; **A.J. Bird, *Arcole, *E.F. Lewis, *T.D. Wagner, *Vapor,* 3 Nov 1864.

Later history: British merchant *Amelia,* 1866. Renamed *Haya Maru* (British or German flag) 1867. Struck a rock and sank between Kobe and Yokohama, 17 Jun 1869.

Texas

Name	Builder	Launched	Comm.
Texas	Glasgow, Scotland (Thomson)	29 Oct 1863	Never
ex-*Pampero*			
Tonnage	2,090 tons D, 1,000 tons		
Dimensions	230' × 32' × 20'; also reported as 220'6" × 33'2" × 19'8"		
Machinery	1 screw, 2-cyl. horizontal back-acting (56' × 2'6") (Greenock Foundry), 4 boilers, NHP 330, 13 knots		
Armament	Never armed		

Notes: Composite hull, lifting screw, bark rig. Never sailed for CSN. Cover name *Canton*. Seized by British government 10 Dec 1863.

Later history: Sold to Chile 1866. Seized at sea by Spanish frigate *Gerona,* 22 Aug 1866; comm in Spanish Navy as *Tornado*. Captured filibuster *Virginius,* 1873. Stricken 1896, BU after 1939.

Fig 10.4: The cruiser *Tallahassee* at Halifax, August 18, 1864. Notice the guns aft. She survived the war to resume her merchant career until lost off Japan in 1869. (Collection of the Maritime Museum of the Atlantic, Halifax, N.S., Canada)

Ajax Class

Name	Builder	Launched	Comm.
Ajax	Dumbarton, Scotland (Denny)	15 Dec 1864	Never
Hercules	Dumbarton, Scotland (Denny)	29 Dec 1864	Never
Tonnage	515 tons B, 341 GRT		
Dimensions	176' × 25' × 7'6"		
Machinery	2 screws, 2 horizontal back-acting engines (28" × 1'6"), IHP 525, 12 knots		
Armament	1–9" MLR, 1–8" MLR (intended)		

Notes: Ordered by Bulloch 1864. Completed too late for CSN service. Were to be converted at Wilmington, N.C. Brigantine rig.

Service records:

Ajax: Was to be named **Olustee**. Sailed for Wilmington, N.C., 12 Jan 1865, but returned to Britain.

Hercules: Was to be named **Vicksburg**.

Later history: Both probably sold to Argentine Navy.

Adventure Class

Name	Builder	Launched
Adventure	Dumbarton, Scotland (Denny)	1865
Enterprise	Dumbarton, Scotland (Denny)	1865
Tonnage	972 tons, 1,600 tons D, 776 GRT	
Dimensions	250' × 30' × 12'; also reported as 258'4" (bp) × 30'6" × d16'	
Machinery	2 screws. 2 horizontal direct-acting engines (42" × 1'9"), IHP 1175, 14 knots	
Armament	(U)	

Notes: Iron hulls, bark rig. Ordered by Captain Bulloch, 1863. Cover names *Tientsin* and *Yangtze,* respectively.

Later histories:

Fig 10.5: The steamer *Hercules* was built in England to become a Confederate gunboat. Her later history is a matter of conjecture. (Huntington Library, San Marino, Calif.)

Fig 10.6: The Peruvian corvette *Union* was built for Confederate Navy in France and would have been named *Texas*. (U.S. Naval Historical Center)

Adventure: Completed as *Amazonas*. Sold to Argentina 1866 as gunboat, renamed *General Brown*. Renamed *Chacabuco*, 1884; school ship. Hulked 1893. BU 1910.

Enterprise: Completed as *Brasil*. Sold to Brazil 1866 as transport, probably renamed *Leopoldina*. Decomm 1877.

Louisiana Class

Name	Builder	Launched
Louisiana ex-*Osacca*	Bordeaux, France (Arman)	May 1864
Mississippi ex-*Yeddo*	Bordeaux, France (Arman)	1864
Texas ex-*San Francisco*	Nantes, France (Jollet)	1864
Georgia ex-*Shanghai*	Nantes, France (Dubigeon)	1864
Tonnage	1,827 tons D	
Dimensions	243′ × 35′6″ × 18′ (*Texas*, as *Union*); in Prussian service: 267′ (oa) 246′8″ (bp) × 36′6″ × 18′	
Machinery	1 screw, single expansion, 4 boilers, IHP 1300, 13.5 knots. (Mazeline)	
Complement	230	
Armament	14–30pdr MLR	

Notes: Ordered by Captain Bulloch in Apr 1863 but embargoed by French government, Feb 1864. Later sold by builders to Prussian and Peruvian Navies.

Later histories:

Louisiana: Prussian *Victoria*, May 1864. BU 1892.

Mississippi: Prussian *Augusta*, May 1864. Foundered with all hands in hurricane in Gulf of Aden, 2 Jun 1885.

Texas: Peruvian *Union*. Scuttled to prevent capture by Chilean forces at Callao, Jan 1881.

Georgia: Peruvian *America*. Wrecked in tidal wave at Arica, 13 Aug 1868.

In addition to the above, four *Alabama*-class cruisers were begun at McIntosh Bluff, Ala.

SAILING VESSELS

Name	Builder	Launched	Comm.
Clarence ex-*Coquette*	Baltimore, Md.	1857	6 May 1863
Tonnage	253 tons B		
Dimensions	114′ × 24′ × 11′		
Rig	Brig		
Armament	1–12pdrH		

Notes: Captured at sea by CSS *Florida* en route to Baltimore, 6 May 1863, and armed as a raider.

Service record: Burned at sea 12 Jun 1863, crew transferred to *Tacony*.

Ships captured: **Whistling Wind*, 6 Jun 1863; *Alfred H. Partridge*, 7 Jun 1863; **Mary Alvina*, 9 Jun 1863; *Kate Stewart*, **Mary Schindler*, *Tacony*, 12 Jun 1863.

Name	Builder	Launched	Comm.
Tacony	Newcastle, Del.	1856	12 Jun 1863
Tonnage	296 tons B.		
Dimensions	(U)		
Rig	Bark		
Armament	1–12pdrH		

Notes: Captured at sea by CSS *Clarence*, whose commander transferred his crew to this vessel, 12 Jun 1863. Also called *Florida No. 2*.

Service record: Captured 15 vessels while cruising off New England coast. Burned to prevent capture, 25 Jun 1863; crew transferred to prize *Archer*.

Ships captured: **Arabella*, 12 Jun 1863; **Umpire*, 14 Jun 1863; *Isaac Webb*, **L.A. Micawber*, 20 Jun 1863; **Byzantium*, **Goodspeed*, 21 Jun 1863; **Elizabeth Ann*, *Florence*, **Marengo*, **Ripple*, **Rufus Choate*, 22 Jun 1863; **Ada*, **Wanderer*, 23 Jun 1863; *Archer*, *Shatemac*, 24 Jun 1863.

Name	Builder	Launched	Comm.
Tuscaloosa ex-*Conrad*	Philadelphia, Pa.	1850	20 Jun 1863
Tonnage	500 tons		
Dimensions	(U)		
Rig	Bark		
Armament	3–12pdr		

Notes: American bark *Conrad* captured off Brazil by CSS *Alabama*, 20 Jun 1863 and commissioned at sea as a cruiser.

Service record: Cruised in South Atlantic 1863, taking several prizes. Seized at Capetown by British authorities 26 Dec 1863 as an uncondemned prize.

Ships captured: *Santee*, 31 Jul 1863; *Living Age*, 13 Sep 1863.

GUNBOATS

Chattahoochee Class

Name	Builder	Laid down	Launched	Comm.
Chattahoochee	Saffold, Ga. (Johnston)	Dec 1861	1862	1 Jan 1863
(Unnamed)	Elizabeth City, N.C. (Martin & Elliott)	1861	Never	Never

Tonnage	(U)
Dimensions	130' (bp) × 30' × 7'3", d10'; also reported as 150' × 25' × 8'
Machinery	2 screws. 2 horizontal direct-acting LP engines (28" × 1'8"), 12 knots
Complement	120
Armament	4–32pdr SB, 1–32pdr MLR, 1–9" SB

Notes: Designed by J.L. Porter. Three-mast schooner rig.

Service records

Chattahoochee: Georgia coast. Sunk by boiler explosion at Blountstown, Fla., 27 May 1863 (18 killed). Raised and repaired at Columbus, Ga. Destroyed to prevent capture in Apalachicola River, Fla., Dec 1864.

(Unnamed): Destroyed incomplete to prevent capture.

Macon Class

Name	Builder	Laid down	Launched	Comm.
Macon	Savannah, Ga. (Willink)	1861	1863	3 Aug 1864
ex-*Ogeechee* (Jun 1864)				
Peedee	Peedee (S.C.) NYd	(U)	1862	20 Apr 1864

Tonnage	(U)
Dimensions	*Macon*: 150' × 25' × d10'
Peedee	170' × 26' × d10'
Machinery	10 knots
Complement	91
Armament	*Macon*: 6 guns. *Peedee*: 1–7"R, 1–6.4"R, 1–9" SB

Notes: Seven of this class ordered.

Service records:

Macon: Defense of Savannah. Surrendered at Augusta, Ga., May 1865. FFU

Peedee: Destroyed to prevent capture in the Peedee River above Georgetown, S. C., 18 Feb 1865.

Hampton Class

Name	Builder	Laid down	Launched	Comm.
Hampton	Norfolk NYd	(U)	1862	(U)
Nansemond	Norfolk NYd	(U)	1862	May 1862

Tonnage	(U)
Dimensions	116' × 18' × 8'
Machinery	1 screw, 2 engines
Complement	(U)
Armament	(U)

Notes: Designed by Porter.

Service records:

Hampton: James River. Action at Trent's Reach, Va., 21 Jun 1864. Action at Dutch Gap, Va., 13 Aug 1864; Action against Ft. Harrison, Va., 29 Sep–1 Oct 1864. Engagement at Chapin's Bluff, Va., 22 Oct 1864. Burned to prevent capture on evacuation of Richmond, 3 Apr 1865.

Nansemond: James River. Action at Trent's Reach, Va., 21 Jun 1864. Action at Dutch Gap, Va., 13 Aug 1864. Action against Ft. Harrison, 29 Sep–1 Oct 1864. Burned to prevent capture on evacuation of Richmond, 3 Apr 1865.

"Maury Gunboats"

Name	Builder	Laid down	Launched	Comm.
Norfolk	Norfolk NYd	1861	Never	Never
Portsmouth	Norfolk NYd	1861	Never	Never
Escambia	Norfolk NYd	1861	Never	Never
Elizabeth	Norfolk NYd	1861	Never	Never
Yadkin	Norfolk NYd	1861	Never	Never

Tonnage	166 tons
Dimensions	106' × 21' × 5'd 8'dpth
Machinery	2 screws
Armament	1–9" SB, 1–32pdr

Notes: Maury gunboats designed by Capt. Matthew Fontaine Maury. Wood hull. One hundred were planned, fifteen laid down in Virginia yards. Others, being built at Pensacola, Fla., Edwards Ferry, N.C., and Elizabeth City, N.C., were destroyed before naming or completion. *Isondiga* (see p. 180), *Torch* (see p. 178) and perhaps *Yadkin* (see p. 164) were commenced as units of this class.

Service records:

All Norfolk boats burned on ways to prevent capture, 10 May 1862.

Dixie Class

Name	Builder	Laid down	Launched	Comm.
Dixie	Norfolk NYd	1862	Never	Never
(Unnamed)	Norfolk NYd	1862	Never	Never
(Unnamed)	Portsmouth, Va (Graves & Nash)	1862	(U)	Never
(Unnamed)	Portsmouth, Va (Graves & Nash)	1862	(U)	Never

Tonnage	(U)
Dimensions	112' × 20' × 8'
Machinery	1 screw
Armament	(U)

Note: Similar to Maury gunboats with sail rig. First two destroyed on fall of Norfolk, 10 May 1862. One being built at Portsmouth, Va., became U.S. Army gunboat *General Jesup*. The second may have been towed to Richmond and completed as *Drewry* (see p. 184).

Gaines Class

Name	Builder	Laid down	Launched	Comm.
Gaines	Mobile, Ala. (Bassett)	Sep 1861	1862	1862
Morgan	Mobile, Ala. (Bassett)	Sep 1861	1862	early 1862

Tonnage	863 tons
Dimensions	202' × 38' × 7'3", d13' dr 13' dpth

Fig 10.7: The gunboat *Gaines*, from a contemporary drawing. Built at Mobile in 1962 with partial armor, she was sunk after the Battle of Mobile Bay. (U.S. Naval Historical Center)

Machinery	Side wheels, 2 noncondensing engines (23″ × 7′), 10 knots.
Armament	1–7″ MLR, 1–6″ MLR, 2–32pdr MLR, 2–32pdr SB

Notes: Built of unseasoned wood with partial 2″ iron plating.

Service record

Gaines: Run aground to prevent capture following Battle of Mobile Bay, 5 Aug 1864
Morgan: Battle of Mobile Bay, 5 Aug 1864. Damaged in engagement near Blakely, Ga., Apr 1865. Surrendered, 4 May 1865. Sold Dec 1865.

Later history: Merchant *Morgan* 1865. Lost, cause unknown, 10 Oct 1866.

Carondelet Class

Name	Builder	Laid down	Launched	Comm.
Bienville	Bayou St. John, La. (Hughes)	1861	Feb 1862	5 Apr 1862*
Carondelet	Bayou St. John, La. (Hughes)	1861	Jan 1862	16 Mar 1862
Tonnage	(U)			
Dimensions	196′ × 38′			
Machinery	Side wheels			
Armament	5–42pdr, 1–32pdr MLR			

Notes: *Bienville* delivered 5 Apr 1862.

Service record

Bienville: Destroyed to prevent capture prior to completion in Lake Pontchartrain, La., 21 Apr 1862.
Carondelet: Engagement at Pass Christian, Miss., 4 Apr 1862. Destroyed to prevent capture in Lake Pontchartrain, La., 21 Apr 1862.

TORPEDO BOATS

Spar Torpedo Boats

Name	Builder	Laid down	Launched	Comm.
Torch	Charleston, S.C. (F.M. Jones)	1863	Summer 1863	1863
Tonnage	(U)			
Dimensions	About 150′ long			
Machinery	Screw			

Complement	11
Armament	Triple spar torpedo

Notes: Ironclad. Not fully completed because of lack of armor. Machinery unreliable. May have been begun as a Maury gunboat.

Service record: Defense of Charleston. Attacked USS *New Ironsides* off Charleston, 10 Aug 1863. Immobilized thereafter. Taken to Washington NYd, 1865.

Name	Builder	Laid down	Launched	Comm.
David	Charleston, S.C.	1863	1863	1863
Dimensions	48′6″ (oa) × 6′ × 5′			
Complement	4			
Armament	1 spar torpedo			

Notes: Built by Theodore Stoney, designed by F.D. Lee. Cigar shape. Four more were built at Charleston, of which two were completed. Others of this type were under construction later in the war: two at Columbus (Ga.) NYd, two more at Charleston (Ferguson & Jones), two at Wilmington, N.C. (by the Army), five at Savannah (including one for Mobile), and one each at Houston, Tex., and Shreveport, La. None of these were completed.

Service record: Attacked USS *New Ironsides* off Charleston, 5 Oct 1863. Attacked USS *Memphis* in North Edisto River, 6 Mar 1864, and USS *Wabash* off Charleston, 18 Apr 1864. FFU.

Name	Builder	Laid down	Launched	Comm.
Viper	Columbus (Ga.) NYd	1864 31	31 Mar 1865	Never
Dimensions	50′ × 6′ × 4′6″			

Notes: Twelve of this type were ordered in 1864, including four at Richmond, two at Columbus, Ga, and one on Peedee River, S.C. Designed by Graves. Machinery ordered from abroad. Six sets of 2-cylinder engines were believed to have been on the blockade runner *Susan Beirne*, which was never able to reach her destination.

Name	Builder	Laid down	Launched	Comm.
Hornet	Richmond NYd	(U)	1864	(U)
Scorpion	Richmond NYd	(U)	1864	(U)
Squib	Richmond NYd	(U)	1864	(U)
Wasp	Richmond NYd	(U)	1864	(U)

Fig 10.8: A captured Confederate torpedo boat at Washington Navy Yard, alongside the monitor *Saugus* (with stripe on turret). (Paul H. Silverstone Collection)

Fig 10.9: The torpedo boat *David* aground at Charleston, 1865. Notice the long spar protruding from the bow. (National Archives)

Tonnage	(U)
Dimensions	46′ × 6′3″ × 6′9″ dpth; *Squib*: 30′ × 6′ × 3′
Machinery	1 screw, condensing engines. (7″ × 6″), 1 boiler
Armament	1–18′ spar torpedo

Notes: Wood hulls built at Richmond late 1864.

Service records

Hornet: Sank after collision with flag-of-truce steamer *Allison* in James River, 26 Jan 1865.
Scorpion: Damaged by ammunition explosion on CSS *Drewry* near Trent's Reach, Va., 24 Jan 1865. Captured by Federal forces or burned in James River, 24 Jan 1865.
Squib: Attacked USS *Minnesota* off Newport News, 7 Apr 1864. Sent by rail to Wilmington, N.C. FFU
Wasp: Served in James River 1864–65. FFU

Name	Builder	Laid down	Launched	Comm.
Midge	Charleston, S.C.	1864	1864	1864
Dimensions	30′ × 12′			

Notes: Similar to *David* type.

Later history: Taken to Brooklyn NYd and put on display Jun 1865. Sold 4 May 1877 and BU. In addition, the Navy instructed Captain Bulloch to order twelve torpedo boats to be built in England.

Names	Builder	Built
No.1, No.2, No.3, No.4, No.5, No.7, No.8	Charleston, S.C.	1864–65
Dimensions	50′ × 5′6″	

Notes: Screw propulsion. Captured at fall of Charleston, 1865.

Name	Builder	Built
No. 6	Charleston, S.C.	1864-65
Dimensions	160′ × 11′7″	

SUBMARINE TORPEDO BOATS

Name	Builder	Laid down	Launched	Comm.
Pioneer	New Orleans, La.	1861	1862	12 Mar 1862
Dimensions	34′ × 4′ × 4′			
Complement	2			

Notes: Designed by J.R. McClintock.

Service record: Comm as privateer 12 Mar 1862. Sunk to prevent capture in Bayou St. John, La. 1862. Now at Louisiana State Museum.

Fig 10.10: The torpedo boat *Midge* on display at Brooklyn Navy Yard during the 1870s.

Notes: Designed by J.R. McClintock and H.L. Hunley.

Service record: Swamped while attempting to attack Federal ships off Mobile, 14 Feb 1863.

Name	Builder	Laid down	Launched	Comm.
St. Patrick	Selma, Ala.	(U)	1864	(U)
Dimensions	50′ × 6′ × 10′			
Complement	6			

Notes: Built by J.P. Halligan. Transferred to CS Army under CSN command.

Service record: As a surface gunboat, attacked USS *Octorara* off Mobile, 28 Jan 1865. FFU.

Name	Builder	Laid down	Launched	Comm.
H.L. Hunley	Mobile, Ala. (Park & Lyons)	Spring 1863	1863	1863
Dimensions	40′ × 3′6″ × d4′			
Complement	9			

Notes: Designed by H.L. Hunley. Hand-cranked propeller. Ballast tanks could be filled or emptied. Mercury depth gauge.

Service record: Taken by rail to Charleston, Aug 1863. Foundered at her dock 29 Aug 1863 (5 killed). Raised and recomm. Failed to surface during test, 15 Oct 1863 (all 8 aboard lost); again raised and fitted with spar torpedo. Sank USS *Housatonic* off Charleston and apparently foundered returning to base, 17 Feb 1864 (9 lost). Wreck raised 9 Aug 2000 and put on display at Charleston.

11
AREA DEFENSE FORCES

LOUISIANA AREA

In addition to the following vessels, the ironclads *Manassas*, *Mississippi*, and *Louisiana* operated in the Louisiana area.

Mississippi River Defense Fleet

Fourteen vessels were purchased at New Orleans and armed by the Confederate War Dept to defend the Mississippi River. These were converted to cottonclad rams, protected by compressed cotton bales, with a ram of 4″ oak and 1″ iron. They were under command of CSN officers, but were not part of the Navy. Former identities of most of these are not known. Among ships seized at New Orleans in 1861, the following sidewheel steamers are otherwise unaccounted for and could be among those converted to cottonclads: *Anglo-American* (454 tons, built 1849 in New York), *A.J. Whitmore* (432 tons, built 1857 in New York), *James L. Day* (414 tons, built 1843 in New York), *James M. Whann* (417 tons, built 1859 in Shousetown, Pa.), and *St. Charles* (379 tons, built 1849 in Jeffersonville, Ind.). Also mentioned, otherwise not identified were *Defiance*, *Panther*, *J.P. Whitney* and *Texas*, These are mentioned in the reports of May 4, 1861 by John H. Loper, and June 27, 1861 by Commander W.W. Hunter and others.

Name	Builder	Launched	Acquired	Comm.
Colonel Lovell ex-*Hercules*	Cincinnati, Ohio	1845	1861	1861
Tonnage	521 tons, also reported as 371 tons			
Dimensions	162′ × 30′10″ × d11′			
Machinery	Side wheels			
Armament	4–8″ guns			

Service record: Engagement off Ft. Pillow, 10 May 1862. Rammed by USS *Queen of the West* and *Monarch* and sank off Memphis, 6 Jun 1862.

Name	Builder	Launched	Acquired	Comm.
Defiance	Cincinnati, Ohio	1849	End 1861	Mar 1862
Tonnage	544 tons			
Dimensions	178′ × 29′5″ × d10′11″			
Machinery	Side wheels, HP engines			
Complement	40			
Armament	1–32pdr			

Service record: Defense of New Orleans. Burned to prevent capture north of New Orleans, 28 Apr 1862.

Name	Builder	Launched	Acquired	Comm.
General Beauregard ex-*Ocean*	Algiers, La.	1847	5 Apr 1862	5 Apr 1862
Tonnage	454 tons			
Dimensions	161.8′ × 30′ × 10′			
Machinery	Side wheels			
Armament	4–8″, 1–42pdr			

Notes: Converted from towboat at New Orleans.
Service record: Engagement off Ft. Pillow, 10 May 1862. Hit by gunfire, exploded, and sank at Battle of Memphis, 6 Jun 1862.

Name	Builder	Launched	Acquired	Comm.
General Bragg ex-*Mexico*	New York, N.Y. (Westervelt)	1850	15 Jan 1862	25 Mar 1862

Service record: Damaged by ramming at engagement off Ft. Pillow, 10 May 1862. Captured after running aground at Battle of Memphis, 6 Jun 1862. Comm in USN as USS *General Bragg*. (See p. 119.)

Name	Builder	Launched	Acquired	Comm.
General Breckinridge	(U)	(U)	15 Jan 1862	22 Apr 1862
Tonnage	(U)			
Dimensions	(U)			
Machinery	Stern wheel			
Complement	35			
Armament	1–24pdr			

Service record: Defense of New Orleans. Burned to prevent capture below New Orleans, 24 Apr 1862.

Name	Builder	Launched	Acquired	Comm.
General Earl Van Dorn	(U)	(U)	1862	Mar 1862
Tonnage	(U)			
Dimensions	(U)			
Machinery	Side wheels			
Armament	1–32pdr			

Notes: May have been the former *Junius Beebe*; see *General Sumter*.
Service record: Mississippi River Defense Fleet. Engagement off Fort Pillow, 10 May 1862, sank USS *Mound City* by ramming. Engagement of 1 Jun 1862. Only survivor of Confederate force after Battle of Memphis, 6 Jun 1862. Burned to prevent capture at Yazoo City, Miss., 26 Jun 1862.

Name	Builder	Launched	Acquired	Comm.
General Lovell	(U)	(U)	1862	Apr 1862
Tonnage	(U)			
Dimensions	(U)			
Machinery	Side wheels			
Complement	50			
Armament	1–32pdr			

Notes: Former Mississippi tug converted to ram.
Service record: Burned to prevent capture below New Orleans, 24 Apr 1862.

Name	Builder	Launched	Acquired	Comm.
General M. Jeff Thompson	(U)	(U)	Jan 1862	11 Apr 1862
Tonnage	(U)			
Dimensions	(U)			
Machinery	Side wheels			
Armament	(U)			

Service record: Engagement off Ft. Pillow, 10 May 1862. Hit by gunfire, ran aground, and burned to water's edge; then exploded and sank during Battle of Memphis, 6 Jun 1862.

Name	Builder	Launched	Acquired	Comm.
General Sterling Price	Cincinnati, Ohio	1856	25 Jan 1862	1862

ex-*Laurent Millaudon*
Service record: Damaged by gunfire at engagement off Ft. Pillow, 10 May 1862. Damaged in collision with CSS *General Beauregard* during Battle of Memphis and later sank in shallow water, 6 Jun 1862. Salved and comm. in USN as USS *General Price*. (See p. 120.)

Name	Builder	Launched	Acquired	Comm.
General Sumter	Algiers, La.	1853	1861	1862

ex-*Junius Beebe*
Notes: River towboat converted to cottonclad with 4″ wood and 1″ iron ram. Some sources say *Junius Beebe* became *General Earl van Dorn*.
Service record: Defense of Ft. Pillow, 10 May 1862. Hit by gunfire, ran aground on Arkansas shore during Battle of Memphis, 6 Jun 1862. Refloated and comm. in USN as USS *Sumter*. (See p. 120.)

Name	Builder	Launched	Acquired	Comm.
Little Rebel	Belle Vernon, Pa.	1859	1861	1862

ex-*R. & J. Watson*
Notes: Also known as *R.E. & A.N. Watson*.
Service record: Engagement off Ft. Pillow (flagship), 10 May 1862. Beached after being damaged at Battle of Memphis, 6 Jun 1862. Comm in USN as USS *Little Rebel*. (See p. 131.)

Name	Builder	Launched	Acquired	Comm.
Resolute	(U)	(U)	25 Jan 1862	31 Mar 1862
Tonnage	(U)			
Dimensions	(U)			
Machinery	Side wheels			
Complement	40			
Armament	2–32pdr MLR, 1–32pdr SB			

Notes: Former tugboat
Service record: Run ashore by crew and abandoned during engagement at Ft. Jackson, La., 24 Apr and burned to prevent capture, 26 Apr 1862.

Name	Builder	Launched	Acquired	Comm.
Stonewall Jackson	(U)	(U)	16 Mar 1862	1862
Tonnage	(U)			
Dimensions	(U)			
Machinery	Side wheels			
Complement	30			
Armament	1–32pdr or 1–24pdr SB			

Service record: Rammed and sank USS *Varuna* during engagement below New Orleans, then run aground in sinking condition and burned, 24 Apr 1862.

Name	Builder	Launched	Acquired	Comm.
Warrior	(U)	(U)	16 Mar 1862	1862
Tonnage	(U)			
Dimensions	(U)			
Machinery	Side wheels			
Complement	40			
Armament	1–32pdr			

Service record: Damaged by gunfire of USS *Brooklyn*; driven ashore and burned during action below New Orleans, 24 Apr 1862.

Fig. 11.1: The cottonclad *Stonewall Jackson* was a unit of the Mississippi River Defense Fleet, which sank the USS *Varuna* below New Orleans, April 24, 1862, then was destroyed herself.

Gunboats

Name	Builder	Launched	Acquired	Comm.
A.B. Seger	(U)	(U)	1861	1861

Tonnage	30 tons
Dimensions	55' × (U)
Machinery	Side wheels, 2 locomotive engines
Armament	2 guns

Note: Gunboat and dispatch vessel in Berwick Bay.

Service record: Ran aground and abandoned in Berwick Bay, Atchafalaya River, 1 Nov 1862. Placed in Union service.

Name	Builder	Launched	Acquired	Comm.
Anglo-Norman	Algiers, La.	1850	15 Jan 1862	1862

Tonnage	558 tons
Dimensions	176'2" × 29'5" × 9'
Machinery	Side wheels
Complement	35
Armament	1–32pdr

Notes: Towboat seized at New Orleans, Jan 1862.

Service record: Burned at New Orleans, 7 Apr 1862.

Name	Builder	Launched	Acquired	Comm.
Anglo-Saxon	New York, N.Y. (Collyer)	1848	15 Jan 1862	1862

Tonnage	508 tons
Dimensions	120'3" × 28' × d11'
Machinery	Side wheels
Armament	(U)

Notes: Seized at New Orleans, Jan 1862

Service record: Defense of New Orleans. Caught fire and drifted downstream in sinking condition at defense of New Orleans forts, 24 Apr 1862. Later U.S. transport.

Name	Builder	Launched	Acquired	Comm.
Arrow	(U)	(U)	Spring 1861	1861

Tonnage	(U)
Dimensions	(U)
Machinery	Screw
Armament	1–32pdr

Notes: Seized 1861 and converted to gunboat.

Service record: Defense of New Orleans. Burned to prevent capture in West Pearl River after capture of New Orleans, 4 Jun 1862.

Name	Builder	Launched	Acquired	Comm.
Barataria	Barataria, La.	1857	(U)	(U)

Notes: Lytle* lists a vessel of this name built at Barataria, La., 1857. Little known about this vessel; believed to have been ironclad. Often spelled *Barrataria*.

Service record: Captured at New Orleans by U.S. Army, Apr 1862. Comm in USN as USS *Barataria*. 1 Jan 1863 (See p. 69.)

---

* See *Merchant Steam Vessels of the United States, 1790-1868: The Lytle-Holdcamper List*, edited by B. Mitchell (Staten Island, NY: Steamship Historical Society of America, 1975.

Name	Builder	Launched	Acquired	Comm.
Calhoun	New York, N.Y. (Sneeden)	1851	1861	15 May 1861

Notes: Built as *Cuba* but renamed before completion.

Service record: Comm as privateer, captured six prizes, 1861. Ran blockade two times. Attack on Federal sqn at Head of Passes, 12 Oct 1861. Captured by USS *Samuel Rotan* off South West Pass, La., 23 Jan 1862. Comm as USS *Calhoun*. (q.v.)

Ships captured: *John Adams, Mermaid*, May 1861; *Panama*, 29 May 1861.

Name	Builder	Launched	Acquired	Comm.
Diana ex-USS *Diana*	Brownsville, Pa.	1858	Apr 1863	Apr 1863

Tonnage	239 tons
Dimensions	(U)
Machinery	Side wheels

Notes: Ironclad, transport, disabled and captured at Bayou Teche, La., 28 Mar 1863. Previously seized by Union forces, 27 Apr 1862.

Service record: Attack on Federal troops at Bayou Teche, La., 11 Apr 1863. Severely damaged by gunfire, and burned to prevent capture at Franklin, La., 12 Apr 1863.

Name	Builder	Launched	Acquired	Comm.
Dollie Webb	Wheeling, Va.	1859	(U)	(U)

Tonnage	139 tons
Dimensions	125' × 27' × 4.5'
Machinery	Stern wheel
Armament	5 guns

Notes: Probably a converted towboat; little information exists. Reported burned at Algiers, La., 5 May 1861, but this must be an error or a different ship.

General Polk (See p. 187.)

Name	Builder	Launched	Acquired	Comm.
General Quitman (I) ex-*Galveston*	New York, N.Y. (Simonson)	1857	1862	1862

Tonnage	945 tons
Dimensions	230' (wl) × 37' × 6' or 233'3" × 34'3" × 9'
Machinery	Side wheels, vertical beam engine, 1 boiler (Allaire)
Complement	90
Armament	2–32pdr

Notes: Converted to cottonclad ram with iron ram. Two masts.

Service record: Defense of New Orleans. Burned to prevent capture below New Orleans, 24 Apr 1862.

Name	Builder	Launched	Acquired	Comm.
Governor Moore ex-*Charles Morgan*	New York, N.Y. (Westervelt)	1854	Jan 1862	1862

Tonnage	1,215 tons
Dimensions	220'2" × 34' × 15'6"
Machinery	Side wheels, 1 vertical beam engine (60" × 11'), 2 boilers (Morgan)
Complement	93
Armament	2–32pdr MLR

Notes: Cottonclad ram. Schooner rig.

Fig 11.2: The cottonclad gunboat *Governor Moore*, from a drawing by R.G. Skerrett, was sunk defending New Orleans in April 1862.

Service record: Sank USS *Varuna*, later burned after being severely damaged during Federal attack on the New Orleans forts, 24 Apr 1862 (64 killed).

Name	Builder	Launched	Acquired	Comm.
Ivy	Brooklyn, N.Y. (Burtis)	1845	1861	1861

ex-*V.H. Ivy*, ex-*El Paraguay*, ex-*Roger Williams*

Tonnage	447 tons B.
Dimensions	191' × 28' × d9'
Machinery	Side wheels, 1 vertical beam engine (44" × 11')
Complement	60
Armament	1–8" SB, 1–32pdr MLR, 2–24pdr brass H (as privateer)

Notes: Originally comm as a privateer, 16 May 1861.
Service record: Attack on Federal squadron at Head of Passes, 12 Oct 1861. Destroyed to prevent capture at Liverpool Landing, Yazoo River, Miss., May 1863.

Name	Builder	Launched	Comm.
J.A. Cotton	Jeffersonville, Ind.	1861	1862

Tonnage	549 tons
Dimensions	229' × 36' × 7'
Machinery	side wheels
Armament	1–32pdr SB, 1–9pdr MLR

Notes: Partially ironclad gunboat. Also spelled *J.A. Cotten*.
Service record: Engagement off Brashear City, Berwick Bay, La., 3 Nov 1862. Engagement off Brashear City, 13 Jan and burned to prevent capture, 15 Jan 1863.

Name	Builder	Launched	Acquired	Comm.
James L. Day	New York, N.Y. (Simonson)	1843	May 1861	1861

Tonnage	414 tons
Dimensions	187' × 25'6" × 6'
Machinery	Side wheels
Armament	(U)

Notes: Mississippi River towboat seized at New Orleans and converted to a gunboat.
Service record: Defense of New Orleans. Engagement at Head of Passes, 12 Oct 1861. FFU

Name	Builder	Launched	Acquired	Comm.
McRae	Philadelphia, Pa. (Cramp)	1852	17 Mar 1861	1861

ex-*Marquès de la Habana*, ex-*Carolina*

Tonnage	680 tons
Dimensions	188' × 30' × 11'
Machinery	1 screw, 2 vertical condensing engines (40" × 3') (Bldr)
Complement	119
Armament	1–9" SB, 6–32pdr SB, 1–6pdr MLR

Notes: Former Mexican rebel steamer *Marquès de la Habana* seized as a pirate by USS *Saratoga*, 7 Mar 1860, a seizure later declared illegal by a U.S. court. Bark rig, wood hull.

Fig 11.3: The gunboat *McRae* took part in the defense of New Orleans. As the *Marques de la Habana*, this ship was operated by Mexican rebel forces when captured by the USS *Saratoga* in 1860. (U.S. Naval Historical Center)

Service record: Defense of New Orleans. Attack on Federal squadron at Head of Passes, 12 Oct 1861. Severely damaged in action below New Orleans, 24 Apr 1862. Sank at New Orleans' wharf, 27 Apr 1862.

Name	Builder	Launched	Acquired	Comm.
Mobile	Philadelphia, Pa.	1860	Jul 1861	(U)

Tonnage	283 tons
Dimensions	(U)
Machinery	Side wheels (or screw)
Armament	3–32pdr SB, 1–32pdr MLR, 1–8″ SB

Notes: Wood hull, three masts. Identity and chronology of this ship subject to conjecture. Protection: 12″ timber and iron.
Service record: Ran blockade several times 1861–2. Engaged USS *Hatteras* in Atchafalaya Bay, La., 1 Feb 1862. Burned to prevent capture at Yazoo City, 21 May 1863.

Name	Builder	Launched	Acquired	Comm.
Memphis	(U)	(U)	1861	Feb 1862
New Orleans	(U)	(U)	1861	1862

Tonnage	(U)
Dimensions	(U)
Armament	17–8″ SB, 1–9″ SB, 2–32pdr MLR.

Notes: Similar floating batteries, converted from floating dry docks.
Service records
Memphis: Destroyed at capture of New Orleans, Apr 1862.
New Orleans: Defense of Island No. 10, sunk to avoid capture, 7 Apr 1862.

Name	Builder	Launched	Acquired	Comm.
Oregon	New York, N.Y. (Collyer)	1846	1861	1861

Tonnage	532 tons
Dimensions	216′10″ × 26′6″ × 9′6″
Machinery	Side wheels
Armament	1–8″, 1–32pdr, 2 how

Notes: Wood hull, one mast. Seized in 1861 for blockade running, then converted to gunboat.
Service record: Ran blockade many times 1861. Engaged USS *New London* at Pass Christian, Miss., 25 Mar 1862. Defense of New Orleans. Destroyed to prevent capture on evacuation of New Orleans, Apr 1862.

Name	Builder	Launched	Acquired	Comm.
Pamlico	New York, N.Y. (Englis)	Mar 1856	10 Jul 1861	2 Sep 1861

Tonnage	218 tons
Dimensions	(U)
Machinery	Side wheels
Armament	3–8″ SB, 1–6.4″R

Notes: Purchased at New Orleans.
Service record: Defense of New Orleans. Engaged Federal vessels off Horn Island, Miss., 4 Dec 1861. Engaged USS *New London* at Pass Christian, Miss., 25 Mar 1862. Burned to avoid capture in Lake Pontchartrain, 4 Apr 1862.

172 Civil War Navies, 1855-1883

Name	Builder	Launched	Acquired	Comm.
Tuscarora	(U)	(U)	1861	1861

Tonnage	(U)
Dimensions	(U)
Machinery	Side wheels.
Armament	1–32pdr MLR, 1–8″ columbiad

Notes: Purchased and converted at New Orleans.

Service record: Attack on Federal sqn at Head of Passes, 12 Oct 1861. Accidentally destroyed by fire near Helena, Ark., 23 Nov 1861.

Name	Builder	Launched	Acquired	Comm.
Webb	New York, N.Y. (Webb)	6 Sep 1856	17 May 1861	1862

ex-*William H. Webb*

Tonnage	655 tons B.
Dimensions	206′ ( ) 190′ (dk) 179′7″ (bp) × 32′ × 9′6″
Machinery	Side wheels, 2 vertical overhead beam engines (44″ × 10′), 2 boilers (Allaire)
Armament	1–130pdr MLR, 2–12pdr H

Notes: Wood hull. Issued privateer commission but used as a transport. Converted to cottonclad ram, January 1862.

Service record: Engaged USS *Indianola* near New Carthage, Miss., 24 Feb 1863. Ran blockade past Red River, 23 Apr and past New Orleans, but, pursued by Federal warships, was run ashore and burned to prevent capture south of New Orleans, 24 Apr 1865.

Transports and Other Steam Vessels (Louisiana Area)

Name	Builder	Launched	Acquired	Comm.
St. Philip	New York, N.Y. (Simonson)	17 Jun 1852	Apr 1861	1861

ex-*Star of the West*, ex-*San Juan*

Tonnage	1,172 tons
Dimensions	228′4″ × 32′8″ × d24′6″
Machinery	Side wheels, 2-cyl. vertical beam engine (66″ × 11′) (Allaire)
Armament	2–68pdr, 4–32pdr guns

Service record: Employed by Federal government to supply Ft. Sumter in Charleston harbor, Jan 1861. Captured by Confederate steamer *General Rusk* off Texas, 17 Apr 1861. Receiving ship, New Orleans, 1861–62. Taken up Mississippi and Yazoo River. Scuttled to obstruct channel of the Tallahatchie River, Mar 1863.

Name	Built at	Launched/Acquired	Tons	Dimensions	Type	Armament
Belle Algerine	Philadelphia, Pa.	1855	45	(U)	Screw	(U)
Boston	(U)	(U)	(U)	(U)	Screw	(U)
Dan	Calcasieu, La.	1858	112	(U)	S/w	(U)
Darby	(U)	(U)	(U)	(U)	(U)	(U)
Empire Parish	New Albany, Ind.	1859	279	170′ × 32′ × d6′2″	S/w	(U)
General Quitman (II)	New Albany, Ind.	1859	615	246′ × 36′ × 7′3″	S/w	(U)
Gossamer	Pittsburgh, Pa.	1863	144	122.5′ × 23.1′	St/W	
Hart	Paducah, Ky.	1860	175		S/w	
Landis	Cincinnati, Ohio	1853	377	190′ × 30′ × d9′	S/w	
ex-*Joseph Landis*						
Mosher	Philadelphia, Pa.	1857	45		Screw	None
ex-*C.A. Mosher*						
Music	Jeffersonville, Ind.	1857	330	175′ × 32′3″ × 6.2	S/w	2–6pdr
Orizaba	New York, N.Y. (Simonson)	1858	595	210′ × 30′ × 6′	S/w	
Phoenix					S/w	
Star	New Albany, Ind.	1840	250 (420 tons)		HP	Unarmed
Tennessee	New York, N.Y. (Robb)	1853	1,275			
Texas	New York, N.Y. (Westervelt)	1852	1,152		S/w	
W. Burton	New Albany, Ind.	1857	253	151′ × 25′ × 5′6″	S/w	Unarmed
ex-*William Burton*						

* *Types:* screw = screw propeller driven; st/w = sternwheel steamer; s/w = sidewheel steamer.

Notes and service records

Belle Algerine: Screw tug. Defense of New Orleans. Rammed and sunk by CSS *Governor Moore* as a hazard during engagement off Fort Jackson, 24 Apr 1862. Unfit for service and landed guns.

Boston: Screw tug. Former USN towboat captured at Pass à l'Outre, La., 8 Jun 1863. Reported fitted as privateer, possibly lengthened. May be the ship captured by USS *Fort Jackson* off Bermuda, 8 Jul 1864.

Dan: Captured by a launch from USS *Kensington* in Calcasieu River, La., Oct 1862. Sunk in Mississippi River while in Union service, Feb 1863.

Darby: Transport. Captured at Bayou Teche, La., 14 Apr 1863.

Empire Parish: Tow and dispatch boat. Captured at fall of New Orleans, Apr 1862 and burned there 28 May 1864.

General Quitman: Troop and supply ship on western rivers 1862–65.
    Later history: Sold 1865. Merchant *General Quitman*. Snagged and lost at New Texas Landing, La., 22 Oct 1868.

Gossamer: Transport in Bayou Teche, 1863. Burned at Franklin, La.
    Later history: Rebuilt after the war. Lost in Red River at Campti, La., 22 Sep 1869.

Hart: Name may have been *Ed R. Hart*. Transport in Bayou Teche and Berwick Bay, 1862–63. Sunk to avoid capture at Bayou Teche, La., 14 Apr 1863.

Landis: Acquired as tender to ironclad *Louisiana.* Defense of New Orleans. Damaged in engagement below New Orleans, 24 Apr 1862. Surrendered off Fort St. Philip, 28 Apr 1862.
  Later history: Used as tug and transport by U.S. Army 1862-65. FFU
Mosher: Tug. Sunk by gunfire from USS *Hartford* while towing fireboat during engagement below New Orleans, 24 Apr 1862.
Music: Two horizontal HP engines (20″ × 8′). Mississippi towboat, commissioned as a privateer. Later disarmed tender to Forts Jackson and St. Philip. Active in Atchafalaya and Red Rivers, 1863. FFU
Orizaba: Vertical beam engine, 1 boiler. Seized at Galveston, Tex., Sep 1861. Used as blockade runner, 1862–65.
  Later history: Lost by stranding at Liberty, Tex., 15 Jun 1865.

Phoenix: Sidewheel tug. Tender to CSS *Manassas.* Sunk during engagement below New Orleans, 24 Apr 1862.
Star: Steam tug. Sunk by Union gunboat during action below New Orleans, 24 Apr 1862.
Tennessee: Seized at New Orleans, Jan 1862, for use as blockade runner. Made one voyage. Captured at fall of New Orleans, 25 Apr 1862. Comm in USN as USS *Tennessee.* (q.v.)
Texas: Seized at New Orleans, Jan 1862.
W. Burton: Tender to CSS *Louisiana.* Damaged in engagement below New Orleans, 24 Apr 1862. Surrendered to U.S. Navy below New Orleans, 28 Apr 1862.
  Later history: Served with U.S. Army.

Armed Sailing Vessels (Louisiana Area)

Name	Builder	Launched	Acquired	Tons	Dimensions	Type	Armament
Corypheus	Brookhaven, N.Y.	1859	1861	81	72′ × 20′ × 6′	schr	
Morgan	(U)	1861	1861	(U)	(U)	schr	3 guns
ex-USRC *Morgan*							
Pickens	Somerset, Mass. (Hood)	11 Jun 1853	18 Feb 1861	153	100′ × 23′	schr	5 guns
ex-USRC *Robert McClelland*							
Washington	Baltimore	1837	1861	(U)	91′2″ × 22′1	Brig	1–42pdr
ex-USRC *Washington*							
William B. King	(U)	(U) 13 Jul 1861	13 Jul 1862	(U)	(U)	Schr	

Notes and service records
Corypheus: Operated in Lake Pontchartrain and Lake Borgne. Captured in Lake Pontchartrain by USS *Calhoun*, 13 May 1862. Comm in USN as USS *Corypheus.* (q.v.)
Morgan: U.S. Revenue Cutter seized 1861. FFU

Pickens: U.S. Revenue Cutter seized at New Orleans, 29 Jan 1861. Engagement at Head of Passes, La., 12 Oct 1861. FFU.
Washington: U.S. Revenue Cutter seized at New Orleans 1861.
William B. King: Schooner. Active service at Berwick, La., 1861

TEXAS AREA

Gunboats (Texas Area)

Name	Builder	Launched	Acquired	Comm.
Bayou City	Jeffersonville, Ind.	Aug 1859	26 Sep 1861	1861

Tonnage (U)
Dimensions 165′ × 28′ × 5′
Machinery Side wheels
Complement 135
Armament 1–32pdr

Notes: Operated by State of Texas as cottonclad gunboat until taken over by War Dept, Oct 1862.
Service record: Rammed and captured USS *Harriet Lane* at Battle of Galveston, 1 Jan 1863. FFU

Name	Builder	Launched	Acquired	Comm.
Clifton	New York, N.Y. (Simonson)	1861	8 Sep 1863	1863

ex-USS *Clifton*
Notes: Captured at Sabine Pass, Tex., 8 Sep 1863.
Service record: Went aground and burned to prevent capture off Sabine Pass while running blockade, 21 Mar 1864.

Name	Builder	Launched	Acquired	Comm.
Corpus Christi	(U)	(U)	(U)	1864

Notes: No design information available.
Service record: Operated in Texas in 1864.

Name	Builder	Launched	Acquired	Comm.
Diana	(U)	(U)	1862	1862

Complement 61
Armament 2–12pdr guns
Armor 1″ iron
Notes: Ram.
Service record: Defense of Galveston, 1862-63.

Name	Builder	Launched	Acquired	Comm.
General Bee	(U)	(U)	(U)	Jul 1862

Service record: Gunboat at Corpus Christie, 1862

Name	Builder	Launched	Acquired	Comm.
Harriet Lane	New York, N.Y. (Webb)	20 Nov 1857	1863	1863

ex-USS/USRC Harriet Lane
Notes: Captured at Galveston, 1 Jan 1863.
Service record: Defense of Texas coast 1863–64. Converted to blockade runner early 1864.
Later history: Merchant *Lavinia* 1864. Ran blockade and remained at Havana. Converted to bark and renamed *Elliott Richie* 1867. Foundered off Pernambuco, Brazil, 13 May 1884.

Name	Builder	Launched	Acquired	Comm.
Josiah H. Bell	Jeffersonville, Ind. (Howard)	1853	Summer 1862	1862

ex-*J.H. Bell*

174 Civil War Navies, 1855-1883

Tonnage	412 tons
Dimensions	171' × 30' × 6.7'
Machinery	Side wheels
Complement	35
Armament	1–8" columbiad; (Jun 1863) 1–24pdr, 1–12pdr H

Notes: Cottonclad gunboat.

Service record: Engagement at Sabine Pass, captured USS *Morning Light* and *Velocity*, 20 Jan 1863. Operated off Sabine Pass 1863–65. Scuttled 1865.

Name	Builder	Launched	Acquired	Comm.
Mary Hill	Smithfield, Tex.	1859	(U)	(U)
Tonnage	234 tons			
Dimensions	(U)			
Machinery	Side wheels			
Armament	1–24pdr, 1–12pdr			

Notes: Cottonclad gunboat.

Service record: Operated between Matagorda and Galveston.

Later history: Merchant *Mary Hill* 1865. Lost by snagging in Trinity River, Tex., 22 Nov 1865.

Name	Builder	Launched	Acquired	Comm.
Sachem	New York, N.Y.	1844	8 Sep 1863	Sep 1863
ex-USS *Sachem*				

Notes: Captured at Sabine Pass, Tex., 8 Sep 1863.

Service record: Operated at Orange and Sabine Pass. Reported converted to blockade runner. FFU.

Name	Builder	Launched	Acquired	Comm.
Uncle Ben	(U)	(U)	(U)	(U)
Armament	3–12pdr			

Notes: Cottonclad gunboat.

Service record: Engagement at Sabine Pass, captured USS *Morning Light* and *Velocity*, 20 Jan 1863.

Other Steam Vessels (Texas Area)

Name	Built at	Launched	Acquired	Tons	Dimensions	Type	Armament
A.S. Ruthven	Cincinnati, Ohio	1860		144	127' × 30' × 4'8"	S/w	
Colonel Stelle	Pittsburgh, Pa.	1860		199	138' × 24' × d4'8	S/w	
Dime		(U)	1863				
Era No. 3	Freedom, Pa.	1858		144	129' × 28.3' × d4.3'	St/W	
Florilda	Louisville, Ky.	1857		304		S/w	
General Rusk	Wilmington, Del. (Harlan)	1857	1861	417	200' × 31' × 5'7"	S/w	
Grand Bay	Mobile, Ala.	1857		135	121' × 26'5" × 4'5"	St/W	
Island City	Brownsville, Pa.	1856		245		S/w	
Jeff Davis		(U)	1863				
John F. Carr		(U)					2 guns
Lone Star	Louisville, Ky.	1854	Jul 1863	126	112' × 26' × 4.7'	S/w	
Lucy Gwin	Freedom, Pa.	1859		152		St/W	
Neptune		(U)					2 guns
Roebuck	Brownsville, Pa.	1857		164	147' × 23' × d5'	S/w	
Sun Flower	Louisville, Ky.	1857		105	121'6" × 25' × 3'9"	S/w	

* *Types:* screw = screw propeller driven; st/w = sternwheel steamer; s/w = sidewheel steamer.

Notes and service records

A.S. Ruthven: Transport, Galveston Bay.
    Later history: Merchant *A.S. Ruthven* 1865. Lost 1869.
Colonel Stelle: Transport. Sunk by accident off Pelican Island, Galveston, 10 Feb 1864. Raised.
    Later history: Lost at sea, 31 Dec 1867.
Dime: Tender and transport, 1863. Reportedly "very small."
Era No. 3: River patrol and transport on Brazos River.
    Later history: Merchant *New Era No. 3*, 1865. RR 1875.
Florilda: Troop transport. Battle of Sabine Pass, 8 Sep 1863.
General Rusk: Iron hull. Beam engine (44"x11'). Seized at Galveston 1861. Reconnaissance and signal boat. Captured steamer *Star of the West* off Indianola, Tex., 17 Apr 1861. Defense of Buffalo Bayou in San Jacinto River, Dec 1861. Transferred to Confederate Army, 1862.
    Later history: Merchant *Blanche* 1862, as blockade runner. Chased ashore at Marianao, Cuba, by USS *Montgomery*, 7 Oct 1862, and lost during salvage attempt, causing an international incident.

Grand Bay: Transport, Sabine River. FFU
Island City: Supply boat, Galveston 1863–65.
Jeff Davis: Transport.
John F. Carr: Transport and cottonclad gunboat, 1863. Battle of Galveston, 1 Jan 1863. Wrecked in Matagorda Bay, Tex., early 1864.
Lone Star: Transport 1863–65.
Lucy Gwin: Transport. Battle of Galveston, 1 Jan 1863. Surrendered at Matagorda, May 1865 but removed to Mexican side of the Rio Grande.
Neptune: Wood tug. Transport in Galveston Bay. Sank after ramming USS *Harriet Lane* during engagement at Galveston, 1 Jan 1863.
Roebuck: Cottonclad transport.
Sun Flower: Unarmed cottonclad. Transport in Sabine River area.
    Later history: Merchant *Sun Flower* 1865. Wrecked in Galveston harbor, 3 Oct 1867.

Sailing Vessels (Texas Area)

Name	Builder	Launched	Acquired	Tons	Dimensions	Type	Armament
Anna Dale				70		Schooner	1–12pdr
Breaker						Schooner	
Dodge	Page & Allen	1856	1861	153	100'4" × 23' × 8	Schooner	1–9pdr
ex-USRC *Henry Dodge*							
Elma			Jul 1862			Schooner	
ex-*Major Minter*							
Fanny Morgan			22 Oct 1861	8	26' × 11'	Fast sailboat	
George Buckhart						Schooner	1–6pdr
Julia A. Hodges				8		Schooner	
Lecompt						Schooner	
Royal Yacht			Oct 1861	40		Schooner	1–12pdr
Velocity						Schooner	
ex-USS *Velocity*							

Notes: *Anna Dale:* Captured by USS *Pinola* off Pass Cavallo, Tex., Feb 1865, ran aground and burned.

Breaker: Pilot boat. Chased ashore by USS *Corypheus* at Pass Cavallo, 12 Aug 1862, salved by U.S.

Dodge: U.S. Revenue Cutter seized at Galveston, 2 Mar 1861. Defense of Texas coast 1861-63.

Later history: Merchant *Mary Sorley* 1864. Captured as a blockade runner by USS *Sciota* off Galveston, Tex., 4 Apr 1864. FFU

Elma: Acquired for conversion to patrol ship. Run aground in Nueces Bay and burned, 12 Aug 1862.

Fanny Morgan: Guard and dispatch boat at Galveston.

George Buckhart: Operated in Matagorda Bay area. Captured as blockade runner by USS *Quaker City* off Brazos Santiago, 17 Mar 1865.

Julia A. Hodges: Dispatch boat. Captured by USS *Estrella* near Indianola, Tex., 6 Apr 1864.

Lecompt: Patrol ship, Matagorda peninsula 1862. Captured by USS *Westfield* and *Clifton* in Matagorda Bay, Oct 1862. Recaptured by Confederates at Galveston, 1 Jan 1863. Chased ashore by USS *Cornubia* in Galveston Bay, 24 May 1865.

Royal Yacht: Seriously damaged by fire after being attacked off Galveston, 8 Nov 1861. Captured as blockade runner off Galveston by USS *William G. Anderson*, 15 Apr 1863.

Velocity: Captured at Sabine Pass, Tex., 23 Jan 1863.

GULF COAST AREA

This section lists Confederate vessels that operated in the waters off Alabama, Mississippi, and the west coast of Florida. In addition to the ships listed, the ironclads *Huntsville, Tuscaloosa, Jackson, Tennessee,* and *Nashville* also operated in these waters.

Gunboats (Gulf Coast Area)

Name	Builder	Launched	Acquired	Comm.
Baltic	Philadelphia, Pa.	1860	1862	May 1862

Tonnage	624 tons
Dimensions	186' × 38' × 6'5"
Machinery	Side wheels, 5 knots
Complement	86
Armament	2 Dahlgren, 2–32pdr, 2 others

Notes: River towboat converted to armored ram at Mobile. Unfit for service and dismantled in 1864. Armor used for CSS *Nashville*.

Service record: Operated in Mobile Bay area 1862–65. Captured at Nanna Hubba Bluff in Tombigbee River, Ala., 10 May 1865. Sold by USN 31 Dec 1865.

Name	Builder	Launched	Acquired	Comm.
Danube	Bath, Me. (Hall Snow)	1854	May 1861	(U)

Tonnage	980 tons
Dimensions	170'4" × 30'11" × 16'11"
Armament	4–42pdr

Notes: Full rigged ship seized 1861 and converted to floating battery.

Service record: Anchored at Apalachee Battery in Mobile Bay, 1864. Sunk as a blockship in Mobile Bay, Nov 1864.

Name	Builder	Launched	Acquired	Comm.
Gunnison	Philadelphia, Pa.	1856	1862	1862
ex-*A.C. Gunnison*				

Tonnage	54 tons
Dimensions	70' × 15' × d7'
Machinery	1 screw, 2 engines (16" × U), HP 80
Complement	10
Armament	2–6pdr (1 spar torpedo added)

Service record: Comm as privateer, 25 May 1861. Dispatch and torpedo boat 1862. Surrendered Apr 1865. FFU

Name	Builder	Launched	Acquired	Comm.
Phoenix	Mobile, Ala	(U)	1863	(U)

Armament	6 guns

Service record: Ironclad floating battery. Sunk as a blockship at Mobile, Aug 1864.

Name	Builder	Launched	Acquired	Comm.
Selma	Mobile, Ala.	1856	22 Apr 1861	Nov 1861
ex-*Florida* (Jul 1862)				

Notes: Converted coastal packet steamer. Armor: plated 3/8" iron. Renamed Jul 1862.

Service record: Engaged USS *Massachusetts* off Mobile, 19 Oct 1861. Engaged USS *Montgomery*, 4 Dec 1861. Hit a snag and sank at Mobile, 5 Feb 1863; refloated. Surrendered after Battle of Mobile Bay, 5 Aug 1864 (7 killed). Comm in USN as USS **Selma**.

176 Civil War Navies, 1855-1883

Fig 11.4: An impression of the gunboat *Selma*, a converted packet steamer, which surrendered after the Battle of Mobile Bay. (U.S. Naval Historical Center)

Other Steam Vessels (Gulf Coast Area)

Name	Built at	Launched	Acquired	Tons	Dimensions	Type	Armament
Bradford	Louisville, Ky.	1844		152			
Crescent	Mobile, Ala.	1858		171		S/w	
Dalman	Jeffersonville, Ind.	1851		364		S/w	
ex-*Peter Dalman*							
Dick Keys	Cincinnati, Ohio	1853	8 May 1861	369	177' × 30.5' × 7.1'	S/w	
General Sumter	Palatka, Fla.	1859		41		S/w	
Governor Milton				68	85' × 20' × 4'8"	S/w	
ex-*G.W. Bird*							
Gray Cloud	Elizabeth, Pa.	1854					
Great Republic							
Helen							
Henry J. King	New Albany, Ind.	1856		409		S/w	
Iron King							
J.H. Jarvis							
James Battle	New Albany, Ind.	1860		407	225' × 35' × 7.5'	S/w	
Marianna						S/w	
Neafie	Philadelphia, Pa. (Reaney Neafie)	1856		103		#screw	
ex-*Jacob G. Neafie*							
Nelms							
Spray							
Swan	(U)			487			
Time	Elizabeth, Pa. ?	1860		263		S/w	
Turel							
William H. Young	Brownsville, Pa.	1860		179		S/w	

Notes and service record:
Bradford: Storeship at Pensacola, Fla., 1862.
Crescent: Tug at Mobile, Ala., 1861

Dalman: Receiving ship, Mobile 1862–65.
Dick Keys: Assisted blockade runners out of Mobile. Transport.
General Sumter: Also known as *General Sumpter*. Transport. Captured by USS *Columbine* in Big Lake George, Fla., 23 Mar 1864

Governor Milton: (May be the *George M. Bird*, 75 tons, built at Covington, Fla. in 1858.) Transport. Captured by a boat from USS *Darlington* above Hawkinsville, Fla., 7 Oct 1862.

Gray Cloud: For details see USS **Kinsman,** p. 70. Former Army steamer sold into merchant service 1859. Operated near Ship Island and Biloxi, 1861–62. Captured before Jul 1862 as *Kinsman.*

Great Republic: Cottonclad steamer. Captured late 1864.

Helen (I): Steamer, guard boat, and transport. Burned to prevent capture at Pensacola, May 1862.

Henry J. King: Transport. Operated between Selma and Mobile, Ala. 1864. Captured in Coosa River, Ala., 14 Apr 1865.

Iron King: Coal transport. Operated between Selma and Mobile 1864.

J.H. Jarvis: Little information known, possibly a new steamer built at Columbus, Ga., 1864.

James Battle: Transport. HP engines, 5 boilers. Captured by USS *De Soto* running blockade 70 miles southeast of Mobile, 18 Jul 1863. Used by U.S. Army.
Later history: Merchant *James Battle* 1865, RR 1867.

Marianna: Towboat and transport.

Neafie: Iron hull. Transport and tug. Damaged during engagement off Fort Pickens, Fla., 22 Nov 1861. Captured before 1863.
Later history: U.S. War Dept, 1864. Merchant *Neafie*, 1866. RR 1876.

Nelms: Steamboat at Fort McRae, Fla., 1861. Remained at Pensacola until Mar 1862. FFU

Spray: (May be the screw steamer, 106 tons, built at Wilmington, Del. 1852) Operated at St. Marks, Fla., 1863-65.

Swan: Tender at Mobile, Ala. 1861. Captured as blockade runner by USS *Amanda and Bainbridge* off Key West, Fla., 24 May 1862.
Later history: Merchant 1863. Foundered en route Key West–New Orleans, 19 Feb 1863.

Time: Steamer used at Pensacola NYd 1862.

Turel: Transport used at Pensacola, Fla., 1862.

William H. Young: Transport and store ship in Gulf area, 1862–65. Captured by U.S. Army, Jun 1865.

Sailing Vessels (Gulf Coast Area)

Name	Builder	Launched	Acquired	Tons	Dimensions	Type	Armament
Aid						Schr	
Alert							1–32pdr
Helen (II)						Sloop	
Isabella						Sloop	
Lewis Cass	Page & Allen	1856	1861	153	100' × 23'	Schr	1–68pdr gun
ex-USRC *Lewis Cass*							

Notes and service records

Aid: Captured by boat from USS *Niagara* off Mobile, 5 Jun 1861.

Alert: Lighthouse tender, seized at Mobile, 18 Jan 1861. Served at Mobile, Ala. 1861–62.

Helen (II): Transport, Florida coast. Captured by boat from USS *Sagamore* near Bayport, 2 Apr 1863 and destroyed by fire.

Isabella: Captured by USS *Fort Henry* in Waccasassa Bay, Florida Keys, 22 May 1863.

Lewis Cass: U.S. Revenue Cutter seized at Mobile, 30 Jan 1861. FFU

ATLANTIC COAST AREA

This section lists Confederate vessels that operated in the waters off Georgia, South Carolina, North Carolina, and the east coast of Florida. In addition to the ships listed, the ironclads *Atlanta* and *Savannah* operated in Georgia; *Chicora, Palmetto State, Charleston,* and *Columbia* at Charleston; and *Albemarle, Neuse, North Carolina,* and *Raleigh* in North Carolina.

Gunboats (Atlantic Coast Area)

Name	Builder	Launched	Acquired	Comm.
Arctic	Wilmington, N.C.	1863	1863	1863

Notes: Lightship, converted to ironclad floating battery. Machinery removed late in 1862 for CSS *Richmond*.
Service record: Cape Fear River 1863–64. Sunk as blockship, 24 Dec 1864

Name	Builder	Launched	Acquired	Comm.
Ellis	Wilmington, Del.	1860	1861	1861
ex-*Fairfield*				

Service record: Defense of Forts Hatteras and Clark, 28–29 Aug 1861. Defense of Roanoke Island, N.C., 7–8 Feb 1862. Captured during defense of Elizabeth City, N.C., 10 Feb 1862. Commissioned as USS *Ellis*. (q.v.)

Name	Builder	Launched	Acquired	Comm.
Fanny	(U)	(U)	1861	1861
Machinery	Screw			
Complement	49			
Armament	1–32pdr, 1–8pdr MLR			

Notes: Former U.S. Army vessel, seized at Loggerhead Inlet, N.C., 1 Oct 1861.
Service record: Battle of Roanoke Island, N.C., 7–8 Feb 1862. Defense of Elizabeth City, N.C. Run aground and blown up, 10 Feb 1862.

Name	Builder	Launched	Comm.
Fisher	Edwards Ferry, N.C.	1865	Never
Tonnage	66 tons		
Machinery	Screw steamer		

Service record: Captured while building, 1865, and taken to Norfolk.
Later history Merchant *Alexander Oldham*, 1865. Lost (cause unknown) 1873.

Name	Builder	Launched	Acquired	Comm.
Georgia	Savannah, Ga.	Mar 1862	May 1862	Jul 1862
Dimensions	250' × 60'			
Complement	200			
Armament	4 to 9 guns			

Notes: Ironclad floating battery. Also known as *State of Georgia* and *Ladies' Ram*.
Service record: Defense of Savannah 1863–64. Destroyed to prevent capture at Savannah, 21 Dec 1864.

Name	Builder	Launched	Comm.
Halifax	Halifax, N.C.	1865	never
Dimensions	Length 91'		

Notes: Steamer. Converted from towboat.

Service record: Captured on the ways at Halifax, N.C., 12 May 1865. Launched and towed to Norfolk, Jun 1865. FFU.

Name	Builder	Launched	Comm.
Isondiga	Savannah, Ga. (Krenson & Hawkes)	1863	Apr 1863
Tonnage	(U)		
Dimensions	(U) × (U) × 6'6"		
Machinery	Stern wheel, 5 knots		
Complement	60		
Armament	1–9" shell gun, 1–6.4"R		

Notes: Wood gunboat, no masts. Probably begun as a "Maury gunboat."
Service record: Defense of Savannah. Burned to prevent capture after fall of Savannah, 21 Dec 1864.

Name	Builder	Launched	Acquired	Comm.
Raleigh	(U)	(U)	May 1861	1861
Tonnage	65 tons			
Machinery	screw			
Armament	2–6pdr H			

Note: Iron hull.
Service record: Defense of Forts Hatteras and Clark, N.C., 28-29 Aug 1861. Defense of Roanoke Island and Elizabeth City, N.C., 7-10 Feb 1862. Tender to CSS *Virginia* at Hampton Roads, Mar 1862. Renamed ***Roanoke***, late 1864. Action at Trent's Reach, James River, 21 Jun 1864. Destroyed to prevent capture in James River, 4 Apr 1865.

Name	Builder	Launched	Acquired	Comm.
Sampson	Savannah, Ga.	1856	1861	1861
Tonnage	313 tons			
Dimensions	(U)			
Machinery	Side wheels			
Complement	49			
Armament	1–32pdr SB, 1–12pdr			

Notes: Tugboat. Converted to gunboat.
Service record: Defense of Port Royal, S.C., 4-7 Nov 1861. Engagements at Fort Pulaski, Ga., Dec 1861, and Jan 1862, damaged. Receiving ship, Savannah 1862–63. Damaged during expedition to destroy railway bridge over Savannah River, Dec 1864.
Later history: Merchant *Samson* 1868. Lost (cause unknown) 1870.

Name	Builder	Launched	Acquired	Comm.
Savannah	Greenpoint, N.Y. (Sneeden & Whitlock)	Sep 1856	1861	1861

ex-*Everglade*

Tonnage	406 tons B
Dimensions	173' (dk) × 28'8" × 4'6", d8'
Machinery	Side wheels, 1 inclined engine, 1 boiler, NHP 90 (Morgan)
Armament	1–32pdr

Notes: Purchased by Georgia in 1861 and converted to gunboat. Wood hull.
Service record: Defense of Port Royal, S.C., 5–6 Nov 1861, damaged. Defense of Fort Pulaski, Ga., 16 Nov 1861, 28 Jan 1862, and 10–11 Apr 1862. Receiving ship, Savannah, 1862–63. Renamed ***Oconee***, 28 Apr 1863. Sold, summer 1863. Sailed as blockade runner *Savannah* but foundered at sea in a gale, 19 Aug 1863.

Name	Builder	Launched	Acquired	Comm.
Sea Bird	Keyport, N.J. (Terry)	1854	1861	1862
Tonnage	202 tons			
Dimensions	(U)			
Machinery	Side wheels			
Complement	42			
Armament	1–32pdr SB, 1–30pdr MLR			

Notes: Purchased by North Carolina 1861.
Service record: Defense of Roanoke Island, N.C., 7–8 Feb 1862. Rammed and sunk by USS *Commodore Perry* at Elizabeth City, N.C., 10 Feb 1862.

Name	Builder	Launched	Acquired	Comm.
Stono	Brooklyn, N.Y. (L & F)	1861	1863	1863

ex-USS *Isaac Smith*
Notes: Captured in Stono River, S.C., 30 Jan 1863.
Service record: Wrecked on breakwater near Fort Moultrie, S.C., while attempting to run blockade, 5 Jun 1863.

Name	Builder	Launched	Acquired	Comm.
Uncle Ben	Buffalo, N.Y.	1856	1861	1861
Tonnage	155 tons			
Dimensions	(U)			
Machinery	1 screw			
Armament	1 gun			

Notes: Lake Erie tug used to reinforce Fort Sumter, but seized by Confederates at Wilmington, N.C., Apr 1861. Engines removed for CSS *North Carolina*, 1862.
Service record: Defense of Wilmington, N.C. Fitted as privateer ***Retribution***.
Ships captured (as *Retribution*): *J.P. Elliott*, 10 Jan 1863; *Hanover*, 31 Jan 1863; *Emily Fisher*, 19 Feb 1863.
Later history: Renamed *Etta*. Lost off Cape Hatteras, 1865.

Name	Builder	Launched	Acquired	Comm.
Winslow	New York, N.Y. (Terry)	1846	1861	

ex-*Joseph E. Coffee*

Tonnage	207 tons
Dimensions	143' × (U) × (U)
Machinery	Side wheels
Armament	1–32pdr, 1–6pdr R

Notes Also known as ***Warren Winslow***. Purchased by North Carolina.
Service record: Patrolled in Hatteras area, 1861. Struck sunken object and burned to prevent capture in Ocracoke Inlet, N.C., 7 Nov 1861, while going to aid of wrecked French corvette *Prony*.
Ships captured: *Mary Alice*, *Priscilla*, Jul 1861; *Transit*, 15 Jul 1861; *Herbert*, 18 Jul 1861; *Itasca*, 4 Aug 1861.

Name	Builder	Launched	Acquired	Comm.
Yadkin	Wilmington, N.C.	1863	1863	1864
Tonnage	300 tons			
Dimensions	(U)			
Machinery	screw			
Armament	1 or 2 guns			

Notes: May have been begun as a "Maury gunboat."
Service record: Operated in North Carolina. Burned to prevent capture on fall of Wilmington, Feb 1865.

Other Steam Vessels (Atlantic Coast Area)

Name	Built at	Launched	Acquired	Tons	Dimensions	Type	Armament
Aid	Philadelphia, Pa.	1852	1861	147		Screw	1–42pdr
Albemarle	Wheeling, Va.		1861			St/W	
Amazon	Wilmington Del. (Harlan)	1856		372	157'6" × 45' × 5'6"	#S/w	
Appomattox ex-*Empire*	Philadelphia, Pa.	1850	1861	120		S/w	1–32pdr
Beaufort (See p. 185.)							
Beauregard						S/w	
Berosa							
Bombshell			1864		90' × (U) × 3'5"		1–20pdr, 3–H
Caswell		1861				S/w	
Catawba							
Chesterfield	Charleston, S.C.	1853	1861	204		S/w	
Clarendon	Portsmouth, Va.	1860		143		Screw	
Colonel Hill							
Cotton Plant	Philadelphia, Pa.	1860		85	107' × 18'9" × 4.5'	Screw	
Curlew	Wilmington Del. (Harlan)	1856		350	135' × 23' × 8	S/w	1–32pdr
Currituck	Norfolk, Va.	1860		44		screw	
Darlington	Charleston, S.C.	1849		298		S/w	
Dolly							
Egypt Mills	Poplar Neck, Md.	1856		70		Screw	
Equator	Philadelphia, Pa.	1854		64		#Screw	
Etiwan	Charleston, S.C.	1834		132		S/w	
Firefly			May 1861			S/w yacht	1 gun
Forrest ex-*Edwards*			1861				1–32pdr
General Clinch	Charleston, S.C. (J. Poyas)	1839	Jan 1861	256	131' × 24' × 8'8"	S/w	2 guns
General Lee							
Governor Morehead						St/W	
Helen ex-*Juno*	Glasgow, Scotland (Tod)	1860	Dec 1863	185		S/w	
Huntress	New York, N.Y.	1838	Mar 1861	500	230' × 24'6" × 6'6"	S/w 16 knots	1 to 3
Ida						S/w	
Indian Chief							
Jeff Davis (i)							
Junaluska ex-*Younalaska*	Philadelphia, Pa.	1860		79		Screw	2 guns
Kahukee	Wilmington, Del. (Harlan)	1855	Jul 1861	150	85' × 17'6" × 7'	Screw	
Kate L. Bruce	GB ?	(U)		310			
Lady Davis ex-*James Gray*	Philadelphia, Pa.	1858	May 1861	161		Screw	1-24pdr,1–12pdr MLR guns
Leesburg							
M.E. Dowing							
Marion	Charleston, S.C.	1850		258		S/w	
Moultrie	New York, N.Y. ?	1856		381			
Planter	Charleston	1860		313		S/w	1–32pdr, 1–24pdr How
Post Boy						S/w	
Queen Mab						S/w	
Rebel							
Resolute	Savannah, Ga.	1858		322		S/w	
Robert Habersham	Savannah, Ga.	1860		173		S/w	
Skirwan							

Name	Built at	Launched	Acquired	Tons	Dimensions	Type	Armament
Sumter	Charleston, S.C.	1863					
Talomico						S/w	
Transport	(U)	1864		40		S/w HP engine.	
Waterwitch							
ex-USS *Waterwitch*							
Weldon N. Edwards							
Wilson	Beaufort, N.C.	1856		58		#St/W	

Notes and service records

Aid: Engine removed for ironclad building at Charleston. Tender, Charleston, S.C. 1861–62. BU 1862.

Albemarle: Transport and cargo ship in North Carolina 1861. Captured by USS *Delaware* off New Bern, N.C., 15 Mar 1862.
Later history: Transport, wrecked in New Bern harbor, 5 Apr 1862.

Amazon: Iron hull. HP engine (22″ × 6′) Transport, Savannah area. Surrendered to USS *Pontiac*, 2 Mar 1865.
Later history: Merchant *Amazon* 1865. Snagged and sunk in Savannah River, Ga., Feb 1866.

Appomattox: Tug. Engagement at Roanoke Island, N.C., 7–8 Feb 1862. Defense of Elizabeth City, N.C., 10 Feb 1862; scuttled to prevent capture later that day.

Beauregard: Transport, operated at Savannah. Captured at Savannah, Jan 1865.

Berosa: Cargo vessel. Foundered off Florida coast east of St. Mary's River, 8 Apr 1863.

Bombshell: Two inclined HP engines (33″ × 10′). Erie Canal steamer sunk as U.S. Army transport in Albemarle Sound, N.C., 18 Apr 1864 and raised by Confederates. Recaptured by USS *Mattabesett* and *Sassacus* during battle in Albemarle Sound, 5 May 1864.

Caswell: Tender at Wilmington, N.C. Burned to avoid capture at Wilmington, Feb 1865.

Catawba: Tender at Charleston, 1861.

Chesterfield: Transport, South Carolina 1861–65. FFU.

Clarendon: Former ferryboat. Dispatch vessel and transport, Fort Fisher, N.C., Dec 1864. Captured and burned by Union forces at Fayetteville, N.C., 14 Mar 1865.

Colonel Hill: Transport, Cape Hatteras area. Burned by U.S. Army forces near Tarborough, N.C., 20 Jul 1863.

Cotton Plant: Iron hull. Operated at Plymouth, N.C. with CSS *Albemarle*, Apr–May 1864. Surrendered May 1865 at Halifax, N.C.
Later history: Merchant *Cotton Plant* 1865. Barge 1881.

Curlew: Iron hull. Tug, LP engine (29″ × 9′). Disabled during attack on Roanoke Island, 7 Feb 1862, and destroyed to prevent capture, 8 Feb 1862.

Currituck: Dispatch vessel and towboat, North Carolina. FFU.

Darlington: Captured by USS *Pawnee* near Fernandina, Fla., 3 Mar 1862.
Later history: Army transport 1862. Merchant *Darlington* 1866. RR 1874.

Dolly: Steamer in Roanoke River; sunk near Edwards Ferry, N.C., May 1865.

Egypt Mills: Transport. Captured in Roanoke River, N.C., 22 May 1865.
Later history: Merchant *Alida* 1865. RR 1869.

Equator: Torpedo boat. Defense of Cape Fear River area, 1864. Burned to prevent capture at Wilmington, N.C., Jan 1865.

Etiwan: Transport and cargo ship, Charleston harbor. Struck a torpedo (mine) and run ashore, spring 1863. Sunk by Federal batteries off Fort Johnson, 7 Jun 1864.
Later history: Salved. Merchant *St. Helena* 1867. RR 1894.

Firefly: ex-U.S. Coast Survey, seized 29 Dec 1860. Wood steam yacht. Tender, Savannah. Burned to prevent capture at Savannah, 21 Dec 1864.

Forrest: Steam tug. Disabled during defense of Roanoke Island, 7–8 Feb 1862. Burned to prevent capture at Elizabeth City, N.C., 10 Feb 1862.

General Clinch: Crosshead engine. Tender and transport, Charleston harbor 1861–64. Sank in Charleston harbor 1864. Raised and used as blockade runner. FFU

General Lee: Transport at Savannah 1864.

Governor Morehead: Transport and towboat, Pamlico and Neuse Rivers. Destroyed by U.S. Army, Jul 1863.

Helen: Lost in gale as blockade runner, 10 Mar 1864. (See Blockade runners)

Huntress: Fast (16 knots) mail packet purchased by Georgia 1861. Battle of Port Royal, 7 Nov 1861. Transport, Charleston harbor 1862. Sold 29 Oct 1862.
Later history: Blockade runner *Tropic*. Accidentally burned off Charleston, 18 Jan 1863.

Ida: Former U.S. Government vessel. Transport, dispatch boat, and towboat in Savannah River, 1862–64. Captured and burned near Argyle Island, 10 Dec 1864.

Indian Chief: Receiving ship, Charleston, 1862–65. Tender for torpedo (mine) operations. Burned on evacuation of Charleston, 18 Feb 1865.

Jeff Davis (II): Steamer, Savannah area, 1864.

Junaluska: Helped capture USS *Fanny* in Loggerhead Inlet, N.C., 1 Oct 1861. BU 1862.

Kahukee: Tug. Vert HP engine (24″ × 1′8″), 9 knots. Iron hull. Operated around Hatteras Inlet, N.C., 1861. FFU

Kate L. Bruce: Former schooner, converted to steamer and armed at Columbus, Ga., 1862. Sunk as blockship in Chattahoochee River. 1864.

Lady Davis: Iron hull. Engine removed for CSS *Palmetto State*, 1862. Defense of Savannah 1861. Battle of Port Royal, S.C., 7 Nov 1861. Used as blockade runner 1862. Captured as hulk at Charleston, Feb 1865.
Ship captured: *A.B. Thompson*, 19 May 1861.
Later history: U.S. Lighthouse Board 1865.

Leesburg: Transport, Savannah R 1862-65. FFU

M.E. Downing: Dispatch boat, North Carolina, 1861.

Marion: Transport, Charleston, 1861–63. Sunk accidentally by Confederate mine in Ashley River, 6 Apr 1863.

Moultrie: (May be screw steamer *General Moultrie* built in 1856 at New York and sold foreign in 1866.) Charleston station 1862–63. Returned to owner, 24 Aug 1863.

Planter: Dispatch boat and transport, Charleston. Spirited out of Charleston harbor by Robert Smalls, 13 May 1862 and turned over to USS *Onward*. Commissioned as USS *Planter*. (q.v.)

Post Boy: Dispatch boat, North Carolina, 1861–62.

Queen Mab: Transport, Charleston area. Captured, 18 Feb 1865.

Rebel: Transport, North Carolina and Virginia.

Resolute: Transport and tender to CSS *Savannah*. Defense of Port Royal, S.C., Nov 1861. Damaged during engagement in Savannah River, 12 Dec 1864; ran aground and was captured.
Later history: Merchant *Ajax* 1867. RR 1881.

Robert Habersham: Transport, Savannah area. Lost with all hands by explosion in Savannah River, 19 Aug 1863.

Skirwan: Captured at Halifax, N.C., May 1865.

Sumter: Transport and munitions carrier, Stono River and Charleston 1863. Sunk in error by gunfire from Fort Moultrie, 30 Aug 1863 (40 killed).

Talomico: Transport 1861–63. Sunk accidentally at Savannah, 1863.

Transport: Tug. Captured at Charleston, Feb 1865. Transferred to U.S. Army Jul 1865.

Treaty: Tug. Captured by boat from USS *Albatross* in Santee River, 20 Jun 1862.

Waterwitch: For details, see USS *Waterwitch* p. 14. Captured in boarding attack in Ossabaw Sound, Ga., 3 Jun 1864. Remained at White Bluff, Ga., and burned to prevent capture, 19 Dec 1864.

Weldon N. Edwards: Defense of North Carolina 1861. Hulked Aug 1861.

Wilson: Transport. Captured by USS *Commodore Perry*, *Shawsheen*, and *Ceres* at Hamilton, N.C., on Roanoke River, 9 Jul 1862. Transferred to U.S. Army.

Sailing Vessels (Atlantic Coast Area)

Name	Built at	Launched	Acquired	Tons	Dimensions	Type	Armament
Black Warrior						Schr	2–32pdr
Gallatin	New York NYd	1831	1861	112	73'4" (pp) × 20'6" × d7'4"	Schr	2–12pdr
ex-USRC *Gallatin*							
Hawley						Schr	
Isabella Ellis			1861	340		Schr	
J.J. Crittenden						Schr	
Jeff Davis (ii)						Schr	
Kate L. Bruce				310		Schr	
M.C. Etheridge	Plymouth, N.C.	1859			144 92' × 24' × 7'	Schr	2 guns
Manassas						Schr	
ex-USRC *Minot*							
Memphis	New York, N.Y.	1851		100	111' × 25'	yt	
ex-*Camilla*, ex-*America*							
Petrel	(U)		Dec 1860	82			1–42pdr + 1
ex-USCS, ex-USRC *William Aiken*, ex-*Eclipse*							
Renshaw		1862		80	68' × 20'	schr	
ex-*R.T. Renshaw*							

*Types: schr - schooner; yt = yacht

Notes and Service records

Black Warrior: Defense of Roanoke Island and Elizabeth City, N.C., 7–10 Feb 1862. Burned to prevent capture, 10 Feb 1862.

Gallatin: U.S. Revenue Cutter seized in Georgia 1861. Commissioned as privateer, Apr 1861. FFU.

Hawley: Transport, North Carolina 1861.

Isabella Ellis: Transport 1861. In Union service 1864.

J.J. Crittenden: Captured by USS *Whitehead* off Newbegun Creek, S.C., June 1864, and later sunk.

Jeff Davis (II): Captured off New Berne, N.C., June 1864.

Kate L. Bruce: Blockade runner 1861–62.

M.C. Etheridge: Storeship, North Carolina. Burned to prevent capture when attacked by USS *Whitehead* in Pasquotank River, 10 Feb 1862.

Manassas: Reportedly seized as U.S. Revenue Cutter at New Berne, N.C., 27 Aug 1861 (though no such revenue cutter has been found). Operated off North Carolina 1861. BU 1862.

Memphis: Blockade runner as *Camilla*, 1861. Discovered scuttled in St. Johns River, Fla., Mar 1862. Salved and comm in USN as USS *America*. (q.v.)

Petrel: Seized Dec 1860, comm as privateer 1861. Sunk by USS *St. Lawrence* off Charleston, 28 Jul 1861.

Renshaw: Captured by launch from USS *Louisiana* in Tar River, N.C., 20 May 1863. See USS **Renshaw**. (q.v.)

VIRGINIA AREA

In addition to the following vessels, the ironclads *Virginia, Richmond, Brandywine, Texas, Fredericksburg,* and *Virginia II* operated in the Virginia area.

Gunboats (Virginia Area)

Name	Builder	Launched	Comm.
Drewry	(U)	1863	1863

Tonnage 166 tons
Dimensions 106' × 21' × 5', d8'
Machinery (U)
Armament 1–6.4" MLR, 1–7" MLR

Note: Wood hull. May have been started as a *Dixie* class gunboat.

Service record: Tender and gunboat, 1863. Action at Trent's Reach, 21 Jun 1864. Destroyed by two hits from artillery fire in Trent's Reach, James River, 24 Jan 1865 (2 killed).

Name	Builder	Launched	Acquired	Comm.
Jamestown	New York, N.Y. (Westervelt)	1852	Apr 1861	Jul 1861

Tonnage 1,500 tons
Dimensions 240'3" (dk) × 33'6" × 23'5", d17'
Machinery Side wheels, 2 vertical beam engines (42" × 10'), 2 boilers
Complement (U)
Armament 1–10" SB, 1–64pdr, 6-8", 2–32pdr MLR

Notes: Seized by Virginia 1861. Brigantine rig. Built for New York–Richmond run.

Service record: Renamed *Thomas Jefferson*, July 1861. Battle of Hampton Roads, 8–9 Mar 1862. Captured three ships at Hampton Roads, 11 Apr 1862. Sunk as a blockship in James River, 15 May 1862.

Name	Builder	Launched	Acquired	Comm.
Patrick Henry	New York, N.Y. (Webb)	May 1859	Apr 1861	1861
ex-*Yorktown*				

Tonnage 1,300 tons
Dimensions 250' (dk) × 34' × 13', d17'
Machinery Side wheels, 2 vertical beam engines (50" × 10'), 2 boilers (Morgan)
Complement 150
Armament 1–10" SB, 1–64pdr, 6-8", 2–32pdr MLR

Notes: Seized by Virginia 1861. Brigantine rig. Built for New York–Richmond run.

Service record: Engaged gunboats above Newport News, Va., 13 Sep and 2 Dec 1861. Damaged at battle of Hampton Roads, 8–9 Mar 1862 (4 killed). Housed the Confederate Naval Academy at Drewry's Bluff, Va., Oct 1863–5. Burned on evacuation of Richmond, 3 Apr 1865.

182 Civil War Navies, 1855-1883

Fig 11.5: The gunboat *Patrick Henry*, from a drawing by Clary Ray, was the school ship for the Confederate Naval Academy at Richmond.

Name	Builder	Launched	Acquired	Comm.
Satellite	New York, N.Y.	1854	23 Aug 1863	1863
ex-USS *Satellite*				

Service record: Captured by boarders at mouth of Rappahannock River, 23 Aug 1863. Captured three schooners in Chesapeake Bay. Stripped and scuttled, 2 Sep 1863.

Name	Builder	Launched	Acquired	Comm.
Teaser	Philadelphia, Pa.	1855?	1861	1861
ex-*Wide Awake*				

Notes: Wood tug purchased by Virginia 1861. Prior identity conjectural.

Fig 11.6: The *George Page* operated in Virginia in 1862. From a contemporary sketch in *Harpers Weekly*.

Service record: Battle of Hampton Roads, 8–9 Mar 1862. Used as balloon tender and torpedo (mine) layer. Damaged in action with USS *Maratanza* at Haxall's on James River, 4 Jul 1862, and captured. Comm as USS *Teaser*. (q.v.)

Name	Builder	Launched	Acquired	Comm.
Torpedo	(U)	(U)	(U)	1863
Tonnage	150 tons			
Dimensions	70′ × 16′ × d6′6″			
Machinery	Screw			
Armament	2–20pdr			

Service record: Torpedo boat tender, James River. Burned and sunk to prevent capture at Richmond, Apr 1865. Raised and sent to Norfolk NYd.

Other Steam Vessels (Virginia Area)

Name	Built at	Launched	Acquired	Tons	Dimensions	Type	Armament
Allison							
Beaufort	Wilmington, Del.	1854	9 Jul 1861	85	85′ × 17′5″ × d6′11″		1–32pdr MLR
ex-*Caledonia*							
Curtis Peck	New York, N.Y.	1842	1861	446		S/w	
General Scott							
George Page	New York, N.Y. (Collyer)	1853	1861	410	128′ × 26′ × 4′, d7′	S/w	2 guns
Harmony	Philadelphia, Pa.	1859		78		S/w	2–32pdr MLR
John B. White	Buffalo, N.Y.	1857		39		Screw	
Logan	Wilmington, Del. (Harlan)	1855	1861	296	160′ × 26′ × 7′6″	S/w	
Northampton	Baltimore, Md.	1860	1861	405		S/w	
Powhatan							
Rappahannock	Brooklyn, N.Y. (Burtis)	1845	1861	413		S/w	1 gun
ex-*St. Nicholas*							
Reliance	Keyport, N.J. (Terry)	1860	23 Aug 1863				
ex-USS *Reliance*							
Roanoke (I)							
Roanoke (II)							
ex-*Raleigh*							
Rondout	Poughkeepsie, N.Y.	1828		40		S/w	
Schultz	New York, N.Y.	1850		164		S/w	
ex-*A.H. Schultz*							
Seaboard	Philadelphia, Pa.	1859		59		S/w	

Name	Built at	Launched	Acquired	Tons	Dimensions	Type	Armament
Shrapnel							
Towns	Philadelphia, Pa.	1855		89		S/w	
ex-*W.W. Towns*							
Young America	Gloucester, N.J.	1857	1861				

Notes and service records

Allison: Transport. Attempt to pass obstructions at Trent's Reach, 23–24 Jan 1865. Sank torpedo boat *Hornet* in collision, 26 Jan 1865. FFU. (Possibly *William Allison*: screw; 301 tons, built in 1854 at Baltimore, Md., abandoned in 1892)

Beaufort: 1 vertical direct acting engine (22″ × 1′10″). Battles of Roanoke Island and Elizabeth City, N.C., Feb 1862. Tender to CSS *Virginia* at Hampton Roads, 8–9 Mar 1862. James River 1862–65. Action at Trent's Reach, 21 Jun 1864. Captured 3 Apr 1865. Sold 15 Sep 1865
Later history Merchant *Roanoke* 1865. Barge 1878.

Curtis Peck: Patrol and flag-of-truce boat. Sunk as blockship in James River, Sep 1862.

General Scott: Transport. Burned to prevent capture in York River, May 1862.

George Page: Vertical beam engine. Built as U.S. Army transport; captured in Aquia Creek, Va., May 1861. May have been renamed. *City of Richmond*: River defense service. Burned to prevent capture at Quantico, Va., 9 Mar 1862.

Harmony: Tug, ordnance transport. Attacked USS *Savannah* off Newport News, 30 Aug 1861. FFU.

John B. White: Tug. Surrendered near Hampton Roads, 8 May 1862.
Later history: Served with U.S. Army. Sunk by torpedo (mine), 1 Jan 1864.

Logan: Transport. Burned to prevent capture in Pamunkey River above White House, Va., 1862.

Northampton: Cargo ship, James River, 1861–62. Sunk as a blockship at Drewry's Bluff, Va., Sep 1862.

Powhatan: Tug acquired for defense of Roanoke Island 1861.

Rappahannock: Merchant passenger steamer seized by passengers in Potomac River, 28 Jun 1861, and turned over to CSN. Operated in the Rappahannock River 1861–62. Burned to prevent capture at Fredericksburg, Apr 1862.

Reliance: For details see USS *Reliance*, p. 90. Captured by Confederate boarders in Rappahannock River, 19 Aug 1863. Destroyed to prevent recapture at Port Royal, Va., 28 Aug 1863.

Later history: Apparently salved. Merchant 1865. Lost (U), 26 Apr 1883.

Roanoke (I): Chartered steamer in Nansemond River, Va. 1861 and North Carolina 1862.

Roanoke (II): See **Raleigh**, p. 180, transferred from North Carolina Feb 1862.

Rondout: Transport. Captured by Potomac Flotilla in Rappahannock River, 20 Apr 1862.

Schultz: Flag-of-truce boat in James River. Blown up by Confederate torpedo (mine), 19 Feb 1865. [Also reported as USS *Columbine* (q.v.)]

Seaboard: Tug operated by CSA Engineer Corps. Captured by USS *Lilac* in James River below Richmond, 4 Apr 1865. Snagged and run aground, May ? 1865.

Shrapnel: Picket boat, James River. Destroyed to prevent capture at Richmond, 3 Apr 1865.

Towns: Sunk as blockship in Warwick River, Va., Sep 1861.

Young America: Captured off Fortress Monroe, Va. by USS *Cumberland*, 24 Apr 1861. Comm as USS **Young America**.

Sailing Vessels Notes:

Alena: Seized by USS *Mount Vernon* in Pamunkey River, Jun 1861.

Beauregard: Transport. Burned by Union forces off Ragged Island, Va., 4 May 1862.

Confederate States: For details see USS *United States*. p. 95. USN frigate seized at Norfolk NYd 1861. Receiving ship Norfolk 1861–62. Sunk as a blockship in Elizabeth River, Apr 1862. Raised and BU.

Duane: U.S. Revenue Cutter seized at Norfolk, 18 Apr 1861.

Gallego: Cargo and store ship, James River. Ran aground at Drewry's Bluff, late 1864, refloated 18 Jan 1865. FFU

Germantown: For details see USS *Germantown*, p. 95. USN sloop, sunk at Norfolk NYd and raised by Confederates, Jun 1861. Sunk as blockship in Elizabeth River, May 1862.

Plymouth: For details see USS *Plymouth*, p. 96. USN sloop scuttled at Norfolk NYd, Apr 1861. Raised by Confederates. Hulk scuttled to avoid capture at Norfolk, 10 May 1862.

Sailing Vessels (Virginia Area)

Name	Builder	Launched	Acquired	Tons	Dimensions	Type	Armament
Alena						Sloop	
Beauregard						Schr	
Confederate States	Philadelphia, Pa.	1797	1862		175′ × 43′	Frigate	
ex-USS *United States*							
Duane	Philadelphia, Pa. (Teas)	1849	Apr 1861	153	102′ × 23′ × 9′7″	Schr	
ex-USRC *William J. Duane*							
Gallego	Newburyport, Mass.	1855		596	144′ × 30′ × d15′	Schr	
Germantown	Philadelphia NYd	1843	1861		150′ x 36′	sloop	
ex-USS *Germantown*							
Plymouth	Boston NYd	1843	1861		147′ x 38′	sloop	
ex-USS *Plymouth*							

MISSISSIPPI RIVER AREA

In addition to the ships listed, the ironclads *Arkansas*, *Eastport*, and *Missouri* also operated in the inland riverways.

Gunboats

Name	Builder	Launched	Acquired	Comm.
General Polk ex-*Ed Howard*	New Albany, Ind.	1852	1861	Dec 1861
Tonnage	390 tons			
Dimensions	280' × 35' × 8'			
Machinery	Side wheels			
Armament	2–32pdr MLR, 1–32pdr SB.			

Notes: Purchased and converted at New Orleans, 1861.
Service record: Operations off New Madrid, Mo., Dec 1861. Escaped up Yazoo River after fall of Island No.10. Burned at Liverpool, below Yazoo City, 26 Jun 1862.

Name	Builder	Launched	Acquired	Comm.
Grand Duke	Jeffersonville, Ind. (Howard)	1859	Feb 1863	1863
Tonnage	508 tons			
Dimensions	205' × 35' × 7'6"			
Machinery	Side wheels, (24" × 7') 4 boilers			
Armament	(U)			

Notes: Cottonclad gunboat.
Service record: Attacked by Union vessels on Atchafalaya River, La., 14 Apr 1863. Damaged in action with USS *Albatross* at Fort de Russy, La., 4 May 1863. Burned by accident at Shreveport, La., 25 Sep 1863.

Name	Builder	Launched	Acquired	Comm.
J.A. Cotton ex-*Mary T.*	Jeffersonville, Ind.	1861	19 Mar 1863	1863
Tonnage	372 tons			
Dimensions	185' × 34'6" × 4'10"			
Machinery	Side wheels (22" × 8'), 4 boilers			
Armament	2–24pdr, 2–12pdr, 1 H.			

Notes: Cottonclad gunboat. Seized in Red River, early 1863. Also known as *Cotton Jr.*
Service record: Engaged USS *Albatross* at Fort DeRussy, La., 4 May 1863. Operated in Red River area 1863–65. Surrendered May 1865. BU at Pittsburgh, hulk crushed by ice Feb 1867.

Name	Builder	Launched	Acquired	Comm.
Jackson ex-*Yankee*	Cincinnati, Ohio	1849	9 May 1861	1861
Tonnage	297 tons			
Dimensions	(U)			
Machinery	Side wheels			
Complement	75			
Armament	2–32pdr			

Notes: Purchased at New Orleans, converted, and sent up river.
Service record: Engaged Federal gunboats off Hickman, Ky., 4 Sep 1861. Hit by gunfire at Lucas Bend, Mo., 10 Sep 1861. Engagement near Head of Passes, Miss., 12 Oct 1861. Engagement below New Orleans, 24 Apr 1862. Destroyed to prevent capture above New Orleans, Apr 1862.

Name	Builder	Launched	Acquired	Comm.
James Johnson	Jeffersonville, Ind.	1856	1861	(never)
Tonnage	526 tons			
Dimensions	(U)			
Machinery	Side wheels			
Armament	(U)			

Service record: Destroyed to prevent capture while undergoing conversion at Nashville, Tenn., 23 Feb 1862.

Name	Builder	Launched	Acquired	Comm.
James Woods	Jeffersonville, Ind. (Howard)	1860	1861	(never)
Tonnage	585 tons			
Dimensions	257' × 37' × 7'			
Machinery	Sidewheels			
Armament	(U)			

Service record: Destroyed to prevent capture while undergoing conversion at Nashville, Tenn., 23 Feb 1862.

Name	Builder	Launched	Acquired	Comm.
Livingston	New Orleans, La. (Hughes)	1861	1862	1 Feb 1862
Tonnage	(U)			
Dimensions	180' × 40' × 9'			
Machinery	Side wheels			
Armament	2–30pdr MLR, 4 shell guns			

Notes: Ferry or towboat converted to a gunboat while under construction. Taken up river for fitting out at Columbus, Ky.
Service record: Defense of Island No. 10, Jan 1862. Burned to prevent capture in Yazoo River, 26 Jun 1862.

Name	Builder	Launched	Acquired	Comm.
Maurepas ex-*Grosse Tete*	New Albany, Ind.	1858	1861	1861
Tonnage	399 tons			
Dimensions	180' × 34' × 7'			
Machinery	Side wheels			
Armament	7 guns			

Service record: Operations at Island No.10 and New Madrid, Mo., 12 Mar–7 Apr 1862. Sunk to obstruct White River near St. Charles, Ark., 16 Jun 1862.

Name	Builder	Launched	Acquired	Comm.
Pontchartrain ex-*Lizzie Simmons*	New Albany, Ind.	1859	12 Oct 1861	Mar 1862
Tonnage	454 tons			
Dimensions	204' × 36'6" × 10'			
Machinery	Side wheels			
Armament	2–32pdr MLR and 5 others			

Notes: Purchased at New Orleans. Also known as *Eliza Simmons*.
Service record: Defense of Island No.10, and New Madrid, Mo., Mar–Apr 1862. Engagement at St. Charles, Ark., 17 Jun 1862. Burned to prevent capture near Little Rock, Ark., 9 Oct 1863.

Name	Builder	Launched	Acquired	Comm.
Queen of the West	Cincinnati, Ohio	1854	Feb 1863	Feb 1863

Notes: Ellet ram captured off Fort de Russy, La., 14 Feb 1863. (See p. 118.)

Service record: Engaged USS *Indianola* near New Carthage, Miss., 24 Feb 1863. Caught fire and blew up during engagement in Atchafalaya River, 14 Apr 1863.

Name	Builder	Launched	Acquired	Comm.
St. Mary ex-*Alexandria*	Plaquemine, La.	1862	1862	

Notes: Cottonclad gunboat.

Service record: Operated in Yazoo and Tallahatchie Rivers, 1863. Captured by joint Army–Navy expedition at Yazoo City, 13 Jul 1863. Comm as USS ***Alexandria***.

Fig 11.7: A drawing of the Ellet ram *Queen of the West* with added notes following her capture by the Confederates. (U.S. Naval Historical Center)

Name	Builder	Launched	Acquired	Comm.
Tom Sugg	Cincinnati, Ohio	1860	early 1862	(U)

Notes: Cottonclad gunboat.

Service record: Operated in White River. Captured by USS *Cricket* in Little Red River, 14 Aug 1863. Comm as USS ***Tensas***.

Other Steam Vessels (Mississippi River Ares)

Name	Built at	Launched	Acquired	Tons	Dimensions	Type	Armament
A.W. Baker	Louisville, Ky.	1856		112	95' × 25' × d4'6"	S/W	
Acacia			1862				
Admiral						S/W	
Alamo							
Alfred Robb	Pittsburgh Pa.	1860		86	114'9" × 20' × 4'6"	St/W	
Appleton Belle	West Newton, Pa.	1856		103		St/W	
Argo	Freedom, Pa.	1856		99	136' × 21' × 4'	#St/W	
Argosy							
Argus						St/W	
B.M. Moore	(U)			38	81'5" × 17'1" × 3'	S/W	
Beauregard							
Ben McCulloch	Cincinnati, Ohio	1860		80	100' × 22' × 3.9'	St/W	
Berwick Bay	Plaquemine, La.	1857		64		S/W	
Blue Wing				170			
Bracelet	Louisville, Ky.	1857		169		S/W	
Charm	Cincinnati, Ohio	1860	1861	223		S/W	
Cheney ex-*B.P. Cheney*	Pomeroy, Ohio	1859	1861	247		S/W	
Clara Dolsen	Cincinnati, Ohio	1861		939	268' × 42' × d8'9"	S/W	
Cotton Plant	Rochester, Pa.	1859	1862	59		S/W	
Countess	Cincinnati, Ohio	1860		198	150' × 30' × d4'8"	S/W	
De Soto	New Albany, Ind.	1860		390	180' × 35' × 7'	S/W	
Dew Drop	Cincinnati, Ohio	1858		184		S/W	
Doubloon	Cincinnati, Ohio	1859	1861	293	165' × 33' × 5'	S/W	
Dr. Batey	Louisville, Ky.	1850		281	171' × 28'9" × d6'	S/W	1–6pdr gun
Dunbar	Brownsville, Pa.	1859		213		S/W	
Edward J. Gay	St. Louis, Mo.	1859	1 Feb 1863	823	277' × 39' × 8.5'	S/W	
Elmira	Pittsburgh, Pa.	1858	1861	139	125 × 27 × 4'6"	St/W	
Emma Bett	Pittsburgh, Pa.	1858	1862	79		St/W	
Era No. 5	Pittsburgh, Pa.	1860		115		St/W	
Fairplay	New Albany, Ind.	1859		162	138'8" × 27' × 4'9"	S/W	
Ferd Kennett	St. Louis, Mo.	1861	May 1861	591	238' × 40.5' × 6.5	S/W	
Frolic	Wheeling, Va.	1860		296 or 393		S/W	
Gordon Grant			1861				

Name	Built at	Launched	Acquired	Tons	Dimensions	Type	Armament
Grampus	McKeesport, Pa.	1856	1862	252		St/W	2–12pdr
ex-*Grampus No.2*							
Grand Era	Louisville, Ky.	1853		323	171' × 33' × 6.1'	S/W	
ex-*R.W. McRea*							
H.D. Mears	Wheeling, Va.	1860		338	214' × 34' × 5.5'	#S/W	
H.R.W. Hill	New Albany, Ind.	1852	1861	602		S/W	
Hartford City	McKeesport, Pa.	1856	May 1862	150		S/W	
Hope	Louisville, Ky.	1855	1862	193	128' × 34' × 5'	#St/W	
J.D. Clarke						S/W	
J.D. Swain	Jeffersonville, Ind.	1859		228	150'6" × 30' × d6	S/W	
Jeff Davis							
John Simonds	Freedom, Pa.	1852		1,024	295' × 40.5' × 8'	S/W	
John Walsh	Cincinnati, Ohio	1858		809	275' × 38' × d8	S/W	
Julius	Paducah, Ky.	1859		224		St/W	
ex-*Julius H. Smith*							
Kanawha Valley	Wheeling, Va.	1860		147		#St/W	
ex-*Kanawha Valley No.2* (identity conjectural).							
Kaskaskia	Cincinnati, Ohio	1859		49		S/W	
Kentucky			1861			S/W	
Lady Walton	Cincinnati, Ohio	1858		150		St/W	
Le Grand	New Albany, Ind.	1856		235	198' × 35'6" × 5'6"	S/W	
Linn Boyd	Paducah, Ky.	1859		227		#S/W	
Louis D'Or	Cincinnati, Ohio	1860		343	180.9' × 32.6' × d7.2'	S/W	
Louisville	New Albany, Ind.	1861	Feb 1863	572	227'6" × 38' × 7'	S/W	
Magenta	New Albany, Ind.	1861		782	269' × 39' × 7'9"	S/W	
Magnolia	New Albany, Ind.	1859		824	258' × 44' × 7.5	S/W	
Mars	Cincinnati, Ohio	1856		329	180' × 34',	S/W	
Mary E. Keene	New Albany, Ind.	1860		659	238' × 38' × d7'8"	S/W	
Mary Patterson	Grand Glaize, Ark.	1859		105		#St/W	
May							
Merite			1865				
Mohawk	Elizabeth, Pa.	1860		100		St/W	
Moro	Louisville, Ky.	1858	1862	132	122' × 24'10" × d4'9"	S/W	
Muscle	Allegheny, Pa.	1856		125		St/W	
Natchez	Cincinnati, Ohio	1860		800	273' × 38' × d8'	S/W	
Nelson							
New National							
Nina Simmes	New Albany, Ind.	1860	1861	327	177' × 33' × 6'	S/W	
Ohio Belle	Cincinnati, Ohio	1855		406	185.8' × 39.6' × 7.8	S/W	
Osceola	Louisville, Ky.	1858	1861	157		S/W	
Pargoud	Jeffersonville, Ind.	1860		522	219' × 36' × d7'	S/W	
ex-*J. Frank Pargoud*							
Paul Jones	McKeesport, Pa.	1855		353	172' × 34' × 6'6"	S/W	
Peytona	New Albany, Ind.	1859	17 Apr 1862	685	256' × 37' × 7'6"	S/W	
Prince	Cincinnati, Ohio	1859	1861	223		S/W	
Prince of Wales	Cincinnati, Ohio	1860		572	248' × 40' × 7'	S/W	
R.J. Lackland	Cincinnati, Ohio	1857		710	265' × 40' × d7'	S/W	
Red Rover	Cape Girardeau, Mo.	1859	7 Nov 1861				
Republic	Jeffersonville, Ind.	1855		689	249' × 40' × 7.3'	S/W	
Robert Fulton	California, Pa.	1860		158	137' × 29' × 4.3'	S/W	
St. Francis No.3	Jeffersonville, Ind.	1858		219	160' × 29' × 6	S/W	
Sallie Wood	Paducah, Ky.	1860					

Name	Built at	Launched	Acquired	Tons	Dimensions	Type	Armament
Sam Kirkman	Paducah, Ky.	1857		271	157' × 36.5	St/W	
Samuel Hill							
Samuel Orr	New Albany, Ind.	1861		179	150' × 29' × 5'	St/W	
ex-Sam Orr							
Scotland	Jeffersonville, Ind.	1855		567	230' × 27' × d7'	S/W	
Sharp	Jeffersonville, Ind.	1859		218	147' × 29' × 6.5	S/W	
ex-J.M. Sharp							
Slidell	New Orleans, La.	1862	1862				
Sovereign	Shousetown, Pa.	1855		336	228'6" × 37' × 6.4"	S/W	
Starlight	Jeffersonville, Ind.	1858		280	162' × 31' × 6'	S/W	
T.D. Hine	Jeffersonville, Ind.	1860		205	147' × 30' × 6'	S/W	
ex-T.D.Hine No.2							
35th Parallel	Cincinnati, Ohio	1859		419		S/W	
Trent							
Twilight	(U)			392	215' × 33' × 6'	S/W	
Vicksburg	New Albany, Ind.	1857		625	244.5' × 36' × 7.5	S/W	
Victoria	Elizabeth, Pa.	1858					
Volunteer	Monongahela, Pa.	1862					
W.W. Crawford	Cincinnati, Ohio	1861		123		S/W	
Wade Water Belle							
White Cloud							
Yazoo	Jeffersonville, Ind.	1860		371		S/W	

Notes and service records

A.W. Baker: Cargo ship. Run ashore by USS *Queen of the West* and burned 15 miles below mouth of Red River, 2 Feb 1863.

Acacia: Transport. Captured near Memphis, June 1862. Sunk Aug 1862. (May be side-wheel steamer *Acacia Cottage*, 109 tons, built at California, Pa., 1857, snagged 25 miles above Helena, Ark., 21 Aug 1862.)

Admiral: Picket boat. Captured at New Madrid, Mo., 7 Apr 1862.

Alamo: Transport, Arkansas River and Matagorda Bay, Tex.

Alfred Robb: Transport, Upper Tennessee River. Captured by USS *Tyler* in Tennessee River, 19 Apr 1862. Comm as tinclad USS **Alfred Robb**.

Appleton Belle: Burned to prevent capture at Paris, Tenn., 7 Feb 1862.

Argo: Burned on Sunflower River, Miss. by USS *Linden*, 25 May 1863.

Argosy: Cargo ship or transport. Burned to prevent capture in Sunflower River, Miss., May 1863.

Argus: Army transport. Captured and burned in mouth of Red River, La., 7 Oct 1863.

B..M. Moore: Captured in Hatchee River by USS *Pittsburg*, 9 Jun 1862. Comm as USS **General Pillow**.

Beauregard: Transport. Captured at Mound City, 6 Jun 1864.

Ben McCulloch: Transport. Escaped up Tallahatchie River after fall of Yazoo City, Miss. Burned to avoid capture on Tchula Lake, Jul 1863, or captured as Confederate steamer and burned at Monroe, La., 26 May 1868.

Berwick Bay: Transport. Captured and destroyed by Ellet's rams at mouth of Red River, 3 Feb 1863.

Blue Wing: Seized by Federals at Helena, Ark., Dec 1862.

Bracelet: Transport on White and Arkansas Rivers 1863. Burned at Little Rock, Ark., 10 Sep 1863.

Charm: Transport, ammunition, and gun carrier. Battle of Belmont, Mo., 7 Nov 1861. Burned in Big Black River, Miss., Jul 1863.

Cheney: Cottonclad. Burned at Yazoo City, Miss., 14 Jul 1863.

Clara Dolsen: Captured by Union ships in White River, 14 Jun 1862. Comm as USS **Clara Dolsen**.

Cotton Plant: Transport on Tallahatchie and Yazoo Rivers. Burned to prevent capture in Tallahatchie River, 23 Jul 1863.

Countess: Burned to prevent capture at Alexandria, La., 15 Mar 1864.

De Soto: Surrendered at Island No. 10, 7 Apr 1862. Comm as USS *De Soto* later renamed **General Lyon**.

Dew Drop: Transport. Burned to prevent capture on Sunflower River, Miss., 30 May 1863.

Doubloon: Transport. Scuttled in Red River, May 1864. Raised and repaired. **Later history:** Burned at New Orleans, 24 Jun 1867.

Dr. Batey: (Also spelled *Dr. Beatty*) Engaged USS *Indianola* near New Carthage, Miss., 24 Feb 1863. Escaped capture at Harrisonburg, La., Jul 1863. FFU.

Dunbar: Transport. Sunk to prevent capture in Tennessee River during defense of Fort Henry, Tenn., 6 Feb 1862. **Later history:** Raised and used by U.S. Army. Sold 1865, converted to barge.

Edward J. Gay: Scuttled and burned to avoid capture in Yalobusha River, Miss., 17 Jul 1863.

Elmira: Transport. Captured in Tensas River by USS *Forest Rose* and *Cairo*, 13 Jul 1863. FFU

Emma Bett: Transport. Captured by U.S. and burned in Quiver Bayou, 30 May 1863.

Era No. 5: Transport. Captured by USS *Queen of the West* in Red River, 14 Feb 1863. Lost 1863 while serving Army as dispatch boat. FFU.

Fairplay: Transport. Captured near Vicksburg by Federal gunboats, 18 Aug 1862. Comm as USS **Fairplay**.

Ferd Kennett: Transport. Burned and scuttled in Yalobusha River, Miss., 17 Jul 1863

Frolic: Operated in Red River above Fort de Russy, 1863-64. Captured 1864. **Later history:** Merchant *Frolic*. RR 1873.

Gordon Grant: Tug. Served in Mississippi River near Columbus, Ky. 1861–62. Went aground and burned by accident above Memphis, 5 Jun 1862.

Grampus: Transport. Sunk to prevent capture at Island No.10, 7 Apr 1862. Raised by U.S. Probably the same ship which burned and sank, 11 Jan 1863.

Grand Era: Cottonclad tender in Red River 1863. Engaged USS *Indianola* near New Carthage, Miss., 24 Feb 1863. Dismantled 1864, machinery used in ram *Missouri*.

H.D. Mears: Scuttled to avoid capture in Sunflower River, 25 Jul 1863.

H.R.W. Hill: Transport. Battle of Belmont, Mo., 7 Nov 1861. Captured after Battle of Memphis, 6 Jun 1862. Used by U.S. Army until 1865. BU

Hartford City: Transport. Operated around Vicksburg, Miss. 1862-63. Burned to prevent capture in Tallahatchie River, 18 Jul 1863.

Hope: Transport. Operated in Mississippi and Yazoo Rivers 1862-63. Burned to prevent capture at Fort Pemberton, Miss., 25 May 1863.

J.D. Clarke: Transport. Captured and scuttled in mouth of Red River, 10 Apr 1863.

J.D. Swain: Built by Howard. Transport. Sunk in mouth of McCall's River 1862. Raised Apr 1864 and put in Union service.
   Later history: Merchant *J.D. Swain* 1865. Stranded in Escambia River, Fla., 1869.

Jeff Davis: Steam gunboat. Captured at Memphis, 6 Jun 1862. May have been taken into Union service.

John Simonds: Army support ship. Sunk after capture of Island No.10, 6 Apr 1862.

John Walsh: Transport. Operated in Mississippi and Yazoo Rivers 1862-63. Burned to block Yazoo River below Greenwood, Miss., 22 May 1863.

Julius: Burned to prevent capture at Florence, Ala., 7 Feb 1862.

Kanawha Valley: Hospital boat. Burned at Island No.10, 6 Apr 1862.

Kaskaskia: Transport and towboat. Operated in White and Little Red Rivers. Captured by USS *Cricket* in Little Red River, 14 Sep 1863.
   Later history: U.S. transport 1863. Stranded at Grand Chain, Ill., 20 Feb 1864.

Kentucky: Transport. Operated at Columbus, Ky., Nov 1861 and Island No. 10, Mar 1862. Captured by Western Gunboat Flotilla at Memphis, 6 Jun 1862.
   Later history: Advertised for sale Oct 1862, and probably returned to owners. May be same vessel which was destroyed, perhaps by a boiler explosion, near mouth of Red River, Jun 1865.

Lady Walton: Transport. Surrendered at mouth of White River, 6 Jun 1863.
   Later history: Merchant 1864. Sunk in collision with steamer *Norman* at Warsaw, Ky., 2 Aug 1864.

Le Grand: Transport or storeship.

Linn Boyd: (Also known as *Lynn Boyd.*) Transport. Burned to prevent capture in Tennessee River at mouth of Duck River, Fort Henry, 7 Feb 1862.

Louis D'Or: Cargo ship. Operated on Mississippi and Red Rivers.
   Later history: Merchant *Louis D'Or*, 1865. BU 1867.

Louisville: Cargo ship. Captured on Little Red River by USS *Manitou* and *Rattler*, 13 Jul 1863. Comm as USS **Ouachita**.

Magenta: Transport. Burned to prevent capture above Yazoo City, Miss., in Yazoo River, 14 Jul 1863.

Magnolia: Transport. Burned to prevent capture above Yazoo City, Miss., in Yazoo River, 14 Jul 1863.

Mars: Transport. Captured at Island No.10, 7 Apr 1862.
Later history: Taken into Union service 1862. Merchant *Mars* 1863. Snagged and sunk at Cogswell Landing, Mo., 8 Jul 1865.

Mary E. Keene: Transport. Scuttled or burned at Yazoo City, 24 Jul 1863.

Mary Patterson: Transport. Sunk to obstruct White River near St. Charles, Ark., 16 Jun 1862.

May: Cottonclad transport, 1863.

Merite: Steamer employed as gunboat above New Orleans, Apr 1865.

Mohawk: Watch boat. Sunk at Island No. 10, 7 Apr 1862.

Moro: Transport. Almost captured near Vicksburg, Nov 1862. Captured near mouth of Red River by USS *Queen of the West*, 4 Feb 1863, and burned.

Muscle: Also known as **Cerro Gordo**. Transport, Tennessee River. Captured north of Eastport, Miss., 8 Feb 1862. Foundered in Tennessee River while under tow.

Natchez: Cottonclad. Burned in Yazoo River near Burtonia, Miss., 13 Mar 1863.

Nelson: Mentioned in 1863 in Red River.

New National: Transport. Captured at Memphis, Jun 1862.

Nina Simmes: Transport. Operated near Port Hudson, La., 1861.
   Later history: Merchant *Nina Simmes* 1865. Snagged and lost 60 miles below Bayou Sara, La., 17 Apr 1869.

Ohio Belle: Watch boat. Captured at Island No. 10, 7 Apr 1862.
   Later history: Army transport 1864. Merchant *Alabama Belle*, 1866. BU 1867.

Osceola: Transport. Operating around Shreveport, La., 1864. FFU.

Pargoud: Built by Howard. Cargo ship or transport. Burned to prevent capture in Yazoo River, 14 Jul 1863.

Paul Jones: Transport. Burned with *Charm* in Big Black River, Miss., Jul 1863.

Peytona: Tender to CSS *Mississippi* at New Orleans, 1862. Burned and scuttled to avoid capture at Satartia, Miss. in Yazoo River, 14 Jul 1863.

Prince: Transport. Battle of Belmont, Mo., 7 Nov 1861. Sunk to prevent capture at Island No.10, 27 Feb 1862. Also reported snagged and sunk at Hickman, Ky.

Prince of Wales: Transport. Burned to prevent capture at Yazoo City, 14 Jul 1863.

R.J. Lackland: (Also called *R.J. Lockland.*) Transport. Burned to prevent capture in Yazoo River below Fort Pemberton, Miss., 22 May 1863 (or sunk below Greenwood, Miss., 14 Jul 1863).

Red Rover: Accommodation ship New Orleans, 1861. Defense of Columbus, Ky., 1861. Damaged by gunfire at Island No. 10, 15 Mar 1862. Captured by USS *Mound City* at Island No. 10, 7 Apr 1862. Comm as USS **Red Rover**.

Republic: Transport. Burned to prevent capture at Yazoo City while undergoing conversion to a ram, 21 May 1863.

Robert Fulton: Transport. Captured by USS *Osage* and burned in Red River, 7 Oct 1863.

St Francis No. 3: Built by Howard. Transport. Burned at Little Rock, Ark., 10 Sep 1863.

Sallie Wood: Transport, Tennessee River. Captured by USS *Conestoga* while laid up at Florence, Ala., 8 Feb 1862. Comm as USS **Sallie Wood.**

Sam Kirkman: Cargo ship. Burned to prevent capture at Florence, Ala., 8 Feb 1862.

Samuel Hill: Transport, Mississippi and Yazoo Rivers.

Samuel Orr: Hospital boat, Tennessee River. Burned to prevent capture and blew up at mouth of Duck River, 7 Feb 1862.
   Later history: Rebuilt 1865. Towboat *Robert J. Young* 1875.

Scotland: Transport. Burned to prevent capture at Fort Pemberton, Miss. and to block channel in Yazoo River, Jul 1863.

Sharp: Transport and dispatch boat in Tallahatchie River. Burned to prevent capture in Sunflower River, Aug 1863 or in Yalobusha River, Feb 1864.
   Later history: Rebuilt 1865 as *J.M. Sharp*. RR 1871.

Slidell: Gunboat, 8 guns Destroyed in Tennessee River before 6 Feb 1863.

Sovereign: Transport. Ran aground and captured near Island No.37, 5 Jun 1862. Comm as USS **Sovereign**.

Starlight: Transport. Captured in Thompson's Creek north of Port Hudson, 26 May 1863.
   Later history: Burned at Algiers, La. , 23 Apr 1868.

T.D. Hine: Transport, Mississippi and Red Rivers. Captured 1865.
   Later history: Merchant *T.D.Hine* 1865. RR 1871.

35th Parallel: Cottonclad. Burned to prevent capture after running aground in Tallahatchie River, 13 Mar 1863.

Trent: Transport, Mississippi and Red Rivers 1862-63.

Twilight: Transport. Ouachita River, 1864-65.
   Later history: Merchant *Twilight* 1865. FFU.

Vicksburg: (Also known as *City of Vicksburg.*) Rammed and damaged by USS *Queen of the West* at Vicksburg, 2 Feb 1863. Machinery removed; later went adrift and burned, 29 Mar 1863.

Victoria: Transport. Captured after battle of Memphis, 6 Jun 1862. Comm as USS **Abraham**.

Volunteer: Transport. Captured off Natchez Island, Miss., 25 Nov 1863. Comm as USS **Volunteer**.

W.W.Crawford: Transport. Captured Aug 1863.
   Later history: Merchant 1865. RR 1868.

Wade Water Belle: Captured by USS *Conestoga*, prior to Sep 1862.

White Cloud: Transport. Captured near Island No.10 by USS *New Era*, 13 Feb 1863.

Yazoo: Transport. Captured and sunk at Island No. 10, 7 Apr 1862.

12
PRIVATEERS

The Confederate government granted letters of marque and reprisal to a number of individuals. All ships which received such letters are listed below.

Name	Type	Tons	Dimensions	Built	Issued at	Described
A.C. Gunnison	Steam tug	54	70' × 15' × d7'	1861	Mobile, Ala.	p. 178
Beauregard	Schooner	101		1862	Charleston, S.C.	
Bonita	Steamer	1,110		1862		
Boston	Steamer			1863	Mobile, Ala.	
Charlotte Clark	Steamer	1,100		1863		
Chesapeake	Schooner	60		1863		
Dixie	Schooner	110		1861	Charleston, S.C.	
Dove	Steamer	1,170		1862		
F.S. Bartow	Schooner	74				
Gallatin	Schooner	150		1861		p. 184
General N.S. Reneau	Steamer			1861		
Gibraltar	Schooner	60		1864	Mobile, Ala.	
Gordon	Steamer	518	175' × (U) × 7'	1861		p. 199
Governor A. Mouton	Steamer	125		1861	New Orleans, La.	
Hallie Jackson	Brig			1861		
Isabella	Steamer	801		1861	New Orleans, La.	
J.C. Calhoun	Sidewheel steamer	508		1861	New Orleans, La.	p. 61
J.M. Chapman	Schooner	90				
J.O. Nixon	Schooner	95		1861	New Orleans, La.	
Jefferson Davis ex-Echo, ex-Putnam	Brig	187		1861	Charleston, S.C.	
Joseph Landis	Steamer	400		1861		
Josephine	Schooner			1861		
Lamar	Schooner			1861		
Lorton	Schooner	95		1861	Baltimore, Md.	
Manassas	Ram	387		1861	Algiers, La.	p. 152
Mariner	Steamer	135		1861	Wilmington, N.C.	

Name	Type	Tons	Dimensions	Built	Issued at	Described
Matilda	Bark	400		1861	New Orleans, La.	
Mocking Bird	Steamer	1,290		1862	New Orleans, La.	
Monticello	Ironclad steamer	460		1861		
Music	Sidewheel steamer	273	172' × 29' × 6'	1861	New Orleans, La.	p. 175
Onward	Schooner	70		1861		
Paul Jones	Schooner	160		1864		
Pelican	Steamer	1,479		1862		
Petrel	Schooner	82		1861	Charleston, S.C.	p. 184
ex-*William Aiken*, ex-*Eclipse*						
Phenix	Steamer	1,644	245' × 34' × d19'	1861	Wilmington, Del.	
Pioneer	Submarine			1861		p. 167
Pioneer II	Submarine			1863		
Rattlesnake	Sidewheel steamer	1,221	215'6" × 34'6" × d21'9"	1862		p. 161
ex-*Thomas Wragg*, ex-CSS *Nashville*						
Rescue	Schooner	120	150' ×(U)			
Sallie	Schooner	170		1861	Charleston, S.C.	
Savannah	Schooner	53		1861	Charleston, S.C.	
Sealine	Brig	179		1861	Baltimore, Md.	
Stephen R. Mallory	Schooner	74		1864		
ex-*Don Jose*						
Stonewall Jackson	Schooner			1864		
Texas	Sidewheel steamer	800		1863		
Triton						
V.H. Ivy	Sidewheel steamer	454	191' × 28'	1861	New Orleans, La	p. 172
William H. Webb	Sidewheel steamer	656	195' × 31'6" × 9'6"	1861		p. 174
York	Schooner	68		1861	Norfolk, Va.	

13
BLOCKADE RUNNERS

The blockade runners listed below are believed to have been owned fully or in part by the government of the Confederate States of America or of individual states. There were many other privately owned blockade runners.

Name	Builder	Launched
Colonel Lamb	Liverpool, England (Jones Quiggin)	1864
Hope	Liverpoolm, England (Jones Quiggin)	1864
Tonnage	1,788 tons, 1132 GRT (Hope)	
Dimensions	281'6" (oa) 279'6" (bp) × 26' (40' oa) × 11'	
Machinery	Side wheels, 2-cyl. oscillating engines (72" × 6'), 4 boilers, NHP 350, 16 knots (Victoria Engine Works)	

Notes: Near sisters, steel hulls. *Colonel Lamb* was the largest steel ship built to date. Two funnels.

Service Records

Colonel Lamb: Ran blockade two times.
Later history: Merchant *Colonel Lamb* 1865. Became Greek *Ariel*, then *Bomboulina*. Blew up while loading munitions for Greece at Liverpool, 17 Nov 1867.
Hope: Captured by USS *Eolus* in Cape Fear River, 22 Oct 1864.
Later history: Merchant *Savannah* 1865. Sold 1866 to Spanish Navy, as paddle frigate, renamed *Churruca*. Stricken 1880, BU 1885.

Name	Builder	Launched
Bat	Liverpool, England (Jones Quiggin)	21 Jun 1864
Deer	Liverpool, England (W.H. Potter)	31 Aug 1864
Owl	Liverpool, England (Jones Quiggin)	21 Jun 1864
Stag	Liverpool, England (Bowdler Chaffer)	1 Aug 1864
Tonnage	771 tons B	
Dimensions	250' (oa) 230' (bp) × 26' × 6'6"	
Machinery	Side wheels, 2-cyl. vertical oscillating engines (52" × 4'6"), 2 boilers, NHP 180, 13 knots (Watt)	

Notes: Schooner rig, two funnels, steel hull. Government-owned British register ships. *Deer* and *Stag* subcontracted by Jones & Quiggin.

Service Records

Bat: Captured by USS *Montgomery* in Cape Fear River on first voyage, 10 Oct 1864. Commissioned as USS **Bat**.
Deer: Captured by USS *Canonicus, Catskill*, and *Monadnock* off Charleston, on second voyage, 18 Feb 1865.
Later history: Merchant *Palmyra* 1865. Sold foreign (Argentina) 1869. FFU.
Owl: Ran blockade seven times from Sep 1864 into Wilmington, to May 1865 to Galveston. Sold in Britain 1865.
Later history: Merchant *Owl* 1865.
Stag: Ran blockade three times. Captured by USS *Monticello* off Wilmington, N.C., 20 Jan 1865. Sold 1865,
Later history: Merchant *Zenobia* 1865. Sold foreign (Argentina) 1867. Probably transport *Cenobia*, renamed *Villeta* 1875, then *Santa Fe*, converted 1875 to three-mast schooner *Maria Luisa*.

Name	Builder	Launched
Lark	Birkenhead, England (Laird)	Oct 1864
Wren	Birkenhead, England (Laird)	Nov 1864
Tonnage	390 tons GRT	
Dimensions	211'2" × 23'2" × 6' (Wren), 210'8" (Lark)	
Machinery	Side wheels, 2 oscillating engines (44" × 3'6"), 2 boilers, HP 150, 12 knots	

Notes: Steel hull. Two funnels. Designed for use in isolated harbors.
Later history:
Lark: Ran blockade eight times.
Later history: Merchant *Port Said* 1869 and lengthened, *Hankow*, 1870; became two ships 1873, 1) *Lilian*, RR 1886 and 2) *Bergen*, renamed *Marseilles*, 1873; *Baron Pahlen*, 1874; *Friede*, 1886; *Citta di Riposto*, 1895. BU 1896.
Wren: Ran blockade seven times. Captured 1865.
Later history: Merchant *Tartar* 1865. Sold foreign 1868.

Fig 13.1: The blockade runner *Colonel Lamb*, built in Liverpool in 1864, which made two successful runs. She was the largest steel ship built up to that time. (U.S. Naval Historical Center)

Name	Builder	Launched
Condor	Glasgow, Scotland (Elder)	Jul 1864
Falcon	Glasgow, Scotland (Elder)	12 May 1864
Flamingo	Glasgow, Scotland (Elder)	26 May 1864
Ptarmigan	Glasgow, Scotland (Elder)	Jun 1864
Tonnage	284 tons GRT, also reported as 446 tons	
Dimensions	270' × 24' × 7'	
Machinery	Side wheels, 15 knots	
Complement	50	

Notes: Long low iron hull with straight stem, three tall raked funnels, single mast. Owned by Collie & Co.

Service Record

Condor: Went aground at entrance to Wilmington, N.C., evading wreck of stranded *Night Hawk* on maiden voyage, 1 Oct 1864. Captained by A. C. Hobart-Hampden, RN, VC. The famous courier and spy Rosa Greenhow was among those lost.
Falcon: Ran blockade five times.
Flamingo: Ran blockade two times 1864–65. Possibly wrecked off Charleston 1865.
Ptarmigan: Ran blockade three times 1864–65. Possibly renamed *Evelyn*. Sold to Argentina as naval transport *Pampa*.

Name	Builder	Launched
Curlew	Liverpool, England (Jones Quiggin)	15 Feb 1865
Plover	Liverpool, England (Jones Quiggin)	15 Feb 1865
Snipe	Liverpool, England (Jones Quiggin)	15 Feb 1865
Widgeon	Liverpool, England (Jones Quiggin)	15 Feb 1865
Tonnage	645 tons, 409 GRT	
Dimensions	225' × 24' × 6', d11'	
Machinery	Side wheels, HP 160, 12 knots (*Curlew, Plover*: Forrester; *Snipe, Widgeon*: Watt)	

Notes: Steel hull. Were to be turned over to Confederate States when paid for in cotton. Delivered too late for service. FFU

Name	Builder	Launched
Albatross	Birkenhead, England (Laird)	Mar 1865
Penguin	Birkenhead, England (Laird)	Mar 1865
Tonnage	1,063 tons, 659 GRT	
Dimensions	249' × 30'1" × 10', d13'2"	
Machinery	Side wheels, 2 oscillating engines, NHP 260, 12 knots	

Notes: Steel hull, ordered by Bulloch. Were to be turned over to Confederate States when paid for in cotton.

Later history:

Albatross: Sold to Brazil 1865, as transport *Isabel*. Sold 1876.
Penguin: Greek royal yacht *Amfitriti*, 1869. Hulk 1906, sold 1909.

Name	Builder	Launched
Rosine	Liverpool, England (Jones Quiggin)	15 Oct 1864
Ruby	Liverpool, England (Jones Quiggin)	1865
Tonnage	1,391 tons. 900 GRT	
Dimensions	270' (oa) 260'3" (bp) × 33' × 9', 15'6"d	
Machinery	Side wheels. NHP 300, 14 knots	

Notes: Steel hulls. *Ruby* not launched at the end of the war. Four funnels. Were to be turned over to Confederate States when paid for in cotton.

Later history:

Rosine: Sold to Turkey 1869. Turkish dispatch vessel *Eser-i-Nusret*. RR 1890.
Ruby: Sold to Turkey 1869. Turkish dispatch vessel *Medar-i-Zafer*. RR 1890.

Name	Builder	Launched
Louisa Ann Fanny	London, England (Dudgeon)	1865
Mary Augusta	London, England (Dudgeon)	1865
Tonnage	972 tons GRT	
Dimensions	250' × 25'6" × 10'	
Machinery	2 screws, 2 2-cyl. (40" × 1'10"), 1750 HP, 16.2 knots	

Notes: Contracted by Captain Bulloch. Planned names *Waccamaw* and *Black Warrior*. *Adventure* and *Enterprise*, also ordered as commerce raiders, were similar in size. The ultimate disposition of these four ships has been the subject of much speculation.

Service Record:

Louisa Ann Fanny: Supplied CSS *Stonewall* at Lisbon, Mar 1865. Arrived Havana too late to run blockade. May have been sold to Venezuela as naval transport *Bolivar* or Brazilian transport *Werneck*. Also reported wrecked on Sandhammaren Reef, near Ystad in Sweden, 9 Nov 1880.
Mary Augusta: Completed too late.

Later history: May have been sold to Brazil as naval transport and renamed *Vassimon*.

Name	Builder	Launched
Advance ex-*Lord Clyde*	Greenock, Scotland (Caird)	3 Jul 1862

Notes: Name often written *A.D. Vance*. Owned by state of North Carolina.

Service record: Ran blockade 18 times. Captured by USS *Santiago de Cuba* off Wilmington, N.C., 10 Sep 1864. Comm in USN as *Advance*. (See p. 45.)

Fig 13.2: An artist's sketch of the blockade runner *Flamingo*, one of four sisters built at Glasgow. (U.S. Naval Historical Center)

Name	Builder	Launched	Acquired
Arizona	Wilmington, Del. (Harlan)	1859	15 Jan 1862

Notes: Taken for public service at New Orleans.
Service Record: Ran blockade two times, renamed ***Caroline*** Oct 1862. Captured by USS *Montgomery* off Mobile, 29 Oct 1862. Comm in USN as ***Arizona***. (See p. 46.)

Name	Builder	Launched	Acquired
Atlantic	New York, N.Y. (Collyer)	1852	14 Jan 1862
Tonnage	623 tons		
Dimensions	217' × 27'6" × d10'6"		
Machinery	Side wheels. vertical beam engines		

Notes: Seized at New Orleans. Wood hull
Service Record: Ran blockade eight times under British flag, renamed *Elizabeth*, 1863. Ran aground and burned to prevent capture in Cape Fear River, 24 Sep 1863.

Name	Builder	Launched	Acquired
Austin	Wilmington, Del. (Harlan)	1860	14 Jan 1862

Notes: Seized at New Orleans.
Service Record: Ran blockade ten times. Renamed *Donegal*. Captured by USS *Metacomet* off Mobile Bay, 6 Jun 1864. Comm in USN as ***Donegal*** (see p. 77.)

Name	Builder	Launched	In service
Beauregard ex-*Priscilla C. Ferguson*	Charleston, S.C.	1850	14 Oct 1861

Notes: Privateer brig (or schooner)
Service Record: Captured by USS *William G. Anderson* in Bahama Channel, 12 Nov 1861, one week after sailing. Comm in USN as USS ***Beauregard***.

Name	Builder	Launched
Bahama	Stockton, England (Pearse)	24 Jan 1862
Bermuda	Stockton, England (Pearse)	9 Jul 1861
Tonnage	*Bahama*: 888 tons GRT; *Bermuda*: 897 GRT, 1003 n/r.	
Dimensions	*Bahama*: 226' × 29'2" × 19'	
	Bermuda: 211' × 30'3" × 16'	
Machinery	1 screw, vertical condensing direct-acting engine (45" × 2'6"), 135 HP, 11 knots (Fossick & Hackworth)	

Notes: Near sisters. Iron hull, brig rig. Three masts, one funnel. Bark rig.
Service records:

Bahama: Rendezvous with CSS *Florida* in Bahamas with armaments, Apr 1862. Rendezvous with CSS *Alabama* at sea near Madeira, with guns, stores, and crew members, Aug 1862.
Later history: Merchant *Bahama* 1864. Sold in Japan and renamed *Meiko Maru* 1864; *Bahama* 1868, *Meiko Maru* 1870; engines removed and renamed *Sumanoura Maru* 1877 (Japanese bark). Sunk in collision with *Yamashiro Maru*, 1884.
Bermuda: Blockade runner, ran blockade 2 times. Captured by USS *Mercedita* northeast of Abaco Island, Bahamas, 27 Apr 1862. Comm. in USN as USS ***Bermuda***. (See p. 79.)

Blanche, see CSS General Rusk (p. 174)
Camilla, see USS America (p. 106)
Chameleon, see CSS Tallahassee (p. 161)

Name	Builder	Launched
City of Richmond ex-*Avalon*	London, England (Dudgeon)	1864
Tonnage	829 GRT	
Dimensions	230' × 27' × 14.6'	
Machinery	Side wheels	

Notes: Iron hull.
Service record: Diverted as tender to CSS *Stonewall*, Jan 1865, and never ran blockade.
Later history: Merchant *Agnes Arkle*. Sold to Brazil 1866.

Name	Builder	Launched
Coquette	Renfrew, Scotland (Henderson)	23 Jun 1863
Matilda	Renfrew, Scotland (Henderson)	1863
Tonnage	531 tons; 390 tons reg.	
Dimensions	228' × 25' × 10'	
Machinery	2 screws, 13.5 knots (Bldr)	

Notes: Iron hull. Purchased Dec 1863.
Service Records:

Coquette: Ran blockade 13 times. Ran aground off Wilmington, N.C., 8 Mar 1864 and damaged propeller. Damaged in collision with HMS *Vesuvius* in Bermuda, Apr 1864. Sold Jul 1864 but continued as blockade runner.
Later history: Merchant *Maryland*. Sold foreign 1873.
Matilda: Wrecked on Lundy Island in River Clyde, Scotland, in thick fog on passage to Nassau, 4 Apr 1864.

Name	Builder	Launched
Cornubia	Hayle, England (Harvey)	27 Feb 1858

Notes: Cornwall packet steamer.
Service Record: Ran blockade 23 times 1861–63. Renamed ***Lady Davis***, Jun 1863. Captured by USS *James Adger* and *Niphon* at New Inlet, N.C., 8 Nov 1863. Comm in USN as ***Cornubia***. (See p. 48.)

Name	Builder	Launched
Ceres	London, England (Dudgeon)	1863
Dee	London, England (Dudgeon)	1863

Fig 13.3: The blockade runner *Robert E. Lee* was captured in 1863 after 15 successful runs. It later became the USS *Fort Donelson*.

Don	London, England (Dudgeon)	1863
Flora	London, England (Dudgeon)	1862
Hebe	London, England (Dudgeon)	1863
Vesta	London, England (Dudgeon)	1862
Tonnage	353 to 449 GRT	
Dimensions	175′ × 22′6″ × d12′3″ (average)	
Machinery	2 screws, 2 2-cyl. horizontal direct-acting engines (26″ × 1′9″), 4 boilers	

Notes: *Don* owned by North Carolina. Others of this group of similar twin-screw fast ships were *Annie* (later USS *Preston*), *Kate*, and *Venus*, privately owned.

Service Record:

Ceres: Run aground off Old Inlet, N.C., 6 Dec 1863. Set on fire but captured by USS *Violet*.

Dee: Ran blockade seven times. Chased ashore by USS *Cambridge* and destroyed near Masonboro Inlet, 5 Feb 1864.

Don: Captured by USS *Pequot* off Wilmington, N.C., 4 Mar 1864. Comm in USN as *Don*.

Flora: Ran blockade 11 times. Sold to Confederate government, Oct 1863; renamed *Virginia* and then *Cape Fear*. Used as a transport on Cape Fear River. Scuttled off Smithville, 16 Jan 1865.

Hebe: Ran blockade three times. Chased ashore by USS *Shokokon* at New Inlet, N.C., and destroyed, 18 Aug 1863.

Vesta: Run aground and destroyed while trying to enter Little River Inlet, N.C., on first voyage, 11 Jan 1863.

Name	Builder	Launched
Eugenie	Hull, England (Samuelson)	1862
Tonnage	428 GRT	
Dimensions	235′ × 24.2′ × 11.9′	
Machinery	Side wheels, 2-cyl. oscillating engines (58″ × 4′6″), 13 knots	

Notes: Iron hull

Service record: Ran blockade 10 times. Ran onto a sandbar and was badly damaged running blockade into Wilmington, N.C., 7 Sep 1863. Repaired and sent to Nassau.

Later history: Merchant *Hilda*, 1868. BU 1889.

Fingal, see CSS *Atlanta* (p. 151)
Gibraltar, see CSS *Sumter* (p. 160)

Name	Builder	Launched
Granite City	Dumbarton, Scotland (A. Denny)	11 Nov 1862

ex-USS *Granite City*

Notes: For details see USS *Granite City*, p. . Captured at Calcasieu Pass, La., 28 Apr 1864.

Service Record: Possibly renamed *Three Marys*. Run ashore off Calcasieu River by USS *Penguin* and destroyed, 21 Jan 1865.

Name	Builder	Launched
Greyhound	Glasgow, Scotland (Kirkpatrick)	19 Oct 1863
Tonnage	290 tons, 583 tons n/r	
Dimensions	201.4′ × 22.7′ × 13′	
Machinery	1 screw, 2 oscillating engines (Caird)	

Notes: Three masts, iron hull.

Service Record: Captured by USS *Connecticut* off Wilmington, N.C., 10 May 1864.

Later history: Merchant *Greyhound* 1864. Lost by stranding at Beaver Harbour, Nova Scotia, 14 Nov 1865. [A ship of this name was reported sunk by a torpedo (mine) near Bermuda Hundred, Va., while serving as floating headquarters of General Ben Butler, but this was a different ship and not a Navy ship.]

Name	Builder	Launched
Hansa	Glasgow, Scotland	1858
Tonnage	257 tons	
Dimensions	177′6″ × 22′3″ × d12′2″, also reported as 209′8″ in length	
Machinery	Side wheels, 12 knots	

Notes: Owned by State of North Carolina. Two funnels.
Service record: Ran blockade 21 times.
Later history: Lengthened 1864. FFU.

Name	Builder	Launched
Harriet Pinckney	Middlesboro, England (Richardson)	Jul 1862
Tonnage	715 tons GRT	
Dimensions	191.3′ × 28.9′ × d17.6′	
Machinery	1 shaft, 2-cyl. engines	

Notes: Brig rig. Wood hull with iron frame. Owned by Confederate Army, carried supplies from England to West Indies.
Service record: Assigned as tender for CSS *Rappahannock*.
Later history: Merchant *Leda*. Wrecked near Bayonne, France, 12 Jun 1896.

Name	Builder	Launched
Juno (I)	Glasgow, Scotland (Tod)	1860
ex-*Helen* (III), ex-*Juno*		
Tonnage	185 tons	
Dimensions	(U)	
Machinery	Side wheels	

Note: Previously used as a gunboat at Charleston, S.C.
Service Record: Foundered in gale after leaving Charleston, 10 Mar 1864.

Name	Builder	Launched
Juno (II)	Bristol, England (G.K. Stothert)	1853
Tonnage	298 tons GRT	
Dimensions	163′2″ × 19′7″ × 11′4″	
Machinery	Side wheels, 2-cyl. engine (46″ × 4′), 13.5 knots	
Complement	50	

Note: Iron hull, schooner rig.
Service Record: Captured by USS *Connecticut* off Wilmington, N.C., 22 Sep 1863.
Later history: Merchant *Dacotah* 1864. Sold foreign 1867.

Lavinia, see *Harriet Lane* (p. 173).

Name	Builder	Launched
Lynx	Liverpool, England (Jones Quiggin)	1864
Tonnage	372 tons GRT	
Dimensions	219′ × 21′ (36′oa) × d12′	
Machinery	Side wheels. HP 150, 12 knots	

Notes: Two funnels and two masts, steel hull.
Service Record: Ran blockade ten times. Damaged by gunfire of USS *Howquah* and forced aground 6 miles below Ft. Fisher when leaving Wilmington, N.C., 25 Sep 1864.

Blockade Runners 195

Name	Builder	Launched	Acquired
Magnolia	New York, N.Y. (Simonson)	22 Aug 1854	Jan 1862

Notes: Seized at New Orleans.
Service record: Captured on first trip by USS *Brooklyn* and *South Carolina* off Pass a l'Outre, La., 19 Feb 1862. Comm in USN as *Magnolia*.

Name	Builder	Launched	Acquired
Matagorda	Wilmington, Del. (Harlan)	1858	Jan 1862
ex-*Alice*			
Tonnage	616 tons, 1,250 GRT		
Dimensions	220′ × 30′ × d10′6″		
Machinery	Side wheels, beam engine (44″ × 11′)		

Notes: Seized at New Orleans. Iron hull.
Service Record: Ran blockade 19 times. Captured 75 miles off Cape San Antonio, Cuba, by USS *Magnolia*, 10 Sep 1864.
Later history: Merchant *Matagorda*, 1864. RR 1871.

Name	Builder	Launched
Merrimac	London, England (Mare)	Sep 1862
ex-*Nangis*		

Service Record: Ran blockade two times. Sold to private interests after first voyage. Captured by USS *Iroquois* off Cape Fear, 24 Jul 1863. Comm. in USN as *Merrimac*.

Name	Builder	Launched
Nita	Mobile, Ala.	1856
ex-*Crescent*		

Service record: Captured by USS *De Soto* en route Havana–Mobile, 17 Aug 1863. Comm in USN as *Nita*. (See p. 64.)

Name	Builder	Launched
Phantom	Liverpool, England (Fawcett Preston)	1862
Tonnage	266 tons, 322 tons GRT	
Dimensions	192′9″ (bp) × 22′ × 8′6″, d12′	
Machinery	1 screw, HP 170, 14 knots (Bldr)	
Complement	33	

Notes: Steel hull, schooner rig. Owned by Dept of Ordnance.
Service Record: Ran blockade five times. Wrecked off Cape Fear while being pursued by USS *Connecticut*, 23 Sep 1863.

Name	Builder	Launched	Acquired
Robert E. Lee	Glasgow (Thomson)	16 May 1860	Fall 1862
ex-*Giraffe* (Dec 1862)			

Notes: Also known as *R.E. Lee*. Built as Irish Sea ferry.
Service Record: Ran blockade 15 times. Captured by USS *James Adger* and *Iron Age* off Bermuda, 9 Nov 1863. Comm in USN as *Fort Donelson*. (See p. 49.)

Name	Builder	Launched
Theodora	New York, N.Y. (Sneeden)	1852
ex-*Gordon*, ex-*Carolina*		
Tonnage	518 tons B.	

Dimensions	175' × U × 7'
Machinery	Side wheels, vertical beam engine
Armament	3 guns

Notes: Fitted out as privateer *Gordon,* July 1861. Sold to CSN as ***Nassau***. Carried Confederate envoys Mason and Slidell to Cuba, where they boarded the steamer *Trent*, Oct 1861. (see *San Jacinto*)

Service Record: Ran blockade seven times. Captured by USS *Victoria* and *State of Georgia* off Wilmington, N.C., 28 May 1862.

Tropic (*Huntress*, see p. 180)

Name	Builder	Launched	Acquired
Virgin	Glasgow, Scotland (Aitken Mansel)	1864	(U)
Tonnage	442 tons		
Dimensions	216' × 24'5" × 10'9"		
Machinery	Sidewheels		

Note: Iron hull.

Service Record: Seized by U.S. at Mobile, 12 Apr 1865.

Later history: Turned over to Revenue Cutter Service but was not suitable. Merchant *Virginius* 1870. Captured as gun-runner by Spanish cruiser *Tornado*, 31 Oct 1873; captain and 39 others were executed causing an international incident almost leading to war with Spain. Turned over to USN but foundered in storm off North Carolina, 26 Dec 1873.

Name	Builder	Launched	Acquired
Victoria	Mystic, Conn. (Greenman)	1859	Jan 1862
Tonnage	487 tons B.		
Dimensions	180' × 29.5' × 9.6'		
Machinery	Side wheels, inclined direct engines		

Notes: Seized at New Orleans.

Service Record: Ran blockade six times 1861–62.

Later history: Merchant *Victoria* 1863. Lost by stranding at Bayou d'Arbonne, La., Jan 1866.

Name	Builder	Launched
William G. Hewes	Wilmington, Del. (Harlan)	15 Oct 1860

Notes: Iron hull. Seized at New Orleans, Apr 1861. Name sometimes misspelled "Heines," "Hawes," or "Jewess."

Service Record: Ran blockade twelve times 1861–63. Renamed ***Ella and Annie***, Apr 1863. Captured off New Inlet, N.C. by USS *Niphon*, 9 Nov 1863. Comm in USN as ***Malvern***.

14
TENDERS

See also blockade runners *Bahama*, *City of Richmond*, and *Harriet Pinckney*.

Name	Builder	Launched
Agrippina	Scarborough, (Tindall)	1834
Tonnage	285 tons	
Dimensions	97' × 24'4" × d16'5"	

Service record: Bark. Tender to CSS *Alabama*. Supplied her in Caribbean, Azores, and other places. Blockaded by USS *Mohican* & *Onward* at Bahia, Brazil, May–Jun 1863.

Name	Builder	Launched
Alar	Neath, Wales	1847
Tonnage	150 tons	
Dimensions	134' × 17' × 9'3"	

Service record: Steamer. Tender to CSS *Georgia*.

Name	Builder	Launched
Castor	Malta	1851
Tonnage	252 tons	

Service record: Bark. Tender to CSS *Georgia*.

Name	Builder	Launched
Lapwing	(U)	(U)

Service record: Bark. Captured by CSS *Florida* in South Atlantic, 28 Mar 1863; armed as tender with two howitzers. Burned at Rocas, west of Fernando de Noronha, Brazil, after *Florida* failed to appear, 20 Jun 1863.

Name	Builder	Launched
Laurel	Glasgow, Scotland (Inglis)	3 Sep 1863
Tonnage	565 tons GRT	
Dimensions	185' × 25'2" × 12'2"	
Machinery	1 shaft, HP 140, 13 knots	

Notes: Former Liverpool packet purchased 1864.

Service Record: Armed and brought officers to CSS *Shenandoah* at Funchal, Madeira Is., Oct 1864. Ran blockade twice then sold in 1864.

Later history: Merchant *Confederate States*, Dec 1864. Lengthened (to 207') and converted to screw 1869. Renamed *Walter Stanhope*, later *Niobe*.

Appendix
LIST OF SHIPBUILDERS

Abrahams	John J. Abrahams, Baltimore, Md.	Collier	Hambleton, Collier, Peoria, Ill.
Adams	Aquila Adams, Boston, Mass.	Collyer	Thomas Collyer, New York, N.Y.
A. Denny	Archibald Denny, Dumbarton, Scotland	Columbus NYd*	Columbus Navy Yard (CSN), Columbus, Ga.
Aitken Mansel	Aitken & Mansel, Greenock, Scotland	Colwell	Joseph Colwell, Jersey City, N.J.
Allaire	Allaire Iron Works, New York, N.Y.	Coney	James Coney, Boston, Mass.
Allen	G.B. Allen & Co., St. Louis, Mo.	Continental	Continental Iron Works, Greenpoint, N.Y.
Arman	L'Arman Freres, Bordeaux, France	Corliss	Corliss Steam Engine Co., Providence, R.I.
Ash	James Ash, Millwall, London, England	Cramp	C.H. & W.H. Cramp, Philadelphia, Pa.
Atlantic	Atlantic Iron Works, Boston, Mass.	Curtis	Paul Curtis, Boston, Mass.
Barclay Curle	Barclay Curle & Co., Whiteinch, Glasgow, Scotland	Curtis & Tilden	Curtis & Tilden, Boston, Mass.
Bassett Selma*	Henry D. Bassett, Selma, Ala.	Curtis, Medford	James O. Curtis, Medford, Mass.
Bassett*	Bassett & Gates, Mobile, Ala.	Delamater	C.H. Delamater Iron Works, New York, N.Y.
Bell	David Bell, Buffalo, N.Y.	Denmead	A. & W. Denmead & Son, Baltimore, Md.
Berry	Berry & Bros., Wilmington, N.C.	Denny	Wm. Denny & Bros. Ltd., Dumbarton, Scotland
Birely	Jacob Birely, Kensington, Philadelphia, Pa.	Dialogue	J.H. Dialogue & Son, Camden, N.J.
Birely Lynn	Jacob Birely & John W. Lynn, Philadelphia, Pa.	Dolan	Dolan & Farron, Williamsburg, N.Y.
Boston NYd	Boston Navy Yard, Charlestown, Boston, Mass.	Donahue	Donahue, Ryan & Secor, San Francisco, Calif.
Boston Loco	Boston Locomotive Works, Boston, Mass.	Dubigeon	Chantiers Dubigeon, Nantes, France
Brooklyn NYd	Brooklyn Navy Yard, Brooklyn, N.Y.	Dudgeon	J.& W. Dudgeon, Millwall, London, England
Brown	Joseph Brown, Cincinnati, Ohio	Dunham	R.H. Dunham & Co., New York, N.Y.
Brown & Bell	Brown & Bell, New York, N.Y.	Dyer	Joseph W. Dyer, Portland, Me.
Burtis	Devine Burtis, Brooklyn, N.Y.	E. Webb	Eckford Webb, Greenpoint, N.Y.
Caird	Caird & Co. Ltd., Greenock, Scotland	Eads	James B. Eads, Mound City, Ill. & St. Louis, Mo.
Cameron*	Cameron & Co., Charleston, S.C.	Eason*	James M. Eason, Charleston, S.C.
Capes	Capes & Allison, Hoboken, N.J.	Elder	Randolph Elder & Co., Glasgow, Scotland
Carondelet	Union Iron Works, Carondelet, Mo.	Elliot*	Gilbert Elliot, Edwards Ferry, N.C.
Carter	C.P. Carter, Belfast, Me.	Ellis	William M. Ellis, Washington, D.C.
Cassidy*	J.L. Cassidy, Wilmington, N.C.	Englis	John Englis, New York, N.Y.
City Point	City Point Works, Boston, Mass.	Esler	Henry Esler & Co., New York, N.Y.
Cobb	Cobb & Fields, Jersey City, N.J.	Etna	Etna Iron Works. New York, N.Y.

Fardy	J.J. Fardy & Bros., Baltimore, Md.	McKay	Donald McKay, Boston, Mass.
Fletcher	Fletcher Harrison & Co., New York, N.Y. (Later W.A. Fletcher North River Iron Works)	McKnight	John L. McKnight, Bordentown, N.J.
		McLeod	Daniel McLeod, Brooklyn, N.Y.
Fulton	Fulton Iron Works, New York, N.Y.	Means*	Gilbert Means, Peedee Navy Yard (CSN), Mars Bluff, S.C.
Fulton IW	Fulton Iron Works, St. Louis, Mo.		
Gardner	C.F. & H.D. Gardner, East Boston, Mass.	Mehaffy	A. Mehaffy & Co., Portsmouth, Va.
Gatz	Gatz McClune & Co., St. Louis, Mo.	Merrick	Merrick & Sons, Philadelphia, Pa.
Gaylord	T. G. Gaylord, St. Louis, Mo.	Merrick & Towne	Merrick & Towne, Philadelphia, Pa.
Gildersleeve	Gildersleeve & Sons (Portland), East Haddam, Conn.	Mershon	D.S. Mershon, Jr., Bordentown, N.J.
Globe	Globe Iron Works, Boston, Mass.	Miller	William C. Miller, Liverpool, England
Goodspeed	E.G. & W.H. Goodspeed, East Haddam, Conn.	Moore	Moore & Richardson, Cincinnati, Ohio
Gray	J. & R.I. Gray, New York, N.Y.	Morgan	Morgan Iron Works, New York, N.Y.
Greenman	George Greenman & Co., Mystic, Conn.	Morris	J.P. Morris & Co., Philadelphia, Pa.
Greenwood	Miles Greenwood, Cincinnati, Ohio	Morris Towne	Morris Towne & Co., Philadelphia, Pa.
Hall, Boston	Samuel Hall, Boston, Mass.	Murphy	James Murphy, New York, N.Y. (Murphy McCrady & Worden)
Harlan	Harlan & Hollingsworth Co., Wilmington, Del.		
Harvey	Harvey & Son, Hayle, England	Murray	Murray & Hazelhurst, Baltimore, Md.
Hazelhurst	Hazelhurst & Wiegard, Baltimore, Md.	Mystic	Mystic Iron Works, Mystic, Conn.
Hews	Hews & Philips, Belfast, Ireland	Napier	R. Napier & Sons Ltd., Dalmuir, Glasgow, Scotland
Hickson	Robert Hickson & Co., Belfast, Ireland	Neafie	Neafie & Levy, Philadelphia, Pa.
Highland	Highland Iron Works, Newburgh, N.Y.	Neilson	Neilson & Co., Glasgow, Scotland
Hill	Lawrence Hill, Renfrew, Scotland	Neptune	Neptune Works, New York, N.Y.
Hillman	Hillman & Streaker, Philadelphia, Pa.	Niles	Niles Tool Works, Niles, Ohio
Hood	J.M. Hood, Somerset, Mass. & Bristol, R.I.	Norfolk NYd	Norfolk Navy Yard, Norfolk, Va.
Hughes *	John Hughes & Co., Bayou St. John, La.	Novelty	Novelty Iron Works, New York, N.Y.
Inglis	A. & J. Inglis Ltd., Glasgow, Scotland	Oregon	Oregon Iron Works, Portland, Ore.
Jackman	George W. Jackman, Jr., Newburyport, Mass.	Oswald	T.R. Oswald & Co., Sunderland, England
Jackson	Jackson & Watkins, London, England	Pacific	Pacific Iron Works, Bridgeport, Conn.
Jewett	James C. Jewett & Co., Brooklyn, N.Y.	Page & Allen	Page & Allen, Portsmouth, Va.
Jollet	Jollet & Babin, Nantes, France	Page & Bacon	Page & Bacon, New Albany, Ind.
Jones Quiggin	Jones Quiggin & Co., Liverpool, England	Patapsco	Patapsco Steam Tug Co., Baltimore, Md.
Junger	McCord & Junger, New Albany, INInd.	Pearse	Pearse & Lockwood, Stockton–on–Tees, England
Kirkpatrick	Kirkpatrick & McIntyre, Glasgow, Scotland	Pease	Pease & Murphy, New York, N.Y.
L & F	Lawrence & Foulkes, Brooklyn, N.Y.	Peck	Peck & Kirby, Cleveland, Ohio
Laing	Sir James Laing & Sons Ltd., Sunderland, England	Pensacola NYd	Pensacola Navy Yard, Pensacola, Fla.
Laird	Laird Brothers, Birkenhead, England	Perine	Perine's Perine's Iron Works, Williamsburg, N.Y.
Larrabee	Larrabee & Allen, Bath, Me.	Philadelphia NYd	Philadelphia Navy Yard, Philadelphia, Pa.
Lawrence	George W. Lawrence, Thomaston, Me.	Pile	W. Pile & Co., Sunderland, England
Lawrie	Lawrie & Co., Whiteinch, Glasgow, Scotland	Poillon	C. & R. Poillon, New York, N.Y.
Loring	Harrison Loring, Boston, Mass.	Pook	S.H. Pook, Fairhaven, Conn.
Lupton	Edward Lupton, Brooklyn, N.Y.	Pook Mystic	S.H. Pook Iron Works, Mystic, Conn.
Lynn	John W. Lynn, Philadelphia, Pa.	Poole	Poole & Hunt, Baltimore, Md.
Mallory	Charles H. Mallory, Mystic, Conn.	Portland	Portland Locomotive Works, Portland, Me.
Mare	Mare & Co., Blackwall, London, England.	Portsmouth NYd	Portsmouth Navy Yard, Kittery, Me.
Mare Island NYd	Mare Island Navy Yard, Vallejo, Calif.	Providence	Providence Steam Engine Works, Providence, R.I.
Marvel	T.S. Marvel, Newburgh, N.Y.	Pusey	Pusey & Jones, Wilmington, Del.
Maxson Fish	Maxson, Fish & Co., Mystic River, Conn.	Quintard	Quintard Iron Works, New York, N.Y.
Mazeline	Mazeline Engine Works, Le Havre, France	Reaney	Reaney, Son & Archbold, Chester, Pa.
McCord	Charles W. McCord, St. Louis, Mo.	Reaney Neafie	Reaney & Neafie, Chester, Pa.

Reeder	Charles Reeder, Baltimore, Md.	Thatcher	W. & A. Thatcher, Wilmington, Del.
Reliance	Reliance Machine Co., Mystic, Conn	Thompson	Nathaniel W. Thompson, Kennebunk, Me.
Richmond NYd*	Richmond Navy Yard (CSN), Richmond, Va.	Thomson	J. & G. Thomson Ltd., Clydebank, Glasgow, Scotland
Risdon	Risdon Iron Works, San Francisco, Calif.	Tift*	N. & A. Tift, Jefferson City, La.
Roach	John Roach & Son, Chester, Pa.	Tod	Tod & McGregor, Glasgow, Scotland
Robb	John A. Robb, Baltimore, Md.	Tomlinson	Tomlinson, Hartapee & Co., Pittsburgh, Pa.
Robinson	J.A. & E.T. Robinson, Baltimore, Md.	Tredegar*	Tredegar Iron Works, Richmond, Va.
Rodman	Rodman & Co., New York, N.Y.	Tucker	F.Z. Tucker, Brooklyn, N.Y.
Roosevelt	Roosevelt, Joyce & Co., New York, N.Y.	Tufts	Otis Tufts, Boston, Mass.
S. Brooklyn	South Brooklyn Engine Works, Brooklyn, N.Y.	Underhill	J.S. Underhill Dry Dock & Iron Works, New York, N.Y.
S. Smith	Sylvanus Smith, Boston, Mass.	Union DD	Union Dry Dock Co., Buffalo, N.Y.
Sampson	A. & G.T. Sampson, Boston, Mass	Union IW	Union Iron Works, San Francisco, Calif.
Samuelson	Martin Samuelson & Co., Hull, England	Van Deusen	J.B. & J.D. Van Deusen, New York, N.Y.
Secor	Zeno Secor & Co., Jersey City, N.J.	Vaughn & Lynn	Vaughn & Lynn, Philadelphia, Pa.
Shirley*	J.T. Shirley, Memphis, Tenn	Vulcan	Vulcan Iron Works, New York, N.Y.
Simons	William Simons & Co. Ltd., Renfrew, Scotland	W.Collyer	William Collyer, Greenpoint, N.Y.
Simonson	Jeremiah Simonson, New York, N.Y.	Wash IW	Washington Iron Works, Newburgh, N.Y.
Sneeden	Samuel Sneeden, New York, N.Y.	Washington NYd	Washington Navy Yard, Washington, D.C.
Sneeden Whitlock	Sneeden Whitlock & Co., Greenpoint, N.Y.	Watts	Watts & Co., England
Snowden & Mason	Snowden & Mason, Pittsburgh, Pa.	Webb	William H. Webb, New York, N.Y.
Stack	Thomas Stack, New York, N.Y.	Webb & Bell	Webb & Bell, New York, N.Y.
Stack & Joyce	Stack & Joyce, Brooklyn, N.Y.	Weidner	Charles A. Weidner, Philadelphia, Pa.
Stackhouse	Stackhouse & Tomlinson, Pittsburgh, Pa.	West Point	West Point Foundry, Newburgh, N.Y.
Steers	Henry Steers, Greenpoint, N.Y.	Westervelt	Jacob A. Westervelt, New York, N.Y.
Stephen	A. Stephen & Sons Ltd., Govan, Glasgow, Scotland	Whitlock	E.S. Whitlock, Greenpoint, N.Y.
Stevens	Robert L. Stevens, Hoboken, N.J.	Wilcox	Wilcox & Whiting, Camden, N.J.
Stillman	Stillman, Allen & Co., New York, N.Y.	Williams	E.F. Williams, Greenpoint, N.Y.
Stover	Stover Machine Co., New York, N.Y.	Willink*	Henry F. Willink, Savannah, Ga.
Sutton	James T. Sutton & Co., Philadelphia, Pa.	Winson	Winson & Co., Philadelphia, Pa.
Swift	Alexander Swift & Co., Cincinnati, Ohio	Woodruff	Woodruff & Beach, Hartford, Conn.
Taunton	Taunton Locomotive Works, Taunton, Mass.	Wright	Wright & Whitaker, Buffalo, N.Y.
Teas	Teas & Birely, Philadelphia, Pa.	Wm. Wright	William Wright & Co., Newburgh, N.Y.
Terry	B.C. Terry, Keyport, N.J.		
Tetlow	James Tetlow, Boston, Mass.		

*Confederate shipyards

BIBLIOGRAPHY

SERIAL PUBLICATIONS:

American Neptune
Annual Reports of the Navy Department
Journal of the Franklin Institute (1845–1865)
Merchant Vessels of the United States (various from 1870)
New York Times (1861–1869)
The Original American Lloyds Register of American and Foreign Shipping (1860 and 1868)
Record of American and Foreign Shipping, American Bureau of Shipping (various from 1870)
Warship International

BOOKS:

Bauer, K. Jack. *Ships of the Navy 1775–1969*. Troy, NY: Rensselaer Polytechnic Institute, 1969.

Bennett, Frank M. *The Steam Navy of the United States*. Pittsburgh, PA: Warren & Co., 1896.

Bourne, John A. *A Treatise on the Screw Propeller*. London: Longmans Green, 1867

Canney, Donald L. *U.S. Coast Guard and Revenue Cutters 1790–1935*. Annapolis, MD: Naval Institute Press, 1995.

Canney, Donald L. *The Old Steam Navy: Frigates, Sloops and Gunboats, 1815–1885*. Annapolis, MD: Naval Institute Press, 1990.

Canney, Donald L. *The Old Steam Navy: The Ironclads, 1842–1885*. Annapolis, MD: Naval Institute Press, 1993.

Cooney, David M. *Chronology of the United States Navy 1775–1965*. New York: Franklin Watts, 1965.

Heyl, Erik. *Early American Steamers*. 6 vols. Buffalo, NY: author, 1953–59.

Milligan, John D. *Gunboats Down the Mississippi*. Annapolis, MD: Naval Institute Press, 1965.

Mitchell, C. Bradford, ed., *Merchant Steam Vessels of the United States 1790–1868: The Lytle–Holdcamper List*. Staten Island, NY: Steamship Historical Society of America, 1975.

Neeser, Robert W. *Statistical and Chronological History of the United States Navy 1775–1907*. New York: Macmillan, 1909.

Ridgely–Nevitt, Cedric. *American Steamships on the Atlantic*. Newark, NJ: University of Delaware, 1981.

Scharf, J. Thomas. *History of the Confederate States Navy. 1887*. Columbia, MD: Fairfax Press, reprint 1977.

U.S. Coast Guard. *Record of Movements, Vessels of the U.S. Coast Guard. 1790–1933*. Washington D.C.: U.S. Coast Guard Headquarters, 1935.

U.S. Navy. *Civil War Naval Chronology, 1861–1865*, 6 vols. Washington, D.C.: Navy Department, 1961–66.

U.S. Navy. *Dictionary of American Naval Fighting Ships*, 8 vols. Washington, D.C.: Naval Historical Center, Department of the Navy, 1959–81.

U.S. Navy. *Official Records of Union and Confederate Navies in the War of the Rebellion*, Edited by Richard Rush. 30 vols. Washington, D.C.: GPO, 1895–1921.

Ward, J.H. *Steam for the Million:* A Popular Treatise on Steam and Its Application to the Useful Arts, Especially to Navigation ... New York,1876.

Way, Frederick, Jr. *Way's Packet Directory, 1848–1983*. Athens, OH: Ohio University Press, 1983.

Wise, Stephen R. *Lifeline of the Confederacy: Blockade Running during the Civil War*. Columbia, S.C.: University of South Carolina, 1988.

INDEX

**CIVIL WAR INDEX
PLAN OF THE BOOK**

**Part I United States
Navy warships**

I. Contents
   Introduction ix
   Explanation of data xi
   USN Chronology xiii
   Abbreviations used xvii
   Naval ordnance xix
1. Armored vessels 3
   Monitors 4
   Ironclads 11
2. Unarmored steam vessels 13
   Ships on Navy List 1855 13
      sidewheel frigates 14
      sidewheel sloops 14
      sidewheel gunboat 15
      screw frigate 15
      screw gunboat 15
   Screw frigates 15
   Screw cruisers 18
   Screw sloops 20
   Screw gunboats 29
   Sidewheel sloop 34
   Sidewheel gunboats 34
   Spar torpedo boats 40
   Submarine 41
   Picket boats 42
3. Acquired combatant vessels 43
   Prewar merchant acquisitions . 43
   Acquired merchant vessels
   Large sidewheel combatants .. 45
   Large screw combatants 53
   Coastal sidewheel comb. 61

   Coastal s/w ferryboats 66
   Coastal combatants 69
   Coastal screw comb. 70
4. Service vessels 77
   Sidewheel auxiliaries 77
   Screw auxiliaries 79
   Tugs 81
      Navy-built steam tugs 81
      Acquired s/w tugs 81
      Acquired screw tugs 83
5. Sailing ships 93
   Ships on the Navy list 1855 .. 93
      Ships of the line 93
      Frigates 93
      Sloops 95
      Brigs 96
      Storeships 97
   Wartime acquisitions 97
      Mortar schooners 97
      Ships 100
      Barks 101
      Brigs 104
      Schooners 104
6. Mississippi River Fleet 109
   Armored vessels 109
      River monitors 109
      River ironclads 112
      Converted river iron. 114
   Unarmored vessels 116
      Timberclads 116
      Ellet rams 117
      Rams 119
      River gunboats 119
      Large tinclads 120
      Tinclads 121
         Sidewheelers 121
         Sternwheelers 124

      Other tinclads 131
      River service craft 131/132
      Tugs 134
7. US Revenue Cutter Service .. 137
   Steamers 137
   Small schooners 143
8. US Coast Survey 145

**Part II Confederate
States Navy**

Introduction to Part II
   Confederate Navy 147
9. Armored vessels 149
   Seagoing armored ships 149
   Casemate ironclads 150
10. Unarmored steam vessels ... 157
   Cruisers 157
   Gunboats 163
   Torpedo boats 164
   Submarine torpedo boats ... 165
11. Area defense forces 167
   Louisiana 167
      Miss. River Defense 167
      Gunboats 169
   Texas 173
   Gulf coast 175
   Atlantic coast 177
   Virginia 181
   Mississippi River 184
12. Privateers 189
13. Blockade runners 191
14. Tenders 197

List of shipbuilders 199
Bibliography 203

CIVIL WAR INDEX - UNION SHIPS

(*Note: Revenue cutters indexed by last name*)

A.C. Powell, 83
A. Houghton, 101
Abeona, 121
Abraham, 132
Acacia, 70
Achilles, 10, see Modoc
Active (USRC), 141
Adams, 34, illus.36
Adela, 45
Adirondack, 24
Admiral, 79
Adolph Hugel, 97
Advance, 45
Aetna, 10, see Nausett
Agamenticus, 8, illus.8
Agassiz (USRC), 141, 143
Agawam, 38
Aitken, William (USRC), 141
Ajax, 7, see Manayunk
Alabama (armed steamer), 45
Alabama (ship-of-the-line), 93
Alarm, 41
Alaska, 27, illus.29
Albany, 27, see Contoocook
Albatross, 53
Albemarle, 104
Alert (USRC), 142
Alert, 33
Alert, 83, see A.C. Powell
Alexandria, 121
Alfred Robb, 124
Algoma, 10, see Squando
Algoma, 27, see Benicia
Algonquin, 38
Allegheny, 14
Allen, Philip (USRC), 141
Alliance, 34
Alligator, 41
Alpha, 83
Althea, 84
Amanda, 101
Amaranthus, 84
America, 106, illus.107
Ammonoosuc, 18
Amphitrite, 8, see Tonawanda
Anacostia, 43
Anemone, 84
Anna, 106
Antelope, 69
Antietam (USRC), 141
Antietam, 17
Antona, 53
Appleton, John (USRC), 141
Arago (USRC), 141, 143
Arapaho, 26,

Arethusa, 79
Argos, 10, see Koka
Argosy, 124
Ariel, 106
Aries, 53
Arizona, 46
Arkansas, 79
Arletta, 97
Aroostook, 29, illus.33
Arthur, 102
Ascutney, 38
Ashuelot, 40
Ashuelot (USRC), 136
Aster, 84
Astoria, 27, see Omaha
Atlas, 6, see Nahant
Augusta, 46
Augusta Dunsmore, 53
Avenger (bark), 102
Avenger (ram), 119
Azalea, 84

Bache (USCS), 143
Bailey (USCS), 143
Bainbridge, 96
Baltimore, 77
Bancroft (USCS), 143
Banshee, 46
Barataria, 69
Baron de Kalb, 113, illus.113, see St. Louis
Bat, 46, illus.47
Beauregard, 106
Belle, 84
Ben Morgan, 100
Benefit, 132
Benicia, 27
Benton, 114, illus.114
Bermuda, 79
Beta, 85
Bibb, George M. (USRC), 138, see Moccasin
Bibb (USCS), 143
Bienville, 46
Bignonia, 85
Black, Jeremiah S. (USRC), 141
Black Hawk, 120, illus.120
Bloomer, 69
Blue Light, 81
Bohio, 104
Bon Homme Richard, 19
Boutwell, George S. (USRC), 139
Bowditch (USCS), 143
Boxer, 52, see Tristram Shandy
Brandywine, 93
Braziliera, 102
Brilliant, 124
Britannia, 47
Bronx (USRC), 136
Brooklyn, 20, illus.21

Brown, Aaron V. (USRC), 141
Buckthorn, 85

C.P. Williams, 97
Cactus, 77
Cairo, 112
Calhoun, 61, illus.62
California, 17
Calypso, 53
Camanche, 5, illus.5
Cambridge, (sloop) 26, see Congress
Cambridge (armed steamer), 54
Camelia, 85
Campbell, James (USRC), 141
Campbell (USRC), 141, see Lane
Canandaigua, 25
Canonicus, 6, illus.7
Carmita, 106
Carnation, 85
Carondelet, 112
Carrabasset, 121
Casco, 9, illus.3, 11
Cass, Lewis (USRC), 141
Castor, 7, see Mahopac
Caswell (USCS), 143
Catalpa, 85
Catawba, 6
Catskill, 5, illus.6
Cayuga, 29
Centaur, 7, see Saugus
Ceres, 61
Champion, 122
Chandler, William D. (USRC), 138, see Jasmine
Charles Phelps, 100
Charlotte, 106
Charybdis, 10, see Cohoes
Chase, Salmon P. (USRC) (1865), 137, illus.138
Chase, Salmon P. (USRC) (1878), 140
Chatham, 77
Chattanooga, 20
Chenango, 38
Cherokee, 54
Chickasaw, 111
Chicopee, 38
Chillicothe, 113
Chimo, 9
Chippewa, 29
Choctaw, 116, illus.116
Chocura, 29, illus.32
Chotauk, 106
Cimarron, 37
Cincinnati, 112
Circassian, 79
Circe, 112, see Marietta
Clara Dolsen, 132
Clematis, 85
Clifton, 66
Clinton, 85

Clover, 85
Clyde, 47
Cobb, Howell (USRC), 141, 143
Coeur de Lion, 61, illus.63
Cohasset, 86
Cohoes, 9
Colfax, Schuyler (USRC), 139
Collier, 125
Colorado, 17
Colossus (tinclad), 125
Colossus (monitor), 9, see *Kalamazoo*
Columbia (armed steamer), 54
Columbia (frigate), 93
Columbine, 81
Columbus, 93
Commodore, 61
Commodore Barney, 66
Commodore Hull, 67
Commodore Jones, 67
Commodore McDonough, 67
Commodore Morris, 67
Commodore Perry, 66, illus.68
Commodore Read, 67
Conemaugh, 38, illus.39
Conestoga, 116, illus.117
Confiance, 27
Congress (sloop), 26, illus.28
Congress (frigate), 94
Connecticut (cruiser), 19,
    see *Pompanoosuc*
Connecticut (armed steamer), 47, illus.48
Constellation, 95
Constitution, 94
Contoocook, 26
Cornubia, 48
Corwin, Thomas (USRC), 140
Corwin (USCS), 143
Corypheus, 106
Courier, 100
Covington, 122
Cowslip, 61
Coxe, Tench (USRC), 140
Crawford (USCS), 143
Crawford, William H. (USRC) (1861), 141
Crawford, William H. (USRC), (1873), 138,
    see *Nansemond*
Cricket, 125
Crocus, 86
Crusader, 43, illus.44
Cumberland, 95
Curlew (armed steamer), 70
Curlew (tinclad), 125
Currituck, 70
Cushing, Caleb (USRC), 141
Cuyahoga (USRC), 136
Cyane, 95
Cyclops, 111, see *Kickapoo*

Dacotah, 24
Daffodil, 82

Dahlia, 134
Dai Ching, 70
Daisy, 134, illus.134
Dale, 95
Dallas, Alexander J. (USRC), 139
Dan Smith, 98
Dana (USCS), 143
Dana, 104
Dandelion, 86
Darlington, 77
Dart, 106
Davis, Jefferson (USRC), 141
Dawn, 70
Daylight, 71
De Soto, 46, illus.47
Decatur, 95
Delaware (armed steamer), 61
Delaware (frigate), 18, illus.18
    see *Piscataqua*
Delaware (USRC), 138
Delta, 86
Despatch, 44
Detroit, 27
Dexter, Samuel (USRC), 139
Diana, 70
Dick Fulton, 119
Dictator, 8, illus.9
Discover (USRC), 142
Dix, John A. (USRC) (1865), 137
Dix, John A. (USRC) (1873), 138,
    see *Wilderness*
Dobbin, James C. (USRC), 141
Dodge, Henry (USRC), 141
Dolphin, 97
Don, 71
Donegal, 77
Dragon, 71
Duane, William J. (USRC), 141
Dumbarton, 48
Dunderberg, 12, illus.12

E.B. Hale, 71
Eastport, 115, illus.116
Elfin, 125
Elk, 122
Ella, 78
Ellen, 67
Ellis, 82
Emerald, 86
Emma Henry, 48
Emma , 55
Enterprise, 34
Eolus, 10, see *Shawnee*
Eolus, 48
Epervier, 33
Epsilon, 86
Erebus, 10, see *Squando*
Essex (river ironclad), 114, illus.115
Essex (gunboat), 34
Estrella, 71

Ethan Allen, 102, illus.102
Etlah, 9
Eugenie, 104
Eureka, 71
Eutaw, 38,
Ewing, Thomas (USRC), 136,
    see *Northerner*
Exchange, 125

Fahkee, 79
Fairplay, 122, illus.122
Fairy, 125
Falmouth, 95
Farallones, 102
Fauntleroy (USCS), 143
Fawn, 125, illus.126
Fearnot, 100
Fern, 134
Fernandina, 102
Fessenden, William P. (USRC) (1883), 140
Fessenden, William Pitt (USRC) (1865), 137
Fire Fly (USCS), 143
Flag, 55
Flambeau, 55
Florida (cruiser), 19, illus.20
    see *Wampanoag*
Florida (armed steamer), 45
Floyd, John B. (USRC), 141
Forest Rose, 126, illus.126
Fort Donelson, 49
Fort Henry, 67
Fort Hindman, 123, see *James Thompson*
Fort Jackson, 49
Fort Morgan, 79, see *Admiral*
Fortune, 81
Forward, Walter B. (USRC) (1842), 141
Forward, Walter (USRC) (1882), 140
Fox, 106, F
Franklin, 15, illus.15
Fredonia, 97
Frolic, 45, see *Advance*
Fuchsia, 71, illus.72
Fulton, 14
Fury, 10, see *Umpqua*

G.L. Brockenborough, 106
G.W.Blunt, 104
Galatea, 55
Galena (ironclad), 11, illus.12
Galena (sloop), 28
Gallatin, Albert (USRC), 139
Gamage, 126
Gamma, 86
Gazelle, 122
Gem of the Sea, 103
Gemsbok, 103
General Bragg, 119, illus.120
General Burnside, 122
General Grant, 122

Index

General Lyon, 132
General Pillow, 123
General Price, 120, illus.120
General Sherman, 122
General Thomas, 122
Genesee, 37
George Mangham, 98
George W. Rodgers, 106, see *Shark*
Geranium, 82
Gerdes (USCS), 143
Germantown, 95
Gertrude, 55
Gettysburg, 49
Gladiolus, 86
Glance, 87
Glasgow, 78
Glaucus, 55
Glide (I), 127
Glide (II), 127
Goliath, 6, see *Catskill*
Gorgon, 10, see *Naubuc*
Governor Buckingham, 56
Grampus, 132
Grand Gulf, 56
Granite, 106
Granite City, 62
Grant, U.S. (USRC), 139
Great Western, 132
Grossbeak, 123
Guard, 101, see *National Guard*
Guerriere, 18
Guthrie, James (USRC) (1882), 140
Guthrie, James (USRC) (1868), 139
Guthrie (USCS), 143

Hall, James (USCS), 143
Hamilton, Alexander (USRC), 139
Hamlin, Hannibal (USRC), 139
Harcourt, 87
Harpy, 10, see *Klamath*
Harriet Lane, 62, illus.64;(USRC), 135
Hartford, 20, illus.20
Hartley, John F. (USRC), 140
Harvest Moon, 49
Hassalo, 18
Hassler (USCS), 143
Hastings, 123
Hatteras, 49
Hecate, 10, see *Etlah*
Hecla, 9, see *Shackamaxon*
Heliotrope, 82
Hendrick Hudson, 56, illus.57
Henry, Joseph (USCS), 143
Henry Andrew, 72
Henry Brinker, 72
Henry Janes, 98
Hercules, 9, see *Quinsigamond*
Hercules (USRC), 135
Hero, 10, see *Casco*
Hetzel, 62, illus.64

Hibiscus, 72
Hollyhock, 83
Home, 80
Honduras, 78, illus.78
Honeysuckle, 87
Hope, 105
Horace Beals, 98
Hornet, 50, illus.50, see *Lady Sterling*
Housatonic, 24
Howell Cobb, 106
Howquah, 72
Hoyt, 87
Humboldt (USCS), 143
Hunchback, 68
Huntress, 127
Huntsville, 56
Huron (1861), 29
Huron (1874), 33
Huron (1876), 34, illus.35, see *Alliance*
Hyacinth, 134
Hydra, 10, see *Tunxis*
Hydrangea, 87

Ibex, 123
Ice Boat, 78
Ida, 83
Idaho, 20
Illinois, 18,
Independence, 94
Indianola, 113
Innis, 87
Ino, 100
Intrepid, 41
Iosco, 38
Iowa, 18, see *Ammonoosuc*
Iris (monitor), 10, see *Shiloh*
Iris (tug), 87
Iron Age, 57
Ironsides Jr., 103
Iroquois, 22
Isaac N. Seymour, 63
Isaac Smith, 72
Isilda, 106
Island Belle, 83
Isonomia, 63
Itasca, 29
Iuka, 57
Ivy, 134

J.C. Kuhn, 103
J.W.Wilder, 106
Jackson, Andrew (USRC), 141
Jacob Bell, 63
James Adger, 49
James L. Davis, 103
James S. Chambers, 105
James Thompson, 123
Jamestown, 95
Jasmine, 87, (USRC), 138
Jason, 6, see *Sangamon*

Java, 18
Jean Sands, 87
John Adams, 95
John Griffith, 98
John Hancock, 44
John L. Lockwood, 63
John P. Jackson, 68
Johnson, Andrew (USRC), 137, illus.138
Jonquil, 87
Judge Torrence, 132
Julia, 106
Juliet, 127
Juniata, 24, illus.25
Juniper, 88

Kalamazoo, 9
Kalmia, 87, see *Innis*
Kanawha, 29
Kankakee (USRC), 136
Kansas, 32
Katahdin, 29
Kate, 127
Kearsarge, 22
Kennebec, 29
Kenosha, 27
Kensington, 80
Kenwood, 127
Keokuk, 12
Keosauqua, 26
Kewanee (USRC), 136
Kewaydin (river monitor), 111,
    see *Kickapoo*
Kewaydin (frigate), 18, see *Pennsylvania*
Key West, 127
Keystone State, 50
Kickapoo, 111
Kineo, 29
King Philip, 78
Kingfisher, 103
Kinsman, 70
Kittatinny, 105
Klamath, 10
Koka, 10

Laburnum, 88
Lackawanna, 26
Lady Sterling, 50
Lafayette, 115, illus.116
Lancaster (Ellet ram), 117
Lancaster (sloop), 21, illus.23
Lane, Joseph (USRC), 141
Larkspur, 88
Laurel, 134
Lavender, 88
Lavinia Logan, 132
Lehigh, 5
Lenapee, 38
Leslie, 88
Levant, 96
Lexington (timberclad), 117, illus.117

Lexington (sloop), 96
Leyden, 81
Lightning, 106
Lilac, 88
Lilian, 50
Lily, 134
Lincoln (USRC), 138
Linden, 127
Lioness, 118
Little Ada, 73
Little Rebel, 131
Lodona, 57
Louisiana, 73
Louisville, 112, illus.113
Lupin, 88

Macedonian, 96
Mackinaw, 38
Madawaska, 19
Madgie, 73
Magnolia, 50, illus.51
Mahaska, 35
Mahoning (USRC), 136
Mahopac, 6
Malvern, 51
Manayunk, 6
Manhattan, 7
Manhattan (USRC), 139
Manitou (sloop), 26, see *Worcester*
Manitou (tinclad), 123, see *James Thompson*
Maratanza, 35, illus.37
Marblehead, 29
Marcy, William L. (USRC), 141
Marcy (USCS), 143
Maria, 81
Maria A. Wood, 98
Maria Denning, 132
Maria J. Carlton, 98
Marietta, 112
Marigold, 88
Marion (1873), 28
Marion (1839), 96
Marmora, 128
Martin, 89
Mary Sanford, 80
Mason, John Y. (USCS), 143
Massachusetts (bark), 102, see *Farallones*
Massachusetts (armed steamer), 57
Massachusetts (monitor), 9, see *Passaconaway*
Mattabesett, 38
Matthew Vassar, 98
Maumee, 32
Mayflower, 81
McClelland, Robert (USRC), 141
McCulloch, Hugh (USRC) (1865), 137
McCulloch, Hugh (USRC) (1877), 139, see *Mosswood*

McLane, Louis (USRC), 138, see *Delaware*
Medusa, 6, see *Nantucket*
Memphis, 58, illus.59
Mendota, 38
Mercedita, 58
Mercury, 64
Meredith (USCS), 143
Meredosia, 27
Merrimac (armed steamer), 51
Merrimack (frigate), 15, illus.16
Metacomet, 38
Meteor, 128
Miami (USRC), 136
Miami, 34
Miantonomoh, 8
Michigan, 15
Midnight, 103
Mignonette, 134
Milwaukee, 111, illus.112
Minerva, 112, see *Sandusky*
Mingo (Ellet ram), 118
Mingoe (gunboat), 38
Minnesota, 16, illus.17
Minnetonka (monitor), 10, see *Naubuc*
Minnetonka (frigate), 18, see *California*
Mississippi, 14
Mist, 128
Mistletoe, 134
Mobile, 52, see *Tennessee*
Moccasin, 89, (USRC) 138
Modoc, 10
Mohawk, 44
Mohican (1859), 22
Mohican (1883), 28
Mohongo, 40, illus.41
Monadnock, 8
Monarch, 118
Mondamin, 26
Monitor, 4, illus.4
Monocacy, 40
Monongahela, 26, illus.28
Montauk, 5
Monterey, 89
Montgomery, 56
Monticello, 58
Moodna, 12, see *Keokuk*
Moose, 128
Morning Light, 100
Morris (USRC), 141
Morse, 68
Mosholu, 26, see *Severn*
Mosswood (USRC), 139
Mound City, 112
Mount Vernon, 58
Mount Washington, 64
Muscoota, 40
Myrtle, 134
Mystic, 44

Nahant, 5
Naiad, 128
Nansemond, 64, (USRC) 138
Nantasket, 33
Nantucket, 5
Napa, 10
Narcissus, 89
Narragansett, 24
National Guard, 101
Naubuc, 10
Naugatuck, 73
Naumkeag, 128
Nausett, 10
Nebraska, 9, see *Shackamaxon*
Nemaha (USRC), 135
Nemesis, 10, see *Napa*
Neosho, 109, illus.110
Neptune (armed steamer), 55
Neptune (monitor), 7, see *Manhattan*
Nereus, 55
Neshaminy, 18
Nettle, 134
Nevada, 18, see *Neshaminy*
New Berne, 80
New Era (tinclad), 128
New Era (river ironclad), 114, see *Essex*
New Hampshire, 93, see *Alabama*
New Ironsides, 11, illus.11
New London, 73
New National, 133
New Orleans, 93
New York (frigate), 18
New York (ship of the line), 93
Niagara, 17, illus.17
Nightingale, 101
Nina, 81
Niobe, 10, see *Waxsaw*
Niphon, 59
Nipsic (1863), 32
Nipsic (1878), 34
Nita, 64
Norfolk Packet, 99
North Carolina, 93
Northerner (USRC), 136
Norwich, 74, illus.73
Nyack, 32
Nyanza, 123
Nymph, 128

O.M. Pettit, 83
Octorara, 35
Ohio, 93
Oleander, 83
Oliver H. Lee, 99
Omaha, 27, illus.30
Oneida, 22
Oneota, 7
Onondaga, 5, illus.5
Ontario, 18, see *New York*
Onward, 101

210 Index

Oregon, 9, see *Quinsigamond*
Oriole, 129
Orion, 10, see *Chimo*
Orvetta, 99
Osage, 109, illus.111
Osceola, 110, see *Neosho*
Osceola, 38
Ossipee, 24, illus.25
Otsego (monitor), 10, see *Tunxis*
Otsego (gunboat), 38
Ottawa, 29
Ouachita, 120, illus.121
Owasco, 29
Ozark, 110, illus.111

Pampero, 101
Pansy, 134
Para, 99
Passaconaway, 9
Passaic, 5, illus.6
Patapsco, 5
Patroon, 74
Paul Jones, 36
Paw Paw, 131
Pawnee, 24, illus.24
Pawtucket, 38
Pawtuxet (USRC), 136
Peacock, 27
Peirce (USCS), 143
Pembina, 29
Penguin, 59
Pennsylvania (frigate), 18
Pennsylvania (ship of the line), 93
Penobscot, 29
Pensacola, 21
Peony, 89
Peoria, 38
Peosta, 123
Pequot, 32
Percy Drayton, 106
Peri , 129
Periwinkle, 89
Perry, 97
Perry, Commodore (USRC), 136
Peterhoff, 59,
Petrel (USCS), 143
Petrel (USRC), 141
Petrel, 129
Philadelphia, 78
Philippi, 64
Phlox, 79
Pilgrim, 81
Pink, 89
Pinola, 29
Pinta, 81, illus.82
Piscataqua (monitor), 10, see *Chimo*
Piscataqua (frigate), 18
Pittsburg, 112
Planter, 65

Plymouth (1869), 28, illus.29,
  see *Kenosha*
Plymouth (1843), 96
Pocahontas, 44, illus.44, see *Despatch*
Polaris, 89, see *Periwinkle*
Pompanoosuc, 19
Pontiac, 38
Pontoosuc, 38
Poppy, 89
Port Fire, 81
Port Royal, 37
Portsmouth, 96
Potomac, 94
Potomska, 74
Powhatan, 14, illus.14
Prairie Bird, 129
Preble, 96
Preston, 59
Primrose, 90
Princess Royal, 59
Princeton, 15
Proteus, 55, illus.57
Pulaski, 45
Puritan, 9,
Pursuit, 103
Purveyor, 103, see *J.C. Kuhn*
Pushmataha, 26, see *Congress*

Quaker City, 51
Queen, 80
Queen City, 123
Queen of the West, 118
Quinnebaug (1875), 28, illus.30
Quinnebaug (1866), 33
Quinsigamond, 9

R.B.Forbes, 90
R.R.Cuyler, 60
Racer, 99
Racer (USRC), 141
Rachel Seaman, 105
Ranger, 33
Raritan, 94
Rattler, 129, illus.129
Red Rover, 133, illus.133
Reindeer, 129
Release, 97
Reliance, 90
Reliance (USRC) (1861), 135
Reliance (USRC) (1867), 141
Relief, 97
Relief (USRC), 141
Renshaw, 106
Resaca, 33
Rescue, 90
Rescue (USRC), 141
Resolute, 90
Resolute (USRC), 141
Restless, 103
Rhode Island, 51

Richmond, 21, illus.22
Roanoke (monitor), 4, illus.4, (frigate) 17
Rocket, 90
Rodolph, 130
Roebuck, 104
Roman, 101
Romeo, 130
Rosalie, 106
Rose, 90
Rush, Richard (USRC), 139

Sabine, 94
Sachem, 74
Saco, 32, illus.34
Sacramento, 25, illus.26
Saffron, 90
Sagamore, 29
Saginaw, 34, illus.37
St. Clair, 130
St. Lawrence, 95
St. Louis (sloop), 96
St. Louis (river ironclad), 112
St. Mary's, 96
Sallie Wood, 133
Sam Houston, 106
Samson (river monitor), 111,
  see *Chickasaw*
Samson (river steamer), 133
Samuel Rotan, 105
San Jacinto, 15
Sandusky, 112
Sangamon, 5
Santee, 95
Santiago de Cuba, 52
Sarah Bruen, 99
Saranac, 14, illus.14
Saratoga, 96
Sassacus, 38
Satellite, 68
Saugus, 7
Savannah, 95
Saville (USRC), 141
Sciota, 29
Scylla, 7, see *Canonicus*
Sea Bird, 106
Sea Foam, 99
Search (USRC), 142
Sebago, 35
Selma, 65
Seminole, 24
Seneca, 29
Serapis, 27
Severn, 26
Seward, William H. (USRC), 136
Shackamaxon, 9
Shamokin, 40
Shamrock, 38
Shark, 106
Shawmut, 32, illus.34
Shawnee, 10, illus.10

Index   211

Shawsheen, 65
Shenandoah, 25, illus.27
Shepherd Knapp, 101
Sherman, John (USRC), 137
Shiloh, 10
Shokokon, 68
Shubrick (USRC), 135
Sibyl, 130
Sidney C. Jones, 100
Signal, 130
Silver Cloud, 130
Silver Lake, 130
Siren, 131
Snowdrop, 90
Somerset, 69
Sonoma, 38
Sophronia, 100
Sorrel, 91
South Carolina, 57
Southfield, 69
Sovereign, 133
Speedwell, 81
Spirea, 72
Spitfire, 10, see Suncook
Springfield, 124
Spuyten Duyvil, 40, illus.41
Squando, 10
Standish, 81
Star, 58, see Monticello
Stars and Stripes, 60
State of Georgia, 52
Stepping Stones, 69
Stettin, 60
Stevens, E.A. (USRC), 136
Stevens Battery, 11
Stockdale, 131
Stonewall, 106
Stromboli, 10, see Wassuc
Stromboli, 40, see Spuyten Duyvil
Sumter (river gunboat), 120
Sumter (armed steamer), 45
Suncook, 10
Sunflower, 74
Supply, 97
Susan A. Howard, 106
Susquehanna, 14
Suwanee, 40
Swatara (1873), 28
Swatara (1865), 33
Sweet Brier, 91
Switzerland, 118, illus.119

T.A. Wood, 100
T.D. Horner, 119
Tacony, 38
Taghkanic, 27
Tahgayuta, 26
Tahoma, 29
Talladega, 27

Tallahatchie, 131
Tallahoma, 38
Tallapoosa, 38, illus.41
Tartar, 10, see Yazoo
Tawah, 124
Teaser, 74
Tecumseh, 7, illus.7
Tempest (monitor), 10, see Yuma
Tempest (tinclad), 131
Tennessee (cruiser), 19, see Madawaska
Tennessee (armed steamer), 52
Tensas, 124
Terror, 8, see Agamenticus
Thistle, 134
Thomas Freeborn, 65
Thompson, Jacob (USRC), 141
Thunder, 106
Thunderer, 9, see Passaconaway
Ticonderoga, 26, illus.28
Tiger (USRC), 135
Tigress, 91
Tioga, 37
Tippecanoe, 7
Tonawanda, 8, illus.9
Tornado, 111, see Winnebago
Torrey (USCS), 143
Toucey, Isaac (USRC), 141
Trefoil, 80
Trenton, 18, illus.19
Triana, 81
Tristram Shandy, 52
Tritonia, 65
Tulip, 71
Tunxis, 10
Tuscarora, 23
Tuscumbia, 114, illus.114
Twilight (USCS), 143
Two Sisters, 106
Tyler, 117, illus.118

Umpqua, 10
Unadilla, 29
Uncas, 74
Underwriter, 65
Undine, 131
Union, 81
Unit, 84
United States, 95
Uno (USRC), 137
Valley City, 75
Valparaiso, 104
Vandalia, 28
Vandalia, 96
Vanderbilt, 52, illus.54
Vanderbilt (USRC), 142
Varina (USRC), 141, 143
Varuna, 60
Velocity, 106
Verbena, 91

Vermont, 93,
Vesuvius, 7, see Tippecanoe
Vicksburg, 60
Victoria, 75
Victory, 124
Vigilant (USRC), 141
Vincennes, 96
Vindicator, 119, illus.119
Violet, 91
Virginia (armed steamer), 60
Virginia (ship of the line), 93
Vixen (river monitor), 110, see Neosho
Vixen (armed steamer), 65
Volunteer, 133

Wabash, 16
Wachusett, 22
Walker (USCS), 143
Wampanoag, 19
Wamsutta, 75
Wanderer, 105
Wando, 53
Warren, 96
Washington (USRC), 141
Washington, Peter G. (USRC), 137, see Uno
Wasp, 48, see Emma Henry
Wassuc, 10, illus.10
Watauga, 18
Watch, 83, see A.C. Powell
Water Witch, 14, illus.15,
Wateree, 38
Wave, 131
Waxsaw, 10
Wayanda (USRC), 136
Weehawken, 5
Western World, 75
Westfield, 69
Whitehall, 69
Whitehead, 75
Wildcat, 106
Wilderness, 66, (USRC) 138
Willamette, 26
William Bacon, 100
William Badger, 101
William G. Anderson, 104
William G. Putnam, 66
William H. Brown, 133
Winnebago, 111
Winnipec, 40
Winona, 29
Winooski, 38
Wissahickon, 29
Wolcott, Oliver (USRC), 139
Woodbury, Levi (USRC), 136, illus.137
Worcester, 26
Wyalusing, 38
Wyandank, 79
Wyandotte (armed steamer), 45

Wyandotte (monitor), 7, see *Tippecanoe*
Wyoming, 23

Yankee, 83, illus.84
Yantic, 32
Yazoo, 10
Young America, 91
Young Rover, 61
Yucca, 80
Yuma, 10

Zeta, 91
Zouave, 91

INDEX - CONFEDERATE SHIPS

35th Parallel, 187
A.B. Seger, 169
A.C. Gunnison(privateer), 189
A.S. Ruthven, 174
A.W. Baker, 185
Acacia, 185
Admiral, 185
Advance (B/R), 192
Adventure, 161
Agrippina, 197
Aid (Gulf), 177
Aid (Atlantic), 179
Ajax, 161
Alabama, 157, illus. 158
Alamo, 185
Alar, 197
Albatross, 192
Albemarle (ironclad), 153
Albemarle (Atlantic), 179
Alena, 183
Alert, 177
Alexandra, 157
Alfred Robb, 185
Allison, 182
Amazon, 179
Anglo-Norman, 169
Anglo-Saxon, 169
Anna Dale, 175
Appleton Belle, 185
Appomattox, 179
Arctic, 177
Argo, 185
Argosy, 185
Argus, 185
Arizona (B/R), 193
Arkansas (ironclad), 150, illus. 151
Arrow, 169
Atlanta, 151, illus. 152
Atlantic (B/R), 193

Austin (B/R), 193

B.M. Moore, 185
Bahama (B/R), 193
Baltic, 175
Barataria, 169
Bat (B/R), 191
Bayou City, 173
Beaufort, 182
Beauregard (Atlantic), 179
Beauregard (Virginia), 183
Beauregard, 185
Beauregard (privateer), 189
Beauregard (B/R), 193
Belle Algerine, 172
Ben McCulloch, 185
Bermuda (B/R), 193
Berosa, 179
Berwick Bay, 185
Bienville, 164
Black Warrior, 181
Blue Wing, 185
Bombshell, 179
Bonita (privateer), 189
Boston, 172
Boston (privateer), 189
Bracelet, 185
Bradford, 176
Breaker, 175

Calhoun, 169
Caroline, 193, see *Arizona*
Carondelet, 164
Castor, 197
Caswell, 179
Catawba, 179
Ceres (B/R), 193
Chameleon, 161, see *Tallahassee*
Charleston (ironclad), 153
Charlotte Clark (privateer), 189
Charm, 185
Chattahoochee, 163
Cheney, 185
Cheops, 150
Chesapeake (privateer), 189
Chesterfield, 179
Chickamauga, 157
Chicora, 152, illus. 153
City of Richmond (B/R), 193
Clara Dolsen, 185
Clarence, 162
Clarendon, 179
Clifton, 173
Colonel Hill, 179
Colonel Lamb (B/R), 191, illus. 192
Colonel Lovell, 167
Colonel Stelle, 174
Columbia (ironclad), 154
Condor (B/R), 192

Confederate States, 183
Coquette (B/R), 193
Cornubia (B/R), 193
Corpus Christi, 173
Corypheus, 173
Cotton Plant, 185
Cotton Plant (Atlantic), 179
Countess, 185
Crescent, 176
Curlew (Atlantic), 179
Curlew (B/R), 192
Currituck, 179
Curtis Peck, 182

Dalman, 176
Dan, 172
Danube, 175
Darby, 172
Darlington, 179
David, 164, illus. 165
De Soto, 185
Dee (B/R), 193
Deer (B/R), 191
Defiance, 167
Dew Drop, 185
Diana,La, 169
Diana, 173
Dick Keys, 176
Dime, 174
Dixie, 163
Dixie (privateer), 189
Dr. Batey, 185
Dodge, 175
Dollie Webb, 169
Dolly, 179
Don (B/R), 194
Doubloon, 185
Dove (privateer), 189
Drewry, 181
Duane, 183
Dunbar, 185

Eastport, 151
Edward J. Gay, 185
Egypt Mills, 179
El Monassir, 149, see *Mississippi*
El Tousson, 149, see *North Carolina*
Elizabeth, 163
Ellis, 177
Elma, 175
Elmira, 185
Emma Bett, 185
Empire Parish, 172
Enterprise, 161
Equator, 179
Era No. 3, 174
Era No. 5, 185
Escambia, 163
Etiwan, 179

Eugenie (B/R), 194

F.S. Barlow (privateer), 189
Fairplay, 185
Falcon (B/R), 192
Fanny, 177
Fanny Morgan, 175
Ferd Kennett, 185
Fingal (B/R), 151, see *Atlanta*
Firefly, 179
Fisher, 177
Flamingo (B/R), 192, illus. 193
Flora (B/R), 194
Florida (cruiser), 158, illus. 159
Florilda, 174
Forrest, 179
Fredericksburg, 154
Frolic, 185

Gaines, 163, illus. 164
Gallatin, 181
Gallatin (privateer), 189
Gallego, 183
General Beauregard, 167
General Bee, 173
General Bragg, 167
General Breckinridge, 167
General Clinch, 179
General Earl Van Dorn, 168
General Lee, 179
General Lovell, 168
General M. Jeff Thompson, 168
General N.S. Reneau (privateer), 189
General Polk, 184
General Quitman (Louisiana), 169
General Quitman II (Louisiana), 172
General Rusk, 174
General Scott, 182
General Sterling Price, 168
General Sumter, 168
General Sumter (Gulf), 176
George Buckhart, 175
George Page, 182, illus. 182
Georgia (cruiser), 159
Georgia (cruiser), 162
Georgia, 177
Georgiana, 159
Germantown, 183
Gibraltar (privateer), 189
Gibraltar (B/R), 160, see *Sumter*
Gordon (privateer), 189
Gordon Grant, 185
Gossamer, 172
Governor A. Mouton (privateer), 189
Governor Milton, 176
Governor Moore, 169, illus. 170
Governor Morehead, 179
Grampus, 186
Grand Bay, 174

Grand Duke, 184
Grand Era, 186
Granite City (B/R), 194
Gray Cloud, 176
Great Republic, 176
Greyhound (B/R), 194
Gunnison, 175

H.D. Mears, 186
H.L. Hunley, 166
H.R.W. Hill, 186
Halifax, 177
Hallie Jackson (privateer), 189
Hampton, 163
Hansa (B/R), 195
Harmony, 182
Harriet Lane, 173
Harriet Pinckney (B/R), 195
Hart, 172
Hartford City, 186
Hawley, 181
Hebe (B/R), 194
Helen (Gulf), 176
Helen (Gulf), 177, sloop
Helen (Atlantic), 179
Henry J. King, 176
Hercules, 161, illus. 162
Hope, 186
Hope (B/R), 191
Hornet, 164
Hunley, 166
Huntress, 179
Huntsville (ironclad), 153

Ida, 179
Indian Chief, 179
Iron King, 176
Isabella (Gulf), 177
Isabella (privateer), 189
Isabella Ellis, 181
Island City, 174
Isondiga, 178
Ivy, 170

J.A. Cotton (Louisiana), 170
J.A. Cotton, 184
J.C. Calhoun (privateer), 189
J.D. Clarke, 186
J.D. Swain, 186
J.H. Jarvis, 176
J.J. Crittenden, 181
J.M. Chapman (privateer), 189
J.O. Nixon (privateer), 189
Jackson (ironclad), 153
Jackson, 184
James Battle, 176
James Johnson, 184
James L. Day, 170
James Woods, 184

Jamestown, 181
Jeff Davis, Tex, 174
Jeff Davis (Atlantic), 179
Jeff Davis (Atlantic), 181
Jeff Davis, 186
Jefferson Davis (privateer), 189
John B. White, 182
John F. Carr, 174
John Simonds, 186
John Walsh, 186
Joseph Landis (privateer), 189
Josephine (privateer), 189
Josiah H. Bell, 173
Julia A. Hodges, 175
Julius, 186
Junaluska, 179
Juno I (B/R), 195
Juno II (B/R), 195

Kahukee, 179
Kanawha Valley, 186
Kaskaskia, 186
Kate L. Bruce (Atlantic), 179
Kate L. Bruce (Atlantic), 181
Kentucky, 186
Lady Davis, 179
Lady Walton, 186
Lamar (privateer), 189
Landis, 172
Lapwing, 197
Lark (B/R), 191
Laurel, 197
Lavinia (B/R), 173, see *Harriet Lane*
Le Grand, 186
Lecompt, 175
Leesburg, 179
Linn Boyd, 186
Little Rebel, 168
Livingston, 184
Logan, 182
Lone Star, 174
Lorton (privateer), 189
Louis Cass, 177
Louis D'Or, 186
Louisa Ann Fanny (B/R), 192
Louisiana (ironclad), 151
Louisiana (cruiser), 162
Louisville, 186
Lucy Gwin, 174
Lynx (B/R), 195

M.C. Ethridge, 181
M.E. Dowing, 179
Macon, 163
Magenta, 186
Magnolia, 186
Magnolia (B/R), 195
Manassas (ram), 150, 189
Manassas (Atlantic), 181

214 Index

Marianna, 176
Mariner (privateer), 189
Marion, 179
Mars, 186
Mary Augusta (B/R), 192
Mary E. Keene, 186
Mary Hill, 174
Mary Patterson, 186
Matagorda (B/R), 195
Matilda (privateer), 190
Matilda (B/R), 193
Maurepas, 184
May, 186
McRae, 170, illus. 171
Memphis (Louisiana), 171
Memphis (Atlantic), 181
Merite, 186
Merrimac (B/R), 195
Midge, 165, illus. 166
Milledgeville, 154
Mississippi (ironclad), 149, illus. 149
Mississippi (ironclad), 151
Mississippi (cruiser), 162
Missouri, 153
Mobile, 171
Mocking Bird (privateer), 190
Mohawk, 186
Monticello (privateer), 190
Morgan, 163
Morgan (Louisiana), 173
Moro, 186
Mosher, 172
Moultrie, 179
Muscle, 186
Muscogee, 153, see *Jackson*
Music, 172
Music (privateer), 190

Nansemond, 163
Nashville (ironclad), 154
Nashville (cruiser), 159
Nassau, 195, see *Theodora*
Natchez, 186
Neafie, 176
Nelms, 176
Nelson, 186
Neptune, 174
Neuse, 153
New National, 186
New Orleans, 171
Nina Simmes, 186
Nita (B/R), 195
Norfolk, 163
North Carolina (ironclad), 149
North Carolina, 152
Northampton, 182

Oconee, 178, see *Savannah*
Ohio Belle, 186
Olustee, 161, see *Tallahassee*

Olustee, 161, see *Ajax*
Onward (privateer), 190
Oregon, 171
Orizaba, 172
Osacca, 162, see *Louisiana*
Osceola, 186
Owl (B/R), 191

Palmetto State, 152
Pamlico, 171
Pargoud, 186
Patrick Henry, 181, illus. 182
Paul Jones, 186
Paul Jones (privateer), 190
Peedee, 163
Pelican (privateer), 190
Penguin (B/R), 192
Petrel (Atlantic), 181
Petrel (privateer), 190
Peytona, 186
Phantom (B/R), 195
Phenix (privateer), 190
Phoenix (Louisiana), 172
Phoenix (Gulf), 175
Pickens, 173
Pioneer, 165
Pioneer (privateer), 190
Pioneer II (privateer), 190
Planter, 179
Plover (B/R), 192
Plymouth, 183
Pontchartrain, 184
Portsmouth, 163
Post Boy, 179
Powhatan, 182
Prince, 186
Prince of Wales, 186
Ptarmigan (B/R), 192

Queen Mab, 179
Queen of the West, 185, illus. 185

R.J. Lackland, 186
Raleigh (ironclad), 152
Raleigh (Atlantic), 178
Rappahannock, 159
Rappahannock (Virginia), 182
Rattlesnake (privateer), 159, 190, see *Nashville*
Rebel, 179
Red Rover, 186
Reliance, 182
Renshaw, 181
Republic, 186
Rescue (privateer), 190
Resolute, 168
Resolute (Atlantic), 179
Richmond (ironclad), 152
Roanoke I (Virginia), 182
Roanoke II (Virginia), 182

Robert E. Lee (B/R), 195, illus. 194
Robert Fulton, 186
Robert Habersham, 179
Roebuck, 174
Rondout, 182
Rosine (B/R), 192
Ruby (B/R), 192

Sachem, 174
St. Francis No. 3, 186
St. Mary, 185
St. Patrick, 166
St. Philip, 172
Sallie (privateer), 190
Sallie Wood, 186
Sam Kirkman, 187
Sampson, 178
Samuel Hill, 187
Samuel Orr, 187
San Francisco, 162, see *Texas*
Santa Maria (ironclad), 149
Satellite, 182
Savannah (ironclad), 152
Savannah (Atlantic), 178
Savannah (privateer), 190
Schultz, 182
Scorpion, 164
Scotland, 187
Sea Bird, 178
Seaboard, 182
Sealine (privateer), 190
Selma, 175, illus. 176
Shanghai, 162, see *Georgia*
Sharp, 187
Shenandoah, 159, illus. 160
Shrapnel, 183
Skirwan, 179
Slidell, 187
Snipe (B/R), 192
Sovereign, 187
Sphinx, 150, see *Stonewall*
Spray, 176
Squib, 164
Stag (B/R), 191
Star, 172
Starlight, 187
Stephen R. Mallory (privateer), 190
Stonewall, 150, illus. 150
Stonewall Jackson, 168, illus. 168
Stonewall Jackson (privateer), 190
Stono, 178
Sumter (cruiser), 160
Sumter (Atlantic), 180
Sun Flower, 174
Swan, 176

T.D. Hine, 187
Tacony, 162
Tallahassee (cruiser), 161, illus. 161
Talomico, 180

Teaser, 182
Tennessee (Louisiana), 172
Tennessee (ironclad), 150, illus. 151
Tennessee II (ironclad), 154
Texas (ironclad), 154
Texas (cruiser), 161
Texas (cruiser), 162, illus. 162
Texas (Louisiana), 172
Texas (privateer), 190
Theodora (B/R), 195
Thomas Jefferson, 181, see *Jamestown*
Tientsin, 161, see *Adventure*
Time, 176
Tom Sugg, 185
Torch, 164
Torpedo, 182
Towns, 183
Transport, 180
Trent, 187
Triton (privateer), 190
Tropic (B/R), 179 see *Huntress*
Turel, 176
Tuscaloosa (ironclad), 153
Tuscaloosa, 162
Tuscarora, 172
Twilight, 187

Uncle Ben, 174
Uncle Ben (Atlantic), 178

V.H. Ivy (privateer), 190
Velocity, 175
Vesta (B/R), 194
Vicksburg, 161, see *Hercules*
Vicksburg, 187

Victoria, 187
Victoria (B/R), 196
Viper, 164
Virgin (B/R), 196
Virginia (Merrimack), 150
Virginia (1862), 154
Volunteer, 187

W. Burton, 172
W.W.Crawford, 187
Wade Water Belle, 187
Warren Winslow, 178, see *Winslow*
Warrior, 168
Washington, 173
Wasp, 164
Waterwitch, 180
Webb, 172
Weldon N. Edwards, 180
White Cloud, 187
Widgeon (B/R), 192
William B. King, 173
William G. Hewes (B/R), 196
William H. Webb (privateer), 190
William H. Young, 176
Wilmington, 154
Winslow, 178
Wison, 180
Wren (B/R), 191

Yadkin, 163 178
Yangtze, 161, see *Enterprise*
Yazoo, 187
Yeddo, 162, see *Mississippi*
York (privateer), 190
Young America, 183

Printed in Great Britain
by Amazon